A GIFT OF PRESENCE

A GIFT OF PRESENCE

The Theology and Poetry of the Eucharist in Thomas Aquinas

Jan-Heiner Tück

TRANSLATED BY SCOTT G. HEFELFINGER

Foreword by Bruce D. Marshall

 The Catholic University of America Press Washington, D.C.

Originally published as *Gabe der Gegenwart: Theologie und Dichtung der Eucharistie bei Thomas von Aquin*
Copyright © 2014 Verlag Herder GmbH, Freiberg im Breisgau

English translation copyright © 2018
The Catholic University of America Press
All rights reserved

Library of Congress Cataloging-in-Publication Data
Names: Tück, Jan Heiner, author.
Title: A gift of presence : the theology and poetry of the Eucharist in Thomas Aquinas / Jan-Heiner Tück ; translated by Scott G. Hefelfinger ; foreword by Bruce D. Marshall.
Other titles: Gabe der Gegenwart. English
Description: Washington, D.C. : The Catholic University of America Press, 2018. |
Includes bibliographical references and index.
Identifiers: LCCN 2018011982 | ISBN 9780813230399 (cloth)
Subjects: LCSH: Thomas, Aquinas, Saint, 1225?–1274. | Lord's Supper—History— Middle Ages, 600–1500.
Classification: LCC B765.T54 T8313 2018 | DDC 234/.163092—dc23
LC record available at https://lccn.loc.gov/2018011982

CONTENTS

Foreword by Bruce D. Marshall   vii

Translator's Preface   xi

Author's Preface to the Third Edition   xvii

Author's Preface to the First Edition   xix

Abbreviations   xxi

Introduction   1

Part A. Systematic Reconstruction: The Eucharistic Theology of the *Summa theologiae*

1. Preliminaries   23
2. "*Hoc est corpus meum*": The Transformation of the Gifts   55
3. "*Quod pro vobis tradetur*": The Passion of Christ and Its Representative Realization in the Celebration of the Eucharist   94

Part B. The Poetic Distillation of Eucharistic Theology in the Hymns

4. Preliminaries   163
5. The Mystery of Eucharistic Conversion: The Hymn *Pange lingua gloriosi*   175
6. A Poetic Theology of Gift: The Hymns *Sacris solemniis* and *Verbum supernum*   194
7. Commemoration—Making-Present—Expectation: The Sequence *Lauda Sion*   209

8. Hidden Presence and Contemplative Adoration: The Hymn *Adoro te devote* 229

9. Summary: The Poetic Distillation of Eucharistic Theology in the Hymns 244

Part C. Eucharistic Passages

10. An Interim Reflection: Epochal Forms of Eucharistic Theology 253

11. The Self-Gift of Jesus Christ in the Signs of Bread and Wine 274

12. Eucharistic Passages 301

Bibliography 341

Index 377

FOREWORD

After Vatican II the theology of Thomas Aquinas went into nearly total eclipse in the Catholic world, where it had long been best known and loved. This sudden occultation had various causes.

The teaching of the Council itself was not one of them. The texts of Vatican II cite Aquinas as an authority more than they cite any other individual figure in the Catholic theological tradition. A passion for "updating" Catholic thought, encouraged by the Council but in its aftermath not always wisely pursued, is surely one cause of disregard for the figure who had been most central to Catholic intellectual life for generations before Vatican II. The "ressourcement" likewise encouraged by the Council is another. Renewed engagement with the biblical and patristic sources of Catholic faith and theology has often been undertaken not—in the spirit of the Council—as a complement to continued study of the great medieval doctors, but as an alternative to it. The much-derided neo-Thomistic "manuals" through which Catholic theology was largely taught in the first half of the twentieth century were a further cause; whatever their merits, it has to be granted that these textbooks were generally not helpful as an entry into Thomas's own world of thought. For these and other reasons, Aquinas has effectively been a closed book to a great many of the Catholic theologians trained since Vatican II.

In the theology of St. Thomas there are, of course, many matters of philosophical interest. Outside the Catholic world as well as within it, philosophers never widely shared the post-Conciliar disregard for Aquinas to which Catholic theologians became subject. The considerable growth of interest in medieval thought among philosophers and historians of philosophy schooled in the analytic tradition has, in fact, led to a much wider engagement with, and intellectual regard for, Aquinas and other medieval theologians than would have been common among philosophers fifty years ago. In the nature of the case, this has meant that much of the work on Aquinas over the last several generations has stopped short at those matters which, because they seemed strictly theological, were assumed to be most remote from the interest and competence of philosophers—above all the Trinity, the Incarnation, and the Eucharist. Thus, paradoxically, the Christian teachings that form the heart of Thomas's whole intellectual enterprise have lain virtually untouched for decades. Philosophers think, understandably, that Thomas's treatment of these teachings is essentially the business of theologians, and theologians are hardened against it.

When it comes to Thomas's Trinitarian theology and his Christology this peculiar state of affairs has begun to change in the last decade or two. Until the appearance of Jan-Heiner Tück's *Gabe der Gegenwart* in 2009, however, there had been no book-length study of Aquinas on the Eucharist since the Second Vatican Council. The book has been quite successful in Germany, having gone into a third edition within five years of its original appearance. The Catholic University of America Press has done a valuable service to theology by making the book available to English-speaking readers, among whom interest in St. Thomas is surely wider than it now is in Germany or France.

The book opens with a brief discussion of why, and how, we should read Aquinas today. Here Tück locates his project within the current spectrum of Thomas interpretation and of Catholic theology more generally, distancing himself both from a "repristinating" Thomism hostile to contemporary theological concerns and from the widespread indifference to Aquinas, and with him all forms of scholasticism, in Catholic theology after Vatican II. His aim is to offer a full-bodied interpretation of Aquinas on the Eucharist which is at once historically responsible and consistently attentive to modern and contemporary questions. He wants to let contemporary theology question Aquinas, but, equally, to have Aquinas question contemporary theology.

This means that the book, while offering a close reading of Thomas throughout, is not primarily a historical study of Thomas's Eucharistic theology. Such a study would have to examine all of Aquinas's texts on the Eucharist, in particular the major systematic treatments in Book IV of the *Scriptum* on the *Sentences* and in *Summa Contra Gentiles*, Book IV, tracing out their interrelationships, locating their historical sources, and identifying the places where Thomas follows established views and those where he breaks new ground. Well informed as he is about St. Thomas, Tück makes no claim to undertake this kind of comprehensive historical study (which would be a truly massive enterprise). His book is very much a "retrieval" of Thomas on the Eucharist for contemporary theology, based on two quite different textual strains in Thomas's treatment of the topic: the *Summa theologiae*'s *Tertia pars*, and Thomas's Eucharistic poetry.

In the first major section of the book Tück offers a well-crafted "systematic reconstruction," as he puts it, of the most central claims in Thomas's Eucharistic theology, attentive to the historical background of what Thomas is doing and sensitive to many questions contemporary readers are likely to ask. Christ's "somatic real presence" in the Eucharist; Eucharistic conversion, or transubstantiation; the eternal high priesthood of Christ, who makes present in a representative manner the once-for-all reality of his saving passion though the Church's action; the relationship of the last supper to the Cross and the Eucharist; the sacrificial character of the Eucharist—these foundational features of Aquinas's Eucharistic theology all receive perceptive and detailed analysis. Anyone interested in Thomas's theology will find much here to interest them and provoke their own reflection, whether they agree with Tück's reading of Thomas or want to offer alternative interpretations.

But today there are far fewer theologians—to say nothing of students and other interested readers—who have even a basic grasp of Thomas on the Eucharist than there would have been two or three generations ago. One of the great merits of this book is its success at offering a sympathetic (though not uncritical) presentation of Aquinas on the Eucharist to a generation of students and scholars who have lost touch with this deeply formative moment of the Catholic theological tradition. By presenting it in a way both substantive and accessible, Tück offers a needed good to contemporary theology—especially, but not only, Catholic theology. If the book consisted only of this opening section on the Eucharistic questions of the *Summa theologiae*, it would be quite welcome.

Tück, however, offers much more. The middle section of the book is a detailed, theologically rich analysis of Thomas's Eucharistic hymns, precisely as the poetic complement that reveals the "spiritual undercurrent" of his technical Eucharistic theology. As Tück observes, the hymns themselves remain to some extent familiar to practicing Catholics (especially *Pange lingua* and *Adoro te devote*, and to a lesser extent the sequence *Lauda Sion*), and they have been well studied by Pierre-Marie Gy and others. The literature on Aquinas's poetry sometimes makes helpful comments on its theological content, but so far as I know Tück is the first writer deliberately to bring Thomas's Eucharistic poetry into detailed and systematic conversation with his Eucharistic theology. This is a great contribution of the present work, and sets it apart from any other modern treatise on the Eucharist in Aquinas. Especially in the present situation of Catholic theology, where entrance into Thomas's thinking about the Eucharist by way of the *Tertia pars* creates particularly daunting challenges, offering access by way of the hymns (without neglecting the technical theology) is an inspired thought.

The third and final major portion of the book moves to a contemporary "translation" (Tück's term) of Aquinas's Eucharistic theology and spirituality. Here Tück offers a series of admittedly "fragmentary" reflections that represent steps toward a contemporary understanding of the Eucharist consonant with Thomas and informed by him, but intelligible to contemporary readers for whom Thomas's technical language has become opaque or positively misleading. This third section of the book is likely to provoke animated reactions from readers, not least those who know Thomas well. Some will no doubt contest Tück's historical judgments as well as his claims about what a contemporary "translation" of Thomas on the Eucharist ought to look like. This simply adds to the interest of Tück's book. What he says in this section is often debatable, but it is both thoughtful and thought-provoking, and it will contribute significantly to the overall aim of the book: a renewed and more widespread engagement with St. Thomas on the Eucharist.

Bruce D. Marshall
Lehman Professor of Christian Doctrine
Perkins School of Theology
Southern Methodist University

TRANSLATOR'S PREFACE

To the student coming for the first time to Thomas Aquinas and his Eucharistic theology, it might not be far-fetched that he or she pose the rhetorical question: which is the greater mystery, Thomas and his terse scholastic style or the Eucharistic sacrament itself? And although those who enjoy a fairly extensive familiarity with Aquinas's work will perhaps think the question humorous, this is not because the mystery of Aquinas's thought fails to impress itself on us; no, it is precisely this mystery, this slightly alien and otherworldly character, that has become fruitful for us, in our thinking and, we may hope, in our lives as well. If there has been an underlying and uniting force in the recent ressourcement movement among Thomistic thinkers, it has much to do with rediscovering the distance and strangeness of the Angelic Doctor's life and thought—not to reduce or dismiss its worth, but rather to rediscover and render fruitful the richness in, and sometimes precisely in virtue of, this mysterious distance.

Given the relative prominence of this line of Thomistic thought in the English-speaking world, it is my hope that Jan-Heiner Tück's work, *A Gift of Presence*, will in many ways feel right at home in our hands, despite the fact this edition marks the first time it appears in English. Professor Tück shares the impulse of many current disciples of Thomas to dive deeply into the "otherness" of Thomas's texts and thought—not only the historical and cultural aspects of this otherness, but also the otherness of the lived unity between theology, on the one hand, and everyday life, devotion, and spirituality, on the other. That the author embraces this strangeness and wrestles with it in a Eucharistic context suggests the richness of the present work: it is a carefully historical project that does not shy away from substantive issues of theology and spirituality, but instead marshals historical analysis to think in a robustly theological way about the Eucharist, and then explores the fecund interplay between this theology and the lived, vibrant sphere of spirituality. Given this depth and breadth, I can only hope in this brief preface to highlight but a few of its aspects, ones that seem to me significant especially in light of our English-speaking scholarly context.

In Anglophone theology today, Aquinas appears as a frequent and appreciated interlocutor. Whether referred to sympathetically or critically, the Angelic Doctor remains very much a part of the broader theological conversation, particularly but not exclusively within the broad ambit of Catholic theology. This is much less the case in the Germanic theological world. Consequently, the first word to be spoken in Professor Tück's work is a rationale for reading Thomas today and how one ought to do just that. Such an argument may seem a well-trodden path in the English-speaking theological world; in fact, however, Tück's thoughtful and highly readable account of Thomas's place in contemporary theology paints a carefully contoured and delicately shaded portrait of thinking theologically with Thomas today. Much more than a mere apologia for Thomas and his continuing relevance, Tück's approach could be considered a manifesto for Thomistic thinkers of all stripes who see—or who want to see—that fruitful and rigorous work with Thomas's texts involves paying close attention to wide differences between the medieval and contemporary contexts, and then striving to render these differences fruitful, edifying, and challenging. For a clear and powerful example of precisely this sort of scholarship, one need simply continue beyond the introductory chapter, after which three lines of inquiry are undertaken.

The first might be said to pick up after Vatican II brought an end to neoscholastic styles of doing theology and the use of manuals fell largely out of practice. While many positives may be ascribed to this turn of events, it has brought with it the consequence that primers in Thomistic theology are fewer and further between. This of course applies to some areas more than others. It is not that introductory texts in Thomistic philosophy or theology are hard to come by—a number of good texts are on offer. Nor is it that highly specific and specialized topics fail to draw significant writing efforts—they continue to thrive, and happily so. Rather, it is the space between broad overview and specialized monograph that has fallen by the wayside in post-neoscholastic, Thomistic theology. And this, perhaps, in no area more than Aquinas's sacramental theology.

Into this yawning gap steps Professor Tück's work, and it bridges the divide with aplomb and insight. Attentive as always to the relevant historical details, but without attempting—and getting lost in—an historical research project, Tück crafts what he aptly styles a "systematic reconstruction" of Aquinas's theology of the sacraments in general, as well as, and in much greater depth, his treatment of the Eucharistic sacrament. For both the novice and seasoned reader of Aquinas, this primer—a "handbook" in the best of the Germanic scholarly tradition—on the sacrament of the Eucharist is bound to enlighten. In this way it fills a conspicuous need in Anglophone Thomistic theology and does a great service for those seeking a lucid and insightful presentation of Aquinas's sacramental theology, with the Eucharist holding pride of place.

The second line of inquiry finds Tück taking this already solid contribution and amplifying it by setting it in conversation with a wholly different genre of Thomas's writing: his Eucharistic poetry. In many ways, this move exemplifies and crowns the work's efforts to bring together once more things formerly united but now disparate, as a way of challenging and augmenting our contemporary conversation and sensibilities, all by respecting and drawing on the historical distance between ourselves and the scholastic period. It is true that contemporary theology, aware of the divergence between theory and practice, between academic and lived theology, often tries to unite them; but it is also true that almost as never before, theology remains a highly specialized and often wildly speculative discipline. Thus, the careful theological reading of Thomas's poetry, deeply rooted in his methodical sacramental theology, marks a rare and welcome statement of the possible unity between theology and spirituality, as well as the beauty and richness flowing therefrom. At the very least, there is no work in English that, in this respect, is similar to Tück's project here, let alone that can rival it. There is, suffice it to say, a wealth of new insights here to be appreciated, reflected upon, and discussed further and more broadly in the academy.

Such a discussion would surely branch out quickly to touch upon two lines of thought that in recent years have posed a challenge to standard Thomistic accounts of the Eucharist in the English-speaking world. The first, represented by Louis-Marie Chauvet, puts forward a decidedly anti-metaphysical and symbolist understanding of the Eucharist. Because Aquinas's discussion of the sacraments in general relies on classical metaphysical conceptions, central among which is that of causality, other aspects of the sacraments fall by the wayside, in particular those dimensions that are truly symbolic and cannot be placed within a causal framework. The second line of thought begins in Rene Girard's mimetic theory and its resulting critique of sacrifice. Girard's work in literary and cultural criticism gets taken up by Edward Kilmartin, Robert Daly, and David Power, among others, to call attention to the manifold underpinnings of the Eucharist that go beyond its merely sacrificial dimensions. Here, themes of the Eucharistic meal, Christ's presence, and various other liturgical considerations are brought into play and assembled into a fuller account of the Eucharistic liturgy and sacrament.

Similar themes and questions mark the German theological landscape and thus, even without drawing on these authors explicitly, Tück tackles a third line of inquiry that takes up many of these motifs. As it happens, his engagement with the thought of Johannes Betz puts him indirectly in conversation with Kilmartin and Daly, who trace their theological lineage to Betz in highly significant ways. But what stands out above all in the engagement with more recent thinkers—Betz as well as others, including Karl Rahner, Edward Schillebeeckx, Joseph Ratzinger, and the like—is that, although Thomas was not confronted by the same set of questions confronting us today, his own approach to the Eucharist suggests much common ground. For there is a breadth to Thomas's account that exceeds a merely sacrificial perspective and goes far beyond merely Aristotelian metaphysics. Indeed, as the title of this work indicates, there are highly personalistic, deeply biblical, and thoroughly liturgical themes at play in Thomas's treatment, especially the motifs of personal presence and absence. In tandem with the keen insights of the foregoing sections, the last section offers a highly significant intervention within contemporary discussions of the Eucharist. The learned, pacific, and generous nature of Tück's entrance into these debates will offer much food for thought for those working in the area of sacramental theology, for Tück's constructive project draws connections between the Angelic Doctor and the pressing questions raised by Chauvet, Girard, and others with respect to Eucharistic theology.

For all of these reasons and more besides, it is my hope that this work will find a welcoming audience within the English-speaking world. In this English edition, I have tried to stay close to the original German, which demonstrates the rare combination of being both sophisticated and elegant; at the same time, I have aimed to stay well within the limits of idiomatic English expression. This, of course, is what every translator tries to do. But I think it important to note further that there is, happily, not merely *one* style of idiomatic English. Accordingly, I have tried to render it in a style that seeks to reflect something of the original style in German, for this too is a creation of the author and, in my view, the responsibility and challenge of the translator to articulate. In order to realize this work, I have relied on much support from many collaborators; while many thanks are therefore in order, I am here able to thank only a very few. My gratitude to Jan-Heiner Tück for his wise and beautiful work, and for his tremendous help and unfailing patience throughout the project; to John Martino at CUA

Press for his unflagging and adept support and flexibility; to Bernhard Dolna for initiating the project through a simple, small request; to Joseph Wawrykow for his enthusiastic interest and support, as well as his scholarly example; and to Simone, my wife, who is not only my best and most faithful textual editor and interlocutor, but also and in countless ways the *sine qua non* of this project and the larger, most joyful project of family life and discipleship.

Scott G. Hefelfinger
Notre Dame, Indiana, Holy Thursday, 2016

AUTHOR'S PREFACE TO THE
THIRD EDITION

The Irish author James Joyce greatly esteemed Thomas Aquinas as a poet. In his book *A Portrait of the Artist as a Young Man*, there is a passage in which Joyce has his alter ego—Stephen Dedalus—argue about beauty and truth in Thomas's thought. When his interlocutor cannot entirely follow the train of thought, Dedalus says: "Perhaps Aquinas would understand me better than you. He was a poet himself. He wrote a hymn for Maundy Thursday [sic]. It begins with the words *Pange lingua gloriosi*. They say it is the highest glory of the hymnal. It is an intricate and soothing hymn. I like it." Even if Joyce erred in his placement of the hymn within the liturgical year—as is well known, *Pange lingua* was not written for Holy Week but for the solemnity of Corpus Christi—still his aesthetic judgment remains notable: "I like it."

This judgment appears to be shared by not a few of our contemporaries. At any rate, there is a delightfully animated interest in the Eucharistic theology and poetry of Thomas Aquinas. This continuing demand has prompted Herder Publishing House to have the present study published in a third edition. For the new edition, supplementary bibliographic references have been added here and there, remaining errors have been rectified, and a passage has been inserted on the Eucharist as a source of joy, which does not separate itself from the suffering of others. I would like to note with gratitude the benevolent and quite polyphonic resonance that the book has found in academic discussions: Karl-Heinz Menke, in *Theologische Revue* 105 (2009): esp. 470–73; Werner Löser, in *Theologie und Philosophie* 131 (2009): 613–14; Erich Garhammer, in *Lebendige Seelsorge* (6/2010): 68–69; Christoph Amor, in *Zeitschrift für Katholische Theologie* 132 (2010): 224–25; Thomas Marschler, in *Theologie und Glaube* 101 (2011): 155–58; Iso Baumer, in *Schweizer Kirchenzeitung* 180 (2012): 103–4; Matthias Mühl, in *Christ in der Gegenwart* 64.13 (2012): 138; Ivica Ragus, in *Ephemerides Theologiae*

Diacovenses 4 (2013): 765–69. Finally, heartfelt thanks goes out to my colleagues at the Institute for Systematic Theology, René Hofmann and Britta Mühl, for reviewing the manuscript once more, as well as to Dr. Stephan Weber for his reliably delightful collaboration.

                              Jan-Heiner Tück
                              Vienna, on the Feast of St. Thomas Aquinas, 2014

AUTHOR'S PREFACE TO THE FIRST EDITION

A Gift of Presence—bearing this title the present study considers the relation between the theology and the poetry of the Eucharist in the thought of Thomas Aquinas. The real presence of Jesus Christ in the signs of bread and wine, which Peter Handke once called *that which is most real*, is not the product of a human act of recollection but a gift, a sacrosanct gift of the resurrected crucified one himself. On the night before his death, Jesus left his disciples a twofold sign of his friendship; he, who was soon to be absent, bound his presence to this sign. Thomas speaks of a *maximae caritatis signum*, in which is distilled Jesus' giving of his life. In each Eucharistic celebration, this gift of life is made newly present in signs. Bread and wine are transformed through words into the body and the blood of Jesus Christ. Physical food becomes a sign of another sort of food which imparts a share in a life that no longer knows of death. The consecration, however, takes place by means of words that make real what they say. It is not a matter of word magic, for the words are spoken by the priest in the name of another—*in virtute et persona Christi*—and precisely for this reason do they have their transforming power. The ontological penetration of this transformative process, carried out by Thomas Aquinas in his doctrine of transubstantiation, and the poetic celebration of the Eucharistic presence of Christ, reflected in the hymns for the Divine Office on the feast of Corpus Christi—these two aspects are brought together in the present study. The thesis runs thus: in the hymns for Corpus Christi, a poetic distillation of Thomas's Eucharistic theology presents itself and, moreover, discloses the spiritual subtext of his reflections on the theology of the Eucharist. Doctrine and life, scientific theology and spirituality, do not go their separate ways in Thomas. The speculative thinker who put himself in the service of the reception of the *corpus aristotelicum* and established the standards for theological reflection was at the same time a contemplative man of prayer who reflected upon Scripture and celebrated Holy Mass daily.

The present work was accepted as *Habilitationsschrift* in July 2006 by the theological faculty of Albert Ludwig's University of Freiburg in Breisgau. The text was slightly revised for the publication process, which was delayed by my taking up professorships at the universities of Vienna, Osnabrück, and Freiburg. I had the privilege of working under the direction of Prof. Helmut Hoping from 2000 to 2007 as scholarly assistant at the Freiburger working area for dogmatic and liturgical theology, and I would like to thank him for many and diverse inputs and conversations. Prof. Peter Walter undertook the task of being my second reader and from him I was able to take several additional pointers.

Theological reflection has a certain background in the lived-in world, and here I would like to mention my own with gratitude. My wife, Gabriele, has accompanied my theological work from the beginning with great interest. Whenever I succumbed to the temptation to devote myself too much to theology, my children Elias, Johanna, Greta-Maria, and Julius called me back into our family ensemble at just the right moment. I would like to dedicate this work to my parents, Paul and Hildegard Tück, from whom I have received the fundamental orientation of faith that I am privileged today to reflect upon and hand on.

Jan-Heiner Tück
Freiburg, on the Feast of St. Thomas Aquinas, 2009

ABBREVIATIONS

AAS	*Acta Apostolicae Sedis*
BSLK	*Die Bekenntnisschriften der evangelisch-lutherischen Kirche*
Cath	*Catholica*
CIC	Codex iuris canonici
CCL	Corpus Christianorum Latinorum
CCCM	Corpus Christianorum. Continuatio Mediaeualis
Conc	*Concilium*
DH	*Enchiridion Symbolorum Definitionem et Declarationem de rebus Fidei et Morum*
DT	*Divus Thomas*
FC	Fontes Christianes
FKTh	*Forum Katholische Theologie*
FZThPh	*Freiburger Zeitschrift für Theologie und Philosophie*
HDG	Handbuch der Dogmengeschichte
HPhBMA	*Herders Philosophische Bibliothek des Mittelalters*
HWPh	*Historisches Wörterbuch der Philosophie*
JVK	*Jahrbuch für Volkskunde*
JRGS	*Joseph Ratzinger Gesammelte Schriften*
KatBl	*Katechetische Blätter*
LJ	*Liturgisches Jahrbuch*
LThK	*Lexikon für Theologie und Kirche*
MThZ	*Münchener Theologische Zeitschrift*
MySal	*Mysterium Salutis*
PG	Patrologiae Cursus Completus: Series Graeca
PhJ	*Philosophisches Jahrbuch der Görres-Gesellschaft*
PL	Patrologiae Cursus Completus: Series Latina

RevSR	Revue des sciences religieuses
RGG	Religion in Geschichte und Gegenwart
RSPhTh	Revue des sciences philosophiques et théologiques
RSR	Recherches de science religieuse
StZ	Stimmen der Zeit
ThG	Theologie der Gegenwart
ThGl	Theologie und Glaube
ThPh	Theologie und Philosophie
ThPQ	Theologisch-Praktische Quartalsschrift
ThQ	Theologische Quartalschrift
ThRv	Theologische Revue
ThWNT	Theologisches Wörterbuch Neues Testament
TRE	Theologische Realenzyklopädie
UVK	UVK Verlagsgesellschaft (ehem. Universitätsverlag Konstanz)
WuW	Wirtschaft und Wettbewerb
ZAM	Zeitschrift für Aszese und Mystik
ZKaTh	Zeitschrift für Katholische Theologie
ZKG	Zeitschrift für Kirchengeschichte
ZNW	Zeitschrift für die neutestamentliche Wissenschaft und die Kunde der älteren Kirche
ZThK	Zeitschrift für Theologie und Kirche

A GIFT OF PRESENCE

Introduction

1. Why and How to Read Thomas Today

Until the middle of the twentieth century, the work of Thomas Aquinas was largely determinative for the treatises of scholastic theology. With a more open posture toward modern questions and the dissolution of neoscholastic theology, theological engagement with the work of Thomas Aquinas has declined significantly, at least in the German-speaking world. Already in 1970, Karl Rahner offered the diagnosis that there is a "strange silence" concerning Thomas Aquinas, and he felt moved to offer a "call to contemporary Catholic theologians not to forget" the *Doctor communis*.[1] In recent years, a certain renaissance of historical *research* into Thomas has produced notable studies on aspects of the philosophy and theology of his work; yet despite this, when it comes to the concrete enterprise of *teaching*, the observation is apposite that the work of the *Doctor communis* no longer plays a privileged role in contemporary systematic theology. The assessment can hardly be exaggerated that it is possible to receive a diploma or Master's degree in Catholic theology without ever having read one article of the *Summa theologiae*. Since the dogmatic handbooks have carried out the requisite paradigm shift from a neoscholastic to a hermeneutical, salvation-historical conception of theology,[2] Thomas Aquinas has become one reference author among many. The new interest in the *biblical* foundation of all theology, the appreciation of *patristic* theology initiated by the *nouvelle*

---

1. K. Rahner, *On Recognizing the Importance of Thomas Aquinas*, in his *Theological Investigations*, vol. 13: *Theology, Anthropology, Christology* (New York: Darton, Longman and Todd Ltd., 1975), 3–12, here 3.

2. This hermeneutical method is followed, for example, in the handbooks by M. Kehl, *Eschatologie*, 3d ed. (Würzburg: Echter, 1996), esp. 20–22; idem, *Die Kirche: Eine katholische Ekklesiologie* (Würzburg: Echter, 1992), esp. 53–60; and then the respective fascicles in Th. Schneider, ed., *Handbuch der Dogmatik*, vol. 2 (Mainz: Matthias-Grünewald, 1992); W. Beinert, ed., *Glaubenszugänge: Lehrbuch der katholischen Dogmatik*, vol. 3 (Paderborn: Schöningh, 1995). The take away point from this roll call is that Thomas Aquinas is not at all reckoned among the dominant reference authors.

théologie, the sharpened awareness of the *ecumenical* dimension of theological issues, but also the critical-constructive engagement with non-theological sciences—all of these have contributed to the fact that the theology of high Scholasticism, in particular the work of Thomas Aquinas, has forfeited its preeminent place in research and teaching.

In view of the challenges facing theology today, this development may well be irreversible, even though there is an entire series of magisterial statements that explicitly recommend the philosophical and theological work of Aquinas as the standard for teaching. Only a few prominent witnesses are here recalled in passing:[3] Pope Leo XIII, in his encyclical *Aeterni Patris* (August 4, 1879), underlined the outstanding significance of Thomas's philosophy and called for "the golden wisdom of St. Thomas to be established once again and disseminated as widely as possible, for the defense and adornment of the Catholic faith, for the good of society, and for the increase of all sciences."[4] Neo-Thomism, which gained increasing influence beginning in the middle of the eighteenth century, had earlier already occasioned a return of Catholic theological faculties to Thomism broadly understood.[5] Theological awakenings such as the Tübingen school in Catholic theology, which sought to consider the dimension of historicity in conversation with German idealism, were repressed. Undoubtedly, the magisterial endorsement of neo-Thomism enabled the achievement of a certain stabilization and uniformity of Catholic theology *ad intra*. At the same time, the

---

3. On the background, see L. Bendel-Maidl, *Tradition und Innovation: Zur Dialektik von historischer und systematischer Perspektive in der Theologie. Am Beispiel von Transformationen in der Rezeption des Thomas von Aquin im 20. Jahrhundert* (Münster: LIT, 2004), 66–89.

4. See *AAS* 12 (1879): 97–115. Excerpts also found in DH 3135–3140, here 3140: "ut ad catholicae fidei tutelam et decus, ad societatis bonum, ad scientiarum omnium incrementum auream sancti Thomae sapientiam restituatis et quam latissime propagetis." See R. Aubert, *Die Enzyklika "Aeterni patris" und die weiteren päpstlichen Stellungnahmen zur christlichen Philosophie*, in E. Coreth, ed., *Christliche Philosophie im katholischem Denken des 19. Und 20. Jahrhundert: Rückgriff auf scholastiches Erbe*, vol. 2 (Graz: Styria, 1988), 310–32.

5. Of course Thomism exists only in a plurality of different forms, as pointed out in G. Prouvost, *Thomas d'Aquin et les thomismes* (Paris: Cerf, 1996). I understand here, by the umbrella term "Thomism," the teaching tradition of those schools which, since the thirteenth century, took the doctrine of Thomas and defended it against criticism, related it to new inquiries, and attempted to interpret it more exactly. Following O. H. Pesch, four epochs of Thomism can be distinguished: (1) the epoch of the *defensiones* (thirteenth to fifteenth centuries), which defended Thomas's doctrine against the Franciscan school in particular; (2) the epoch of the *commentaries*, which is tightly interconnected with the introduction of the *Summa theologiae* as a theological course book in the universities (from the end of the fifteenth century until the Council of Trent); (3) the epoch of the *disputationes*, in which questions of Reformation theology led to notable developments in Thomism, above all in the realm of positive theology through the integration of so-called scriptural proofs (from the Council of Trent until the middle of the eighteenth century); (4) the epoch of *neo-Thomism*, which brings especially the philosophical but then also the theological work of Thomas into engagement with modern questions and issues (from the middle of the eighteenth century until the Second Vatican Council). See the article of O. H. Pesch, *Thomas von Aquino / Thomismus / Neuthomismus*, in *TRE* 33 (2002): 433–74; P. Engelhardt, "Thomismus," in idem, *Thomas von Aquin: Wegweisungen in sein Werk* (Leipzig: St. Benno, 2005), 57–73.

magisterial promotion of Thomism was at least ambivalent considered *ad extra*, as it risked a defensive apologetic response to the challenges posed by the philosophy of German idealism—Kant, Fichte, Schelling, Hegel—and the nineteenth-century critics of religion—Feuerbach, Marx, Nietzsche. The questions fermented, but Pius X sharpened Leo XIII's program once again, as he called for a return to scholastic metaphysics as a remedy against modernism—a position anchored not only in the 24 Theses of Thomistic Philosophy,[6] but also juridically in the *Codex iuris canonici* of 1917.[7] After the crisis of modernism, Pope Pius XI wrote the encyclical *Studiorum Ducem*, thereby strengthening the significance of Thomas's theology in particular.[8] The document, which appeared for the occasion of the 600th anniversary of his canonization, on June 29, 1923, put a central focus on the personal holiness of Thomas as the most fundamental reason for his clarity and the decisiveness of his theological and philosophical teaching.[9] The Second Vatican Council also overcame "the neuroses of anti-modernism, perceptible and debilitating in ways ever new,"[10] by means of a dialogical opening up to the important concerns of modern man; in so doing, it emphasized the exemplary importance of Thomas, admittedly "much more quietly"[11] and in the context of a new structuring of a theological course of studies which parted ways with the neoscholastic method.[12] In the Decree on Priestly Formation, *Optatam Totius*, we read that students of theology "ought to learn, with St. Thomas as their master, to penetrate contemplatively and more profoundly the mysteries of salvation in their wholeness and to understand their interconnections, in order that they may illumine the mysteries of salvation as completely as possible."[13] In order to appraise

6. See DH 3601–3624.
7. See CIC (1917) can. 1366 §2: "Philosophiae rationalis ac theologiae studia et alumnorum in his disciplinis institutionem professores omnino pertratent ad Angelici Doctoris rationem, doctrinam et principia, eaque sancte teneant." Significantly, CIC (1983) can. 252 still adduces the authority of Thomas only in the context of formation in dogmatic theology.
8. See *AAS* 15 (1923): 323f.; *DH* 3665–3667.
9. On this point, see Bendl-Maidl, *Tradition und Innovation*, 82: "It seems an irony of fate that the theology of a man who devoted himself with zeal against the protests of monastic theology and for the place of theology as a science within the university is now withdrawn from the dispute, once again under the aspect of holiness."
10. J. Ratzinger, *Die erste Sitzungsperiode des Zweiten Vatikanischen Konzils: Ein Rückblick* (Cologne: Bachem, 1983), 20.
11. Rahner, *Recognizing the Importance of Thomas*, 11.
12. See the commentary by O. Fuchs and P. Hünermann, found in P. Hünermann and B. J. Hilberath, eds., *Herders Theologischer Kommentar zum Zweiten Vatikanischen Konzil*, vol. 3 (Freiburg: Herder, 2005), 436f.
13. See *LThK*, 2nd edition, Ergänzungsband 13 (1967): 347f. See also the Declaration on Christian Education, *Gravissimum Educationis*, §10, as well as *CIC* (1983) can. 252 §3: "Lectures are to be given in dogmatic theology, based always on the written word of God and on sacred Tradition; through them the students are to learn to penetrate more deeply into the mysteries of salvation, with St. Thomas in particular as their teacher."

this valuation correctly, one must not skip over the fact that a proposal bearing the title *De doctrina S. Thomae servanda* and tending toward canonizing the philosophy of Thomas was drafted in the run-up to the Council and then dismissed by the Council fathers—an event that was interpreted as "the end of Thomism's narrowly and mechanistically wielded normativity."[14] More than three decades after the Council, Pope John Paul II continued the magisterial esteem for the *Doctor communis* in his encyclical *Fides et Ratio* (September 14, 1998) and designated him as the "leading master and paragon for the study of theology," without however ascribing to him an exclusive monopoly.[15] In addition to (neo-) Thomism, other philosophical streams are also explicitly acknowledged.[16]

What is conspicuous in surveying these magisterial statements—consulted here somewhat in isolation from their context—is, on the one hand, the continuity of lofty estimation and, on the other, a certain attenuation in Thomas's authority that has been discernible since Vatican II. This attenuation remains unnoticed when isolated voices, having recourse to the magisterial statements quoted earlier, recall the "singular authority and perennial validity"[17] of the *Doctor angelicus* and promote the "timeless wisdom"[18] of his thinking, holding it up as a therapeutic agent for a theology that is losing its own standing more and more in the nexus of engagements with the human and philosophical sciences. However, just as one rightly acknowledges the Gothic cathedrals and the scholastic *summae* as paradigmatic expressions of the high Middle Ages,[19] so also neo-Gothic architecture of the nineteenth century is attended by overtones of anachronism,

---

14. Pesch, *Thomas von Aquino / Thomismus / Neothomismus*, 462.

15. John Paul II, *Fides et Ratio*, §78. See also §57f.

16. Ibid., §59. Benedict XVI, whose own theology is without doubt characterized more by Augustine and Bonaventure, made the appraisal, little noticed up to this point but certainly noteworthy, that Thomas Aquinas is "the greatest theologian of the west" ("Address at the Cathedral of Cologne," 20th World Youth Day [18 August 2005]).

17. See D. Berger, *Was ist ein Sakrament? Der hl. Thomas von Aquin und die Sakramente im allgemeinen* (Sieburg: Franz Schmitt, 2004), 19.

18. See D. Berger, *Thomas Aquinas and the Liturgy*, 2nd edition (Naples: Sapientia Press, 2005), 10: "The relevance of the angelic teacher's doctrine shows itself in its unfamiliarity; where it breaks through those superficial plausibilities which support the faith propositions of the zeitgeist and which have created their own language in the widespread, daily jargon of the Church; where its timeless wisdom [sic] puts us into a state of painful and yet salutary unrest, which forces open the strictures of our thinking, drags us out of our house of timeliness in order to lead us to a timeless [sic] progress lying far above present controversies and scandals in theology as well as Church politics." This text is taken up in an identical fashion in *Was ist ein Sakrament?* 20.

19. See E. Panofsky, *Gothic Architecture and Scholasticism* (New York: Archabbey Press, 1957; Cologne: DuMont, 1989). The thesis that Gothic architecture is Scholasticism become stone has admittedly been received in art history rather reservedly or even negatively. See the summary review by W. Beckermann, in *Concilium Medii Aaevi* 1 (1998): 1000–1013.

despite all of its handiwork and precision.[20] Something analogous may be said of the neoscholastic effort to take up again a "philosophy of earlier times" (Joseph Kleutgen), an effort that indeed presents a distinctive and consciously chosen strategy to react to the challenges of the Enlightenment; it is a strategy, however, that relies less upon dialogical exchange and testing the opposing arguments in a soberly critical way and more upon marking various positions in an apologetic manner—thus differing from its principal witness, Thomas Aquinas. Those who represented neo-Scholasticism and neo-Thomism indisputably deserve credit for launching a serious and intensive engagement with the medieval traditions of philosophy and theology, as well as for initiating new critical editions of the most important thinkers of the scholastic period. The way that neo-Scholasticism is often presented in the newer histories of theology—as a negative foil for the new theological awakenings of the twentieth century—may therefore be partially in need of revision. All the same, neo-Scholasticism brought along with it what was "to a large extent a dry formalism and an overemphasis on arguments from authority, as well as an unhistorical way of thinking which failed furthermore to integrate adequately—or even at all, in some cases—modern currents in thinking."[21]

In light of this background, the present study shifts the work of Thomas Aquinas into a historical perspective. In an exemplary way, Thomas undertook an engagement with the questions of *his* time, with the texts of the *corpus aristotelicum* leading the way, texts that were forbidden at the time and were discussed with great controversy. The challenges to theology *today* arose more than 700 years later through thinkers such as Kant, Hegel, Nietzsche, Freud, Heidegger, Habermas, and Derrida, to name a few. But these were *not* the challenges faced by Thomas, and one should not assume he gave answers to questions that were posed only centuries later and with clearly altered intellectual presuppositions. This *historical difference* in hermeneutical points of departure is emphatically stressed in this work in order to make clear that current efforts to establish a new iteration of Thomism (which, as already implied, is itself a complex entity)[22] still present a project that is doubtless *anachronistic*. Even if the *anachronism* is promoted in the sense of "unseasonable,"[23] such a characterization still re-

---

20. Giving a reappraisal of church architecture is the recent contribution by Chr. K. Steger, *Nur neugotisch? Das pastorale Programm im historistischen Kirchenbau 1870 bis 1914* (Regensburg: Pustet, 2013).
21. P. Walter, "Neuscholastik, Neuthomismus," *LThK* 7 (1997, 3d edition): 779–82, here 781.
22. See the instructive article offering an overview: K. Obenauer, "Thomas von Aquin—IV. Thomism," *LThK* 9, 3d edition (2000): 1517–22 (Lit.).
23. See D. Berger, "'S. Thoma praesertim magistro ...': Überlegungen zur Aktualität des Thomismus,"

mains vague if the productive unseasonability of Thomas is not brought to bear on a concrete engagement with contemporary questions. At any rate, Berger's plea for a resuscitation of the Thomistic *philosophia et theologia perennis* falls short of his principal witness, Thomas Aquinas, since it largely disregards the open-ended dispute with the current *signa temporis*, or else carries on its diagnosis of the times under auspices that are a priori negative. To take up our earlier comparison once again, as Gothic quotations in the design prose of postmodern architecture can certainly be appealing, so too neo-Thomism can augment the current spectrum of theories with a position that finds resonance with some, precisely because of its contrast to contemporary currents of thought that are skeptical of the truth. All things considered, we may say with Joseph Ratzinger that, in today's world, "a simple repristination of a thoroughgoing Thomism" is "certainly not the way."[24]

It would be just as much a mistake, however, to suppose that the abandonment of neo-Scholasticism renders the theological heritage of Thomas Aquinas obsolete. There is among some systematic theologians of the present time a noticeable tendency to transition from the historical-critical exaltation of the so-called biblical "evidence" immediately into systematic-theological penetration without consulting the epochal mediating figures of the theological tradition—this could lead to a peculiar forgetfulness of tradition and history. Thus it is profitable to call to mind the Rahnerian exhortation and to attempt a *rereading* of a thinker who shaped the theological tradition of the Occident as perhaps no other did. It is conceivable that the present hour is indeed especially opportune for such a *rereading*, for since neo-Scholasticism is now considered a thing of the past and has itself become strongly appreciated as a subject of theological-historical research, the engagement with Thomas Aquinas has been freed from the constraint of reading his work forward in time as manifesting prospective answers relevant to modern questions. It was years ago that the epistemological interest of certain interpreters of Thomas, trying to instill his thought with modern relevance, occasioned the ironic remark of the philosopher Odo Marquard: "The Thomists have interpreted Thomas so differently, perhaps it is time to change him."[25]

LThK 15 (1999) 180–92, here 185–87. The figure of the "contemporaneity of the non-contemporaneous," which Berger also develops elsewhere (see *Thomas Aquinas and the Liturgy*, 9; *Was ist ein Sakrament?* 20), traces back to Ernst Bloch, who interprets it in the sense of a (neo)Marxist theory of history, a discussion in which Thomas Aquinas certainly does not have the standing that Berger aims to ascribe to him. See E. Bloch, *Heritage of Our Times*, trans. Neville and Stephen Plaice (Berkeley/Los Angeles: Wiley, 1991), 104–16.

24. Benedict XVI (J. Ratzinger), *Eschatology: Death and Eternal Life*, 2nd edition (Washington, D.C.: The Catholic University of America Press, 2007), 181.

25. Thus—in dependence on the eleven theses of K. Marx regarding Feuerbach—O. Marquard,

Beyond this, the historical research into Thomas, which goes back further than Thomism to reveal the authentic teaching of Aquinas, has produced impressive results that can be built upon.[26] This research has not only taken a closer look at the genesis of his thinking in relation to particular questions, but also elaborated more precisely the context in which his work is embedded. In particular, greater attention is given today to the long-neglected connection between theology and spirituality, between doctrine and life.[27]

Finally, a renewed engagement with a classical figure such as Thomas Aquinas is enriching for contemporary dogmatic theology for yet another reason: in such an engagement, not only does contemporary theology learn high formal standards for the theological enterprise, but also it can think with and through a paradigmatically speculative penetration of the deposit of faith. None other than Karl Barth highlighted these qualities in his *Church Dogmatics*: "In the two *Summae* of Thomas we enter the sphere of the most calm and sober enquiry and teaching, of the strictest method and of corresponding statement—a sphere where nothing unnecessary, but everything necessary is said, and what is said is controlled by everything else and by its immediate and remote contexts, so that there are no mere assertions, but every statement ventured is proved with refreshing conscientiousness."[28] The hermeneutical difference between the age of high Scholasticism and our own can be made use of productively in theological discourse if the current questions of interest are articulated candidly. Instead of measuring Thomas's work immediately in terms of whether and to what extent it holds the potential to answer the questions posed today, the present study will attempt—with all the unfamiliarity of language and form of

---

Schwierigkeiten mit der Geschichtsphilosophie, 4th ed. (Frankfurt/Mainz: Suhrkamp, 1994), 170 (in the view of J. B. Metz, *Christliche Anthropozentrik: Über die Denkform des Thomas von Aquin* [Munich: Kösel, 1962]).

26. For just an overview of the research, see the following summary works: J. A. Weisheipl, *Friar Thomas d'Aquino: His Life, Thought, and Works* (Garden City, N.Y.: Doubleday, 1983); O. H. Pesch, *Thomas von Aquin: Grenze und Größe mittelalterlicher Theologie: Eine Einführung* (Mainz: Matthias-Grünewald, 1988); J.-P. Torrell, *Saint Thomas Aquinas*, vol. 1: *The Person and His Work*, trans. Robert Royal (Washington, D.C.: The Catholic University of America Press, 2005); T. F. O'Meara, *Thomas Aquinas Theologian* (Notre Dame, Ind.: Notre Dame University Press, 1997); etc.

27. See J.-P. Torrell, *Saint Thomas Aquinas*, vol. 2: *Spiritual Master* (Washington, D.C.: The Catholic University of America Press, 2003).

28. K. Barth, *Church Dogmatics* III/3: *The Doctrine of Creation*, ed. Bromiley/Torrance (Edinburgh: T&T Clark Ltd, 1960), 391. See also the appreciation of J. Habermas in conversation with E. Mendieta, found in J. Manemann, ed., *Befristete Zeit* (Jahrbuch Politische Theologie 3) (Münster: LIT, 1999), 190–209, here 194: "When I look into the 'Summa contra Gentiles' of Thomas Aquinas, I am spellbound by the complexity, the level of differentiation, the seriousness and rigor of the dialogically constructed argumentation. I am an admirer of Thomas. He represents an intellectual figure who was able by himself to vouch for his own authenticity. That there is no longer such a bluff today amidst the surf of dissolving religiosity is also simply a fact."

argumentation[29]—first of all to trace Thomas's own movement of thinking. Only after attending to a close textual reconstruction can and should the conversation with contemporary questions of interest be taken up. In the course of this procedure, it will become apparent that certain limits of Thomas's theology will reveal themselves in light of contemporary theology, as well as the reverse, that certain limits of contemporary theology will reveal themselves in light of Thomas's theology. With a view to Eucharistic theology, for example, the hermeneutical pre-judgment that is current today—that Thomas Aquinas foreshortened the view of the Eucharistic mystery with his theological concentration on the when and how of consecration—would need to be examined in light of the texts and, to turn the tables, cross-examined with the question of whether a Eucharistic theology that one-sidedly picks up on the communal and prandial aspects is not also in danger of curtailing the mystery of the Eucharistic presence of Jesus Christ in the gifts of bread and wine.

2. The Theology and Poetry of the Eucharist in Thomas Aquinas

> Let us make our own the words of St. Thomas Aquinas, an eminent theologian and an impassioned poet of Christ in the Eucharist.
>
> John Paul II[30]

In the present work, the central focus of our attention is the Eucharistic theology of Thomas Aquinas as it is found, in its most mature conceptual expression, in the *Tertia pars* of the *Summa theologiae*. As a complement to this, the Eucharistic hymns from the Divine Office for the solemnity of Corpus Christi, as well as the hymn *Adoro te devote*, will be drawn into the investigation. In this way, the relationship between theology and poetry in Thomas Aquinas will become an explicit object of inquiry. While the relationship between theology and poetry has been extensively discussed in recent years under the headings "literary theology" and "theo-poetry," it has been first and foremost the literary output of modern writers that has

---

29. "Invariably, at first contact with a scholastic text"—writes Chenu—"a modern reader cannot get away from the impression that he has just entered into a strange world. Even if he is familiar with Latin, he is baffled by any of the following: the machinery through which the author conveys his thought; the line of argument that he follows throughout; his parcelling out of his subject matter; his monotonous repeating of formulas; his ever-recurring use of divisions, subdivisions, and distinctions; the distressing impersonality of his style" (M.-D. Chenu, *Toward Understanding Saint Thomas*, trans. A.-M. Landry and D. Hughes [Chicago: Regnery Publishing, 1964], 59). Similarly, Pesch, *Thomas von Aquin*, 49ff.

30. John Paul II, Encyclical Letter *Ecclesia de Eucharistia*, §62.

stood front and center;[31] the viewpoint of the present work, however, will be directed to the theo-poetic potential of a medieval theologian, whose hymns have thus far garnered little attention in academic theology.[32] Moreover, it should also be highlighted that these hymns were written for the Divine Office of Corpus Christi at the express instruction of Pope Urban IV and thus they each fulfill a particular function in the liturgical texts of the solemnity. All the same, it would be false simply to subsume them under the rubric of customary religious poetry or to dismiss them as secondary commissioned work of the *Doctor communis*—for all liturgy disrupts the purposes of the workaday world. It serves for "the glorification of God and therein the salvation of man."[33] Man's liturgical service to God, which responds to God's service to man, transcends the present to reach the time of salvation, which spans past, present, and future. Grateful remembrance of the divine acts of salvation is intertwined with a plea for the making present of salvation and hope of eschatological consummation. In the hymns for Corpus Christi, the Eucharistic structure of time plays an important role. Corresponding to the meaning of the solemnity, it is above all joy and thanks regarding the gift of Jesus Christ's presence in the Eucharist that are expressed. But the other motifs characterizing the Eucharistic theology of Aquinas are also poetically brought together here. Thus, the present work will attempt to show that the hymns can be read as a *poetic distillation of the Eucharistic theology* of Thomas Aquinas.

The integration of the hymns demands, moreover, that we consider more precisely the *literary genus* and keep before our eyes the methodological difference between theology as scientific speech *about* God and prayer as

---

31. See K.-J. Kuschel, *Im Spiegel der Dichter: Mensch, Gott und Jesus in der Literatur des 20. Jahrhunderts* (Düsseldorf: Patmos, 1997); H. Schröer, G. Fermor, and H. Schroeter, eds., *Theopoesie. Theologie und Poesie in hermeneutischer Sicht* (Rheinbach: CMZ Verlag, 1998); J.-H. Tück, "Gelobt seist du Niemand." Paul Celans Dichtung—eine theologische Provokation (Frankfurt/Mainz: Josef-Knecht, 2000); J. Bauke-Ruegg, *Theologishe Poetik und literarische Theologie? Systematisch-theologische Streifzüge* (Zurich: Theologischer Verlag, 2004); G. Langenhorst *Theologie und Literatur. Ein Handbuch* (Darmstadt: Wissenschaftliche Buchgesellschaft, 2005); M. Kutzer, *In Wahrheit erfunden. Dichtung als Ort theologischer Erkenntnis* (Regensburg: Pustet, 2006); J.-H. Tück, *Hintergrundgeräusche. Liebe, Tod und Trauer in der Gegenwartsliteratur* (Ostfildern: Matthias-Grünewald, 2010); J.-H. Tück and A. Bieringer, eds., "Verwandeln allein durch Erzählen." Peter Handke im Spannungsfeld von Theologie und Literaturwissenschaft (Freiburg: Herder, 2014).

32. See however: A. Stock, *Poetische Dogmatik. Christologie*, vol. 3: *Leib und Leben* (Paderborn: Schöningh, 1998), 305–24; O.-Th. Venard, *Thomas d'Aquin. Poète théologien*, vol. 2 (Genf: Ad Solem, 2003–2004), who undertakes rather a discursive analysis of the *Summa theologiae* and only sporadically deals with the hymns; so also R. Cantalamessa, *This is My Body : Eucharistic Reflections Inspired by Adoro Te Devote and Ave Verum*, trans. A. Neame (Boston: Pauline Books and Media, 2005) and A. Stock, *Mittelalterliche Hymnen* (Berlin: Insel Verlag, 2012).

33. See W. Kasper, *Sakrament der Einheit. Eucharistie und Kirche* (Freiburg-Basel-Vienna: Herder, 2004), 16 [Eng.: *Sacrament of Unity: The Eucharist and the Church* (New York: The Crossroad Publishing Company, 2004)]: this corresponds quite well to the view of Aquinas, who distinguishes the *cultus divinus* and the *santificatio hominis* in the performance of the sacraments. See S. *th.* III, q. 60, a. 5 c.

faithful speaking *with* God. The Italian poet Boccaccio (1313–75) once noted in his work *Vita di Dante*: "I say that theology and poesy may be called nearly the same thing, for their object is one and the same. Furthermore, I even say that theology is nothing more than a poem about God."[34] This remark can well be applied to the relationship between theological reflection on the Eucharist and poetic hymnody in Thomas Aquinas. Both forms agree on the fact that they have one and the same object: Jesus Christ, who bequeathed to man a *gift of his presence* in the form of bread and wine. Whereas, on the one hand, theology—supported first by revelation as attested in the biblical writings—considers the sacramental self-gift of Jesus in the Eucharist and reflects on the conditions of its realization, the hymns, on the other hand, as religious activities in speech, occupy themselves with praising the Eucharistic presence of Jesus Christ and giving thanks to God for this gift. Unlike Boccaccio, therefore, one will have to designate the reflections of the *Summa theologiae* not simply as "poetry about God,"[35] but rather as a discursive effort of *intellectus fidei*,[36] whereas the hymnic poetry articulates theology's consciously scaled-back posture of one praying before God. Precisely in the hymns it becomes conspicuous that Thomas "was not only a philosophical and theological thinker, not only a university professor, but also a mystic visionary, a saint."[37]

In his book *Introduction à l'étude de saint Thomas d'Aquin*, Marie-Dominique Chenu drew attention to the difference between literary genres, a difference of which Thomas availed himself in his writings.[38] Plato authored dialogues; Augustine, *Confessiones*; Thomas Aquinas, commentaries and *summas*, above all. This is no accident. Thomas is a Master of Theology; nearly everything he writes and publishes is a fruit of his teaching, first as *baccalaureus biblicus* and then as *magister in theologia et sacra pagina*. This

---

34. G. Boccaccio, *Tutte le opere*, vol. 3, *Vita di Dante*, ed. V. Branca (Milan: Mondadori, 1974), 475: "Dico che la teologia e la poesia quasi una cosa si possono dire, dove uno medesima sia il suggetto; anzi dico più: che la teologia niuna altra cosa è che una poesia di Dio." See, by the same, *Das Leben Dantes*, trans. O. Frhr. von Taube (Frankfurt/Mainz: Insel Verlag, 1987), 57.

35. See also the word of F. Petrarca: "Poesy certainly does not stand in opposition to theology. I would almost like to say that theology is a poesy coming forth from God" (quoted from W. Barner in the epilogue to G. Boccaccio, *Das Leben Dantes*, 85–99, here 98. See also E. R. Curtius, *Europäische Literatur und lateinisches Mittelalter* (Tübingen et al.: Francke, 1993, 11th edition). Eng.: *European Literature and the Latin Middle Ages*, trans. W. R. Trask (Princeton, N.J.: Princeton University Press, 1991).

36. On the understanding of theology as *sacra doctrina* in Thomas, see the explanation by H. Hoping, *Weisheit als Wissen des Ursprungs. Philosophie und Theologie in der "Summa contra gentiles" des Thomas von Aquin* (Freiburg: Herder, 1997), 71–94.

37. J. Pieper, *Guide to Thomas Aquinas*, trans. Richard and Clara Winston (London: Faber and Faber, 1962), 16. On July 18, 1323—so not even fifty years after his death—Thomas Aquinas was canonized by John XXII, and on April 15, 1567—certainly also in view of the Counter-Reformation—he was designated as *Doctor ecclesiae*.

38. M.-D. Chenu, *Toward Understanding Saint Thomas*, 79–125.

has ramifications on language. Thomas does not speak and write the classical Latin of antiquity. The Ciceronian eloquence brought to life again by the humanists of the sixteenth century is alien to Thomas. He writes—as Chenu says—"the 'barbaric' Latin of the Middle Ages."[39] It is a technical language, a scholastic language that is spoken in the context of the university and must be beneficial for the university's linguistic community, which is composed of participants of the most diverse origins; it is formal, impersonal, and without aesthetic appeal. Utility and conceptual precision stand in the foreground;[40] the ideal of scientific knowledge, which finds a congenial instrument in the *quaestio disputata*, demands a diction that is *breviter et dilucide*.[41] Literary prolixity and stylistic means of rhetoric such as metaphor, parable, and allegory do not agree with the scholastic understanding of science. Thomas explicitly criticizes Plato's poetic language.[42] "In like manner, he reduced to rational factors what the mystics had to say about mystical experience and their amplified description of affective states, doing the same with the tropes and figures of Scripture."[43] When Thomas composes a *lectio*, it is devoted entirely to the explanation of a text at hand; when he crafts a *quaestio*, it goes beyond textual exposition to deal with the conflict between diverse positions on a particular problem and then to advance a unique solution (*solutio / responsio*) after weighing the *pro* and *contra* arguments. It is not surprising that the literary genus of both requires a conceptually precise, academically oriented language that neutralizes subjective or even affective moments. The same holds for the strictly regulated procedure of the public *disputatio*, which found its literary reflection *en miniature* in the articles of the *Summa theologiae*.[44] "The *Summa* was not written and [therefore] cannot be read as a sermon of St. Bernard or a chapter from *The Imitation of Christ*."[45]

39. Ibid., 104.
40. See J. Leclercq, *L'amour des letters et le désir de Dieu* (Paris: Cerf, 1957). In German: *Wissenschaft und Gottverlangen. Zur Mönchstheologie des Mittelalters* (Düsseldorf: Patmos, 1963), 166f.: "The scholastic language knows nothing of adornment, it is abstract and uses words from a unique technical language inattentive to beauty; the only thing that matters is that the words are conceptually precise."
41. S. th. I, prol.
42. See *In An*. I, 8 (nn. 3–13); *In Phys*. I, 15 (n. 138); *In Cael*. I, 22 (n. 228); *In Met*. I, 15 (n. 231); *De div. nom*., prol.
43. Chenu, *Toward Understanding Saint Thomas*, 119.
44. See F. A. Blanche, "Le vocabulaire de l'argumentation et la structure de l'article dans les ouvrages de S. Thomas," *RSPhTh* 14 (1925): 167–87. The structure of an article images in miniature form the course of a scholastic disputation. First, the objections (*obiectiones*) are listed with the precursor *videtur quod*, after which there follows in the *sed contra* an alternative to the objections—generally in the form of a quotation that brings an *auctoritas* into play—whereupon, finally, the answer of the master (*respondeo dicendum*) ensues in the *corpus articuli*, which amounts to a *determinatio magistralis* and simultaneously provides the basis for rebuttal of the objections adduced at the beginning.
45. Chenu, *Das Werk des hl. Thomas von Aquin*, 121.

12   INTRODUCTION

All the more remarkable is the fact that Thomas Aquinas, in whose work the speculative penetration of the truths of faith found a most elevated form, also composed hymns and prayers. The spirituality of Thomas, which in any case is noticeable in a hidden way in his scientific works, is articulated more openly in his hymns. Here also the treatment of language is bound up with particular regularities. Meter and rhyme provide a formal structure, which presents demands on the poetic diction that are far from easy to fulfill. The conciseness of the form requires a thematic concentration, but also opens up the possibility of considering diverse aspects through a single lens and of undertaking a distillation of references. It is precisely in the poetic art of paucity that we find a likely reason for the tremendous history of the reception enjoyed by the Eucharistic hymns of Thomas. Over the course of centuries, the hymns have belonged to the festive treasury of Catholic Eucharistic piety; not a few composers have drawn inspiration from them to create impressive musical settings; such a poet as Dante emphatically honored Thomas's poetic qualities in the *Divina Commedia*;[46] and in his *Autos sacramentales* the Spanish Baroque playwright Calderón de la Barca staged a poetic competition in which Thomas Aquinas and his hymn *Pange lingua* do not take second place even to the rhetorical power of the Church fathers Ambrose, Augustine, Gregory the Great, and Jerome.[47] If the estimation of George Steiner is accurate, wherein he states that poets have a particularly marked sense for the quality of poetry and that literary works that comment on other works of literature (as Calderón did on the hymns *Pange lingua*) belong to the most important witnesses of literary criticism,[48] then in the case of Aquinas we have occasion to ask whether the widespread image of "unmusical Thomas"[49] ought to be submitted to a revision. At any rate, the Eucharistic hymns reveal another side of the *Doctor communis*, a side of which too little notice has been taken in academic theology. He was not only a philosophically and likewise theologically adept thinker but also a man of profound prayer, who brought his speculative considerations into his meditative contemplation as well. Precisely his prayers enable the spiritual subtext of his theology to be unveiled. In this respect, an inquiry into his poetic theology always has the additional task of raising the question of the relationship between dogma

46. See Dante Alighieri, *Divina Commedia* [Eng.: *Paradise*, trans. Anthony Esolen (New York: Modern Libary, 2004)], Paradiso X–XIV.
47. See Calderón de la Barca, *Geistliche Festspiele*, vol. 7, ed. and trans. H. Lorinser (Regensburg: Manz, 1888), 223–333: St. Parnass (*El sacro Parnasso*).
48. Thus G. Steiner, *Real Presences* (London: University of Chicago Press, 1989), 24–39.
49. See O. H. Pesch, *Thomas von Aquin*, 343–52.

and life, between theology and holiness, a relation that since the thirteenth century has become precarious.[50]

3. Theme and Interest in the Question

It would be methodologically naïve to believe that one could present the main features of Eucharistic theology "objectively" without "subjective" pre-selections and interests flowing into the treatment of the material. The central interest of this work should therefore be expressly stated.

This study bears the title *Gift of Presence*. In this title, two aspects of Eucharistic theology are bound together: reflection on the real *presence* of Jesus Christ in the Eucharist together with its character as sacrosanct *gift*, indeed the self-gift of the glorified Christ. Indeed, the *verba testamenti* articulate both aspects, when they place after the *hoc est corpus meum* (real presence) the further determination *quod pro vobis tradetur* (self-gift of Jesus Christ). It is well known that Thomas conceptually designated the mode of the sacramental making present using the explanatory model of transubstantiation. To this end, he referred to the Aristotelian concepts of "substance" and "accident," in order to pursue a theological way toward the Eucharist that weaved between the Scylla of a crude sacramental realism, on the one hand, and the Charybdis of a spiritualistic symbolism, on the other. This middle way alone corresponds to the meaning of the words of institution as witnessed by the New Testament. All the same, he did not— as is so often remarked—falsify or alienate the biblical guidelines by using Aristotelian philosophy; the contrary is rather the case, as he transformed Aristotle's intellectual tools to make them adequate to the meaning of the *verba testamenti* as witnessed to in the biblical deposit. Accordingly—and this can hardly be underscored clearly enough—the doctrine of transubstantiation follows a fundamental impulse that is profoundly *biblical*.

Beyond conceptually clarifying the mode of sacramental presence, Thomas Aquinas also indicated that the Eucharist is a *memoriale passionis Christi*. This designation contains a hint that the Eucharistic theology of Aquinas can be adequately understood only if it is tied back to the theology of the Passion. Now, while transubstantiation seeks to describe the *modus* of the sacramental making present and thus the *how* of the real presence, the characterization of the Eucharist as *memoriale passionis Christi* identi-

---

50. See H. U. von Balthasar, "Theology and Sanctity," in *Explorations in Theology*, vol. 1: *The Word Made Flesh* (San Francisco: Ignatius Press, 1989), 181–209. On this point also, see J. Servais, "'Weisheit, Wissen und Freude.' Zur Überwindung einer verhängnisvollen Diastase," in *Die Kunst Gottes verstehen. Hans Urs von Balthasars theologische Provokationen*, ed. M. Striet and J. H. Tück (Freiburg: Herder, 2005), 320–48.

fies the *contents*, hence the *what* of the sacrament. The relationship between the last supper, Passion, and Eucharist calls therefore for further investigation. Already at the last supper, Jesus interpreted—in anticipation of the Passion—his death in meaningful words and gestures as an act of self-gift. This promissory self-gift was honored on the cross and is further elucidated in the soteriological passages of the *Summa theologiae*, which draw on the complex motif of *traditio*. In this respect, it is also constitutive for the Eucharist, as Jesus Christ himself imparts ever anew his salutary presence in the forms of bread and wine through the ongoing course of history. The interim between ascension and parousia is bridged, as the giver, who *in propria specie* is himself absent, imparts his presence *in specie sacramenti*. Simultaneously, however, the living bread (*panis vivus et vitalis*) offers a foretaste of impending glory.

Tied up with viewing these conceptual linkages is a certain correction of current judgments regarding Aquinas's Eucharistic theology. Thus, the "tendency to a progressive 'reification' of the understanding of the Eucharist" is attributed to him.[51] Through focusing on the question of the real presence and working out the doctrine of transubstantiation—so runs an oft-uttered accusation[52]—Thomas abetted a consequential constriction that led to a neglect of other central aspects of the Eucharist. The *presence of the glorified Lord*, which Johannes Betz comprehended under the concept of "principal actual-presence" [*prinzipale Aktualpräsenz*],[53] recedes into the background in Thomas's thinking on Eucharistic theology just as much as the *remembrance of his salvific deeds*, the "commemorative actual-presence." In the end, the theological concentration on the moment of consecration has dulled the *communio* and prandial character as well as stunted the awareness of the liturgy of the Eucharist.[54]

---

51. See, for example, G. Koch, *Sakramentenlehre*, in *Glaubenszugänge. Lehrbuch der Katholischen Dogmatik*, vol. 3, ed. W. Beindert (Paderborn: Schöningh, 1995), 434.

52. Thus B. J. Hilberath and Th. Schneider speak of "the considerable *constriction* of perspective which came about through the *fixation* on the somatic real presence in the posing of the question" ("Eucharistie. Systematisch," in P. Eicher, ed., *Neues Handbuch Theologischer Grundbegriffe* [Munich: Kösel, 2005], 313–23, here 318). See also H. B. Meyer, *Eucharistie. Geschichte, Theologie, Pastoral* (Regensburg: Pustet, 1989), 227f.: "But the doctrine of transubstantiation also remained *fixated* on the somatic real presence. What was and remained forgotten was the actually present dimension of the Eucharistic celebration, which was bound up with reflection on the sacramental making present" (emphasis added).

53. J. Betz, "Eucharistie," in *LThK* 3, 2nd edition (1959), 1142–57, here 1154: "If the unity of the Eucharistic event is to be terminologically articulated in the multiplicity of its aspects, then the bodily presence of the person of Christ may be designated as *somatic real-presence*, the presumptive making present of the work of redemption as *commemorative actual-presence*, and the spiritually effective presence of the glorified Kyrios (of the *minister principalis*) as *principal actual-presence*" (emphasis added).

54. The division of the treatise on the Eucharist in *S. th.* III, qq. 73–83 appears to allow this assessment: after the question, whether the Eucharist is a sacrament (q. 73), Thomas raises the question about matter (q. 74) and the mode of Eucharistic conversion (q. 75), and then the manner of Christ's bodily presence

By way of contrast, the goal of the present study is to show that Thomas Aquinas did indeed shift the aspect of the "somatic real presence" of Christ in the consecrated bread and wine into the foreground, but in no way did he dismiss the other aspects—principal and commemorative actual-presence; celebration of the Eucharist in the course of a meal; the liturgy of the Eucharist. The *concentration* on the motif of real presence not only is theologically and historically conditioned by the general question that arose through the Eucharistic controversies of the ninth and eleventh centuries, a question Thomas and his contemporaries were given to solve; this concentration also has its source in the conviction that the biblically witnessed *verba testamenti* designate the essential *center* of the Eucharist—a conviction that is indeed hotly contested today.[55] At the same time, the fact that Thomas likewise designated the Eucharist as *memoriale passionis Christi* shows that he definitely held in view the aspect of the commemorative actual-presence. Furthermore, for him it is indisputable that Jesus Christ's somatic real presence in the consecrated gifts depends on the principal actual-presence of Jesus Christ, inasmuch as the priest executes the speech act precisely not in his own name but *in persona Christi*. Finally, the fact that Thomas devoted an entire *quaestio* to the rite of the Eucharist makes it profitable to ask the question whether the going image of scholastic theology's forgetfulness of the liturgy must at the very least be modified. After all, it could be that the diagnosis of a constriction of Eucharistic theology brought about by Thomas Aquinas is, in fact, a manifestation of a constricted reception of his work.

A further point demanding clarification is the question of the *personal* understanding of the Eucharist. The accusation is often levied upon Thomas—and scholastic sacramental theology generally—that by taking over Aristotelian categories and the strongly pronounced interest in questions of efficacy and validity of the sacraments, "the personal and dialogical dimen-

---

(q. 76) and the problem of the accidents remaining without a subject (q. 77), continuing with form (q. 78) and effect (q. 79) as well as use (q. 80), reception (q. 81), and the correct administration of the sacrament (q. 82). Only the closing question pertains to the rite of the Eucharist (q. 83). The question is, however, whether the thematic concentration on the moment of consecration and the ontological illumination of the event of Eucharistic conversion has, in fact, as its consequence that the other aspects of the Eucharist are lost.

55. Thus, parts of the German-speaking area of liturgical studies are dominated by the assessment that the post-patristic tradition of the Western, Latin liturgy was essentially an aberration. The fixation on the *verba institutionis*, the development of the doctrine of transubstantiation and the corresponding liturgical gesture of elevation—all of this obscured the fundamentally anamnetic and epicletic character of the Eucharistic prayer. See the exemplary study by R. Messner, *Die Meßreform Martin Luthers und die Eucharistie der Alten Kirche. Ein Beitrag zu einer systematischen Liturgiewissenschaft* (Innsbruck: Tyrolia, 1989). On the criticism that the Occidental liturgical development was an error, see the meta-critique carried out by D. Wendenbourg, "Den falschen Weg Roms zu Ende gegangen? Zur gegenwärtigen Diskussion über Martin Luthers Gottesdienstreform und ihr Verhältnis zu den Traditionen der Alten Kirche," in *ZThK* 94 (1997): 437–67.

sions of the [sacramental] event tend to be underexposed."[56] At first glance, this impression may apply to the systematic theological treatment of the Eucharist in the *Summa theologiae*. However, the perspective changes when one calls upon soteriology to clarify the term *passio Christi*, which—in a way different from the doctrine of satisfaction found in Anselm of Canterbury—relies more heavily upon the factual happenings of salvation history and seeks to unfold a perspective of personal freedom regarding the events of redemption. Casting a glance at the Eucharistic hymns also makes it nearly impossible to sustain the judgment of an impersonal and technical approach to the Eucharist. The poetic structure of a hymn such as *Adoro te devote* is dialogics become speech. This could point to the fact that beneath Thomas's austerely and technically worked out theology of the Eucharist lies a spiritual subtext characterized by a profoundly personal engagement that is rooted in a lived-in world of prayer, daily reading of Scripture, and the celebration of the Eucharist.

4. The Structure of the Work

This work is divided into three parts. Part A takes up a systematic reconstruction of the main lines in the *Summa theologiae*'s presentation of Eucharistic theology. The primary textual foundation is thus provided by the *Summa theologiae*, which was composed between 1265 and 1273 and in which Aquinas's theological reflection on the Eucharist found its most mature elaboration. In matters essential, the main features of Thomas's Eucharistic theology remained constant, and thus a genealogical approach to his works will be waived; all the same, the *Sentences* commentary, the *Summa contra gentiles*, as well as the scriptural commentaries will be drawn in to round out the perspective. The reconstruction itself comprises three sections: after preliminary clarifications on sacramental theology in general, which introduce pertinent categories and locate the Eucharist within the order of the sacraments, a second section entitled *"Hoc est corpus meum*—the Conversion of the Gifts" will work out the centerpiece of Thomas's Eucharistic theology: the doctrine of transubstantiation. The Eucharistic controversies of the ninth and eleventh centuries established the canon of questions at that time: *when, how,* and *by what means* bread and wine are transformed into the body and the blood of Christ, and *whether* Jesus Christ is present in the Eucharist *in signo* or *in veritate*. Thomas Aquinas took up these

---

56. See E.-M. Faber, *Einführung in die katholische Sakramentenlehre* (Darmstadt: Wissenschaftliche Bugesellschaft, 2002), 40.

questions and his attempt to solve them resulted in working out the doctrine of transubstantiation. This explanatory model has recourse to the categories of Aristotle in order to illuminate ontologically the mode of the sacramental making present; it is a model that has the ambition, which is not to be underappreciated, of standing in precise correspondence to the biblical meaning of the *verba testamenti*.[57] Thomas seeks to carry out this ambition in what is virtually a linguistic analysis of the formula of consecration, whose meaning he elucidates in contrast to other potential formulae. Finally, he illuminates the role of the priest, who performs the speech act of consecration not in his own name but *in persona Christi* and thus makes use of the principal actual-presence of the glorified Lord.

That Thomas's Eucharistic theology nonetheless does not admit of being reduced to the topic of Eucharistic conversion is what the third section attempts to show. Bearing the title "*Quod pro vobis tradetur*—the Representative Making Present of the Passion of Jesus Christ," it first works out the motif of Jesus Christ's self-gift. Over and over again, Thomas characterized the Eucharist as *memoriale passionis Christi* and thus expressly emphasized that the Eucharist is also a matter of making the salvific deeds of Jesus Christ sacramentally present, and hence the "commemorative actual-presence." After a historical flashback to the last supper, where Jesus, in the presence of his disciples, anticipates and interprets his upcoming death, there follow explications of the fittingness and drama of the Passion. In order to trace more precisely the semantic contours of the term *passio Christi*, we will call upon the interpretive categories drawn from the soteriological passages of the *Summa theologiae*, which seek to manifest the suffering of Christ in its salvific relevance. Through this analysis, it will become clear that Thomas draws upon a plurality of categories in order to illuminate the mystery of redemption from various vantage points, thus definitively breaking up the Anselmian conceptual monopoly related to the term *satisfactio*. At the same time, through a stronger interpretation based on personal freedom, the voluntary self-gift of Jesus Christ, his sacrifice on the cross, will be shown as the center of the event of redemption. The question of how this

---

57. Thomas is definitely conscious of the fact that the words of consecration used in the Church's liturgy present discrepancies when compared with the New Testament witness—indeed, that the New Testament tradition itself is not uniform (see *In Matth* XXVI, l. 4, n. 2200 and n. 2002; *In I Cor* XI, l. 6, n. 680). He ascribes the *verba consecrationis* to the tradition of the apostles (*S. th.* III, q. 78, a. 3 ad 9). It would be anachronistic to presuppose in the case of a theologian of high Scholasticism a consciousness of the problem engendered through the historical-critical inquiry into the genesis of the last supper tradition. For Thomas, it is certain that the consecration comes about through the fact that the minister recites the words of Jesus Christ himself: "If, therefore, the consecration would not have taken place then using these words, then it also would not take place now" (*S. th.* III, q. 78, a. 1 ad 1).

event, historically past and carried out once for all, can be upheld as actually present in the progress of history motivates a final inquiry into the way Christ's sacrifice is representatively made present in the celebration of the Eucharist. The explanation of the rite in the treatise on the Eucharist has been hitherto little noted, but it can reveal that Thomas sees the sacrifice of Christ as primarily represented in the act of consecration. Sacrament and sacrifice thus do not yet go their separate ways in his interpretation of the Eucharist, as would increasingly be the case in the Eucharistic theology of the late Middle Ages.

Part B stands under the heading "The Poetic Distillation of Eucharistic Theology in the Hymns." Some preliminary clarifications cast light upon the historical background of the Eucharistic hymns, before they briefly take up the genesis of the solemnity of Corpus Christi and recall that Thomas Aquinas was commissioned by Pope Urban IV to compose the liturgical texts for the Divine Office of Corpus Christi. It is stated early on that the liturgical texts of the Office gather nearly all of the Old Testament figures who point to the Eucharist.[58] But instead of examining the entire arrangement of the Divine Office in view of its biblical and patristic influences or commenting on it from the viewpoint of liturgical studies, the present examination concentrates on a theological interpretation of the hymns.[59] The long-debated question of authorship can be considered as settled after Pierre-Marie Gy's detailed study, which approaches the matter from the viewpoint of both theological and liturgical history. After a presentation of the arguments supporting the authenticity of the hymns, individual theological interpretations follow; the subjects of these interpretations are the hymns *Pange lingua*, *Sacris solemniis*, *Verbum supernum*, as well as the sequence *Lauda Sion* and, standing apart from the Office, the hymn *Adoro te devote*. In addition to analyses of the linguistic form, which seek to draw attention to the poetic *surplus*, we find here above all an interpretive working out of the main Eucharistic and theological motifs.

Part C presents *Eucharistic passages* that go beyond the theological and historical reconstruction and attempt to make them fruitful for a herme-

---

58. See C. le Brun-Gouanvic, ed., *Ystoria sancti Thome de Aquino de Guillaume de Tocco (1323)* (Toronto: Pontifical Institute of Mediaeval Studies, 1996), 133: "Scripsit officium de corpore Christi, de mandato Vrbani, in quo omnes que de hoc sunt sacramento ueteres figures exposuit, et ueritates que de noua sint gratia compulauit."

59. The study by R. Zawilla, "The Biblical Sources of the *Historiae Corporis Christi* Attributed to Thomas Aquinas" (PhD diss., University of Toronto, 1985) undertook a detailed examination of the Office of Corpus Christi, composed by Thomas, focusing upon the biblical verses referenced therein; that he explicitly excluded the hymns, however, provides additional motivation for a theological engagement with the Eucharistic poetry of Thomas.

neutical disclosure of the Eucharist today. First, an outline serves to illustrate both the significance of the epochal figures of Eucharistic theology as well as the limits of high Scholasticism in comparison with other historical manifestations of theology. A return to the last supper tradition of the New Testament as the normative foundation of theological reflection on the Eucharist should make it apparent that Jesus summarized his life and death in the twofold symbolic action over the bread and wine. Given this background, the question of whether the scholastic concentration on the *verba testamenti* ought to be criticized as a historical derailing of theology or liturgy or whether it can be appreciated as a proper unfolding of Jesus' self-gift as the Scriptures bear witness to it, is a question of its own. Jesus Christ makes himself pneumatically present in the Eucharistic signs—this provides the basis from which a certain reformulation of the doctrine of transubstantiation will be suggested, one which leans more heavily on categories of personal freedom. The glorified Lord himself is the one who draws the gifts of bread and wine into his own sphere of reality and thus makes them into pure signs of his presence. The "material" presence of these gifts can be kept free of the suspicion that an idol is involved if it is made clear *who* gives himself in them. A humble contribution toward overcoming the fateful diastasis between doctrine and life, theology and spirituality should thereby be achieved. In the hymns, we repeatedly encounter the idea that the Eucharist is a *viaticum* for the *homo viator*—provision, as it were, for man, who often hungers and thirsts spiritually en route to the "land of the living." According to Thomas, the *veiled* presence of the resurrected crucified one in the sacrament of the Eucharist is marked by a dynamic that tends toward the *unveiled*, face-to-face encounter. Thomas sang the praises of this dynamic in a language of longing and thus made plain that the Eucharist points beyond itself. It is not only a remembrance of suffering but also a reminder of a future that no longer knows of pain. In just this way, it can help us to traverse the way into the *terra viventium*: the passage from death to a life that no longer knows of death.

PART A

SYSTEMATIC RECONSTRUCTION

The Eucharistic Theology of the *Summa theologiae*

I

Preliminaries

> Without body: without sacrament. Angels only: no sacrament.
> Beasts only: no sacrament. Man: ... no escape from sacrament.
>
> David Jones

The Setting of the Treatise on the Eucharist in the Structure of the *Summa theologiae*

The writing of *summae*, which had its golden age between the twelfth and fourteenth centuries, may be considered "a paradigmatic manifestation of Scholasticism."[1] These *summae* offer a collection of traditional teaching material made as complete as possible using a rather additive method. But what Thomas undertakes differs from these *summae*; it differs also from the summary presentations or compendia in a particular area of teaching, which were kept very brief (*abbreviatio*). Instead, what Thomas attempts in his *Summa theologiae* is nothing less than to put forward a systematically ordered presentation of the whole science of faith. The pedagogical aim is to convey everything that belongs to the Christian religion in such a way that it serves the formation of beginners—the *eruditio incipientium*.[2] Before Thomas, there were—typologically oversimplified[3]—two principles of

---

Epigraph is from D. Jones, "Art and Sacrament," *Epoch and Artist: Selected Writings*, ed. H. Grisewood (London: Faber and Faber, 1972), 143–79, here 167.

1. R. Imbach, "Summa, Summenliteratur, Summenkommentare," *LThK* 9 (2000, 3rd edition): 1112–17, here 1112.

2. See *S. th.* I, prol.: "propositum nostrae intentionis in hoc opere est, ea quae ad Christianam religionem pertinent, eo modo tradere, secundum quod congruit ad eruditionem incipientium."

3. A rough overview sketching the contours of the twelfth century is offered by R. Heinzmann, "Der Plan der Summa Theologiae des Thomas von Aquin in der Tradition der frühscholastischen Systembildung," in *Thomas von Aquin. Interpretation und Rezeption: Studien und Texte*, ed. W. P. Eckert (Mainz: Matthias-

division. The one followed the model of salvation history and is found in an exemplary way in the summa *De sacramentis christianae fidei* by Hugh of St. Victor. In the first book, he treats of salvation history, from creation to Incarnation, and in the second, the events from the Incarnation to the consummation of the world.[4] The advantage of being oriented toward salvation history comes to Hugh at the price of a disadvantage, namely, a poor overview—no *ordo disciplinae* ever really becomes clear in the handling of the material. The second way of constructing a presentation follows not salvation history but a rational systematization. Abelard is certainly the most prominent representative of this type. He founded his *Theologia scholarium* on a logical, structured blueprint oriented toward the sequence *fides— caritas—sacramentum*.[5] After the mysteries of faith—Trinity, Creation, Incarnation—the fundamental characteristics of a Christian way of life are treated (*caritas*); in conclusion, Abelard goes into the theology of the sacraments. The merit of this logical and systematic principle of division is bound up with the disadvantage that the relevant *gesta divina* of salvation history recede from view.

With this as background, Thomas Aquinas put forward a complete outline in the *Summa theologiae*, an outline that avoided both a purely additive treatment of the material as well as an unordered presentation. His *ordo disciplinae* seeks to correspond to the *ordo rerum* and forms a unique synthesis of speculative penetration of the faith paired with biblical salvation history. To what extent the *Summa theologiae* owes its structure to its predecessors can remain an open question here.[6] Without elaborating once more the complex discussion concerning the structural plan of the theological *Summa*,[7] we may, following Marie-Dominique Chenu, Max Seckler,

---

Grünewald, 1974), 455–69 (which traces the contours of Peter Lombard, Peter of Poitiers, Simon of Tournai, Praepositinus, Master Hubertus).

4. See Hugh of St. Victor, *De sacramentis christianae fidei*, in PL 176, 173–618. In the *Prologus*, we read: "Primus liber a principio mundi usque ad incarnationem narrationis seriem ducit. Secundus liber ab incarnatione Verbi usque ad finem et consummationem omnium ordine procedit" (ibid., 173). See Hugh of St. Victor, *On the Sacraments of the Christian Faith*, trans. R. J. Deferrari (Cambridge, Mass.: The Mediaeval Academy of America, 1951), 3.

5. See Abaelard, *Theologia Scholarium*, I, 1, in *Opera theological*, vol. 3, ed. E. M. Buytaert, CCCM 13, 318, 1–2: "Tria sunt, ut arbitror, in quibus humanae salutis summa consistit, fides uidelicet, caritas et sacramentum." That this classificatory scheme—dogma, ethics, sacraments—worked to build up the school surrounding Abelard is shown by A. M. Landgraf, *Écrits théologiques de l'école d'Abélard. Textes inédits Louvain* (Louvain: Spicilegium Sacrum Lovaniense, 1934). See also D. E. Luscombe, *The Influence of Abaelard's Thought in the Early Scholastic Period* (Cambridge: Cambridge University Press, 1969), esp. 231ff.

6. R. Heinzmann pointed out that the *Summa "Colligite fragmenta"* of Master Hubertus is similarly structured, and he thus advocated the difficult to refute thesis that the plan of the *Summa theologiae* is already anchored in a specific tradition of teaching. See, by the same, "Der Plan der Summa Theologiae des Thomas von Aquin."

7. The last larger-scale contribution to the architectonic scheme of the *Summa theologiae* came from

and Otto Hermann Pesch,[8] affirm that Thomas developed his *ordo disciplinae* in dependence on the neoplatonic *exitus-reditus* scheme,[9] but not without tying the question of the origin and end of all things to a decisively salvation-historical perspective. Theology is science concerning God, and all things are considered in reference to God—*sub ratione Dei*—whether it be with a view to their origin (*principium*) or to their end (*finis*).[10] Into this formal scheme of *exitus* and *reditus*, which Thomas had already invoked as the principle dividing the material in his *Sentences* commentary,[11] each thing, each being, each action can be inscribed in the ultimate foundational context, recognized within it, and considered in view of it. To this it can be added that the scheme—despite its fundamental cyclical structure[12]—is open to the contingent events of salvation history. In this way, Thomas integrates the teaching about diverse states of salvation—*status naturae, gratiae,*

W. Metz, *Die Architektonik der Summa theologiae des Thomas von Aquin. Zur Gesamtansicht des thomasischen Gedankens* (Hamburg: Meiner, 1998). Metz seeks to replace what had until then been the generally agreed upon threefold interpretive key—namely the triad, the *exitus* of creatures from God (I), the *reditus* of creatures to God (II), and Christ as the way of *reditus* (III)—with the Aristotelian triad, *theoria—praxis—poiesis*. This comes with the price, however, of qualifying as peripheral accessories the salvation historical passages, such as the treatise on the work of the six days, the theology of the old law, and the mysteries of Jesus' life. On this point, see M. von Perger, "Theologie und Werkstruktur bei Thomas von Aquin. Wilhelm Metz' Studie zur *Summa theologiae*," *FZThPh* (2001): 191–208, as well as the review by O. H. Pesch that oscillates between approval and critique, in *ThRv* 97 (2002): 60–63.

8. See M.-D. Chenu, "Le plan de la Somme théologique de Saint Thomas," *Revue Thomiste* 47 (1939): 93–107 [in German: *Der Plan der 'Summa'*, found in *Thomas von Aquin*, vol. I, ed. K. Bernath (*Chronologie und Werkanalyse*) (Darmstadt: Wissenschaftliche Buchgesellschaft, 1978), 173–95]; Chenu, *Introduction à l'étude de saint Thomas d'Aquin* (Paris: Institut d'Études Médiévales, 1950) [Eng.: *Toward Understanding Saint Thomas* (Chicago: Regnery Publishing, 1964), 301–18]; U. Horst, "Über die Frage einer heilsökonomischen Theologie bei Thomas von Aquin," *MThZ* 12 (1961) 97–111; M. Seckler, *Das Heil in der Geschichte. Geschichtstheologisches Denken bei Thomas von Aquini* (Munich: Kösel, 1964), 33–47; O. H. Pesch, "Um den Plan der Summa Theologiae. Zu Max Secklers neuem Deutungsversuch," in *Thomas von Aquin*, vol. I, ed. K. Bernath, 411–37; Pesch, *Thomas von Aquin*, 381–400.

9. E. Schillebeeckx takes another point of view, disputing the influence of the cyclical *exitus-reditus* scheme and wanting instead to discern in the sequence creation, gracing, and sacraments a step-wise advancing, and thus progressive line of development. See, idem., *De sacramentale heilseconomie* (Antwerp: Bilthoven, 1952), 1–18 (also recently accessible in French translation: *L' économie sacramentelle du salut* [Fribourg: Academic Press Fribourg, 2004]). R. Heinzmann, who called attention to similarly structured *Summae* in the theology of the twelfth century, passes judgment rather reservedly on the *exitus-reditus* scheme; see his *Die Theologie auf dem Weg zur Wissenschaft. Zur Entwicklung der theologischen Systematik in der Scholastik*, found in *MThZ* 25 (1974) 1–17.

10. See *S. th.* I, q. 1, a. 8: "Omnia autem pertractantur in sacra doctrina sub ratione Dei: vel quia sunt ipse Deus; vel quia habent ordinem ad Deum, ut ad principium et finem." In view of the doctrine of the four causes, speaking of God as *principium omnium* can also be related to the *causa efficiens*, while speaking of God as the *finis omnium* can be related to the *causa finalis*.

11. In the *Sentences* commentary, the division of the material already can be recognized as a linguistic echo of the *exitus-reditus* scheme: "Cum enim sacrae doctrinae intentio sit circa divina, divinum autem sumitur secundum relationem ad Deum vel ut principium vel ut finem, consideratio huius *doctrinae* erit de *rebus* secundum quod exeunt [sic!] a Deo ut a principio, et secundum quod referentur in ipsum ut in finem. Unde in prima parte determinat de rebus divinis secundum exitum [sic!] a principio; in secunda secundum reditum ad finem" (*In I Sent.*, d. 2, div. text., emphasis mine). See also the prologues of *In I Sent.* and *In III Sent.*

12. See on this point M. Seckler, *Das Heil in der Geschichte*, 28–31.

gloriae—and also times in salvation history—*tempus ante legem, sub lege, sub gratia*—into the *exitus-reditus* scheme. To be sure, he also made corrections to the neoplatonic idea of emanation, thereby allowing us to catch sight of a *theological* recasting of the scheme. Unlike the neoplatonic conception, according to which the plurality of the created world is understood as a sort of catastrophic falling away from the One, Thomas emphasizes that creation's going forth from God is an expression of his *free* agency as Creator. Thomas traces the motif of creation back to divine goodness and love.[13] The world is therefore not to be construed as a mobile likeness of an immobile prototype; rather, it has a share in the life of God himself, whose essence is understood in a Trinitarian way. Precisely on account of the concept of creation, a rather different view of the world now becomes possible: while corporality and temporality are regarded in neoplatonic thought as deficient and thus as intermediate stages to be superseded, a contrarily positive judgment emerges when man's body belongs to a creation affirmed by God and when time springs from a free divine initiative. A Christian transformation of the cyclical scheme, which is characterized by the structural moments of descent, conversion, and ascent, emerges moreover through the real sequence of salvation-historical events. Accordingly, in the presentation of creation, fall, and redemption found in the *Summa theologiae*, Thomas repeatedly draws out the fittingness of these events, that is, he undertakes an *a posteriori* theological reflection on the plausibility of God's actions and in no way brings the necessity (*necessitas*) of a cosmic law into play *a priori*, so to speak. The presence of Scripture in the *Summa theologiae*—especially in the passages concerning the work of the six days (*S. th.* I, qq. 67–74), the old law (*S. th.* I-II, qq. 98–105), the mysteries of the life of Jesus (*S. th.* III, qq. 27–59), etc.—shows furthermore that biblical salvation history is not relegated to an ornamental appendix of the *ordo disciplinae*, but rather it plays a determinative role in this very *ordo*.[14]

Regarding the concrete structure of the *Summa theologiae*, a threefold division is found. After a theoretical introduction concerning the scientific character of the whole enterprise,[15] the first part treats of God's existence, his essence, as well as the creation of the world from God. The second part describes the "motion of the rational creature to God,"[16] that is, the way of

---

13. *S. th.* I, q. 47, a. 1: "produxit enim res in esse propter suam bonitatem communicandam creaturis."
14. The prologue to the commentary on Matthew shows, by the way, that Thomas's *exitus-reditus* scheme can also be transferred to the realm of Christology. There, during the division of the gospel, it reads: "Et ideo dividitur totum Evangelium in tres partes. Primo enim agit Evangelista de Christi humanitatis in mundum *ingressu*, secundo de eius *processus*; tertio de euis *egressa*" (*In Matth* I, l. 1, n. 11, emphasis mine).
15. See *S. th.* I, q. 1.
16. See *S. th.* I, q. 2, prol.: "Quia igitur principalis intentio huius sacrae doctrinae est Dei cognitionem

man, gifted with reason and freedom, to God, his Creator and Perfecter; in the center stand the actions of man, his virtues and vices, but also the aid of grace granted by God. With its teaching on Jesus Christ, the third part presents the principle, as it were, of the mediation of salvation, by which the *reditus* of man to God is carried out. Christ is the way along which man can attain to the *ultimus finis*.[17] The treatise on Christology essentially adduces arguments from fittingness, which do not hold an inferior status in relation to the logical arguments of necessity on account of the fact that they correspond to the free action of God in history. Beyond the fittingness of place and point in time, Thomas also discusses the fundamental question of the fittingness of the Incarnation. In doing so, he has recourse to the theme of the self-communication of the good. As it belongs to the essence of the good to communicate itself to others—*se aliis communicare*—so it is most fitting that God, the *summum bonum*, communicate himself to his creatures in the highest way. The Incarnation is, as the highest concentration of this *communicatio boni*, profoundly reasonable.[18] In view of the structure of the revelatory event, Thomas notes further that here the invisible things of God are shown in visible things—*per invisibilia monstrentur invisibilia Dei*. The historical self-disclosure of God, his communication with men, takes place *per visibilia*. The central Christological thought—that the human nature of Christ is an instrument conjoined (*instrumentum coniunctum*) to the divinity—attains concrete vividness in the theology of the mystery of Jesus' life. The Christology of the *Summa theologiae* treats first of questions regarding the hypostatic union and its ramifications for the mystery of the person of Jesus Christ (qq. 1–26); then it turns to the *acta et passa* of the incarnate Son of God: after a section on questions of Mariology (qq. 27–34), the mysteries of Jesus' life are pursued in detail (qq. 35–45), before soteriology itself is thematized in the Passion, death, resurrection, and glorification

---

tradere, et non solum secundum quod in se est, sed etiam secundum quod est rpincipium rerum et finis earum, et specialiter rationalis creaturae, … ad huius doctrinae expositionem intendentes: primo tractabimus de Deo; secundo de motu rationalis creaturae in Deum; tertio, de Christo, qui secundum quod homo, via est nobis tendendi in Deum." In the introduction to the *Secunda pars*, the discussion is about God as exemplar and man as image—a terminology that also reveals a neoplatonic influence.

17. See *S. th.* III, prol.: "Quia Salvator noster Dominus Iesus Christus, teste Angelo, populum suum salvum faciens a peccatis eorum, viam veritatis nobis in seipso demonstravit, per quam ad beatitudinem immortalis vitae resurgendo pervenire possimus, necesse est ut, ad consummationem totius theologici negotii, post considerationem ultimi finis humanae vitae et virtutum ac vitiorum, de ipso omnium Salvatore ac beneficiis eius humano generi praestitis nostra consideratio subsequatur." See also *Comp. theol.*, c. 2: "Christi humanitas via est qua ad Divinitatem pervenitur."

18. M. Scheuer, "Aliis communicare. Zum Offenbarungsverständnis des Thomas von Aquin," found in "*Wozu Offenbarung?" Zur philosophischen und theologischen Begründung von Religion*, ed. B. Dörflinger et al. (Paderborn: Schöningh, 2006), 60–83. See C. Berchtold, *Manifestatio veritatis. Zum Offenbarungsbegriff bei Thomas von Aquin* (Münster: LIT, 2000), 245–37, where the idea of Christ's self-manifestation in the commentary on John and the *Summa theologiae* is worked out.

of Christ (qq. 46–59). The extensive treatment of the mysteries of Jesus' life—"unique in the whole of medieval literature"[19]—indicates that Thomas seeks to reveal the invisible mystery of Jesus Christ in visible actions. He ascribes redemptive significance to the individual stages of Jesus' life, and so the reproach that is occasionally raised, that Thomas's teaching on redemption is a staurocentric reduction, cannot be maintained. Nevertheless, as is still to be shown, Thomas sees the Passion as a culmination of Jesus' life and deeds inasmuch as it condenses in itself the voluntary self-gift to the will of the Father, which frees men from the burden of sin.

The motif, that the invisible reality of God becomes perceptible in visible signs, can be translated into the realm of the sacraments, which are designated by Thomas as *instrumenta separata* of the divine salvific work. In them, the event of communication between God and men is carried forward, so to speak. At any rate, it is no accident that the reflections on general sacramental doctrine are subsequent to Christology, without a theological reflection on the essence of the Church—*De ecclesia*—coming before or in the midst of the treatment of the sacraments. "Therefore, what has become visible in the savior has passed over into the sacraments."[20] This insight of Leo the Great seems to align itself with Thomas, so that an implicit ecclesiology ought to be extracted from his reflections on Christology (see *S. th.* III, q. 8) and sacramental theology (see qq. 60–90). The sevenfold sacraments, however, are elucidated by Thomas following an analogy with basic anthropological experiences.[21] After dealing with the sacraments in general (see *S. th.* III, qq. 60–65), Thomas goes into the individual sacraments and considers them in the catechetical order still customary today: Baptism, Confirmation, Eucharist, Penance, "Extreme Unction," Ordination, and Matrimony, although the *Tertia pars* breaks off with the treatment of the sacrament of Penance (*S. th.* III, q. 90). The theology of the remaining sacraments is found in the volumes of the *Supplementum* (*Suppl. I*, qq. 1–58), which in all probability was based on the material already present in the *Sentences* commentary and put together by Reginald of Piperno, the *so-*

---

19. T. Marschler, *Auferstehung und Himmelfahrt Christi in der scholastischen Theologie bis zu Thomas von Aquin*, v. 1 (Münster: Aschendorff, 2003), 73. On the theology of the mysteries of the life of Christ, see: G. Lohaus, *Die Geheimnisse des Lebens Jesu in der "Summa Theologiae" des heiligen Thomas von Aquin* (Freiburg: Herder, 1985); J.-P. Torrell, *Le Christ en ses mystères. La vie et l'auvre de Jésus selon Thomas d'Aquin* (Paris: Desclée, 1999).

20. Leo the Great, *De Ascensione Domini. Sermo II* (SC 74, ed. R. Dollw, 274–87, here 278): "Quod itaque Redemptoris nostri conspicuum fuit, in sacramenta transivit."

21. On the interrelation of Christology and ecclesiology, or sacramental theology, see the explanation in M. Dauphinais and M. Levering, *Knowing the Love of Christ: An Introduction to the Theology of St. Thomas Aquinas* (Notre Dame, Ind.: Notre Dame University Press, 2002), 109–18.

cius continuus of Thomas, to whom the *Compendium theologiae* is also dedicated.[22] The treatise on the Eucharist, the sacrament of sacraments, takes up a relatively good deal of space (*S. th.* III, qq. 73–83). But before we take this up in more detail, we must first of all sketch the main features of general sacramental theology, since interpretational categories are developed here that are also determinative for the interpretation of the Eucharist.

The Main Features of General Sacramental Theology

Whoever seeks today to draw closer to the sacramental theology of Thomas Aquinas will not be able to dismiss his own preconceptions, nor will he be able to ignore reservations present in the general theological discussion.[23] It belongs to a hermeneutically reflective approach to disclose the distance between time periods rather than conceal them in a harmonizing way. Thus it is disconcerting from today's perspective that the theology of the Scholastics makes an immediate connection between Christology and sacramental theology without expressly considering the ecclesiological embeddedness of the sacraments in the Church. Whoever holds in the back of his mind the teaching of Christ as primordial sacrament, the Church as the fundamental or root sacrament, and the special sacraments as exercises of the Church's life,[24] will have to ask whether the ecclesiological dimension of the sacraments is perhaps underdeveloped in the *Summa theologiae*.

---

22. On this point, see J.-P. Torrell, *Saint Thomas Aquinas*, vol. 1: *The Person and His Work*, 272–75.

23. On this theme, see the following works: H.-F. Dondaine, *La définition des sacrements dans la Somma Théologique*, in *RSPhTh* 31 (1947) 213–28; O. H. Pesch, *Besinnung auf die Sakramente. Historische und systematische Überlegungen und ihre pastoralen Konsequenzen*, in: *FZPhTh* 18 (1971) 266–321; K. Rahner, "Introductory Observations on Thomas Aquinas' Theology of the Sacraments in General," in K. Rahner, *Theological Investigations* XIV (1976), 149–60; J. Finkenzeller, *Die Lehre von den Sakramenten im allgemeinen. Von der Schrift bis zur Scholastik* (Freiburg: Herder, 1980), 38–42; O. H. Pesch, "Die Kunst Gottes oder: Sakrament und Wort—und die Kirche," in Pesch, *Thomas von Aquin*, 343–80; L. G. Walsh, "The Divine and the Human in St. Thomas' Theology of Saraments," in *Ordo sapientiae et amoris: Hommage au Professeur Jean-Pierre Torrell*, ed. C.-J. Pinto de Oliveira (Fribourg: Éditions Universitaires, 1993), 321–51; H.-J. Röhrig, "'Realisiernde Zeichen' oder 'Zeichen einer heiligen Sache.' Das Sakramentverständnis des hl. Thomas von Aquin als Anfrage an gegenwärtige Sakramententheologie," *Lebendiges Zeugnis* 58 (2003) 101–16; D. Berger, *Was ist ein Sakrament? Der hl. Thomas von Aquin und die Sakramente im allgemeinen* (Siegburg: Franz-Schmitt, 2004); K. Hedwig, "'Efficiunt, quod figurant.' Die Sakramente im Kontext von Natur, Zeichen, und Heil," in *Thomas von Aquin: Die Summa theologiae. Werkinterpretationen*, ed. A. Speer (Berlin: De Gruyter, 2005), 401–25.

24. See, for example, the related works by E. Schillebeeckx, *Christus: Sakrament der Gottbegegnung* (Mainz: Matthias-Grünewald, 1960), 23–26 [Eng.: *Christ the Sacrament of the Encounter with God* (New York: Sheed and Ward, 1963), 13–17]; O. Semmelroth, *Die Kirche als Ursakrament* (Mainz: Josef-Knecht, 1963); Semmelroth, *Die Kirche als Sakrament des Heils*, in: *MySal* IV/1, 309–56, as well as R. Schulte, *Die Einzelsakramente als Ausgliederung des Wurzelsakraments*, in *MySal* IV/2, 46–155; E. Jüngel and K. Rahner, *Was ist ein Sakrament?* (Freiburg: Herder, 1971); T. Schneider, *Zeichen der Nähe Gottes. Grundriß der Sakramententheologie* (Mainz: Matthias-Grünewald, 7th edition, 1998), 36–53.

The next point to be taken into account is that medieval sacramental theology follows a standardized catalog of questions; thus, the medieval approach appears perhaps to be of only limited plausibility to an anthropologically oriented theology which seeks points of contact with human self-understanding. Scholasticism—and with it also Thomas Aquinas—took as self-evident themes such as sacramentality, institution,[25] matter and form, agency, minister and recipient; accordingly, precisely these questions were raised. It would be wrong to assume that this same catalog of questions is also self-evident for contemporary theology. Thus, a historical hermeneutic of unfamiliarity will candidly take note of both difference and distance from contemporary questions, without therefore assuming contemporary issues to be canonical and beyond dispute.

Third, the notion that God would encounter us bodily in material signs hits upon some discomfort. "Our race, supposedly so enamored of the world and of the body"—thus Otto Hermann Pesch in refreshingly clear prose—"quickly revealed itself as a host of 'Platonists,' where one has to imagine that God and his love could encounter us in material, bodily signs, in other words, 'wrapped up' in material things."[26] At this point, the suspicion of reifying grace quickly slips into the room. The doctrine concerning the objective efficacy of the sacraments *ex opere operato* and the theological concentration on the words of consecration appears to foster an occult understanding of the sacraments, which is unacceptable today (and perhaps it always was). However, the accentuation of the objective character of the sacraments could also be an indispensable indication of the fact that "redemption and salvation cannot be brought about by men," thus presenting a fundamental "difference from magic (repeatedly practiced in the waves of esotericism)."[27] It is beyond dispute, however, that today one rather tends to interpret the sacraments as "signs of God's closeness,"[28] as privileged places of encountering God. A theology of the sacraments that has recourse primarily to categories of causality and is interested above all in the efficacious realization of the sacraments as well as their validity and fruitfulness, appears by the same token to have a rather weakly pronounced sensibility for the personal dimension of the sacraments and their liturgical context.[29] Af-

---

25. At the same time, it is immediately to be noted that the institution of the seven sacraments was already problematized by the Reformers, and completely so by historical-critical exegesis. This still holds if one takes into account that the concept of *institutio* for the scholastic theologians was rather broadly understood and included, beyond the deeds of Jesus, those also of the apostles and the Holy Spirit in the Church.

26. Pesch, *Thomas von Aquin*, 357.

27. H. Vorgrimler, "Sakrament," *LThK* 8, 3rd ed. (1998): 1440–45, here 1443.

28. See Schneider, *Zeichen der Nähe Gottes*.

29. See F.-J. Nocke, *Sakramententheologie. Ein Handbuch* (Düsseldorf: Patmos, 1997), 60.

ter making our way through the general sacramental theology of Thomas, we will have to return to the soundness of these objections.

The Sacrament as *signum sacrum sanctificans*

At the juncture between Christology and the general theology of the sacraments stands the observation that the sacraments *of the Church*[30] receive their efficacy through the *verbum incarnatum*.[31] Thus the origin of every salvific reality mediated by the Church lies in Jesus Christ.

It has been repeatedly observed that Aquinas's reflections on a general theology of the sacraments are permeated by a unique tension. On the one hand, he appears to follow the Augustinian notion that the sacraments belong in the genus of signs: "... sacramentum ponitur in genere signi."[32] On the other hand, he bases himself on the Aristotelian doctrine of causes and teaches that the sacraments not only signify but also bring about something sacred, and indeed as *causae instrumentales*.[33] Both aspects are simply central for his theology of the sacraments.

Thomas seeks first to clarify by way of definition *what* a sacrament is, and he asks whether it is to be placed in the genus of signs. The fact that a significant theological tradition designates a sacrament following the Augustinian concept of *signum sacrae rei* appears to work infelicitously with the etymological meaning of the word. In the objections, Thomas lists off a veritable bundle of definitional suggestions, which bring before the reader's eyes the equivocity of the word *sacramentum*. *Sacramentum* is etymologically bound up with *sacrare* (to make holy)—something that rather suggests a relation *in genere causae*, since it is here employed to ascribe a salvific effect to the sacrament. Beyond that, *sacramentum* is used in the Vulgate and in

---

30. This point itself is already a clue to the thesis that even though a stand-alone treatise *De ecclesia* is missing, at least an "indirect" ecclesiology is still displayed in Thomas's thought.

31. See the introduction to the treatise on the sacraments: S. *th.* III, q. 60: "Post considerationem eorum quae pertinent ad mysteria Verbi incarnati, considerandum est de Ecclesiae sacramentis, quae ab ipso Verbo incarnato efficaciam habent." See also *S. c. G.* IV, c. 56.

32. See *S. th.* III, q. 60, a 1. In Augustine, the classic definition of signs is found in *De doctrina christiana*, 2, 1, 1 (CCL 32, 32, 5–7): "Signum est enim res praeter speciem, quam ingerit sensibus, aliud aliquid ex se faciens in cogitationem venire." See, on this point, J. Finkenzeller, *Die Lehre von den Sakramenten im allgemeinen* (Freiburg: Herder, 1980), 40–43. As is well-known, Augustine distinguishes between *signa naturalia*—such as the tracks of an animal or the smoke that points to a fire—and *signa data*—signs that are exchanged by living beings in order to share with each other movements of soul or feelings, and in man's case, also knowledge. Among *signa data*, words (*verba*) are of singular significance, since they themselves enable all other signs to be expressed. Thus they are indispensable for human communication. See G. Wenz, *Einführung in die evangelische Sakramentenlehre* (Darmstadt: Wissenschaftliche Buchgesellschaft, 1988), 13–21.

33. On the Aristotelian doctrine of causes see *Phys.* II, 3 (195a29 ff.); *Metaph.* I, 3–10 (983a26ff.); as well as the systematic reconstruction in Thomas: *De princ. nat.* 3 (42–58) and 4 (1–127). As will be shown later, the category of instrumental causality is decisive for sacramental theology.

the Latin Church fathers as an equivalent to the Greek word μυστήριον, in which we find inscribed the meaning "things concealed and covert."[34] If, however, the sacrament is defined as a *sacrum secretum* (following Isidore of Seville), then the relation to the genus of causes appears to be misplaced, for a *signum* is obviously and clearly related to a *res significata*. Finally, Thomas references the *Decretum Gratiani* to say that the sacrament is also understood as an oath or unconditional voluntary commitment[35]—a meaning that again makes its placement *in genere signi* appear problematic. Nevertheless, Augustine's nearly classical definition is handed on, according to which the sacrament is a *signum sacrum*. In the *sed contra*, therefore, Thomas gives Augustine's authority the appropriate space with the following quotation: *Sacrificium visibile invisibilis sacrificii sacramentum, idest sacrum signum, est*.[36]

Faced with this evident ambiguity and in order to avoid equivocity in the notion of sacrament, Thomas orders—good Aristotelian[37] that he is—the diverse aspects to *one* central viewpoint (*ad unum*). In doing so, he firstly takes up the example of health, which Aristotle brings in to clarify the πρὸς ἕν structure of knowledge in metaphysics. "Thus, from the health which is in an animal, not only is the animal said to be healthy through being the subject of health: but medicine also is said to be healthy through producing health (*sanitas effectiva*); diet through preserving it (*conservativa*); and urine, through being a sign of health (*significativa*)."[38] With the sacraments, the central point of view is the *res sacra*, to which the signified aspects are related. Accordingly—as Thomas writes—"a thing may be called a 'sacrament,' either from having a certain hidden sanctity, and in this sense a sacrament is a 'sacred secret' (*sacrum secretum*); or from having some

---

34. On the conceptual background, see A. Schilson, "Symbol und Mysterium als liturgiewissenschaftliche Grundbegriffe," in *Liturgische Theologie*, ed. H. Hoping and B. Jeggle-Merz (Paderborn: Schöningh, 2004), 57–84.

35. See *Decretum Gratiani* p. II, causa 22, q. 5, can. 14, in *Corpus iuris canonici*, ed. E. Friedberg, vol. 1 (Leipzig: Bernhard Tauchnitz, 1879), cols. 886f. See also Tertullian, who connected Christian initiation through Baptism with the oath of allegiance taken by recruits (*mart.* 3; Corpus Scriptorum Ecclesiasticorum Latinorum 76, 1–8, ed. V. Bulhart and J. W. Ph. Borleffs)—an analogy also used by Isidore: "Tria sunt militiae genera: sacramentum, evocatio, coniuratio. Sacramentum, in quo post electionem iurat unusquisque miles se non recedere a militia, nisi post completa stipendia, i.e., militiae tempora." *Etymol.* IX, cap. 3, n. 53 (ed. W. M. Lindsay = PL 82, 547).

36. ["The visible sacrifice is the sacrament, i.e., the sacred sign, of the invisible sacrifice"—Translator.] Quoted in *S. th.* III, q. 60, a. 1 sed contra and a. 2 sed contra. See Augustinus, *De civitate Dei*, X, 5 (CCL 47, ed. B. Dombart, 277). See also *Sermo* 272 (PL 38, 1247): "Ideo dicuntur sacramenta, quia in eis aliud videtur, aliud intelligitur. Quod videtur, speciem habet corporalem, quod intelligitur, fructum habet spiritualem." [They are therefore called sacraments because in them one thing is seen, another is understood. What is seen has a bodily appearance and what is understood bears spiritual fruit.]

37. See *Metaph.* IV, 2 (1003a, 36–1005a, 18): "Being is said in many ways (πολλαχῶς), but always in reference to *one* (πρὸς ἕν)."

38. *S. th.* III, q. 60, a. 1 c.

relationship to this sanctity, which relationship may be that of a cause, or of a sign or of another relation."[39] Through this rather broad understanding of the concept of sacrament, which refers the diverse aspects analogously to the viewpoint of holiness (*sanctitas*),[40] Thomas can speak of sacraments in the old covenant or also of sacraments *in voto*.[41] In contrast, when it comes to the more precise definition of the sacraments in the new covenant, Thomas clings to—and here he differs from his earlier *Sentences* commentary[42]—the Augustinian placement of sacraments in the genus of signs, but not without immediately including their sanctifying character as the *differentia specifica*. The sacraments not only reveal the sacred, and thus are not limited to an index function, but are—as Thomas elucidates—"signs of a holy thing *insofar as it makes men holy*."[43] In this definition, which indicates the specific difference of the sacraments in the new covenant, we find the three components sign, cause, and sanctification taken together. Through its sanctifying power, a sacrament distinguishes itself from the many things manifest to the senses in the created world, which point to the wisdom of the Creator (see Rom 1:20) but do not possess a sanctifying character.

But also a sanctifying sign can—if it is complex—end up being suspiciously ambiguous. Ambiguity, however, would be precarious when it comes to the description of the sacred and sanctifying. Therefore, Thomas gives a clear definition of the various ways in which the sacraments designate man's sanctification: as *signum rememorativum*, the sacrament refers back to the *cause* of sanctification, the Passion of Christ; as *signum demonstrativum*, to the *form* of sanctification, hence grace and the virtues brought about by Christ's Passion; and finally, as *signum prognosticum*, it points ahead to the *end* of our sanctification, future glory.[44] This definition of a sacrament of-

---

39. *S. th.* III, q. 60, a. 1 c: "Sic igitur sacramentum potest aliquid dici, vel quia in se habet aliquam sanctitatem occultam, et secundum hoc sacramentum idem est quod sacrum secretum; vel quia habet aliquem ordinem ad hanc sanctitatem, vel causae, vel signi, vel secundum quamcumque aliam habitudinem." See on this point also K. Hedwig, '*Efficiunt quod figurant*', 404.

40. See *S. th.* III, q. 60, a. 1 ad 3: "non tamen aequivoce, sumpto nomine sacramenti, sed analogice, scilicet secundum diversam habitudinem ad aliquid unum, quod est res sacra."

41. See *S. th.* III, q. 60, a. 2 ad 2. See also *S. c. G.* IV, c. 57.

42. See Dondaine, *La définition des sacraments dans la Somma Théologique*, 214–20.

43. *S. th.* III, q. 60, a. 2: "proprie dicatur sacramentum ... signum rei sacrae, inquantum est *sanctificans homines*" (emphasis added). See also q. 61, a. 3, where the sacraments are designated as "quaedam sensibilia signa invisibilium rerum quibus homo *sanctificatur*" (emphasis added).

44. See *S. th.* III, q. 60, a. 3. The oft quoted passage reads: "sacramentum proprie dicitur quod ordinatur ad significandum nostram sanctificationem. In qua tria possunt considerari: videlicet ipsa causa sanctificationis nostrae, quae est passio Christi; et forma nostrae sanctificationis, quae consistit in gratia et virtutibus; et ultimus finis nostrae sanctificationis, qui est vita aeterna. Et haec omnia per sacramenta significantur. Unde sacramentum est et signum rememorativum euis quod praecesit, scilicet passionis Christi; et demonstrativum eius quod in nobis efficitur per Christi passionem, scilicet gratiae; et prognosticum, idest praenuntiativum, futurae gloriae." A comparable definition is also to be found in Bonaventure, *Breviloquium*, VI, 2.

fers a theological configuration of three layers in time. The past, the saving deed of Christ, is not simply past; through the operation of the sacramental signs, it extends into the present and qualifies it. The saving and redeeming power of the Passion is passed on through the sacraments and determines the present life of the faithful. At the same time, the sacraments are taken up into an eschatological dynamic that foreshadows the *finis ultimus* of coming glory. "The sacraments are the form in which the Christ event, transcending all times, acquires duration and can always become present in the now for individual men."[45] The sacraments bridge, so to speak, the historical distance between the past saving deed of Christ, the present of the faithful, and their future in the consummation of all things, which will no longer lie along the timeline of a historically immanent chronology. Thus the sacraments themselves will be without function in the eschaton. What is decisive is that Thomas roots the present agency of the sacrament in salvation history. Without the redemptive act of Jesus Christ, the sacraments would have no sanctifying power. They are what they are not of themselves but through Christ the author of sanctification (*auctor sanctificationis*).[46] Through this memorial aspect oriented toward the past, however, the sacraments of the new covenant are distinguished from those of the old covenant, which serve, according to Thomas, as prefigurations of things to come. At the same time, written into the sacraments of the new covenant is also an abiding promissory surplus: they usher in the final consummation and even offer a foretaste of the world to come, for which reason one cannot simply qualify the time of the Church with her sacramental order of salvation as the time of fulfillment.

Going further, Thomas pursues the question concerning the elements of which a sacrament is composed. Through the specific coming together of a natural element (matter) with a significant word (form), a sacrament becomes a sacrament. At the same time, it is important that the sign function of the sacraments corresponds to a basic anthropological given, inasmuch as men are led by means of signs from things known to things unknown.[47] Thomas speaks of nothing less than a certain connaturality, when he holds to the proposition that it is in accord with the nature of man to attain to the knowledge of intelligible realities through those things manifest to the

---

45. Pesch, *Thomas von Aquin*, 370.
46. See *S. th.* I-II, q. 110, a. 4 ad 2, where Christ is designated as *sanctificationis auctor* (see also *S. th.* I, q. 43, a. 7).
47. *S. th.* III, q. 60, a. 2: "signa proprie dantur hominibus, quorum est per nota ad ignota pervenire." Likewise: *S. th.* III, q. 72, a. 1.

senses.[48] The selection of sensible things to be used in the performance of the sacraments does not, in Thomas's view, belong to man, but rather it belongs to God to regulate. In this context, Aquinas distinguishes between two aspects in the performance of the sacraments: *cultus divinus*, which pertains to the relation of man to God, and *sanctificatio hominis*, which refers to the relation of God to man.[49] The sanctification of man is, however, proper to God. Thus, it falls to his power to determine the means by which he desires to sanctify man. It is not given to man to choose according to his own judgment or whim the means by which he wants to be sanctified. Therefore, just as Christian cult is not a product of human inspiration or creative power, neither is the meaning of the symbolic actions set up by an act of collective ascription of meaning. For Thomas, it is much more appropriate to acknowledge with gratitude that God enacted the institution of particular signs that bring about the sanctification of man. In the sacraments of the new covenant, therefore, those things are to be used that are appointed to the task by divine institution (*institutio divina*). If the New Testament witnesses allow an explicit determination to be overlooked, what is required is a hermeneutic art of mediation in order at least to trace ecclesial practice back to an implicit *institutio divina*.[50] On this point, one must emphasize that in scholastic theology, the concept of *institutio* was not construed in the modern sense of historical-critical inquiry.

Nevertheless, the visible elements, the *res sensibilis*, certainly can be interpreted in many ways. The symbolism of water, for example, can be variously understood: as source of life, as a means of purification, but also as a life-threatening force. It requires therefore an interpretive word that joins the visible element so that the sacramental action clearly separates itself from other symbolic actions.[51] Through the statement "I baptize you," it is immediately clear, says Thomas, that the water is being used here as a sign of purification.[52]

48. See *S. th.* III, q. 60, a. 4: "Est autem homini connaturale ut per sensibilia perveniat in cognitionem intelligibilium." Similarly, *S. c. G.* IV, c. 56.

49. See *S. th.* III, q. 60, a. 5 c.

50. *Institutio divina* is an important point of inquiry in the discussion of each of the individual sacraments. See *S. th.* III, q. 66, a. 2 (Baptism); q. 72, a. 1 ad 1 (Confirmation); q. 73, a. 5 (Eucharist); q. 84, a. 7 (Penance); etc. For the sacrament of Confirmation, for example, a direct *institutio divina* is not biblically demonstrable, and so Thomas lays down that Christ instituted the sacrament *non exhibendo, sed promittendo*.

51. *S. th.* III, q. 60, a. 6: "[...] per verba magis distincte possumus exprimere quod mente concipimus. Et ideo ad perfectionem significationis sacramentalis necesse fuit ut significatio rerum sensibilium per aliqua verba determinatur." See Augustine's definition, which became significant in the reception history: "detrahe uerbum, et quid est aqua? Accedit uerbum ad elementum, et fit sacramentum" (*Io. ev. tr.* 80, 3 [CCL 36, ed. R. Willems, 529]).

52. See *S. th.* III, q. 66, a. 1 ad 3. Not the water itself but the use of water, the washing off (*ablutio*), is

But there is also another reason that a special meaning belongs to the word. It is, in fact, related to the *causa sanctificans*, the Word become flesh (*verbum incarnatum*).[53] Here Thomas crafts an analogy to the Incarnation: as sensible flesh (*caro sensibilis*) was united with the Word of God (*verbum Dei*) in the mystery of the Incarnation, so the sacrament is configured in a way similar to the *verbum incarnatum* through the fact that the word joins the matter in question. Finally, the coming together of the material element and the word in the sacrament also corresponds to the body-soul composition of man. The *medicina sacramentalis* refers to the whole man, when the *res sensibilis* touches the body and then the *verbum* is taken up in faith by the soul.[54]

Now, there are sacraments, such as Penance or Matrimony, which are conferred without a visible element. Thus, Thomas refines the Augustinian terminology of *verbum* and *elementum* by falling back on Aristotelian hylomorphism, and he distinguishes between the matter and form of a sacrament. The words indicating the distinctive meaning of the symbolic action are the *form*; in contrast, what stands in need of determination is the *matter* of the sacrament (and which therefore may not be construed within the contemporary horizon of a tangible, material substrate). Compared to the concept of element, the advantage of the Aristotelian concept of matter therefore consists in the fact that it is semantically broader and not limited to the level of a *res sensibilis*; it can—as in the case of Penance—also encompass sins as the matter of the sacrament. On the other hand, a certain priority thus accrues to the form, as it is the principle of determination.[55] Should the form be contravened by the minister in an intentional way, for example through an utterance that distorts the meaning or through changing the words, then the sacrament does not come about.[56]

---

accordingly the outward sign that signifies the inner content, justification (*iustificatio*). That the symbolism of water is suitable for designating the essence and effect of Baptism is shown by Thomas in S. *th*. III, q. 66, a. 3.

53. See also: *De ver.*, q. 27, a. 4 ad 10.

54. See S. *th*. III, q. 60, a. 6 c.

55. S. *th*. III, q. 60, a. 7 c: "In omnibus compositis ex materia et forma principium determinationis ex parte formae, quae est quodammodo finis et terminus materiae. Ideo principalius requiritur ad esse rei determinata forma quam determinata materia; materia enim determinata requiritur ut sit proportionata determinatae formae. Cum igitur in sacramentis requirantur determinatae res sensibiles, quae se habent in sacramentis sicut materia multo magis requiritur in eis determinata forma verborum."

56. Thomas discusses the question whether the sacraments are accomplished in cases of linguistic deviations from the formula of consecration (incorrect pronunciation, additions and omissions, whether by mistake or deliberately: see S. *th*. III, q. 60, a. 7 ad 3 and a. 8). In general, the rule is that a sacrament fails to occur when the semantics of the form are affected, or are contravened by an utterance that distorts the meaning. Thomas gives the example of saying "in nomine matris" instead of "patris."

The Anthropological Fittingness of the Sacraments

Beyond this, Thomas raises the question of why the sacraments are necessary. Here, it is necessary to bear in mind that various forms of necessity were discussed in high Scholasticism. In addition to simple or absolute necessity, which belongs only to God, there is the relative necessity of means, without which an end cannot be attained (*necessitas ex suppositione finis*).[57] Since it is quite within the power of God to grant salvation to a man even without the sacraments,[58] the concept of necessity in the realm of the sacraments is to be understood in yet a different way. They are necessary only in the sense that in the present order of salvation, God willed salvation to men in no other way than precisely through the sacraments. An attitude of respect before the divine will demands, however, that one not arbitrarily bypass the sacramental order of salvation. If God has tied his grace to certain signs, then man can ignore this only to his own detriment. To this extent, the theology of the sacraments is fundamentally characterized by a certain positivism: it is oriented to the datum of the divine ordinance, the *institutio divina*.

The primary task of theology as *sacra doctrina* is to plumb the depths of God's will as it is made manifest in the testimonies of revelation. Therefore, for the one who wants to understand the will of God in a profound way, the question of the necessity of the sacraments transforms itself into the question of the fittingness of the sacraments.[59]

Because God willed the sacraments, because Christ instituted the sacraments, one can only invoke aptness, "reasons for fittingness." In this context, the Scholastics—indeed from the early Scholastics right up to Thomas—are seen to speak matter-of-factly and terminologically of a *necessitas* of the sacraments and they treat this *necessitas* predominantly according to the necessity of receiving the sacraments. When they do so, here as in other similar cases, they employ an exaggerated mode of expression and mean in substance the fittingness or the good sense of the fact that the sacraments exist.[60]

---

57. See K. Hedwig, "*Efficiunt quod figurant*," 409 (with reference to pertinent passages in Aristotle).
58. See *In IV Sent.*, d. 1, q. 1, a. 2, qc. 2: "Deus potentiam suam non alligavit sacramentis." Similarly: *S. th.* III, q. 64, a. 7: "Deus virtutem non alligavit sacramentis, quin possit sine sacramentis effectum sacramentorum conferre." See *S. th.* III, q. 72, a. 6 ad 1; *De ver.*, q. 28, a. 3, arg. 3.
59. *S. th.* III, q. 61. See also: *In IV Sent.*, d. 1, q. 2, a. 1; *S. c. G.* III, c. 119 und IV c. 55f. With regard to the individual sacraments, the question of salvific necessity is treated in detail when considering Baptism (*S. th.* III, q. 68, a. 1–4; 9–12), in less detail regarding the Eucharist (*S. th.* III, q. 73, a. 3) and Penance (*S. th.* III, q. 85, a. 5–10), and merely indirectly concerning Confirmation (*S. th.* III, q. 72, a. 7–9) and Extreme Unction or Anointing of the Sick (*S. th.* Suppl., q. 30, a. 1). See the doctrine of *votum sacramenti*, which can take the place of real reception of the sacrament.
60. Pesch, *Besinnung auf die Sakramente*, 275.

In explaining this fittingness, Thomas refers not only to the analogy of the Incarnation: as God's eternal Word made himself visible and tangible in the Incarnation, so in the sacraments invisible grace is made visible and tangible in signs manifest to the senses.[61] Furthermore, Thomas adduces three separate arguments for the anthropological fittingness of the sacraments:

1. First, he invokes the already mentioned anthropological argument, according to which man, on account of his body-soul composition, requires sensible signs to be led from visible to invisible things.[62] In the *Summa contra gentiles*, Thomas joins this anthropological argument with a reference to the Incarnation. There is a similarity (*similitudo*) between the *verbum incarnatum* as the first cause of salvation and the sacraments as the instruments of salvation, insofar as both make visible the invisible reality of the divine.[63]

2. In addition, Thomas brings forward an argument we might rather call salvation-pedagogical. This argument makes reference to the fact of sin, which is a precarious matter for man: when on account of sin man subjugates himself to bodily things through the passions (*per affectum*), then the salvific antidote must be applied at the same place where the sickness is located. The healing of the sick person cannot take place while bypassing the patient. Therefore, it is fitting (*conveniens*), holds Thomas, that God administered man a spiritual remedy (*medicina spiritualis*) by means of *signa corporalia*. And, taking up Augustinian motifs, he adds that it is a school of humility for man to have to recognize that he can be helped up from his excessive inclination toward bodily things only by means of bodily things.[64]

3. A third argument makes reference to man's inclination to occupy himself chiefly with bodily activities. It would have been too difficult, says

---

61. See *S. th.* III, q. 60, a. 6.
62. See *S. th.* III, q. 60, a. 4. Similarly also Bonaventure, *In IV Sent.*, d. 1, p. 1, a. un., q. 1.
63. See *S. c. G.* IV, c. 55.
64. See on this point the critical remarks of Pesch, *Thomas von Aquin*, 319–20: "Thus we find in Thomas an argument from fittingness for the necessity of the sacraments, which today might amuse rather than convince and indeed is also somewhat below Thomas's level: on account of the fact that salvation is bound up with sensible symbols, man should be humbled, since he also sinned through his being excessively inclined toward the sensible world. So sacrament as punishment." Similarly already in Pesch, *Besinnung auf die Sakramente*, 278. The thought that the sacraments have a humbling function for man is, however, of Augustinian origin and was received into the Middle Ages by Hugh of St. Victor, for example (see idem, *De sacramentis*, I, p. 9, c. 3 = PL 176, 319–22), and was disseminated by the *Sentences* of Peter Lombard. There we find the brief determination: "Triplici autem ex causa sacramenta instituta sunt: propter humilitatem [sic], eruditionem, exercitationem" (*Sent. IV*, d. 1, c. 5). See on this point the commentary of Bonaventure, who accepts this division approvingly: *In IV Sent.*, d. 1, p. 1, c. 5; see also *Breviloquium*, VI, 1. In spiritual theology, *humilitas*, as a practical form of conformity with the *Christus humilis*, holds a high status. For background, see S. Ernst, "Die bescheidene Rolle der Demut. Christliche und philosophische Grundhaltungen in der speziellen Tugendlehre (S. th. II-II, q. 161)," in *Thomas von Aquin. Die Summa theologiae*, ed. A. Speer, 343–76, esp. 344–47.

Thomas, had man been burdened with completely abstaining from the bodily sphere. Thus, in the sacraments bodily practices are presented, which he can implement to salutary effect. These *exercitationes* have, in Thomas's view, the salutary side effect of being a preventive for superstitious practices, demonic cult, and other deleterious things.[65]

In his commentary on the *Sentences*, Thomas brought in another argument, which touches upon the ecclesiological dimension of the sacraments. Every religion requires external signs that serve the worship of God when its members come together in assembly, the *cultus divinus*. Therefore, the sacraments are also necessary as visible signs for the Church as *verissima religio*.[66] In this context, Thomas does not expressly reflect upon the function had by the signs in establishing identity for a religious collective, although precisely circumcision in the old covenant and Baptism in the new would have suggested such thoughts.[67]

The Sacraments in the Economy of Salvation History

Thereafter, Thomas elucidates the sacraments' embeddedness in the economy of salvation history.[68] These explanations are important for the connection between the old and the new covenant. Already in the theology of early Scholasticism, history was divided into three differing periods. Thus Hugh of St. Victor, for example, distinguishes (1) the time of the natural law (*lex naturae*), which stretched from the Fall of Adam to the Mosaic Law; (2) the time of the written law (*lex scripta*), which spanned from Moses to Christ; and (3) the time of grace (*tempus gratiae*), which commenced with the coming of Christ and will continue until the parousia.[69] According to this con-

---

65. By way of summary, Thomas holds: "Sic igitur per sacramentorum institutionem homo convenienter suae naturae eruditur per sensibilia; humiliatur, se corporalibus subiectum cognoscens, dum sibi per corporalia subvenitur; praeservatur etiam a noxiis corporalibus per salubria exercitia sacramentorum" (S. th. III, q. 61, a. 1). See also S. th. II-II, q. 82, a. 19, where a threefold significance is attested of the exterior signs in view of the exercise of religion: (1) it leads the spirit to the easier acquisition of supersensible reality; (2) it also works on the affective side of man; (3) it offers the possibility of expressing the inner movement and emotion in a bodily way as well. See on this point the commentary to the German edition of Thomas's works, v. 29 (1935), 489.

66. See *In IV Sent.*, d. 1, q 1, a. 2, s.c.

67. The teaching that a sacrament is a *signum unitivum et distinctivum*, that an identity-establishing but also delimiting function for the Church accrues to it, is found explicitly in Duns Scotus Ord. IV, d. 1, q. 3, n. 2. See J. Finkenzeller, *Die Lehre von den Sakramenten im allgemeinen*, 147. Nevertheless, in the Quaestio concerning circumcision, one finds Thomas making the passing suggestion: "Populus autem fidelium congregandus erat aliquo signo sensibili: quod est necessarium ad hoc quod homines in quacumque religione adunentur." See S. th. III, q. 70, a. 2 ad 2.

68. See S. th. III, q. 61, a. 2–4. On the difference between the sacraments of the old and the new law, see also S. c. G. IV, c. 57.

69. *De sacramentis christianae fidei*, I, 8, 11 (PL 176, 312–13).

ception, man, bearing the burden of *peccatum originale*, requires a certain medicine, which assumed a more concrete form from time period to time period. Thomas also takes up, along with his predecessors' periodization of salvation history, the medicinal metaphor, but he holds at the start that the sacraments, as remedial for sin, were not yet necessary in the *status innocentiae*.[70] It was proper to the constitution of prelapsarian man that the higher powers ruled over the lower, with the former being in no way dependent on the latter. As the spirit (*mens*) was subordinated to God, so also the lower powers of the soul were subordinated to the spirit, and the body to the soul. It would then have contravened this order if the soul were to be perfected through something bodily;[71] the communication of grace, therefore, would have ensued *spiritualiter et invisibiliter*.[72]

The situation presents itself differently for the period of salvation history before Christ, which again is divided into the times of *lex naturae* and *lex scripta*. Already for the time stretching from the Fall to the Mosaic Law, it was necessary that certain helps were imparted to man sickened by sin. Thus, in the period of the natural law, there were first *indeterminate* sacraments,[73] which on account of the increase of sin were replaced by the *more determined* sacraments of the written law (circumcision, ritual prescriptions, sacrifices, etc.).[74] Thomas speaks of "certain visible signs, through which man manifests his faith in the future coming of the redeemer."[75] In contrast to the sacraments of the new covenant, those of the old covenant point not to something present or past, but rather to something still to come. Precisely the future orientation of the "sacraments" of the old covenant, however, indicates that for Thomas the economy of salvation history is *Christologically* structured. Faith in the coming of Christ justifies the man of the old covenant, and he bears witness to this faith in certain determined signs;[76]

---

70. See *S. th.* III, q. 61, a. 2.

71. Regarding marriage, says Thomas, in paradise it would have been instituted as an *officium naturae* but not as a sacrament. See *S. th.* III, q. 61, a. 2 ad 3.

72. *S. th.* III, q. 61, a. 2 ad 1.

73. On the so-called natural sacraments, see *S. th.* I-II, q. 103, a. 1.

74. See *S. th.* III, q. 61, a. 3 ad 2: "Et ideo etiam necesse fuit quod in vetere lege quaedam sacramenta fidei quam habebant de Christo venturo, determinaretur; quae quidem comparantur ad sacramenta quae fuerunt ante legem, sicut determinatum ad indeterminatum, quia scilicet ante legem non fuit determinate praefixum homini quibus sacramentis uteretur, sicut fuit per legem."

75. *S. th.* III, q. 61, a. 3: "quaedam signa visibilia, quibus homo fidem suam protestaretur de futuro Salvatoris adventu." In other places, Thomas explained more precisely how he understands the sacraments of the old covenant. See *S. th.* I-II, q. 101, a. 4, where distinctions are made between *sacrifices* that constitute the cult, *sacred objects* that serve the cult (*sacra*), *instructions* that determine moral conduct (*observantiae*), and *sacred signs*, through which the people and priests are consecrated wo the *cultus divina* (*sacramenta*).

76. In his reflections on circumcision as *protestatio fidei*, Thomas can even say: "Eadem autem est fides nostra et antiquorum patrum." Filling out the picture, he adds in view of the faith of the fathers: "fides eorum erat de futuro" (*S. th.* III, q. 70, a. 1).

the sacraments of the new covenant, however, not only testify to faith in Christ's coming, but also vouchsafe a participation in his grace. Accordingly, the sacraments of both periods in salvation history are diversely qualified. Whereas the signs of the old covenant were essentially heralds of the one to come, the signs of the new covenant are efficacious signs of the one already come.[77] Not until the *status gloriae* will they be superseded, when the sacramental order will give way to the immediate and consummate manifestation of truth.[78] Standing behind this historical periodization, Thomas discerns a divine pedagogy, which he captures in an impressive image in the *Summa contra gentiles*: "Just as the father of a family gives one set of orders to a small child and another to one already grown, so also God harmoniously gave one set of sacraments and commandments before the Incarnation to point to the future, and another set after the Incarnation to deliver things present and bring to mind things past."[79] Consequently, the theologically decisive difference between the sacraments of the old covenant and those of the new consists in the fact that the latter not only designate but also contain and cause grace.[80] Not until the consummation of history will the sacramental economy be superseded.

With this teaching, Thomas breaks from the theology of history offered by Joachim of Fiore, who formulated a further epoch of salvation history (Holy Spirit), which went beyond the epoch of the old covenant (Father) and that of the new covenant (Son); in this further epoch, the Sermon on the Mount would be observed in a literal fashion and the Church's sacramental order would be superfluous. Thomas has sharp criticism for the thesis that a qualitatively new time within history itself is still to be expected. It is exceedingly foolish (*stultissimum*) not to hold the Gospel of Christ as the definitive one, for God's revelation in Jesus Christ has an eschatolog-

---

77. See *S. th.* III, q. 61, a. 4.

78. See *S. th.* III, q. 61, a. 4 ad 1, where Thomas undertakes to situate precisely the sacraments of the new covenant in salvation history: "status novae legis medius est inter statum veteris legis, cuius figurae implentur in nova lege, et inter statum gloriae, in qua omnis nude et perfecte manifestabitur veritas."

79. *S. c. G.* IV, c. 57. See also *S. th.* III, q. 61, a. 4 ad 3.

80. Bonaventure also expresses similarly the difference between the sacraments of the old and new covenant: "Illa promittebant tantum et significabant, haec autem dant salutem" (*In IV Sent.*, d. 1, p. 1, c. 6). See also *S. th.* III, q. 62, a. 6. Here we can ignore that in the theology of Early and High Scholasticism circumcision (*circumcisio*) is treated specifically as the primary sacrament of the old covenant. It is to be noted only *en passant* that Thomas advocates in his *Sentences* commentary the thesis that no sacrament of the old covenant works *ex opere operato*, with the exception of circumcision: "Et ideo alii dicunt et melius, quod nullo modo sacramenta ispa veteris legis, id est opus operatum in eis, gatiam conferebant, excepta circumcisione" (*In IV Sent.*, d. 1, q. 1, a. 5, qc. 1). With more reservation, we find in *S. th.* III, q. 62, a. 6 ad 3, that circumcision is a "sign of justifying faith" (*signum fidei iustificantis*). For background, see J. Finkenzeller, *Die Lehre von den Sakramenten im allgemeinen*, 154–57.

ical character and cannot be superseded.[81] The Spirit keeps the work of the Son present in history, but the sacraments will be mediating instruments of salvation until the *status novae legis* is superseded by the *status gloriae*.

The Instrumental Causality of the Sacraments

With the motif of salvific mediation, however, we touch upon the efficacy of the sacraments, which Thomas pursues in a distinct *quaestio*.[82] The considerations regarding the effect of grace in the sacraments are significant because they plumb further and more precisely the relation between sign (*signum*) and cause (*causa*). Thomas emphasizes that the sacraments of the new covenant are not only vessels of grace or God's making grace visible,[83] but also causes of grace. At the same time, he abandons—and this is worth noting explicitly—the phrase *ex opere operato*, which he had still used in the *Sentences* commentary to characterize the objective efficacy of grace independent of previous human achievements.[84] In the *Summa theologiae*, Thomas breaks from the so-called "divine pact" theory of the Franciscan theologians (William of Auxerre, Summa Halensis, Bonaventure),[85] a theory which held that in the administration of the sacrament what takes place is merely a superficial parallelism of exterior sign and interior grace. The foundation of the sacramental effect of grace is a contract (*pactum*) in which God has obligated himself to give his grace each time a certain symbolic action is performed—then and only then. In the background of the pact theory is (1) the thesis that something spiritual cannot be mediated through something bodily, as well as (2) the widely held notion that grace can be produced in the soul only by a generic act of creation. In this conception, efficient causality does not belong to the sacraments—they dispose

---

81. *S. th.* I-II, q. 106, a. 4 ad 4: "stultissimum est dicere quod Evangelium Christi non sit Evangelium regni." See also q. 106, a. 4 ad 2: "excluditur quorumcumque vanitas qui dicerent esse expectandum aliud tempus spiritus sancti. Docuit autem spiritus sanctus apostolos omnem veritatem de his quae pertinent ad necessitatem salutis, scilicet de credendis et agendis." See W. J. Schachten, *Ordo salutis. Das Gesetz als Weise der Heilsvermittlung. Zur Kritik des hl. Thomas von Aquin an Joachim von Fiore* (Münster: Aschendorff, 1980).

82. *S. th.* III, q. 62 as well as q. 64, a. 1.

83. Hugh of St. Victor taught that the sacraments are vessels (*vasa*) of grace, and thus drew a clear dividing line between the efficacy of the material element and the inner effect of grace. See idem., *De sacramentis christianae fidei*, 1, 9, 4 (PL 176, 323): "Si ergo vasa sunt spiritualis gratiae sacramenta, non ex suo sanant, quia vasa aegrotum non curant, sed medicina."

84. See E. Schillebeeckx, *L'économie sacramentelle du salut* (Fribourg : Academic Press Fribourg, 2004), 518: "Saint Thomas use une vingtaine de fois en contexte sacramentaire de la terminologie ,ex opere operato' dans le *Scriptum super Sententiis*, alors que nous ne l'avons découverte nulle part dans la Somme. Ceci signale, qu'il n'estime pas ce terme technique."

85. See Bonaventure, *In IV Sent.*, d. 1, a. un., q. 1. On the particular characteristics, see J. Finkenzeller, *Die Lehre von den Sakramenten im allgemeinen*, 196–201.

the soul for the reception of grace, to be sure, but grace itself is imparted directly and immediately by God. Thomas sees at work here a subtle devaluation of the sacramental order: in the context of this theory, the sacraments are nothing but mere signs of grace.[86]

In contrast to this, he insists in the *Summa theologiae* that the sacraments are not only signs but also causes of grace, and he grounds his understanding on a conceptual distinction that derives from the Aristotelian theory of causes.[87] There are two distinct efficient causes, the principal cause (*causa principalis*) and the instrumental cause (*causa instrumentalis*).[88] The principal cause operates in virtue of its form, through which it determines the effect and makes it similar to itself. In this way, however, only God can cause grace, for "grace is nothing other than an imparted semblance of the divine nature."[89] The concern of the pact theory to designate God as the exclusive author of grace is thus addressed. At the same time, however, the externally abiding parallelism is corrected and bettered through the doctrine of instrumental causality, according to which the sacraments operate not through their form but only through the motion they receive from the principal cause. Therefore, the effect is assimilated not to the instrument but to the principal cause—as for example a table resembles not the hatchet with which it was fashioned but the idea of the table in the carpenter's designing mind. In this way, Thomas holds that the sacraments of the new covenant cause grace; they are required by divine ordination (*ex ordinatione divina*) so that *in their performance* grace is caused. Thus they are not downgraded to mere signs, to which divine grace is added merely because of a pact; rather, they are at once cause and sign of grace. Precisely through their connection with the principal cause—God—the instrumental causes—the sacraments—generate a far greater effect than they could of their own nature. The reservation held by the Franciscan school of thought, that something bodily cannot act upon something spiritual,[90] can be cleared up if the

---

86. See *S. th.* III, q. 62, a. 1: "iste modus non transcendit rationem signi ... Secundum hoc igitur sacramenta novae legis nihil plus essent quam signa gratiae."

87. See R. M. Schultes, "Die Wirksamkeit der Sakramente," in: *Jahrbuch für Philosophie und spekulative Theologie* 20 (1906): 409–49; J. Stufler, "Bemerkungen zur Lehre des hl. Thomas über die virtus instrumentalis," in *ZKTh* 42 (1918): 719–62.

88. See *S. th.* III, q. 62, a. 1: "duplex est causa agens, principalis et instrumentalis. Principalis quidem operatur per virtutem suae formae cui assimilatur effectus ... ; et hoc modo nihil potest causare gratiam, nisi Deus, quia gratia nihil est aliud quam quaedam participata similitudo divinae naturae." See also L. Elders, *The Metaphysics of Being of St. Thomas Aquinas in a Historical Perspective*, trans. John Dudley (Leiden: Brill, 1993), 297: "The principal cause makes the effect by its own power, while the instrumental cause does so through the power it receives (by way of a passing entity) from the principal cause."

89. *S. th.* III, q. 62, 4.

90. *S. th.* III, q. 62, a. 1, obj. 2: "Nullum corporale agere potest in rem spiritualem." See also *S. th.* III, q. 62, a. 1 ad 1.

spiritual sphere is interwoven with the bodily within the sacrament. This, however, is precisely the point of the Thomistic move of drawing from the category of instrumental cause: to the extent that the sacraments belong to the corporeal sphere, a proper operation (*propria operatio*) is assigned to them, and it is through this operation that they reach the corporeal and sensible world. Simultaneously, however, they perform an instrumental operation (*instrumentalis operatio*) on the soul by the power of God (*in virtute divina*). The invisible principal cause acts concretely in signs and thus also visibly through the sacraments, which mediate grace to men by way of instrumental causality.

Thomas clarifies further the sacraments' mode of operation, by distinguishing between the concepts *instrumentum coniunctum* and *instrumentum separatum*. To do this, he employs the following analogy: as the hand is for man an instrument conjoined by nature (*instrumentum coniunctum*), while the staff moved by the hand is a separated instrument (*instrumentum separatum*); so also the humanity of Christ is, on account of the hypostatic union, an instrument of salvation bound up with the divinity,[91] while the sacraments are *instrumenta separata* that are moved by the humanity of Christ. In reference to the teaching on causes, this can be stated thus: the principal cause (*principalis causa*) of grace is ascribed to the divinity of Christ. The humanity of Christ is related thereto as an *instrumentum coniunctum*,[92] which for its part uses the sacraments as *instrumenta separata*. This is schematized in the figure on p. 45. The salvific power of the sacraments transmits itself *from* the divinity of Christ, who *through* his humanity (as *instrumentum coniunctum*) brings about grace *in* the sacraments (as *instrumenta separata*).[93] Through this interpretation of the sacraments in terms of instrumental causality, Thomas is able to bring further specifica-

---

91. In this treatise on Christology, Thomas had already presented the humanity of Christ as an instrument of the Word hypostatically united to it. See *S. th.* III, q. 13. He interprets the unity of divine and human nature in the sense of the *subsistence theory*, according to which the eternal Word takes on an individual human nature that is not itself a person. This non-personality of human nature (*anhypostasis*) does not therefore indicate any deficit, since it finds fulfillment of its openness through being taken up into the Person of the eternal Word. See O. H. Pesch, *Gottes Wort in der Geschichte*, in: idem., *Katholische Dogmatik aus ökumenischer Erfahrung*, v. I/1 (Ostfildern: Matthias-Grünewald, 2008), 735–62. Furthermore, Thomas stresses that the human nature, as instrument of salvation, emcompasses body, soul, and reason (*S. th.* III, q. 5).

92. On the Christological doctrine, according to which the *humanitas Christi* is an *instrumentum coniunctum divinitati in persona*, see *S. th.* III, q. 13, a. 2; q. 19, a. 1. For background, see the instructive presentation in Th. Marschler, *Auferstehung und Himmelfahrt Christi*, 169–79.

93. *S. th.* III, q. 62, a. 5: "Et ideo opportet quod virtus salutifera derivetur a divinitate Christi per eius humanitatem in ipsa sacramenta." At the same time, Thomas makes clear that deliverance from sin takes place through Christ's passion. In *S. th.* III, q. 64, a. 3, Thomas explains: "interiorem sacramentarum effectum operatur Christus et secundum quod est Deus, et secundum quod est homo: aliter tamen et aliter. Nam secundum quod est Deus, operatur in sacramentis *per auctoritatem*. Secundum autem quod est homo, operatur ad interiores effectus sacramentorum *meritorie, et efficienter, sed instrumentaliter*" (emphasis added).

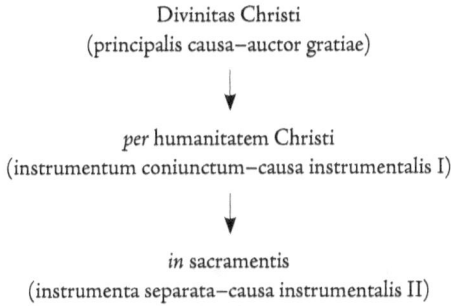

tion to the vessel theory of grace, a theory developed by Hugh of St. Victor, widely handed on in Scholasticism and certainly prone to being suspected of reifying grace. Aquinas explicitly teaches that grace in the sacrament is not contained in a vessel as a place.[94] Rather, speaking of the sacraments as *vasa gratiae* can be maintained only if they are understood in the sense of instrumental causality, that is, if they are interpreted as instruments of divine grace.[95]

But sacramental grace, on the one hand, is ordained as a remedy for the defects of past sin—for though the act of sin be but cursory and limited to a discrete moment, the guilt remains and encumbers man (*reatus culpae*). On the other hand, sacramental grace should dispose man for the celebration of the liturgy, the *cultus Dei*. Both tasks, however, are most intimately bound up with the Passion of Christ. Thus, Thomas refers to the fact that the sacraments draw their power above all from the Passion of Christ, the soteriological meaning of which will be presented in detail later on. At this point, however, an abbreviated version can already be put forward: on the cross, Christ redeemed men from their sins once and for all. At the same time, he laid the foundation for the rite of the Christian religion through his Passion, in that he presented himself to God as gift and sacrifice, as

---

94. See *S. th.* III, q. 62, a. 3 ad 1: "gratia non dicitur esse in sacramento sicut in subiecto, neque sicut in vase, prout vas est locus quidam, sed prout vas dicitur instrumentum alicuius operis faciendi."

95. The teaching of Aquinas on the sacraments' instrumental mode of operation is unanimously recognized; what is contested, however, is how Thomas understands this instrumental mode of operation in a more detailed way. While he explicitly teaches a dispositive efficacy in the *Sentences* commentary and *De veritate* (see *In IV Sent.*, d. 1, q. 1, a. 4 as well as d. 5, q. 1, a. 3, qa. 1; *De veritate*, q. 27, a. 4 ad 3; *De potentia*, q. 3, a. 4 ad 8), no such corresponding discussions are found in the *S. th.* One group then has wanted to read from this absence in the *S. th.* a late self-correction by Thomas. For other interpreters, on the contrary, a change in teaching is not assumed based on the mere fact of not discussing the matter explicitly; thus they assume a continuity in teaching. On this complex discussion, see: M. Gierens, "Zur Lehre des heiligen Thomas über die Kausalität der Sakramente," *Scholastik* 9 (1934): 321–345, who casts his vote for doctrinal continuity.

Thomas repeatedly asserts on the basis of Ephesians 5:2.[96] It is no accident that Thomas recalls the common symbolism of water and blood flowing from the side of Christ (see Jn 19:34). Water points to Baptism, blood to the Eucharist, and Thomas names them both as the most important sacraments (*potissima sacramenta*).[97] This reference to the priority of the *sacramenta maiora* is significant inasmuch as it offers a point of contact with the churches and ecclesial communities stemming from the Reformation.

Minister and Recipient of the Sacraments

Now, just as the instrument conjoined by nature can impart its power to the separated instrument, so also could Christ, insofar as he is a man, communicate the power or ability (*potestatem communicare*) to confer the sacraments.[98] Already in his remarks on general sacramental theology, Thomas holds that valid administration of the sacraments is not tied up with the moral disposition or personal sanctity of the minister. Here too he appeals to a figure of argumentation based on instrumental causality.[99] Because the ministers of the Church administer the sacraments *not from their own power* but rather as exercising an instrumental function, the effect of the sacrament is no better on account of a better minister nor worse on account of a worse one. The fundamental assertion remains valid that the action is actually ascribed not to the instrument but rather to the principal agent.[100] Christ, however, is the principal agent (*principalis agens*), and he works through good ministers as living members and through bad ministers as inanimate instruments.[101] What is presupposed is simply that the delegated ministers observe the prescribed rite and intend to do what the Church does.[102]

---

96. Eph 5:2b: "[Christus] tradidit se ipsum pro nobis oblationem et hostiam Deo in odorem suavitatis."

97. See *S. th.* III, q. 62, a. 5: "sacramenta Ecclesiae specialiter habent virtutem ex passione Christi, cuius virtus quodammodo nobis copulatur per susceptionem sacramentorum. In cuius signum, de latere Christi pendentis in cruce fluxerunt aqua et sanguis, quorum unum pertinet ad baptismum, aliud ad Eucharistiam, quae sunt potissima sacramenta." See also *S. th.* III, q. 66, a. 3 ad 3.

98. See F. Morgott, *Der Spender der heiligen Sacramente nach der Lehre des heiligen Thomas von Aquin. Eine theologische Studie* (Freiburg: Herder, 1886).

99. See *S. th.* III, q. 64, a. 1 and 5.

100. *In IV Sent.*, d. 5, q. 2, a. 2, qc. 2: "Actio non attribuitur instrumento proprie sed principali agenti." See *S. th.* III, q. 64, a. 8, obj. 1: "actio non perficitur secundum intentionem instrumenti, sed secundum intentionem principalis agentis."

101. *S. th.* III, q. 64, a. 5 ad 2.

102. See *S. th.* III, q. 64, a. 8. The *intentio faciendi quod ecclesia facit* is manifested through words. Through these words, the minister bestows determinacy and singularity of meaning to a sacramental action that, in itself, admits of many meanings and is thus ambiguous: "Ea vero quae in sacramentis aguntur, possunt diversimode agi: sicut ablutio aquae, quae fit in baptismo, potest ordinari et ad munditiam corporalem et ad sanitatem corporalem, et ad ludum, et ad multa alia huiusmodi. Et ideo opportet quod determinetur

Because the conferral of the sacrament is independent of the personal worthiness of the minister, the salvific effect is secured and guaranteed (*securitas salutis*). Were, in fact, "the validity of the sacrament dependent upon the sanctity of the minister, man could never be secure with respect to his salvation, for no one can judge the moral condition of another, except for God, who sees through the mysteries of the heart."[103] Moreover, a man would then place his hope not in Christ but in another man.

The minimal stipulation, that the minister intend "to do what the Church does," presupposes that he is not a dead, mechanical instrument, but rather a person gifted with reason and will. Thomas thus also distinguishes between inanimate instruments, which receive merely mechanical impulses from the principal agent (as the axe from the hand of the carpenter), and animate instruments, which not only are moved from without but also display a certain proper motion. In this way, a man moves his members to particular actions by means of his will. In the realm of administering the sacraments, therefore, it is necessary that the minister subordinate his intention to that of the principal agent, thus having the intention to do what Christ and the Church do.[104] Accordingly, the intentional act of the minister is not the expression of a subject who desires to take command of salvation; instead, it is the expression of voluntary subordination to the *ordo* of the sacraments ultimately decreed by God. It should be added that the minister acts in the person of the whole Church (*in persona totius ecclesiae*), whose minister he is; but in the words spoken, the intention of the Church finds expression, and this suffices for the execution of the sacrament, as long as the contrary is not outwardly made known.[105] Thomas notes that if concentration is impaired or thoughts wander, no explicit intention is given; nevertheless, an implicit one is present, which he calls *intentio habitualis*, because the original resolution to confer the sacrament continues to have an effect in it.[106]

A validly dispensed and objectively efficacious sacrament becomes fruitful in the recipient if he sets no obstacle (*obex*) against it. In other words, the recipient—above all, of the Eucharist—is urged to be free of grave sins

---

ad unum, idest ad sacramentalem effectum, per intentionem abluentis. Et haec intentio exprimitur per verba quae in sacramentis dicuntur." Elsewhere, Thomas notes that morally indisposed ministers, who nevertheless administer the sacraments, sin personally: see *S. th.* III, q. 64, a. 6 ad 1.

103. Finkenzeller, *Die Lehre von den Sakramenten im allgemeinen*, 189.
104. *S. th.* III, q. 64, a. 8 ad 1.
105. See *S. th.* III, q. 64, a. 8 ad 2.
106. As a rule, the administration of Confirmation is reserved to the bishop (see *S. th.* III, q. 72, a. 11, and q. 65, a. 3 ad 2)—similarly, Holy Orders. Baptism, Eucharist, Penance, and Extreme Unction are administered by a priest. In exceptional cases, an emergency Baptism can be administered by a lay person.

in order not to receive the sacrament unworthily. By contrast, the sacrament of Penance is ordered to absolving the sinner of grave sins. Baptism, Confirmation, and Ordination, which can be received only *once*, impress an abiding sign on the recipient, an indelible mark (*character indelebilis*). In Baptism, this mark is the sacramental expression of definitively belonging to Christ; in Confirmation, of being sealed with the Holy Spirit; and in Ordination, of being commissioned by Jesus Christ as a minister.

The Order of the Sacraments and the Preeminence of the Eucharist

It is well known that the term "sacrament"—considered within the history of theology—was rather broadly construed for a long period of time. Narrowing the term down to the seven sacraments of the Church took place only relatively late, namely, in the twelfth century.[107] The seven sacraments were codified by the magisterium at the Council of Lyon in 1274 (see DH 860); this was reinforced in 1439 by the Armenian decree of the Council of Florence, which relies essentially on the opusculum of Thomas Aquinas entitled *De articulis fidei et Ecclesiae sacramentis* (see DH 1310);[108] finally, in 1547, the Tridentine decree on the sacraments defended the sevenfold numbering against the objections of the Reformers (see DH 1600–1613). When the theology of High Scholasticism speaks of the necessity of precisely seven sacraments, this can only be understood in the sense of fittingness.

Unlike Albert the Great or Bonaventure, who present the seven sacraments in "somewhat forced symbolism"[109] as remedies for diverse sins,[110]

---

107. We cannot go into the early scholastic classification of the sacraments here. The consensus in the research is that the number seven gained acceptance in the middle of the twelfth century, as can be gathered from the *Sententiae divinitatis* and the treatise *De sacramentis* of Master Simon (see Finkenzeller, *Die Lehre vom den Sakramenten im allgemeinen*, 123–25). In the reception history, the *Sentences* of Peter Lombard can hardly be overestimated, the composition of which is dated by M. Grabmann (*Geschichte der Katholischen Theologie seit dem Ausgang der Väterzeit*, 2nd ed. [Darmstadt: Wissenschaftliche Buchgesellschaft, 1961], 40) to the years 1150–1152 and influence of which—particularly canonically—touched the glosses of the *Decretum Gratiani*, which incidentally was not yet familiar with the sevenfold numeration of the sacraments. In Lombard, we find a complete listing of the seven sacraments, which are theologically subdivided into three groups: "Iam ad sacramenta novae legis accedamus, quae sunt baptismus, confirmatio, panis benedictio, id est eucharistia, poenitentia, unctio extrema, ordo, coniugium. Quorum alia remedium contra peccata praebent et gratiam adiutricem conferunt ut baptismus, alia remedium tantum sunt, ut coniugium, alia gratia et virtute nos fulciunt, et eucharistia et ordo" (*Sent.* IV, d. 2, c. 1).

108. *De articulis fidei et ecclesiae sacramentis*, in *Opuscula theologica*, vol. 1 (Rome: Marietti, 1954), nn. 612–29.

109. Thus J. Pieper, *Guide to Thomas Aquinas* (London: Faber and Faber, 1962), 124.

110. See Bonaventura, *In IV. Sent.*, d. 2, a. 1, q. 3; idem., *Breviloquium* VI, 3. In both places, the fittingness of each of the seven sacraments is explained with its healing character. In the explanation, Baptism is ordered to original sin, Penance to mortal sin, Holy Anointing to venial sin, Order to ignorance, the Eucharist to an evil will (*malitia*), Confirmation to weakness, and Matrimony to concupiscence.

Thomas offers an *anthropological* justification for the number seven. He recalls first of all the twofold end to which the sacraments are ordered: on the one hand, perfecting man with a view to all that belongs to the *cultus Dei* within the Christian religion, and on the other, offering a remedy for the defects of sin.[111] In line with both perspectives, Thomas tries to make plausible the assertion that the institution of seven sacraments is most reasonable, drawing upon the appropriate anthropological points of connection. His thesis is that there is a fundamental correspondence between bodily and spiritual life, and this should be understood to refer to both the *individual* and the *social* dimensions of human life.[112]

Concretely, he distinguishes three moments by which the bodily life of the individual attains to its perfection: firstly, through *procreation* (*generatio*), on account of which man first begins to live. Corresponding to corporeal procreation is Baptism, which is interpreted as "spiritual rebirth" (*spiritualis regeneratio*) based on Titus 3:5. As corporeal birth is a one-time process, through which man enters into life, so also is spiritual rebirth through the sacrament of Baptism singular and unrepeatable.[113] Thereafter, corporeal life requires growth, through which man is led to his full size and power. To this corresponds the sacrament of Confirmation in the spiritual life, which imparts the power of the Holy Spirit.[114] Thomas certainly relates Confirmation to the spiritual growth process when he explains the sacrament as the sign of distinction (*signum distinctivum*) between children and those who have come of age.[115] Just as no one can be brought to a state of maturity

---

111. See *S. th.* III, q. 65, a. 1. Already in *S. th.* III, q. 62, a. 5 we find something similar: "Gratia autem sacramentalis ad duo praecipue ordinari videtur: videlicet ad tollendos defectus praeteritorum peccatorum, inquantum transeunt actu et remanent reatu; et iterum ad perficiendum animam in his quae pertinent ad cultum Dei secundum religionem Christianae vitae." And again: *S. th.* III, q. 63, a. 1.

112. A summary anticipation of this argumentation is already found in *S. c. G.* IV, c. 58.

113. See *S. th.* III, q. 66, a. 9. Here, beyond the analogy to physical birth, three further reasons for the unrepeatability of Baptism are adduced. First, the fact that Baptism is into the death of the Lord, who died only once; second, the consideration that Baptism confers an indelible mark (*character indelibilis*); third, calling to mind that Baptism is administered principally as a remedy for original sin (*peccatum originale*), which is also unrepeatable.

114. See *S. th.* III, q. 72, a. 1 c.

115. See *S. th.* III, q. 72, a. 5 c: "character confirmationis est signum distinctivum, non infidelium a fidelibus, sed spiritualiter provectorum ab his quibus dicitur: *Sicut modo geniti infantes* [I Petr 2,2]." Thomas presupposes nevertheless the classical order of the sacraments of initiation (Baptism, Confirmation, Eucharist). It would thus be anachronistic to attempt to employ Thomas Aquinas as the principal witness for the thesis, brought forward in the theology of the twentieth century, that Confirmation is to be seen as the sacrament of maturity, of conscious decision or adolescence. Although one can discuss its anthropological soundness, this thesis reverses the original order of the sacraments of initiation when it places the conferral of the sacrament of Confirmation *after* First Holy Communion. Thus, liturgists in these parts have criticized this completely accepted inversion of Confirmation and Eucharist, calling it an aberration and speaking of a "decomposition of the sacraments of initiation." See M. Kunzler, *Die Liturgie der Kirche* (Paderborn: Bonifatius, 1995), 396–401; R. Messner, *Einführung in die Liturgiewissenschaft* (Paderborn: Schöningh, 2001), 136–42,

without first being born, so the sacrament of Confirmation presupposes Baptism. Only one who is spiritually reborn is able to be led to perfect spiritual maturity (*aetas perfecta spiritualis*). Finally—as Thomas argues—corporeal life requires continual sustenance in order to be preserved in strength.[116] Hunger and thirst are basic anthropological functions that serve self-preservation. Following on this line of thought, it is the Eucharist that comes into play at the sacramental level, with Thomas designating the Eucharist as spiritual nourishment (*spirituale nutrimentum*) that joins the recipient with Christ. Already this relation to fundamental human needs for food and drink[117] shows that it is necessary to revise the common assessment of Thomas, which holds that he simply overlooks or underrates the Eucharist's prandial character because of his interest in the consecration and conversion. Nevertheless, it is to be noted that, under the rubric of *individual* perfection, the communal character of the Eucharist cannot be properly appreciated; elsewhere in the *Summa theologiae*, Thomas refers to this communal character, for example when he designates the Eucharist as *paschale convivium*.[118] Thus, to summarize the foregoing way of argumentation, an individual's initiation into the *vita spiritualis* of the Christian faith comes about through the triad of Baptism, Confirmation, and the Eucharist.[119]

Generation, growth, and nourishment—in the realm of corporeal things, these moments make possible the perfection of human life; but beyond these, corporality also demands that we reckon with illnesses requiring healing treatments. Corresponding to these in the spiritual life is the weakness owing to sins. As a remedy to restore health in the *vita spiritualis*, the cosmos of the sacraments provides two aids: first, the sacrament of Penance (*poenitentia*), which takes away personal sins committed after Baptism; second, Extreme Unction (*extrema unctio*), which clears up the last vestiges of sins (*reliquiae peccatorum*) that, on account of carelessness or ignorance, have not yet been completely blotted out through Penance. Furthermore, the sac-

---

here 140; H. Hoping, *Das Mysterium der Taufe. Heilszeichen und Grund christlicher Identität*, in *Wiederkehr der Rituale*, ed. B. Kranemann, et al. (Stuttgart: Kohlhammer, 2004), 99–117, here 100.

116. See *In I Cor*, XI, 24, lect. 5 (n. 650), where the analogy between *vita corporalis* and *vita spiritualis* is likewise drawn out.

117. See *S. th.* III, q. 73, a. 2 c.

118. See *S. th.* III, q. 66, a. 10 ad 5.

119. See *S. th.* III, q. 65, a. 1 c: "Per se autem perficitur corporalis vita tripliciter. Primo quidem, per generationem, per quam homo incipit esse et vivere. Et loco huius in spirituali vita est baptismus, qui est spiritualis regeneratio: secundum illud ad Tit. 3, [5]: *Per lavacrum regenerationis*, etc. – Secundo, per augmentum, quo aliquis perducitur ad perfectam quantitatem et virtutem. Et loco huius in spirituali vita est confirmatio, in qua datur Spiritus Sanctus ad robur. Unde dicitur discipulis iam baptizatis, Luc. 24, [49]: *Sedete in civitate quousque* [Vulg.: *quoadusque*] *induamini virtute ex alto*.—Tertio, per nutritionem, qua conservatur in homine vita et virtus. Et loco huius in spirituali vita est Eucharistia. Unde dicitur Ioan. 6, [54]: *Nisi manducaveritis carnem Filii hominis et biberitis eius sanguinem, non habebitis vitam in vobis*." See also *S. th.* III, q. 73, a. 1 c.

rament of Extreme Unction prepares the old or sick person for final glory (*finalis gloria*).[120]

In addition to these sacraments pertaining to the *vita spiritualis* of the individual (even if they are celebrated within the community of the Church), there are also sacraments that correlate with the *social* dimension of human coexistence. Here we find, first of all, the ability to lead the people and carry out public actions. This ability (*potestas*) is imparted through the sacrament of Order (*sacramentum ordinis*). It is hardly by chance that this *potestas regendi et actus publicos exercendi* is undergirded by a biblical verse from the letter to the Hebrews, which states that the priest offers sacrifices not only for himself but also for the people (see Heb 7:27). Furthermore, the body politic is potentially endangered by the mortality of its members and thus requires a corresponding fertility for its continual preservation. Related to natural propagation (*naturalis propagatio*), which serves the preservation of the species, is the sacrament of Matrimony, encompassing both the bodily and the spiritual life of man. Matrimony, Thomas adds, is not only a sacrament but also a natural obligation (*officium naturae*).[121] Finally, it functions as a remedy (*remedium*) for concupiscence of the sexual instinct, which, on account of its intensity, can injure both person and nature, as well as affect reason.[122]

Within the entire context of the cosmos of the sacraments, the Eucharist has an elevated status, for which Thomas adduces three reasons: first, he draws attention to a fundamental difference. Whereas Christ himself is substantially (*substantialiter*) contained in the Eucharist, the other sacraments merely participate in the power of Christ. Even Aristotle, however, underlined that an ontological priority accrues to what is *per essentiam* when compared to what is merely *per participationem*.[123] Second, Thomas asserts that all the other sacraments are ordered to the Eucharist as to an end (*finis*). It is obvious that ordination takes place for the sake of consecrating the Eucharist, whereas Baptism is ordered to receiving the Eucharist. Confirmation is a reassurance not to keep oneself from the Eucharist out of an all too great timidity. Through Penance and Extreme Unction,

---

120. See also *S. th.* III, q. 65, a. 1 ad 4: "in extrema autem unctione praeparatur homo ut recipiat immediate gloriam."
121. See *S. th.* III, q. 65, a. 1 and a. 2 ad 1.
122. *S. th.* III, q. 65, a. 1 ad 5: "contra concupiscentiam venereorum oportuit specialiter remedium adhiberi per aliquod sacramentum: primo quidem, quia per huiusmodi concupiscentiam non solum vitiatur persona, sed etiam natura; secundo propter vehementiam eius, qua rationem absorbet."
123. See *S. th.* III, q. 65, a. 3: "in eo continetur ipse Christus substantialiter: in aliis autem sacramentis continetur quaedam virtus instrumentalis participata a Christo." See *S. th.* III, q. 62, a. 4 ad 3; a. 5. On the ontological priority of *essentia*, see Aristotle, *Physica*, I. VIII, c. 5 (257a30–31). See also Thomas, *In Phys.*, l. 9 (n. 1049). See also Thomas, *In librum Boethii De trinitate*, prol. (HPhBMA 3).

one is prepared to receive the Eucharist worthily. At least through its symbolism, Matrimony is related to the Eucharist in that it signifies the union of Christ with the Church (see Eph 5:32). Finally, Thomas refers to the liturgical rite and points out that nearly all the other sacraments are administered and brought to an end in the celebration of the Eucharist.

A Preliminary Reflection

In summary, we can say that Thomas undergirds the seven sacraments with a conceptual system that makes reference to the anthropological requirements of individual life first and then to social life as well.[124] Thus, Eberhard Jüngel is to be agreed with when he states: "When it comes to the sacraments, Thomas Aquinas justified their sevenfold number, as affirmed in the Roman Catholic Church, with, among other reasons, the anthropological disposition for divine grace given in the liminal experiences of human life—an argument to which even Goethe granted high plausibility."[125] The *rites de passages* that were universally developed for the occasions of birth, adolescence, *unio coniugalis*, sickness, and nearing death receive the character of sacraments in the Church. The thesis that the sacraments ritually embellish anthropological junctions of life can, in its basic tendency, already find support in Thomas; still, with a view to painting a complete picture, Thomas suggests an alternative interpretive possibility, wherein the sevenfold number of the sacraments refers to the three theological virtues (*fides, spes, caritas*) on the one hand, and the four cardinal virtues (*prudentia, iustitia, temperantia, fortitudo*) on the other.[126] But Thomas leaves this correlation to stand without further commentary, which could indicate that it seemed to him to be ultimately hypothetical.

Precisely the more recent sacramental theology, which comments on the work of Thomas Aquinas rather reservedly or even critically, would certainly find in the *Summa theologiae* points of connection with an anthropologically oriented sacramental theology—something it has itself largely overlooked.[127] Not only the insight that the sacraments correspond in a

---

124. In *S. th.* III, q. 65, a. 2 this conceptual system is once again expressly presented. The sacraments of Baptism, Confirmation, and Eucharist are positively ordered to the perfection of the individual and thus deserve once again a priority over the sacraments of Penance and Extreme Unction, which tend—now negatively—to the removal of defects.

125. E. Jüngel, "Gottes Passage: Schwellenängste und weihnachtliche Selbstvergessenheit," *Neue Zürcher Zeitung*, December 24, 2005 (Supplement: Literatur und Kunst). Jüngel refers to J. W. von Goethe, *Aus meinem Leben. Dichtung und Wahrheit*, 4th ed. (Berlin: H. G. Bohn, 1976), 313–17, a passage from the seventh book, in which Goethe bemoans the poverty of "protestant cult" and impressively illuminates the seven sacraments with recourse to anthropological realities.

126. Just such a correlation is offered by Bonaventure, *Breviloquium*, VI, 3.

127. See most recently H. Verweyen, *Warum Sakramente?* (Regensburg: Pustet, 2001), esp. 11–16.

certain way to fundamental situations of human life, but also the foundational principle that man is led to knowledge of intelligible truth through sensible things, could be hermeneutically appropriated today. At the same time, Thomas does not simply derive the sacraments from human necessities. The anthropological *horizon of discovery*, which can lay down a first point of entry into the sacraments, may not overlook the theological and Christological *horizon of justification*.[128] The sacraments trace back to God as origin, who brings about grace *through* Jesus Christ *in* concrete signs. As the invisible eternal Word of God became visible and tangible in the life and death of Jesus, so the invisible grace of Christ becomes efficaciously present in and through very determined, visible symbolic actions. With Thomas, we ought to hold fast to the sacraments' Christological foundation, which tends to recede somewhat when the sacraments are spoken of as "self-performances of the Church."[129]

Moreover, when Thomas ascribes to the sacraments an instrumentally causal meaning over and above a significative meaning, he appreciates the bodily-material aspect of the proper reality of the sacraments more than the "divine pact" theory of the Franciscan school does. In the final analysis, in asserting that God *immediately* pours grace into the soul whenever the external symbolic action is performed in proper form, the Franciscans do not get beyond a parallelism, which remains superficial, between the effect of grace and the symbolic action.[130]

In addition, placing the emphasis on God as the Creator of sacramental grace finally permits the suspicion of magic to be staved off. In Thomas's sacramental theology, it is not man who takes possession of God through some formulae; it is rather the reverse, for God imparts grace to man through decreeing the sacraments. It may be that the theological concentration on the *forma sacramenti* could encourage misunderstanding the Eucharistic consecration itself as involving some secret spell—the linguistic history of the made-up word "hocus-pocus" can be derived from the Latin *forma sacramenti* "hoc est corpus meum." In particular, the scholastic phrase *ex opere operato*, which, tellingly, is not found in the sacramental theology of the *Summa theologiae*, elicited criticism, even though its original intention was to underscore precisely the primacy of God's action. The objective efficacy of the sacrament does not depend on the personal integrity of the min-

---

128. See E.-M. Faber, *Einführung in die katholische Sakramentenlehre* (Darmstadt: Wissenschaftliche Buchgesellschaft, 2002), 20.
129. See K. Rahner, *The Church and the Sacraments*, trans. W. J. O'Hara (London: Herder and Herder, 1974), 39.
130. See, in an exemplary way, Bonaventure, *Breviloquium*, VI, 1.

ister, whose moral disposition or other subjective qualities are insignificant when it comes to the realization of the sacrament. He needs simply to use the right matter, adhere to the prescribed form, and have the intention of the Church. All the same, one will have to judge with nuance the reception of the Aristotelian doctrine of causes in the sacramental theology of Aquinas. To the degree that the material aspect of the sacrament's proper reality can be emphasized by the category of instrumental causality, the personal, and above all ecclesial, side of the sacraments tends rather to recede. The discovery of this weak point remains valid even if the personal dimension of the sacraments in Thomas is suggested time and again. On this particular point, the analysis and interpretation of the Eucharistic hymns—especially of *Adoro te devote*—will open up another avenue of approach.

What is decisive for the wider context is the difference between the Eucharist and the other sacraments, to which Thomas refers at the conclusion of his reflections on general sacramental doctrine. Thus, it is not just any power whatsoever of Christ that is conveyed in the Eucharist, but rather the Eucharist contains a *sacrum absolute*, namely Christ himself.[131] Whoever receives the consecrated gifts—the body and blood of Christ—receives Christ himself.[132] This is the emphatic meaning of Eucharistic communion, which stands out qualitatively from the allocation of grace conferred by the other sacraments.

But how can Christ himself be received in the gifts of bread and wine? One property of Thomas's Eucharistic theology that is always emphasized is that he defined with conceptual precision the *somatic real presence of Christ* in the consecrated gifts as well as the mode of sacramental making present. His doctrine of transubstantiation, which relies upon the preparatory work of his teacher Albert the Great,[133] was adopted by the magisterium at the Council of Trent, and it definitively characterized scholastic theology's treatment of the Eucharist well into the twentieth century. A more precise consideration of this topic—in close dependence on the presentation of the *Summa theologiae*—will be undertaken in the following chapter.

---

131. See the statement of the difference in *S. th.* III, q. 73, a. 1 ad 3: "Haec est differentia inter Eucharistiam et alia sacramenta habentia materiam sensibilem, quod Eucharistia continet aliquid *sacrum absolute*, sicilicet ipsum Christum: aqua vero baptismi continet *aliquid sacrum in ordine ad aliud*, scilicet virtutem ad sanctificandum, et eadem ratio est de chrismate et similibus. Et ideo sacramentum Eucharistiae perficitur in ipsa consecratione materiae: alia vero sacramenta perficiuntur in applicatione materiae ad hominem sanctificandum" (emphasis added).

132. See the definition of the Eucharist as "sacramentum quod ipsum Christum coniugit homini" (*S. th.* III, q. 65, a. 4 ad 3).

133. See on this point H. Jorissen, *Der Beitrag Alberts des Großen zur theologischen Rezeption des Aristoteles am Beispiel der Transsubstantiationslehre* (Münster: Aschendorff, 2002).

2

"Hoc est corpus meum"

The Transformation of the Gifts

> A tremor went through the world, as the bread was transformed into the divine body,
> And, "simili modo," the wine, into the divine blood.
>
> Peter Handke

The Somatic Real Presence of Jesus Christ through Transubstantiation

In scholastic theology before Thomas Aquinas, treatments of the Eucharist were governed by the question of how Christ's presence in the gifts of bread and wine is to be understood. Two interpretative variants can be typologically distinguished: the first softened Christ's presence in a spiritualistic way and interpreted the consecrated gifts of bread and wine merely as commemorative; in contrast, the second championed a crass sacramental realism, identifying the consecrated gifts immediately with the flesh and blood of the historical Christ. These two interpretations trace their historical roots to the tension between Augustinian spiritualism and Ambrosian realism,[1] a

---

Epigraph is from P. Handke, *Langsame Heimkehr. Erzählung* (Frankfurt.: Suhrkamp, 1984), 206. The text continues: "Resolutely, the adult kneels down."

1. The characterization of Augustine's Eucharistic theology as spiritualism is of course debated. In contrast to the older Protestant research (Harnack, Loofs, Seeberg, Holl, etc.), Catholic authors such as Schanz and Lecordier put forward the (admittedly difficult to validate) thesis that Augustine's Eucharistic theology is to be interpreted in the sense of realism and metabolism. A modified position is presented in the following works: K. Adam, *Die Eucharistielehre des hl. Augustinus* (Paderborn: Schöningh, 1908); F. Hoffmann, *Der Kirchenbegriff des hl. Augustinus* (Munich: Max Hueber, 1933); J. Ratzinger, *Volk und Haus Gottes in Augustins Lehre von der Kirche* (St. Ottilien: Herder, 1992) (now *JRGS* [Joseph Ratzinger Gesammelte Schriften] 1 [Freiburg: Herder, 2012]); W. Gessel, *Eucharistische Gemeinschaft bei Augustinus* (Würzburg: Augustinus-Verlag, 1966); W. Simonis, *Ecclesia visibilis et invisibilis* (Frankfurt: Knecht, 1970), 109ff. The

tension that flared up again later as the substance of the Eucharistic controversies in the ninth and eleventh centuries.[2] With these interpretations as a back drop, one will have to praise the effort made by Thomas Aquinas to determine precisely the mode of the Eucharistic making present, and indeed in such a way that the *traditio* of Jesus' legacy remains free from falsifications in one or another direction. For Thomas, the final criterion of any Eucharistic theology is the testimony of Scripture. More precisely, he questions whether the diverse theories of making Christ present take into account the words of institution, *Hoc est corpus meum*. The commonly voiced suspicion that the model of transubstantiation, with its Aristotelian concepts, reshapes or simply falsifies the biblical testimony finds itself confronted with Aquinas's claim that only the doctrine of transubstantiation is able to conform to the content of the biblically attested words of institution.

---

tendency to devalue the visible in relation to the invisible—the Platonic heritage in Augustine's thought—may make his Eucharistic theology susceptible, at least, to interpretations along the lines of later symbolism.

2. It will be necessary to go into the Eucharistic controversies once more, taking into account the different ways of thinking operative in different contexts. Here, the only point to be made is that Paschasius Radbertus, in his work *Liber de corpore et sanguine Domini*, championed a massive realism in which the elements were transformed (*commutari*) into the flesh and blood of Christ by the power of a divine miracle of omnipotence. Following the Ambrosian line of metabolism, Radbertus insists on the *that* of Eucharistic conversion without being able to determine more precisely the *how*. He takes as his point of departure that the Eucharistic body is the same as that which was born, suffered, resurrected, and now sits in heaven. See *Liber de corpore et sanguine Domini*, 1,2 (CCCM XVI, ed. B. Paulus, 14,44–15,55 = PL 120, 1269 B) as well as 21,9 (122, 298–302 = 1340 C). The assertion of a total identification of the Eucharistic with the historical body of Christ, which the symbolic function of the sacramental forms is not able to fulfill, has called forth criticism. Radbertus's sharpest critic, Rathramnus, emphasizes—more in the line of Augustine—the difference between sign and signified, when he interprets bread and wine as *figura* or *similitude* of the body and blood of Christ, without however denying the real presence. See idem, *De corpore et sanguine Domini*, 74 (PL 121, 158 BC). He presupposes the Platonic way of thinking about exemplar and participation, according to which the consecrated elements are real signs of the exemplar—Christ sitting enthroned in heaven. Radbertus has obviously already broken away from this background, this Platonic way of thinking in terms of exemplars, for which reason the "crisis of the sacramental idea" was spoken of. When the *imago* or *figura* no longer participates in the exemplar of *veritas*, when it is therefore no longer understood as a sign fulfilled in reality but rather merely as pointing toward something else, then there arise difficulties in thinking about the Eucharistic real presence. A new edition and intensification of the controversy took place in the eleventh century at the hands of Berengar of Tours (†1088), who rejected the conversion of bread and wine into the body and blood of Christ and promoted a spiritualistic interpretation of the Eucharist, all of which derived from a sensualistic understanding of substance. Berengar was invited to recant his position several times (1050 at Vercelli; 1051 at Paris; 1054 at Tours). After that, he put before Pope Nicholas II in 1059 a confession of faith composed by Humbert of Silva Candida. See L. Hödl, "Die confessio von 1059," in *Scholastik* 37 (1962): 370–94. Berengar's critics, Lanfranc of Bec and Guitmund of Aversa, related the concept of substance to a metaempirical level and taught that the earthly substance of bread and wine are transformed into the body and blood of Christ while the visible species remain. See Lanfranc, *De sacramento corporis et sanguinis Christi*, in PL 150, here 430 C; additionally Guitmundus, *De corporis et sanguinis Christi vertitate*, in PL 149, here 1444 B, 1450 B, 1481 B. With respect to content, the later doctrine of transubstantiation is anticipated here *in nuce*. The thesis of a substantial transformation finds its magisterial expression in the formula of faith demanded of Berengar by the Roman synod of 1079: *panem et vinum ... substantialiter converti in veram et propriam ac vivificatricem carnem et sanguinem Jesu Christi* (DH 700). For background, see J. Betz, "Eucharistie als zentrales Mysterium," in *MySal* 4/2 (1973): 231–43; H. Jorissen, *Die Entfaltung der Transsubstantiationslehre bis zum Beginn der Hochscholastik* (Münster: Aschendorff, 1965).

At the same time, it is notable that the focus of scholastic Eucharistic theology on the event of consecration was rendered problematic by the liturgical movement's return to patristic sources. If all attention is devoted to the questions of *when* and *why* the gifts of bread and wine are able to become the flesh and blood of Jesus Christ, then other aspects of the mystery are placed in the background. The theological focus placed upon what Johannes Betz called the "somatic real presence"[3] of Jesus Christ in the consecrated gifts can allow—so it appears, at least—not only the motif of table fellowship (*communio*), but also the "principal actual presence" of the exalted one as well as the remembrance of the saving deeds of Jesus Christ—the "commemorative actual presence"—to recede into the background. Aquinas's Eucharistic doctrine presents a dogmatic and historical high point within the horizon of neoscholastic theology, inasmuch as the problem of Eucharistic conversion found sufficient ontological illumination; all the same, a contrary judgment will be rendered by a theology adopting a biblical and patristic orientation. From the vantage point of a biblical and patristic theology of the Eucharist, for which the mystical presence of the exalted *Kyrios* and the *anamnesis* of his saving deeds occupy the central place, scholastic Eucharistic theology appears to succumb to an ultimately fatal constriction.[4] It was hardly an accident that one could speak of a "wariness toward the medieval"[5] in recent sacramental theology.

In addition, there is the fact that the concentration placed upon the event of conversion provoked a critique from liturgical theology. From this vantage point, it appears as if scholastic theology isolated *one* segment, that is, the canon, from its liturgical context; moreover, within the canon itself, it focused once again all the attention on the formula of consecration.[6] In fact, one can hardly deny that there exist striking correspondences between the guiding intellectual interest of scholastic Eucharistic theology to illuminate the event of conversion ontologically and the liturgical praxis of the time. For in the liturgy, too, the moment of Eucharistic conversion was

---

3. On this terminology, see J. Betz, "Eucharistie," *LThK* 3, 2nd ed. (1959): 1142–57; idem, *Die Aktualpräsenz der Person und des Heilswerkes Jesu im Abendmahl nach der vorephesinischen, griechischen Patristik* (Freiburg: Herder, 1955). See also L. Lies, "Zur Eucharistielehre von Johannes Betz (1914–1984)," *ThPh* 128 (2006): 53–80.

4. An example is the assessment of H. B. Meyer, *Eucharistie*, 227f.: "But it [the doctrine of transubstantiation] also remains *fixated* on the somatic real presence. What was and remains lost is that dimension of the Eucharistic celebration called actual presence, which is bound up with the commemoration that also makes present" (emphasis added). See also idem, 202, where we find a similar instance.

5. S. Winter, *Eucharistische Gegenwart* (Regensburg: Pustet, 2002), 48.

6. See, for example, the criticism of A. Schmemann, "The Sacrament of Anaphora," in his *The Eucharist: Sacrament of the Kingdom* (Crestwood, N.Y.: St. Vladimir's Press, 1988), 159–70.

increasingly emphasized and framed with sensible *signals of alterity*. The fact that the canon was prayed silently by the priest, that is, the congregation not participating, generated a quasi-sacral aura that underscored the significance of the moment precisely through the withdrawal of words.[7] Furthermore, the elevation of the consecrated host is to be mentioned, an ostentatious gesture that corresponded to the medieval desire for show— the *désir de voir l'hostie*[8]—and was interpreted as a new epiphany of the God-man.[9] Beyond this, the pious bow (*inclinatio*) of the priest after the consecration indicated the presence of the *corpus dominicum*[10]—a gesture that was identified with the "worship ceremonial" of a servant before his king and lord. Finally, and not to be forgotten, is the ringing of the bells, both inside and outside the Church, which made the moment of Eucharistic conversion acoustically apparent not only *intra* but also *extra muros ecclesiae*. All of this made it possible for a piety to arise that was focused entirely on the transitory moment of the elevation.[11] In short: a whole ensemble of nonverbal signs marked the high significance of the event of consecra-

---

7. See J. A. Jungmann, *Missarum Sollemnia*, vol. 2, 126f., who brings in evidence that the "holy silence" during the canon already begins to appear in the eighth century and is indeed bound up with the Carolingian reception of the Roman Ordo.

8. See E. Dumoutet, *Le désir de voir l'hostie et les origines de la dévotion au Saint—Sacrement* (Paris: Beauchesne, 1926), who designates the desire for optic communion as "sentiment, qui du XIIe au XVIe siècle fut un des principaux elements de la devotion eucharistique" (7).

9. On the historical background, see the individual study, rich in material, by P. Browe, "Die Elevation im Mittelalter," in idem, *Die Eucharistie im Mittelalter. Liturgiehistorische Forschungen in kulturwissenschaftlicher Absicht*, with an introduction by H. Lutterbach and Th. Flammer (Münster: LIT, 2003), 475–508. (See also in this work the historical attestations of the emergence of the bells and candles at the consecration, as well as the celebrant's bowing and genuflecting.) On the basis of historical sources, Browe can show that the elevation of the consecrated host does not emerge until the end of the twelfth century, spreading rapidly and widely thereafter in the first half of the thirteenth century (the *elevatio calicis* does not appear until later, in the fourteenth and fifteenth centuries). See also J. A. Jungmann, *Missarum Sollemnia*, vol. 2, 256–71; A. Angenendt, *Geschichte der Religiosität im Mittelalter*, 2nd ed. (Darmstadt: Wissenschaftliche Buchgesellschaft, 2002), 488–515, esp. 505f. Already Albert the Great considers the *elevatio hostiae* a general custom of the Church: "Videmus quod universalis usus ecclesiae habet, quod facta consecratione elevatur hostia, a populo videnda et adoranda" (*In IV Sent.*, d. 13, a. 18). Thomas also presupposes the elevation as self-evident: "hostia consecrata proponitur populo adoranda" (*S. th.* III, q. 78, a. 6 s.c.; see also *In I Cor*. XI, l. VI, n. 673). Thomas himself is—as his biographer Bernard Guidonis hands on—supposed to have personally prayed during the elevation: "Tu rex gloriae Xriste, Tu patris sempiternus es filius" (see Guidonis, *Vita S. Thomae Aquinatis* (Fontes vitae S. Thomae Aquinatis III—Documents inédits publiés par la Revue Thomiste), ed. D. Prümmer, o. O. (1926), 182.

10. See *S. th.* III, q. 83, a. 5 ad 5, where Thomas interprets the bow of the head as a ritual representation of Christ's Passion. The genuflection (*genuflexio*) after the consecration came into being, according to Browe, only later, in the fourteenth and fifteenth centuries.

11. The Augustinian hermit Gottschalk Hollen expressed himself critically in the fifteenth century regarding this practice: "They come when they hear the bells: then they enter, see the elevation; if it has passed, they go away, running or fleeing as if they had seen the devil" (cited from D. Burkard, "Nähe und Distanz. Eucharistische Frömmigkeit im Mittelalter," in *Mehr als Brot und Wein*, ed. W. Haunerland [Würzburg: Echter, 2005], 73–96, here 84).

tion,[12] which, beginning in the thirteenth century, not only stood "at the center of the people's piety,"[13] but also set free a productive energy in the spirituality of the time that is not to be underestimated.[14] For the Eucharistic elevation, prayers such as the *Ave verum* were written and songs were composed, indeed visions of the saints have been handed on.[15] To be sure, the ritual staging of the act of consecration would have remained an empty formalism if what took place in the Eucharistic conversion could not be theologically stated with greater accuracy. Thus, the doctrine of transubstantiation attempts to indicate more precisely *when*, *how*, and *by what means* the presence of the *Christus passus* comes into being in the forms of bread and wine. On this point, a sensualistic understanding of the Eucharistic real presence is just as much avoided as a symbolistic one, which is ready to see in the consecrated gifts merely a commemoration of Jesus Christ.

In signo or *in veritate?* Setting Up the Problem for Eucharistic Theology

In his *quaestio* devoted to the real presence,[16] Thomas puts the question whether the body of Christ is contained in the sacrament *secundum veritatem* or *solum secundum figuram vel sicut in signo*. The question, which is posed in light of the Eucharistic controversies of the ninth and eleventh centuries, implies a conceptual alternative: either *veritas* or *figura/signum*. In this way of setting up the question—let it be explicitly noted—what remains hidden or unmentioned is that *signum* can itself be an image of *veritas*, as was manifestly the case for the Platonically inspired, real-symbolic thinking of the patristic period.[17] Aquinas is clear on the fact that faith in the real presence of Christ in the Eucharist is exposed to manifold questions. The objections reflect that what is self-evident for faith is in no way self-evident. It is no accident that Thomas begins with the *locus classicus*

---

12. The ostentatious gesture of elevation, which was often accompanied by acclamations and songs (see Ph. Harnoncourt, *Gesamtkirchliche und teilkirchliche Liturgie. Studien zum liturgischen Heiligenkalender und zum Gesang im Gottesdienst unter besonderer Berücksichtigung des deutschen Sprachgebiets* (Freiburg: Herder, 1974), 294–305), can also be proven to be, since the beginning of the thirteenth century, an iconographic topos of book illuminations (see M. Rubin, *Corpus Christi. The Eucharist in Late Medieval Culture* [Cambridge: Cambridge University Press, 1991], 131–34).

13. Thus Browe, *Eucharistie im Mittelalter*, 498, who states further: "in this moment, the most intimate prayer took place and the most ardent expression of one's faith in the incarnate and crucified God was manifested."

14. See A. Stock, *Poetische Dogmatik: Christologie*, vol. 3 (Paderborn: Schöningh, 1998), 320–24.

15. See, as an example, the testimonies of St. Gertrude of Helfta, or those of Bl. Margareta Ebner, among others, which are mentioned by Browe, *Eucharistie im Mittelalter*, 498–502.

16. See S. th. III, q. 75, a. 1. See also *In IV Sent.*, d. 10, q. 1, a. 1.

17. For background, see A. Gerken, *Theologie der Eucharistie* (Munich: Kösel, 1973), 61–96.

i. e., of the Eucharistic discourses in John's Gospel (Jn 6:53–58). The hard realism of the words—"Unless you eat the flesh of the Son of Man and drink his blood, etc."—is attenuated by Jesus himself, when he responded to the objection, "this teaching is difficult":[18] "It is the spirit that gives life; the flesh is useless." Jesus' response thus clearly appears to refute a total identification of the Eucharistic with the historic *corpus Domini*.[19] Moreover, the authority of Augustine seems to speak for a symbolistic interpretation of the Eucharist, when he advocates for a spiritual understanding of the Eucharist in his commentary on the Psalms.[20] Augustine's vote in the matter is significant in the history of theology, inasmuch as Berengar of Tours refers to Augustine in his critique of crude sacramental realism and claims the authority of the bishop of Hippo for the thesis that the body of Christ is present in the sacrament *in signo* but not *in veritate*.[21]

A further difficulty in considering the real presence arises in relation to *space*. The body of the exalted one, so it is asserted, can be in only *one* place. Jesus' pledge, "I am with you always, until the end of the age" (Mt 28:20), cannot therefore be understood to refer to the real presence but only to a symbolic presence, for the *corpus Christi verum* is bound to one spatial limit.[22] Here also the authority of Augustine is cited for a symbolic interpretation of the Eucharist, who in his commentary on John's Gospel establishes that the body of the risen one is *in uno loco* whereas his truth is everywhere.[23]

In the same troubling direction a third problem can be pointed out,

---

18. "durus est hic sermo / quis potest eum audire?" (Jn 6:60).

19. In the *Sentences* commentary, Thomas also raises the concern that if the *corpus Christi verum* is contained in the sacrament of the Eucharist, it insinuates a sublime cannibalism; the consumption of human flesh is a "bestial atrocity," which is unable to be brought into accord with the adoration of the sacrament. See *In IV Sent.*, d. 10, q. 1, a. 1, obj. 1 (n. 7): "In his enim quae ad pietatem et reverentiam pertinent divinam, nihil debet esse quod in crudelitatem vel irreverentiam sonet. Sed manducare carnes hominis sonat in quamdam bestialem crudelitam et irreverentiam manducati. Ergo et in sacramento pietatis, quod ad manducationis usum ordinatur, non debet esse verum corpus Christi quod manducatur."

20. Augustine, *En. In Ps* 98 (CCL 39, ed. D. E. Dekkers et I. Fraipont, 1386 = PL 37, 1265): "Spiritualiter intelligite quod locutus sum; non hoc corpus quod videtis, manducaturi estis, et bibituri illum sanguinem quem fusuri sunt qui me crucifigent. Sacramentum aliquod vobis commendavi, spiritualiter intellectum vivificabit vos. Etsi neccese est illud visibiliter celebrari, oportet tamen invisibiliter intellegi.—Understand spiritually, what I say [Augustine has Christ say]. It is not this body you see that you will eat, nor is it the blood spilled by those who crucify me that you will drink. It is a sacrament that I have entrusted to you. Understood spiritually, it will vivify you. If it is also necessary to celebrate it in a visible way, still it must be understood spiritually." See also *Decretum Gratiani*, p. III, d. 2, can. 44, ed. Richter-Friedberg, I, 1330; Peter Lombard, *IV Sent*, d. 10.

21. See the commentary in the German edition of Thomas's works [*Thomas-Ausgabe*], vol. 30 (1938), 406f.

22. See *S. th.* III, q. 75, a. 1, obj. 2. Similarly, and earlier, see: *In IV Sent.*, d. 10, q. 1, a. 1, obj. 4 and 5.

23. See Augustinus, *In Io. Ev. tr.* XXX, 1 (CCL 36, ed. R. Willems, 289 = PL 35, 1632): "donec saeculum finiatur. Sursum est Dominus; sed hic est ueritas Dominus. Corpus enim Domini in quo resurrexit, uno loco esse potest: ueritas eius ubique diffusa est."

that of *multilocality*, which calls attention to the impossibility of *one* body being present simultaneously in *several* places. Because, however, the body of Christ, after the ascension, has its place in heaven and thus at the right hand of the Father, it cannot be truly in the sacrament of the altar, but only symbolically.[24]

Finally, the motif of the sending of the Spirit is brought into play. The disciples could receive the Spirit only after their emotions were no longer fixed upon the bodily presence of Jesus Christ. Referring to John 16:7, it is asserted that the *physical* absence of Jesus Christ is so to speak the precondition for his *pneumatic* presence (see Rom 5:5). With this as background, we ought not to speak of a *praesentia corporalis* in the sacrament of the altar.

Against this sequence of objections, Thomas juxtaposes the authority of Hilary[25] and Ambrose,[26] who emphasize the real presence of the body and blood of Christ in the Eucharistic gifts. In the *Sentences* commentary, moreover, Thomas appeals to Scripture and the Pauline admonition that he who eats the Eucharistic bread and drinks the cup of salvation without considering that it is the body of the Lord calls judgment upon himself (see 1 Cor 11:29)—a statement that, in Thomas's view, presupposes the real body of the Lord (*corpus Christi verum*) to be contained in the sacrament.[27]

The exposition of the problem shows on the one hand the difficulties with which the faith sees itself confronted when it comes to the real presence; on the other hand, *auctoritates* such as Scripture, and also Hilary and

---

24. See *S. th.* III, q. 75, a. 1, obj. 3. Similarly, and earlier, see: *In IV Sent.*, d. 10, q. 1, a. 1, obj. 6.

25. Thomas cites the following statements of Hilary, *De Trinitate*, VIII, 14: "De veritate carnis et sanguinis Christi non est relictus ambigendi locus. Nunc, et ipsius Domini professione, et fide nostra, caro eius vere est cibus et sanguis eius vere est potus. – Concerning the reality of the flesh and blood of Christ, there is no more room for doubt. For now, according to the teaching of the Lord and our faith, his flesh is truly a meal and his blood truly a drink." The form of the text in the Marietti edition differs from the critical edition of SC, where it reads: "De ueritate carnis et sanguinis Christi non relictus est ambigendi locus. Nunc enim et ipsius Domini professione et fide nostra uere caro est et uere sanguis est." Hilary of Poitier, *La trinité*, vol. 2, bks. IV–VIII. Texte critique par G. M. de Durand, Ch. Morel, et G. Pelland (SC 448) (Paris: Cerf, 2000), 398.

26. Ambrose, *sacr.* VI, 1 (in *S. th.* III, q. 75, a. 1, s.c., cited in abbreviation, according to Gratian, *Decretum*, p. III, d. 2, can. 84): "Sicut verus est Dei Filius Dominus Iesus Christus, ita vera Christi caro est, quam accipimus, et verus sanguis eius est potus.—As the Lord Jesus Christ is truly the Son of God, so it is also the case with the true flesh of Christ, which we receive, and likewise the drink his true blood." The whole passage reads: "Sicut verus est dei filius dominus noster Iesus Christus, non quemadmodum homines per gratiam, sed quasi filius dei ex substantia patris, ita vera caro, sicut ipse dixit, quam accipimus, et verus eius est potus" (idem, *De sacramentis—De mysteriis* (Fontes Christiani [FC] 3, ed. J. Schmitz) (Freiburg: Herder, 1990), 180f.). Ambrose transmits the justification for this understanding of the Eucharist in *sacr.* 4, 14–23, where he develops his understanding of the Eucharistic conversion, the so-called metabolic approach (ibid., 143–50).

27. Additionally, the salvation-historical nexus *figura—veritas* is touched upon in the *Sentences* commentary: as the Paschal lamb (*agnus paschalis*) in the old covenant pointed ahead to Christ and was consumed as a meal, so correspondingly in the new covenant the true body of Christ (*corpus Christi verum*) must be eaten. See *In Iv Sent.* d. 10, q. 1, a. 1 (n. 9), s.c.

Ambrose, are adduced who clearly bear witness to this faith. The question now is whether Thomas will affiliate himself rather with a symbolistic interpretation, which can mitigate the stated objections, since it posits a presence *solum in signo*; or whether he will develop a solution that is able to preserve the position—attested by Hilary and Ambrose and granted magisterial approbation by the Fourth Lateran Council[28]—that takes as its point of departure a real presence of Christ's body and blood in the Eucharistic gifts.

In his response, Thomas affirms first of all that the real presence of Christ's body and blood in the sacrament is *not able to be grasped by the senses (non sensu)*. This sensory deficit regarding the Eucharistic mystery, which can be designated as a "lack of sensory verification,"[29] will be poetically expressed by Thomas in the hymn for the Office of Corpus Christi.[30] Only faith, which rests on hearing the divine word—and here the word reads: *Hoc est corpus meum, quod pro vobis tradetur* (see Lk 22:19; 1 Cor 11:24)—offers entrance into the *Mysterium fidei*.[31] For clarification, Thomas quotes a passage from Cyril of Alexandria, who commented upon the *verba testamenti* in the following way: "Do not doubt whether it is true. Rather, accept the Savior's word in faith. For he is the truth, he does not lie."[32] In addition, the *Commentary on the Sentences* brings in the argument that the faithful would not be joined to Christ in holy communion at all if he were not contained *per suam essentiam* in the forms of bread and wine.[33]

In order to understand the meaning of the words of institution and thus make plausible faith in Christ's real presence in the Eucharist, Thomas adduces diverse reasons of fittingness. His *first consideration* places the *ver-*

---

28. See DH 802: "Iesus Christus, cuius corpus et sanguis in sacramento altaris sub speciebus panis et vini *veraciter continentur*" (emphasis added).

29. A. Stock, *Poetische Dogmatik: Christologie*, vol. 3: *Leib und Leben* (Paderborn: Schöningh, 1998), 317.

30. In the vesperal hymn *Pange lingua gloriosi*, the text runs: *et si sensus deficit, / ... sola fides sufficit*, or again, *praestet fides supplementum / sensuum defectui*. And in the sequence *Lauda Sion*, we find: *Quod non capis, quod non vides, / animosa firmat fides*. See, on this point, my work "Die Sequenz *Lauda Sion* als poetische Verdichtung der Eucharistietheologie des Thomas von Aquin," *ThGl* 93 (2003): 475–97, as well as the remarks in Part B.

31. *S. th.* III, q. 75, a. 1: "verum corpus Christi et sanguinem esse in hoc sacramento, non sensu [DThA, vol. 30, 52, offers a textual form diverging from the Marietti edition: neque sensu neque intellectu] deprehendi postest, sed sola fide, quae auctoritati divinae innititur."

32. In the Marietti edition (p. 466), the reference for Cyril, *In Luc.* XX, 19, is wrongly given as PG 72, 909 B. The passage can be found rather at PG 72 (1864), 911 B, where it reads: "Neque dubites; id quippe verum est, ipso manifeste dicente: 'Hoc est corpus meum,' et, 'Hic est sanguis meus.' Imo potius Servatoris verba cum fide recipe; qui cum sit veritas, non mentitur." In the version found in the *S. th.*, the passage runs slightly differently: "Non dubites an hoc verum sit, sed potius suscipe verba Salvatoris in fide; cum enim sit veritas, non mentitur." See also Ambrose, who, after he ascribed the event of consecration to the operative power of the word of Christ, observed: "Deinde ipse dominus Iesus testificatus est nobis, quod corpus suum accipiamus et sanguinem. Numquid debemus de eius fide et testificatione dubitare?" (*sacr.* IV, 23 [FC 3, ed. J. Schmitz, 150]).

33. See *In IV Sent.*, d. 10, q. 1, a. 1, n. 12.

ba testamenti within the horizon of salvation history and quotes the passage from the letter to the Hebrews, the Law is only a shadow of good things to come and does not contain the image (*imago*) of the things themselves (see Heb 10:1). If, however, the manifold sacrifices of the old covenant signify only by way of anticipatory types, then the fulfillment of these types must acquire an added theological value (*aliquid plus*) in the new covenant. From this *figura-veritas* schema,[34] Thomas concludes that the sacrifice instituted by Christ contains the *Christus passus* not only in signs but also in truth; that is to say, Christ is present *non solum in significatione vel figura, sed etiam in rei veritate*. Accordingly, Thomas follows Dionysius in naming the sacrament that contains Christ himself the "consummation of all other sacraments," which only participate in the power of Christ.[35] The Eucharist is not exhausted therefore in the communication of grace but rather finds its end in communion with Jesus Christ. As the faithful communicate with Christ, so they become members of his body ever anew, thus forming the *corpus Christi mysticum*.[36]

The *second* argument Thomas presents for the real presence of Christ appears at first glance to speak of a total identification between the Eucharistic and the historical body of Christ, when it traces the *praesentia corporalis* back to the *caritas Christi*. It was out of love that the eternal Word became man and for our salvation took on a body.[37] A *proprium* of friendship, however, consists in living and eating together with friends (the semantics of *convivere* emcompasses both aspects).[38] Therefore, Christ promised his

---

34. See *S. th.* I-II, qq. 99–105. On this point, see O. H. Pesch, *Thomas von Aquin*, 285–317; idem, "Sittengebote, Kultvorschriften, Rechtssatzungen. Zur Theologiegeschichte von Summa Theologiae I-II 99, 2–5," in *Thomas von Aquino. Interpretation und Rezeption: Studien und Texte* , ed. W. P. Eckert (Mainz: Matthias-Grünewald, 1974), 488–518.

35. *S. th.* III, q. 75, a. 1: "Et ideo hoc sacramentum, quod ipsum Christum realiter continet, ut Dionysius dicit cap. 3 *Eccles. Hierar.*, est *perfectivum omnium sacramentorum aliarum*, in quibus virtus Christi participatur" (emphasis added). The quotation from Pseudo-Dionysius can be found frequently in Thomas (see *S. th.* III, q. 65, a. 3; *In IV Sent*, d. 8, q.1, a. 1; d. 10, q. 1, a. 1, etc.)

36. See *S. th.* III, q. 82, a. 9 ad 2: "Unitas corporis mystici est fructus corporis veri percepti." See also *In IV Sent*, d. 8, q. 1, a. 2, sol. 2 ad 4: "Ad perfectionem corporis exigitur, quod membra capiti coniunguntur. Sed per hoc sacramentum membra Ecclesiae suo capiti coniunguntur." For background, see M. Grabmann, *Die Lehre des heiligen Thomas von Aquin von der Kirche als Gotteswerk* (Regensburg: Manz, 1903), 267–94.

37. At this point it is important to recall that Aristotle had ruled out in a radical way friendship between gods and, more importantly, between God and men, because he did not see the criteria for mutual love and *communication* fulfilled. It is otherwise with Thomas, *S. th.* II-II, q. 2, a. 1, who points out that the infinite God communicated himself to finite men in Jesus Christ, thereby fulfilling the conditions of *communicatio*. For background, see H. Dörnemann, *Freundschaft als Paradigma der Erlösung* (Würzburg: Echter, 1997), 105–29; E. Schockenhoff, "Die Liebe als Freundschaft des Menschen mit Gott. Das Proprium der Caritaslehre des Thomas von Aquin," *IKaZ Communio* 36 (2007): 232–46; idem, *Bonum hominis. Die anthropologischen und theologischen Grundlagen der Tugendethik des Thomas von Aquin* (Mainz: Matthias-Grünewald, 1987), 493–501.

38. Living together grows stronger in a common meal (*convivium*). See Aristotle, *Nicomachean Ethics*

friends his *praesentia corporalis* as a reward. Thomas hints here at the motif of the heavenly wedding banquet and thus makes clear that the sacramental presence will be surpassed once again by the fullness of the eschatological presence. Nevertheless, in the meantime—the "interim" between ascension and parousia—Christ has not entirely withheld from his friends his bodily presence. Distinguishing himself from those who espouse a crude sacramental realism—who speak for a *manducatio corporalis* and thereby confirm the suspicion of anthropophagy—Thomas differentiates his explanation, holding that Christ binds himself to us through the truth of his body and blood, and indeed in this sacrament (*in hoc sacramento*).[39] This, however, means that the presence of Christ *in proprie specie* must be distinguished from his presence *in specie sacramenti*:[40] in the time of his physical absence, Christ offers himself in the forms of bread and wine, which remain behind after the consecration as subject-less accidents. In the reception of the consecrated gifts, what takes place is the true and real—thus not merely symbolic—unification with Christ, so that following Thomas the Eucharist can be designated as the enactment of friendship with Christ. This is already expressed in the Eucharistic discourse of John's Gospel, where being with and next to each other in a spatial way is surpassed by a mutual being in each other: "Those who eat my flesh and drink my blood abide in me, and I in them" (Jn 6:56).[41] For this reason, Thomas characterizes the Eucharist as *signum maximae caritatis* and at the same time sees in it an indication of the human hope for perfection. Pointing to the bodily presence of friends may not therefore be thought of "*according to the conceptual model of bodily presence in a place*," as Josef Wohlmuth correctly observed.[42] Such spatial connotations are to be kept at bay from the sacramental presence of Christ.

This confirms the third argument, which likewise attenuates talk of the *praesentia corporalis* by emphasizing that the bodily presence in the Eucharist is given to faith *in an invisible manner* (*invisibili modo*). The real presence is neither empirically comprehensible nor rationally demonstrable. It is only plausible in faith, and this faith as such would be made void if it

---

IX, 12 [1171b32–33]. See A. W. Keaty, "Thomas's Authority for Identifying Charity as Friendship: Aristotle or John 15:15?" *The Thomist* 62 (1998): 581–601.

39. *S. th.* III, q. 75, a. 1: "Interim tamen nec sua praesentia corporali in hac peregrinatione destituit, sed per veritatem corporis et sanguinis sui nos sibi coniugit in hoc sacramento."

40. On this distinction, see also *S. th.* III, q. 73, a. 5 c.

41. On the analysis of reciprocal formulas of immanence, see K. Scholtissek, *In ihm sein und bleiben. Die Sprache der Immanenz in den johanneischen Schriften* (Freiburg-Basel-Vienna: Herder, 2000).

42. J. Wohlmuth, "Eucharistie als liturgische Feier der Gegenwart Jesu Christi. Realpräsenz und Transsubstantiation im Verständnis katholischer Theologie," in *Eucharistie. Positionen katholischer Theologie*, ed. Th. Söding (Regensburg: Pustet, 2002), 87–119, here 95.

could be undergirded with visible proofs. Beyond that, something rather gruesome would be asked of the senses were they in fact required to see, touch, and taste the flesh and blood of the sacrificed Christ.[43]

To the objections cited, Thomas answers in the following way: a spiritual construal of the Eucharist, which could find expression in the formula *Hoc significat corpus meum*, would not do justice to the sense of the words of institution, since they assert a true presence of the Lord in the forms of bread and wine (*Hoc est corpus meum*). For this reason, Augustine's teaching is enlisted to counter a symbolistic interpretation. Berengar of Tours wrongfully appeals to the bishop of Hippo. Augustine did not advocate an empty symbolism but rather called attention to the fact that Christ is not carved up like a slaughtered animal and sold to the butcher's shop; instead, his body and blood are truly received, even if *in a spiritual manner*, that is, invisibly.[44] Analogously, Thomas will point out in other passages that the violent event of crucifixion is not repeated in the celebration of the Eucharist. The rite of the Eucharist is an image representing (*imago representativa*) the suffering of Christ; it makes present not the act of crucifixion but that of Christ's self-giving.[45]

43. In the end, Thomas gives a theological and historical reference to the magisterium's judgment of Berengar, who ruled out a transformation of the gifts of bread and wine, thereby appearing to dispute the real presence of Christ in the Eucharist (see DH 690 and 700). That Berengar of Tours did not advocate a mere symbolism but rather took Augustine's understanding of *signum sacrum* and used it to criticize a crude sacramental materialism, without himself denying the real presence, has been recently argued—as was mentioned—by H. Jorissens, "Berengar von Tours," *LThK* 2, 3rd ed. (1994): 244–46. For a different view, see F. Courth: "By means of the consecration, bread and wine become the *figura* of the Lord's body. Berengar excludes a real presence because the glorified body of Christ cannot be called down upon earthly gifts" (*Die Sakramente. Ein Lehrbuch für Studium und Praxis* [Freiburg: Herder, 1995], 185).

44. See Augustine, *In Io Ev tr.* XXVII, n. 5 (CCL 36, ed. R. Willems, 272 = PL 35, 1617): "Non prodest quidquam, sed quomodo illi intellexerunt: carnem quippe sic intellexerunt, quomodo in cadauere dilaniatur, aut in macello uenditur, non quomodo spiritur uegetatur." The *Sentences* commentary as well counters the suspicion of anthropophagy with the proposition that the body of Christ is not eaten after the fashion of bodily food (*ad modum cibi corporalis*), chopped up and ground down by the teeth; it is rather a matter of *sacramental* eating. The passage runs: "dicendum quod in crudelitatem sonaret et maximam irreverentiam, si corpus Christi ad modum cibi corporalis manducaretur, et scilicet ipsum verum corpus Christi dilaniaretur et dentibus atteretur. Hoc autem non contingit in sacramentali manducatione" (*In IV Sent.*, d. 10, q. 1, a. 1 ad 1 [n. 14]). In these words, one can observe a careful correction of the crude sensualism found in the *Professio Fidei* that was presented to Berengar in 1059. The document states "that the bread and wine laid upon the altar are, after the consecration, not only a sacrament but also the true body and the true blood of our Lord Jesus Christ, and are sensuously [sic]—not only in sacrament but also in truth—touched and broken by the priest's hands and ground up [sic] with the teeth of the faithful.— ... scilicet panem et vinum, quae in altari ponuntur, post consecrationem non solum sacramentum, sed etiam verum corpus et sanguinem Domini nostri Iesu Christi esse, et sensualiter, non solum sacramento, sed in veritate, manibus sacerdotum tractari et frangi et fidelium dentibus atteri, iurans per sanctam et homousion Trinitatem et per haec sacrosancta Christi evangelia" (DH 690). See also Bonaventure, *Breviloquium*, VI, 9, who argues that it is not acceptable to masticate Christ's flesh with the teeth, first, because it makes one shudder at the thought, and secondly, because his body is incorruptible.

45. See *S. th.* III, q. 83, a. 1. When A. Vonier (*A Key to the Doctrine of the Eucharist* [Bethesda, Md.: Zaccheus Press, 2003], 80ff.) speaks of a "slaughtering [*Schlachtung*; Vonier's original English has *immolation*]

It is not visibly, like the terrestrial body of the Lord (*in propria specie*), that the *Christus passus* is present wherever the sacrament is celebrated, but rather invisibly (*in specie sacramenti*). For the problem of multi-locality as well, Thomas refers to the *sacramental* mode of presence in order to find his way to a solution. Sacramental presence is not to be grasped *according to the mode of a body*, which occupies one place by means of its extension. The body of Christ is not present upon different altars as if in different places, but rather *sicut in sacramento*. This sacramental presence is not to be understood as merely symbolic, even though sacrament is placed in the genus of signs.

But how can the mode of making present be more precisely described? How can the body and blood of Jesus Christ come to be from bread and wine? In medieval theology there were three basic explanatory approaches already referred to in Peter Lombard's *Sentences*, from which Thomas also draws in his explications: first, impanation (later also designated with the term consubstantiation), second, annihilation, and third, transubstantiation.[46] It will be seen that the reception of Aristotelian philosophy opened up new possibilities of overcoming the crisis of sacramental ideas. It is precisely the distinction between substance and accident that allowed both extremes—a crude sacramental materialism (*res*) in the understanding of the real presence and a purely symbolistic interpretation—to be left behind.

Impanation as an Explanatory Model and Its Critique

One possible explanation for the real presence of Christ in the Eucharist is the doctrine of impanation.[47] According to this teaching, the substance of the body and blood of Christ enters into the substance of bread and wine. Thus, Christ becomes present in that he unites himself to the substance of bread (*impanatio* = becoming bread). Guitmund of Aversa had already engaged this doctrine in his work *De corporis et sanguinis Christi veritate*,

---

of Christ in the Eucharistic sacrifice," he obviously brings post-Tridentine theories of sacrifice into Thomas's treatise on the Eucharist. The term *mactatio* certainly does not appear in the *Summa theologiae*. All the same, Vonier also excludes the idea of a ritual repetition of "slaughtering" in the Eucharist, when he states: "We do not say that Christ is slaughtered anew in the Eucharistic sacrifice, for this would mean a substantial process of disintegration in the very Person of Christ such as He is now, a thing not to be admitted. But we do say that He is slaughtered, because the slaughter on Calvary is represented so truly, and is applied so directly, through the Eucharistic Body and Blood" (83, replacing "immolated" with "slaughtered").

46. See H. Jorissen, *Die Entfaltung der Transsubstantiationslehre bis zum Beginn der Hochscholastik* (Münster: Aschendorff, 1965), who offers an instructive overview of this triad of theories describing how the Eucharist is made present and also presents the diverse qualifications of these theories in the scholastic theologians of the twelfth and thirteenth centuries. See also G. Macy, "The Dogma of Transubstantiation in the Middle Ages," *Journal of Ecclesiastical History* 45 (1994): 11–41, esp. 13ff.

47. See *S. th.* III, q. 75, a. 2, as well as *In IV Sent.*, d. 11, a. 1, qa. 1 and *S. c. G.*, c. 63.

though without identifying its exponents by name.[48] *After* Thomas Aquinas, there are considerable witnesses to this theory, such as Duns Scotus, who did not consider the theory of consubstantiation unscriptural,[49] or John Wyclif and Martin Luther, both of whom supported this theory.[50] Thomas himself first registers arguments that seem to speak for impanation. *Prima facie* this theory corresponds better to the testimony of the senses—eyes, touch, and taste—which perceive the forms of bread and wine to be unchanged even after the consecration. Moreover, there is the consideration of John of Damascus that the sacrament of the Eucharist corresponds to the human practice of eating bread and drinking wine, for which very reason God joined his divinity to these signs and made them into his body and blood.[51] Another aspect of sacramental theology that appears to support the explanatory model of impanation is that in Baptism and Confirmation as well, the substance of the matter remains in existence (water, chrism, etc.). Analogously, this would need to apply to the Eucharist as well. Finally, there are symbolic reasons why it would be important for the substance of bread and wine to remain intact in this sacrament: as bread is obtained from many grains and wine from many grapes, so also does the Church, the *corpus Christi mysticum*, consist of many members.

To this vote for the model of impanation Thomas opposes the authority of Ambrose, who states that, even if after the consecration the forms of bread and wine continue to be seen, one may still not believe in anything other than the flesh and blood of Christ.[52]

In the *corpus articuli*, the *Doctor communis* repudiates impanation as an explanatory model, since it is opposed by the truth that the true body of

---

48. See Guitmundus, *De corporis et sanguinis Christi veritate in Eucharistia*, in: PL 149, 1427–1512, here 1430: "Alii vero, rectis Ecclesiae rationibus cedentes, nec tamen a stultitia recedentes, ut quasi aliquo modo nobiscum esse videantur, dicunt ibi corpus et sanguinem Domini revera, sed latenter contineri, et ut sumi possint quodammodo, ut ita dixerim, *impanari*" (emphasis added).

49. See *Oxon.*, d. 11, q. 3, n. 9, 14–15 (= *Opera omnia*, XVII, ed. Vivès, 357, 375f.). But the authentic interpretation of the magisterium professes that the *verba testamenti* are to be interpreted in the sense of transubstantiation. In itself, consubstantiation would certainly also accommodate the semantic content of the words of institution. As is well known, a similar position is advocated by William of Ockham. On this point, see E. Iserloh, *Gnade und Eucharistie in der philosophischen Theologie des Wilhelm von Ockham* (Wiesbaden: Verlag Phillip von Zabern in Wissenschaftliche Buchgesellschaft, 1956), 155–60.

50. See H. Jorissen, "Konsubstantiation," *LThK* 6, 3rd ed. (1997): 323f. See also J. R. Geiselmann, *Die Eucharistielehre der Vorscholastik* (Paderborn: Schöningh, 1926), 302.

51. See *S. th.* III, q. 75, a. 2, obj. 1. Even earlier there is a reference to this quotation from John of Damascus (*De fide orthodoxa*. I, IV, c. 13 [ed. E. M. Buytaerd, 316f.] in: *In IV Sent.*, d. 11, q. 1, a. 1 (n. 14).

52. *S. th.* III q. 75, a. 2, s.c.: "Licet figura panis et vini videatur, nihil tamen aliud quam caro Christi et sanguis post consecrationem credenda sunt." The Marietti edition gives as the source: Ambrosius, *De sacr.* IV, 5. Following the critical edition of Fontes Christiani, the passage reads: "Antequam consecratur, panis est; ubi autem verba Christi accesserint, corpus est Christi. Denique audi dicentem: 'accipite et edite ex hoc omnes: hoc est enim corpus meum.' Et ante verba Christi calix est vini et aquae plenus; ubi verba Christi operata fuerint, ibi sanguis efficitur, qui plebem redemit" (FC 3, ed. J. Schmitz, 148–50).

Christ is contained in the sacrament.[53] He grounds his negative judgment first of all by a line of thought that refers crucially to change of place, which is implied in the process of becoming bread. Were the doctrine of impanation to be accurate, Christ, who is not present before the consecration, would then have to join with the substances of bread and wine through a local motion (*per motum localem*).[54] Such a motion, however, includes the following three difficulties, which Thomas already cites in the *Summa contra gentiles*:[55]

1. The glorified Christ would cease to be in heaven, because the arrival *in loco altaris* is possible only by leaving the *locus coelesti*.[56] But the imaginative assumption that Christ would leave heaven every time the Eucharist is celebrated on earth contradicts the Creed, which speaks of his sitting at the right hand of the Father.

2. Every body moved in place that leaves its point of origin (*terminus a quo*), in order to reach its destination (*terminus ad quem*), must pass through some place in between before it reaches its end (which can likewise be asserted of Christ only with difficulty).

3. Such a motion cannot have its destination (*terminus ad quem*) at several places simultaneously. Because, however, it is certainly possible that Christ's body begins to exist sacramentally on different altars, only the alternative explanation can be valid, namely, that he begins to exist there by means of the transformation of the substance of bread and wine (*relinquitur quod non posit aliter corpus Christi incipere esse de novo in hoc sacramento nisi per conversionem substantiae panis in ipsum*).[57] But what is transformed does not remain after the transformation, for which reason the substance of bread does not remain in existence after the consecration.

---

53. The rehabilitation of impanation, or consubstantiation, by John Wyclif was condemned by the Council of Constance (DH 1151), while that by Martin Luther—who, as is well known, relied on the Eucharistic understanding of Pierre d'Ailly—was condemned by the Council of Trent. See DH 1652: "Si quis dixerit, in sacrosancto Eucharistiae sacramento remanere substantiam panis et vini una cum corpore et sanguine Domini nostri Iesu Christi, negaveritque mirabilem illam et singularem conversionem totius substantiae panis in corpus et totius substantiae vini in sanguinem, manentibus dumtaxat speciebus panis et vini, quam quidem conversionem catholica Ecclesia aptissime transsubstantiationem appellat: anathema sit.—Whoever says that the substance of bread and wine perdure together with the body and blood of our Lord Jesus Christ in the most holy sacrament of the Eucharist, and denies that wonderful and singular conversion of the whole substance of bread into the body and the whole substance of wine into the blood, leaving only the species of bread and wine ... : anathema sit."

54. See G. Ardley, "The Physics of Local Motion," *The Thomist* 17 (1954): 145–85.

55. See *S. c. G.* IV, c. 63.

56. It is notable here that Thomas understands the exalted Christ's way of being present in a quite spatial manner.

57. *S. th.* III, q. 75, a. 2, c. See also, on the problem of multi-locality, q. 76, a. 5.

A further argument against impanation given by Thomas, which demonstrates his orientation toward the biblical witness, is the *form of the sacrament*, which runs: *Hoc est corpus meum*. If the substance of bread would in fact perdure in the sacrament, these words of Jesus would not be accurate and instead it would have to read: *Hic est corpus meum* ("This [bread] is my body").[58] We will see later that Thomas attempts to unfold more exhaustively the semantics of the *verba testamenti* by analyzing other potential formulas of consecration. Precisely on account of the strict orientation toward the biblical *verba testamenti*, Thomas even expresses here—as he already did in the *Commentary on the Sentences*[59]—the suspicion of idolatry: the worship of the sacrament of the altar, liturgically expressed both in the elevation of the consecrated gifts and in the priest's bowing,[60] would be problematic if there remained behind a created substance, which would be illegitimately worshiped with the adoration due to God alone.[61]

Differing from his teacher Albert the Great—who did not yet classify impanation as heretical but rather left it as a valid, even if less convincing, explanatory model for the Eucharistic presence[62]—Thomas lays down in closing that the doctrine of impanation is heretical.[63] Following Hans Jorissen, it can therefore be established: "For Thomas, what is heretical about the doctrine of consubstantiation emerges directly from the truth of the literal interpretation of the Lord's words which is demanded by Holy Scripture. As these words testify to the real presence of Christ in their immediate literal sense, so they express that what is given in the sacrament is the body of Christ in an exclusive sense; they thus include also the fact that the substance of bread does not remain and, in consequence, the substan-

---

58. See also on this point *S. c. G.* IV, c. 63: "si substantia panis simul est in hoc sacramento cum vero corpore Christi, potius Christo dicendum fuit; 'Hic est corpus meum', quam, 'Hoc est corpus meum': cum per 'hic' demonstretur substantia quae videtur, quae quidem est substantia panis, si in sacramento cum corpore Christi remaneat."

59. See *In IV Sent.*, d. 11, q. 1, a. 1 (n. 24): "Esset enim idololatriae occasio, si hostiae veneratio latriae exhiberetur, substantia panis ibi remanente."

60. See P. Browe, *Die Eucharistie im Mittelalter*, 475–509.

61. Finally, impanation runs contrary to the Church's sober precept disallowing the reception of the body of Christ after a normal meal but allowing a second consecrated host to be received after already receiving a first. For background, see P. Browe, "Die Nüchternheit vor der Messe und Kommunion im Mittelalter," *Die Eucharistie im Mittelalter*, 33–38.

62. See Albert the Great, *De corpore Domini*, d. 3, tr. 8, c. 1 n. 4, where the doctrine of consubstantiation is censured in the following way: "dico sine praeiudicio, quod numquam mihi placuit ista opinio, quae quamvis non iudicetur esse haeretica, tamen est valde incauta, et haeresi valde vicina." Also in the earlier *Sentences* commentary, impanation is qualified merely as "false," but not as heretical (see *In IV Sent.*, d. 11, a. 8 ad 1). Thus, it is not entirely accurate when G. Macy asserts that Albert the Great repudiated impanation as heretical (see Macy, "The Dogma of Transubstantiation in the Middle Ages").

63. Already earlier in his *Sentences* commentary (*In IV Sent.*, d. 11, q. 1, a. 1 ad qc. 1 resp.), Thomas had characterized as heretical the thesis that the substances of bread and wine coexist with those of flesh and blood.

tial change of the whole substance of bread and wine into the substance of Christ's body and blood."[64]

When taking up the arguments *for* impanation cited at the outset, Thomas first puts forward a correct interpretation of the quotation from John of Damascus, who indeed taught that God joined his divinity with bread and wine, without however wanting this to be understood as the substance of bread and wine remaining behind in the sacrament. Furthermore, the species of bread and wine, in which Christ is present in a hidden way, are sensibly perceptible even after the consecration. The counterargument that the substance of the matter remains in existence in the other sacraments is without cogency, for Christ himself is not contained in the other sacraments.[65] In the final analysis, the subject-less accidents remaining after the consecration are fully adequate for the *modus significandi*. The species of bread and wine, which are accessible to the senses, are pregnant signs of what is contained in them: on the one hand, the *corpus Christi verum*, the *nutrimentum spirituale*, which strengthens and nourishes the faithful; on the other hand, the *corpus Christi mysticum*, which consists of many members and is expressed symbolically by the many grains and many grapes that make up the bread and wine.[66]

Annihilation as an Explanatory Model and Its Critique

In order to clarify how bread and wine are changed into the flesh and blood of Jesus Christ,[67] the thesis was put forward in the theology before Thomas that, through the consecration, the substance of bread and of wine is either dissolved into the *materia praeiacens* or rather destroyed, that is, annihilated.[68] *Materia praeiacens*, into which *corpora mixta* can dissolve, comprises

---

64. H. Jorissen, *Die Entfaltung der Transsubstantiationslehre*, 51. See also *In IV Sent*, d. 11, q. 1, a. 1 (nn. 23 and 26). Bonaventure reaches the same judgment, although he does not bring the charge of heresy directly into play. See Bonaventure, *In IV Sent.*, d. 11, p.1 a un q. 1 concl.: "haec positio aufert sacramenti veritatem..., quia ponit ex hoc falsitatem in forma; ... Propter hoc igitur haec positio est reprobanda et neminem habet ex doctoribus defensorem; immo communiter tenet Ecclesia, quod est ibi conversio panis in corpus Christi."

65. See on this point *S. th.* III, q. 73, a. 1 ad 3, where the difference between the Eucharist and the other sacraments is explained as follows: "Haec est autem differentia inter Eucharistiam et alia sacramenta habentia materiam sensibilem, quod Eucharistia continet *sacrum absolute*, scilicet *ipsum Christum*: aqua vero baptismi continet aliquid *sacrum in ordine ad aliud*, scilicet *virtutem ad sanctificandum* et eadem ratio est de chrismate et similibus. Et ideo sacramentum Eucharistiae perficitur in ipsa consecratione materiae: alia vero sacramenta perficiuntur in applicatione materiae ad hominem sanctificandum" (emphasis added).

66. See, even earlier, *In IV Sent.*, d. 11, q. 1, a. 1 (n. 28): "species sic remanentes repraesentant aliquo modo substantiam quam prius afficiebant, et per se consequens proprietates ejus; et ita habent rationem significandi per quamdam similitudinem corpus Christi verum et mysticum."

67. See *S. th.* III, q. 75, a. 3, as well as *In IV Sent.*, d. 11, q. 1, a. 2; *Quodl.* V, q. 6, a. 1 and *S. c. G.* IV, c. 63.

68. According to H. Jorissen, *Die Entfaltung der Transsubstantiationslehre*, 26–55 (which includes a list of sources), this theory finds numerous proponents, some famous, in the twelfth and the first part of the

the four elements (earth, water, fire, air). It is not to be confused with *materia prima*, which is without form and, as pure potency, presents a limit concept for speculative thinking.[69] But is a dissolving or annihilation of the substances of bread and wine theologically conceivable?

With a view to the explanatory model of *dissolving* into the four elements, Thomas first of all states the proposition that, after the consecration, nothing remains behind under the species except the substances of the body and blood of Christ. If the substances of bread and wine were in fact to dissolve into the four elements, they would have to be removed by a local motion, because indeed after the consecration nothing but the substance of Christ's body and blood remains under the species. This removal of the four elements would have to be perceivable by the senses, but this is not the case. In addition, there is a temporal and theological difficulty that speaks against the model of the substances of bread and wine dissolving into the four elements. The transformation does not take place gradually and incrementally, but instantaneously.[70] This means: the substances of bread and wine remain in existence until the last moment of consecration. Only when the last syllable of the *verba testamenti* is spoken by the priest does the transformation ensue, so that there is no moment in which the bread and wine could dissolve into *materia praeiacens*.

Thomas brings similar deliberations to bear on the explanatory model of *annihilation*,[71] which includes two changes that take place simultaneously but are quite distinct from each other: first, the annihilation of the substances of bread and wine, which cease to exist; and second, an appearance of the substances of the body and blood of Christ, which begin to exist in place of the bread and wine. Already in the *sed contra*, Thomas called to mind Augustine's assertion that God, Creator and preserver of all things,

---

thirteenth centuries: Peter Abelard (in all likelihood), Roland Bandinelli, Magister Udo, the *Glossa ordinaria* to the *Decretum Gratiani*, the canonist Huguccio, the school of Peter Cantor (slight preference for annihilation), Robert of Courson, Gaufred of Poitiers, William of Auvergne, and Roland of Cremona.

69. See Aristotle, *Met.* 7, 3 1029a20f. See also the explanation: "By the term prime matter, Aristotle understands what one stumbles upon when the process of becoming is, so to speak, traced back to its origin (e.g. house, stone, clay, earth, prime matter). In speaking of this πρώτη ὕλη, one can no longer say what it is made out of or whence it comes into existence. Thus, it is never really present: the term πρώτη ὕλη is a sort of limit concept" (C. von Bormann, W. Franzen, A. Krapiec, and L. Oeing-Hanhoff, "Form und Materie," in *HWPh* 2 [1972]: 977–1030, here 983). The Aristotelian doctrine of an uncreated *materia prima* is, however, taken into the horizon of faith in creation (see *S. th.* I, q. 44, a. 2).

70. Thomas presents this in *S. th.* III, q. 75, a. 7, as well as earlier in *In IV Sent.*, d. 11, a. 3, qa. 2 and *Quodl.* 7, q. 8. See also K. Hedwig, "Über das 'Jetzt' (nunc) bei Thomas von Aquin," *PhJ* 109 (2002): 114–29, esp. 127f.

71. This explanatory model was later advocated by the Nominalists. God first annihilates the substance of bread and wine in order then to make present the substance of Christ's body and blood. See J. Finkenzeller, "Annihilation," *LThK* 1, 3rd ed. (1993): 697f.

cannot be the cause of the annihilation of something created. The *transitus* of a transformation aims from one thing to another; it does not aim at nothing. If the substances of bread and wine were to be annihilated, however, we could no longer speak of a change (*conversio*). Apart from that—and here Thomas once again returns to the biblical foundation of the Eucharist—the hypothesis of a dissolving or annihilation contradicts the form of the sacrament. The *verba testamenti*, "this is my body," do not denote in any way a dissolving or annihilation of the substance, and so therefore they cannot bring it about.

Thus, after impanation and annihilation are ruled out, only the last member in the triad of traditional theories concerning how Christ is made present remains promising for adequately explaining the real presence of the *Christus passus* in the Eucharist: the explanatory model of transubstantiation. Because it relocates the event of conversion to the level of substance, it evades the difficulties of a physical explanation of the Eucharistic presence. Just as it affords a middle way between the two extremes of sacramental realism and a spiritual interpretation of the Eucharist, so also it is able to open up a *via media* between consubstantiation and annihilation, through the conceptual distinction between substance and accident, for it teaches neither a substantial permanence nor an annihilation of the gifts of bread and wine.

Transubstantiation as an Explanatory Model

Thomas Aquinas was not simply the inventor of transubstantiation, a doctrine later proclaimed by the Council of Trent as dogma.[72] Without delving once again into the complex prehistory of the concept of transubstantiation,[73] let it merely be recalled that Berengar's criticism of the Eucharistic conversion forced his objectors to define the process of conversion with greater conceptual precision. Especially the theologians Lanfranc of Bec and Guitmund of Aversa took up the Ambrosian line of metabolism in the eleventh century and defined the Eucharistic *conversio* as a substantial change, though without yet coining the technical term *transsubstantiatio*.[74]

---

72. See *S. th.* III, q. 75, a. 4, and earlier *In Sent IV*, d. 11, q. 1, a. 3, qa. 1, as well as *S. c. G.* IV, c. 63; *C. grace. Arm.*, c. 8.

73. See G. Macy, *The Dogma of Transubstantiation in the Middle Ages*; H. Jorissen, "Transsubstantiation," *LThK* 10 (2001): 177–82. On the contemporary discussion, see H. Seidl, *Zum Substanzbegriff in der katholischen Transsubstantiationslehre*, *FKTh* 11 (1995) 1–18.

74. See B. Neunheuser, *Eucharistie im Mittelalter und Neuzeit* (Freiburg: Herder, 1963); J. Betz, *Eucharistie als zentrales Mysterium*, in *MySal* 4/2 (1973): 231–43; M. Vaillantcourt, "Guitmund of Aversa and the Eucharistic Theology of St. Thomas," *The Thomist* 68 (2004): 577–600.

The main lines of their concerns in Eucharistic theology find magisterial expression in the Synod of Rome (1079), convened against Berengar and giving rise to the expression *substantialiter converti*.[75] *Transsubstantiatio* as a technical term—which, according to an anonymous disciple of Berengar, was supposedly introduced by Robert Pullus in 1140—is first attested in the Sentences ascribed to Roland Bandinelli, as the current scholarship would have it.[76] The concept was accepted only hesitatingly in the twelfth century but was later widely received;[77] at the Fourth Lateran Council it was the object of a magisterial decision,[78] from which both Albert the Great[79] and his disciple Thomas Aquinas were able to take their bearings, even if in their explanations of Eucharistic doctrine—unlike the later Duns Scotus,[80] Ockham,[81] and Gabriel Biel[82]—"a reference to the magisterial sanctioning of the doctrine of transubstantiation by the Fourth Lateran Council is nowhere to be found."[83] This observation of Hans Jorissen applies to the Eucharistic *doctrine* of Aquinas, even though when it comes to the *poetic* theology contained in the hymns we must add the supplementary remark that a reference is readily apparent in the sequence *Lauda Sion*, where the text runs: *Dogma datur Christianis / Quod in carnem transit panis / Et vinum in sanguinem*.

In the article on transubstantiation, the insights of the preceding arti-

75. It was demanded of Berengar that he accept the doctrinal formula "panem et vinum ... substantialiter converti in veram et propriam ac vivificatricem carnem et sanguinem Jesu Christi" (DH 700).

76. See J. Goering, "The Invention of Transubstantiation," *Traditio* 46 (1991): 147–70, here 148, where—next to a text of John Beleth—reference is made to the *Sentences of Roland*, subsequently Pope Alexander III (ed. A. M. Gietl [Freiburg, 1891—Wiederabdruck Amsterdam, 1969], 231): "Verumtamen si necessitate imminente sub alterius panis specie consecraretur, profecto fieret transsubstantiatio [sic], sanguinis autem numquam fit nisi de vino transsubstantiatio [sic]. – If, out of necessity, some other type of bread were consecrated, there would indeed be a transubstantiation, but a transubstantiation of the blood happens only from wine."

77. See J. de Ghellinck, "Eucharistie au XIIe siècle en occident," *Dictionnaire de Théologie Catholique* V/2 (1913): 1233–3102; L. Hödl, "Der Transsubstantiationsbegriff in der scholastischen Theologie des 12. Jahrhunderts," *Recherches de Théologie ancienne et médiévale* 31 (1964): 230–59.

78. See DH 803: "There is, however, a general Church of the faithful, outside of which none at all are saved, in which the priest himself is at once the sacrifice, Jesus Christ, whose body and blood are truly contained in the sacrament of the altar under the signs of bread and wine, when by divine power the bread is substantially converted into the body and the wine into the blood (*transsubstantiatis pane in corpus, et vino in sanguinem potestate divina*)."

79. See H. Jorissen, *Der Beitrag Alberts des Großen zur theologischen Rezeption des Aristoteles am Beispiel der Transsubstantiationslehre* (Münster: Aschendorff, 2002).

80. Duns Scotus, *Oxon.*, d. 11, q. 3, n. 15 (*Opera omnia* XVII [Paris: Vivès, 1894], 376).

81. See W. Ockham, *In IV Sent.*, q. 6 D, where the doctrine of transubstantiation is accepted, based on the "determinatio ecclesiae," even though the attempted solution of consubstantiation had earlier been presented as more reasonable ("rationabilior"), since it avoided the problem of the continued existence of accidents without a subject. See Iserloh, *Gnade und Eucharistie in der philosophischen Theologie des Wilhelm von Ockham*, 157–59.

82. Gabriel Biel, *Sacrosancti Canonis Missae expositio*, f. 99b.

83. H. Jorissen, *Die Entfaltung der Transsubstantiationslehre*, 62.

cles are retained. The body of Christ cannot begin to exist in the sacrament as a result of local motion, nor can its mode of presence be determined locally. By excluding these explanatory possibilities, the only remaining possibility for Thomas is the consequence that the body of Christ begins to exist in the sacrament by conversion of the substance of bread (*per conversionem substantiae*) into itself.[84]

In order to grasp more precisely this *conversio substantialis*, whose character is altogether supernatural (*omnino supernaturalis*), Thomas works out the difference between this and natural changes.[85] In the created realm, there can only be changes in view of the *form*, whereas with God the *substance* of a thing can also be changed. In order to illuminate this distinction, Thomas relies upon the scholastic axiom: *omne agens agit, inquantum est actu*.[86] Every creature is limited in its actuality, since it belongs to a determined genus and species. Thus, every action of a created agent depends upon a *determined* actuality (*actus determinatus*). Each thing, however, receives its determination in actuality from its form. For this reason, in the context of created reality there can be only a *change of form*, thus a transformation.

In contrast to this, God is unlimited actuality (*actus infinitus*),[87] and his agency reaches to the whole nature of an existing thing—Thomas speaks of God as the *auctor entis*.[88] Therefore, not only can he effect a change of form (*immutatio formae*), so that one form replaces another in the same subject (*subiectum*), but he can also bring about the conversion of an entire existing thing (*conversio totius entis*)[89]—with the result that the whole substance of *one thing* is transformed into the whole substance of *another thing*: *et hoc agitur divina virtute in hoc sacramento*. When it comes to the Eucharistic conversion, it is not only a matter of *conversio formalis*, nor is it

---

84. See *S. th.* III, q. 75, a. 4: "Respondeo dicendum quod, sicut supra dictum est, cum in hoc sacramento sit verum corpus Christi, nec incipiat ibi esse de novo per motum localem; cum etiam nec corpus Christi sit ibi sicut in loco, ut ex dictis patet, necesse est dicere quod incipiat esse per conversionem substantiae panis in ipsum. Haec tamen conversio non est similis conversionibus naturalibus, sed est *omnino supernaturalis, sola Dei virtute* effecta" (emphasis added). On the concept of substance, see *S. th.* I, q. 29, a. 2.

85. On this point, see S. L. Brock, "St. Thomas and the Eucharistic Conversion," in: *The Thomist* 65 (2001): 529–65, here 546f.

86. "Every agent acts insofar as it is in act." See L. Elders, *Die Metaphysik des Thomas von Aquin in historischer Perspektive*, vol. 1: *Das ens commune* (Salzburg: Anton Pustet, 1985), 129f.

87. See *S. th.* I, q. 5.

88. *S. th.* III, q. 75, a. 4 ad 3.

89. See *S. th.* I, q. 65, a. 3: "quanto aliqua causa est superior, tanto ad plura se extendit in causando. Semper autem id quod substernitur in rebus invenitur communius quam id quod informat et restringit ipsum; sicut esse quam vivere, et vivere quam intellegere, et materia quam forma. Quanto ergo aliquid est magis substratum, tanto a superiori causa directe procedit. Id ergo quod est primo substratum in omnibus, proprie pertinet ad causalitatem supremae causae."

an act ascribing a new meaning from a human perspective, as one could add in view of contemporary discussions of Eucharistic theology; rather, it is a matter of *conversio substantialis* brought about by divine power, for which Thomas uses the term *transsubstantiatio*.[90] Like the act of creation, *creare ex nihilo*, a conversion of substance embodies a divine rather than a human possibility.[91]

The doctrine of transubstantiation seeks to conform to the meaning of the *verba testamenti*; at the same time, there is bound up with it a certain reshaping of Aristotelian resources, which prompted Edward Schillebeeckx to comment: "The Aristotelianism that was applied to the Eucharist by Catholic theologians is incidentally a radical 'transubstantiation' of the authentic, historical Aristotelianism, which does not countenance such a separation of substance and accidents."[92] According to Aristotle, there cannot be accidents without a subject (*subiectum*). Following Thomas, however, it is precisely the accidents of bread and wine that remain behind, without a subject, after the consecration, since the substance of bread and the substance of wine were converted.[93]

It should by now be seen clearly that the doctrine of *transubstantiation* does not refer to the empirical level but instead aims at an ontological reality. The conversion of substance remains invisible. Here, there is a yawning gap between the testimony of the eyes, which see the properties remaining behind, and the reality claimed by faith: that under the signs of bread and wine the substance of Jesus Christ's body and blood are present. The suspicion of deceiving the senses (*deceptio*) could be raised here, insofar as the witness of the senses—through which the intellect can move from the accidents to the substance—appear to be misled. But Thomas refutes this suspicion of deception or simulation by relying on Aristotle's distinguishing between the witness of the senses and the function of the intellect. While the senses are oriented to the accidents, the intellect aims at knowledge of the substance (*intellectus, cuius est proprium obiectum substantia*).[94] Through

---

90. The term is found explicitly in only a few passages: *S. th.* III, q. 75, a. 4 c. and a. 8 c., as well as q. 78 a. 4 c.

91. On the distinction between divine creating (*creare*) and human making (*facere*), see *Coll. In Symb. Apost.* 1 (n. 881): "In hoc enim differunt creare et facere, quia facere est de nihilo aliquid facere: facere autem est de aliquo aliquid facere." See also *S. th.* I, q. 45, a. 2 c. The difference between the act of creation and the act of transubstantiation consists in the fact that the latter takes as its point of departure a created substance, whose accidents remain intact even after the substantial conversion.

92. E. Schillebeeckx, *Die eucharistische Gegenwart. Zur Diskussion über die Realpräsenz* (Düsseldorf: Patmos, 1967), 37.

93. See *S. th.* III, q. 75, a. 5, as well as *In IV Sent.*, d. 11, q. 1, a. 1, qa. 2.

94. See *S. th.* III, q. 75, a. 5 ad 2 (with reference to Aristotle, *De anima*, III, 6, 430 b, 14 sq.). See the earlier work: *In IV Sent.*, d. 11, q. 1, a. 1, aq 2 ad 1: "in hoc sacramento non est aliqua deceptio neque fictio. Non

faith, however, which does not set itself against sensory knowledge yet still reaches beyond it, the intellect is preserved from deception.[95]

That the real presence of Jesus Christ's body and blood remains *hidden* under the sacramental signs was fittingly arranged by divine providence (*per divinam providentiam*), Thomas holds. It would be awful (*horribile*) to consume a man's flesh and drink his blood during the *usus sacramenti*. Here, Thomas takes up a patristic *topos* found as early as Ambrose.[96] In addition, through the accidents of bread and wine that remain behind, the sacrament is protected from possible opprobrium by unbelievers, who could justly raise the accusation of anthropophagy, if Christ were to be consumed in his own species (*in propria specie*) and violence thereby be done to the impassibility of the glorified one.[97] In another passage, Thomas holds expressly that when there is a Eucharistic miracle—when the body of Christ miraculously appears on the altar under the form of flesh and the blood under the form of blood—the Eucharistic species may *not* be received.[98] A further argument of fittingness for the discrepancy between the witness of the senses and faith is seen by Thomas ultimately in the merits of faith (*meritum fidei*)—an aspect already foreshadowed in the Gospel of John.[99] Were the *Christus passus* to be sensibly perceived in the sacrament of the Eucharist, then faith, which alone makes known the hidden presence of the exalted Lord, would be unnecessary: *Visus, tactus, gustus, in te fallitur, / sed auditu solo tute creditur*, runs the hymn *Adoro te devote*.[100]

---

enim sensus decipitur, quia non habet judicare nisi de sensibilibus speciebus, quae quidem ibi vere sunt sicut et sensui ostenduntur: *neque etiam intellectus*, qui habet judicium de substantiis rerum per fidem juvatus."

95. On the relation between faith and knowledge, see *S. th.* II-II, qq. 1–9. See also A. Zimmermann, "Glaube und Wissen," in *Thomas von Aquin* ed. A. Speer (Berlin: De Gruyter, 2005), 271–97. In the treatise on faith, Thomas elucidates Heb 11:1 (*S. th.* II-II, q. 4, a. 1). Thomas holds to the fact that faith includes a twofold relation to God: it relates first to God as good and end, inasmuch as the will (*voluntas*) is involved, and second to God as truth (*prima veritas*), inasmuch as the intellect is concerned. "To the extent that, in faith, the understanding accepts God in his self-revelation without insight, faith has to do with knowledge of the truth: God convinces the believer's understanding of that which he does not see." Thus Pesch, *Thomas von Aquin*, 123.

96. See already Ambrose, *sacr.*, IV, 20: "thus you also drink the symbol of the precious blood, so that no aversion to blood (*horror cruoris*) arises." See also VI, 3.

97. See *S. th.* III, q. 77, a. 1: "Manifestum est etiam quod huiusmodi accidentia non sunt in substantia corporis et sanguinis Christi sicut in subiecto: quia substantia humani corporis nullo modo potest his accidentibus affici; neque etiam est possibile quod corpus Christi, gloriosum et impassibile existens, alteretur ad suscipiendas huiusmodi qualitates."

98. See also *S. th.* III, q. 82, a. 4 ad 3.

99. See Jn 20:29: "dicit ei [sc. Thomae] Iesus / quia vidisti me credidisti / beati qui non viderunt et crediderunt."

100. See J.-P. Torrell, "Adoro te. La plus belle prière de saint Thomas," *Recherches thomasiennes. Études revues et augmentées* (Paris: Librairie Philosophique, 2000), 367–75; J.-H. Tück, "Verborgene Gegenwart und betrachtendes Verweilen. Zur poetischen Theologie des Hymnus Adoro te devote," *IKaZ Communio* 34 (2005): 401–18. In *S. th.* III, q. 75, a. 7, Thomas goes into the theological and temporal problem of whether the Eucharistic conversion takes place gradually (*successive*) or in a moment (*in instanti*). He adduces three

Accordingly, we can say in summary: Thomas explains the somatic real presence of Jesus Christ in the sacrament of the Eucharist by means of the theory of transubstantiation. In order to clarify ontologically the conversion of bread and wine into the flesh and blood of Christ—brought about only by divine power (*virtute divina*) and thus qualified as *omnino supernaturale*—Thomas avails himself of Aristotelian resources. At the same time, he orients himself toward the *verba testamenti* as the criterion for any theological attempt at elucidation. Alternative explanatory models such as impanation or annihilation are ultimately rejected by Thomas because they are not adequate to the semantic content of the words of institution. Moreover, the definition of Jesus Christ's Eucharistic mode of presence as *per modum substantiae* excludes corporality, spatiality, and extension. Thus, despite a verification deficit in the empirical order—the substance of Christ's body and blood is inaccessible to the senses—the explanatory model of transubstantiation attempts to speak of a real presence of the *Christus passus*, without pigeonholing it as a thing in place and time. Seen against the background of the Eucharistic controversies of the ninth and eleventh centuries, the doctrine of transubstantiation pursues a middle way between crude sensualism and mere spiritualism. Through teaching the permanence of subjectless accidents, it is able to preserve the symbolic character of bread and wine —the valid concern of sensualism. By interpreting the conversion as transubstantiation, Thomas can hold fast to the true and real presence of Jesus Christ's body and blood in the Eucharist—the *particula veri* of sacramental realism—without lapsing into an undifferentiated total identification of the historical Christ (*in propria specie*) with the Eucharistic *Christus passus* (*in specie sacramenti*).

The Meaning of the *verba testamenti* and the Analysis of Alternative Formulas of Consecration

In his reflections on Eucharistic theology, Thomas Aquinas bases his thought on the givens of the Bible. Thus he attempts to draw out the meaning of the *verba testamenti* and undertakes a subtle analysis of the words of institution, "*Hoc est corpus meum.*" In a first step, he teases out the unique-

---

reasons for the instantaneous character of conversion: firstly, the substance of Christ's body, the end of this *conversio*, does not suffer degrees of greater or lesser; secondly, there is no subject in this conversion which must be gradually prepared; thirdly, the *conversio* is brought about all at once, hence *subito*, by God's infinite power. More precisely, the conversion is accomplished by the word of Christ spoken by the priest in such a way that the last moment of the word's being pronounced is the first moment in which the sacrament of Christ's body is present (see *S. th.* III, q. 75, a. 7 ad 1).

ness of the *verba testamenti*, comparing them with the formulas for the administration of other sacraments. In doing so, he underscores that the *forma sacramenti* has a constitutive meaning for the coming to be of the sacrament. Beyond the semantic level, he also takes the practical execution of the sacrament into account by emphasizing that the enunciation of the form by the authorized minister of the sacrament is—to put it in the terminology of the philosophy of language[101]—not only a constative speech act but a reality positing, that is, a *performative*, speech act. Through simultaneously bringing about the reality it signifies, the consecration performed by the priest *in persona Christi* is distinguished from a literary quotation, which repeats Jesus' speech act at the last supper.

In a second step, Thomas elucidates the meaning of the *verba testamenti* by way of contrast. He investigates potential alternatives for the *forma sacramenti* and questions their implications. He shows thereby that only the words of institution witnessed to by the New Testament bring about the reality of Christ's body and blood. Alternative consecratory formulas—considered in a linguistic-pragmatic fashion—do not achieve the same effect.

The *forma sacramenti* of the Eucharist in Contrast to the Other Sacraments

Bound up with investigating the *form* of the sacrament is a certain constriction of the way of setting up the theological issue of the Eucharist; this is easily seen if one considers a short typological comparison with the patristic conception of the Eucharist. In the ancient Church, the Eucharist was understood as a mysterious deed, in which one tried to conform to Jesus' action at the last supper by celebrating his presence *and* the remembrance of his salvific deeds in the liturgy of the Eucharist. Giving thanks, calling down the Spirit upon the gifts (*epiclesis*), remembering the salvific deeds (*anamnesis*), and taking part in the holy gifts (*koinonia*) were essential for the performance of the sacrament.

In contrast, along with the distinction in sacramental theology between word and element, and the Aristotelian terminology of matter and form

---

101. See J. L. Austin, *How to Do Things with Words* (Cambridge: The William James Lectures, 1962); J. R. Searle, *Sprechakte. Ein sprachphilosophischer Essay* (Frankfurt/M.: Suhrkamp, 2000). Regarding its reception in more recent sacramental theology, see: A. Moos, *Das Verhältnis von Wort und Sakrament in der deutschsprachigen Theologie des 20. Jahrhunderts* (Paderborn: Bonifatius, 1993), 204–11; H. O. Meuffels, *Kommunikative Sakramententheologie* (Freiburg–Basel–Vienna: Herder, 1995), 26f.; D. Sattler, "Wandeln Worte Wirklichkeit? Nachdenkliches über die Rezeption der Sprechakttheorie in der (Sakramenten-)Theologie," *Cath* 51 (1997): 125–38. See H.-G. Nissing, *Sprache als Akt bei Thomas von Aquin* (Leiden-Boston: Brill Academic Publishers, 2006), esp. 447–84.

(hylomorphism), we find a concentration of theological interest on the act of consecration, which tends to shift the anamnetic and epicletic character of the sacrament into the background. With a view to the Eucharist, this means that the aspect of somatic real presence—that is, the presence of Christ's flesh and blood in the consecrated gifts of bread and wine—is decidedly prioritized over the aspect of commemorative actual presence, that is, the remembrance of the Lord's salvific deeds. At any rate, this impression stands out when Thomas says that in cases of necessity, pronouncing the words of institution as *forma sacramenti* is sufficient for confecting the sacrament of the Eucharist.[102] But how can the meaning of the form be more precisely determined? How is this form distinguished from the formulae for administering other sacraments?

Thomas elaborates a twofold difference. Firstly, he states that the Eucharist comes to be through the consecration of the matter (*consecratio materiae*), whereas the other sacraments come about through the use of the consecrated matter (*usus materiae consecratae*)—as for example Baptism, through the rite of washing, and Confirmation, through the rite of sealing.[103] Thereafter, he emphasizes that in the other sacraments it is only a blessing (*benedictio materiae*) that is conferred. Through the blessing, the consecrated matter, like any instrument, receives a certain spiritual power (*quaedam spiritualis virtus*), which can pass into inanimate instruments through the minister operating as an animate instrument. With the Eucharist, however, the consecration of the matter consists in a wonderful *conversion of substance*, which can be brought about by God alone.[104] For this reason, the minister carrying out this sacrament has only to pronounce the words of Christ (*prolatio verborum*).[105]

---

102. See *S. th.* III, q. 78, a. 1 ad 4: "si sacerdos sola verba praedicta proferret cum intentione conficiendi hoc sacramentum, perficeretur hoc sacramentum, quia intentio faceret ut haec verba intelligerentur quasi ex persona Christi prolata, etiamsi verbis praecedentibus hoc non recitaretur." Thomas, however, does not neglect to add that a priest would sin mortally were he to undertake to consecrate the gifts outside of the liturgical context: "Graviter tamen peccaret sacerdos sic conficiens hoc sacramentum, utpote ritum Ecclesiae non servans" (ibid.). Just a bit earlier, Thomas also explicitly pointed to the fact that the reception of the Eucharist (*usus*) belongs to the perfection of the sacrament: "ad quamdam perfectionem sacramenti pertinet materiae consecratae usus" (*S. th.* III, q. 78, a. 1 ad 2). Still, the focus placed on the act of consecration can nevertheless count as the specific feature of the Eucharistic theology of the west, since the early Middle Ages at the latest. In fact, already in the ninth century we find the remarkable statement of Amalar of Metz: "satis esset ... sola benedictio episcoporum aut presbyterorum ad benedicendum panem et vinum, quo reficeretur populus ad animarum salutem" (*Liber Officialis*, III praef. [ed. Hanssens, 257]).

103. See *S. th.* III, q. 78, a. 1. See also *In I Cor XI*, l. V (n. 660).

104. See *S. th.* III, q. 78, a. 1: "in hoc sacramento consistit in quadam miraculosa conversione substantiae, quae a solo Deo perfici potest."

105. Certainly, Thomas does not forget to point out that the *manducatio* also belongs to the perfection of this sacrament, fulfilling Jesus' instruction, "take and eat." But, for Thomas, the *usus materiae consecratae* does not belong to the form of the sacrament, for which reason there can be adoration of the Eucharist

This twofold difference between the Eucharist and the other sacraments can be confirmed by an analysis of the *form*: the form of the other sacraments signifies the use of matter (*ego baptizo te*), whereas the form of the Eucharistic sacrament expresses only the consecration of the matter, namely by it being said: "This is my body." In the analysis of form, Thomas distinguishes the following modes of assertion:

1. The form of execution (*modus exercentis*) in the sacraments of Baptism ("I baptize you in the name of the Father, and of the Son, and of the Holy Spirit") and Confirmation ("I sign you with the sign of the cross, I strengthen you through the chrism of salvation, in the name of the Father, and of the Son, and of the Holy Spirit"). In both sacraments—Baptism[106] and Confirmation[107]—a speech act and a sacramental act are simultaneously carried out.[108]

2. The form of command (*modus imperantis*): through the imperative formula, "Receive the authority to offer the sacrifice in the Church for both the living and the dead," the transmission of consecratory power is expressed in the sacrament of Ordination.[109]

3. The form of deprecation (*modus deprecantis*), for example in the sacrament of Extreme Unction (*extrema unctio*).[110]

At the same time, what is to be noted is *who* speaks and *in whose name* he speaks. An analysis of the modes of assertion also reveals distinctions here:

---

bread outside of the Eucharistic celebration. See *In IV Sent*, d. 8 q. 2 aq. 2 n. 144: "usus materiae in hoc sacramento non est de essentia sacramenti, sicut in aliis, ideo illa verba quae ad usum pertinent, non sunt de forma, sed tantum illa quae ad consecrationem materiae pertinent, scilicet,'Hoc est corpus meum.'" See also *In Math*, c. XXVI, l. 3 (n. 2182).

106. See *S. th*. III, q. 66, a. 5.

107. See *S. th*. III, q. 72, a. 4, where the then customary formula for administering Confirmation—"Consigno te signo crucis, confirmo te chrismate salutis, in nomine Patris et Filii et Spiritus sancti"—is explained. More precisely, Thomas distinguishes three components: first, the cause that imparts the fulness of the Spirit's power: the holy Trinity ("in nomine Patris et Filii et Spiritus sancti"); second, the fact that spiritual power is imparted to men through a visible sign ("confirmo te chrismate salutis"); third, the fact that the faithful are given a sign for the spiritual battle ("consigno te signo crucis"). On the bishop as the ordinary minister of Confirmation, see *S. th*. III, q. 72, a. 11.

108. In this respect, the *modus exercentis* corresponds to the sacramental happening. See *S. th*. III, q. 78, a. 1 ad 3: "in sacramento baptismi minister aliquem actum *exercet* circa usum materiae, qui est de essentia sacramenti" (emphasis added). Regarding Baptism, Thomas has recourse to Mt 28:19 and thus emphasizes that the *forma sacramenti* must explicitly name the case of the sacrament. This happens in two ways: on the one hand, the words "ego baptizo" designate the minister as *causa instrumentalis*, while on the other, the words "in nomine Patris et Filii et Spiritus sancti" designate the triune God as *causa principalis*.

109. See *S. th*. III, q. 82, a. 1 ad 1: "Accipe potestatem offerendi sacrificium in Ecclesia tam pro vivis quam pro mortuis." See *S. th*. Suppl., q. 34, a. 4: "in forma ordinis exprimitur usus ordinis per actum, qui imperatur; et exprimitur traductio potestatis per imperativum modum."

110. See *S. th*. Suppl., q. 29, a. 7 and 8. The then customary formula for administering the sacrament, which had the character of a deprecative prayer, ran: "Per istam sanctam unctionem, et suam piissimam misericordiam, indulgat tibi Dominus quidquid deliquisti per visum, etc."

if one considers the form of the other sacraments, what is conspicuous is that this is spoken in the person of the minister (*in persona ministri*). By way of contrast, the form of the Eucharist professes the *person of the speaking Christ himself*.[111] Thomas recalls a passage by Ambrose that reflects on the liturgical context of the words of institution and emphasizes the linguistic-pragmatically decisive surroundings of the consecration, namely, the priestly discourse: "The consecration is accomplished by the words and expressions of the Lord Jesus. Because, by all the other words spoken, praise is rendered to God, prayer is put up for the people, for kings, and others; but when the time comes for perfecting the sacrament, the priest uses no longer his own words, but the words of Christ. Therefore, it is Christ's words that perfect this sacrament."[112] Thus it is given to understand that the minister, who brings the prayers before God *in persona ecclesiae*, changes his perspective in speaking while performing this sacrament; this means, in fact, that he does nothing but utter the words of Christ.[113]

But is the form apposite? The form must signify what is effected in the sacrament. It has not only a significative but also a factitive function. With regard to the Eucharist, this means that the words of consecration spoken over the bread must denote the conversion of the bread into the body of Christ. This is precisely what the form "*Hoc est corpus meum*" does, which Thomas analyzes further in the *Summa theologiae*. In his commentary on the First Letter to the Corinthians, Thomas explains that the words spoken by Jesus at the last supper encompass more than the actual words of consecration. He subdivides into three sequences the utterance that Jesus made while instituting the sacrament: (1) He refers the instruction "take and eat – *accipite et manducate*" to the use of the sacrament, concerning which he has already pointed out that a preeminent meaning is ascribed to being united with Christ *in the manner of a meal*.[114] (2) Then, Thomas identifies

---

111. *S. th.* III, q. 78, a. 1 c: "Sed forma huius sacramenti profertur *ex persona Christi loquentis*: ut datur intellegi quod minister in perfectione huius sacramenti nihil agit nisi quod profert verba Christi" (emphasis added). See also *In IV Sent.*, d. 8, q. 1, a. 3.

112. See *S. th.* III, q. 78, a. 1 s.c. The passage can be found in Ambrose, *De sacr.* IV, 14 (FC 3, ed. J. Schmitz), where it runs: "Consecratio igitur quibus verbis est et cuius sermonibus? Domini Iesu. Nam reliqua omnia, quae dicuntur in superioribus, a sacerdote dicuntur: laus deo, defertur oratio, petitur pro populo, pro regibus, pro ceteris. Ubi venitur, ut conficiatur venerabile sacramentum, iam non suis sermonibus utitur sacerdos, sed utitur sermonibus Christi. Ergo sermo Christi hoc conficit sacramentum."

113. *S. th.* III, q. 78, a. 1 c. For Thomas, the performative power of the words of institution, spoken *virtute divina*, would bring about a substantial conversion even *outside* of the liturgical celebration. Even so, he underscores—as already emphasized—the point that a priest who carries out the sacrament without heeding the rite of the Church would sin mortally. See *S. th.* III, q. 78, a. 1 ad 4.

114. See *In I Cor* XI, l. V (n. 651): "Est autem notandum quod generans non coniungitur genito secundum substantiam sed solum secundum virtutem, sed cibus coniungitur nutrito secundum substantiam. Unde in sacramento baptismi, quo Christus regenerat ad salutem, non est ipse Christus secundum suam

the ensuing self-identification of Jesus with the prandial gifts ("This is my body – *hoc est corpus meum*") as the essential truth of the sacrament (*veritas sacramenti*). (3) Through the explanatory clause "which will be given up for you—*quod pro vobis tradetur*," the mystery of the sacrament is finally indicated, which consists in the symbolic presentation of the Lord's suffering. The memorializing mandate concluding the discursive sequence, "*Hoc facite in meam commemorationem*," forms an appeal to the apostles and their successors to celebrate the sacrament frequently.

In contrast to this, Thomas concentrates his treatment in the *Summa theologiae* entirely on the form of the sacrament and ignores the other parts of the words of institution. In the words of institution, "*Hoc est corpus meum*," which express the *veritas sacramenti*, Thomas distinguishes three moments more precisely: first, the conversion itself (*conversio*); second, the point of origin (*terminus a quo*); and third, the end point of the conversion (*terminus ad quem*).

The conversion can be considered in two ways: either in its becoming, thus as a process (*in fieri*), or in its having become, thus as a result (*in facto esse*). In Thomas's mind, however, the Eucharistic conversion need *not* be considered in its becoming, but only in its having become. This is so first because, through God's infinite power, the conversion takes place instantaneously (*in instanti*) rather than gradually;[115] and second because the intention of the conversion anticipates the result (*in facto esse*). To illustrate this, Thomas calls upon an analogy from architecture. As the artistic idea or form in the mind of the architect is directed primarily to the form of the completed house and only secondarily to the execution of building, so also in the form of the Eucharistic sacrament what is expressed is the primary intention, which is directed to the result of the conversion.

Accordingly, in the form of the Eucharistic sacrament, it is the result of the conversion (*in facto esse*) that finds expression, and therefore the external members of the transformation must be signified as they relate to each other *after the execution* of the conversion. *Post consecrationem*, however, the *terminus ad quem* has the characteristic of a substantial reality (*corpus Christi*); on the other hand, the *terminus a quo*—the species of bread and wine—remain not in the manner of substance but only in the manner of subjectless accidents, which can be perceived by the senses. The *terminus a quo* is therefore appropriately expressed by the pronoun *hoc*, without fur-

---

substantiam, sed solum secundum suam virtutem. Sed in sacramento Eucharistiae, quod est spirituale alimentum, Christus est secundum suam substantiam." See also *S. th.* III, q. 78, a. 1 ad 2.

115. See *S. th.* III, q. 75, a. 7.

ther determination, since this refers to substance in general.[116] The *terminus ad quem*, however, is expressed through the substantive *corpus meum*, the result of the conversion. With this as background, the form "*Hoc est corpus meum*" designates precisely the substantial conversion of bread into the body of Christ.[117]

The Meaning of the *verba testamenti* in Contrast to Alternative Formulae for Administering the Sacraments

The form of a sacrament brings about what it signifies; it is a *verbum efficax*. If the essence of the sacrament of the Eucharist consists in substantial conversion, then this must be expressed exactly in the form. In order to make clear the adequacy of the form "*Hoc est corpus meum*," Thomas examines potential alternatives and questions their implications:

1. "*Hoc fit corpus meum*: This *is becoming* my body." For this formula, one could make the argument that it better expresses the *happening* of conversion, which is expressed by *fit* rather than by *est*. Thomas counters this formula by pointing out that the final effect of *consecratio* is accounted for not by the *process* of conversion (*fieri*) but rather by the *result* of conversion (*in facto esse*). Thus, the result (*in facto esse*) must be expressed in the form.[118]

2. "*Hoc sit corpus meum*: Let this be my body." For this formula, one could make the argument that—in analogy to the words of creation (see

---

116. On this point, see also *S. th.* III, q. 78, a. 5, where—after a detailed report of the doctrinal positions advocated prior to Thomas—it is indicated that the semantically undetermined pronoun "this" (*hoc*) must be referred to the sensibly perceptible species, under which is contained, firstly, the bread and wine, and then after the conversion, the substance of Christ's body and blood.

117. For the sake of completion, let it be mentioned that Thomas undertakes an analogous analysis for the form "*Hic est calix sanguinis mei* etc." See *S. th.* III, q. 78, a. 3. It is notable that Thomas—differently, for example, from Bonaventure (see *IV Sent.*, d. 8, p. 2, a. 1, qu. 2; *Breviloquium*, VI, 9)—explains not only the formula "*Hic est calix sanguinis mei*" as belonging to the *forma sacramenti*, but also the additional modifier "*novi et aeterni testamenti, mysterium fidei, qui pro vobis et pro multis effundetur in remissionem peccatorum.*" While the *transformation* (*conversio*) of the wine into the blood of Christ is indicated by the first part of the formula, the apposition states more precisely the *soteriological effect* of the blood spilled in the Passion. For Thomas, this is ordered to three ends: (1) the attainment of the eternal inheritance (*ad adipiscendam aeternam haereditatem*—referring to Heb 10:19); (2) the justification coming from faith (*mysterium fidei*—referring to Rom 3:25f.); and (3) the remission of sins (*in remissionem peccatorem*—referring to Heb 9:14). Held by Thomists since Cajetan, the view that Thomas ultimately considered necessary only the phrase "Hic est calix sanguinis mei," with the remaining words not belonging in the strict sense to the *forma sacramenti* (see F. Diekamp, *Katholische Dogmatik nach den Grundsätzen des heiligen Thomas von Aquin*, ed. K. Jüssen, 12th ed. [Münster: Sarto, 1954], 130), is not only opposed to Aquinas's assertion that the whole unity of the speech is *de substantia formae* (*S. th.* III, q. 78, a. 3 c.), it also contradicts the commentary on 1 Cor 11:25, where Thomas holds: "totum pertinet ad vim effectivam formae" (*In I Cor* XI, 25, l. VI, n. 681).

118. See *S. th.* III, q. 75, a. 8 c., as well as the earlier: *In IV Sent.*, d. 8, q. 1, a. 3 aq. 3, where the formula "Hoc fit corpus meum," or "Hoc mutetur in corpus meum" are excluded by showing that they do not signify the "esse vel non esse" of that which is the "principaliter intentum" in this sacrament.

Gen 1: *fiat* [subjunctive present])—it better expresses the imperative character of the words of institution spoken *in persona Christi*. The parallel between the creative and the Eucharistic word, upon which Ambrose had earlier reflected,[119] would indeed be worth considering to the extent that in both cases an efficient speech act of God is involved. Nevertheless, Thomas validates this analogy to God's creative speaking only in a conditional way: in the sacramental consecration (*consecratio*), God's speech operates *effective et sacramentaliter*, that is, the level of signs is not superseded and the effect follows rather *secundum vim significationis*. Thus, the bread and wine's character as sign, which symbolizes the ecclesial dimension of the Eucharist, remains intact even after the substantial conversion (*transsubstantiatio*). For this reason, the final effect in the consecration must be expressed by the indicative present (*est corpus meum*). In the *creatio rerum*, however, God's speech is operative only effectively and not *sacramentaliter*; it is not bound to any given thing, but rather takes place *ex nihilo*, and for this reason the mode of speaking is imperative: *"fiat lux et facta est lux"* (Gen 1:3).[120]

3. "Hic panis *est corpus meum—This bread* is my body." A vote for this formula could be justified by indicating that, since the result of conversion is designated by *corpus meum*, its origin must similarly be named concretely with *hic panis*. But, according to Thomas, this suggestion fails to recognize that the *terminus a quo*, that is, the bread and the wine, does not retain its substantial being after the conversion. As a result, the formula *hic panis est corpus meum* approaches the explanatory model of consubstantiation,[121]

---

119. See Ambrose, De *sacr*., IV, 15 (FC 3, ed. J. Schmitz): "Quis est sermo Christi? Nempe is, quo facta sunt omnia. Iussit dominus, facta est terra, iussit dominus, facta sunt maria, iussit dominus, omins creatura gemerata est. Vides ergo, quam operatorius sermo sit Christi. Si ergo tanta vis est in sermone domini Iesu, ut inciperent esse, quae non erant, quanto magis operatorius est, ut sint, quae erant, et in aliud commutenatur.—Which word is the word of Christ? It is that word by which everything was created. The Lord gave a command, and the earth was created; the Lord gave a command, the seas were created; the Lord gave a command, and whole of creation was brought forth (see Gen 1:1–31). Thus, you see how efficacious the word of Christ is. So if such power is contained in the word of the Lord Jesus that what was not could be made to be, then how much more can it bring about that something remains what it was and is simultaneously transformed into something." Ambrose thus discusses not only the divine power of the word as it is highlighted in both the act of creatioin and the process of Eucharistic conversion, but also the difference between *creatio* and *commutatio*. Admittedly, his theory of conversion, often referred to as metabolism, lacks the conceptual precision of the later doctrine of transubstantiation.

120. On this point, see S. *th*. III, q. 75, a. 8 c., where Thomas discusses in greater detail the difference between *conversio substantialis, creatio ex nihilo,* and *mutatio naturalis*.

121. See also S. *th*. III, q. 75, a. 2 c. It is interesting that M. Luther did in fact explain the *verba testamenti* in this sense, in order to undergird his understanding of the real presence as consubstantiation: "Et maior est verbi dei auctoritas quam nostri ingenii capacitas. Ita in sacramento ut verum corpus verusque sanguis sit, non est necesse, panem et vinum transsubstantiari, ut Christus sub accidentibus teneatur, sed utroque simul manente vere dicitur 'hic [sic!] panis est corpus meum, hoc vinum est sanguis meus,' et econtra.— And the authority of God's word is greater than our powers of comprehension. Thus, for the true body and true blood to be in the sacrament, it is not neecessary that bread and wine be transubstantiated, so that Christ is contained under the accidents; rather, since both remain simultaneously it is truly said: 'This

which—as Thomas states—not only is "heretical" but also encourages idolatry, since it commends adoration of the body of Christ along with the bread. In contrast, the semantic indeterminateness of the demonstrative pronoun "*hoc*" refers to neither the substance of the bread nor the substance of the body, but rather the substance contained under the properties, which first was bread and then is the body of Christ.[122]

4. "*Hoc est corpus* Christi—This is the body *of Christ*." The preference for this formula could be argued from the fact that the express declaration of the person is indispensable in order to exclude any confusion with the officiating priest who acts *in persona Christi*. But, for Thomas, the person of Christ is expressed clearly enough by the context of recounting the institution of the Eucharist and by the pronoun "*meum*."

5. "*Hoc* erit *corpus meum*—This *will be* my body." The option for a formula in the future tense could be motivated by looking to the twofold form of the Eucharist. As long as the consecration over the wine has not taken place, it can be argued that the consecration of the bread cannot take effect. Thomas opposes to this view the position that the words of institution, which trace back to Jesus, would not be true if they did not bring about exactly what they signify. But the indicative present of the copula *est* signifies that the effect takes place *simul tempore* with the enunciation of the form.[123] Moreover, the elevation of the consecrated host would be an idolatrous act, were the presence of Christ's body to come to be only after the consecration of the wine. The problem raised by the twofold form of the Eucharist is

---

bread is my body, this wine is my blood,' and conversely" (idem, *De captivitate Babylonica ecclesiae praeludium* [1520] = WA 6, 511, 38 – 512, 2). For background, see L. Grane, "Luthers Kritik an Thomas von Aquin in *De captivitate Babylonica*," ZKG 80 (1969): 1–13. Notwithstanding the distinction between the doctrine of transubstantiation and that of consubstantiation, or ubiquitarianism, the Lutheran and Roman Catholic understandings of the last supper agree on emphasizing the real presence. On the convergence in ecumenical dialogue, see the important study *Lehrverurteilungen—kirchentrennend?* vol. 1, ed. K. Lehmann and W. Pannenberg (Freiburg-Göttingen: Herder, 1986), 89–124, esp. 94–108.

122. See *S. th.* III, q. 78, a. 5 c., where a subtle analysis of the demonstrative pronoun is carried out, which agrees substantially with the *Commentary on the Sentences*. See *In Sent.* IV, d. 8, q. 2, a. 1, qa. 4. See also the concise determination: *In Math. XXVI*, l. III (n. 2184): "Dicendum quod sensus est: *Hoc est corpus meum*, idest contentum sub accidente est corpus meum. Vel hoc fit quod contentum sub accidentibus sit corpus meum. Unde in fine posuit nomen, sed in principio pronomen, quod substantiam indeterminatam significat; sed per nomen forma determinata. Unde in principio non est forma, sed in fine."

123. See *S. th.* III, q. 78, a. 6, where the question is discussed, whether the consecration of bread takes effect only when the wine also is consecrated. In fact, the position holding that the conversion of the bread takes place only after the consecration of the wine was supported in the theological tradition prior to Thomas by authors such as Petrus Comestor, Peter Cantor, and Stephen Langton (a list of sources is found in P. Browe, *Die Eucharistie im Mittelalter*, 477). Thomas critiques this conception by emphasizing the *veritas* of the Eucharistic formula. The manner of speaking, "*Hoc est corpus meum*," includes the point that the effect takes place simultaneously with the conclusion of the consecratory speech act. If the effect were not expected until a future moment, then the *forma sacramenti* would have to be changed and the indicative present (*est*) replaced with the future (*erit*).

solved by Thomas elsewhere by means of the so-called doctrine of concomitance, according to which the *Christus totus* is present under each of the two forms. After the conversion of bread, the body of Christ is present *ex vi sacramenti*, but the blood *ex reali concomitantia*. After the consecration of the wine, the blood of Christ is also present *ex vi sacramenti*.[124]

6. "*Hoc* significat *corpus meum*—This *signifies* my body." This formula, which amounts to a merely symbolic interpretation of the Eucharistic presence, is alleged by Thomas to be "heretical" in *Summa theologiae* III, q. 75, a. 1 and already earlier in the *Sentences* commentary.[125] Also in his commentary on John 6:52, this formula is expressly ruled out. There, we find that Christ's statement, "The bread that I will give you *is* my flesh (*caro mea est*)," designates with precision the *veritas* of the sacrament of the Eucharist. "*Caro mea est*" may not be weakened into the sense expressed in the formula, "*carnem meam significat*."[126]

In conclusion, it is to be said that in the consecratory formula, "*Hoc est corpus meum*," three dimensions coinciding in the performance can be distinguished. The formula is first of all uttered *recitatively*, because the priest does not employ his own words but rather speaks the *verba testamenti* as handed on by the custom of the Church. In addition, the Eucharistic formula has a *significative* dimension, since it designates the conversion of bread into the body of Christ and of wine into the blood of Christ. Finally, the formula is also *effective* inasmuch as it brings about through divine power (*virtute divina*) what it signifies.

After going through the doctrine of transubstantiation as found in the *Summa theologiae*, one could find the suspicion confirmed that scholastic theology of the Eucharist encouraged a fixation on the somatic real presence in the consecrated gifts of bread and wine, even to the point of definitively solidifying its staying power. At the same time, it is to be admitted

---

124. With the aid of the doctrine of concomitance (see on this point J. J. Megivern, *Concomitance and Communion* [Fribourg–New York: Herder, 1963]), Thomas also explains the presence of the soul and the divine nature of Christ: the direct goal of the sacramental conversion of bread and wine is the flesh and blood of Christ, not his soul or his divinity. These are contained in the converted gifts, so to speak, indirectly and "by natural consequence," and indeed this is so because the divine Logos never abandoned the assumed body, and the soul is joined to the glorified body through the resurrection. Thus, in each of the two Eucharistic species the *totus* Christus is always present. See *S. th.* III, q. 76, aa. 1 and 2.

125. See *In IV Sent.*, d. 8, q. 2 a. 1 aq. 4 (n. 163); *S. th.* III, q. 78, a. 5.

126. See *In Ioan. VI*, l. VI (n. 962). See also the commentary (n. 974) on the saying. "Caro enim mea vere est cibus et sanguis mea vere est potus" (Jn 6:56). Thomas sees the firm emphasis of *vere est* as excluding the view that enigmatic or parabolic speech is exhibited here. In order to reinforce the claim to truth made by the statement and to eliminate a purely figurative interpretation, Thomas cites the *verba testamenti* in the version given in Mt 26:26: "Hoc est corpus meum ... et hic est sanguis meus novi testamenti." See also *In I Cor*, l. V (n. 663), where a symbolic construal of the *verba testamenti* in the sense of "hoc est signum vel figura corporis mei" is explicitly qualified as heretical.

that the scholastic period—as with every epoch—could not step outside the historical context in which it was embedded. The way the question was framed by Eucharistic controversies of the ninth and eleventh centuries—whether Jesus Christ is present in the Eucharist *in signo* or *in veritate*—needed to be conceptually worked out and clarified. Offering an ontological penetration of Christ's mode of presence, the doctrine of transubstantiation presented a solution to the question. It adopted a *via media* between crude sensualism and pure spiritualism, by shifting the event of conversion to an intelligible level. Empirically seen, nothing happens to the gifts of bread and wine; but from the vantage point of faith everything is changed, as the substance of bread and wine gives way to the substance of Christ's body and blood. Through this solution, Thomas is indeed able to take up the *particula veri* of crude sacramental realism, when he decisively emphasizes the real presence of Christ. But to the extent that he defines this real presence as *substantial*, he extracts it from the realm of empirical validation: *substantia non est visibilis oculo corporali*.[127] The *signum* of bread is broken and masticated by the teeth, but the *res significata* of Christ's body remains untouched: *Nulla rei fit scissura, / Signi tantum fit fractura, / Qua nec status nec statura / Signati minuitur*—thus the Sequence *Lauda Sion*.[128]

At the same time, the doctrine of transubstantiation is able to take up what is partially correct in spiritualism, which concluded to a merely symbolic presence from the fact that nothing changes on the visible level of the *signum*—at the cost of underhandedly falsifying the meaning of the *verba testamenti* and having to translate *hoc est corpus meum* into *hoc significat corpus meum*. Even Thomas concedes that one cannot conclude to the real presence of Jesus Christ from the level of sign. What really matters is the reality-positing power of the word alone, a word spoken *in persona Christi* and accepted in faith. The word alone institutes the real presence of Christ's body and blood in the gifts of bread and wine—a reality accessed not by the senses but through faith.

Even if it is the case that the doctrine of transubstantiation shows a way between the Scylla of crude sacramental realism and the Charybdis of mere spiritualism, its solution still remains bound up in a certain way with the difficulty of how the problem is framed: the concentration on the event of conversion. Set against this background, it appears that the allegation of the Eucharistic theology of the Scholastics limiting itself totally and exclu-

---

127. *S. th.* III, q. 76, a. 7.
128. Guitmund of Aversa had already taught that the body of Christ is substantially contained in each part of the host and is not separated by breaking the host. See idem, *De corporis et sanguinis Christi veritate*, in PL 149, 1450 C.

sively to the somatic real presence in the consecrated gifts and backgrounding other aspects of the Eucharistic mystery can hardly be dismissed. At the same time, the allegation does not, through its continual repetition in the literature, gain plausibility. Rather, if one pays attention to the premises of the event of conversion, the further question poses itself, whether the common allegation must not be submitted to a revision. If one considers in particular that the conversion of the gifts does not come about through the priest's personal contribution but through the fact that he speaks the words of consecration *in persona Christi*, then a thoroughly personal actual presence of Christ is claimed. As Thomas emphasizes repeatedly, the author of the *conversio substantialis* is Christ, the eternal, incarnate, crucified, and resurrected Word of the Father; the priest speaking the words of consecration *in persona Christi* is a delegated instrument. Only through the actual presence of Jesus Christ does the priest's recitation of the words of institution become an *effective* speech act bringing about the reality it signifies. In this way, relying on the terminology of Johannes Betz, we can speak of a "principal actual presence" of the divine Word, without which the conversion of the Eucharistic gifts and thus the somatic real presence would not come to be at all. At the same time, applying the doctrine of concomitance, it becomes clear that the *Christus totus* and thus also his deeds are present in the Eucharist. Indeed, person and work are not to be separated, so that the Eucharistic real presence of Jesus Christ at least implicitly encompasses the moments of life, death, resurrection, and ascension. In the consecratory formula spoken over the wine, the soteriological meaning of Christ's Passion is explicitly brought into play, when it is said: "*Hic est calix sanguinis mei, novi et aeterni Testamenti, mysterium fidei, qui pro vobis et pro multis effundetur in remissionem peccatorum.*"[129] Given this, it should still be briefly indicated that the conversion of gifts presupposes the actual presence of the person Jesus Christ, before the next part of this work presents in more detail the suggestion that Thomas's Eucharistic theology offers points of contact for what is designated as "commemorative actual presence" in contemporary Eucharistic theology: the somatic real presence of Christ in the consecrated gifts and the re-presentation of his self-gift in the sacrifice of the Eucharist belong together.

---

129. See *In I Cor* XI, 25, l. VI (n. 681f). See also *S. th.* III, q. 78, a. 3.

The Principal Actual Presence of Jesus Christ in the Priest's Consecratory Speech Act

If the priest were to speak only on his own authority, then uttering the *verba testamenti* in the Eucharistic celebration would remain a literary quotation lacking the power to consecrate. His word becomes a *verbum efficax* by and only by being spoken *in persona Christi*. The priestly speech act *in persona Christi*, however, claims the actual presence of Jesus Christ and brings it effectively to bear on the sacramental action.[130] "The priest can recite the words of consecration 'as if they were said by Christ,' because the 'infinite (divine) power of Christ' brings it about that these words, after the Lord once spoke them, possess transformative power whenever a priest repeats them."[131] Already in his reflections on general sacramental theology, Thomas made use of causal-theoretical categories to elucidate more precisely how the sacraments come about. He distinguishes—as already pointed out—between principal and instrumental cause. The divinity of Christ works in the sacraments as principal cause (*principalis causa*) and author of grace (*auctor gratiae*). On account of the hypostatic union, the humanity of Christ is an instrument conjoined to the divinity (*instrumentum coniunctum divinitati*), and this conjoined instrument serves the sacraments, which are *instrumenta separata*. The salutary power of the sacraments derives *from* the divinity of Christ, which operates *through* his humanity *in* the sacraments (as *instrumenta separata*).[132]

Applied to the sacrament of the Eucharist, this means: when the priest acts *in persona Christi* and says the words of consecration over the gifts of bread and wine, he claims Christ, inasmuch as he is God, as the *auctor gratiae*.[133] The reality signified by the words *Hoc est corpus meum* is made present at just the moment when the priest performs the consecration *in persona Christi*.[134] Claiming the person of Christ is indispensable also for a temporal

---

130. This event is poetically encapsulated in the hymn *Pange lingua*: "Verbum caro panem verum / verbo carnem efficit."
131. Th. Marschler, *Auferstehung und Himmelfahrt Christi*, vol. 1, 537.
132. See *S. th.* III, q. 64, a. 1.
133. See *S. th.* III, q. 64, a. 3: "interiorem sacramentorum effectum operatur Christus, et secundum quod est Deus, et secundum quod est homo, aliter tamen et aliter. Nam secundum quod est Deus, operatur in sacramentis per auctoritatem; secundum autem, quod est homo, operatur ad interiores effectus sacramentorum meritorie et efficienter, sed instrumentaliter."
134. See *S. th.* III, q. 78, a. 1: "in hoc sacramento consecratio materiae consistit in quadam miraculosa conversione substantiae, quae *a solo Deo* perfici potest; unde minister in hoc sacramento perficiendo non habet alium actum nisi prolationem verborum.... Forma huius sacramenti profertur quasi ex persona ipsius Christi loquentis, ut detur intelligi quod minister in perfectione huius sacramenti nihil agit, nisi quod profert verba Christi" (emphasis added).

and theological reason: only Christ's person can bring it about that the recitation of the words spoken at the last supper *back then* also effectuates Christ's making himself present *today* in the gifts of bread and wine.

Not everyone is authorized to speak the consecratory formula of the Eucharistic sacrament.[135] Whoever acts not in their own name but in the name of another person requires—according to Thomas—the proper power (*potestas*). As power is granted by Christ to the baptized to receive the sacrament of the Eucharist, so is the power (*potestas*) conferred on the priest through Ordination to consecrate this sacrament *in persona Christi*.[136] Through Ordination, he is added—as Thomas explicitly holds—to the rank of those to whom Christ said: "Do this in remembrance of me" (Lk 22:19).[137] Thomas places the proper attribute of the priestly office in the *potestas consecrandi*; leading the parish and preaching the word are, for Thomas, subordinate functions, which he already took into consideration in the context of general sacramental theology.[138]

One could reply that the sacrament also comes to be when a nonordained layperson speaks the words of institution. For the words of institution, which make up the form of the sacrament, do not change whether spoken by a layperson or a priest. To this sort of question, which levels out the difference between laypeople and ministers, Thomas offers for consideration the thought that the sacramental power (*virtus sacramentalis*) depends not only on the correct recitation of the words of institution, but also on the competence of the one reciting. As Baptism is carried out through both the words themselves and the use of water, so does the *virtus consecrativa* in the Eucharistic sacrament similarly lie not only in the words themselves but also in the *potestas* conferred on the priest at his Ordination. This conferral of power finds expression in the formula for administering sacramental Ordination when the bishop says: "Receive the power (*potestas*) to offer the sacrifice in the Church for both the living and the dead."[139] Conse-

---

135. *S. th.* III q. 82, a. 1: "Hoc sacramentum est tantae dignitatis quod non conficitur nisi in persona Christi."

136. The Romano-Germanic Pontifical (tenth century) defines the office as "potestas offere sacrificium Deo missamque celebrare." This definition greatly influenced medieval theology. The question to what extent this and similar definitions led to a cultic and sacerdotal constriction of understanding the priestly ministry, which was only revised at the Second Vatican Council, must remain open here.

137. On this point, see the detailed study by J. Ternus, "Dogmatische Untersuchungen zur Theologie des hl. Thomas über das Sakrament der Weihe," *Scholastik* 7 (1932): 161–86 and 354–86 (continuation), as well as *Scholastik* 8 (1933): 161–202 (conclusion).

138. See the earlier Hippolytus, *trad. apost.* 10 (FC 1, ed. W. Geerlings, 240): "Ordinatio autem fit cum clero propter liturgiam."

139. *S. th.* III q. 82, a. 1 ad 1: "Accipe potestatem offerendi in Ecclesia sacrificium tam pro vivis quam pro mortuis." See also *S. th.* III (Suppl.), q. 34, a. 4 c.

quently, Thomas joins the administration of the Eucharist to the conferral of power through Christ, which is sacramentally sealed in priestly Ordination through the laying on of hands and prayer (and at that time as well, the handing over of the vessels); in this way, self-authorization to administer the Eucharist is excluded.

If we consider this theological background of Ordination, the speech act of consecration is once more differently illuminated. The priest does not speak here in his own name but *in persona Christi loquentis*.[140] This means, he claims in a certain way the identity of Christ when he, as it were, lets Christ himself act in the consecratory speech act.[141] The priest's claiming the identity of Christ is not an act of presumption; rather, it is justified by the sacramental conformity with Christ, which takes place as early as Baptism but in a special way through Ordination.[142] In his ministerial action, the priest participates in the eternal priesthood of Christ.[143] Nevertheless, these speech performances *in persona Christi* are identifiable as such only in faith and, precisely as such, they cannot be perceived acoustically. From a purely phonetic standpoint, nothing changes whether the priest at one moment reads the Gospel, at another utters the prayers *in persona ecclesiae*, or at another recites the words of institution *in persona Christi*; the vocal pitch, timbre, and speech melody of the celebrant remain the vocal pitch, timbre, and speech melody of the celebrant, even if Christ himself speaks through his mouth. One could speak therefore—taking up the Aristotelian terminology—of a "transubstantiation" of the consecratory speech act.[144] The "accidents," that is, the acoustically perceptible and phonetically describable signals, *remain*, while the "substance," that is, the speaking person, *changes*. This "conversion of substance" reveals the grammatical change from an account of the institution of the Eucharist deemed narrative to a performative utterance *in persona Christi*. But the assertion of faith, that in a certain sense Christ himself speaks in the *forma sacramenti*, removes itself from the realm of empirical validation, as does also faith in the real

---

140. See *S. th.* III, q. 78, a. 1 c: "forma huius huius sacramenti profertur ex persona Christi loquentis: ut detur intellegi quod minister in perfectione sacramenti nihil agit nisi quod profert verba Christi."

141. See *In Matth*, XXVI, l. 3 (n. 2181). "Unde sacerdos peragit in persona Christi, et non utitur verbis in persona propria, sed in persona Christi."

142. *S. th.* III, q. 63, a. 3 ad 2: "illi qui deputantur ad cultum Christianum, cuius auctor est Christus, characterem accipiunt quo Christo configurantur."

143. *S. th.* III, q. 22, a. 4 c: "Christus est fons totius sacerdotii. Nam sacerdos legalis erat figura ipsius; sacerdos autem novae legis in persona ipsius operatur."

144. See P. M. Candler, "Liturgically Trained Memory. A Reading of Summa theologiae III.83," *Modern Theology* 20 (2004): 423–45, here 428: "the words of the priest are only made worthy by themselves being *transubstantiated*, by being transformed from the mere recitation of a textual narrative into the performative utterance *in persona Christi*."

presence of Christ in the consecrated gifts of bread and wine. At the same time, the attempt to set up an analogy with transubstantiation is of limited value. For the proper activity of the priest as *instrumentum animatum* is not exhausted in the correct recitation of the words of conversion; it includes as well the right *intention* to do what Christ and the Church do.[145]

Simply for the sake of completeness, let it be emphasized once more that the coming to be of the sacrament is independent of the moral disposition of the priest. "The servants of the Church can administer the sacraments even if they are unworthy."[146] Thomas cites Augustine explicitly, who set the theological course for the Catholic understanding of the priestly ministry during the Donatist controversy: "Within the Catholic Church, in the mystery of the Lord's body and blood, nothing greater is done by a good priest, nothing less by an evil priest, because it is *not by the merits of the consecrator* that the sacrament is accomplished, but by the Creator's word, and by the power of the Holy Spirit."[147] The priest consecrates this sacrament not *virtute propria* but as *minister Christi*.[148] Thus, he does not cease to be a minister of Christ because he is bad, for "the Lord has good and bad ministers."[149]

Finally, let it be noted that understanding the consecratory speech act of the priest could still be greatly deepened from the perspective of the philosophy of language. In particular, the insight that Thomas, in contrast with Aristotle, conceived his discussions of language from the *speaker's perspective* could be made fruitful for interpreting the sacramental speech act. Beyond that, the various dimensions of Thomas's doctrine of *verbum* could be further thought out, allowing an inner coherence to be discerned between Trinitarian theology, a theology of creation, a theology of Incarnation, and sacramental theology.[150] Within the horizon of Thomas's teaching on *ver-*

---

145. S. th. III, q. 64, a. 8 ad 1: "Instrumentum animatum, sicut est minister, non solum movetur, sed etiam quodammodo movet seipsum, in quantum sua voluntate movet membra ad operandum; et ideo requiritur eius intentio, qua se subiiciat principali agenti, ut scilicet intendat facere, quod facit Christus et ecclesia."

146. See S. th. III, q. 64, a. 5.

147. Cited in S. th. III, q. 82, a. 5 s.c.: "Intra ecclesiam catholicam, in mysterio corporis et sanguinis Domini, nihil a bono maius, nihil a malo minus perficitur sacerdote, quia *non in merito consecrantis*, sed in verbo perficitur Creatoris, et virtute Spiritus sancti" (emphasis added).

148. See S. th. III, q. 82, a. 1 and a. 2 ad 2, as well as a. 3.

149. On this point, see the fundamental study by H. G. Nissing, *Sprache als Akt bei Thomas von Aquin* (Leiden-Boston: Brill Academic Publishers, 2006), who works out the operative understanding of speech in Thomas's thought—relying especially on his commentary on Aristotle's *Peri hermeneias*.

150. For background, see the exposition of the prologue of John's Gospel in *In Ioan.*, I, l. 1 and 2 (nn. 23–94); S. th. I, q. 34, as well as the rich list of sources in Nissing, *Sprache als Akt bei Thomas von Aquin*, 159, who likewise reconstructs the doctrinal development in Thomas's works of his doctrine of *verbum* (see ibid., 121–60).

bum, God the Father is thought of as *speaker* from eternity, and the consubstantial Word, in which he speaks *himself*, is not only the second person of *Deus trinitas* but also the principle of creation, out of which is created *everything that is* (*creatio ex nihilo*). Moreover, the eternal Word of the Father is the principle by which everything that exists is conserved in its being (*creatio continua*). Lastly, the reality-causing power of the creative Word, which was incarnated in Jesus Christ (*verbum incarnatum*), is also called upon as *verbum efficax*—albeit differently—in the administration of the Eucharist, and indeed in that moment when the priest speaks *in persona Christi*. In the interpretation of the hymns, we will have to return to these connections.

3

"*Quod pro vobis tradetur*"
The Passion of Christ and Its Representative Realization in the Celebration of the Eucharist

The Historical Origin: Jesus' Last Supper and the *Passio Christi*

While the explanatory model of transubstantiation attempts to determine conceptually the mode (that is, the *how*) of Christ's being made present, the motif of the *passio Christi* indicates the content (that is, the *what*) of that which is rendered sacramentally present in the celebration of the Eucharist. Both moments belong together. Even the formula of consecration, "*Hoc est corpus meum*," is more precisely determined by the relative clause, "*quod pro vobis tradetur*."[1] The somatic real presence of Christ in the consecrated gifts of bread and wine cannot therefore be separated from the memory of Jesus Christ's suffering and death, the commemorative actual presence. The danger of treating the holy gifts as cultic objects and objectifying them obtains to the extent that *who* it is that gives himself—and *what* this self-giving means—is not considered, or is simply forgotten. It is Jesus Christ's surrendering of his own life that is made present in the Eucharist in a representative way, and this gift of his own life has saving and redeeming power. The formula of consecration spoken over the chalice brings the soteriological effect of Christ's dying explicitly into words, when it states that the blood "is poured out for you and for many for the forgiveness of sins."

With that said, it is important to consider how Christ's abandoning his

---

1. Something analogous applies to the formula of consecration: "Hoc est calix sanguis mei, novi et aeterni testamenti, mysterium fidei, qui pro vobis et pro multis effundetur in remissionem peccatorum." On this point, see S. th. III, q. 78, a. 3, where Thomas also gives an account of the inhomogeneity found in New Testament's written report and analyzes more exactly the individual segments of the formula.

life, his *sacrificium* on the cross, can be relevant for salvation at all times, given its historical and onetime character. His surrender to the will of the Father *and* to humanity in need of redemption, which Thomas lets coalesce in the multilayered term *traditio*, must be made present ever anew if it is to be efficacious today as well. This takes place first of all through an act of remembrance (*commemoratio*), which goes back to the explicit commission of Christ as he parts with his disciples: "Do this in memory of me." (1 Cor 11:25; Lk 22:19). Nevertheless, the sacramental making-present of Christ's suffering in the Eucharist is distinguished from a mere cult of the dead. It is not the product of the human capacity for remembering, which is always characterized by the ambivalence of, on the one hand, being able to bring something past into present consciousness, but, on the other, then having to experience the absence of what is recalled as all the more painful.[2] The point of this sacramental making-present consists rather in the fact that Jesus Christ himself as the *eternal* high priest institutes ever anew the reminder of his self-surrender *in the stream of time*. It is therefore a further question, through what words and symbolic actions this making-present takes place, and thus which basic liturgical conditions must be fulfilled, so that the *Christus passus* can give himself in the gifts of bread and wine. Whereas in the preceding part, the *how* of the real presence stood primarily in the foreground, that is, the conversion of gifts in the event of consecration, in this part our concern is the gift itself: *what* is imparted in the Eucharist? Or more precisely, in order to avoid impersonal connotations: *whose* surrendering of life is made present—and what ramifications does *communio* with Christ, the giver of this gift, have for the receiver? In particular, the direction of the questions pursued here will move toward examining the relationship between the last supper, the Passion, and the celebration of the Eucharist. Thus, the historical origin of the Eucharist will first of all be taken up. Subsequently, attention will be given to the suffering and death of Jesus Christ, which, following Thomas, can certainly be understood as an incarnate commentary on the pro-existence of Jesus expressed in the *verba testamenti*. Through reliance on the soteriological passages of the *Summa theologiae*, it can moreover be shown how the almost formulistically used term *passio Christi* is more precisely determined by Thomas. Finally, we will sketch the way Thomas illuminates the representative making-present of Christ's sufferings in the celebration of the Eucharist. Through this process, it will become clear that the somatic real presence of the *Christus passus* and the sacramental representa-

2. For background, see my reflections, "Gedenken und danken. Einleitende Bemerkungen," in A. Schmemann, *Eucharistie. Sakrament des Gottesreiches* (Freiburg: Johannes-Verlag, 2005), 7–25.

tion of his self-giving in the ritual performance belong most closely together. The dimensions of sacrament and sacrifice do not yet go their separate ways.

The *Novum Testamentum*—The "Institution" of the Eucharist

The last supper is the place where Jesus Christ himself pointed to his impending suffering in the company of his apostles. The still-present Christ peered ahead to his death and the time of his absence and left behind the testament of his love for his disciples remaining behind. The difference here between temporal circumstances is certainly to be noted: whereas the sacrament of the Eucharist presents a *memoriale passionis Christi*, the last supper interpretively *anticipates* the event of the cross. Without this anticipatory interpretation, the crucifixion as a brutal act of execution would remain semantically dumb; conversely, without Jesus' self-surrender unto death, the *verba testamenti* would have remained *flatus vocis*. The words spoken at the last supper and the suffering on the cross are reciprocally illuminating.

Thomas repeatedly takes up the scene of the last supper as the historical origin of the sacrament.[3] In the presentation of the farewell scene, we can glimpse in his otherwise austere diction a certain affective coloration, which is even more clearly expressed in the poetic hymns. For him, it is a matter of theologically thinking through the last testament, that is, the testament of Jesus who parts ways with his disciples. In the *Summa theologiae*, the question is formulated, whether the time of the institution of the Eucharist was fitting. Thomas brings forward three arguments from fittingness.

First, he points to the fact that the institution was fitting on account of its content, for, in contrast to the other sacraments, Christ himself is contained in the Eucharist. When he prepared himself *before his suffering* (*in propria specie*) to leave his disciples, he left behind for them *his very self* in sacramental form (*in sacramentali specie seipsum reliquit*). It would have been a sign of insufficient love, so to speak, if Christ had withheld from his friends a sign of his presence in the time of his absence.[4] The withdrawal of his bodily presence at the ascension, his disappearing from the disciples' sight,[5] is—and this is decisive for this context—the presupposition for a

---

3. See the passages: *S. th.* III, q. 73, a. 5; q. 83, a. 2 ad 3, as well as *In IV Sent.*, d. 8, q. 1, a. 3, and the scriptural commentaries *In Matth* XXVI; *In I Cor* XI, l. IV and V.

4. See *S. th.* III, q. 75, a. 1.

5. This becomes clear indirectly in a quotation Thomas uses here from Eusebius, which discusses the visible disappearance of Christ: "Quia corpus assumptum ablaturus erat ab oculis et illaturus sideribus, necesse erat ut die Cenae sacramentum corporis et sanguinis sui consecraret nobis, ut coleretur iugiter per mysterium quod semel offerebatur in pretium" (*S. th.* III, q. 73, a. 5, drawing on *Decretum Gratiani*, p. III, d. 2, can. 35 [ed. Richter-Friedberg I, 1325]).

new, pneumatically qualified presence. For this reason, Thomas can even hold that the withdrawal of the bodily presence (*subtractio praesentiae corporalis*) at Christ's ascension is beneficial for the faithful: it enhances faith, which is directed to things invisible; it bolsters the hope that Christ is preparing a place in heaven; and it directs the affect of love toward heavenly things.[6] Certainly, the presence of Christ's divinity, which is always and everywhere present (see Mt 28:20),[7] is distinguished from the sacramental presence of the *Christus passus*. In order to make the mode of this presence clearer, Thomas employs an analogy with the picture of the emperor, which in his absence is presented to his subjects for reverence. This analogy is admittedly lacking, inasmuch as the *Christus passus* is himself contained in the sacrament, in contrast to which the absent emperor is merely symbolically represented in the picture, and this in a diminished sense. Moreover, in the cult of the emperor the activity lies one-sidedly with the subjects, who render their reverence to the picture; in the Eucharist, however, it is first Christ who offers the gift of his presence. He left himself behind for the faithful, and indeed in another form (*in alia specie*). This distinction is important, because it is able to avert a misunderstanding of the relation between the historical and the Eucharistic body of Christ as an undifferentiated total identification. It is not the case that Christ's flesh is directly masticated by the teeth. The flesh and blood of Christ are consumed not *in propria* but rather *in alia specie*. The charge of anthropophagy or cannibalism, which goes beyond the *ordo significationis*, is thus inappropriate.[8]

In and under the species of bread and wine, Christ left behind the gift of his presence.[9] Thomas clarifies the duplicity of signs by referring not only to the point that the Eucharist is understood as spiritual food (*alimentum spirituale*) that satisfies spiritual hunger and thirst, in an analogy to basic anthropological needs. As *memoriale dominicae passionis*, it likewise represents the Lord's blood, spilled and separated from the body at the violent execution

---

6. See *S. th.* III, q. 57, a. 1 ad 3, where the *corpus articuli* makes clear that the withdrawal of the *praesentia corporalis* in no way implies the withdrawal of the *praesentia divinitatis*—thus the assurance: "I am with you always, to the end of the age" (Mt 28:20).

7. See *In Matth* XXVIII (n. 2469). Here the "ego vobiscum" is connected with the name "Emmanuel" (see Is 7:14 [Vulg.]: "virgo concipiet et pariet filium et vocabitis nomen eius Emmanuel"), which is interpreted, "God with us (*Deus nobiscum*)."

8. See *In I Cor* XI, l. 14 (n. 652): "Continetur autem sub alia specie propter tria. Primo quidem ne esset horribile fidelibus sumentibus hoc sacramentum, si *in propria specie* carnem hominis ederent, et sanguinem biberent; secundo ne hoc ipsum esset derisibile infidelibus; tertio ut cresceret meritum fidei, quae consistit in hoc quod creduntur ea quae non videntur" (emphasis added).

9. Thomas made this aspect clear in the legend *Immensa* of the Office. See *Officium de festo corporis Christi*, l. II, 276f.: "Ut autem tanti beneficii iugis in nobis maneret memoria, corpus suum in cibum et sanguinem suum in potum sub specie panis et vini sumendum fidelibus dereliquit."

on the cross.¹⁰ With the term representation (*repraesentatio*), which requires further clarification, the transition to the second perspective is carried out, a perspective that will show the fittingness of the sacrament's institution.

This has to do with the symbolic representation of Christ's Passion. Because there is not and cannot be salvation apart from faith in the suffering of Christ—as Thomas notes, drawing on Romans 3:25—a fitting representation of the Passion (*aliquid repraesentativum dominicae passionis*) is required at all times. In the old covenant, the Paschal lamb had the function of pointing ahead to the *passio Christi*. Thus, we read: "*etenim pascha nostrum immolatus est Christus*—for our Paschal lamb, Christ, has been sacrificed" (1 Cor 5:7). In place of the paschal lamb, which designated the Passion in an *anticipatory* way, the sacrament of the Eucharist steps into the scene in the new covenant and by *looking back* recalls the past suffering of Christ (*sacramentum quod est rememorativum praeteritae passionis*). According to Thomas, it was therefore fitting that *after* the celebration of Passover and shortly *before* the Passion a new sacrament was instituted.¹¹

Finally, Thomas explores the *farewell situation* more closely and notes, not without a keen psychological intuition: "last words, chiefly such as are spoken by departing friends, are committed most deeply to memory; since then especially affection for friends is more enkindled."¹² Precisely the approaching Passion of their master moved the hearts of the disciples (*corda discipulorum*) profoundly, so that they were especially receptive at this moment for a sign of the highest love (*signum maximae caritatis*). If the institution of the Eucharist had not taken place until after the resurrection, then—as Thomas remarks in the *Sentences* commentary—the joy concerning the resurrection would have made the afflictions of the Passion easily forgotten.¹³

---

10. See *In I Cor*, XI, 23 (n. 653): "Est enim memoriale dominicae passionis, per quam sanguis Christi fuit separatus a corpore; et ideo in hoc sacramento seorsum offertur sanguis a corpore."

11. See *In IV Sent.*, d. 8, q. 1, a. 2 (n. 53), where Thomas relates the figures of the Old Testament to the three aspects of the sacrament: "Et sic *quantum ad id quod est tantum sacramentum* in eucharistia, fuit figura eius oblatio Melchisedech; *quantum autem ad id, quod est res et sacramentum*, scilicet ipsum Christum passum, fuit figura agnis paschalis; *quantum autem ad id quod est res tantum*, scilicet gratiam, fuit signum manna quae reficiebat, omnem saporem suavitatis habens" (emphasis added). See *S. th.* III, q. 73, a. 6, where this division is modified and a preferential meaning is ascribed to the *agnus paschalis*. Earlier in *S. th.* III, q. 60, a. 2 ad 2, we find: "immolatio agnis paschalis significabat immolationem Christi, qua sanctificati sumus."

12. *S. th.* III, q. 73, a. 5: "ea quae ultimo dicuntur, maxime ab amicis recedentibus, magis memoriae commendantur: praesentim quia tunc magis *inflammatur affectus ad amicos*"—and Thomas continues—"ea vero ad quae magis afficimur, profundis animo imprimuntur" (emphasis added). See earlier *In IV Sent.*, q. 1, a. 1 ad 4 (n. 98): "Quanto autem aliquis ad amicum diutius conversatur, fit maior dilectio; et quando ab amicis separamur, sentitur motus dilectionis ferventior propter dolorem separationis; et ideo verba amicorum a nobis recedentium finaliter dicta magis memoriae imprimuntur." For background on the theme of testamentary farewell, see G. Steiner, *Lessons of the Masters* (Cambridge, Mass.: Harvard University Press, 2005).

13. See *In IV Sent*, d. 8, q. 1, a. 2, qa. 3 (n. 93): "dicendum quod imminente passione corda discipulorum

At this point we should note that the testament of Jesus is not a *written* and fixed document but rather an ensemble of words and symbolic actions, in which his last intention is articulated. Written words—whose signs outlast both writer and addressee, and can still be deciphered when lifted out of their original context—are not the medium Christ employs to express the spoken word in relation to two significant gestures that reveal his self-gift for the many with sensible incisiveness. Passing on the *novum testamentum*, which was handed on to the disciples, is therefore itself bound up with bodily performances. The *traditio* set in motion by Jesus is transferred to humans, who put themselves at its disposal; it demands that the *verba testamenti* are spoken orally and the bread broken manually and shared with others (see Acts 2:42, 46; 20:7). The Eucharistic making-present of Christ's Passion is thus joined with the priest's living voice and the activity of his hands; the priest does not act from his own authority but *in persona Christi*. Christ's surrender should be written into the bodily actions of those who ministerially carry out the remembrance of Christ.

This self-gift is expressed in a condensed way in the phrase "*quod pro vobis tradetur*," in which Thomas sees the mystery of the Eucharist touched upon.[14] The Eucharist, however, is the remembrance (*commemoratio*) of Jesus Christ's Passion, which Thomas interprets as a multi-layered event of the *traditio*. Because the term *passio Christi* pervades the *Summa*'s theological reflections on the Eucharist, and because it is almost shorthand for *what* is recalled in the sacrament of the altar, in what follows we will work out more precisely the soteriological meaning of Christ's suffering in the theology of Thomas Aquinas. To do this, we will draw from the pertinent passages of the *Tertia pars* of the *Summa theologiae*, which is structured so that the whole of it has Christ as its theme, Christ as the way of man's return (*reditus*) to God.[15] Unlike interpretive attempts that do not follow Thomas's division of the material but rather try to open up the matter from a systematic perspective,[16] I am taking my orientation from the structure of the *Summa theologiae*, which first treats of the fittingness of Christ's suf-

---

magis erant affectata ad passionem, quam passione jam peracta, quando jam erant immemores pressurae passionis propter gaudium resurrectionis."

14. *In Matth* XXVI, l. V (n. 671): "tangit mysterium huius sacramenti."

15. See *S. th.* III, prol.

16. See M. Levering, *Christ's Fulfillment of Torah and Temple: Salvation according to Thomas Aquinas* (Notre Dame, Ind.: Notre Dame University Press, 2002), who uses the motif of fulfilling the Mosaic law through Christ as a hermeneutic key for analyzing the soteriology of Thomas. According to Levering, the soteriology sketched in qq. 46–49 attempts to show that through his Passion, Christ fulfilled once for all the moral, ceremonial, and juridical prescriptions of the Torah. Simultaneously, Christ thereby manifests himself as prophet, priest, and king.

fering, then investigates the diverse efficient causes of the Passion, and finally interprets the event of the Passion by means of central soteriological concepts.

The Self-Gift of Jesus Christ in the Passion: Fittingness and Drama

Faith in the saving power of the cross has provoked questions since day one. Why did Jesus have to suffer a disgraceful death on Golgotha? Could not God have used other means and ways to free humans from sin and guilt? Does not the fact of the Father's not sparing his only Son from a brutal execution cast a shadow on the concept of God?

Already Anselm of Canterbury engaged himself with these and similar questions in his work *Cur Deus homo*. In accord with his programmatic position of faith seeking understanding (*fides quaerens intellectum*) and in conversation with the "unbelievers" of his time,[17] Anselm seeks, *remoto Christo*, to offer necessary reasons for God's Incarnation.[18] All the same, the scope of his argumentation is decidedly soteriological in its orientation. Man, whose destiny lies in the recognition of God's glory but who in fact violated God's glory by sinning,[19] must make satisfaction if he is to reach the end of eternal beatitude despite his sin. The soteriological aporia of sinful man consists in the fact that the fitting satisfaction he ought to undertake lies beyond his powers, for there is simply nothing that he could offer to God, the Creator, which he does not already owe him. Even if he were to give everything he had to give, it would not be sufficient to make good the infinite violation of God's glory that took place in sinning. Now, if God's salvific counsel concerning creation is not to be frustrated by human sin—and God's glory forbids this—then God himself must undertake the reparation otherwise impossible for men. Only God can make compensation for the infinite violation of glory, but he must do this as man, because the specifically human need for satisfaction must not be overlooked. Thus, the God-man (*Deus-homo*) is the one who can resolve the soteriological aporia, in that he gives his infinitely worthy life as satisfaction and thereby restores the glory of God and with it the order of creation. Because Christ, as a

---

17. The "infideles" are literarily represented by the questions of Bosos. On the historical background and the method of "religious disputations," see K. Kienzler, "Die Erlösungslehre Anselms von Canterbury. Aus der Sicht des mittelalterlichen jüdisch-christlichen Religionsgesprächs," in *Versöhnung in der jüdischen und christlichen Liturgie*, ed. H. Heinz (Freiburg: Herder, 1990), 88–116.

18. See the programmatic statement in the prologue: "Ac tandem *remoto Christi*, quasi numquam aliquid fuerit de illo, probat *rationibus necessariis* esse impossibile ullum hominem salvari sine illo (Anselm, *Cur Deus Homo*, praefatio [ed. Schmitt, 2], emphasis added).

19. For Anselm, to sin means to not recompense God what he is owed. See *Cur Deus Homo*, I, 11 (ed. Schmitt 40): "Non est ... aliud peccare quam non reddere Deo debitum."

man without sin, does not owe God death, he can apply the merits of his satisfactory death to men and in just this way realize "another mercy" concordant with justice.[20]

It would take us too far afield here to go further into the details of the epistemological presuppositions, the fundamental concepts (*honor, ordo, satisfactio*, etc.) as well as the individual steps of the argumentation, or for that matter to enter into a critical engagement with Anselm's doctrine of redemption.[21] For our proximate context, the one thing that is decisive is that within the framework of his *ordo*-thinking, Anselm claims to be able to demonstrate the strict necessity of Christ's redemptive deed. At this point, however, a certain correction takes place through Thomas, whose soteriology is more strongly oriented toward salvation history.[22] For Aquinas, the suffering of Christ is *not* strictly speaking necessary for the salvation of men, as if there would have been absolutely no other possibilities for God.[23]

In the *Summa theologiae*, three modes of necessity are distinguished:[24] Set apart by Thomas from (1) strict logical necessity, which derives from intrinsic causes, is (2) relative necessity, which results from either an efficient cause or (3) a final cause. Because an efficient cause causes a coercive necessity (*necessitas coactionis*), it is out of the question for Thomas as an explanation of Christ's suffering and death. No one compelled God to will the Passion of his Son. Rather, Thomas emphasizes—taking the factual events of salvation history as his point of departure—that the suffering of Christ must be designated as necessary *in virtue of a posited end* (*neces-*

---

20. See the statement in *Cur Deus Homo*, II, 20 (ed. Schmitt 152): "Nempe quid misericordius intelligi valet, quam cum peccatori tormentis aeternis damnato et unde se redimat non habenti deus pater dicit: accipe unigenitum meum et da pro te; et ipse filius: tolle me et redime te?—For what could be thought more merciful than if God the Father speaks to the sinner, who has been sentenced to eternal torment and who has nothing with which to free himself: take my only child and give him for yourself; and the Son: take me and save yourself."

21. See G. Greshake, "Erlösung und Freiheit. Zur Neuinterpretation der Erlösungslehre Anselms von Canterbury," *ThQ* 153 (1973): 323–45; G. Gäde, *Eine andere Barmherzigkeit. Zum Verständnis der Erlösungslehre Anselms von Canterbury* (Würzburg: Echter, 1989); P. Hünermann, *Jesus Christus. Gottes Wort in der Zeit* (Münster: Aschendorff, 1994), 197–203; S. Schaede, "Anselms von Canterbury Satiskfationslehre und das Stellvertretungsmotiv," in *Stellvertretung. Begriffsgeschichtliche Studien zur Soteriologie* (Tübingen: Mohr Siebeck, 2004), 274–309.

22. See W. J. Bracken, "Thomas Aquinas and Anselm's Satisfaction Theory," *Angelicum* 62 (1985): 503–30; R. Cessario, *The Godly Image: Christ and Satisfaction in Catholic Thought from Anselm to Aquinas* (Petersham, Mass.: St. Bede's Publications, 1990).

23. The concept of absolute necessity (*necessitas absoluta*) is understood by Thomas in the following way (*S. th.* I, q. 82, a. 1): "Necesse est enim quod non potest non esse." Distinguished from this is relative necessity, which is subdivided into *necessitas finis*, without which an end cannot be reached very well, and *necessitas coactionis*, which determines action in such a way that alternative actions become impossible. See also *S. th.* I, q. 19, a. 3. The Passion of Christ falls under the category of *necessitas finis*.

24. See Aristotle, *Metaph.* V, 5 (1015 a20–b15). In addition, see the commentary of Thomas, *In Metaph.* L. VI (n. 827–41).

sarium ex suppositione finis).²⁵ Thus, speaking of the Passion's necessity is bound up with certain presuppositions; it is *relative*. Only on the supposition that God, in sovereign freedom and from eternity, set for himself the end of liberating men from sin; only on the supposition that he wanted to set this end in motion through a very particular means, namely the suffering of Christ, can it be said that the Passion had to become a reality and in this sense was necessary.²⁶

This understanding of the relative necessity of the Passion, which is traced back to and bound up with God's eternal salvific counsel, forms the horizon in which the sayings of the New Testament can be interpreted—sayings that speak of needing to undergo suffering. Thomas orders these sayings according to three points of view. First, the Passion is necessary from *the perspective of men*, for men are saved by Christ's suffering. For biblical reference, Thomas calls upon John 3:14f., which reads: "so must [*oportet*] the Son of Man be lifted up, that [*ut*]²⁷ whoever believes in him is not lost but may have eternal life." After that, we can speak of a relative necessity of the Passion *in view of Christ himself*, inasmuch as he merited (*meruit*) the glory of exaltation through his humiliation in suffering.²⁸ As a biblical reference, Thomas here cites not the hymn of Philippians, where Christ's exaltation follows his humiliation unto death on the cross (see Phil 2:6–11), but rather a statement used by the risen Lord himself to open up the meaning of the Scriptures for his disciples at Emmaus. "Was it not necessary [*opportuit*] that the Messiah should suffer these things and then enter into his glory?" (Lk 24:26). Finally, this suffering was also necessary *from God's perspective*, since the prefigurations of the *passio Christi* found in the Old Testament Scriptures had to be fulfilled. On this matter, Thomas sees the following reference points in the New Testament: (1) Luke 22:22—"The Son of Man is going as it has been determined"; Luke 24:44—"Everything written about me in the Law of Moses, the prophets, and the psalms must be fulfilled" (see also Lk 24:46). Unlike Anselm, who held the de facto mode of redemption to be necessary strictly speaking, Thomas takes as his point of departure that God potentially could have pursued other ways, but that he chose this way because it was most fitting. Beginning from revelation as laid down in Scripture, Thomas arrives at the conclusion that the

---

25. See the earlier *S. th.* III, q. 1, a. 2, where the *relative* necessity of the Incarnation for the restoration of mankind is worked out.
26. In the *Sentences* commentary, Thomas was more closely aligned with Anselm and spoke then for a strict *necessitas*. See *In III Sent.*, d. 16, q. 1, a. 1, 2. See also M.-R. Hoogland, *God, Passion and Power: Thomas Aquinas on Christ Crucified and the Almightiness of God* (Leuven: Peeters, 2003), 35.
27. The conjunction *ut* expresses the sense of finality, i.e., the positing of an end.
28. This will be considered more precisely below.

Passion was necessary in three ways: first, for the salvation of men; second, for the exaltation of Christ; and third, for fulfilling the divine will.

In this context, Thomas addresses the objection that Christ's suffering was not really requisite for our redemption. Against the thesis of the relative necessity of Christ's suffering, the view can be advanced that, *from the viewpoint of divine mercy*, which also distributes other gifts for free, it is certainly conceivable that it could reduce human guilt without any corresponding satisfaction. One could indeed imagine a sovereign, declarative act of God pronouncing human guilt to be nugatory; in this scenario, mercy would render superfluous the function of Christ's satisfactory suffering as an appeal to justice.[29] On the other hand, so continues the objection, *from the perspective of divine justice* as well, Christ's Passion was not actually necessary, because man earned eternal damnation on account of his sin. But what can mercy still bring about if justice requires eternal punishment for the sinner anyway?

Instead of pitting mercy and justice against each other, Thomas attempts to consider both aspects in their interaction.[30] It is significant that in discussing the objections critically, Thomas once again does not allow himself to entertain theological possibilities, but rather presupposes salvation history as it factually unfolded, and from this vantage point he sees justice and mercy equally realized in the Passion of Jesus Christ: "That man should be delivered by Christ's Passion was in keeping with both his mercy and his justice. With his justice, because by his Passion Christ made satisfaction for the sin of the human race; and so man was set free by Christ's justice: and with his mercy, for since man of himself could not satisfy for the sin of all human nature, God gave him his Son as *satisfactor*."[31] Here

---

29. Anselm had already taken up this objection. See *Cur Deus Homo*, I, 12 (ed. Schmitt, 43f.). He offers for consideration that a reduction of the penalty stemming from pure mercy would leave sin "disordered." Moreover, the just and sinners would stand before God as equals, which would place God himself under the suspicion of injustice; finally, forgiving sins with a decree of the divine will would not restore human nature corrupted by sin. On the ontological impossibility of forgiving sins *sola misericordia*, see Schaede, *Stellvertretung*, 285f.

30. Already Anselm attempted to show in his theory of satisfaction how the attributes of justice and mercy illuminate each other reciprocally. See H. Verweyen, "Die Einheit von Gerechtigkeit und Barmherzigkeit bei Anselm von Canterbury," *IKaZ* 14 (1985): 52–55; G. Gäde, *Eine andere Barmherzigkeit*.

31. *S. th.* III, q. 46, a. 1 ad 3: "quod hominem liberari per passionem Christi, conveniens fuit et misericordiae et iustitiae eius. Iustitiae quidem, quia per passionem suam Christus satisfecit pro peccato humani generis: et ita homo per iustitiam Christi liberatus est. Misericordiae vero, quia, cum homo per se satisfacere non posset pro peccato totius humanae naturae, ut supra habitum est [*S. th.* III, q. 1, a. 2 ad 2], Deus ei satisfactorem dedit Filium suum: secundum illud Rom. 3: *Iustificati gratis per gratiam ipsius, per redemptionem quae est in Christo Jesu, quem proposuit Deus propitiatorem per Fidem in sanguine ipsius.* Et hoc fuit abundantioris misericordiae quam si peccata absque satisfactione dimisset." On the relation between justice and mercy, see *S. th.* I, q. 21, a. 4.

Thomas holds that the *satisfactio* of the Son is a *gift* of the Father to men, so that the reservation circulating since Adolf von Harnack can be invalidated, that is, that the doctrine of satisfaction presupposes a mythological concept of God, "who was angry on account of his offended glory and would not give up his anger until he obtained some kind of equivalent of at least the same measure."[32] The strict logic of equivalence, which finds its origin in satisfaction thinking, always requires that guilt be balanced with a correlative compensation. This logic is burst open *theologically*. Indeed, the fact that God the Father makes the satisfaction of the guiltless Son to benefit guilty men can no longer be explained by means of the logic of equivalence. The *satisfactor* is the gift, a gift given for free. But behind the gift we find here God's immemorial salvific counsel.

Even if divine omnipotence requires holding that in principle there could have been alternative ways of redemption—and, in contrast to Anselm, Thomas insists on these potential alternatives[33]—this possibility is nevertheless to be discarded de facto in light of God's foreknowledge and ordinances. For it is, according to Thomas, impossible that the *praescientia Dei* be deceived and the divine will or his *dispositio* be abrogated. If, however, the *passio Christi* was foreknown by God and likewise appointed from eternity, then it is ultimately impossible that man could have been saved in any other way than by the suffering of Jesus Christ.[34] Thomas attempts to manifest the profound fittingness of the way of salvation laid down concretely by the suffering of Christ and in so doing brings in a whole slew of arguments from fittingness.[35] Let us highlight two of them here. First, man recognizes through Christ's Passion how much God loves him, and is thereby prompted to love God in return, which comprises the perfection of human salvation. One has to keep in mind that "Christ died for us, while we were still enemies" (see Rom 5:8f.). The insight into a love that goes to the extreme encompasses an affective dimension, to which Thomas also returns—as we have already seen—when elucidating the farewell situation of the last supper. Second, Thomas sees in the suffering of Christ an example of the virtues necessary for human salvation. *Christus passus est pro nobis,*

---

32. A. von Harnack, *Lehrbuch der Dogmengeschichte*, 3rd ed., vol. 3, (1909; repr., Tübingen: J. C. B. Mohr, 1932), 402.

33. See *S. th.* III, q. 46, a. 2 ad 3: "haec enim iustitia dependet ex voluntate divina ab humano genere satisfactionem pro peccato exigente. Alioquin, *si voluiset* absque omni satisfactione hominem a peccato liberare, contra iustitiam non fecisset ... si dimittat peccatum, quod habet rationem culpae ex eo quod contra ipsum committitur, nulli facit iniuriam" (emphasis added).

34. On the doctrine of divine foreknowledge, see *S. th.* I, q. 14, a. 13 and I, q. 22, a. 4. See also W. L. Craig, "Aquinas on God's Knowledge of Future Contingents," *The Thomist* 54 (1990): 33–79.

35. See *S. th.* III, q. 46, a. 3. See also Torrell, *Le Christ en ses mystères*, 321f.

nobis relinquens exemplum, ut sequamur vestigia eius.[36] That this *exemplum* cannot be imitated from one's own resources but only by participating in the grace of Christ is self-evident.[37]

Thomas holds that, if one wants to understand the Passion rightly, one must distinguish between the protagonists involved.[38] If one fails to do this, false interpretations of the Passion can arise—for example, that Christ directly killed himself and thus is to be seen as committing suicide, or that those who murdered Christ offered a sacrifice demanded by God, etc.

Unlike Peter Lombard in his *Sentences* or theologians of the time such as Albert the Great or Bonaventure, Thomas devotes himself with great care to the question of the *efficient causes* of Jesus' suffering and death (S. *th.* III, q. 47).[39] He distinguishes the following agents involved in the event of the Passion:

1. *Jesus Christ* is the one who took the Passion upon himself. Thomas does not see him simply as a passive victim of an external, violent deed, for he was not coerced into suffering but rather handed himself over (*se tradidit*), out of love and in obedient conformity to the Father's will. He did this freely (*voluntarie*). Put otherwise: he did not hinder what he could have hindered.[40] Even if he thus *indirectly* co-caused his suffering, it would be misguided to speak of suicide when viewing the Passion. Christ freely exposed himself to the situation of death, but he did not kill himself.[41] Thomas places great value on the fact that Christ remained the sovereign subject of what came to pass, also in the Passion, for he emphasizes that none of this could have happened without Christ's consent.[42] Freely ac-

---

36. S. *th.* III, q. 46, a. 3.

37. In the following articles of q. 46, Thomas goes into the questions, whether Christ had to suffer crucifixion (a. 4); whether he had to endure all suffering (a. 5); whether the pain (*dolor*) of Christ's Passion was greater than all other pains (a. 6); whether he suffered with his entire soul (a. 7); whether the soul of Christ delighted in the beatific vision in the moment of suffering (a. 8); whether he suffered at the right time (a. 9) and at the right place (a. 10); whether it was fitting that he was crucified together with the two thieves (a. 11); and whether suffering can be ascribed to his divinity (a. 12). On this topic, see the commentary in Torrell, *Le Christ en ses mystères*, 323–47, where he points out, among other things, that in these passages of the *Summa*, not only does Thomas's personal spirituality of the cross find expression, but a notable *theologia crucis* also is developed. In addition, the much-discussed problem of how the crucified one could delight in the beatific vision is worked out in a nuanced fashion.

38. In what follows, the concern is to trace the fundamental contours, not to offer a detailed commentary. See Hoogland, *God, Passion and Power*, esp. 1–81; Torrell, *Le Christ en ses mystères*, 348–79.

39. See Torrell, *Le Christ en ses mystère*, 349. See, for example, Bonaventure, *Breviloquium*, IV, 8, who discusses the *status patientis*, the *modus patiendi*, and the *exitus passionis*; he does not take up, however, the complex web of agents participating in the Passion.

40. In this respect, Thomas can say that Christ himself was an *indirect* cause of his suffering and death. See *S. th.* III, q. 47, a. 1.

41. See *S. th.* III, q. 22, a. 2 ad 1: "Christus non se occidit, sed seipsum voluntarie morti exposuit."

42. See *S. th.*, III, q. 47, a. 1 ad 3.

cepting and undertaking the Passion, however, is an expression of *obedience* toward the Father (*ex obedientia Patris*).[43] One could suppose here that this obedience (see Jn 10:18) does injury to Christ's human freedom, that it degrades the Son to a sort of executive organ of the Father's will. But Thomas holds that the freedom of the human will is perfectly realized when it is realized in conformity with its divine origin. In his words and deeds, Jesus accomplished the will of the Father, without so much as one single deviation; with this same attitude, he takes death upon himself. The purpose of his suffering, however, consists in redeeming sinful humanity. In order to express a love that goes to the extreme, Christ even begged that his persecutors and tormentors be forgiven (see Lk 23:24).[44] In this way, the commandment concerning love of God and neighbor, which for the sake of God considers even an enemy as a potential neighbor, is fulfilled in a paradigmatic way on the cross.[45]

2. *God, the Father,* also had a part in the event of the Passion. He handed over (*tradidit*) his Son, which raises the question of whether it is not barbaric and unjust that God the Father exposed his innocent Son to suffering.[46] How can God, the Creator of life who does not desire the death of any of his creatures (see Ex 18:23, 32),[47] hand over his Son to the Passion? Against this sadistic suspicion *avant la lettre*,[48] Thomas holds first that the *traditio* by the Father is already expressed in Paul's letter to the Romans: "God did not withhold his own Son, but gave him up for all of us" (*tradidit*; Rom 8:32).[49] The Father did not do this so that something would accrue (*aliquid accresceret*) to the Son that he did not have before, but rather for

---

43. See *S. th.* III, q. 47, a. 2, where Thomas adduces three reasons for the fittingness of Christ's obedience. First, the Adam-Christ typology: just as the many became sinners through the disobedience of one man, so the many become justified through the obedience of one man (Rom 6:19); second, already the sacrifices of the old covenant require obedience as a disposition. Because, however, obedience was carried out only approximately and therefore inadequately by the priests of the old covenant, Christ fulfilled it overabundantly; third, victory over the devil could be achieved only in obedience to God.

44. See *S. th.* III, q. 47, a. 4 ad 1. Admittedly, Thomas later restricts Jesus' dying plea for forgiveness to the uneducated Jewish people. See *S. th.* III, q. 47, a. 6 ad 1.

45. See *S. th.* III, q. 47, a. 2 ad 1, where Thomas goes further to make clear that Christ fulfilled all the commandments of the old covenant through his suffering: (1) the moral, (2) the ceremonial, and (3) the juridical commandments. See M. Levering, "Israel and The Shape of Thomas Aquinas's Soteriology," *The Thomist* 63 (1999): 65–72.

46. See *S. th.* III, q. 47, a. 3 obj. 1. As is well known, Anselm had earlier raised this question. See *Cur Deus Homo*, I, 8 and I, 10. (ed. Schmitt, 24–28 and 34–38).

47. See *S. c. G.* IV, c. 52 n. 15.

48. With respect to the theological opinion that God the Father handed over Jesus Christ to suffer, D. Sölle (*Suffering* [Philadelphia: Fortress Press, 1975]) raised the charge of sadism. A similar criticism is mounted by feminist theology. See R. Strobel, "Feministisch-theologische Kritik an Kreuzestheologien," *KatBl* 123 (1998): 84–90.

49. See *S. th.* III, q. 47, a. 3 s. c. See *Lauda Sion*: "In figuris praesignatur / Cum Isaac immolatur."

the sake of our redemption.⁵⁰ But does the goal of redeeming mankind justify handing over the Son to henchmen? Thomas insists that the Son suffered freely (*voluntarie*) and out of obedience to the father (*ex obedientia Patris*). Therefore, it is legitimate to speak of a threefold *traditio* at the Father's hands: *first*, in his eternal will, God preordained Christ's suffering for the redemption of mankind. God the Father is bound to this preordination (*praeordinatio*), which Thomas sees declared in the prophetic predictions of the old covenant (see Is 53:6, 10). *Second*, God is not a barbaric despot, who hands over an innocent man to suffer against his will, "for he inspired him with the will to suffer for us by infusing him with charity."⁵¹ Thus, the Father's handing over the Son is matched on the Son's part by a free giving of himself over to the will of the Father. Because of this unconditional conformity of will and deed between Father and Son, which is preserved and concentrated on the cross, harboring the suspicion of a barbaric God must be rejected as unwarranted.⁵² *Third*, we also speak of a *traditio* in the sense that God did not protect Christ from being transferred to his executioners but abandoned him to their violence. This is the reason for the cry on the cross: "My God, my God, why have you abandoned me?" (Mt 27:46).⁵³ The sin of the executioners is thus integrated into an overarching plan of salvation. Without their knowing it, their conduct helps to make redemption possible.

3. Finally, Thomas also addresses the historical agents who caused the crucifixion, and discusses their guilt—in a much more differentiated way than he did in the *Sentences* commentary.⁵⁴ Here also the motif of *traditio* plays a roll. The Jewish authorities handed Jesus over to Pilate, the representative of Roman authority, so that he would inflict the death penalty and order his soldiers to enforce it. According to Thomas, it is profound-

---

50. See *In Rom* VIII, 32, l. VI (nn. 712–14, here 713): "Non tamen Deus pater filio suo non perpecit, ut ei aliquid accresceret, qui est per omnia Deus perfectus, sed propter nostram utilitatem eum passioni subiecit: Et hoc est quod subdit *sed pro nobis omnibus tradidit illum*, id est, exposuit eum passioni pro expiatione peccatorum nostrorum" (emphasis added).

51. *S. th.* III, q. 47, a. 3: "inquantum inspiravit ei voluntatem patiendi pro nobis, infundendo ei caritatem."

52. See *S. th.* III, q. 47, a. 3 ad 2: "Christus, secundum quod Deus, tradidit semetipsum in mortem eadem voluntate et actione qua et Pater tradidit eum. Sed inquantum homo, tradidit semetispum voluntate a Patre inspirata. Unde non est contrarietas in hoc quod Pater tradidit Christum, et ipse tradidit semetipsum."

53. See *S. th.* III, q. 50, a. 2 ad 1, where it says of Christ's abandonment on the cross: "derelictio illa non est referenda ad solutionem unionis personalis, sed ad hoc quod Deus Pater eum exposuit passioni. Unde *derelinquere* ibi non est aliud quam non protegere a persequentibus." See also *In Matth*, XXVII, lect. 2 (n. 2385): "Quare voluisti ut passioni traderer, et isti obtenebrarentur? Item signat admirationem, unde admirabilis est Dei caritas. Ad Rom V, 8: *Commendat Deus caritatem suam in nobis, quoniam cum adhuc peccatores essemus, secundum tempus Christus pro nobis mortuus est*."

54. See *In III Sent.*, d. 20, a. 5a ad 3, where Thomas still speaks sweepingly of "the Jews."

ly sensible that both Jews and Gentiles were involved in Christ's Passion, since the salvific effect of the Passion is supposed to extend to *all*, Jews and Gentiles alike.⁵⁵ Thomas, however, draws a more nuanced picture than the binary of Jews and Gentiles suggests at first glance. In order to be able to assess correctly the different degrees of responsibility for Jesus' death, he goes into the question of whether the agents involved knew what they were doing,⁵⁶ that is, whether it was clear to them that Jesus was the Messiah and Son of God. *With regard to the Jews*, he presents first the educated ruling elite (*principes et rectores*), who did indeed recognize the signs predicted by the prophets but nevertheless failed to push forward to the mystery of Jesus' divinity: "None of the rulers of this age understood this; for if they had, they would not have crucified the Lord of glory" (1 Cor 2:8).⁵⁷ All the same, Thomas does not see in this ignorance any reason to excuse the Jewish leaders, for among them there prevailed an affected ignorance (*ignorantia affectata*). Out of hate and envy, they did not want to recognize the visible signs pointing to Christ's divinity. For this reason, Thomas holds that the guilt of the *principes* was increased.⁵⁸ He characterizes this guilt as *gravissimum* and classifies it—following Venerable Bede after some hesitation—as unpardonable.⁵⁹ Separated from the Jewish ruling elite, the

---

55. See *S. th.* III, q. 47, a. 4.

56. See *S. th.* I-II, qq. 18–21, where Thomas makes clear that sufficient knowledge of the matter must be present in order for a human act (*actus humanus*) to be qualified as sinful.

57. 1 Cor 2:8: "si enim cognovissent numquam Dominum gloriae crucifixissent" (Vulgate). In Acts 3:17 and Luke 23:34, their ignorance is also emphasized. In *In I Cor* II, 8, Thomas holds—in contrast to Chrysostom—that the Jewish ruling class did indeed recognize Jesus as the promised Christ but did not recognize him as the Son of God with certainty. In Thomas's commentary (n. 93), we read: "principes Iudaeorum pro certo sciebant eum esse Christum promissum in lege, quod populus ignorabat. Ipsum autem esse verum Filium Dei non pro certo sciebant, sed aliqualiter conjecturabant."

58. See *S. th.* III, q. 47, a. 5 ad 3: "ignorantia affectata non excusat a culpa, sed magis videtur culpam aggravare: ostendit enim hominem sic vehementer esse affectum ad peccandum quod vult ignorantiam incurrere ne peccatum vitet. Et ideo Iudaei peccaverunt, non solum hominis Christi, sed tanquam Dei crucifixores." On the charge of murdering God, see also the *sed contra* in q. 47, a. 6. Incidentally, the identification of *crucifixores Christi* and *Dei crucifixores* follows the rules regarding the communication of idioms in exactly the same way as the ascription of Mary's title *theotokos*, Mother of God. One must attend to this—as J.-P. Torrell, *Le Christ en ses mystères*, 376f., rightly indicates—in a careful consideration of the anti-Judaistic statements in the work of Thomas, if one wants to avoid anachronistic misjudgments. It is striking that there are *no polemically colored* statements against the Jews in *S. th.* III, q. 47. As a side note, it is well known that Thomas was decidedly against baptizing Jewish children without the consent of their parents. See U. Horst and B. Faes de Mottoni, "Die Zwangstaufe jüdischer Kinder im Urteil scholastischer Theologen," *MThZ* 40 (1989): 173–99. Likewise on this theme, see: J.-P. Torrell, "Ecclesia Iudaeorum. Quelques jugements positifs de saint Thomas à l'égard des juifs et de judaisme," in *Les Philosophies morales et politiques au Moyen Age*, vol. 3, ed. B. C. Bazán, E. Andújar, and L. G. Sbbrocchi (New York–Ottawa: Legas, 1996), 1732–41.

59. The Venerable Bede thinks the phrase, "Forgive them, they know not what they do" (Lk 23:34), can be restrictively interpreted thus: "that he did not pray for those who, while recognizing him as the Son of God, preferred to crucify him rather than confess him" (*In Luc*, VI [CCL 120, ed. D. Hurst. 402f. = PL 92, 616 D]). Thomas also considers the *principes Iudaeorum* to be unpardonable. See *S. th.* III, q. 47, a. 5, and a. 6 ad 1 and ad 3: "Christus voluit quidem suam passionem, sicut et Deus eam voluit: iniquam tamen actionem

maiores, Thomas distinguishes the uneducated people, the *minores*, whom the Scriptures present as not knowing what was going on and therefore, regarding the great majority of them, following the will of the religious authorities, even if there were selective segments that were certainly profoundly impressed by Jesus' miracles and the authority of his teaching. With a view to the *genus peccati*, the people sinned most gravely through their acquiescence to the crucifixion, but on account of their lesser knowledge this guilt is still reckoned as less. Thomas relates Christ's dying statement to the people: "Father, forgive them for they know not what they do" (Lk 23:34). The distinction between *maiores* and *minores*, between the ruling class and the uneducated people, excludes collectively attributing guilt to *the* Jews.[60] Judas, who handed Jesus over to the high priests out of greed (*ex cupiditate*), is mentioned in a rather marginal way.[61] *With regard to the Gentiles*, however, Thomas first names the Roman governor, Pontius Pilate, who had his executioners crucify Jesus and whose name found its way into the Apostle's Creed. Pilate's motive was fear of the emperor (*timor Caesaris*). Thomas ranks his guilt not as great as that of Judas and the high priests. The Roman soldiers, finally, carried out the execution as commanded and in this way *directly* killed Christ. Because they had no knowledge of the Law, their guilt is minimal.[62]

It is apparent that this nuanced presentation of the events of the Passion is characterized by the term *traditio* as a leitmotif: first, *Jesus Christ* is not simply a passive victim (*victima*) of a violent event that remains external to him; he bore his suffering freely (*voluntarie*) and in obedience to the Father (*ex obedientia Patris*). This salvific event is bound up with love,[63]

Iudaeorum noluit. Et ideo occisores Christi ab iniustitia *non excusantur*" (emphasis added). At the same time, Thomas emphasizes elsewhere: "Maior autem fuit caritas Christi patientis quam iniquitas occisorum. Et ideo passio Christi magis valuit reconciliandum Deum toti humano generi, quam ad provocandum iram" (*S. th.* III, q. 49, a. 4 ad 3).

60. Also Mt 27:25—"His blood be on us and on our children"—is expounded by Thomas without anti-Judaistic overtones and is not interpreted as a collective act of self-damnation. See his *In Matth* XXVI, l. I (n. 2343): "Et ita fiet quod sanguis Christis expetitur ab eis usque hodie; et bene convenit illis quod dictum est Gen. IV, 10: *Sanguis fratris tui Abel clamat ad me de terra*. Sed sanguis Christi efficacior est quam sanguis Abel." The last words hint at the hope for forgiveness (see *In Hebr* XII, l. IV, n. 712). See also Torrell, *Le Christ in ses mystères*, 378.

61. See *S. th.* III q. 47, a. 6 ad 2: "Iudas tradidit Christum, non Pilato, sed principibus sacerdotum, qui tradiderunt eum Pilato." Likewise, *S. th.* III, q. 47, a. 3 ad 3: "Iudas autem tradidit ipsum ex cupiditate ..."

62. The thought that every sinner is in a certain way co-responsible for Christ's suffering is not addressed by Thomas in q. 47; nevertheless, he already remarked earlier that the *sins of all* increase the pain of Christ. See *S. th.* III, q. 46, a. 6 ad 4: "Christus non solum doluit pro amissione vitae corporalis propriae, sed etiam pro peccatis omnium aliorum."

63. See the derivation of salvation history from the motive of love: *In Eph* 3:19 (n. 178): "Ubi sciendum est quod quidquid est in mysterio redemptionis humanae et incarnationis Christi, totum est opus charitatis. Nam quod incarnatum est, ex caritate processit.... Quia vero mortuus fuit, ex caritate processit: ... Propter

and thus with Jesus Christ's free act of self-surrender (*se tradidit*). Second, God the Father handed him over to the power of men in order to set in motion the redemption of sinful humanity through him. The further question, whether a shadow is cast upon our understanding of God on account of this handing over of the Son to the executioners, is answered by Thomas with the indication that the Father simultaneously imparted to the Son the power to fulfill this mission. The *opus redemptionis* is thus initiated by the conformity of will and deed between Father and Son. Third, a graduated scale of responsibility for the crucifixion itself is asserted: *Judas Iscariot*, the disciple of the Lord, betrayed Jesus and handed him over to the high priests—this too is an aspect of *traditio*.[64] The *principes Iudaeorum* transferred Jesus to Pontius Pilate as the representative of the *imperium romanum* and demanded his crucifixion. Their deed is characterized as unpardonable—despite the prayerful supplication of the dying Jesus.[65] Finally, Pilate had him crucified out of fear of the emperor; this was carried out by his soldiers, who merely carried out the order. Therewith, the Passion of Jesus Christ is described as a multilayered *traditio*-event.[66] Leveling the blanket accusation that the Jews murdered God is thus not possible from Thomas's perspective, especially since it is important to him that Jews and Gentiles are similarly involved in Jesus' trial, for in each of them Thomas sees represented human nature in need of redemption.

As is well known, *Nostra Aetate*—to engage in a small excursus into the twentieth century—was the first magisterial document that decisively repudiated the sweeping accusation of deicide leveled upon the Jews: "True,

---

hoc dicit Gregorius: *O inaestimabilis dilectio caritatis! ut servum redimeres, filium tradidisti. Et ideo scire caritatem Christi, est scire omnia mysteria incarnationis Christi et redemptionis nostrae, quae ex immensa caritate Dei processerunt, quae quidem caritas excedit omnem intellectum creatum.*"

64. See Jn 6:65: "Sciebat enim ab initio Iesus ... quis *traditurus* esset" (emphasis added). See also Jn 6:72: "hic enim erat *traditurus* eum" (emphasis added). See also 1 Cor 11:23. In addition, see *S. th.* III, q. 46, a. 5, where it is presented that Jesus took upon himself every human suffering according to genus. There we find a consideration of Peter's denial ("Passus etiam a familiaribus et notis: sicut patet de Iuda eum prodente, et Petro ipsum negante") as well as the disciples' fleeing after Jesus' capture in the garden of Gethsemani ("Passus est enim Christus in suis amicis eum deserentibus").

65. On this point, see the reflections that Thomas undertakes concerning predestination and reprobation (*reprobatio*): *S. th.* I, q. 23. Thomas holds explicitly that God reprobates some (a. 3). Nevertheless, a certain asymmetry exists between predestination and reprobation, inasmuch as God elected those destined for eternal life out of love, while, concerning the reprobate, he merely *allows* that they become guilty of their own volition and thus bring upon themselves the correlative damnation. All the same, this solution can hardly satisfy, since the term "allow" does not silence the further question, why God refuses grace and glory to the one group, while granting grace and glory to the other group *for free*. On this point, see the thoughts of O. H. Pesch, *Thomas von Aquin* (Mainz: Matthias-Grünewald, 1988), 145–59.

66. In recent theology, *tradio*-thinking has been taken up in its multidimensionality by H. U. von Balthasar, *Mysterium Paschale: the Mystery of Easter* (Edinburgh: Ignatius, 1990), 107–11, as well as by H. Verweyen, *Gottes letztes Wort*, 3rd ed. (Regensburg: Pustet, 2000), 51–55 (admittedly without reference to Thomas Aquinas).

the Jewish authorities (*auctoritates Iudaeorum*) and those who followed their lead pressed for the death of Christ; still, what happened in his Passion cannot be charged (*imputari possunt*) against all the Jews, without distinction (*indistincte*), then alive, nor against the Jews of today."⁶⁷ Rejection of the collective guilt of all Jews of all times is clearly expressed, though the document still omits specific mention of the Roman authorities' juridical responsibility, in particular that of the procurator. Thus, the impression can arise that Pontius Pilate was a submissive executive organ of the Jewish authorities, who worked toward Jesus' execution. Just a short while later, the Commission of Faith and Order published the Bristol report, which spoke more clearly to emphasize: "Recent research has generally arrived at the conclusion that it is historically false to hold the Jewish people in Jesus' time wholly responsible for his death. Only a small minority located in Jerusalem conducted themselves with active hostility towards him, and even these cooperated only indirectly to bring about his death: the actual judgment came down from the Roman authorities. Moreover, it is impossible to hold the Jews of today responsible for something that some of their predecessors participated in nearly two millennia ago."⁶⁸ This nuanced view of the historical circumstances surrounding Jesus' trial is absolutely necessary in order to prevent the continuation of the fatal anti-Judaistic reception history of the New Testament accounts of the Passion. There is an observable tendency present in some exegetes to trace Jesus' crucifixion back to merely a political-procedural conflict with the Roman occupying power, and thus wholly to contest some participation by Jewish authorities.⁶⁹ But this maneuver invites the question of whether this does not unbecomingly trivialize the potential for religious conflict contained in Jesus' message and conduct.⁷⁰

The question to be taken up in what follows—returning here to Thomas Aquinas—thus runs: why was the Passion of Jesus necessary at all to redeem mankind, and for what reasons did God hand over his Son to the power of men? Where does the soteriological meaning of this event ultimately lie?

---

67. Vatican II, Declaration *Nostra Aetate*, n. 4.

68. Report "Die Kirche und das jüdische Volk" (1967), in *Die Kirchen und das Judentum. Dokumente von 1945–1985*, ed. R. Rendtorff and H. H. Henrix 2nd ed. (Gütersloh-Paderborn: Kaiser, 1989), 350–63, here 362.

69. See E. W. Stegemann, "Wie im Angesicht des Judentums vom Tod Jesu sprechen? Vom Prozess Jesu zu den Passionserzählungen der Evangelien," in *Wie heute vom Tod Jesu sprechen?* ed. G. Häfner and H. Schmid (Freiburg: Katholische Akademie, 2002), 23–52.

70. On this point, see G. Häfner, "Nach dem Tod Jesu fragen. Brennpunkte der Diskussion aus neutestamentlicher Sicht," in *Wie heute vom Jesu sprechen?* ed. Häfner and Schmid, 139–90, esp. 139–51.

The Soteriological Interpretative Categories of *meritum, satisfactio, redemptio,* and *sacrificium*

In his *theological* interpretation of Christ's Passion, Thomas adopts concepts from the tradition.[71] First and foremost, it is Anselm's doctrine of satisfaction that is present in the background, even though Thomas's thinking relies more heavily on the de facto events of salvation history and tries to transpose Anselm's rather technical-juridical categories into a vision highlighting the personal and freely enacted dimensions of the redemptive event. All of the modes of agency wrapped up in Christ's suffering presuppose *free consent arising out of love.* Thomas elucidates the act of redemption by means of the traditional guiding concepts *meritum, satisfactio, sacrificium,* and *redemptio;* at this point, even the mere plurality of terms signals the complexity of the topic of redemption. The priority of the concept *meritum* is not accidental, inasmuch as it is applicable beyond the cross to the entirety of Jesus' life. According to Thomas, the life of Jesus had a meritorious character already beginning at his conception.[72] While the category of merit relates primarily to the moral dimension—whoever holds to the commandments of the Law acquires merit—the concept of satisfaction stands rather in a juridical context—whoever renders satisfaction for the violation of divine glory reestablishes peace. The category of sacrifice, finally, has cultic and ceremonial connotations—through expiation for the sins of the many, atonement is inaugurated.

The Soteriological Category of Merit (*meritum*)   The first associations called forth by the linguistic game of merit[73] and reward are mercantile ones, since it appears to be entirely determined by the principle of equivalence:[74] whoever renders a certain service acquires the right to a correspond-

---

71. See H. Kessler, *Die theologische Bedeutung des Todes Jesu. Eine traditionsgeschichtliche Untersuchung* (Düsseldorf: Patmos, 1970), 170–226; P. Mitzka, "Das Wirken der Menschheit Christi zu unserem Heil nach dem hl. Thomas von Aquin," *ZKTh* 69 (1947): 189–208; R. Cessario, *Christian Satisfaction in Aquinas: Towards a Personalist Understanding* (Washington: University Press of America, 1982).

72. See *S. th.* III, q. 34, a. 3. See also Torrell, *Le Christ en ses mystères,* 38–41.

73. *S. th.* III, q. 48, a. 1. On the doctrine of merit, see V. Cathrein, "Gottesliebe und Verdienst nach der Lehre des hl. Thomas," *ZAM* 6 (1931): 15–32; O. H. Pesch, *Dogmatik im Fragment,* 377–416; U. Kühn, *Via caritatis* (Göttingen: Vandenhoeck & Ruprecht, 1965), 216–18; and recently W. J. Bracken, "Of What Benefit to Himself Was Christ's Suffering? Merit in Aquinas's Theology of the Passion," *The Thomist* 65 (2001): 385–407.

74. The Latin word *meritum* finds a double correspondence in German. In the context of a relation of service or work, *der Verdienst* (gain, profit) designates the remuneration for the service rendered. One has a juridical right to this remuneration on account of a work contract. In contrast, *das Verdienst* (merit, credit) relates to services freely rendered apart from what is demanded by the Law. One acquires merits in the body politic, for example, through social engagement, without therefore being able to assert a claim to reward. A

ing reward: *merces dicitur quod pro merito redditur*.⁷⁵ But can we earn merit at all in relation to God? Do we not owe him everything anyhow, since we have received everything from him (see 1 Cor 4:7)?⁷⁶ And what advantage could arise for God through human merits? Do not the Scriptures testify: "Who has given a gift to him, to receive a gift in return?" (Rom 11:35).

The questions suggested show that the discussion of merit in theological discourse is anything but self-evident. If it is to be sensible, it must be understood differently than in relations among men, where the principle of equivalence is valid for those of the same rank. "As it is an act of justice to give a just price for anything received from another, so also is it an act of justice to make a return for work or toil."⁷⁷ But even where interpersonal relations are characterized by a certain asymmetry—as for example the relation between father and son or between master and servant—the principle of equivalence is valid, but only in a restricted way. The relation between God and men, however, is completely unequal, for between them stands an infinite distance and man has nothing that he has not received from God. Thus, Thomas speaks of a *maxima inaequalitas*.⁷⁸

If speaking of man meriting something before God is nevertheless to make sense, then certain preconditions must be fulfilled. Thomas sees these preconditions as given in a divine order (*divina ordinatio*),⁷⁹ which directs the actions of men to an end attainable only with divine help. The end of man, however, consists in eternal life. He cannot reach this end without grace, for, on the one hand, eternal life is a good exceeding the capacities of created nature, and on the other, man's sin is an obstacle in the way. In order for man nevertheless to be able to reach, even earn, the end determined for him by God, God must impart grace to him.⁸⁰ The merit accruing to man, who determines himself in action through his power of free choice (*liberum arbitrium*), consists ultimately in making God's determination one's own by accepting this grace. Human merit before God exists, therefore, not *propria virtute* but merely *per auxilium gratiae*.⁸¹

---

service in return is not owed, but it can be granted. This second meaning of *meritum* is notable in that it surpasses the horizon of juridical thinking focused on equivalence.

75. *S. th.* I-II, q. 114, a. 1 s.c.

76. "Quid habes, quod non accipisti?" quoted in *S. th.* III, q. 19, a. 3.

77. *S. th.* I-II, q. 114, a. 1: "meritum et merces ad idem referuntur: id enim merces dicitur quod alicui recompensatur pro retributione operis vel laboris, quasi quoddam pretium ipsius [note the cautious diction: *quasi quoddam* pretium]. Unde sicut reddere iustum pretium pro re accepta ab aliquo, est actus iustitiae; ita enim recompensare mercedem operis vel laboris est iustitiae actus. Iustitia autem aequalitas quaedam [sic] est."

78. *S. th.* I-II, q. 114, a. 1.

79. Ibid.

80. Insofar as the *opus meritorium* derives from man's power of free choice, it merits eternal life *ex congruo*; insofar as it arises from the grace of the Holy Spirit, *ex condigno* (see *S. th.* I-II, q. 114, a. 3).

81. *S. th.* I-II, q. 114, a. 2 ad 1.

The principle of equivalence regarding service and remuneration is here broken through to the extent that it is *unmerited* grace that first makes *meritorious* action possible. Of his own resources, man is not in a position to acquire merit with God, since his nature is weakened as a consequence of sin. This is his powerlessness, out of which he must be helped if he is still to be able to reach the goal set before him by the *divina ordinatio*.

Here is the place where the soteriological motif of Christ's merit (*meritum Christi*) can be introduced. For, as Aquinas has it, through Christ's taking suffering upon himself, he acquired merit not only for himself,[82] but also for all men. The soteriological significance of his suffering and death thus consists in the fact that the reward merited by Christ benefits *all* men. To make clear the universal significance of Christ's merit, Thomas falls back upon the motif of *corpus Christi* and the differentiation between head (*caput*) and members (*membra*), which he already developed elsewhere.[83] Following this and by analogy with the natural body of man, where the different members exercise different functions, the Church can be understood as *corpus Christi mysticum*. In a way that is analogous to the human head, Christ is the *caput ecclesiae*. More precisely, Thomas distinguishes three aspects belonging to the head: the elevated rank (*ordo*) as the highest part of the body; the perfection of the head (*perfectio*) as the seat of the inner and outer senses; and finally the ability and power (*virtus*) of the head, inasmuch as it directs and moves the other members. These virtues of the head also belong to Christ *spiritualiter*. Regarding the *excellent rank*, the grace of Christ is the highest and first, corresponding to his closeness to God; all other men have received grace only in view of his grace (see Rom 8:28). Regarding *perfection*, Christ too has all grace in fullness—as Thomas holds in line with John 1:14. Finally—and this is decisive for the transmission of merit—he is also the *source of power*, from which all grace flows into the members of the Church.[84]

---

82. *S. th.* III, q. 19, a. 3 and a. 4. See also *In III Sent.*, d. 18, a. 5–6; *De ver.*, q. 29, a. 6–7. See P. Glorieux, "Le mérite du Christ selon saint Thomas," *RevSR* 10 (1930): 622–49; B. Catao, *Salut et rédemption chez S. Thomas* (Paris, 1965), 45–77; J. P. Wawrykow, *God's Grace and Human Action: "Merit" in the Theology of Thomas Aquinas* (Notre Dame, Ind.: University of Notre Dame Press, 1995), 239–47; Torrell, *Le Christ en ses mystères*, 384–95.

83. See *S. th.* III, q. 8. See also M. Seckler, "Das Haupt aller Menschen," in *Die schiefen Wände des Lehrhauses. Katholizität als Herausforderung* (Freiburg: Herder, 1988), 26–39, 207–11.

84. See *S. th.* III, q. 8, a. 1: "Haec autem tria competunt Christo spiritualiter. Primo enim, secundum propinquitatem ad Deum gratia eius altior et prior est, etsi non tempore: quia omnes alii acceperunt gratiam per respectum ad gratiam ipsius, secundum illud Rom. 8: *Quos praescivit, hos et praedestinavit conformes fieri imaginis Filii sui, ut sit ipse primogenitus in multis fratribus*.—Secundo vero, perfectionem habet quantum ad plenitudinem omnium gratiarum, secundum illud Ioan. 1: *Vidimus eum plenum gratiae et veritatis*, ut supra ostensum est (sc. q. 7, a. 9).—Tertio, virtutem habuit influendi gratiam in omnia membra Ecclesiae: secundum illud Ioan. 1: 'De plenitudine eius omnes accepimus.'—Et sic patet quod convenienter dicitur Christus caput Ecclesiae."

Of course, the overflow of grace to the members is not an automatic affair but rather is bound up with belonging interiorly to the body of Christ. Thomas avails himself of the Adam-Christ typology in order to illuminate this: "Just as one man's trespass led to condemnation for all, so one man's act of righteousness leads to justification and life for all" (Rom 5:18). Against this background, Thomas can state that Christ was not given grace as an individual person but as the head of the Church (*caput ecclesiae*), so that grace would overflow from him to all the members.[85] Head and members constitute "one mystical person. And hence it is that Christ's merit extends to others inasmuch as they are his members; even as in a man the action of the head reaches in a manner to all his members, since it perceives not merely for itself alone, but for all the members."[86] One may not overlook the fact that, through the transmission of his merit to men, Christ opened up the possibility of acquiring merit, through free acts carried out on the foundation of grace. "De sa part, tout est accompli, mais de la nôtre, tout est à faire [on his part, everything is accomplished, but on ours, everything is to be done]," writes Jean-Pierre Torrell, in order to add immediately that it is here not a matter of some homiletic exhortation but of constant theological doctrine, according to which Christ neither replaces the efforts of believers nor makes them superfluous but, on the contrary, invites them to cooperate (*coopérer*) in attaining to salvation.[87]

The Soteriological Categories of *satisfactio, sacrificium,* and *redemptio*   The other soteriological categories Thomas calls upon to clarify the salvific significance of Christ's death also appear to be closely interwoven with an economy of exchange, which connects the restoration of a faulty order of freedom to the generation of certain services: the violated honor of the one offended can be restored only by adequate satisfaction (*satisfactio sufficiens*); for redemption (*redemptio*) from guilt, a certain price (*pretium*) must be paid; and only a sacrifice (*sacrificium*) pleasing to God seems able to avert God's anger.[88] Thus, the soteriological explanatory models that Thomas adopts from the tradition appear without exception to be bound up with an equivalence-based way of thinking; nevertheless, the theological

---

85. See *S. th.* III, q. 48, a. 1.
86. *S. th.* III, q. 19, a. 4: "in Christo non solum fuit gratia sicut in quodam homine singulari, sed sicut in capite totius Ecclesiae, cui omnes uniuntur sicut capiti membra, ex quibus constituitur *mystice una persona*. Et exinde est quod *meritum Christi se extendit ad alios*, inquantum sunt membra eius; sicut etiam in uno homine actio capitis aliqualiter pertinet ad omnia membra eius, quia non solum sibi sentit, sed omnibus membris" (emphasis added). See also *S. th.* I-II, q. 114, a. 6.
87. See Torrell, *Le Christ en ses mystères*, 390.
88. *S. th.* III, q. 48, a. 2.

point will consist precisely in the fact that at a certain time and at a decisive place, God's antecedent will for salvation and the redeemer's wholehearted self-gift broke through the economy of guilt and reparation in order to make possible man's salvation.

Let us take up first the term *satisfactio*, in relation to which the other two categories, *redemptio* and *sacrificium*, are interpreted.[89] The explanatory model of reparation has been a point of contention in the history of theology, and in contemporary theology it is accused of framing the biblical message of redemption in a primarily juridical way or limiting it to a staurocentric approach. Despite this, we will try to look first at Thomas's presentation with as impartial an eye as possible. Any way we look at it, it is clear that the term *satisfactio* is only one in an ensemble of soteriological categories; thus, it cannot be said to have a monopoly on explaining the mode of causality attributable to Christ's Passion.[90] As Thomas writes in the *Summa theologiae*, the act of satisfaction presupposes an action through which injury was inflicted on another.[91] The initial situation is characterized by

---

89. See A. Patfoort, "Le vrai visage de la satisfaction du Christ selon Saint Thomas," in *Ordo sapientiae et amoris*, ed. C.-J. Pinto de Oliveira (Fribourg: Éditions Universitaires, 1993), 247–66; R. Cessario, *The Godly Image: Christ and Satisfaction in Catholic Thought from Anselm to Aquinas*; D. J. Jamros, "Satisfaction for Sin. Aquinas on the Passion of Christ," *The Irish Theological Quarterly* 56 (1990): 307–28.

90. The term *satisfactio* is encountered not only in q. 48 but also in other passages of the *Tertia pars*. It is not an accident that Thomas speaks of the satisfactory aspect of Christ's Passion as early as q. 1, where the topic is the motive for the Incarnation (see here Torrell, *Maître spirituel*, 139–47). After he begins by introducing reasons of fittingness showing how man is furthered in the good by the Incarnation (see *S. th.* III, q. 1, a. 2), he discusses the usefulness of the Incarnation in view of restraining man from evil. It is here that the motif of satisfaction plays a central role: "The Incarnation frees man from the slavery of sin, which, as Augustine says (De Trin. xiii, 13), 'ought to be done in such a way that the devil should be overcome by the justice of the man Jesus Christ,' and this was done *by Christ satisfying for us*. Now a mere man could not have satisfied for the whole human race, and God was not bound to satisfy; hence it behooved Jesus Christ to be both God and man" (*S. th.* III, q. 1, a. 2 [emphasis added]).

91. On the definition of *satisfactio*, see Torrell, *Le Christ en ses mystères*, 400f., who states the following without offering sources: *Satisfactio* comes from *satis-facere*, doing enough. It has to do with a clause of Roman law, which presented an alternative for settlement of a debt or restitution for an injury inflicted by one upon another. Supposing that the accused person cannot perfectly settle the debt or wholly restore the injustice committed, they can still offer the creditor or the injured person a form of compensation. Through *benevolence*, the injured person can reckon this compensation as sufficient: without demanding a perfect recompense, which would be adequate in the strict sense, the one injured thus judges that the compensation offered is a *satisfactio* and the other person has consequently "done enough." Torrell refers to two moments that are characteristic of this understanding of *satisfactio*: first, the *juridical* fact that guilt cannot be completely blotted out, or the debt forgiven, as long as the debtor has not settled a part of his debt, or the offender has not expressed his compunction to the offended person. Second, the rather *ethical* aspect, which relates to the attitude of the creditor, or the injured person. For it is an act of benevolence that achieves the conciliation. Satisfaction does not have its end in itself but in the rectification of a conflict situation and thus the restoration of normal relations between persons. According to this understanding, it is precisely *breaking through a notion of strict equivalence* between debt and reparation that would constitute the proper element of *satisfactio*—which, however, is difficult to harmonize with the current understanding of the terms. See only J. Kremsmair, "Genugtuung I. Rechtsgeschichtlich," in *LThK* (3rd ed.) 4 (1995): 473: "The term satisfaction (*satisfactio*) is found in Roman law with the meaning, to perform sufficiently, corresponding to the requirements of a person or thing, satisfaction, to make expiation for offenses." For a genuinely *theological*

the offender standing in debt with regard to the offended and the question arises, how he can settle his debt with the offended. The first action, which brought injury to the other, requires a second action, which makes amends with the other. This second action is described by Thomas as follows: "He properly atones for an offense who offers something which the offended one loves equally, or even more than he detested the offense."[92] In relation to the situation of sinful men, the problem is sharpened: how can finite man, who infinitely offended against God's glory by sinning, perform an action that would render adequate satisfaction to God? Can he produce a compensatory remuneration that is adequate to the magnitude of his sin? No, he cannot—and yet he would have to be able to in order to do away with the offense to the divine glory.

The redemptive work of Christ leads out of this soteriological aporia; he came into the world for men and did in their place what they are unable to do. Here we must hold fast to the truth: it is not the guilty who render satisfaction themselves for their guilt, but rather it is an innocent one who stands in their place. With Thomas, we can say: "by suffering out of love and obedience, Christ gave more to God than was required to compensate for the offense of the whole human race."[93] Christ brings more than is required; that means, his satisfaction foils and surpasses the economy of exchange, which connects the mistake with a certain remuneration. Christ, in whom divine and human natures are hypostatically united, rendered not only adequate (*sufficiens*) but also a superabundant satisfaction (*satisfactio superabundans*), as Thomas emphasizes, and indeed, first on account of the great love that moved him to take the Passion upon himself, and second on account of the infinite dignity of his life (it was the life of the God-man), and third on account of the completeness of his suffering and the magnitude of the pain he accepted.[94]

Thomas does not stress here the idea that debt in the sense of strict equivalence must be settled; rather, he accentuates the breaking through of this equivalence in the sense of a reconciliation of friendship, which traces back to the initiative of God himself. Thomas addresses this point in the treatise on the sacrament of Penance: "Here we seek not only the restoration of the equivalence demanded by justice, as in vindictive justice

---

use of the category, see the information in K.-H. Menke, "Genugtuung," in *LThK* (3rd ed.) 4 (1995): 473–75.

92. *S. th.* III, q. 48, a. 2: "ille proprie satisfacit pro offensa, qui exhibet offenso id quod aeque vel magis diligit quam oderit offensam."

93. *S. th.* III, q. 48, a. 2: "Christus autem, ex caritate et oboedientia patiendo, maius aliquid Deo exhibuit quam exigeret recompensatio totius offensae humani generis."

94. See *S. th.* III, q. 46, a. 5–6, where Thomas discusses the extent and magnitude of Christ's suffering.

(*iustitia vindicativa*), but also and still more the reconciliation of friendship (*reconciliation amicitiae*), which is accomplished by the offender making atonement *according to the will of the person offended.*"⁹⁵ The point here is that the offended one himself wills the rescue of the offenders and therefore gives Christ to them as *satisfactory*, who enters the world as an advocate for them. The will of the offended one is specified by a love that wills to save all sinners, a love that took upon itself the most extreme measures in the Passion of Christ. The Passion endured in love and free obedience has a satisfactory effect. For "satisfaction would not be efficacious unless it proceeded from charity."⁹⁶

Now, Thomas distinguishes between sin as deed (*peccatum*) and the debt of punishment (*reatus poenae*) as the deed's consequences burdening the sinner. But what is nullified by satisfaction: the debt of punishment or the sin? And what is the actual satisfying element of satisfaction: going through the suffering of the penalty or love and obedience? According to Otto Hermann Pesch, these question are to be answered: "The satisfaction of Christ *takes place* for the sin and in virtue of this wipes out the *debt of punishment*; materially or in terms of content, it *consists in suffering through the entire penalty* for all the sins of humankind, but it has its *satisfying quality* and *effect* before God on account of the pure obedience of love, which bears the satisfaction and in so doing perfectly fulfills the Law of God (!)."⁹⁷

This answer given by Pesch can be confirmed by calling upon the articles that treat the soteriological categories of *redemptio* and *sacrificium*. In raising the topic of *redemptio*, Thomas reminds us first of all of man's need for redemption. Through sin, man fell into a double slavery, from which he must be liberated. On the one hand, he ended up in slavery to the devil (*servitute diaboli*) on account of his sin; on the other, his sin placed him before the divine tribunal.⁹⁸ Through Jesus Christ, who offered his blood

---

95. See *S. th.* III, q. 90, a. 2: "hic non quaeritur sola reintegratio aequalitatis iustitiae, sicut in iustitia vindicativa, sed magis reconciliatio amicitiae, quod fit dum offendens recompensat secundum voluntatem eius quem offendit." See also Torrell, *Le Christ en ses mystères*, 405, who indicates that *S. th.* III, q. 90 is the last *quaestio* flowing from Thomas's quill.

96. *S. th.* III, q. 14, a. 1 ad 1: "non enim esset satisfactio efficax nisi ex caritate procederet." On this point, see the thematic presentation in L. Scheffczyk, "'Satisfactio non efficax nisi ex caritate.' Zur Frage nach dem Grund der Erlösung in Tod und Auferstehung Jesu Christi," *Annales theologici* 1 (1987): 73–94. In contrast to the *Sentences* commentary, Thomas devotes himself in the *Summa* more to the question of how satisfaction becomes efficacious. To this end, he takes up afresh the motif of *corpus Christi mysticum*. See *S. th.* III, q. 48, a. 2 ad 2.

97. O. H. Pesch, *Thomas von Aquin*, 324.

98. See the first part of the *corpus articuli* in *S. th.* III, q. 48, a. 5: "per peccatum dupliciter homo obligatus erat. Primo quidem, servitute peccati: quia *qui facit peccatum, servus est peccati*, ut dicitur Ioan. 8; et 2 Petr. 2: *A quo quis superatus est, huic et servus addictus est*. Quia igitur diabolus hominem superaverat inducendo eum ad peccatum, homo servituti diaboli addictus erat. —Secundo, quantum ad reatum poenae, quo homo

as the "price of our redemption,"[99] man is freed from both the slavery to sin (*peccatum*) *and* the debt of punishment (*reatus poenae*). It is remarkable that Thomas ultimately explains the event of *redemptio* using the soteriological figure of *satisfactio*, when he writes: "Since, then, Christ's Passion was a sufficient and a superabundant atonement for the sin and the debt of the human race, it was as a price at the cost of which we were freed from both obligations."[100] The carefully restricted diction betrays that the word "price" (*pretium*) does not appear for Thomas to be adequate for explicating the salvific meaning of Jesus' death without certain qualifications. In any event, he holds that speaking about a "price," with its ability to spill over into mercantile associations, is in need of clarification.[101] For he adds at this point that one could call the satisfaction, through which one buys off his debt, precisely a "price" (*pretium*). At the same time, he attempts to exclude the mercantile misinterpretation when he emphasizes that the *satisfactio Christi* does not bring about its redeeming effect through money (*pecunia*) or some similar equivalent that remains *external* (*aurum vel argentum*),[102] but rather through the utmost gift, the gift of his own life: "Christus autem

---

erat obligatus secundum Dei iustitiam. Et haec est servitus quaedam: ad servitutem enim pertinet quod aliquis patiatur quod non vult, cum liberi hominis sit uti seipso ut vult."

99. See *S. th.* III, q. 48, a. 5: "Pretium autem redemptionis nostrae est sanguis Christi, vel vita eius corporalis, quae *est in sanguine* (Lv 17:11, 14), quam ipse Christus exsolvit."

100. See the second part of the *corpus articuli* in *S. th.* III, q. 48, a. 4: "Igitur, quia passio Christi fuit sufficiens et superabundans satisfactio pro peccato et reatu poenae generis humani, eius passio fuit quasi quoddam pretium, per quod liberati sumus ab utraque obligatione. Nam ipsa satisfactio qua quis satisfacit, sive pro se sive pro alio, pretium quoddam dicitur quo se redimit a peccato et a poena: secundum illud Dan. 4, [24]: *Peccata tua eleemosynis redime.* Christus autem satisfecit, non quidem pecuniam dando aut aliquid huiusmodi, sed dando id quod fuit maximum, seipsum, pro nobis. Et ideo passio Christi dicitur esse nostra redemptio."

101. Certain texts from the patristic period ascribed to Jesus Christ the predicate "merchant." See Leo the Great, *Sermones* LIV, 4 (= *De passione Domini.* Sermo III, in SC 74, ed. R. Dolle, 58f = PL 54, 321 A): "For he [i.e., Jesus Christ] came into this world as the rich and merciful merchant [*negotiator*] from heaven, and in a wonderful exchange he entered into a salvific trade [*commercium*], in that he took on what was ours and shared what was his, giving honor for disgrace, salvation for pain, and life for death." See also the following sermon of Augustine: "O good merchant, buy us! This I say, buy us, for we must give thanks that you have purchased us. You pay our purchase price for us, we drink your blood; thus you pay for us our purchase price. And we read the Gospel, our bill of sale. We are your servants, your creation: you have made us, you have paid the price for us. A man can purchase a servant but he cannot create him: but the Lord created and purchased his servants, created, in order that they exist; purchased, so that they will not always be prisoners." Augustine, *Sermo* CXXX, 2 (PL 38, 726). See also A. Angenendt, *Geschichte der Religiosität des Mittelalters* (Darmstadt: Wissenschaftliche Buchgesellschaft, 2001), 374f.

102. Already the *sed contra* obviates a mercantile misconstrual of salvation, specifically redemption (*redemptio*), when it cites two New Testament texts pertinent to this theme: "Non corruptibilibus auro vel argento *redempti estis* de vana vestra conversatione paternae traditionis: sed pretioso sanguine, quasi agni immaculati et incontaminati, Christi" (1 Pt 1:18f.), and also "Christus nos *redemit* de maledicto legis, factus pro nobis maledictum" (Gal 3:13). See also the commentary on a comparable passage: *In Cor VI*, 20, l. III (n. 310): *Empti enim estis pretio magno*—"Dicitur autem pretium redemptionis magnum, quia non est corruptibile, sed aeternam habens virtutem, cum sit sanguis ipsius Dei aeterni."

satisfecit ... dando id quod fuit maximum, seipsum, pro nobis."[103] He, who did not have to pay, paid so that those, who had to pay but where unable to do so, owed him their redemption, which is here characterized as redemption from the slavery of sin and debt. It is apparent that the soteriological explanatory models of satisfaction (*satisfactio*) and redemption (*redemptio*) evoke different intellectual contexts or imaginations, but that both are substantially anchored in the logic of a love that gives itself away—a logic that is legible in Christ's self-gift unto death.

This logic of self-gift (*dando ... seipsum pro nobis*) also determines the soteriological category of *sacrificium*, which, unlike the theological terms *meritum* and *satisfactio*, is of biblical origin and stems from the cultic and ceremonial realm. As Thomas explains elsewhere, we find in the old covenant three types of sacrifices,[104] which anticipate the *sacrificium Christi*, namely, burnt offerings (*holocaustum*), sin offerings (*sacrificium pro peccato*), and peace offerings (*hostia pacifica*).[105] The symbolic function of burnt offerings lies in the fact that the one who makes the offering is ready to give himself *entirely* to God. Sin offerings, in contrast, are an expression of sinful man's need for forgiveness, whether it is the priests who offer the sacrifice or the whole people for whom the sacrifice is offered. Finally, peace offerings testify to the gratitude for blessings received and articulate at the same time an appeal for new acts of benevolence.

Against the backdrop of this classification of Old Testament sacrifices, one can understand better the *sacrificial* dimension of Christ's Passion, which Thomas explains in Summa theologiae III, q. 48, a. 3. "He delivered Himself up for us, an oblation and a sacrifice to God for an odor of sweetness," quotes Thomas from Eph 5:2 in the *sed contra*.[106] The dimension of burnt offering (*holocaustum*) is taken up into the unreserved *total self-gift* of Christ to the will of the Father. But both of the other aspects are also contained in Christ's redemptive work. This is made clear in the conceptual determination of sacrifice that Thomas offers. According to this determination, a *sacrificium* is a deed that renders to God the honor owed to

---

103. *S. th.* III, q. 48, a. 4.
104. *S. th.* I-II, q. 102, a. 3 ad 8.
105. The three types of sacrifices, which are also presented in *S. th.* III, q. 22, a. 2 (see further below the section on the priesthood of Christ), are ordered to diverse levels of perfection; but this can remain bracketed here. See also *In Hebr X*, l. 1 (n. 486), where the offering of Christ's body (*oblatio corporis Christi*) is presented as the fulfillment of the Old Testament sacrifices.
106. *S. th.* III, q. 48, a. 3 s.c.: "Tradidit semetipsum pro nobis oblationem et hostiam Deo in odorem suavitatis." Beyond this, there are significant New Testament statements on the theme of sacrifice: Mt 14:24 ("the blood of the covenant, which will be poured out for many") as well as Heb 9–10 (Christ as mediator of the new covenant, who sacrificed to God once for all).

him, in order to appease him (*ad eum placandum*).¹⁰⁷ The Passion of Christ, however, pleased God to the highest degree, for it took place out of love (*ex caritate proveniens*) and was accepted freely (*voluntarie*). Indeed, Christ himself had no need for a sin offering to reconcile himself with God, for he was without sin; but his Passion is still rightly—indeed even principally— to be understood as a sin offering restoring untarnished communion with God. Thomas augments this position by referring to Augustine's famous definition, which distinguishes four aspects of sacrifice, namely: *to whom* the sacrifice is offered, *by whom* it is offered, *what* is offered, and *for whom* it is offered.¹⁰⁸ As the one, true mediator, Christ—says Augustine—reconciles men through a *sacrificum pacis*. He remained one with the one *to whom* he sacrificed, and united himself with those *for whom* he made the sacrifice, and was both *the one who* offered the sacrifice and *what* he offered.¹⁰⁹

Sacrifice encompasses a material element and—even more important— the inner disposition with which it is offered. In view of the material element, the gift of his own life, the difficulty arises that there are no Old Testament prefigurations in which a man is sacrificed. In fact, the institution of human sacrifice is repudiated as ungodly (see Ps 106:38; Is 57:5). Even the story of Isaac's binding, which Thomas refers to the cross of Christ in other passages, can be interpreted as a critique of human sacrifice. Against this argument, Thomas opposes the principle that the reality (*veritas*) must not only correspond to the prefigurations (*figurae*) but also surpass them. Thus, he finds it reasonable that the flesh of Christ, which was offered for us, was prefigured not by human flesh but by other living creatures. The flesh of Christ, however, which he himself offered, is designated by Thomas as the most perfect sacrifice (*perfectissimum sacrificium*).¹¹⁰ He does not conceal the violent aspect of Christ's sacrifice (*sacrificium*), which is brought about

---

107. See *S. th.* III, q. 48, a. 3: "sacrificium proprie dicitur aliquid factum in honorem proprie Deo debitum, ad eum placandum."

108. See Augustine, *De trin.*, IV, 14 (CCL 50, ed. W. J. Montain, 186f. = PL, 42, 901): "cui offeratur, a quo offeratur, quid offeratur, pro quibus offeratur, idem ipse qui unus verusque mediator per sacrificium pacis reconciliat nos Deo, unum cum illo maneret cui offerebat, unum in se faceret pro quibus offerebat, unus ipse esset qui offerebat, et quod offerebat." See *S. th.* III, q. 48, a. 3.

109. The reconciling character of Christ's Passion is also underlined by Thomas in other passages. See *S. th.* III, q. 49, a. 4: "Et similiter tantum bonum fuit quod Christus voluntarie passus est, quod propter hoc bonum in natura humana inventum, Deus placatus est super omni offensa generis humani, quantum ad eos qui Christo passo conjuguntur secundum modum praemissum [a. 1 ad 4; a. 3 ad 1; q. 48, a. 6 ad 2]."

110. Thomas brings in four reasons for this, which seem rather foreign to today's reader: "[Caro Christi] est perfectissimum sacrificium. Primo quidem quia ex eo quod est humanae naturae caro, congrue pro hominibus offertur, et ab eis sumitur sub Sacramento. Secundo quia, ex eo quod erat passibilis et mortalis, apta erat immolationi. Tertio quia, ex hoc quod erat sine peccato, efficax erat ad emundanda peccata. Quarto quia, ex eo quod erat caro ipsius offerentis, erat Deo accepta propter caritatem suam carnem offerentis" (*S. th.* III, q. 48, a. 3 ad 1). See also the commentary on Heb 8:3, where similar motifs are presented with their respective biblical verses: *In Hebr* VIII, l. 1 (n. 384).

by the infamous act of murder (*maleficium*). It is only from the perspective of one who suffers out of love that it could be designated as a sacrifice, but not from the perspective of the executioners.[111] They have, on the contrary, committed an abominable crime.[112] Because Christ "freely gave himself for us," as Thomas emphasizes like a leitmotif, his crucifixion cannot be interpreted as his being merely a passive victim of violence (*victima*). The free and obedient act of giving his life becomes a *sacrificium*, the memory (*commemoratio*) of which is then celebrated in the Eucharist.

The life of Christ—which is deployed in the soteriological grammar of satisfaction (*satisfactio*) as "substitution" (*recompensatio*) and in the grammar of redemption (*redemptio*) as "price" (*pretium*)—functions in the grammar of sacrifice (*sacrificium*) as "gift" of life, which is offered to God. The self-sacrifice of Jesus Christ, in which gift and giver coincide, brings about the reconciliation between God and men—analogous to the fact that the not only sufficient but also overabundant satisfaction overcomes the offense against God caused by the sin of men.

It is admittedly not at all self-evident that the overabundant satisfaction effected by Christ offering his life also benefits sinful man. That the reward of Christ's obedience is recognized as compensation for the disobedience of mankind cannot be further explained within a way of thinking revolving only around compensation. The sinner does not have any claim to reckon to himself Christ's satisfaction. The fact that it nevertheless accrues to his benefit is founded upon God's offering of Christ as the gift of redemption to men in need of salvation.[113] This, however, presupposes a prior salvific counsel that comes before any economy of debt and reparation. But if God's salvific will is antecedent to the concrete redemptive work of Jesus Christ, then the idea must be finally rejected as misguided that God the Father demanded a compensatory payment in order to appease his wrath concerning the sins of men. Conversely, the point of departure must be that God himself resolved to send his Son for the salvation of men, and that the satisfaction effected by the Son's life and death is the way willed by God to inaugurate the overcoming of mankind's guilt. If one heeds this primacy of God's salvific counsel—apart from the question of how the individual soteriological categories worked out by Thomas are to be assessed—then in the face of the cliché repeatedly circulated about, that God's wrath had

---

111. See *S. th.* III, q. 22, a. 2 ad 2.

112. See *S. th.* III, q. 48, a 3 ad 3. Similarly, earlier in *S. th.* III, q. 22, a. 2 ad 2, where the will of Christ is distinguished from the will of his executioners.

113. See the remarkable formulation: divine mercy was made evident through the fact that, because man could not render satisfaction on his own for the sin of all men, God gave him his Son as *satisfactor*. *S. th.* III, q. 46, a. 1 ad 3: "Deus ei [sc. homini] satisfactorem *dedit* Filium suum" (emphasis added).

to be brought around through the death of Jesus Christ, the point made by Otto Hermann Pesch cannot be emphasized enough: "Christ's satisfaction does not *bring about* the love of God—as if through 'appeasing' an offended and vengeful God—but rather it is *brought about* by God's love, namely as the way along which the love of God, never having ceased, reaches man once more."[114]

The Effects of the Passion of Christ

Here we must briefly discuss the effects of the Passion, which are appropriated through faith and the sacraments, since they are at the same time the effects of the Eucharist.[115] Moreover, categories are brought into play here that have a better ring to them in contemporary soteriology when compared to the terms *meritum, satisfactio, sacrificium,* and *redemptio*. Thomas addresses the aspects of liberation (*liberatio*) and reconciliation (*reconciliatio*)—categories that are preferred for the most part in contemporary soteriology over those of satisfaction and sacrifice.[116] He divides his question *De effectibus Passionis Christi* into two parts: first, he treats in a negative way the question, "from what does Christ's suffering free men?" in order then to consider the positive effects. Thomas goes further into the question of whether we are freed by Christ's Passion from sin (a. 1), from the devil's rule (a. 2), and from the debt of punishment (*reatus poenae*) (a. 3). It is not necessary here to present a detailed commentary on every article; instead, it is more important for us to hold on to certain central thoughts.

The proposition that Christ's Passion brought about forgiveness for our sins appears to be so self-evident that it does not require its own discussion. Nevertheless, a theological question of time presents itself: how can the long past event of Christ's Passion free from sins that were not even committed at that time. It is also unclear how the Passion can be the sufficient cause for the forgiveness of sins if Baptism and Penance are also needful for the *homo viator*. Finally, there are human actions that appear to have the effect of forgiving sins. Thomas cites from Scripture Proverbs 10:12 ("love covers all offenses") and Proverbs 16:6 ("By loyalty and faithfulness iniquity is atoned for"). Accordingly, Christ's suffering does not appear to be the only cause for the forgiveness of sins.[117]

---

114. O. H. Pesch, *Thomas von Aquin*, 325.

115. See *S. th.* III, q. 49, as well as *In III Sent.*, d. 19, q. 1 and 2.

116. See the exemplary works: H. Kessler, *Erlösung als Befreiung* (Düsseldorf: Patmos, 1972); Th. Pröpper, *Erlösungsglaube und Freiheitsgeschehen. Eine Skizze zur Soteriologie*, 3d ed. (Munich: Kösel, 1991); J. Werbick, *Soteriologie* (Düsseldorf: Patmos, 1990).

117. See *S. th.* III, q. 49, a. 1, obj. 3–5.

In his answer, Thomas points out that the suffering of Christ causes the forgiveness of our sins in three ways. *First*, it is a cause in that it incites love (*per modum provocantis ad caritatem*). Thomas cites Rom 5:8f.: "God proves his love for us in that while we still were sinners Christ died for us." *Second*, Christ's Passion causes the forgiveness of our sins as redemption (*per modum redemptionis*). It is to be noted that Thomas employs the motif of Christ's body to explain how redemption is appropriated. In this way, an individualistic constriction of the forgiveness of sins is fundamentally excluded. Sin always affects social and ecclesial reality as well. This is expressed by the pertinent passage underscoring the mystical bond between Christ the head and his members: "Since he [i.e., Christ] is our head, then, by the Passion which he endured from love and obedience, he delivered us as his members from our sins, as by the price of his Passion [one observes once again the qualification *quasi*, which seeks to avoid mercantile misinterpretations]: in the same way as if a man by the good industry of his hands were to redeem himself from a sin committed with his feet. For, just as the natural body is one though made up of diverse members, so the whole Church, Christ's mystic body, is reckoned as one person with its head, which is Christ."[118] The grace won by Christ is communicated to his own in a way that is just as self-evident as the communication of the life of the body to its head and members. *Third*, the Passion works—and here Thomas relies upon the conclusion of the previous *quaestio*—as an efficient cause (*per modum efficientiae*). This is indeed the case to the extent that the flesh, in which Christ took upon himself such suffering, is an "instrument of the divinity" (*instrumentum divinitatis*), by means of which his sufferings and deeds (*passiones et actiones*) work with divine power toward the blotting out of sin.

The responses to the objections afford several additional and worthwhile points. To the objection pertaining to the theological issue of time—how sins not yet committed at the time of Christ's suffering and death can be redeemed by it—Thomas responds by referring to the causal effect of the Passion: "Christ by his Passion delivered us from our sins causally—that is, by setting up the cause of our deliverance, from which cause all sins whatsoever, past, present, or to come, could be forgiven: just as if a doctor were to prepare a medicine by which all sicknesses can be cured even in future."[119] Thomas

---

118. *S. th.* III, q. 49, a. 1: "Quia enim ipse est caput nostrum, per passionem suam, quam ex caritate et obedientia sustinuit, liberavit nos, tamquam membra sua, a peccatis, quasi per pretium suae passionis: sicut si homo per aliquod opus meritorium quod manu exerceret, redimeret se a peccato quod pedibus commisisset. Sicut enim naturale corpus est unum, ex membrorum diversitate consistens, ita tota Ecclesia, quae est mysticum corpus Christi, computatur quasi una persona cum suo capite, quod est Christus."

119. *S. th.* III, q. 49, a. 1 ad 3: "Christus sua passione a peccatis nos liberavit causaliter, idest, instituens

responds to the second point, which reminded us of the need to explain the relation between the Passion and the sacraments of Baptism and Penance, by basically indicating that the general cause of the Passion must be applied to individuals for the blotting out of their sins. But this takes place through Baptism, Penance, and the other sacraments, which draw their power from Christ's Passion.[120] Resolving the last objection involves the notion of faith as the mode of application for the forgiveness of sins. The formula returning time and again—that the grace of the Passion is appropriated through faith and the sacraments—forms the hinge between the *corpus Christi* and the *corpus Christi mysticum*; it articulates the transmission of the Passion and its fruits to the faithful.

Of course, the Passion wrested men from the power of the devil, but does it also dispense them from the penalty resulting from the sin committed? For Thomas, the *positive* effect of the Passion consists in the reconciliation of man with God, an aspect already considered by Thomas in the treatment of Christ's priesthood[121] and his mediatorship.[122] It is worth signaling that in his elucidation of reconciliation (*reconciliatio*), Thomas works out several soteriological categories that he already explicated earlier, so that the motif of man's reconciliation with God appears to be a sort of synthesis of certain motifs pertaining to the doctrine of redemption. Thomas states: *the Passion of Christ is the cause of reconciliation of man with God*—and indeed first of all for the reason that it redresses sins, which are responsible for making men enemies of God. At the same time, however, the Passion is also a sacrifice pleasing to God, as the essential effect of a sacrifice consists in its appeasing God. As has already become clear, what is proper to Christ's sacrifice is that it appeased God for every offense of mankind. Still, this reconciliation accrues to the benefit of all who are joined to Christ through faith and the sacraments.[123] The passage shows that the concepts explained earlier—liberation from sin (*liberatio peccati*), sacrifice (*sacrificium*), and thus implicitly also satisfaction (*satisfactio*)—all converge in the concept of reconciliation.

What remains to be added here is a clearing up of a misunderstanding that has been widely circulated until today. God was not brought over by

---

causam nostrae liberationis, ex qua possent quaecumque peccata quandocumque remitti, vel praeterita vel praesentia vel futura: sicut si medicus faciat medicinam ex qua possint etiam quicumque morbi sanari, etiam in futurum."

120. See *S. th.* III, q. 65, a. 5.
121. See *S. th.* III, q. 22, aa. 1 and 3.
122. See *S. th.* III, q. 26, aa. 1–2.
123. See the elucidation of the theme of *incorporatio*: *S.th.* III, q. 48, a. 6 ad 2, as well as q. 49, a. 1 ad 4; a. 3 ad 1.

the Passion of Christ, his wrath not mollified. The idea that God would have begun to love man anew is inappropriate. Even Scripture attests that God never stopped loving man. Therefore, the very reconciliation brought about by Christ's Passion must be interpreted as an expression of God's love, a love that desired to communicate to men the *bonum divinum*.[124] To be sure, Thomas certainly distinguishes between the love of God the Creator, which he has for the nature of man, and his hatred of the sin of man. The meaning of Christ's Passion consists ultimately in this: that the cause for this hatred was taken away, on the one hand because of the purification from sins (*propter ablutionem peccati*), and on the other because of the recompense offered by a more acceptable good (*propter recompensationem acceptabilioris boni*).[125]

In conclusion, there is one point still to note, that the Passion of Christ also had the effect of opening to men the door to heaven (*ianua caelestis*). The eschatological motif of Christ going ahead into heaven to offer intercession before God will be deepened in the consideration of Christ's priesthood. Here, it is merely to be held firm that sin, which refused man's entry into heaven, was cleared away by the Passion. This applies first to the sin of Adam, which affected the whole of mankind (*peccatum originale*), but then also to actual sins (*peccatum actuale*), which are committed by individual persons. Admittedly, liberation from sin is not an automatic thing. One must participate in the Passion of Christ, must stand in a *communicatio* with Christ the redeemer, in order to be freed from sin and precisely thereby to attain entrance into the heavenly kingdom. The forms of this communication, which constitute the *communicatio* with Christ, are faith and love, as well as the sacraments—above all the Eucharist.[126]

A Preliminary Reflection

The Eucharist is the *memoriale passionis Christi*. In order better to understand the *passio Christi*, and in order to provide the necessary background for the consequent clause of the formula of consecration, *quod pro vobis tradetur*, we first looked back to the historical situation of the last supper. There, as Jesus was departing his disciples, he declared the legacy of his love; there, he offered an anticipatory interpretation of his suffering. This interpretation received its incarnate commentary on Golgotha. Thus, in a further section we took a look at the event of the Passion and illuminated more precisely the

---

124. See *In III Sent.*, d. 19, a. 5, sol. 1. See also Torrell, *Le Christ en ses mystères*, 437f.
125. See *S. th.* III, q. 49, a. 4 ad 2.
126. See *S. th.* III, q. 49, a. 5.

soteriological explication given by Thomas to this event. As we did this, the Passion revealed itself as a multifaceted event of tradition. God the Father hands over (*tradit*) his Son; men, Jews and Gentiles, took part in different ways in the betrayal, handing over, and crucifixion; but the Son gives himself freely and in obedience to the Father (*se tradit voluntarie*)—so that in the Passion he himself realizes the work of redemption (*opus redemptionis*). It is the body of Christ that is handed over to death (*quod pro vobis tradetur*), it is the blood of Christ that is shed on the cross (*qui pro vobis et pro multis effundetur*). The meaning of the Passion, therefore, is not exhausted in its being a datum in the never-ending set of data in the human history of violence and suffering; rather, what takes place on the cross is the inexpressible mystery of redemption from sin and death: Christ, the incarnate and sinless son of God, takes away the sin of the world. By means of the diverse soteriological categories of *meritum*, *redemptio*, *satisfactio*, and *sacrificium*, Thomas attempts to understand more precisely the ultimately incomprehensible mystery of redemption. In so doing, the logic of equivalence and its economy of debt and reparation is broken through by the fact that God, the one offended by sin, himself desires the salvation of the offender and offers to men in Christ the gift of forgiveness, gratis, for free.

The Eucharist is the *visible* sign of this love that goes to the extreme. In the Eucharist, Christ's giving of his own life once-for-all, his death for the many, is further handed on and in the succession of time is made present in every place of the world. According to Thomas, it is Jesus Christ himself, the exalted Lord and eternal high priest, who bestows his presence in the gifts of bread and wine. Alongside the commemorative actual presence, which puts the remembrance of suffering at the center of the Eucharist, the principal actual presence of the exalted Lord himself is also and always in play.[127] But how is his priestly action to be determined more precisely? What distinguishes it from the antecedent forms of priesthood found in the Old Testament? In what relation does it stand to the acting, human priest? And in which ritual signs is the self-offering of Jesus Christ concretely represented in the Eucharist? In what follows, we will take up these questions.

---

127. Once again it is to be recalled that the underlying terminology of J. Betz was developed here. See idem, "Eucharistie," *LThK* (2nd ed.) 3 (1959): 1142–57, here 1154: "Should the unity of the Eucharistic happening also be expressed terminologically in the multiplicity of its aspects, then one may designate the bodily presence of the person of Christ as *somatic real presence*, the realization of the redemptive work to be accepted as *commemorative actual presence*, and the spiritual-efficacious presence of the exalted kyrios (of the *minister principalis*) as *principal actual presence*" (emphasis added).

The Representative Making-Present of the *Passio Christi* in the Eucharistic Celebration

The Eternal Priesthood of Christ as Source and Origin of the Priesthood in Time

Before the doctrine of Christ's priesthood and its relevance for Eucharistic theology is expounded, it seems sensible to offer a preliminary remark that relates to the contemporary discussion. In current systematic theology, the topos of Christ's priesthood really does not come up at all (any more). This lacuna can be explained first by the view that "Jesus Christ did not understand himself and his mission in a priestly way, according to the dominant exegetical opinion."[128] In addition to this, the cultic terminology of priest and sacrifice seems to have already become hermeneutically foreign to the faith consciousness of our time. Theologically speaking, the not-unfounded suspicion is nurtured that the significance of Jesus' pro-existent life and death are disguised rather than exposed by cultic-sacerdotal categories. In neo-scholastic theology, the motif of Christ as high priest played a key role in explaining the Catholic priestly office;[129] today, it has lost this central systematic function. The fact that the motif is broadly unfolded in the letter to the Hebrews and is quite present in magisterial pronouncements up through the documents of Vatican II and continuing through the pontificate of John Paul II[130] appears nevertheless to have been hardly beneficial to its reception in post-conciliar theology.[131] If one nevertheless manages not to be reflexively repelled by the hermeneutic foreignness and instead turns to the subject matter, then one will discover that there are soteriologically decisive questions treated here: what did Christ do for us in his giving of his own life? How can it be that this deed still matters for us? Why can Christ's *one-time* self-gift, his death for us on Golgotha, be made present ever anew in successive times and at every place in the world? An attempt to answer these questions is articulated in the doctrine concerning Christ's priesthood, as Thomas develops it in the *Summa theologiae*,[132] but also in

---

128. G. Greshake, "Priester III. Historisch-theologisch," *LThK* (3rd ed.), 8 (1999): 564–66, here 564.

129. See J. Pohle, *Lehrbuch der Dogmatik*, 8th ed., newly revised by M. Gierens, vol. 3 (Paderborn: Schöningh, 1933), 63f., 553; F. Diekamp, *Katholische Dogmatik nach den Grundsätzen des heiligen Thomas*, ed. K. Jüssen, 13th ed., vol. 3 (Münster: Sarto, 1962), 354.

130. See *Sacrosanctum Concilium* 7 and 83; *Lumen Gentium* 28; *Presbyterorum Ordinis* 5 and 7.

131. See the references in Th. Marschle, "Das Hohepriestertum Jesu Christi nach dem hl. Thomas," *Doctor Angelicus* 3 (2003): 143–64. It is notable that J. Sobrino has recently undertaken a liberation-Christological appreciation of the title "high priest," which principally draws out the advocative entrance of the exalted Christ for the poor and weak. See idem, *Der Glaube an Jesus Christus*, (Ostfildern: Grünewald Verlag, 2008).

132. See the commentary on *S. th.* III, q. 22 in J.-P. Torrell, "Le sacerdoce du Christ dans la Somme de théologie," *Revue Thomiste* 99 (1999): 75–100.

his commentary on Hebrews.¹³³ With the following attempt to trace the basic propositions of this doctrine, a deepening of the motif of *principal actual presence* will also be sought after, a motif already treated in the context of the consecratory speech of the priest *in virtute et persona Christi*. The reconstruction will follow the text as closely as possible, in order to avoid the danger of importing anachronistically into Thomas's exposition the issues of post-Tridentine theories regarding the sacrifice of the Mass.[134]

First of all, it is remarkable that Thomas—unlike his contemporaries Albert the Great, Alexander of Hales, and Bonaventure—posed the question of Christ's priesthood in an in-depth way.[135] Jean-Pierre Torrell propounded the hardly contestable hypothesis that Thomas developed a sense for the significance of this theme in writing his commentary on the letter to the Hebrews. In his *Sentences* commentary, there are still no remarks on the theme, whereas in the *Summa theologiae* the topic of *sacerdotium Christi* is given its own *quaestio*. The fact that this *quaestio* alone weaves in eighteen citations from the letter to the Hebrews speaks to the point that Thomas realized the significance and scope of this theme through commenting on the letter to the Hebrews. Concerning the placement of question 22 on Christ's priesthood within the framework of the Christological treatise, it should be called to mind that this question follows the systematic treatment of the hypostatic union (*S. th*. III, qq. 2–15) and thus does not stand in the actual center of the Christological question. Rather, it constitutes one of the "consequences" that result from the divine-human unity of the person of Jesus Christ (*S. th*. III, qq. 16–26).[136] The goal of the segment on the *sacerdotium*

---

133. On this point, see G. Berceville, "Le sacerdoce du Christ dans le Commentaire de l'épître aux Hébreux de saint Thomas d'Aquin," *Revue Thomiste* 99 (1999): 143–58; M. Caprioli, "Il sacerdozio di cristo nella Somma teologica e nel Commento Super Epistolam ad Hebraeos," *Studi tomistici* 45 (1992): 96–105.

134. See B. Neunheuser, "Messopfertheorien," in *LThK* (2nd ed.) 7 (1962): 350–52. Despite all their differences in individual starting points, the post-Tridentine theories regarding the sacrifice of the Mass are similar in that they stem from a general concept of sacrifice derived from the history of religion. Three basic approaches can be distinguished: (1) the *destruction theory*, which holds that a real change of the sacrificial gifts belongs to the sacrifice. This is either seen in the destruction (*destructio*) of the natural elements of bread and wine through the consecration (F. de Suarez), or placed in the *fractio panis* (M. Cano), or even found in the *sumptio* of the Eucharistic gifts (R. Bellarmine); (2) the *oblation theories*, in contrast, emphatically stress the sacrifical *deed* of Jesus Christ. In each celebration of the Mass, Jesus accomplishes anew his sacrificial self-gift accomplished once for all time on the cross (the French school: P. Bérulle, Ch. de Condren, et al.); (3) finally, following Thomas (see *S. th*. III, q. 82, a. 1), the *immolation* or *mactation theories* construe the double consecration not only as a *repraesentatio* of the sacrifice on the cross (G. Vázquez) but also as a "mystical slaughtering," in which Jesus Christ's still relevant sacrificial self-gift is expressed in the celebration of the Mass (L. Billot et al.). For background, see as well the instructive overview by H. Jorissen, "Messopfer," *LThK* (3rd ed.) 7 (1998): 178–84, esp. 181f. (Lit).

135. See the evidence offered by Torrell, "Le sacerdoce du Christ," 76.

136. This positioning is expressly carried out at the beginning of *S. th*. III, q. 20 in the treatise on Christology. On the structure of Christology, see also J. Boyle, "The Twofold Division of St. Thomas's Christology in the *Tertia Pars*," *The Thomist* 60 (1996): 439–47.

130   PART A

Christi is twofold: first of all, it is shown that Jesus Christ was a priest (aa. 1 and 2); after that, fundamental characteristics of this priesthood are adduced in order to emphasize the superiority of Christ's priesthood with respect to the Levitical priesthood of the old covenant.[137] In this context, the motif of Christ's *eternal priesthood*, which cannot be specified apart from his earthly priesthood, also finds its place.

As is so often the case in the *Tertia pars*—which deals with facts of revelation not to be proven but rather to be illuminated in their plausibility—Thomas begins with the question of *fittingness*: is being a priest to be ascribed to Christ at all? In order to answer this question, a clear definition of the term *sacerdos* is necessary: the essential office of a priest is to be a mediator between God and man. This service of mediation encompasses a *double* movement. First, the priest conveys to men divine gifts—a service that Thomas corroborates with the etymological consideration that the concept *sacerdos* derives from *sacra dans*.[138] This descending-katabatic movement is complemented by an ascending-anabatic movement, when we read that the priest both carries the concerns and requests of men before God and offers sacrifice to make reparation for their sins.[139]

Both functions characterize in an essential way the priest's office of mediation, and they are fulfilled by Christ to the most excellent degree. As *mediator*, the incarnate Son of God institutes God's *communicatio* with men. He bridges the infinite distance between God, the Creator of all things, and men, his creatures, in order to share with them the good and to deliver to them the promise of eternal life.[140] At the same time, however, he has

---

137. See the earlier statement of the theme in *In Hebr* VII, l. I (n. 326): "Apostolus probavit Christum esse sacerdotem.... Intendit enim probare excellentiam sacerdotii Christi ad sacerdotium Leviticum."

138. Medieval theology took the etymological derivation from the encyclopedia by Isidore of Seville, where it reads: "Sacerdos nomen habet compositum ex Graeco et Latino, quasi sacrum dans, sicut enim rex a regendo, ita sacerdos a sanctificando vocatus est; consecrat enim et sanctificat" (see *Isidori Hispalensis Episcopi Etymologiarum sive Originum Libri XX*, ed. W. M. Lindsay [Oxford: Oxford University Press, 1957], lib. 7, c. 12, n. 17). In this derivation, the ending "dos" is wrongly explained as δώς, thus as an aorist participle of δίδομι. See E. J. Scheller, *Das Priestertum Christi im Anschluß an den hl. Thomas von Aquin. Vom Mysterium des Mittlers in seinem Opfer und unserer Anteilnahme* (Paderborn: Schöningh, 1934), 75.

139. *S. th.* III, q. 22, a. 1: "proprium officium sacerdotis est esse mediatorem inter Deum et populum: inquantum scilicet divina populo tradit, unde *sacerdos* dicitur quasi *sacra dans* [Cfr. Isidor, Etymol., l. VII, c. 12, n. 21: PL 82, 292 B], secundum illud Mal. 2,7: *Legem requirent ex ore eius*, scilicet sacerdotis; et iterum inquantum preces populi Deo offert, et pro eorum peccatis Deo aliqualiter satisfacit." It follows logically that the definition of the ordained priest, who functions as an *instrumentum* of Christ's eternal priesthood, encompasses both aspects: "sacerdos constituitur medius inter Deum et populum. Unde, sicut ad eum pertinet dona populi Deo offere, ita ad eum pertinet dona sanctificata divinitus populo tradere" (*S. th.* III, q. 82, a. 3).

140. Thomas incorporates Scripture to a striking degree in q. 22, here quoting 2 Pet 1:4: "per quem, scilicet Christum, maxima et pretiosa nobis promissa donavit, ut per haec efficiamini divinae consortes naturae." See also *S. th.* III, q. 1, where the motif of Incarnation is discussed. Without bringing a necessity to communicate into the concept of God, Thomas holds that it belongs to the *essentia bonitatis* to communicate itself to others (*se aliis communicare*). See M. Scheuer, *Aliis communicare*, 60–83.

shared in the fate of men, has taken on flesh, and was faced with temptation. Had he not faced temptation, he would not have experienced what constitutes the affliction of men, nor would he have been able to sympathize with them. Instead, he made the concerns of men profoundly his own and can be their mediator before God. In his commentary on Hebrews, Thomas holds explicitly that a *promptitudo* and *aptitudo* to assist mankind are said of Christ on account of his *compassio* with men, because he knows man's affliction through experience (*per experientiam*).[141] Further still, even though he faced temptation Christ did not sin, and for this reason he was able to free all men from sin and reconcile them to God through the free sacrifice of his life.[142] Since Christ fulfilled both aspects of his mediatory role, the priesthood belongs to him in preeminent fashion.[143] Unlike Augustine, who acknowledged a participation in Christ's priesthood but wanted simultaneously to reserve the title "mediator" strictly for Christ, Thomas holds the conferral of the title *mediator* on those ordained to the ministerial priesthood to be completely legitimate. This is because their mediatorship is understood as a participation in the unique mediatorship of Christ.[144] It is only to be added that the fundamental determination of the priest as *mediator* also encompasses the dimension of proclaiming the word and leading the community,[145] and therefore certainly cannot yet be simply equated with the later cultic-sacerdotal constriction of the priesthood.

All the same, what is constitutive for the determination of the priest is the sacrificial oblation he offers. The specific mark of priesthood lies in the fact that priest (*sacerdos*) and sacrifice (*hostia*) are here identical. Bound up with this, however, are also a number of conceptual difficulties. That Christ was violently sacrificed on the cross is easy to recognize; it is harder to understand how, in this same event, he should simultaneously be the priest who offers the sacrifice. If one wants to focus solely on the priest's task of offering the sacrifice, and thus killing the victim, then one has to interpret

---

141. See *In Hebr*, IV, l. 3 (n. 235).

142. For the second aspect, the operative scriptural passage is Col 1:19f.: "In ipso ... complacuit omnem plenitudinem inhabitare, et per eum reconciliare omnia."

143. In the third objection (*S. th.* III, q. 22, a. 1 ad 3), there is an additional aspect that deserves to be noted, since it connects Christ's priesthood with the motif of *caput Christi*. The objection holds that in the old covenant, the offices of lawgiver (*legislator*) and priest (*sacerdos*) were separate and could not be exercised by a single person. Christ, who must correspond to the old covenant type, could not therefore be both lawgiver of the new covenant and priest. Against this, Thomas holds that, unlike men, who have merely individual gifts of grace, Christ as the head of all has full possession of all graces and thus can unite all offices—priest, king, and prophet—in himself. See the earlier *S. th.* III, q. 7, a. 7.

144. See Torrell, "Le sacerdoce du Christ," 80.

145. See *S. th.* III, q. 65, a. 1 c: "Perficitur homo in ordine ad totam communitatem dupliciter: uno modo per hoc quod accipit potestatem regendi multitudinem, et exercendi actus publicos; et loco huius in spirituali vita est sacramentum ordinis."

the sacrifice of Christ as an act of suicide, inasmuch as he, as priest, was likewise the sacrificial victim.

It is not by accident that Thomas brings to bear the *reflexive* specification of the concept of sacrifice, a specification already laid out in Scripture, systematically developed by Augustine, and arising from the inner disposition of the one offering the sacrifice. Christ does not offer *just any thing* but rather *himself* (see Eph 5:2; Heb 7:27). The *visible* gift [*Gabe*] is the sign of an *invisible* giving [*Hingabe*].[146] The misunderstanding that the offering of material gifts could make superfluous or simply replace the change of heart of the one sacrificing is deflected by this reflexive specification of the sacrifice. The *external* gift, which is here the body of the Lord nailed to the cross, is an expression of an *inner* giving to God that goes to the extreme. And Thomas adds that everything offered to God with the intention of lifting man's spirit to God could be called a sacrifice (*sacrificium*).[147]

But why are sacrifices necessary at all? And what constitutes the specific nature of a sacrifice? Drawing on the threefold division of Old Testament sacrifices, which is broadly unfolded in *S. th.* II-II, Thomas brings forward three reasons arising from the fundamental need of man for redemption and salvation: *first*, sacrifices are necessary for the forgiveness of sins (*ad remissionem peccati*), by which man turned his back on God (*hostia pro peccato*). Hebrews 5:1 is cited as the biblical reference for the necessity of sin offerings, where the task is assigned to the priest "to offer gifts and sacrifices for sins." *Second*, sacrifices are necessary also for man to remain in the state of grace and to cling consistently to God, in whom his peace and salvation consist (*hostia pacificorum*). As a biblical reference for the necessity of peace offerings, Leviticus 3 is invoked and it is recalled that in the old covenant a peace sacrifice was offered for the salvation of the one sacrificing. *Third*, and finally, sacrifices are necessary for uniting man's spirit perfectly with God, something that will take place in the highest way in glory (*holocaustum*). Leviticus 1 serves as the biblical point of reference, where the discussion includes the sacrifice of a whole animal completely consumed by the fire.

According to Aquinas's position, all three aspects of the Old Testament sacrifices were redeemed and fulfilled by the humanity of Christ. This is because, *first*, the sins of men were destroyed (see Rom 4:25: *Traditus est propter delicta nostra*); *second*, men have received saving grace through him (see Heb 5:9: *Factus est omnibus obtemperantibus sibi causa salutis aeternae*);

---

146. Augustine, *De civ. Dei*, X, 5 (CCL 47, ed. B. Dombart, 277), 447: "omne sacrificium uisibile inuisibilis sacrificii sacramentum, idest sacrum signum."

147. *S. th.* III, q. 22, a. 2: "omne illud quod Deo exhibetur ad hoc quod spiritus hominis feratur in Deum, potest dici sacrificium."

third, they have access to perfection in glory through him (Heb 10:19: *Habemus fiduciam per sanguinem eius in introitum sanctorum, sc. in gloriam caelestum*). Against this background, Thomas can say that, inasmuch as he was a man, Christ was not only priest (*sacerdos*) but also the perfect sacrificial victim (*hostia*), namely sin offering (*hostia pro peccato*), peace offering (*hostia pacificorum*), and whole offering (*holocaustum*) in one.

Thus, Christ is simultaneously priest (*sacerdos*) and sacrificial victim (*hostia*) and this distinguishes him from the Levitical priesthood of the old covenant. As Thomas subsequently makes clear,[148] the effect of his priesthood lies in the atonement for sins, which are referred not to Christ himself but to humanity in need of redemption.[149] Because the effect of the *passio Christi* was already discussed in the presentation of the soteriological interpretive categories, we can accentuate here the issue of how Christ's sacrifice can have the power to wipe out sin *once for all* (see Heb 7:17). In the *obiectiones*, the fact that the sacrifices of the old covenant were offered *time and again* is judged as evidence that the effect of a sacrifice was imperfect. Simultaneously, it is recalled that even within the horizon of Christ's priesthood, forgiveness of sins is routinely prayed for, indeed even in the Church the sacrifice is offered without ceasing. Does the daily sacrifice of Christ in the Holy Mass allow the conclusion that the priesthood of Christ did *not* atone for sins once for all?

The reply to this question is noteworthy.[150] Thomas holds, first, that it is not because of a lack of efficacy in Christ's priesthood that sins are called to mind in the new covenant, as if satisfactory atonement had not been made. Rather it is the case that sins for two groups of people are recalled: on the one hand, nonbelievers, who do not want to participate in Christ's sacrifice; for them, prayers are offered that they turn from their sin and to God. On the other hand, those who, after participating in the sacrifice of Christ, do not conform to him in that they repeatedly sin. For Thomas, the daily sacrifice of the Mass *does not present a supplement or repetition of Christ's once-for-all sacrifice on the cross*, as if this did not suffice; rather, the *passio Christi* is representatively made present in the celebration of the Eucharist. Although it remains to be deepened, the decisive statement asserting the identity of the sacrifice of the cross with the sacrifice of the Mass runs: "The sacrifice which is offered every day in the Church is not distinct from that which Christ himself offered, but is a commemoration thereof (*eius commemoratio*)."[151]

---

148. See *S. th*. III, q. 22, a. 3.
149. See *S. th*. III, q. 22, a. 4.
150. See *S. th*. III, q. 22, a. 3 ad 2.
151. *S. th*. III, q. 22, a. 3 ad 2: "Sacrificium autem quod quotidie in Ecclesia offertur, non est aliud a

But what is the prerequisite for being able to make the unique sacrifice on the cross present in the Eucharist?[152] How can the ordained priest act *in virtute et persona Christi*? How ought one to specify the relation between the eternal priesthood of Christ and its temporal representation?

There is a passage that explicitly unfolds the motif of Christ's *eternal* priesthood and can offer a first answer to this question. The biblical *locus classicus* that drives Aquinas's theological reflection on Christ's eternal priesthood is found in Psalm 109:5 (110:5), or again in Hebrews 5:6. There we find: "You are a priest forever according to the order of Melchizedek." Thomas devotes two articles just to this verse. The first takes up the question of what is eternal and what transitory in Christ's priesthood.[153] The second attempts to figure out how the motif of Melchizedek the priest-king is related to Christ.[154] Let us begin with the first article, since it foregrounds the problem of interest to us.

Within the order of priestly ministries, Thomas distinguishes between offering sacrifices (*oblatio sacrificii*), which, as pertains to Christ, took place once for all and thus is past, and the consummation of the sacrifice (*consummatio sacrificii*), whose effect persists, and thus it merits this designation for eternity. Christ's sacrificial offering in accepting suffering and death is a past historical event that nevertheless retains its significance for the history that follows, because, through it, the perfection of the sacrifice is reached, which then benefits man. In order to explain further the *consummatio sacrificii*, Thomas adds that the goal of Christ's sacrifice consists in communicating an eternal rather than temporal good to man. This goal is achieved by his death, for which reason Thomas cites the statement found in the letter to the Hebrews: "Christ came as a high priest of the good things to come" (Heb 9:11).[155] He entered into the holy of holies, into heaven, in order to intercede there for us. In q. 22, a. 5, it is recalled rather in passing that the Old Testament offers a model for Christ's high priesthood, namely, the high priest who entered into the holy of holies once a year for the feast

---

sacrificio quod ipse Christus obtulit, sed eius commemoratio." This statement is again undergirded by the authority of Augustine: "Sacerdos ipse Christus offerens, ipse et oblatio: cuius rei sacramentum, quotidianum esse voluit Ecclesiae sacrificium" (ibid. = *De civ. Dei* X, 20 = CCL 47, ed. B. Dombart, 294).

152. On this issue, see K. Rahner, *The Celebration of the Eucharist*, Quaestiones Disputatae 31, ed. A. Häussling (London: Herder, 1968).

153. *S. th.* III, q. 22, a. 5.

154. *S. th.* III, q. 22, a. 6.

155. *S. th.* III, q. 22, a. 5: "in officio sacerdotis duo possunt considerari: primo quidem, ipsa oblatio sacrificii; secundo, ipsa sacrificii consummatio, quae quidem consistit in hoc quod illi pro quibus sacrificium offertur, finem sacrificii consequuntur. Finis autem sacrificii quod Christus obtulit, non fuerunt bona temporalia, sed aeterna, quae per eius mortem adipiscimur, unde dicitur, Heb. 9, [11] quod *Christus est assistens pontifex futurorum bonorum*; ratione cuius Christi sacerdotium dicitur esse aeternum."

of atonement. In his commentary on Hebrews, Thomas tries to categorize precisely what constitutes the unique meaning of Christ's priesthood when it is seen in relation to this Old Testament *praefiguratio*. Because this interpretation is not insignificant for the motif of Christ's *eternal* priesthood, it is referenced here.

Within the scope of this interest is the commentary on Hebrews 9:11–14, where we read: "But when Christ came as a high priest of the *good things to come*, then through the greater and perfect tent (not made with hands, that is, *not of this creation*), he entered *once for all* into the Holy Place, not with the blood of goats and calves, but *with his own blood*, thus obtaining *eternal redemption* ... how much more will the blood of Christ, who through the eternal Spirit offered himself without blemish to God, purify our conscience from dead works to worship the living God."[156] In his commentary on this passage, Thomas underlines five aspects:[157]

1. The person who entered into the holy of holies (*qui intravit*)
2. The majesty and state of the place into which the priest attained entry (*quo intravit*)
3. The way in which he entered (*quomodo intravit*)
4. The time when he entered (*quando intravit*)
5. The reason he entered (*quare intravit*)

The meaning of Christ's priesthood is illuminated in contrast with the mundane and provisional antitype of the Levitical priesthood. *First*, regarding the person: in the Old Testament, entrance into the holy of holies was reserved to the high priest alone. The privileged place of the pontifex is transferred to Christ in the letter to the Hebrews. He is the *princeps sacerdotum*—as Thomas can say, drawing on 1 Peter 5:4.[158] Even so, in contrast to the high priests of the old covenant, he is a *pontifex bonorum futurorum*, who imparts to man a share in eternal, everlasting life. Again in contrast to the *many* high priests at work in Israel's history, Christ is the *one* mediator between God and man (see 1 Tim 2:5), himself seated at the Father's right hand "to intercede for us" (Heb 7:25).[159]

---

156. In the Vulgate formulation: "¹¹Christus autem adsistens pontifex futurorum bonorum / per amplius et perfectius tabernaculum non manufactum / id est non huius creationis / ¹²neque per sanguinem hircorum et vitulorum / sed per proprium sanguinem introivit semel in sancta / aeterna redemptione inventa / ¹³si enim sanguis hircorum et taurorum / et cinis vitulae aspersus inquinatos sanctificat ad emundationem carnis / ¹⁴quanto magis sanguis Christi / qui per Spiritum Sanctum semet ipsum obtulit immaculatum Deo / emundabit conscientiam vestram ab operibus mortuis ad serviendum Deo viventi."

157. See *In Hebr* IX, l. III (n. 435–46).

158. See 1 Pt 5:4: "et cum apparuerit *princeps pastorum* percipietis inmarcescibilem gloriae coronam" (emphasis added).

159. See *In Hebr* IX, l. III (n. 436): "Iste pontifex non est negligens, sed assistens. Pontifex enim

Second, regarding the dignity of the place: the *tabernaculum caelestis gloriae* is greater and more perfect than the *tabernaculum* of the old covenant. For Thomas, the tent of meeting is a place for pilgrims (*locus peregrinorum*)—it can be moved and is a product of human hands. In contrast, the tabernacle in heaven is *non manufactum*; rather, it is the house of God and everlasting. The *artifex* and *conditor* of this house is God himself. It is notable that Thomas appears to have a completely local conception of the heavenly temple. For he remarks that the body of Christ (*Christi corpus*) can be recognized through the heavenly tabernacle, in which he fought against the devil.[160] That means, Christ's stigmata, which show that he suffered on the cross and placed himself before the hatred of sinners, are visible on the *corpus gloriosum* for all eternity. The Passion is not forgotten but rather remains written into Christ's glorified corporeality as a trace, so that an important fact remains recognizable: the exalted one *is* the crucified one, and his *transitus* from death to life in heavenly glory does not mark a rupture with his lived history, which took place in the medium of the body, but rather it completes this history. Thus, Thomas can draw on Colossians 2:9 to say that, in fact, the whole fullness of the divinity dwells *bodily* in the *tabernaculum caeleste*.[161]

Third, concerning the way he entered: unlike the high priests of the old covenant, who stood before God with the foreign blood of bulls and rams, Christ stood before God with his own blood poured out for our salvation on the cross, as it is attested in Matthew 26:28: "This is my blood of the new covenant, which is poured out for you and for many for the forgiveness of sins."[162]

Fourth, regarding the time: the high priests entered the holy of holies only once per year, namely, at the feast of atonement. But Christ entered into heaven once for all and that means: for all time (*per totum tempus*).[163] Once in heaven, he is always there (*semper est ibi*).

Fifth, for this reason: he entered into the heavenly temple to make intercession for the sins of the people—not for his own, since he had none, but for the sins of others, as Thomas emphasizes in the pro-existent dimension

---

mediator est inter Deum et populum: Christus vero mediator est I Tim. 2,5: *Mediator Dei et hominum homo Christus Iesus*.... Et ideo ipse assistit Patri *ad interpellandum pro nobis*, supra VII, 25; Rom 8,34: *Christus Iesus qui etiam interpellat pro nobis.*"

160. *In Hebr* IX, l. III (n. 438): "per tabernaculum potest Christi corpus intelligi, in quo contra diabolum pugnavit."

161. Ibid.: "Quod est peramplius, quia in ipso habitat omnis plenitudo divinitatis corporaliter, Col. II, 9."

162. See *In Hebr* IX, l. III (n. 439).

163. *In Hebr* IX, l. III (n. 440): "Quarto quando intrabat, quia semel in anno: Christus autem per totum tempus, quod est quasi annus."

of the high priestly actions. Through his blood, however, all are redeemed, and indeed for eternity, since the atoning power of his blood is infinite.

Thus, according to Thomas, Christ's priesthood is elevated above that of the old covenant in a twofold way. It overcomes the *soteriological* impotence of the Levitical priesthood, which was unable to take away the sins of the people even through many and diverse sacrifices. At the same time, as an eternal priesthood, it accomplishes the *eschatological* entrance to God, which the temporal priesthood of the old covenant was ultimately unable to do. The fact of there being many priests in the old covenant is in Thomas's mind a sign of the impermanence of this priesthood; by way of contrast, Christ's priesthood does not reproduce itself: *iste sacerdos, scilicet Christus est immortalis*.[164] Thomas finds this superiority of Christ's priesthood over that of the old covenant prefigured above all in the character of Melchizedek, who received a tithe from Abraham.[165]

In summary, it can be said that Christ's priesthood and the effect of his sacrifice continue to exist in all eternity; at the same time, this is the presupposition for the *commemoratio sacrificii* in time. As *principalis sacerdos*, Christ is the source of every priesthood. The priest who lets himself be taken into the *traditio*-event and who carries out the sacraments *in virtute et persona Christi*, participates in the eternal high priestly office of Christ. He passes on God's *communicatio* with men, a *communicatio* established in and through Christ—and, conversely, he brings the prayers of men before God. With the resurrection and ascension, the *Christus passus* found definitive access to God. Christ does not die any more (see Rom 6:9), but all the same his scars characterize his glorified existence, so that his self-gift for men remains visible in all eternity. He makes intercession for men, he carries out the "intercession par excellence pour tous les hommes."[166] As Christ stands before God as an advocate for all men, so also should the priest, and with him the faithful, stand before God in prayer for others, indeed *pro vivis et mortuis*. This intercessory solidarity aims at either those who do not want to participate in Christ's sacrifice, such as unbelievers, for whose sins prayers must be offered, that they might convert; or those who, after participating in Christ's sacrifice, have fallen through sin. The community of the faithful gathering around the table of the Lord does not close in on itself but, in the mode of intercession, remains connected with those others standing outside.

---

164. "This priest, namely, Christ, is immortal" (*In Hebr* IX, l. IV [n. 368]). The followup reads: "Manet enim in aeternum, sicut Verbum Patris aeternum. Ex cuius aeternitate redundat enim aeternitatis in corpus eius, quia Christus resurgens ex mortuis iam non moritur (Rom VI, 9)."
165. See *S. th.* III, q. 22, a. 6.
166. Chardonnens, "Éternité du sacerdoce du Christ," 171.

The Celebration of the Eucharist as *imago repraesentativa* of Christ's Passion

The question must be further deepened: how can Christ's Passion, in which sinful man's salvation is established, remain present in the course of history and unfold its efficacy therein? Connected with this question is the already-indicated problem of how the *one* historical sacrifice of Jesus Christ on the cross can be brought into connection with the many celebrations of the Mass, without necessitating speaking of repeating Christ's sacrifice or implicating in it some need for completion—a theme broadly raised in the post-Tridentine discussions concerning the sacrifice of the Mass. Thomas himself—and here our attention should be turned to his statements alone—specified the sacrament of the Eucharist explicitly as a commemoration making-present Christ's Passion, or more precisely, his sacrifice (*sacrificium*).[167] If one searches the *Summa theologiae* for theological elucidation and deepening of this statement, one must take note with astonishment that Thomas barely spoke about this theme. Indeed, in his *Sentences* commentary he already posed the question of whether what the priest does is truly called a sacrifice (*sacrificium*) or immolation (*immolatio*) and whether Christ is sacrificed daily (*quotidie*) or was sacrificed only once (*semel*)—and he answered that what the priest offers and consecrates is called *sacrificium* and *oblatio* because it is the recollection (*memoria*) and representation (*repraesentatio*) of the true sacrifice and of the holy immolation that took place on the altar of the cross.[168] In the *Sentences* commentary, one can also find further statements concerning how the *repraesentatio* of the one sacrifice of Christ is liturgically inaugurated. It is to this context that *Summa theologiae* III, q. 83, a. 1 returns when it raises the question, whether Christ is sacrificed (*immoletur*) in the "celebration of this sacrament" (*celebratio huius sacramenti*).[169] Even in the framing of the question it is noteworthy that the liturgical shape (*celebratio*) of the Eucharist is shifted into the center

---

167. See *S. th.* III, q. 73, a. 4 ad 3, where it is held that this sacrament is called a sacrifice (*sacrificium*), since it makes present Christ's Passion ("dicendum quod hoc sacramentum dicitur *sacrificium*, inquantum repraesentat ipsam passionem Christi. Dicitur autem *hostia*, inquantum continet ipsum Christum, qui est hostia suavitatis, ut dicitur Eph 5, [2]"). See also a. 5: "hoc sacramentum simul est sacrificium et sacramentum." And similarly, a. 7: "hoc sacramentum non solum est sacramentum, sed etiam est sacrificium."

168. See *In IV Sent.*, d. 12, expositio textus (n. 9). There we read further: "Christ died once on the cross …; but in the sacrament he is sacrificed daily, because in the sacrament takes place a recollection (*recordatio*) of what took place once." This is undergirded by quotations from Augustine and Ambrose.

169. But see also the statements in *S. th.* III, q. 79, a. 5: "hoc sacramentum simul est sacrificium et sacramentum: sed rationem sacrificii habet, inquantum offertur; rationem autem sacramenti, inquantum sumitur. Et ideo effectum sacramenti habet in eo qui sumit, effectum autem sacrificii in eo qui offert, vel in his pro quibus offertur."

of attention. Given that this question considers the *celebratio* of this sacrament, perhaps a certain common judgment against Aquinas turns out to be in need of revision, that is, the widespread judgment that Thomas Aquinas was interested almost exclusively in the ontological penetration of the words of consecration and thereby encouraged a fixation on the theme of consecration. Beyond the moment of consecration, the celebration (*celebratio*) as a whole here becomes the object of inquiry.[170]

To be sure, speaking of the Eucharist as a sacrifice (*immolatio*) is clearly in no way self-evident, already in Aquinas's time. How can the liturgical celebration receive the name sacrifice when Christ was sacrificed once for all on Golgotha? Must something be added in a way to this historical sacrifice by the liturgical celebration?[171] And, further, can the Eucharistic celebration really be called an *immolatio* when Christ is obviously *not* crucified during the liturgy?[172] Finally, it ought to be considered that in the *immolatio Christi*, priest and sacrificial offering were identical, which does not apply to the Eucharistic celebration *prima vista*.[173] Would it not therefore be more fitting to reserve the name *immolatio* for the historically unique sacrifice on the cross at Golgotha? The urgency of this problem becomes even more apparent when seen against the background of the Eucharistic controversies: if one teaches—as did the proponents of a massive realism—a total identification of historical and Eucharistic *corpus Domini*, then it follows ineluctably that Christ is sacrificed anew on the altar. In order to avoid this problematic conclusion, Lanfranc of Bec already conceded to his rival Berengar that Christ's suffering is not actually repeated in the Mass but is rather figuratively represented, without departing even one jot from holding that the true body and the true blood of Jesus Christ are contained in and under the species of bread and wine.[174] In this context, Lanfranc commented on Augustine's

---

170. On this point, see the pertinent remark of T.-D. Humbrecht, "L'eucharistie, 'représentation' du sacrifice du Christ, selon saint Thomas," *Revue Thomiste* 98 (1998): 355–86, here 366: "C'est bien la *célébration* du sacrement qui est appelée immolation, et pas seulement le moment de la consécration: ce qui veut dire que le déroulement liturgique, l'action totale, la célébration en son unité, relève de la plénitude du sacrement de l'eucharistie, et non point seulement le moment consécratoire, les seules paroles du sacrement."

171. See *S. th.* III, q. 83, a. 1, obj. 1: "Dicitur enim Hebr. 10,14 quod Christus *una oblatione consummavit in sempiternum sanctificatos*. Sed illa oblatio fuit eius immolatio. Ergo Christus non immolatur in celebratione huius sacramenti."

172. See *S. th.* q. 83, a. 1, obj. 2: "immolatio Christi facta est in cruce, in qua *tradidit semetipsum oblationem et hostiam Deo in odorem suavitatis*, ut dicitur Eph. 5,2. Sed in celebratione huius mysterii Christus non crucifigitur. Ergo nec immolatur."

173. See *S. th.* III, q. 83, a. 1, obj. 3: "in immolatione Christi idem est sacerdos et hostia. Sed in celebratione huius sacramenti non est idem sacerdos et hostia. Ergo celebratio huius sacramenti non est Christi immolatio."

174. See Lanfrancus, *De corpore et sanguine Domini*, cap. 13–15 (PL 150, 407–42, here 422–26).

statement, cited by Thomas as well,[175] that Christ was sacrificed once in himself (*in semetipso*) and yet is sacrificed daily in sacrament (*in sacramento*). His commentary runs as follows: "[The statement:] Christ was sacrificed one time in himself, [is so to be understood] that he ... hung on the cross only one time as true God and true man, and presented himself to the Father as a living, passible, mortal sacrifice that was efficacious for redeeming the living and the dead."[176] True, Lanfranc immediately adds that the flesh of the Lord (*caro Domini*) is sacrificed, distributed, and consumed daily.[177]

But Thomas also concerns himself with clarifying the relation between the one-time sacrifice of the cross and the offering of daily Masses. On this score, he appeals to another text—one that was decisive for the medieval interpretation of the Mass[178]—which interprets the Eucharist as *exemplum*,

---

175. See *S. th.* III, q. 83, a. 1, s.c.: "Augustinus dicit, in libro *Sententiarum Prosperi*: *Semel immolatus est in semetipso Christus, et tamen quotidie immolatur in sacramento.*" The passage is found at Augustine, *Epist.* 98, al. 23, *ad Bonif.* n. 9 (CCL 31 A, ed. K.-D. Daur = PL 33, 363–64). The quotation from Augustine along with the commentary by Lanfranc found its way into the *Decretum Gratiani*, which was used by Thomas. See *Decretum Gratiani*, p. III, d. 2, can. 52, in *Corpus iuris canonici*, ed. Richter-Friedberg, I, col. 1333.

176. Lanfrancus, *De corpore et sanguine Domini*, cap. 15 (PL 150, 425): "In seipso semel immolatus est Christus, quia in manifestatione sui corporis, in distinctione membrorum omnium verus Deus et verus homo semel tantum in cruce pependit, offerens seipsum Patri hostiam vivam, passibilem, mortalem, vivorum ac mortuorum redemptionis efficacem."

177. Ibid.: "In sacramento tamen quod in huius rei memoriam frequentat Ecclesia, caro Domini quotidie immolatur, dividitur, comeditur, et sanguis eius de calice fidelium ore potatur."

178. The citation attributed by Thomas in the *corpus articuli* to Ambrose originally stems from Chrysostom. It circulated under the name of Ambrose beginning with Ivo of Chartres (*Panorm.* I, c. 144; PL 161, 1077) and found its way into the *Decretum Gratiani*, p. III, d. 2, can. 53 (ed. Richter-Friedberg I, 1333), which Thomas used as source material. On account of its importance, it is cited here in its entirety in the version found in the *Decretum Gratiani*, which deviates slightly from Chrysostom: "In Christo semel oblata est hostia ad salutem sempiternam potens. Quid ergo nos? Nonne per singulos dies offerimus? Offerimus quidem, sed ad recordationem mortis eius, et una est hostia, non multae? Quomodo una et non multae? quia semel oblatus est Christus. Hoc autem sacrificium exemplum est illius, et ipsum et semper id ipsum. Proinde unum est hoc sacrificium, alioquin, quoniam in multis locis offertur, multi sunt Christi? Nequaquam, sed unus ubique est Christus, et hic plenus existens, et illic plenus. Sicut enim quod ubique offertur unum est corpus, et non multa corpora: ita et unum sacrificium, Pontifex autem ille est, hostiam obtulit nos mundantem. Ipsam vero offerimus etiam nunc, quae tunc oblata consumi non potest. Quod non facimus, in commemorationem fit eius, quod factum est: *Hoc enim facite*, ait [cf. Lc c 22, vol. 19], *in meam commemorationem.*—The oblation (*hostia*) was offered one time in Christ and it has the power to bring about eternal salvation. What, therefore, regarding us [and our deeds]? Do not we sacrifice every day? Yes, we sacrifice but in memory (*recordatio*) of his death, and the oblation (*hostia*) is one, not many? In what way is it one and not many? Because Christ was sacrificed once. This sacrifice (*sacrificium*) is a model (*exemplum*) of that one, the same, always the same. And thus it is a sacrifice (*sacrificium*); otherwise, since it is offered in many places, are there many Christs? In no way. It is the one Christ everywhere, wholly existing here and wholly there. Just as, for example, what is offered everywhere is one body and not many, so also it is one sacrifice (*sacrificium*). The high priest, however, is the one who offered the sacrifice that cleansed us. But the same sacrifice is offered now, which once sacrificed cannot be exhausted. What we do takes place in memory of what took place then: 'Do this,' he says, 'in memory of me'" (translation J.-H. T.). In Chrysostom (*In Epist. Ad Hebr*, c. X, hom. XVII, in PG 63, 131), the passage closes with a sentence not taken up in the *Decretum Gratiani*: "Οὐκ ἄλλην θυσίαν, καθάπερ ὁ ἀρχιερεὺς τότε, ἀλλὰ τὴν αὐτὴν ἀεὶ ποιοῦμεν μᾶλλον δὲ ἀνάμνησιν ἐργαζόμεθα θυσίας.—It is not another sacrifice that we celebrate, as the high priest did back then, but rather it is always the very same; or rather, we celebrate the memory of the sacrifice" (translation J.-H. T.).

as *recordatio* and *commemoratio* (ἀνάμνησις) of the unique sacrifice on the cross. Thomas takes up this interpretation, modifying it slightly, when he foregrounds the concept of *representation* for determining the relation between the historical sacrifice on Golgotha and its being made sacramentally present. Even if the concept *repraesentatio* contains a wide spectrum of meanings in Thomas's corpus, each of which varies with the context, still the use of the term within the context of Eucharistic theology has a conspicuously close connection to the theme of signs. Each representation depends upon a *modus significandi*. That means, there must be a certain similarity (*similitudo*) between sign and signified in order that what is represented can also be expressed in a recognizable way in what it represents.[179] In what follows, therefore, not only should the bridge function of the term *repraesentatio* be considered, but also the level of liturgical signs should be concretely shown, that is, how and by means of which symbolic actions Christ's sacrifice is made present in the Eucharist.

In the *corpus articuli*,[180] Thomas underlines that the Eucharistic celebration is called *immolatio Christi* for a twofold reason: first, because the celebration of this sacrament is a sort of image (*quaedam imago repraesentativa*) making-present Christ's suffering, which is a true immolation (*vera immolatio*).[181] Thus, the language of *imago repraesentativa*, carefully limited by the term *quaedam*, performs a mediation between the one-time event of Golgotha (*semel*) and the daily sacramental making-present in the Eucharist (*quotidie*). Thomas explains the concept of *imago repraesentativa* through a statement of Augustine, which holds that "images are usually named with the names of the things they image. Thus, when we look upon a painting or mural, we say: That is Cicero, that is Sallust."[182] What is apparent in this explanation is that it at any rate makes possible a first approach to the *imago repraesentativa* in the Eucharistic celebration. For, in the first place, a painted image (*pictura*) depicts its object only externally; there is no in-

---

179. Humbrecht ("L'eucharistie, 'représentation' du sacrifice du Christ selon saint Thomas," 359–61) examined the use of the term *repraesentatio* in Thomas's work and suggested three elements of a definition. The term *repraesentatio* is coupled with three concepts: firstly, the idea of *similitudo*; second, the idea of *significatio*; and third, the concept of exemplar cause. In the realm of Eucharistic theology, the dimension of *significatio* dominates without relegating the other two concepts completely to the shadows. Each representation is dependent on a *modus significandi*. More precisely, only that can be represented which is connected by a relation of similarity, which is once again expressed by the *significatio*.

180. See S. *th*. III, q. 83, a. 1 c.

181. Ibid.: "Celebratio huius sacramenti imago quaedam repraesentativa passionis Christi, quae est vera eius immolatio."

182. S. *th*. III, q. 83, a. 1 cites Augustine, *Ad Simpl*., lib. 2, q. 3, n. 2: "solent imagines earum rerum nominibus appellari quarum imagines sunt: sicut cum, intuentes tabulam aut parietum pictum, dicimus, Ille Cicero est, Ille Sallustius."

trinsic connection between exemplar and likeness—a connection constitutive for the celebration of the Eucharist.[183] It is certainly not accidental that Thomas himself specifies this intrinsic connection a little later on, stating that the one-time sacrifice of Christ is the *exemplum* offered and represented in the manifold Masses.[184] In the second place, a painting, like a coin,[185] is a static item while the *celebratio sacramenti* presents a dynamic event with an obviously ordered sequence of liturgical and symbolic actions. Thus, the comparison with an image seems rather to call forth misunderstandings. For if the celebration of the Eucharist presents an *imago repraesentativa passionis Christi*, but the *passio Christi* is emphatically designated as a real immolation (*vera immolatio*), then one could assert that daily Mass simply presents illustrative representations of the one sacrifice of Christ—a danger strengthened rather than restrained by the allegorical explanations of the Mass in the Middle Ages.[186]

Such a reduction of the Mass to an illustrative simulation of the *passio Christi* is what Thomas obviously wants to rule out, and thus he takes up the concept of *imago repraesentativa* once again and lays down: as the celebration of this sacrament is an *imago repraesentativa* of Christ's Passion, so the altar represents the cross itself, on which Christ (*in propria specie*) was sacrificed.[187] The term *imago* therefore aims at an image filled with reality, which is represented through signs showing a certain similarity (*similitudo*) to what they are supposed to represent. For Thomas, this is also made clear by the role of the priest in the celebration of the Eucharist. Even though he brings forward the prayers for the gathered faithful *in persona ecclesiae* and functions here as the mouth of the Church, in the act of consecration he also acts *in persona Christi*. He does not speak on his own but becomes, as it were, the mouth of Christ when he recites the words of consecration. Thomas speaks in this context, and hardly accidentally, of the priest as an image of Christ (*imago*).[188]

---

183. In *S. th.* I, q. 45, a. 7, Thomas distinguishes between *repraesentatio vestigii* and *repraesentatio imaginis*. The first, as an effect, reveals only the causality but not the form of its cause—as, for example, smoke in relation to fire; the representation of image, in contrast, includes a similarity of form, as, for example, a sculpture that refers back to the person represented in it.

184. *S. th.* III, q. 83, a. 1 ad 1: "Ad primum ergo dicendum quod, sicut Ambrosius ibidem dicit, *una est hostia, quam scilicet Christus obtulit et nos offerimus, et non multae, quia semel oblatus est Christus, hoc autem sacrificium exemplum* [sic] *est illius. Sicut enim quod ubique offertur unum est corpus et non multa corpora, ita et unum sacrificium.*"

185. See *S. th.* III, q. 74, a. 1; q. 76, a. 2 ad 1; and q. 79, a. 1.

186. On the criticism of an illustrative symbolism, see A. Schmemann, *The Eucharist: Sacrament of the Kingdom* (Crestwood, N.Y.: St. Vladimir's Press, 1988), 37f., 44–47, 49f. and *passim*.

187. See *S. th.* III, q. 83, a. 1 ad 2: "Ad secundum dicendum quod sicut celebratio huius sacramenti est imago repraesentativa passionis Christi, ita altare est repraesentativum crucis ipsius, in qua Christus in propria specie immolatus est."

188. *S. th.* III, q. 83, a. 1 ad 3: "sacerdos gerit imaginem Christi in cuius persona et virtute verba pronuntiat

Second, the Eucharistic celebration is also called *immolatio* in view of the *effect* of Christ's suffering. The faithful taking part in the Eucharistic celebration receive, according to Thomas, a share in the fruit of the Passion. Without determining in detail once more the soteriological effect of the Passion,[189] Thomas quotes a liturgical text that clarifies his concern: "Each time the memory (*commemoratio*) of this sacrifice (*hostia*) is celebrated, the work of our redemption is carried out (*exercetur*)."[190] Here Thomas quotes an already weakened reading (*exercetur* instead of *exseritur*) of an offertory prayer, which in its original version reads: "Each time the memory of Christ's sacrifice is celebrated, the work of redemption takes place (*exseritur* = emerges; can be seen, heard, felt; is made manifest)."[191] Merely in passing, let it be noted that the liturgical constitution of Vatican II (SC 2) also took up the weakened reading of this offertory prayer in order to explain the essence of the liturgy, specifically the Eucharist as sacrifice.

The Representation of Christ's Sacrifice through Ritual Symbolic Actions

Concluding his treatise on the Eucharist, Thomas offers an explanation of the Eucharistic rite that brings into play an assortment of nonverbal signs, which are performed by the priest during the Mass and, in Thomas's estimation, not only recall the Passion of Christ in an illustrative way but also represent the Passion as *imagines repraesentativae*. In the first place, Thomas offers an interpretation of the numerous signs of the cross made by the

---

ad consecrandum." Because the priest is interpreted as *imago Christi*, the identity of the priest and the sacrifice on the cross can be figuratively expressed in the Eucharistic celebration. For background, see also q. 82, aa. 1 and 3. The construal of the priest as an icon of Christ within the context of certain liturgical actions is also found in the theology of the East. See, e.g., Theodore of Mopsuestia, *Hom. Cat.* 15,21.

189. *S. th.* III, q. 79, a. 2, where Thomas describes the diverse effects of the Eucharist; thus, he cites the conferral of grace, the remission of sins (*peccata venialia*), the edification of the Church community (building up the body of Christ), as well as the attainment of glory. See also *S. th.* III, q. 78, a. 3 ad 2, where Thomas indicates three effects of the blood poured out: first, the attainment of our eternal inheritance; second, the justice of grace; and third, the removal of sin as an obstacle (with reference to the *forma sacramenti*: "which is poured out for you for the remission of sins").

190. See *S. th.* III, q. 83, a. 1 c: "Alio modo, quantum ad effectum passionis: quia scilicet per hoc sacramentum participes efficimur fructus Dominicae passionis. Unde et in quadam Dominicali oratione secreta dicitur [*Miss. Rom.*, Dom. IX post Pent.]: *Quoties huius hostiae commemoratio celebratur, opus nostrae redemptionis exercetur*." E. M. Faber, *Einführung in die katholische Sakramentenlehre* (Darmstadt: Wissenschaftliche Buchgesellschaft, 2001), 63, cites this prayer to explain the understanding in the early Church of the sacrament as a *commemorative act* and to draw out the restricted view of scholastic sacramental theology. Her thesis is that Thomas's "predominant interest in the actual efficacy" brings it about that "the temporal and profound dimension of the sacrament as a commemoration of the salvation event recedes into the background" (40); but this can hardly be maintained. All the same, Thomas himself cites what is brought against him and he considers the temporal structure of the sacraments in a paradigmatic way, as Faber herself notes approvingly elsewhere (55f.). See *S. th.* III, q. 60, a. 3.

191. H. B. Meyer, *Eucharistie. Geschichte, Theologie, Pastoral* (Regensburg: Pustet, 1989), 448, note 1.

priest over the bread and wine during the Eucharistic canon. He does not see any unnecessary repetition in them but instead aligns himself here with the relatively sober explanation of the Mass advocated by Pope Innocent III in his widely received work *De sacra altaris mysterio*,[192] which prefers the rememorative allegorical interpretation of the Mass. He does this not merely out of respect for the tradition but rather quite deliberately. In contrast, for example, to his teacher Albert the Great,[193] who confronted reservedly the allegorical explanation of the Mass initiated by Amalarius of Metz[194] and then widely disseminated, Aquinas correlated each of the numerous signs of the cross in the Roman canon[195] with a particular event in the ever-increasing drama of Jesus' Passion.[196] After the handing over (*traditio*), being sold (*venditio*), and participating in the last supper, Thomas sees the actual Passion expressed in the five signs of the cross made at the words "Hostiam puram, hostiam sanctam, hostiam immaculatam, panem sanctam vitae aeternae et calicem salutis perpetua"; they are a reference to the five wounds of Christ.[197] Thomas expressly protests against

---

192. For a characterization of the work, see Meyer, *Eucharistie*, 212.

193. See A. Franz, *Die Messe im deutschen Mittelalter* (Freiburg: Herder, 1902), 470–73.

194. On this point, see A. Kolping, "Amalar von Metz und Florus von Lyon. Zeugen eines Wandels im liturgischen Mysterienverständnis in der Karolingerzeit," ZKTh 73 (1951): 424–64; J. Beumer, "Amalar von Metz und sein Zeugnis für die Gestalt der Meßliturgie seiner Zeit," ThPh 50 (1975): 416–26; R. Meßner, "Zur Hermeneutik allegorischer Liturgieerklärung," ZKTh 115 (1993): 284–319, 415–34, here 415–22. For Amalarius of Metz's *Liber officialis*, the concept "memoria" plays a central role, inasmuch as it rememoratively refers the one Mass, sub-divided into "officia," to Jesus' life and death, resurrection and ascension. His allegorical explanation of the diverse rites follows a primarily moral and catechetical line; the ecclesial and eschatological dimension of the liturgy—foregrounded in the Byzantine interpretive tradition—falls noticeably into the background. Contemplation of the Passion is meant to prompt a more perfect discipleship.

195. On the emergence and explanation of the *signa crucis* in the canon, see J. A. Jungmann, *Missarum Sollemnia. Eine genetische Erklärung der römischen Messe*, vol. 2: *Die Opfermesse*, 5th ed. (Freiburg-Basel-Vienna: Herder, 1962), 174–79.

196. As he did earlier in the *Sentences* commentary (see In IV Sent., d. 12, expos. textus), Thomas sets up his elucidations largely following Innocent III's rememorative allegorical interpretation of the sign of the cross. On this point, see A. Franz, *Die Messe im deutschen Mittelalter* (Freiburg: Herder, 1902), 455f., who summarizes Innocent's allegorical exposition as follows: "The first three crosses ('Haec dona') call to mind Judas's betrayal; the second five ('Quam oblationem') recall the betrayer, Jesus, the priests, Sadducees, and Pharisees; the third pair (at 'Qui pridie' and 'Simili modo') initiates the act of consecration; the fourth set of five ('Hostiam puram') indicate the five wounds; the fifth pair ('Sacrosanctum filii tui corpus') points to the scourging and the chains; the sixth triplet ('Sanctificas') refers to the third hour in which the Lord was crucified; finally, the seventh group of five ('Per ipsum') presents the *propassio, passio, compassio* of the Lord and the blood and water from his wounded side." See Innocent III, *De sacro altaris mysterio*, lib. V, c. 14 (PL 217, 773–916, here 896). What is significant is that Thomas does *not* appropriate Innocent's numerical speculations but rather holds modestly: "Potest autem brevius dici quod consecratio huius sacrificii et fructus ipsius procedit ex virtute crucis Christi, et ideo ubicumque fit mentio de aliquo horum sacerdos crucesignatione utitur" (S. th. III, q. 83, a. 5 ad 3). One can surely read this remark as an answer to the question left open by Innocent and often raised in the Middle Ages, namely, why the priest also makes the sign of blessing over the sacrificial gifts *post consecrationem* (see PL 217, 887f.).

197. See S. th. III, q. 83, a. 5 ad 4.

seeing "gesticulationes ridiculae"[198] in the priestly rite and thus interprets, for example, the *orans* posture of the priest while praying the canon as a sign of Christ's spreading his arms on the cross.[199] This gesture reminds the faithful of Christ's death; indeed it not only instructs us—according to Peter M. Candler—about Christ's death as an act of self-sacrifice for us, but moreover attempts *to convince* us to participate in Christ's sacrifice:"Hence in this particular liturgical example, the memory is bound together with understanding and will—the recollection of the crucifixion does not simply remind or recollect, it orients one toward the future, and it draws the soul into participation in the political community of the Body of Christ. By imaging this body, the priest re-performs the divine initiative of making the Church one body through Christ's sacrifice. In other words, the memory is trained to remember rightly."[200]

Thomas trains his attention on other gestures as well. Thus, he sees the humility and obedience of Christ expressed in the folding of the priest's hands;[201] he also interprets the liturgical rite, connected with the consecration, of raising the eyes to heaven as a reminiscence of what Jesus did at the last supper—something, by the way, not attested by the New Testament.[202] The rite of mixing the wine and water makes present for him not only the wound in Jesus' side, out of which flowed blood and water (see Jn 19:34), but also the incorporation of the faithful into Christ.[203] In the fraction rite that follows (*fractio hostiae*), Thomas sees the violent breaking of Christ's body on the cross.[204] Of course, Thomas feels compelled to offer the pre-

---

198. See *S. th.* III, q. 83, a. 5 ad 5.

199. On this point, see Jungmann, *Missarum Sollemnia*, vol. 2, 172: "In the Middle Ages, it frequently became customary for him [i.e., the priest] to stretch out his arms widely in the shape of a cross at least after the consecration, as is still usual today in the Dominican Order, among others." Already in the ancient Church the *orans* posture was interpreted as referring to the crucified one. See F. J. Dölger, *Sol salutis. Gebet und Gesang im christlichen Altertum. Mit besonderer Rücksicht auf die Ostung in Gebet und Liturgie*, 2nd ed. (Münster: Aschendorff, 1925) 319f., note 4.

200. P. M. Candler, "Liturgically Trained Memory: A Reading of *Summa theologiae* III.83," *Modern Theology* 20 (2004): 423–45, here 426.

201. See *S. th.* III, q. 83, a. 5 ad 5.

202. See *S. th.* III, q. 83, a. 5 ad 2. Thomas traces this prayerful gesture back to the *traditio apostolorum*.

203. See *S. th.* III, q. 74, a. 6 and 7. See *De articulis fidei et ecclesiae sacramentis* (n. 602): "aqua significant populum, qui incorporatur Christo."

204. The fraction rite stems originally from Jewish meal practices where it is a rite of dividing; Paul referred to this in addressing the community of those participating in the meal (see 1 Cor 10:16). The admixture of water and wine corresponded likewise to a common drinking custom, something that Thomas himself conjectures (see *S. th.* III, q. 74, a. 6 c.). Only relatively late did one find signs of Christ's death represented in both rites. References can be found in Paschasius Radbertus, *De corpore et sanguine Domini*, cap. IV, 34ff. (ed. B. Paulus: CCM, XVI, 28): "Sed figura esse uidetur dum frangitur, dum in specie uisibili aliud intelligitur quam quod uisu carnis et gustu sentitur, dumque sanguis in calice simul cum aqua miscetur. Porro illud fidei sacramentum iure ueritas appellatur. Veritas ergo dum corpus Christi et sanguis uirtute Spiritus in uerbo ipsius ex panis uinique substantia efficitur, figura uero dum sacerdos [sacerdote] quasi

cision that such a breaking of the host in no way entails a new breaking of Christ's body—a position advocated by some theologians in the anti-Berengar camp.[205] The fraction rite affects the visible form of bread but not the metaempirical bodily substance—as Thomas stresses elsewhere.[206] In addition, Thomas sees contained in the wheat bread, which presents the *propria materia* of the Eucharist, an allusion to the word from the Gospel of John: "Unless a grain of wheat falls into the earth and dies, it remains just a single grain" (Jn 12:24).[207] The fact that the liturgical norms of the Western Church require this wheat bread to be *unleavened* involves a reminiscence of the institution of the sacrament, which took place "on the first day of unleavened bread," according to the synoptics (Mt 26:17; Mk 14:12; Lk 22:7).[208] The *wine*, too, recalls the last supper and the "eschatological outlook" of the Lord as he departs from his disciples: "from now on I will not drink of the fruit of the vine" (Lk 22:18; Mt 26:29; see also Jn 15:1, "I am the true vine").

The nonverbal rites pointed out up to now remain completely at the level of an illustrative clarification of the Mass. There is a different sort of importance, however, that accrues to Thomas's earlier consideration, that the Passion of Christ is represented by the twofold material species of bread and wine, which symbolically express the separation of body and blood on the cross.[209] One may certainly state that, for Thomas, the representative making-present of Christ's suffering is distilled in a pregnant way right in the twofold consecration. He writes explicitly: "Our Lord's Passion is represented in the very consecration of this sacrament, in which the body ought not to be consecrated without the blood."[210] In particular, the consecration

---

aliud exterius gerens [gerente] ob recordationem sacrae passionis ad aram quod semel gestum est, cotidie immolatur agnus." See also Lanfranc, *Liber de corpore et sanguine Domini*, cap. XIII, in PL 150, 407–42, here 423: "Sacramenta enim illarum rerum quarum sacramenta sunt semper similitudinem gerunt, sicut in sacramento, de quo haec quaestio ventilatur, dum frangitur hostia, dum sanguis de calice in ora fidelium funditur, quid aliud quam Domini corporis in cruce immolatio eiusque sanguinis de latere effusio designatur?" By way of contrast, in the East we find as early as Ephrem the Syrian (d. 373) that the fraction rite is referred to the sacrificial death of Christ: "He [Christ] broke the bread with his hands to symbolize the sacrifice of his body" (*Hymn. de azym.* 2, 7 = Corpus Scriptorum Christianorum Orientalium Scriptores Syri 109, 4). For background, see Messner, *Zur Hermeneutik allegorischer Liturgieerklärung*, 302–6, who indicates that in Syriac the words for "to divide, to break bread" (*prs*) and "to spread out" (*pr's*) are written in the same way, for which reason it made sense linguistically speaking to refer the broken bread to the crucified one.

205. See Abbaudus, *De fractione corporis Christi* (PL 166, 1341–48).
206. See *S. th.* III, q. 77, a. 7.
207. *S. th.* III, q. 74, a. 3.
208. See *S. th.* III, q. 74, a. 4.
209. *S. th.* III, q. 74, a. 2 and a. 4 ad 2. See also *S. th.* III, q. 76, a. 2 ad 1: the twofold species of bread and wine is able to make present the separation of body and blood during the Passion: "dicendum quod quamvis totus Christus sit sub utraque specie, non tamen frustra. Nam primo quidem hoc valet ad repraesentandam passionem Christi, in qua seorsum fuit sanguis a corpore separatus, unde et in forma consecrationis sanguinis fit mentio de eius effusione." See also *S. th.* III, q. 79, a. 1.
210. *S. th.* III, q. 80, a. 12 ad 3: "repraesentatio Dominicae passionis agitur in ipsa consecratione huius sacramenti, in qua non debet corpus sine sanguine consecrari."

of the wine brings out the sacrificial dimension of Christ's suffering, which also makes clear that the consecratory formula spoken over the chalice expressly signifies the soteriological effect of the Passion.[211] Granting the doctrine of concomitance and its affirmation that the whole Christ is contained in each of the two Eucharistic species, still Christ is present differently under the species of bread than under the species of wine. Even the duality of the species represents at the sacramental level the separation of body and blood; but the double consecration intensifies this once more to the extent that it presents Christ in his condition immediately after his violent death on the cross. The ritual representation (*repraesentatio*) of Christ's Passion and the real presence of Christ effected by the consecration are intimately connected.

Thomas's Eucharistic theology has been accused of fueling an illegitimate narrowing of focus on the formula of consecration and thus getting bogged down in a conceptual and speculative treatment of the *mysterium fidei*.[212] But this accusation can hardly be maintained when one considers that, beyond the words of consecration, Thomas expressly discussed how these words are embedded in the liturgy. The division of the holy Mass, its individual components, and indeed its words and actions,[213] draw a short commentary from Thomas. This commentary, which does not take up a detailed explanation of the Mass, stands not in the center of the treatise on the Eucharist but at its end, and it would be false to shift it from its marginal position. In Scholasticism, consideration of the rite belongs to the canon of questions counted among those to be treated. At the same time, it is profitable not to overlook these passages in his theology. For under the auspices of *commemoratio*, the individual segments of the Eucharistic liturgy are commented upon.[214]

---

211. *S. th.* III, q. 78, a. 3 ad 2: "sanguis seorsum consecratus expresse passionem Christi repraesentat, ideo potius in consecratione sanguinis fit mentio de effectu passionis quam in consecratione corporis, quod est passionis subiectum." Similarly, see *S. th.* III, q. 78, a. 3 ad 7.

212. See Schmemann, *The Eucharist*, 37f., who criticizes the focus placed by scholastic theology on the formula of consecration, since it encouraged a separation between Eucharist and liturgy.

213. See *S. th.* III, q. 83, aa. 4 and 5. Prior to this, Thomas considers time and place (aa. 2 and 3).

214. For background, see J. Menessier, "L'idée du sacré et le culte d'après S. Thomas," *RSPhTh* 19 (1930): 63–82; J. Travers, *Valeur sociale de la liturgie d'après Thomas d'Aquin* (Paris: Cerf, 1946); J. Lécuyer, "Reflexions sur la théologie du culte selon Saint Thomas," *Revue Thomiste* 55 (1955): 339–62; L. G. Walsh, "Liturgy in the Theology of St. Thomas," *The Thomist* 38 (1974): 557–83; P. Nau, *Le mystère du Corps et du Sang du Seigneur. La messe d'après saint Thomas d'Aquin, son rite d'après l'historie* (Solesmes: Abbaye Saint-Pierre, 1976); D. Berger, *Thomas von Aquin und die Liturgie*, 2nd ed. (Cologne: Books on Demand, 2000); Candler, "Liturgically Trained Memory"; Th. Marschler, *Auferstehung und Himmelfahrt Christi*, 573–80. In his chapter "The Eucharistic Liturgy," A. Vonier limits himself to an elucidation of *S. th.* III, q. 83, a. 1 and waives commenting on the rite. See his *A Key to the Doctrine of the Eucharist* (Bethesda, Md.: Zaccheus Press, 2003), 159–64.

The Celebration of the Eucharist as *ars memoriae*—
The Explanation of the Rite in the *Summa theologiae*

The liturgy is a school of remembrance leading one into the mystery of faith. It is precisely to this mystagogical dimension of the liturgy that Thomas wants to point in his commentary on the rite of the Latin Mass as it was celebrated in the thirteenth century. We cannot forget that the *Summa theologiae* is a book with pedagogical intentions. For this reason, it is hardly accidental that Thomas rounds off his theology of the Eucharist with a commentary on the liturgy. Speculative penetration of the contents of faith and practical performance of the liturgy are ultimately not to be separated (*lex orandi—lex credendi*). It is no great feat to note this correlation within Thomas's own biography, which includes his having been familiarized with the liturgical inheritance of the Latin Church when he was a young oblate in the Benedictine monastery of Monte Cassino.[215] In his later Dominican life, he celebrated the Mass every day; what is more, his biographer attests to his extraordinary Eucharistic piety,[216] with the result that his theological teaching stands in tight correspondence with his life of faith. Theology and spirituality are not diastatically separated in his work.[217]

As his comments suggest,[218] Thomas seems to take as his point of departure the foundational form of the solemn Mass, the high Mass with deacon and subdeacon.[219] At the outset, he refers to the preeminent place of the sacrament of the Eucharist in the *nexus sacramentorum*: because the Eucharist contains the *totum mysterium nostrae salutis*, it is celebrated with greater solemnity (*cum maiore solemnitate*) than the other sacraments. "Watch your behavior when entering the house of the Lord," is the admonishing quotation Thomas takes from Eccl 5:1. Hence, some preparation is required in order to celebrate the mysteries worthily. His elucidations are divided into three parts, devoted first to the more remote preparation (from the Introit to the Oratio), then to the instruction in the faith (from the Epistle to the Creed), and finally to the celebration of the mystery (from Offertory to Communion).[220]

---

215. See Torrell, *Saint Thomas Aquinas*, vol. 1, 4f.
216. See the information in Berger, *Thomas von Aquin und die Liturgie*, 23–31.
217. See H. U. von Balthasar, "Theology and Sanctity," in *Explorations in Theology*, vol. 1: *The Word Made Flesh* (San Francisco: Ignatius Press, 1989), 181–209.
218. See especially *S. th.* III, q. 83, a. 4 ad 6, where the individual segments of the liturgy are assigned to the priest, the *ministri* (i.e., deacon and subdeacon), and the choir as representative of the faithful.
219. See Meyer, *Eucharistie*, 214.
220. In his division of the liturgical structure of the Mass, Thomas relies on the interpretation of Albert the Great, who divided the Mass into three parts, namely (1) *introitus*, (2) *instructio*, and (3) *oblatio*. See

Praeparatio One cannot approach the mystery unprepared. Through his mind and senses, man is prepared by words for the mystery of the Eucharist. This preparation includes four parts, each of which is described in terms of *commemoratio*. *Praeparatio* begins with praising God (*laus divina*) in the sung *Introitus*[221]—in accord with the words of the Psalm: *Sacrificium laudis honorificabit me, et illic iter quo ostendam illi salutare Dei* (Ps 50:23). The entrance song is usually sung from the Psalms or in connection with a Psalm, since the Psalms capture in the form of praise what sacred Scripture as a whole contains—a thought added by Thomas with reference to Dionysius.[222] By reciting the psalms, the individuals praying are taken up into the collective community of faith. It is the diachronic reference to the sacred text that makes possible the synchronic prayer of the believers.

The second part contains the recollection of present suffering (*commemoratio praesentis miseriae*), where divine mercy (*misericordia*) is implored in the recitation of the *Kyrie eleison*. Thomas is less focused on the origins of the *Kyrie* as an acclamation of Christ present in the community; instead, he relates the liturgical custom of praying the *Kyrie eleison* three times to the Father, Son, and Holy Spirit—perhaps a stretch for today's sensibilities—to the threefold affliction of ignorance, guilt, and punishment (*ignorantia, culpa, poena*). Such an interpretation has been described as an "arbitrary construction."[223] Less controversial is the Trinitarian interpretation, according to which naming the Father, Son, and Spirit is correlated with the three divine persons.[224]

After the *Kyrie*, the *Gloria in excelsis Deo* takes place, a *reminder of the future*, when it mentions the heavenly glory (*commemorat caelestam gloriam*) longed for by the faithful.[225] Here we want only to set down that in the liturgy—in a clear departure from classical conceptions of memory as ad-

---

Albert the Great, *Opera omnia*, vol. 38: *Distinctiones in sacramentum eucharistiae. Enarrationes in Apocalypsim S. Joannis*, ed. A. Borgnet (Paris: Vivès, 1899), 1–165, here 3. See also A. Franz, *Die Messe im deutschen Mittelalter* (Freiburg: Herder, 1902), 467.

221. Elsewhere, Thomas mentions in passing that the *Confiteor* is prayed before the Introit. See *S. th.* III, q. 83, a. 5 ad 1.

222. See *Eccl. Hier.*, cap. 3 (*Corpus Dionysiacum* II, Patristische Texte und Studien 36, ed. G. Heil and M. Ritter, 82– 84 = PG 3, 429f.).

223. Thus the commentary of the German Thomas-Ausgabe, vol. 30, 573.

224. Gregory the Great advocated a Trinitarian interpretation of the Kyrie. See *ep.* IX, 12 (CCL 140a, ed. D. Norberg, 574). Admittedly, the alternating call "Kyrie—Christe" is not original. Thus E. Peterson, *Heis theos. Epigraphische, formgeschichtliche und religionsgeschichtliche Untersuchungen* (Göttingen: Vandenhoeck & Ruprecht, 1926), 317 (a new edition in the collected works edited by B. Nichtweiss is currently in preparation).

225. Thomas also uses concepts of *commemoratio* in explaining when the Gloria is sung and when not: the Gloria, he writes, is sung only on feasts on which heavenly glory is commemorated (*in quibus commemoratur caelestis gloria*); it is omitted in Masses characterized by grave sorrow (*in officiis luctuosis*), to which it pertains to commemorate suffering (*quae ad commemorationem miseriae pertinent*). See *S. th.* III, q. 83, a. 4 c.

vanced in ancient rhetoric—a commemoration of future things is carried out; thus, the concept of *memoria* is not restricted to commemorating what is past but rather it also encompasses the eschatological dimension, in good biblical fashion.[226]

What follows is the last part of the *Praeparatio*, the collect. The priest performs the collect for the people, that they may be found worthy of so great a mystery, as it is laconically stated. Certainly included here is that the priest "gathers up" the silent prayers of the faithful and brings them before God in the collect (*collecta*). Catherine Pickstock describes this prayer, which concludes the opening part of the Mass, as "a prayer for emotional preparation, a preparation for preparation, a desire for there to be desire."[227]

Instructio   After the preparatory part, instruction for the faithful follows, a lesson, as it were, consisting essentially of readings from Scripture. The proclamation of the Word leads the faithful into the reality they are celebrating. Thomas says that this instruction of the faithful is put before the celebration of the Eucharist because the sacrament of the Eucharist presents the *mysterium fidei*. The important consideration of Christ's being present in the community in a special way during the proclamation of the Word recedes in Thomas's thought behind the motif of *instructio*. Subsequently, readings from the prophetic books and letters from the Apostle ensue, recited by the lector and subdeacon. Thereafter, the choir, representing the people, sings the so-called *Graduale*, which Thomas interprets allegorically as indicating the "progress of life." Following this is the *Alleluia*, which expresses the joy of the faithful (*exultatio spiritualis*). In grave and sorrowful Masses (*in officiis luctuosis*), a *Tractus* is sung, conveying spiritual groaning (*gemitus spirituale*).[228] These affective dispositions—joy and jubilation or groaning and trembling—should be evoked in the people by the preceding teaching.

The culmination of the faithful's instruction is finally the Gospel, in which the very teaching of Christ is contained. This is read aloud by the highest servers, the deacons. At this point, the Word of Christ himself is called to mind. The catechetical and didactic interpretation of the *liturgia verbi*, which dominates the explanation of the rite, opens up indirectly to an anamnetic point of view when Thomas cites a word of Christ from John's Gospel: "If I tell the truth, why do you not believe me?" (Jn 8:46). The word of truth called to mind in the reading of the Gospel demands an answer.

---

226. See Candler, "Liturgically Trained Memory," 438; Wahle, *Gottes-Gedenken*, 76–90.
227. C. Pickstock, "Thomas Aquinas and the Eucharist," *Modern Theology* 15 (1999): 159–80, here 169.
228. The commentary of the German Thomas-Ausgabe (v. 30, 460) makes the differentiation that the *Tractus* does not necessarily exhibit a penitential or sorrowful character.

Through the recitation of the Creed, the faithful people testify publicly their affirmation of Christ's teaching. The individual "I" of the many consolidates itself into the ecclesial "we" of the confessing community of prayer and faith. It is noteworthy that Thomas does not make express mention of the homily, although he belongs to the *Ordo Praedicatorum*. This could be an indication that the homily had already been separated from the liturgy of the Mass in the thirteenth century.[229] The distribution of liturgical roles is similarly notable: the readings and Gospel were not proclaimed by the priest but by the subdeacon and deacon. According to Thomas, this is a sign "that this teaching was proclaimed to the people by the servants sent by God."[230]

The sequence of readings recapitulates the movement of salvation history, which culminates in the Incarnation of God in Jesus Christ. The composition of readings takes place according to the stipulations of the liturgical calendar, which structures time as a time of salvation and recommends individual events and people worthy of the Church's remembrance. Thomas suggests only indirectly that it is the present Christ who speaks to the congregation through the liturgy of the word. According to his pedagogical and didactic accentuation of the liturgy of the word as *instructio*, the faithful should learn to relate their time to the time of salvation. As the answer to the word spoken by the readings, the Creed marks the conclusion of the preparatory part.[231]

Celebratio After these explications of the liturgy of the word, which do not go any further into the specific presence of Jesus Christ in the proclaimed word, Thomas discusses the celebration of the sacrament in a stricter sense; here, the priest now plays a central role, while the liturgical role of the faithful celebrating along with the priest remains by and large unconsidered. At the outset, we find the meaningful statement that the mystery is "offered as a sacrifice, and consecrated and received as a sacrament."[232] Accordingly, the ritual representation of Christ's suffering in the act of oblation, the somatic

229. For background, see H. B. Meyer, *Eucharistie*, 233–36. There we also find related: "More and more frequently, however, one preached *outside of the Mass*, since the mendicant orders were forbidden to preach during the parish Masses" (ibid. 235).

230. *S. th.* III, q. 83, a. 4 ad 6.

231. From today's vantage point, one might see at work here a problematic devaluation of the *liturgia verba* in favor of the *liturgia eucharistica*; instead of attributing a merely preparatory character to the Word of God in the readings, one must certainly follow *Sacrosanctum Conilium* 7 in acknowledging the specific presence of Jesus Christ in the medium of the word more strongly than Thomas does. Anyway, it seems to me that the *particula veri* lies in the fact that, through the hearing of the Word of God, an introduction into the Eucharistic encounter with Christ takes place, which is then sacramentally concentrated in the reception of communion.

232. *S. th.* III, q. 83, a. 4: "Sic igitur populo praeparato et instructo acceditur ad celebrationem mysterii, quod quidem et offertur ut sacrificium et consecratur et sumitur ut sacramentum."

real presence in the gifts of bread and wine as a result of the consecration, and the reception of communion by the faithful belong intimately together. From this intimate association of elements, Thomas then draws the division of the liturgy, which begins with (1) the offering of the gifts (*oblatio*), then transitions into (2) the consecration of these gifts brought forward (*consecratio oblatae materiae*), in order finally to attain its goal in (3) the reception of the Eucharist (*perceptio*). Thomas also then sees the division of the liturgy as stemming from this intimate association.

In his commentary, Thomas emphasizes the interior disposition and brings into play—*en passant*—a wide spectrum of affective qualities. At the *Offertorium*, the praise contained in the offertory song should express first the *joy* of those offering. In the gifts, they bring themselves to the sacrificial table and inscribe themselves, so to speak, in the self-giving movement of Christ. Bread and wine, prepared from many grains of wheat and many grapes, are a symbol of the offering congregation;[233] in contrast, the *oratio sacerdotalis*, that is, the silent priestly prayer, has the function of *appeal*, that the sacrificial gifts of the people be pleasing to God.

Then, the setting of the actual act of consecration is taken into consideration, at which point it is worth remarking that Thomas designates *the whole canon* as *consecratio*, even if he simultaneously emphasizes that the actual consecration takes place solely through the words of institution.[234] First, the people are called to devotion in the Preface (*excitatur populus ad devotionem*). In the opening dialogue between priest and people, the *Sursum corda* presents the exhortation to let go of all thoughts regarding mundane concerns; in response, *Habemus ad Dominum*, indicates recollecting oneself in order to give oneself to God.[235] Thomas does not expressly mention that this concentration on God in the Preface is expressed in thanksgiving, which is performed *per Christum nostrum Dominum*;[236] for this reason, the reproach has been brought against Thomas that he offers a purely psychological explanation of the preface.[237] But without thanksgiving for the

---

233. See *S. th.* III, q. 74, a. 1; q. 75, a. 2.

234. *S. th.* III, q. 83, a. 4 ad 1.

235. In *S. th.* III, q. 83, a. 4 ad 5, Thomas appeals explicitly to Cyprian, who already in the middle of the third century (ca. 252/53) explicated the *Sursum corda* as follows: "Cogitatio omnis carnalis et saecularis abscedat nec quicquam animus quam id solum cogitet quod precatur. Ideo et sacerdos ante orationem praefatione praemissa parat fratrum mentes, dicendo: 'Sursum corda,' ut dum respondet plebs: 'Habemus ad Dominum,' admoneatur nihil aliud se quam Deum cogitare debere" (idem, *domin. orat.*, c. 31 [Corpus Scriptorum Ecclesiasticorum Latinorum 3, 289]). See also Jungmann, *Missarum Sollemnia*, vol. 2, 133–40.

236. On this point, see Jungmann, *Missarum Sollemnia*, vol. 2, 152, who underscores, in view of the formula *per Christum Dominum nostrum*, that the tremendous distance separating man from God is bridged by the mediatorship of Christ.

237. See the commentary of the German Thomas-Ausgabe, vol. 30, 574.

salvific deeds enacted, the praise breaking out in the *Sanctus* would remain incomprehensible. In the hallowing of the divine name,[238] the people gathered[239] join in with the heavenly choirs of angels (see Is 6:3)—as Thomas explicitly notes[240]—and praise with devotion the divinity of Christ, while in the *Benedictus* his humanity is doxologically extolled.

Thereafter, Thomas takes an extremely brief look at the canon, which in the thirteenth century was already prayed silently by the priest.[241] The silence of the people, who do not actively take part in the prayer of the canon, is explained by Thomas with the indication, certainly not unproblematic, that the oblation and consecration (*oblatio et consecratio*) involve only the priest.[242] He does not comment upon the prayer for acceptance, *Te igitur*, instead stressing only that the priest remembers the whole Church (*ecclesia universalis*) and the "authorities," and thereafter he also includes any who offer the sacrifice, as well as those for whom the sacrifice is offered. Accordingly, the "offering of sacrifice" always has an advocative function as well, which benefits those absent and the dead.[243] After this, the priest remembers the saints in the *Communicantes* and asks their intercession for protection. With this invocation of their names, it becomes clear at the same time that the *communio sanctorum* encompasses not only the living—an aspect that Thomas admittedly explores no further. Instead, he lays out that the priest concludes the petitions by asking that this sacrifice be salutary *for all*.

Subsequent to this, there is the transition to the consecration itself, which is preceded by the prayer *Quam oblationem*. One can certainly interpret this prayer preceding the actual act of consecration as an "implicit epiclesis";[244] even Thomas seems to strengthen this construal, for he says that in

---

238. Already Tertullian (*or.* 3, Corpus Scriptorum Ecclesiasticorum Latinorum 20, ed. Reiferscheid– A. Wissowa, 182) establishes a connection between the petition in the Our Father, *Sanctificetur nomen tuum*, and the *Sanctus* acclamation in the Eucharistic liturgy, in which the faithful participate as *angelorum candidati*, as he formulates it.

239. This point is noteworthy, since Jungmann takes as his point of departure that in the thirteenth century, the singing of the *Sanctus* was already delegated to a special choir of clerics. See idem, *Missarum Sollemnia*, vol. 2, 159.

240. Angels and men make up equally the *corpus Christi mysticum*. See S. *th.* III, q. 8, a. 4 c: "Ad unum finem qui est gloria divinae fruitionis ordinantur et homines et angeli. Unde corpus ecclesiae mysticum non solum consistit ex hominibus sed etiam ex angelis. Totius autem huius multidudinis Christus est caput."

241. See Meyer, *Eucharistie*, 218: "The priest speaks the Eucharistic prayer ... in the middle of the altar, and this he does *in a quiet voice* (with the exception of the Preface with Sanctus and Benedictus, the words 'Nobis quoque peccatoribus,' and the concluding formula of the doxology, 'Per omnia saecula saeculorum'); this custom had been established almost everywhere since the early Middle Ages."

242. See S. *th.* III, q. 83, a. 4 ad 6.

243. See also S. *th.* III, q. 83, a. 4 ad 3.: "Eucharistia est sacramentum *totius ecclesiasticae unitatis*; et ideo specialiter in hoc sacramento, magis quam in aliis, debet fieri mentio *de omnibus* quae pertinent ad salutem totius Ecclesiae" (emphasis added).

244. Jungmann, *Missarum sollemnia*, vol. 2, 235–38, here 238: "The formula presents the transformative petition or—getting to the essence of the matter—the *transformative epiclesis*."

the *Quam oblationem* the priest prays for the effect of the consecration (*consecrationis effectum*).[245] In the *Qui pridie*, there takes place the actual conversion of bread and wine into the flesh and blood of Jesus Christ. After recalling the night of the last supper in the form of a *narrative*, the *verba testamenti* are recited by the priest *in persona Christi*. They encompass first of all the summons to receive, *Accipite et manducate*—a prescriptive speech act—and then the actual words of consecration—a performative speech act effecting what it signifies. Given the oft-repeated charge that Western theology is forgetful of the Spirit, it is worth noting that, according to Thomas, the consecration is definitely to be understood as a pneumatic event. With reference to the *filioque*, he explains in his *Sentences* commentary that Christ's action in the Eucharist is through the Holy Spirit. On the question of whether one can attribute transubstantiation to the Holy Spirit, he answers negatively: it is attributed to Christ, since he is at once priest and sacrifice. But he adds immediately that it is the Holy Spirit through whom Christ works.[246] The observations concerning the following segments of the canon—*Unde et memores, Supra quae*,[247] *Supplices*,[248] *Memento, Nobis quoque*—are hardly more than a list. Here, too, the main point is that the canon presents an act of *commemoratio*, where the commemoration refers not only to past salvific deeds and their redemptive meaning for the present but also to the expectation of coming glory, the foretaste of which is presented by the Eucharist.

245. To the objection that the *Quam oblationem* is superfluous as a prayer over the gifts, since the sacrament will be worked *per certitudinem* by divine power, Thomas responds firstly that the effective power of the *verba sacramentalia* is not at all an automatic thing—it can be most certainly be prevented by the intention of the priest. Also, it is not fitting to ask something of God when one knows with full certainty that he will do it. Finally, Thomas offers an interpretation of the *Quam oblationem*: the prayer is not directed at the fulfillment of the consecration but rather at its becoming fruitful for the faithful. Not without reason, therefore, does it say: *ut nobis corpus et sanguis fiat*. Thomas attempts to undergird this interpretation with an exegesis of the five attributes of an oblation—*benedictam, adscriptam, ratam, rationabilem, acceptabilem,* which refer back to the reflections of Paschasius Radbertus (*De corpore et sanguine Domini*, cap. 12; CCM XVI, ed. B. Paulus, 79, 56–62: "Rogamus autem hanc *oblationem benedictam* per quam nos benedicamur, *adscriptam* per quam nos omnes in caelo conscribamur, *ratam* per quam *in uisceribus Christi* censeamur, *rationabilem* per quam a bestiali sensu exuamur, *acceptabilemque facerer dignetur,* quatinus et nos per hoc quia in nobis displicuimus, acceptabiles in eius unico Filio simus"). See *S. th.* III, q. 83, a. 4 ad 7.

246. *In IV Sent.*, d. 10, exp. textus: "Appropriatur Filio sicut operanti, quia ipse est sacerdos et hostia; Spiritui autem sancto sicut quo operatur, quia ipse est virtus de illo exiens ad sanandum, *Luc.* VI, 19."

247. On this point, see also *S. th.* III, q. 83, a. 4 ad 8. The objection holds that, given the sublimity of Christ's sacrifice, it is unfitting to recall the Old Testament sacrifices of Abel, Abraham, and Melchizedek. Thomas responds that, considering the devotion of the one sacrificing, the sacrifices of the Old Testament were most agreeable to God, for which reason the prayer of the priest in the *Supra quae*—that God might accept the sacrifice as he did that of Abel, Abraham, and Melchizedek—is indeed fitting, considering the devotion of the one sacrificing.

248. On this point, see also *S. th.* III, q. 83, a. 4 ad 9, where Thomas draws on Revelation 8:4 to connect the priest's prayer—that the angel might carry the sacrifice to the exalted altar before the face of divine majesty—to the *corpus Christi mysticum* and its prayers. In Thomas's eschatological interpretation, however, the exalted altar is either the *ecclesia triumphans*, to which we asked to be joined, or God himself, in whom we hope to partake.

In the *Pater noster*, with its well-known petition for the gift of daily bread, the faithful people are prepared to receive the sacrament (*panem nostrum quotidianum da nobis hodie*).[249] Likewise, those gathered are predisposed by the kiss of peace given during the *Agnus Dei* as a sign of reciprocal forgiveness; this corresponds to the fact that the sacrament of the Eucharist is a sign of unity and peace.[250] Thereafter, the distribution of communion takes place. First, the priest receives and then he gives to the others what he himself received, so that those gathered around the table of the Lord become what they are: the body of Christ (*corpus Christi mysticum*). Giving thanks for the gifts received makes up the conclusion of the celebration, with the people's post-communion singing and the final priestly prayer articulating this gratitude.

The liturgy as *ars memoriae* does not remain at the level of cognitive content which is called to mind; it is rather productive, in that it establishes a bond between communicants in virtue of communion with Christ. The term Thomas uses nearly as a leit motif in explaining the rite is *commemoratio*. Recollection is here recollection *with* others—a *commemoratio* that distills itself in the act of communion, in the incorporation of the one recollected who gave himself as gift: through the *manducatio* of the transformed gifts, believers become members in the *corpus Christi mysticum*. Holy Communion establishes communion between Christ and the faithful as members of his body. To the extent that the Church gathers around the altar to remember, "memory becomes truly political by re-membering the formerly broken body of Christ."[251] Now we must go into this aspect briefly.

Eucharist: *communio* and *viaticum*

The Eucharist is a *memoriale passionis Christi*. To be sure, it is not exhausted by the ritual making-present of Christ's sacrifice, but includes as well a communion-building and eschatological dimension.[252] Thomas clarified this dimension earlier in his reflections on the name of the Eucharistic sacrament.[253] There he asserts that the Eucharist is called "sacrifice" (*sacrificium*)

---

249. On this point, see J. A. Jungmann, "Das Pater noster im Kommunionritus," *ZKTh* 58 (1934): 552ff.
250. See *S. th.* III, q. 67, a. 2; q. 73, a. 3 ad 3; and q. 79, a. 1.
251. Candler, "Liturgically Trained Memory," 440.
252. Regarding the motif of *corpus mysticum*, see the remarks of H. de Lubac, "Memorial, Anticipation, Present," in *Corpus Mysticum: The Church and the Eucharist in the Middle Ages*, trans. Gemma Simmonds, CJ, with Richard Price and Christopher Stephens (Notre Dame, Ind.: University of Notre Dame Press, 2006), 55–74, esp. note 61.
253. See *S. th.* III, q. 73, a. 4 c: "Respondeo dicendum quod hoc sacramentum habet triplicem significationem. Unam quidem respectu praeteriti: inquantum scilicet est commemorativum Dominicae passionis, quae fuit verum sacrificium, ut supra dictum est [sc. q. 48, a. 3]. Et secundum hoc nominatur *sacrificium*.—

insofar as it refers back to the cause of our redemption. As explained, Thomas sees in Christ's voluntary self-sacrifice the fulfillment of the old Law realized, and this in a threefold way: first, *morally*, inasmuch as charity toward God and man is lived with complete dedication even unto death on the cross; second, in a *cultic and ceremonial way*, since the prescriptions of the old Law are definitively taken up into and fulfilled in the event of the Passion; and third, *juridically*, in that here an innocent man freely made satisfaction (*satisfactio*) for the sins of all men and thus paid the price of redemption for all (*redemptio*).[254]

Besides the *signum rememorativum*, which is concentrated on the suffering and death of Christ, Thomas likewise sees in the Eucharist a *signum demonstrativum*, which refers to Church unity as an effect, the *unitas mystici corporis*, into which men are incorporated through the sacrament. By communicating with Christ the head, they become members of his body. Thus, the Eucharist is also called *communio* or *synaxis*.[255] Thomas cites John of Damascus here, who aptly expressed both aspects of community, the vertical with Christ and the horizontal with the faithful among each other: "The Eucharist is called communion [i.e., community] because we communicate with Christ through it, both because we partake of His flesh and Godhead, and because we communicate with and are united to one another through it."[256] Thus the Church as *corpus Christi mysticum* exists on account of the participation of the faithful in the *corpus Christi verum*. The charge that scholastic Eucharistic theology began focusing on the words of consecration and the sacrificial character in a problematic way, while at the same time failing to recognize the Eucharist's role in building up the Church—all of this is in need of revision, given the foregoing considerations.[257] Thomas

---

Aliam autem significationem habet respectu rei praesentis, scilicet ecclesiasticae unitatis, cui homines congregantur per hoc sacramentum. Et secundum hoc nominatur *communio* vel *synaxis*: dicit enim Damascenus IV libro [*De fide orthodoxa* IV, c. 13 = PG 94, 1153], quod dicitur *communio, quia communicamus per ipsam Christo; et quia participamus eius carne et deitate; et quia communicamus et unimur ad invicem per ipsam.*—Tertiam significationem habet respectu futuri: inquantum scilicet hoc sacramentum est praefigurativum fruitionis Dei, qui erit in patria. Et secundum hoc dicitur *viaticum*: quia hoc praebet nobis viam illuc perveniendi."

254. See M. Levering, "Israel and the Shape of Thomas Aquinas's Soteriology," *The Thomist* 63 (1999): 65–72.

255. See the theological-historical information regarding this motif in H. de Lubac, *Corpus mysticum*, 17ff. The liturgy as "sacrament of the assembly" (*synaxis*) is impressively unfolded by Schmemman, *Eucharistie*, 29–48. His criticism, however, that scholastic dogmatics "simply overlooked the ecclesiological dimension of the Eucharist and thus also forgot the Eucharistic dimension of ecclesiology, of the doctrine of the Church," is not to be so strictly maintained when it comes to Thomas.

256. *S. th.* III, q. 73, a. 4 c.

257. See also G. Emery, "Le fruit ecclesial de l'eucharistie chez S. Thomas d'Aquin," *Nova et Vetera* 4 (1997): 25–40; G. Geenen, "L'adage 'Eucharistia est sacramentum ecclesiasticae unitatis' dans les oeuvres et la doctrine de S. Thomas d'Aquin," *La Eucaristia y la Paz. Congreso eucarístico internacional (1952). Sesiones de estudio*, vol. 1 (Barcelona: Planas, 1953), 275–81.

Aquinas characterizes the Eucharist as the "sacrament of unity." In the celebration of the Eucharist, the Church reveals what she is; thus, the Eucharist is a *signum demonstrativum* of ecclesial *communio*.

It was already indicated that the species of bread and wine signify the communion of the faithful. This symbolic function remains even after the consecration, with the subject-less accidents of bread and wine. As wheat bread is made from many grains and wine pressed from many grapes, so the mystical body of Christ is made up of many members, who stand in close connection with their head, Jesus Christ.[258] This connection with Christ is expressly accomplished by the act of receiving communion, the *manducatio*. In a little-heeded passage of the *Sentences* commentary, Thomas remarks that it was fitting that the sacrament of the Eucharist was instituted in the form of a meal (*in figura cibi*). He undergirds this remark with a reflection drawing out the specific characteristic of the sense of taste. In contrast to the other sensory organs, which are reached by sensible objects only through external mediation, the sense of taste enters into immediate contact with its object. In tactile perception, it is a matter of certain impressions, such as the temperature or superficial properties of an object; when eating, however, a real unification with the consumed object is carried out. The sense of taste (*gustus*) thus distinguishes itself by accomplishing a direct unification with the perceived object. Eating is an act of incorporation, in which the meal is assimilated to the organism of the eater.[259] Of course, Thomas immediately highlights a decisive difference between communion and normal eating. The Eucharistic body of the Lord is precisely *not* transformed into the human organism of the one receiving communion; rather, it is the case that one who participates in the Eucharistic meal is incorporated into the mystical body of Christ.[260] This difference from a normal meal was already held by Augustine, when in the *Confessions* he put the words into Christ's mouth: "It is not you who

---

258. This is emphasized time and again by Thomas. See *S. th.* III, q 73, aa. 1 and 2; q. 74, aa. 1, 4 and 5; q. 75, a. 8 ad 1; q. 77, a. 6; q. 79, a. 1.

259. See *In IV Sent.*, d. 7, q. 1, a. 3 (n. 76): "Et ideo convenienter in figura cibi hoc sacramentum institutum est; quia inter alios sensus solus tactus est cui suum sensibile realiter coniungitur, similitudinibus tantum sensibilium ad alios sensus per medium pervenientibus. Gustus autem tactus quidam est; et inter alia quae ad tactum pertinent, solus cibus est qui agit per coniunctionem sui ad cibatum, quia nutriens et nutritum fit unum; alia tangibilia agunt efficiendo aliquas impressiones in eo quod tangitur, sicut patet de calido, de frigido et hujusmodi." See also *In IV Sent.*, d. 9, a. 1 (n. 16).

260. See *In IV Sent.*, d. 7, q. 1, a. 3 (n. 77): "Et ideo cum omne sacramentum in figura alicujus rei sensibilis proponi debeat, convenienter sacramentum in quo ipsum Verbum incarnatum nobis conjugendum continetur, proponitur nobis in figura cibi, non quidem convertendi in nos per suam conjunctionem ad nos, sed potius sua conjunctione nos in se ipsum convertens." See also *In Matth XXVI*, l. III (n. 2173): "differt iste cibus ab aliis cibis, quia alii cibi convertuntur in corpus nostrum: unde si Christus ita converteretur, irreverentia esset. Sed non est sic, immo e converso."

transforms me into you, like a meal into your body, but rather you will be transformed into me.—*Non tu me mutabis in te, sicut cibum carnis tuae, sed tu mutaberis in me.*"²⁶¹

On account of unification with Christ, the Eucharist is the sacrament of charity (*sacramentum caritatis*). As friendship between God and man, *caritas* is intensified in the Eucharistic *communio* in a unique way. To be sure, the meaning of the Eucharist would be abbreviated if one were to limit it to the level of an individual relation to Christ. Belonging to Christ the head is something accomplished in receiving the consecrated gifts of the Eucharist, and yet it also unites the receiver with all the other faithful who are members of his body.²⁶² Thus, in addition to the personal dimension, the Eucharist always includes the ecclesial dimension of unifying believers with each other in Christ: "*Eucharistia est sacramentum unitatis ecclesiasticae, quae attenditur secundum hoc, quod multi sunt unum in Christo.*"²⁶³

At the same time, the Eucharist is not exhausted in this function of building up the Church, for through the gift of communion with the exalted Christ, it simultaneously transcends the time of the Church. Therefore, Thomas takes up a third common designation for the Eucharist—*viaticum*—and relates it to the eschatological consummation, in which the sacramental mediation of salvation will give way to the immediate vision of God. As *signum prognosticum*, the Eucharist signifies in an anticipatory way the enjoyment of God *in patria*. It offers a foretaste of future glory and is called *viaticum* because it sustains the *homo viator* in attaining the goal of eternal bliss. As the manna sustained the people of Israel on the way through the wilderness to reach the promised land, so the Eucharistic provisions sustain the faithful up to the threshold of death. As the Corpus Christi hymn *Sacris solemniis* puts it: "*Per tuas semitas duc nos quo tendimus, / ad lucem quam inhabitas*—Along your paths, guide us whither we strive / toward the light in which you live." And elsewhere, the Eucharist is nearly depicted as the key that opens the gate to heaven (*ianua caelestis*) for the faithful:²⁶⁴ "*O salutaris hostia, quae caeli pandis ostium*—O salutary sacrifice, which does unlock the gate of heaven," echoes the words of the

---

261. See Augustine, *Conf.* VII, c. 10.
262. See *In IV Sent.*, d. 8, q. 1, a. 3 s.c.: "Ad perfectionem corporis exigitur quod membra capiti conjugantur. Sed per hoc sacramentum membra Ecclesiae suo capiti conjuguntur; unde Ioan. VI,57 dicitur: *Qui manducat carnem meam et bibit meum sanguinem, in me manet et ego in eo.*"
263. *S. th.* III, q. 80, a. 4 c.
264. See *In IV Sent.*, d. 8, q. 1, a. 1, qua 3 (n. 35): "realiter continet hoc quo janua caeli nobis aperta est, scilicet sanguinem Christi." It should be noticed here that the metaphor of the door represents the eschatological perspective.

hymn *Verbum supernum prodiens*.²⁶⁵ In the antiphon for second vespers on the feast of Corpus Christi, Thomas articulated all three temporal dimensions of the Eucharist in a poetically pregnant way:

O sacred banquet, in which Christ is received,
the memory of his Passion is recalled, the soul is filled with grace,
and the pledge of future glory is given to us. Alleluia.²⁶⁶

---

265. See also *S. th.* III, q. 79, a. 2, s.c.: "If any man eat of this bread, he shall live forever" (Jn 6:52). Thus one of the biblical references that makes clear the Eucharist's eschatological dimension.

266. *Officium de festo corporis Christi ad mandatum Urbani Papae IV dictum Festum instituentis*, in idem, *Opuscula theologica II*, ed. Raymondo M. Spiazzi (Turin-Rome: Marietti, 1954), 275–81, here 280: "O sacrum convivium! In quo Christus sumitur, recolitur memoria passionis eius, mens impletur gratia, et futurae gloriae nobis pignus datur. Alleluia."

PART B

THE POETIC DISTILLATION OF EUCHARISTIC THEOLOGY IN THE HYMNS

4

Preliminaries

In the *Autos sacramentales* written by the Spanish playwright Calderón de la Barca (1600–1681), there is a scene in which the sibyls summon the holy Doctors of the Church, Sts. Augustine, Ambrose, Jerome, Gregory the Great, and Thomas Aquinas, to a singing competition.[1] The winner of the prize will be whoever most felicitously sets to verse a previously assigned theme on the mysteries of the cross or the Eucharist. Thomas composes his hymn *Pange lingua* for the contest[2]—and for this he receives the distinction of a golden sun decorating his chest, the "symbol of illuminated knowledge and ardent love for God."[3] In Dante's *Divina Comedia* as well, Thomas figures as a poet. On his visionary journey through Paradise, and with Beatrice and St. Bernard as his guides, Dante comes upon the "song of lights," which fascinates him extraordinarily yet at the same time remains opaque to his mind. None other than Thomas Aquinas appears as interpreter and explains to Dante which lights stand for which figures in the history of theology and devotional practice. At the same time, the *Divine Comedy* has ready to hand a punch line that gets at the rivalry between the two mendicant orders, when an entire *Canto* is devoted to having the Dominican Thomas sing of the greatness of St. Francis of Assisi, while Bonaventure, the Minister General of the Franciscans, is made to do

---

1. See Calderón de la Barca, *Geistliche Festspiele*, vol. 7, trans. and ed. H. Lorinser (Regensburg: Manz, 1888), 223–333: "The Holy Parnass" (*El sacro Parnasso*), esp. 298–323.
2. See Aquinas, *Officium de festo corporis Christi ad mandatum Urbani Papae IV dictum Festum instituentis*, in: idem, *Opuscula theologica II*, ed. R. M. Spiazzi (Rome: Marietti, 1954), 275–81, here 275f.
3. See M. Grabmann, "Die Theologie der eucharistischen Hymnen des hl. Thomas von Aquin," *Der Katholik* 82 (1902): 385–99, here 385. In the speech accompanying the handing over of awards, an allusion is made not only to Aquinas's reticence, attested in legends and worked out according to the topos of the dumb ox, who bellowed the truth of the faith out into the world. In addition, the symbol of the sun as a trophy is itself explained, when we read: "The son of justice / has commissioned him / to write of him, they say / and thus it is very fitting that now / a golden son has become / the reward for this son." Calderón, *Geistliche Festspiele*, vol. 7, 323. Finally, it is to be recalled that, according to legend, Christ said to Thomas in a vision: "Bene de me scripsisti."

the same for St. Dominic.[4] For both Calderón and Dante—and this is the only point to take away here—Thomas Aquinas is indeed a respectable poet. And James Joyce, one of the most significant authors of the twentieth century, joined in this assessment.[5]

Today, in contrast, Aquinas's name appears to stand rather for the highest form of scholastic thinking, for subtle conceptual distinctions and speculations into a metaphysics of substance. That he simultaneously emerged as a poet of Eucharistic hymns, whose linguistic power and sonority inspired the setting of his poetry to music by such composers as Palestrina, Orlando di Lasso, Mendelssohn-Bartholdy, Anton Bruckner, and Paul Hindemith[6]—all of this is less well known or even totally forgotten.[7] Still, his hymns have characterized Eucharistic devotion far beyond the Middle Ages; even to this day, they are present in the liturgical life of the Catholic Church, even if with decreasing frequency. In contrast with the approximately 4,500 sequences that were removed from the official books by the liturgical reform of the Tridentine Council,[8] *Lauda Sion*, for example, is among the four sequences that passed unscathed through the floodgates of the 1570 reform.[9] Let it be remarked only tangentially that in the meantime there are only three sequences remaining, since the *Dies irae* was eliminated from the Missale Romanum of 1970 because of its pronounced theology of final judgment.[10]

---

4. See Dante Alighieri, *Divina Commedia* [Eng.: *Paradise*, trans. Anthony Esolen (New York: Modern Libary, 2004)], Paradiso X–XII.

5. See James Joyce, *The Portrait of the Artist as a Young Man* (New York: Penguin Books, 1967), 333.

6. See A. Heinz, "Lauda Sion," *LThK* 6, 3rd ed. (1997) 680–81.

7. See the chapter "Der unmusische Thomas," in O. H. Pesch, *Thomas von Aquin*, 343–52. A different perspective: A. Stock, *Poetische Dogmatik. Christologie*, vol. 3: *Leib und Leben* (Paderborn: Schöningh, 1998), 305–24.

8. Most of these sequences are collected in volumes 7–10, 24, 37, 39, 40, 42, 44, 53–55 of the *Analecta Hymnica Medii Aevi*, 55 vols. (Leipzig, 1886–1922).

9. The three other sequences are *Victimae paschalis laudes* (Easter); *Veni, Sancte Spiritus* (Pentecost); and *Dies irae* (first it was the sequence of the first Sunday of Advent, and then beginning with the Missale Romanum of 1570, it became the sequence for the celebration of funeral Masses). The *Dies irae* was removed from the Missale Romanum of 1970, though it nevertheless found its way into the Liturgy of the Hours of 1971, where it can be used, broken up into three parts, as the hymn for the Office of Readings, Lauds, and Vespers on the ferial days during the last week of the liturgical year. On this point, see now the worthwhile commentary by A. Stock, *Lateinische Hymnen* (Berlin: Verlag der Weltreligionen, 2012).

10. See A. Stock, *Poetische Dogmatik. Christologie*, vol. 4: *Figuren* (Paderborn: Schöningh, 2001), 196–209.

On the Historical Background of the Eucharistic Hymns

Before interpreting the Eucharistic hymns of Thomas Aquinas, it seems sensible first of all to illuminate briefly the backstory of the solemnity of Corpus Christi, which forms the context in which these hymns are to be discussed. The feast traces back to a movement in the diocese of Liège. The increased adoration of the Blessed Sacrament of the Altar that arose there in the thirteenth century can be appropriately understood only as a reaction to the controversy concerning the real presence brought about by the Cathars and the Albigensians. In addition, Berengar of Tours and his spiritual interpretation of the last supper must also be seen as a negative foil to the increased adoration of the Eucharistic host. The Eucharistic movement in Liège traced back to the initiative of pious women's groups, especially the Beguines and St. Juliana of Liège (d. 1258).[11] In 1209, Juliana, a canoness regular, began to have repeated visions in which she saw a moon featuring a fracture on the edge. In the *Vita Juliana*, we find it written: "When Juliana gave herself to prayer in her youth, a great and wonderful sign appeared to her. She saw the moon in its splendor, but on the edge was a small crack. She gazed upon it for a long time and knew not at all what it ought to mean. And so she besought the Lord fervently to reveal to her the meaning. He revealed to her that the moon represented the Church, but the dark area at the edge intimated that a feast day was still missing, one which he wished to see celebrated by all the faithful. It was his will that the institution of his Most Holy Sacrament receive its own proper celebration, for the increase of faith, which was now abating at the end of the world, and for the grace-filled progress of the elect; and all of this more than on Holy Thursday alone, when the Church was already occupied solely with the washing of the feet and the commemoration of his Passion. What on ordinary days suffers from neglect on account of too little devotion and carelessness is to be made up on this day. When Christ had revealed this to the virgin, he charged her with the task of beginning this celebration and proclaiming his instruction to the world."[12] Starting in 1240, the feast day of the Holy Sacrament was celebrated in Beguine

---

11. See B. Henze, "Juliana von Lüttich," *LThK* 5, 3rd ed. (1997) 1075–76; J. Cottiaux, *Sainte Juliana de Cornillon, promotrice de la Fête-Dieu. Son pays, son temps, son message* (Lüttich: Carmel de Cornillon, 1991); M. Rubin, *Corpus Christi: The Eucharist in Late Medieval Culture* (Cambridge: Cambridge University Press, 1991); K. Schreiner, "Juliana von Lüttich (1193–1258). Eine Frau 'in den Liliengärten des Herrn,'" *Zur Debatte* 38 (2008): 41–43.

12. Cited from P. Browe, *Die Verehrung der Eucharistie im Mittelalter* (Munich: Sankt Meinrad Reprintverlag, 1933), 71f. See also the translation by B. Newman, *The Life of Juliana of Mont-Cornillon* (*Matrologia Latina* 13) (Toronto: Cistercian Publications, 1990), 83.

communities, and in 1246 Bishop Robert of Liège decreed—against some resistance—that the "Feast of the Holy Sacrament" was to be celebrated in his bishopric on the Thursday after the octave of the Trinity. This he ordered with the explicit intention of refuting Eucharistic heresy (*ad confutandam haereticorum insaniam*), rectifying a lack of devotion, and commemorating gratefully and joyfully the institution of the sacrament.[13] Hugo of Saint-Cher also advocated for an introduction of the feast in his role as cardinal legate, admittedly with little success.

In 1261, Jacques Pantaléon—who had been the archdeacon in Lüttich from 1243 to 1248, and who also stood in close communication with the Beguines as their spiritual director—was elevated to the papacy. Taking up the name Urban IV, he promulgated the Bull *Transiturus de hoc mundo*[14] on August 11, 1264, which introduced the *Festum Sanctissimi Corporis Christi* as a new feast day for the whole Latin Church. It is suspected that this directive was occasioned in part by the Eucharistic miracle of Bolsena.[15] It is said that in 1263, a German priest was saying the Mass and he doubted the conversion of the Eucharistic gifts; then "he saw the host as true flesh sprinkled with blood, and the drops of blood were arranged on the coporal in such a way that they formed the face of the redeemer with blood flowing over it."[16] Since the dating of this miracle as well as its attestation are controversial, the question of influence on Urban IV must indeed remain an open question. What is beyond dispute, however, is that with the exception of but a few dioceses the Bull *Transiturus* was initially hardly adopted, since the successor to Urban IV seemed to show no interest in the implementation of the feast.

After his first teaching stint in Paris, Thomas Aquinas stayed for several years in the immediate vicinity of the papal curia in Orvieto (1261–65);[17] there he maintained a friendly acquaintance with the pope and prepared

---

13. See Browe, *Verehrung*, 72.

14. The Bull is documented in E. Friedberg, ed., *Corpus iuris canonici* II (Leipzig: Bernhard Tauchnitz, 1879–1881), cols. 1174–77. On this point, see the recent commentary by Th. Ruster, *Wandlung. Ein Traktat über Eucharistie und Ökonomie* (Mainz: Matthias-Grünewald, 2006), 18–32.

15. Because the dating of the Eucharistic miracle of Bolsena is not certain, Miri Rubin, for example, speaks against any influence on the Bull *Transiturus* (idem, *Corpus Christi*, 176f.).

16. Browe, *Die Verehrung der Eucharistie im Mittelalter*, 75f. See, in contrast, the carefully sober treatment of Eucharistic miracles in the *Sentences* commentary (see *In IV Sent.*, d. 10, a. 4, qa. 2, nn. 114–21, here 114: "utrum species illa quae ibi apparet, sit species corporis Christi, difficile est determinate") as well as in *S. th.* III, q. 76, a. 8.

17. See J.-P. Torrell, *Saint Thomas Aquinas*, vol. 1: *The Person and His Work*, trans. Robert Royal, 2nd ed. (Washington, D.C.: The Catholic University of America Press, 2005), 118f., who through recourse to newer research emphasizes that Thomas occupied the position of lecturer at the Domincan convent of Orvieto and was not a lecturer in the Roman curia itself, as P. Mandonnet asserts (*Thomas d'Aquin lecteur à la curie romaine. Chronologie du séjour (1259–1268)*, in *Xenia thomistica*, vol. III, ed. L. Theissling, 9–40.

several works commissioned by him. Among these, Thomas was entrusted with the preparation of the Divine Office for Corpus Christi. This is based on the report of Tolomeo of Lucca (1236–1336),[18] Thomas's biographer, who was his student in Naples from 1272 to 1274 and, at the same time, his spiritual father and confessor.[19] William of Tocco confirms this view in his *Vita de Thomaso de Aquino*,[20] certainly the most informative source of Thomas's biographical information.[21]

Thomas as Composer of the Eucharistic Hymns— the Question of Authenticity

The authenticity of the Office of Corpus Christi has been questioned time and again. This is partly because the witnesses of Bartholomew of Lucca and William of Tocco are relatively late and earlier sources do not mention Thomas's authorship. Thus, for example, Reginald of Piperno, who was secretary, *socius*, and friend to Thomas in his last years,[22] does *not* list the Office of Corpus Christi in his overview of Thomas's works. Furthermore, the Office is listed in neither Petrus Calo's biography of Thomas nor the extensive material of the canonization process. Beyond that, it is a conspicuous circumstance that the Dominican Order resolved to adopt the feast of Corpus Christi into its ordinarium only very late, specifically in 1318. Had the Dominicans known that their famous confrere Thomas Aquinas was the author of the Divine Office for Corpus Christi, they would hardly have hesitated so long to introduce the solemnity.

In this context, however, what must be taken into consideration is that Pope Urban IV (1261–64) passed away only a few weeks after the promulgation of his Bull *Transiturus*.[23] The adoption of the Bull was therefore very variable, taking place only haltingly and regionally.[24] In the run-up to the Council of Vienne (1311–12), Pope Clement V (1305–14)[25] made the decision

---

18. See P.-M. Gy, "L'office du Corpus Christi et S. Thomas d'Aquin. État d'une recherche," *RSPhTh* 64 (1980): 491–504, here 492, note 6.
19. See U. Neddermeyer, "Bartholomäus von Lucca," *LThK* 3, 2nd ed. (1994): 43; Torrell, *Saint Thomas Aquinas*, vol. 1, xv.
20. See *Ystoria sancti Thome de Aquino de Guillaume de Tocco* (1323)—édition critique, introduction et notes Claire le Brun-Gouanvic (Toronto: Pontifical Institute of Mediaeval Studies, 1996), cap. XVIII: "Scripsit officium de corpore Christi, de mandato pape Vrbani, in quo omnes, que de hoc sunt sacramento ueteres figuras exposuit, et ueritates, que de noua sunt gratia, compilauit."
21. See the nuanced evaluation by Torrell, *Saint Thomas Aquinas*, vol. 1, xv–xviii.
22. See Torrell, *Saint Thomas Aquinas*, vol. 1, 272–75.
23. The Bull was promulgated on August 11, 1264; on October 2 of that same year, Urban IV died.
24. See A. Häussling, "Literaturbericht zu Fronleichnam," *JVK* 9 (1986): 228–40.
25. See A. Kiesewetter, "Clemens V," *LThK* 2, 3rd ed. (1994): 1221.

to compile all the uncodified laws of the Church since Gregory IX,²⁶ and only at this point was attention given once more to the nearly forgotten Bull of Urban IV. Because Clement V died before implementing his plan, the collection of laws was promulgated in 1317 by Pope John XXII (1316–34).²⁷ The general chapter of the Dominican Order reacted to this promulgation in 1318, when it resolved at its gathering in Lyon to introduce the feast "Corpus Christi" into the ordinarium of the *Ordo Praedicatorum* and commissioned the superior general, Hervé Nédellec, to prepare a new Office for the feast.²⁸ This commission, which took place explicitly on account of the constitutions of the Council of Vienne, which were published only in 1317, reveals that both Urban IV's Bull and the Office for the feast composed by Thomas Aquinas were unknown to the general chapter up to this point. In fact, the Office created by Hervé Nédellec and entitled *Gaude felix parens* was approved by the general chapter of the Order in 1321 and 1322.²⁹ One year later, however, in 1323, the general chapter in Barcelona evidently received word that the *Roman* Office had Thomas Aquinas as its author. It was decided immediately that the Office of Hervé Nédellec was to be replaced by that of Thomas and the latter was to be promulgated in all the provinces of the Order.³⁰

Several years earlier, between 1313 and 1316,³¹ Bartholomew of Lucca noted in his *Historia ecclesiastica* that on the instructions of Pope Urban IV,

---

26. The *Liber extra* is the first authoritative collection of canonical legal sources; they were compiled by Raymond of Peñafort at the mandate of Gregory IX and promulgated in 1234. For background, see R. Puza, "Corpus Iuris Canonici," *LThK* 2, 3rd ed. (1994): 1321–24, here 1323.

27. See L. Vones, "Johannes XXII," *LThK* 5, 3rd ed. (1996) 950–51, here 951: "In terms of canon law, he [John XXII] came to the fore through the publication of the additional decretals up to and including Clement V, the *Clementinen* (Bull *Quoniam nulla*, 1317), which was later added to the Corpus Iuris Canonici."

28. See *Acta Capitulorum generalium Ordinis Praedicatorum*, vol. 2, ed. B. M. Reichert (Rome: Nabu Press, 1899), 109: "Volumus et ordinamus quod per totum ordinem fiat officium de corpore Christi feria vᵃ. infra octava trinitatis, sicut in constitutionibus Viennensis concilii est statutum. De officio vero magister ordinis studeat providere." Cited in P.-M. Gy, *La Liturgie dans l'histoire* (Paris: Éditions Saint-Paul, 1990), 223–45, here 223.

29. See *Acta Capitulorum generalium Ordinis Praedicatorum*, vol. 2, ed. Reichert, 128–29 and 139. See Gy, *La Liturgie dans l'histoire*, 223, who points out that the Office composed by Hervé Nédellec *Gaude felix parens* was published by B.-M. De Rubeis in his *Editio Altera Veneta* of St. Thomas's works, vol. 19, 500–504 (=Editio Leonina, vol. 1, 1882, CCLI–CCLIII).

30. See *Acta Capitulorum generalium Ordinis Praedicatorum*, vol. 2, ed. Reichert, 144: "Cum ordo noster debeat se sancte Romane ecclesie, in quantum est possibile, in divino officio conformare, et in eo precipue, quod per nostrum ordinem de mandato apostolico est confectum, volumus quod officium de corpore Christi per venerabiliem doctorem fratrem Thomam de Aquino editum, ut asseritur, per totum ordinem fiat vᵃ. feria post festum trinitatis usque ad octavas inclusive, et dictum officium in ordinario in locis debitis annotetur." See Gy, *La Liturgie dans l'histoire*, 224, who points out that the Chapter of 1324 specifically mentions again that the Office edited by Thomas was to be sent to all the provinces of the Order. See *Acta Capitulorum generalium Ordinis Praedicatorum*, vol. 2, 152.

31. See the remarks of A. Dondaine, "Les 'Opuscula fratris Thomae' chez Ptolémée de Lucques," *Archivum Fratrum Praedicatorum* 31 (1961): 150–54.

Thomas composed two most notable works: first, the *Catena aurea*, which was a continuous commentary on the Gospels drawn from pertinent patristic citations; and second, the Office for the Solemnity of Corpus Christi. Thomas composed the latter entire, from Matins to Compline—including "what is sung on this day" (*quidquid illa die cantatur*), that is, the hymns. Beyond this, Bartholomew specifically emphasizes—as did William of Tocco after him, by the way—that in the composition of the Office we find represented, "as it were, all the figures of the Old Testament," who point to the sacrament of the Eucharist[32]—an observation that can be fully confirmed by textual analysis.[33] Finally, Bartholomew calls attention to the fact that the pope assigned a great indulgence (*magnam indulgentia*) for all the faithful who participate in the Office[34]—a point that turns up in the Office itself when we read an allusion to the Bull *Transiturus*[35] in the third lesson: "... indulgentiam misericorditer tribuit perpetuis temporibus duraturam."[36]

The testimony of Bartholomew of Lucca, arising fifty years after Thomas's death, is admittedly insufficient to yield proof that the Office is to be attributed to Thomas Aquinas. But there is another historical circumstance that can support the plausibility of his statements. A comparison of the Bull *Transiturus* in the original version of 1264 with the version quoted by Clement V in his Bull *Si Dominum* reveals a critical difference: while the original version of the Bull *Transiturus* speaks of both the Office and the *Missa Cibavit* as being "included" in the papal document,[37] this reference is

---

32. *Historia ecclesiastica nova* (ed. O. Clavuot), XXII, 24: "Tunc frater Thomas rediit de Parisius ex certis causis, et ad petitionem Urbani multa fecit et scripsit, sed precipue duo: unum fuit quod exposuit Evangelia sub miro contextu diversorum doctorum.... Officium etiam de corpore Christi fecit ex mandato Urbani, quod est secundum quod fecit ad petitionem Urbani. Hoc fecit completum et quantum ad totum officium tam diurnum quam nocturnum quam etiam ad missam et quidquid illa die cantatur; in qua historia, si attendiums ad verba scribentis, quasi omnes figure Veteris Testamenti in hoc officio videntum contineri, luculento et proprio stilo adaptata ad eucharistie sacramentum."

33. See R. J. Zawilla, "The Historiae Corporis Christi attributed to Thomas Aquinas. A Theological Study of their Biblical Source," unpublished dissertation (Toronto, 1985).

34. *Historia ecclesiastica nova* XXII, 25: "In quo officio summus pontifex [sc. Urbanus IV] magnam fidelibus tribuit indulgentiam qui dicto interessent officio, perpetuo duraturam. Quod postea sub Clemente V roboratum Domini MCCCX in concilio Viennensi super Rodanum celebrato." The last sentence refers to the Bull *Si Dominum* (documented in: E. Friedberg, ed., *Corpus Iuris Canonici* [Leipzig: Bernhard Tauchnitz, 1881], vol. I, cols. 1174–77), in which Clement V basically quotes the Bull *Transiturus* in its entirety and prescribes its reception for the whole Latin Church. The chronological detail of Bartholomew is, however, in need of correction. The Council of Vienne was indeed convened for October 1, 1310, but it could not assemble until October 16, 1311, because of delays bound up with the investigations into the planned disbanding of the Knights Templar. The Council concluded on May 6, 1312. Additionally, by having recourse to a commentary by Johannes Andreae, E. Müller was able to demonstrate that the Bull *Si Dominum* did not present a conciliar decree but was issued outside of the Council. See idem, *Das Konzil von Vienne 1311–1312. Seine Quellen und seine Geschichte* (Münster: Aschendorff, 1934), 644–48.

35. See L. Dorez, ed., *Registres d'Urbain IV*, v. 2/1 (Paris: A. Fontemoing, 1901), 423–25, here 424.

36. *Officium*, 277.

37. The critical passage reads: "Ideoque universitatem vestram monemus et hortamur in Domino, per

missing in *Si Dominum*, which implies that the Bull *Transiturus* prescribed the feast for the Latin Church in general and, in addition, it regulated the concrete liturgical usage of the Office. The hypothesis that Pope Urban IV sent out the Office to but a small number of addressees without prescribing it generally cannot be maintained. Through intensive archival research, Pierre-Marie Gy was able to trace a whole set of textual witnesses to the original version of the Bull *Transiturus*, witnesses that are also independent of the Bull *Si Dominum*.[38] They are addressed to diverse bishops and contain in each case a pertinent reference prescribing the use of the Office.

Going beyond this historical standpoint, Gy was able to substantiate Thomas's authorship through philologically meticulous studies.[39] In order to be able to track his argument, we must call to mind that already in Liège around the year 1240, the suggestion of St. Juliana of Liège led to conceiving an original version of the Office—*Animarum cibus*.[40] There exist, however, two versions of the Roman Office; a first one circulates under the name *Sapientia aedificavit* and is classified similarly by Cyrille Lambot and Pierre-Marie Gy as a provisional draft of the first celebration of the feast in 1264. It already contains most of the elements of the second Office, which is known by the title *Sacerdos in aeternum* and was disseminated by Pope Urban IV along with the Bull *Transiturus de hoc mundo* on August 11, 1264.[41] Both Offices contain indications internal to the text that suggest Thomas's authorship with a probability bordering on certainty:

1. The verse Mt 28:20 ("Ecce ego vobiscum omnibus diebus usque ad consummationem saeculi") was commonly interpreted by Thomas Aquinas's theological contemporaries as a promise of Jesus' presence in the Eucharist. In the Office *Animarum cibus*, the original version that served Thomas as template, Mt 28:20 functions as an antiphon to Lauds.[42] The

---

apostolica vobis scripta mandantes quatinus tam excelsum et tam gloriosum festum ... cum novem lectionibus, cum responsoriis, versiculis, antiphonis, psalmis, hymnis et orationibus ipsi festo specialiter congruentibus, que cum proprio misse officio uobis sub bulla nostra mittimus *interclusa*, deuote ac sollempniter celebratis" (Dorez, ed., *Registres d'Urbain IV*, 425 [n. 874]). It is otherwise in the version documented in the Bull of Clement V, in which the reference to the included Office is missing. See *Corpus iuris canonici*, Friedberg, ed., vol. 2, cols. 1176f.

38. See Gy, *La Liturgie dans l'histoire* (Paris: Éditions Saint-Paul, 1990), 223–45; here 230 (note 21).

39. See Gy, *La Liturgie dans l'histoire*, 223–45. Summarized by Torrell, *Saint Thomas Aquinas*, 129–36.

40. C. Lambot and I. Fransen, *L'office de la Fête-Dieu primitive. Textes et mélodies retrouvés* (Maredsous: Éditions de Maredsous, 1946).

41. The manuscript, which served as the basis for Pierre-Marie Gy's critical edition of the text in the Leonine version and which counts as original, stems from the library of Pope Boniface VIII. See Gy, *La Liturgie dans l'histoire*, 235f.

42. See Lambot and Fransen, *L'office de la Fête-Dieu primitive*, 83. A reference to Mt 28:20 is also found in the directive of Robert, bishop of Liège, who introduced the feast of Corpus Christi in his diocese in 1246. See P. Browe, *Textus antiqui de festo Corporis Christis* (Münster: Aschendorff, 1934), 22: "qui in hac mirabili

Bull *Transiturus* also adduces this verse as a biblical foundation for the Eucharistic real presence.[43] All the more significant, that verse is missing in the Office *Sacerdos in aeternum*, which otherwise deploys an abundance of biblical verses to orchestrate the manifold aspects of the Eucharistic sacrament. According to Gy, this absence indicates the authorship of Thomas Aquinas. One characteristic of his Eucharistic doctrine consists precisely in the fact that—in contrast to Alexander of Hales,[44] Peter of Tarentaise,[45] and Bonaventure[46]—it does *not* adduce Mt 28:20 as the biblical foundation for the real presence in the Eucharist.[47]

2. What is similarly missing from the Office *Sacerdos in aeternum* is the concept of *praesentia corporalis*, which is worked out in the template *Animarum cibus*[48] as well as in the bull of Urban IV.[49] The legenda of the

---

exhibitione sua [in Eucharistia] non cessat nec cessabit adimplere illam suam dulcissimam promissionem quam pollicitus est dicens: 'Ecce vobiscum sum omnibus diebus usque ad consummationem saeculi.'"

43. See Dorez, ed., *Registres d'Urbain IV*, 423: "Hoc est memoriale dulcissimum, memoriale sanctissimum, memoriale salvificum, in quo gratum redemptionis nostre recensemus memoriam, in quo a malo retrahimur, confortamur in bono, et ad virtutem et gratiarum proficimus incrementa, in quo profecto reficimur ipsius corporali presentia Salvatoris, quia in hac sacramentali Christi commemoratione, ipse Christus presens, sub alia quidem forma sed in propria vere substantia est nobiscum. *Ascensurus enim in celum, dixit apostolis eorumque sequacibus*: 'Ecce ego vobiscum sum omnibus diebus usque ad consummationem seculi,' *benigna ipsos promissione confortans*, quod remaneret et esset cum eis etiam per presentiam corporalem." (emphasis added). With minor variations, the text is taken up again in Friedberg, ed., *Corpus iuris canonici*, vol. 2, col. 1176.

44. See Alexander of Hales, *Quaestiones disputatae antequam esset Frater*, q. 51, disp. 5, 2, 170 (ed. Quarrachi, vol. 2, 1960, 955–56): "Item, in Evangelio habetur significatio huius perpetuitatis [Eucharistiae], ex illo quod dicitur in fine Matthaei: *Vobiscum sum usque ad consummationem saeculi*. Hoc intelligitur de re sub specie sacramenti, et quae erit 'usque ad finem saeculi' et non amplius; et non de ipsa re absolute, scilicet non sub sacramento, scilicet corpus Christi [quod] manet in aeternum." See also q. 51, disp. 7, 2, 204 (ed. Quarrachi, vol. 2, 1960, 968): "cum corpore sub sacramento, quae respondet unioni in natura, quia sub sacramento est praesens nobis usque ad consummationem saeculi, sicut dicitur in Evangelio Matthei, ultimo: *Vobiscum sum usque ad consummationem saeculi*."

45. See *In IV Sent.*, d. 10, q. 1, a. 1 sed contra (Toulouse 1751, IV, 108): "Matthei ultimo: 'Ecce ego vobiscum, etc.' Aut ergo praesentia corporali, aut spirituali tantum. Si spirituali tantum, similiter est cum Ecclesia Pater et Spiritus Sanctus, et ipse a principio mundi usque ad finem saeculi. Si corporali, aut ergo visibili, aut invisibili: non primo modo, ergo secundo; sed non altero modo quam in hoc sacramento. Ergo etc." See Gy, *La Liturgie dans l'histoire*, 238.

46. See Bonaventure, *In IV Sent.*, d. 10, q. 1, who answers the question 'Utrum Christus sit in sacramento altaris secundum veritatem' by appealing to Mt 28:20 and 1 Cor 11: "Item, Matthaei ultimo: 'Ecce ego vobiscum sum usque ad consummationem saeculi.' Constat quod hoc non dicit quantum ad effectum divinitatis et gratiae, quia secundum divinitatem est cum omnibus hominibus, secundum gratiam non est semper cum fidelibus omnibus; intelligit ergo secundum humanitatem, sed hoc non visibiliter, sed sub sacramento." Gy, *La Liturgie dans l'histoire*, 238, points out that, of the seventeen places in Bonaventure's work that refer to Mt 28:20, eleven have a meaning specific to Eucharistic theology.

47. See *In IV Sent.*, d. 10, a. 1. See also the data in Gy, 239 (n. 39).

48. The original version of the Office *Animarum cibus* was conceived through the influence of St. Juliana of Liège. There, the *praesentia corporalis* is explicitly invoked as the object of the feast when we find in the Collect of the Mass: "da nobis, quaesumus, eius praesentiam corporalem ita venerari in terris, ut de eius visione gaudere mereamur in caelis." See C. Lambot and I. Fransen, *L'office de la Fête-Dieu primitive. Textes et mélodies retrouvés* (Maredsous: Éditions de Maredsous, 1946), 97.

49. See Dorez, ed., *Registres d'Urbain IV*, 423: "Hoc est memoriale dulcissimum ... in quo profecto reficimur ipsius corporali presentia Salvatoris." Similarly in *Corpus iuris canonici*, Friedberg, ed., vol. 2, col. 1175.

Office "*Immensa divinae largitatis*" contains a double allusion to this use of the term *praesentia corporalis*. On the one hand, it addresses the situation of Jesus' imminent departure from his disciples and emphasizes that he instituted the sacrament not only as a *memoriale passionis* but also as a special comfort for the disciples, who would be saddened by his *absence*. On the other, the legenda speaks of the "ineffable mode of divine presence in the visible sacrament"[50]—a *modus loquendi* that fully corresponds to Thomas's Eucharistic theology. Unlike his contemporaries Bonaventure[51] and Peter of Tarentaise,[52] Thomas harbors theological reservations regarding the suggestion of a *praesentia corporalis*, since this idea can easily provoke a misunderstanding of local presence. Local presence is assigned, however, solely to the *quantitas dimensiva* of bread (and wine), but not to the substance of Christ's body (and blood).[53]

3. A further indication is provided by a passage that is located in the third *Lectio* of the first nocturne and refers to the judgment of the senses in view of the accidents: "Accidentia etiam sine subiecto in eodem subsistent, ut fides locum habeat dum visibile invisibiliter sumitur, aliena specie occultatum, et sensus a deceptione immunes reddantur, qui de accidentibus iudicant sibi notis."[54] Because of its theological terminology, this passage may seem to some extent misplaced in a liturgical celebration. All the same, according to Jean-Pierre Torrell, it contains "something like a signature" of Aquinas,[55] for whom it is here a matter of appreciation of the senses' judgment in view of the Eucharistic accidents—a good Aristotelian position and wholly in accord with the later teaching of the *Summa theologiae*.[56]

---

50. See the critical form of the text in Gy, *La Liturgie*, 245: "Unde, ut arctius huiusmodi caritatis immensitas cordibus infigeretur fidelium, in ultima coena, quando, pascha cum fidelibus [correct: *discipulis*, see Gy, 241] celebrato, transiturus erat ex hoc mundo ad Patrem, hoc sacramentum instituit tamquam passionis suae memoriale perenne, figurarum veterum impletivum, miraculorum ab ipso factorum maximum, et de sua contristatis absentia solacium singulare. Convenit itaque devotioni fidelium sollemniter recolere institutionem tam salutiferi tamquam mirabilis sacramenti, ut ineffabilem modum divinae presentiae in sacramento visibili veneremur, et laudatur Dei potentia." The motif is found later in *S. th.* III, q. 73, a. 5.

51. *In IV Sent.* d. 12, a. 1, q. 1 (ed. Quaracchi IV, 218): "ex hoc quod Christus est tibi corporaliter praesens, fidei meritum augetur, dum hoc credit quod nullatenus ratione cognoscit. Caritatis etiam devotio inflammatur, quando sentit Dominum sibi praesentem in carne: sicut enim ad praesentiam ignis expellitur frigus, sic ad praesentiam carnis Christi expellitur tepor ... quod dicit Dominus 'Caro non prodest quidquam,' intelligit: carnaliter intelligenti. Ille autem intelligit Christum manducari secundum quod comeditur caro cuiuslibet animalis per frustra.... Similiter patet aliud, quia praesentia corporis non auget Dei virtutem, sed congruum est quod Dominus ex sua praesentia corporali aliquod munus specialus tribuat."

52. See *In IV Sent.*, d. 10, q. 1, a. 1, sed contra (Toulouse 1751, IV, 108).

53. See also the passage quoted by Gy (*La Liturgie dans l'histoire*, 243): "Dicitur, quod est in loco altaris vel in ecclesia, sed hoc verum est quod corpus Christi non est in sacramento ut in loco." See also *S. th.* III, q. 75, a. 1; q. 83, a. 2 ad 4.

54. See *Officium de festo corporis Christi*, 277.

55. Torrell, *Saint Thomas Aquinas*, 131.

56. See *S. th.* III, q. 75, a. 5.

Following the earlier accomplishments of Pierre-Marie Gy—who was joined by such renowned Thomistic researchers as Jean-Pierre Torrell,[57] Wolfgang Kluxen,[58] and Otto Hermann Pesch[59]—the present work will henceforth take as its point of departure that Thomas Aquinas is the composer of the Office for Corpus Christi and thus the Eucharistic hymns, which we hope to explore in greater detail in what follows.

Methodological Preliminaries

In the following, the goal is not an exhaustive assessment of the liturgical composition of the Office or a search through it for biblical or patristic motifs. Rather, what is to be undertaken is a concentration on the hymns, in which Thomas's theology of the Eucharist is poetically distilled. The sequence in which the hymns are approached is keyed to the position they occupy in the Office. That means the hymn for first Vespers, *Pange lingua*, forms the beginning, after which follow the hymn for Matins, and so forth. Concretely speaking, we will first examine the *formal* structure of the hymns. Strophic composition, rhyme scheme, meter, and linguistic features will be worked out and the rough structure will likewise be discussed, all without devolving into a detailed philological analysis. After the formal observations, we will move to *theological* interpretation, and an attempt will be made to call attention to the fundamental themes of the hymns. At the same time, respect should be paid to where the poetic excess, the *surplus* of the hymns lies, especially compared to the conceptually worked out theology of the Eucharist in the *Summa theologiae*. In this way, the spiritual subtext of Thomas Aquinas's theological work will become clear *en passant*.

Finally, let us recall that, situated within their liturgical context, these texts aspire not only to be read silently but also to be spoken, indeed sung, aloud. In this way, they acquire a nearly physical presence. Thomas himself pointed out that, for anthropological reasons, praying audibly makes sense. Thus is interior devotion (*interior devotio*) inflamed and the heart of man lifted up to God. Precisely through external signs, whether the voice or other external actions, the spirit is animated by means of the senses and moved to love. *Oratio vocalis* appears of itself when a powerful *affective* mood flows over from the soul to the body, in accord with the word of the Psalms: "My

---

57. Torrell, *Saint Thomas Aquinas*, vol. 1, 129–31.
58. See W. Kluxen, "Thomas von Aquin," *LThK* 9, 3rd ed. (2000): 1509–17, here 1516.
59. Pesch, *Thomas von Aquin*, 105 (without mentioning the name). See also A. Heinz, "Fronleichnam," *LThK* 4, 3rd ed. (1995): 172–74, here 173, as well as W. Kasper, *Sakrament der Einheit*, 50f.

heart hath been glad, and my tongue hath rejoiced."[60] Because the Office for the feast of Corpus Christi ought to evoke and express above all joy and gratitude for the sacrament of the altar, it is profoundly reasonable for the hymns to be prayed aloud.[61] Their vocal *performance* is not something external to them, for rhythm and tone are poetic qualities that do not take effect in silent prayer and thus they yearn to be realized in an auditory way. The meter of the verse structures the time, while rhymes and assonances fill the space; thus, a hymn that is recited or sung in the liturgy creates for the one praying a presence that is always also physical. It is a presence that is articulated "around the body through the effort of its voice as well as all sensible, affective, and intellectual moments."[62] Moreover, an ecclesial dimension is realized through praying the hymns in common. *Many* voices that may have diverse qualities—tone, pitch, range, timbre, intensity—combine in a certain way together into *one*, so that a collective act of recollection (*re-member*) takes place in the liturgical performance of the Eucharistic hymns, an act corresponding to the meaning of the feast: through praying the hymns, which commemorate the Eucharistic presence of Christ's body and blood with gratitude and joy, those praying realize ever anew what they themselves are: *membra* of the *corpus Christi*.

60. S. *th.* II-II, q. 83, a. 12: "adiungitur vocalis oratio ex quadam redundantia ab anima in corpus ex vehementi affection: secundum illud Psalm [Ps. 15,9]: *Laetatum est cor meum, et exsultavit lingua mea.*"

61. See also S. *th.* II-II, q. 84, a. 2, where Thomas draws out the point that in adoration—in accord with the anthropological constitution of man—inner devotion of the spirit should come to be expressed in external gestures of the body.

62. See P. Zumthor, *Die Stimme und die Poesie in der mittelalterlichen Gesellschaft* (Munich: Fink, 1994), 44.

5

The Mystery of Eucharistic Conversion

The Hymn *Pange lingua gloriosi*

The vesperal hymn, *Pange lingua*, may well be one of the most well known witnesses to medieval Eucharistic spirituality.[1] Since the fifteenth century, the two last stanzas, beginning with the words *"Tantum ergo sacramentum,"* have been sung during Benediction of the Blessed Sacrament, and they are known to most practicing Catholics today. In recent years, moreover, the hymn has been the subject of controversial theological discussion. Here, the central point of attention has been the question of whether a particular verse conveys a problematic anti-Semitism, namely, the phrase running *"et antiquum documentum novo cedat ritui* [and let the old covenant yield to a new rite]."[2] If the verse could be understood only in the sense of substitution theory—according to which the people of Israel were finally replaced by the Church and therefore plummeted to the status of a once-great but now-superseded figure in salvation history—then the hymn would in fact require some correction. It would basically be a case of a text that served as a particularly effective vehicle of anti-Semitism because it was widely disseminated in popular piety over the course of centuries. For a theology sensitive to the reality of the Shoah, one of its tasks is indubitably to work through manifest as well as latent anti-Semitism in the history of theology and the Church, and that also includes liturgical texts.[3] A critical per-

---

1. In what follows, the hymns will be cited from *Officium* 275–87. See the adaptation of *Pange lingua* by Heinrich Bone (printed in A. Stock, *Lateinische Hymnen*, 214f.) and by Liborius O. Lumma (in *Gotteslob* [Stuttgart-Vienna, 2013], n. 493).

2. E. Zenger characterized the verse *et antiqum documentum novo cedat ritui* as an "anti-Semitic campaign slogan" (*Das Erste Testament. Die jüdische Bibel und die Christen* [Düsseldorf: Patmos, 1991], 90). Another estimation is arrived at by J. Wohlmuth, "Eucharistie—Feier des Neuen Bundes," in *Christologie der Liturgie. Der Gottesdienst der Kirche Christusbekenntnis und Sinaibund*, ed. K. Richter and B. Kranemann (Freiburg-Basel-Vienna: Herder, 1995), 187–206, here 187.

3. I distinguish here *ad hoc* between Christian anti-Semitism, which has theological roots, and an anti-

spective on this burdensome heritage must be adopted, even if one must be methodically cautious to avoid an anachronistic approach, wherein medieval texts are simply measured by the problems presenting themselves to a theological consciousness disquieted by Auschwitz. Thus, in the interpretation of the hymn, I will direct attention to how, in the incriminating verses, Thomas Aquinas conceives of the relation between old and new covenants. In the course of this inquiry, the question will also be broached, whether the consequent abandoning of the recitation of this hymn when praying the Office in common, something already practiced in some monasteries, is really justified—or perhaps arises from an inordinate cathartic zeal.[4] The text of the hymn reads as follows:

Pange, lingua, gloriosi	Sing, my tongue, the Savior's glory
Corporis mysterium	of His Flesh, the mystery sing;
Sanguinisque pretiosi,	of the Blood all price exceeding,
Quem in mundi pretium,	shed by our Immortal King,
Fructus ventris generosi	destined, for the world's redemption,
Rex effudit gentium.	from a mortal Womb to spring.
Nobis datus, nobis natus	Of a pure and spotless Virgin
Ex intacta Virgine	born for us on earth below,
Et in mundo conversatus,	He, as man, with man conversing,
Sparso verbi semine,	stayed, the seeds of truth to sow;
Sui moras incolatus	then He closed in solemn order
Miro clausit ordine.	wond'rously His Life of woe.
In supremae nocte cenae	On the night of that Last Supper,
Recombens cum fratribus,	seated with His chosen band,
Observata lege plene	He, the Paschal Victim eating,
Cibis in legalibus,	first fulfills the Law's command;
Cibum turbae duodenae	then as Food to His Apostles
Se dat suis manibus.	gives Himself with His own Hand.

Semitism that arose in the European Enlightenment of the eighteenth century and took on exterminating characteristics with the biologistic and racist thinking of the nineteenth and twentieth centuries. For background, see J.-H. Tück, "'Wer euch antastet, tastet meinen Augapfel an' (Sach 12,2). Theologische Anmerkungen zur Singularität der Shoah," *IKaZ Communio* 39 (2010): 440–53.

4. It is obvious that the German translation by Marie Luise Thurmair, which is found in the *Gotteslob* hymnal, tends rather to convey Thomas's viewpoint in the incriminated verses in a distorted fashion than actually to hit the mark. See on this point the instructive contribution by N. Lohfink, "Das 'Pange Lingua' im Gotteslob," *Bibel und Liturgie* 76 (2003): 276–85.

Verbum caro panem verum	Word-made-Flesh, the bread of nature
Verbo carnem efficit	by His Word to Flesh He turns;
Fitque sanguis Christi merum;	wine into His Blood He changes;
Et si sensus deficit,	what though sense no change discerns?
Ad firmandum cor sincerum	Only be the heart in earnest,
Sola fides sufficit.	faith her lesson quickly learns.
Tantum ergo sacramenentum	Down in adoration falling,
Veneremur cernui	This great Sacrament we hail,
Et antiquum documentum	O'er ancient forms of worship
Nova cedat ritui;	Newer rites of grace prevail;
Praestet fides supplementum	Faith will tell us Christ is present,
Sensuum defectui.	When our human senses fail.
Genitori Genitoque	To the Everlasting Father,
Laus et iubilatio,	And the Son who made us free
Salus, honor, virtus quoque	And the Spirit, God proceeding
Sit et benedictio,	From them Each eternally,
Procendenti ab utroque	Be salvation, honour, blessing,
Compar sit laudatio. Amen.	Might and endless majesty. Amen.

[Fr. Edward Caswall, 1849]

Observations on the Diction and Structure of the Hymn

In anticipation of the interpretation itself, a few formal remarks are in order. The hymn has six strophes that follow the rhyme scheme A-B-A-B-A-B and each is composed of six lines. The strophic structure, meter, and melody depend upon the hymn to the cross written by Venantius Fortunatus in the sixth century, *Pange lingua gloriosi proelium certaminis*,[5] which later (ninth century) found its way into the Divine Office during Passiontide and was used in the veneration of the cross.[6] Thomas took over and transformed certain motifs from this then well-known template, and for this reason the linkage between the Passion and the Eucharist is definitely a prominent theme. In his hymns, finally, the alternation of verse-endings

---

5. See *Analecta hymnica medii aevi*, vol. 50, ed. G. M. Dreves and C. Blume (Leipzig: Fues's Verlag, 1907), 70–73. For more on this hymn, which arose at the impetus of Saint Radegund and poetically foregrounds the cross as a sign of victory, see the information in C. Blume, *Unsere liturgischen Lieder. Das Hymnar der altchristlichen Kirche* (Regensburg: Pustet, 1932), 190–99; A. Stock, *Lateinische Hymnen* (Berlin: Insel Verlag, 2012), 146–57.

6. See B. Fischer, "Pange lingua gloriosi," *LThK* 7, 3rd ed. (1998): 1311–12.

is also to be emphasized.[7] It is precisely the final Trinitarian doxology that stands out phonetically from the other strophes due to its more melodious vocalic endings.

The strophes are so arranged that it is first the mystery of the exalted Christ and his salvific deeds that are invoked. Then in the second strophe there follows a poetically condensed retrospective, contemplating Jesus' birth and life; this backward glance places especially the proclamation of the word front and center by drawing upon the parable of the sower. The fundamentally pro-existent posture of Jesus' life is concentrated in the event of the last supper, which is penned in the third stanza. It is no accident that it flows into the Eucharistic motif of self-gift (*se dat suis manibus*). The fourth stanza takes up a further fine-tuning when it more closely illuminates the mystery of Eucharistic conversion, without relying upon a technical theological terminology, such as the categories of substance and accident. One can see in this stanza what is in fact the climax of the hymn, exceptionally poetically crafted by means of diction rich in assonance. In the fifth stanza, the hymn executes a shift in perspective describable in grammatical terms. After the memorative and narrative diction of the first four stanzas, the "we" of the ones praying is incorporated at this point. This "we" expresses in words the answer of the faithful to the gift of the Eucharist, while the sixth stanza brings the hymn to its conclusion with a final Trinitarian doxology that turns fully assured diction to the praise of the inexpressible mystery of the Trinitarian God.

Theological Interpretation

The institution of the solemnity of Corpus Christi was connected with a threefold intention. It should not only (1) attest vigorously to the real presence of Jesus Christ in the Eucharistic gifts, in the face of Berengar and the Cathars, but also (2) rectify the insufficient devotion and dedication of the faithful, as well as (3) carry out the commemoration of the sacrament's institution with gratitude and joy. Thankful joy, however, requires appropriate forms of expression; thus, the hymn *Pange lingua* begins with the summons: "Sing, my tongue ... the mystery."

---

7. See the overview of the endings: 1st strophe: vocalic—consonantic; 2nd strophe: consonantic—vocalic; 3rd strophe: vocalic—consonantic; 4th strophe: consonantic thoughout; 5th strophe: consonantic—vocalic; 6th strophe: vocalic throughout.

Doxology to the Exalted Christ as *Rex Gentium*[8]

Doxology, employing breath and voice, is able to appeal to the tradition of the Psalms: *Labiis exsultationis laudavit os meum* (Ps 62:6). Against the argument that one should praise God with the heart rather than the lips, Thomas responds that, in fact, the mouth's praise is of no avail if it does not correspond to the impulse of the heart, but exterior praise both arouses the interior emotion of the one praising and incites others to the praise of God as well.[9] It is not a question of moving God by means of prayer, but rather of leading the one praying to the right attitude through the performance of prayer. The interior realm—joy and thanks—ought to find expression in the exterior realm; in this way, the body of the one at prayer becomes itself a medium of doxological praise.

Praise, however, does not come to pass apart from an "occasion." Not only philosophy, but also doxology traces its roots back to an elemental act of wonder. "To praise is, in truth, to wonder."[10] It is no accident that the hymn *Pange lingua* refers to a mystery that offers the occasion to render praise. It is certainly notable here that it is not the mystery of the Eucharist that is first of all addressed.[11] Rather, praise is given to the glorified body (*corpus gloriosum*) of the Lord, which becomes present ever anew in the forms of bread and wine during the celebration of the sacrament of the altar. In the face of the Docetic movements of the twelfth and thirteenth centuries, in particular the Cathars, Thomas both emphasized the true corporeality of the risen Lord and criticized spiritualizing construals that attributed to the glorified Christ a *corpus caeleste* or even a *corpus phantasticum*.[12] Just as it belongs to faith in the Incarnation that Christ took on a complete human nature, to which also belongs a very real body, so also it belongs to faith in the resurrection that Christ is glorified in a bodily way.

---

8. See W. Breuer, *Die lateinische Eucharistiedichtung des Mittelalters* (Wuppertal: Henn, 1970), 253–64; A. Stock, *Poetische Dogmatik*, 305–24; W. Urban, "Das eucharistische Brot in den Fronleichnamshymnen des Thomas von Aquin," in *Panis Angelorum. Das Brot der Engel: Kulturgeschichte der Hostie*, ed. O. Seifert (Ostfildern: Thorbecke, 2004).

9. See *S. th.* II-II, q. 91, a. 1 ad 2: "laus oris inutilis est laudanti si sit sine laude cordis, quod loquitur Deo laudem dum *magnalia eius operum* recogitat cum affectu [cf. Eccli. 17,7–8]. Valet tamen exterior laus oris ad excitandum interiorem affectum laudantis, et ad provocandum alios ad Dei laudem." See L. Maidl, *Desiderii interpres. Genese und Grundstruktur der Gebetstheologie des Thomas von Aquin* (Paderborn: Schöningh, 1994), 268–71.

10. E. Canetti, *Aufzeichnungen 1992–1993* (Munich: Carl Hanser, 1996), 25.

11. Thus, the translation by Marie Luise Thurmair—"Das Geheimnis lasst uns künden / das uns Gott im Zeichen bot [The mystery heralds to us / what God offered to us in symbol]"—disregards the Latin original. See *Gotteslob*, n. 544.

12. See *S. th.* III, q. 54, a. 2 ad 2. See T. Marschler, *Auferstehung und Himmelfahrt in der scholastischen Theologie bis Thomas von Aquin*, 184–91.

At the same time, it is significant that the glorified body remains marked with the traces of the Passion.[13]

Even though the reference to body and blood already directs one's thinking to the duality of the signs of bread and wine, it is still primarily the glorified Christ whom the hymn places into the field of vision; this is the same Christ who—as the text has it—shed his precious blood as "ransom for the world" (*pretium mundi*). Speaking of ransom invokes the soteriological interpretive category of *redemptio*—"ransom/redemption"[14]—which at first glance tends to call up mercantile associations. Certainly, Thomas emphasizes that the redemption from sin wrought by Christ through his death is not to be thought of according to the model of an equivalence that remains external. As he explains in the *Summa theologiae*, Christ did not give just any means of payment to ransom the world, but the highest thing he could: *himself*. Unlike men, who were unable to tender redemption's purchase price (see Ps 48:8f.),[15] Christ's "precious blood" had the power to redeem the world. The first letter of St. Peter already calls this to mind, and thus Thomas weaves the Petrine text into his hymn: "You know that you were ransomed (*redempti estis*) from the futile ways inherited from your ancestors, not with perishable things like silver or gold, but with the precious blood of Christ, like that of a lamb without defect or blemish" (*pretioso sanguine quasi agni immaculati Christi et incontaminati*—1 Pt 1:18f.). The year-old, male lamb without defect, which was slaughtered for the celebration of Passover, is a type for the *Christus passus*. The hymn will return to this later.

In the opening stanza, it is first the mystery of the glorified Lord that

---

13. The characteristics of subtlety (*subtilitas*), agility (*agilitas*), clarity (*claritas*), and impassibility (*impassibilitas*) are attributed to the *corpus gloriosum*. See *S. c. G.* IV, c. 86; *Comp. theol.* 168; *S. th.* Suppl., q. 82 (*impassibilitas*), q. 83 (*subtilitas*), q. 84 (*agilitas*), q. 85 (*claritas*). On this point, it is interesting to note that the glorified body's inability to suffer was related to the institution of the Sacrament of the Altar, and the thesis circulated that the Lord gave his body at the last supper as food without thereby causing injury to his bodily integrity. This was to be an indication of the *impassibilitas* of his body. Thomas rebuts this view and insists that the body of the earthly Jesus was able to suffer (*passibilitas*) from birth until death. With a view to the institution of the Sacrament of the Altar, he holds fast to the view: The body given by Jesus to the disciples at the last supper was not eaten physically *in its proper species*—that would have in fact been an anthropophagous act—but rather symbolically *in specie panis*. The rite of breaking the bread, which took place in a similarly symbolic way, did not affect the physical integrity of the Lord. See *In III Sent.*, d. 16, q. 2, a. 2.

14. On the soteriological interpretative category of "redemption [*Loskauf*]" (*redemptio*), see *S. th.* III, q. 48, a. 4: "Igitur, quia passio Christi fuit sufficiens et superabundans satisfactio pro peccato et reatu poenae generis humani, eius passio fuit quasi quoddam pretium [sic], per quod liberati sumus ab utraque obligatione. Nam ipsa satisfactio qua quis satisfacit sive pro se sive pro alio, pretium quoddam dicitur quo se redimit a peccato et a poena: secundum illud Dan. 4: 'Peccata tua eleemosysis redime.' Christus autem satisfecit, non quidem pecuniam dando aut aliquid huiusmodi, sed *dando id quod fuit maximum, seipsum, pro nobis*. Et ideo passio Christi dicitur esse nostra redemptio" (emphasis added).

15. See Ps 48:8f. (Vulgate): "fratrem redimens non redimet vir / nec dabit Deo propitiationem pro eo / neque pretium redemptionis [sic] animae eorum"—but in verse 16 it then runs: "verumtamen *Deus* redimet animam meam." The motif of redemption stands, moreover, in a certain continuity with Exodus, the liberation of the people of Israel from slavery in Egypt.

is lauded, the same Lord who gave his life for us in the Passion. The reference to blood recalls the sacrificial dimension of his death, which is explicitly signified in the *forma sacramenti* spoken over the wine.[16] Thereafter, he enters into the sphere of consummate perfection by way of resurrection and ascension. The withdrawal of his *praesentia corporalis*, however, is definitely of use for the faithful, as Thomas states.[17] And indeed, first, as regards *faith*, which refers to realities unable to be seen; then, as regards *hope*, which finds support in the fact that Christ prepares a dwelling in heaven for those belonging to him (see Jn 14:3); and finally, as regards *love*, which directs its aspirations toward heavenly things (see Col 3:1f.). At the same time, despite all the discontinuity between historical and eschatological reality, the hymn also stresses the following correlation: the exalted Christ, upon whom the hymn bestows the title "king of nations," is at the same time the one who stems from the womb of Mary (*fructus ventris generosi*).[18] In the poetic interlacing of Christological propositions reflecting both grandeur and lowliness, one is certainly able to discern a "delicate allusion to the doctrine of Christ's two natures."[19] The king of nations was born as a child and shed his blood as ransom (*pretium*) for the world. The marks of his wounds make visible the identity of the *corpus gloriosum* with the historical body of the Lord.[20] But he remains "king" and, in this role, judgment over all the nations is a task that falls to him, the glorified One who sits at the right hand of the Father.[21] The majestic title *rex gentium* widens the *titulus crucis*, "King of the Jews,"[22] to include the Gentiles; it spans the biblical deposit, tracing its roots to the Old Testament,[23] finding expression in the glorified Lamb of St. John's Apocalypse,[24] and sounding a messianic note in the O-Antiphons of Advent.[25] It

---

16. "Hic est calix sanguinis mei, novi et aeterni testamenti, qui *pro vobis et pro multis effundetur* in remissionem peccatorum" (emphasis added). On this point, see *In IV Sent.*, d. 8, q. 2, a. 2; *S. th.* III, q. 78, a. 3.

17. See *S. th.* III, q. 57, a. 1 ad 3: "ascensio Christi in caelum, qua corporalem suam praesentiam nobis subtraxit, magis fuit utilis nobis quam praesentia corporalis fuisset. Primo quidem, propter fidei augmentum, quae est de non visis.... Secundo, ad spei sublevationem.... Tertio ad erigendum caritatis affectum in caelestia."

18. See the allusion to Lk 1:42: "benedicta tu in mulieribus et benedictus fructus ventris tui."

19. N. Lohfink, "Das 'Pange Lingua' im *Gotteslob*," 281.

20. On the identity between the earthly and resurrected body, see *S. c. G.*, c. 84: "Erit ergo idem corpus secundum speciem post resurrectionem et ante."

21. See *S. th.* III, q. 58, a. 2: "Unde 'sedere ad dexteram patris' nihil aliud est quam simul cum patre habere gloriam divinitatis, et beatitudinem, et iudicariam potestatem, et hoc immutabiliter et *regaliter*" (emphasis added).

22. See *In Ioan.* XIX, l. 4 (n. 2419–22).

23. See Jer 10:7; Dan 7:13f.

24. See Rev 15:3f.: "magna et mirabilia opera tua Domine Deus omnipotens / iustae et verae viae tuae *rex saeculorum* / quis non timebit Domine et magnificabit nomen tuum quia solus pius quoniam *omnes gentes* venient et adorabunt in conspectu tuo / quoniam iudicia tua manifesta sunt" (emphasis added).

25. See A. Stock, "O-Antiphonen," *Liturgie und Poesie. Zur Sprache des Gottesdienstes* (Kevelaer: Butzon & Bercker, 2010), 67–92, esp. 85f.

marks the exalted Christ's lordly and judicial status,[26] which will be taken up again in another hymn, *Verbum supernum prodiens*; there, the text dwells upon the incarnate Word of God and formulates it thus: *se regnans* [!] *dat in praemium*. The hymn *Pange lingua*, however, deals less with articulating the eschatological potential of associating glorification, judgment, and consummate perfection; rather, it concerns itself with gratefully and joyfully extolling the mystery of the glorified Lord.[27]

The Life of Jesus and the Handing on of the Word

In the hymn's second stanza, a retrospective on the *life of Jesus* and a whole summary of his earthly existence are offered. The description ranges from his being born of the Virgin Mary, to his public ministry and his work of preaching, all the way to the last supper. What the *Summa theologiae* unfolds *discursively* in the theology of the mystery of Christ's life[28] appears here in, so to speak, time-lapsed *poetic* distillation recalling the decisive events of his life. *Nobis datus, nobis natus*, the opening verse rings out sonorously, as it takes up the mariological motif of the first stanza and carries it further (*fructus ventris generosi*). In the background is the famous passage in the book of Isaiah, where it states: "*Parvulus enim natus est nobis et filius datus est nobis*—unto us a child is born and a son is given" (Is 9:6).[29] A gift is mentioned without the giver being explicitly named. But if the Trinitarian life in God is interpreted as an eternal occurrence of giving and receiving, then the rationale for the Incarnation is passing on life: God desires to share himself with others, *se aliis communicare*.[30] The context of the hymn makes clear that in his Son, God gives himself as gift. The infinite distance

---

26. In the *Invitatorium* to Matins for the Solemnity of Corpus Christi, Thomas takes up the motif again. There, the text runs: "Christum regem adoremus dominantem gentibus." On the doctrine of the three offices, see B.-D. de La Soujeole, "Les *tria munera Christi*. Contribution de saint Thomas à la recherche contemporaine," *Revue Thomiste* 99 (1999): 59–74.

27. In addition to meter and rhyme, several distinctive tonal features are conspicuous: *pretiosi—pretium; generosi—gentium; corporis—sanguinis—ventris*.

28. See S. th. III, qq. 35–45. See also G. Lohaus, *Die Geheimnisse des Lebens Jesu in der Summa Theologiae des heiligen Thomas von Aquin* (Freiburg: Herder, 1985).

29. It may be mentioned *en passant*, that Thomas, as *baccalaureus biblicus*, authored a cursory commentary on the book of Isaiah, his first theological work. Because of his predilection for historical-literal exegesis, he interpreted Isaiah 8:4 to mean that the *puer* announced there is the son of the prophet and his wife. This interpretation comes close to the Jewish rejection, which did not see in this verse a messianic proclamation of Jesus Christ, and caused quite a headache for later Thomistic research. See Torrell, *Saint Thomas Aquinas*, 28f. and 337.

30. Thomas establishes the fittingness of the Incarnation in reference to the goodness of divine being: "Deus est bonitas. Pertinet autem ad rationem boni ut se aliis communicet. Unde ad rationem summi boni pertinet quod summo modo se creaturae communicet" (S. th. III, q. 1). On this motif, see: M. Scheuer, "Aliis communicare."

between God, the Creator, and men, his privileged creatures, is thereby fundamentally bridged and the possibility of friendship with God inaugurated.[31] Even Aristotle in his *Nicomachean Ethics* holds a friendship between God and men to be impossible, since the basis—a reciprocal understanding between friends characterized by benevolence—is ruled out.[32] Yet with the Incarnation of God's Son, God himself gives the basis for a friendship of men with God.[33] The gift of the Incarnation and mission of the Son result from God's love (see Jn 3:16: "*Sic Deus dilexit mundum ut Filium suum unigenitum daret*").

The way along which the gift reached men is being born of Mary—*ex intacta virgine*, as the hymn intones. Here also is an echo from the book of Isaiah, where it is promised that the virgin will conceive a son: *Ecce virgo concipiet*.[34] Mary is designated as "intact" (*intacta*). What is implied by this attribute would be more rigorously developed by having recourse to the mariological passages of the *Summa theologiae*.[35] In these texts, Thomas attempts to argue for the fittingness of the events in salvation history that relate to Mary: in particular, that she was freed from the stain of original sin;[36] that she committed neither mortal nor venial sins;[37] that she did not

---

31. See *S. th.* II-II, q. 23, a. 1.

32. See *Nic. Eth.* 1159a: "but if the distance is very great, as is the case with God, then there can no longer be friendship."

33. See H. Dörnemann, *Freundschaft als Paradigma der Erlösung* (Würzburg: Echter, 1997); E. Schockenhoff, *Bonum hominis. Die anthropologischen und theologischen Grundlagen der Tugendethik des Thomas von Aquin* (Mainz: Matthias-Grünewald, 1987), 501–26.

34. As is well known, Is 7:14 in the Hebrew original speaks of a "young woman." The term *alma* leaves open whether it really pertains in a restricted sense to a "virgin." Already the LXX, by translating *alma* with παρθένος (= virgin), had admittedly disambiguated the semantic openness. The Vulgate is beholden to this translation, as the text there reads: *Ecce virgo concipiet* (Is 7:14). For background, see G. L. Müller, "Jungfrauengeburt," *LThK* 5, 3rd ed. (1996): 1091–95.

35. See *S. th.* III, qq. 27–30, where Thomas unfolds a thematically ordered Mariology (sanctification, virginity, espousal, annunciation).

36. See *S. th.* III, q. 27, a. 1 ad 3: "Beata Virgo sanctificata fuit in utero a peccato originali quantum ad maculam personalem: non tamen fuit liberata a reatu quo tota natura tenebatur obnoxia, ut scilicet non intraret in Paradisum nisi per Christi ostia." Thomas does not yet teach the immaculate conception of Mary (see *S. th.* III, q. 31, aa. 7 and 8 ad 2), as Duns Scotus and the Franciscan school after him do. He presupposes that Mary was sanctified (*santificatio*) while in the womb (*in utero*). The reason for this is that for "Thomas, Mary must be conceived under the law of original sin in order to truly count as being in need of redemption." Thus H. U. von Balthasar, *Theodrama: Theological Dramatic Theory*, vol. 3: *The Dramatis Personae: The Person in Christ* (San Francisco: Ignatius Press, 1992), 322. In addition to the universality of original sin, Thomas argues from the preeminence of Christ: "Christus excellit Beatam Virginem in hoc, quod sine originali [sc. peccato] conceptus et natus est. Beata autem Virgo in originali concepta, sed non nata." Thomas, *In salutationem angelicam*, in idem, *Opuscula Theologica* II, ed. E. Spiazzi (Rome: Marietti, 1954), n. 1116. For background: U. Horst, *Die Diskussion um die Immaculata Conceptio im Dominikanerorden. Ein Beitrag zur Geschichte der theologischen Methode* (Paderborn: Schöningh, 1987).

37. See *S. th.* III, q. 27, a. 4, where Mary's election to be the mother of God is discussed and it is emphasized that she would not have been fitted to this task if she had sinned even once: "Et ideo simpliciter fatendum est quod Beata Virgo nullum actuale peccatum commisit, nec mortale nec venial: ut sic impleatur quod dicitur Cant. 4: 'Tota pulchra es, amica mea, et macula non est in te.'"

know man but rather was overshadowed by the Holy Spirit;[38] that she thus conceived as a virgin[39] and finally gave birth to the Redeemer. The predicate *intacta* sets free this mariological horizon of association and accentuates the mystery of faith we call virgin motherhood.[40] The *Summa theologiae* subsequently traces the contours further, taking up the mysteries of the birth, circumcision, and baptism of Jesus.[41] Instead of going into the *hidden life of Jesus*, the hymn relates the gift of the Redeemer directly to the public ministry: *et in mundo conversatus*.[42] According to Thomas, the purpose of the Incarnation is for the incarnate Son of God to visit the world in order to proclaim the truth (*ad manifestandum veritatem*). Had he permanently retired from the world as a hermit and shunned contact with men, then the divine truth would have remained hidden, the sick would not have found a doctor, nor the sinners and tax collectors a path to God.[43] The time of Jesus' public ministry is therefore conceived of as the time of sowing the Word: *sparso verbi semine*. "In *Pange lingua*, the synoptic parable of the sower becomes an image integrating the various parts of Jesus' whole life."[44] Jesus preaches and teaches, his proclamation is directed toward concrete addressees and takes place in a dialogical face-to-face with his listeners.

Orality is the mode of his teaching, not literality, and this preference is profoundly fitting, holds Thomas. As the most sublime teacher (*excellentissimus doctor*), Jesus wanted to impress his teaching directly on the hearts of his listeners.[45] As the center of the person, the heart is the place at which communication is aimed. In addition, the written word would never have been adequate to capturing the loftiness of Christ's teaching. Even the Gospel of John testifies to Jesus' works having an incommensurability surpassing any attempt to limit them in writing, when it states in conclusion: "There are also many other things that Jesus did; if every one of them were written down, I suppose that the world itself could not contain the books that would be written" (Jn 21:25). Finally, Thomas sees a certain preference

---

38. See *S. th*. III, q. 32.
39. *S. th*. III, q. 28, a. 1: "simpliciter confitendum est matrem Christi virginem concepisse."
40. See *S. th*. III, q. 28 (De virginitate matris Dei).
41. See *S. th*. III, qq. 35–39.
42. The phrase contains a literary reminiscence of the Prologue to John's Gospel, where it says: "in mundo erat et mundus per ipsum factus est" (Jn 1:10, Vulgate).
43. See *S. th*. III, q. 40, a. 1: "conversatio Christi talis debuit esse ut conveniret fini incarnationis, secundum quam venit in mundum, primo quidem ad manifestandum veritatem.... Et ideo non debeat se occultare." See C. Berchtold, *Manifestatio veritatis*, 218.
44. A. Stock, *Poetische Dogmatik*, vol. 3, 315.
45. See *S. th*. III, q. 42, a. 4: "Excellentiori enim doctori excellentior modus doctrinae debetur. Et ideo Christo, tamquam excellentissimo doctori, hic modus competebat, ut doctrinam suam auditorum cordibus imprimeret."

for oral over written teaching in that the disciples of Jesus, who received his teaching in an immediate way, then had to hand on the Gospel themselves. Had Jesus left behind his teaching in a fixed written form, then handing on the faith by means of living instruments would not have been so necessary.[46] Jesus, the *verbum incarnatum*, thus teaches in such a way as to scatter the "seed of the Word" so that this seed—to take up the logic of the parable (see Mt 13:3–23)—would bear fruit many times over in the hearts of those who hear him.[47] Such a fruitful reception rests upon three conditions, which Thomas lays out in his commentary on this passage: first, that it is preserved in memory (*memoria*); second, that it takes root in the heart through love (*caritas*); and third, that it is carefully cultivated (*sollicitudo*).[48] The parable of the sower, however, illustrates that efficacious acceptance of the word is blocked through obstacles that subvert precisely these conditions. The seed falls on the path, where it is trampled upon (see Lk 8:5) and eaten by the birds of the air; this is the case when the *verbum Dei* encounters an empty and fickle heart.[49] Here we see the requisite *memoria* thwarted. The seed then falls on rocky ground where there is but little soil, with the result that it cannot take root and thus withers before the rising sun; this is the case when the *verbum Dei* bumps up against hard-heartedness (*cordis duritia*) rather than love. Finally, the seed falls among thorns that run rampant and choke off the sprouting seed; this is the case when love of riches or concerns of this world prevent an attentive reception. Only where these three obstacles to reception are nullified can the *semen verbi* bear fruit. This is the case where it falls upon good soil and the word can inscribe itself in the heart of its hearer, thereafter to grow and bring a superabundant yield.[50]

It is worth noting that Thomas expressly emphasizes the orality of Jesus' proclamation. Unlike the letter, which always puts an intermediate variable between speaker and receiver (*littera habet interpositionem*),[51] the

---

46. See, in addition, *S. th.* III, q. 42, a. 4 ad 2, where the salvation-historical connection between the old and new covenants is worked out, in order to show the priority of oral over written teaching in terms of fittingness: "quia lex vetus in sensibilibus figuris dabatur, ideo etiam convenienter sensibilibus signis scripta fuit. Sed doctrina Christi, quae est 'lex Spiritus vitae,' scribi debuit 'non atramento, sed Spiritu Dei vivi, non in tabulis lapideis, sed in tabulis cordis carnalibus,' ut Apostolus dicit, 2 Cor. 3."

47. Thomas himself, by the way, brought up the motif of the sowing of the word, in order to make clear the then-controversial role of the mendicant orders. See his sermon, "Exiit qui seminat," in: Th. Käppeli, "Una raccolta di predicheaatribuite a S. Thommaso d'Aquino," *Archivum fratrum praedicatorum* 13 (1943): 75–88. Also on this point, see J.-P. Torrell, "Le semeur est sorti pour semer: L'image du Christ pêcheur chez frère Thomas d'Aquin," *Recherches thomasiennes* (Paris: Librairie Philosophique, 2000), 357–66.

48. See *In Matth* XIII, l. I (n. 1087).

49. Ibid. (n. 1088): "Quando in corde vano et instabili cadit verbum Dei, cadit secus viam."

50. Ibid. (n. 1091): "Positis impedimentis, agitur de seminis fructu *Alia ceciderunt in terram bonam, et dederunt fructum*. Terra quae non secus viam, quae non petrosa, quae non spinosa, est terra bona, scilicet cor bonum; et si ibi seminatur, fructum affert."

51. Ibid. (n. 1123).

orally spoken word enters directly into the hearts of those listening: *audire verbum Dei debet habere effectum unum, ut infigatur in corde.*⁵² Thomas returns time and again to the metaphor of the heart in order to designate the center of the person, to which the *verbum Dei* is directed. The word aims at the transformation of the hearer. Conversion and faith, which urge toward profession, are the processes of reception provoked by hearing the divine word.⁵³ At the same time, the word desires to transform hearers of the word (*auditores verbi*) into doers of the word (*factores verbi*). The hermeneutic of the heart remains incomplete if it is not translated into the practice of discipleship.⁵⁴ The word has a life-determining power; it enters into the life of those who hear it and is thus disseminated. (Only later will the words of the *verbum incarnatum* be addressed, so that the "words of eternal life" remain present in the flow of history; nevertheless, they can be fittingly received only when they are read in the spirit of the word rather than according to the letter.)⁵⁵

But the life of Jesus is itself word become flesh. Not only his words but also his deeds are a manifestation of divine truth. *Dominus in sua conversatione exemplum perfectionis dedit.*⁵⁶ The Lord lived in accordance with the prescriptions of the old covenant in order to confirm and fulfill them; he took upon himself the temptations without falling to them;⁵⁷ he lived, as the hymn puts it, as a sojourner on earth and "concluded the time of his earthly life with an astonishing ordinance (*miro clausit ordine*)." This hints at the transition to the scene of the last supper, which the third stanza recalls.

---

52. Ibid. (n. 1122).

53. Unlike the reception of rational contents, which are bound up with cognitive performance, the communication of the *verbum Dei*, which is directed toward the "heart," also includes the volitional and affective sides of a person. Admittedly, the heart of the addressee can also be so constituted as to hinder the efficacious reception of the *semen verbi*. Possible negative modes of reception are explicitly outlined by Thomas following the three obstacles in the parable of the sower (path, rocky soil, thorns). Thus, we read, for example, "Petra est malum cor" (ibid., n. 1126).

54. *In Matth* XIII, l. I (n. 1125—in reference to Jas 1:22).

55. The hymn does not address the fact that the teaching of the *verbum incarnatum* is authenticated by miracles, which fact brings Jesus' *dicta et facta* into a conspicuous congruence. On the miraculous deeds of Christ and their authenticating function, see *S. th.* III, q. 43.

56. *S. th.* III, q. 40. a. 2 ad 1. See also C. Berchtold, *Manifestatio veritatis. Zum Offenbarungsbegriff bei Thomas von Aquin* (Münster-Hamburg-London: LIT, 2000).—It is notable that Thomas cites poverty as the precondition for Jesus' exemplary way of life. One can certainly see a connection here with the mendicant controversy, when Thomas, who belongs to the *Ordo Praedicatorum*, suddenly passes over from the *conversatio Christi* to generalities and underscores the following: "Oportet praedicatores Dei verbi, ut omnino vacent praedicationi, omnino a saecularium rerum cura esse absolutos. Quod facere non possent qui divitias possident. Unde et ipse Dominus, Apostolos ad praedicandum mittens, dicit eis: 'Nolite possidere aurum neque argentum.' Et ipsi Apostoli dicunt, Act. 6: 'Non est aequum nos relinquere verbum et ministrare mensis'" (*S. th.* III, q. 40, a. 3). On the background, see Torrell, *Saint Thomas Aquinas*, 94–114.

57. See *S. th.* III, q. 41.

Jesus' Self-Gift on the Night of the Last Supper

After the succinct overview of Jesus' life, a fine-tuning is undertaken, concentrating solely on the night of the last supper. With a paucity of words, the historical situation is sketched, and each word brings with it a specific court of meanings that should be pursued. It is the *last* meal Jesus spends with his disciples; the mood is tinged with farewells. Jesus lies at table with his "brothers" (*fratribus*)—as the hymn puts it—and celebrates the Passover meal.[58] He observed the Law (*plene observata*), as Thomas highlights, and therefore he also took up the prescribed meal (*cibis in legalibus*) of the Passover celebration. According to Exodus 12, this entails "a male, one-year-old lamb without blemish," which is slaughtered and then is to be eaten along "with unleavened bread and bitter herbs," all in memory of the nocturnal departure from Egypt. Jesus fulfills the ritual prescriptions of the Passover celebration. Thomas finds it important to underscore this. Only thereafter do we come to the significant new gesture: *se dat suis manibus*. "He no longer scatters himself in many words, but rather gathers himself up and then gives himself with his own hands."[59] He gives himself as food (*cibum*) to the Twelve, who were chosen as representatives of the tribes of Israel. The word *cibus* institutes an association, pregnant with meaning, between the old and new covenants. The Passover feasts as dictated by the Law are the *figura* of the new covenant meal, in which Christ gives himself as food—food that designates in an anticipatory way the heavenly wedding banquet (see Mk 14:25). Jesus gives himself with his own hands, as the hymn states. The covenant of his love becomes perceptible to the senses in the breaking and distributing of the bread, which illuminatingly anticipates the significance of the Passion. With this gesture, the resurrected Lord is recognized by the disciples in Emmaus; with this gesture, the ecclesial *traditio* of the Eucharistic self-gift of Christ remains bound up.

The Poetic Pinnacle: The Mystery of Eucharistic Conversion

It is no accident that the impetus for Jesus' giving of himself with his own hands stands architectonically as the focal point of the hymn. Nor is it an accident that in the fourth stanza the historical fact of this self-gift at the last supper is linked with the question of *how* this self-gift can be made present ever anew by the ecclesial community in the history that follows.

---

58. Thomas thus follows the chronology of the synoptics, which have the last supper as coinciding with the feast of Passover.

59. A. Stock, *Poetische Dogmatik*, vol. 3, 315.

Without the Word that not only created the things of reality but also can transform them, the mystery of the Eucharist is incomprehensible. Following the poetic snapshots of Jesus' life and the central scene of the last supper, the hymn now concentrates on the decisive moment of consecration: *Verbum caro panem verum / Verbo carnem efficit*. In this assonance-rich couplet, the performative power of the divine word is expressed with a linguistic density that finds few parallels in western poetry.[60] The meaning centers around the inner connection between Incarnation and Eucharist, which is formulated here through an allusion to the prologue of John's Gospel. It is the very incarnate Word who gathers himself up and, by the *verbum efficax* (i.e. the *verba testamenti*), transforms bread and wine into the body and blood of Jesus.[61] Articulating the event of Eucharistic conversion without recourse to the theory of transubstantiation, the hymn follows here the internal logic of John's Gospel, in which *caro* is discussed only twice: once in the culminating phrase of the prologue (see Jn 1:14), and then in the Eucharistic discourse, which is included in the Gospel for the feast of Corpus Christi.[62]

At this point, it should also be recalled that the word is the form of the sacrament—*accedit verbum ad elementum, et fit sacramentum* runs the definition Thomas often quotes from Augustine.[63] As the word is spoken, it not only describes the reality but constitutes it at the same time. To formulate it theoretically in terms of a speech act, we might say: for Thomas, the words of institution are not constative but performative. Certainly the institution of the sacrament of the altar is, according to Thomas, brought about by the fact that Jesus spoke *particular words* that had the power to transform reality.[64] However, the true essence of things, their substance, is not perceived through their appearance;[65] rather, it is defined by the word pertaining to the intellect (note the assonance of *verbum* and *verum*). The conversion actualized by the word remains withdrawn from the senses. Sight, touch, and taste correlate with the residual forms of bread and wine. In contrast, the intellect illuminated by faith, to which the divine word alone corresponds,

---

60. See Paul Eluard's *dur désir de durer*, which is also a play on the name Dürer (quoted in G. Steiner, *Der Garten des Archimedes. Essays* [Munich: Carl Hanser, 1996], 12).

61. Stock (*Poetische Dogmatik*, vol. 3, 315) formulates it precisely: "The speech of the incarnate Word is concentrated in one word, the effective word ('hoc est ...'), recreating the bread into flesh and wine into blood."

62. On this point, see M. Reiser, "Eucharistische Wissenschaft. Eine exegetische Betrachtung zu Joh 6,26.59," in *Vorgeschmack. Ökumenische Bemühungen um die Eucharistie*, ed. B. J. Hilberath and D. Sattler (Mainz: Matthias-Grünewald, 1995), 164–77, here 175.

63. Augustinus, *Io. ev. tr.* 80, 3 (CCL 36, ed. R. Willems, 529).

64. See *S. th.* III, q. 60, a. 7 c: "Dominus determinata verba protulit in consecratione sacramenti Eucharistiae, dicens Math. 26: 'Hoc est corpus meum.'"

65. See *S. th.* III, q. 76, a. 7 c: "Substantia non est visibilis oculo corporali, neque subiacet alicui sensui, nec etiam imaginationi, sed soli intellectui, cuius obiectum est 'quod quid est.'"

knows that the body and blood of Christ are really present here.[66] The lack of empirical verification of the sacrament has always been a gateway of doubt and thus is mentioned twice in the hymn. The medieval Eucharistic miracles and the legendary, miraculous tales can certainly be understood as a compensatory phenomenon: possible or actual doubts concerning the real presence of Christ's body and blood were to be overcome by graphic demonstration. As is well known, Thomas Aquinas himself commented rather reservedly on the Eucharistic miracles of his time.[67]

Grateful Appreciation of the Giver's Presence in the Gift

The two concluding stanzas display the grateful reaction of the faithful to this great gift. Sounding rather like a syllogistic deduction, the hymn states: *Tantum ergo sacramentum veneremur cernui*. The gift of the sacrament cannot leave one indifferent—it demands appropriate expression. The recollection of the miraculous, sacramental transformation flows into a doxological acclamation, which is grammatically legible in the change of subject to the first person plural, and then also recognizable in the gestures of adoration: those praying kneel down (*cernui*). The presence of the *Christus passus*— who gave his life on the cross for all people and now sits at the Father's right hand enthroned as *rex gentium*—this presence makes the gesture of kneeling, which is reserved for God alone, appear as reasonable and fitting. Here, God presents the gift of atonement not (or no longer) in the form of animal sacrifices but in the unbloody making present of Jesus Christ's sacrifice on the cross, once for all.[68] Thus, the transition from the old rite to the new one is carried out, something described with precision by Alex Stock in his *Poetische Dogmatik*:

In its unbloody part, in consuming of the unleavened bread and the drinking the wine, the Passover meal is pushed to a new level of reality. The bloody part (the slaughtered

---

66. Over and over again, Thomas adduced reasons for why the empirical deficit in verification makes sense (*horror cruoris*; merit of faith; etc.). Corresponding verses are also found in the other hymns (see *Adoro te devote*:"credo quidquid dixit Dei filius nil hoc verbo veritatis verius").
67. See *S. th.* III, q. 76, a. 8.
68. See also *Officium de festo corporis Christi*, Lectio II, 277, where it states: "Quid enim hoc convivio pretiosius esse potest, in quo non carnes vitulorum et hircorum, ut olim in lege, sed nobis sumendus proponitur Christus verus Deus? Quid hoc sacramento mirabilius? In ipso namque panis et vinum in Christi corpus et sanguinem substantialiter convertuntur. Ideoque Christus Deus et homo perfectus, sub modici panis et vini specie continetur.—What therefore can be more precious than this banquet, *in which is presented to us not the flesh of calves and goats, as once in the Law*, but Christ, true God, to be enjoyed? What is more wonderful than this Sacrament? For in it, bread and wine are essentially transformed into the body and blood of Christ. Therefore, Christ, God and perfect man, is contained under the appearance of bread and wine" (emphasis added).

lamb) disappears. Animal sacrifice is abrogated once and for all in the human sacrifice of the crucifixion, and this sacrifice is made present in a wholly unbloody manner in the eating and drinking of bread and wine. The rite of the Paschal lamb called for the eating of meat, but no drinking of blood; blood was painted apotropaically on the doorposts, or cast upon the altar as the lifeblood belonging to God, but not drunk. Blood became our drink only through the ritual duality of bread and wine taking into itself the reality of the new Paschal lamb, Christ. The logic of pacification contained in the ritual slaughter of the past is now found in the simple eating of bread and drinking of wine, and this logic transfers the blood into a ritual context.[69]

The ritual innovation remains bound up with the presuppositions of salvation history found in the Old Testament; at the same time, it marks a reconfiguration of sacrifice. Apart from the anticipatory significations—the *figurae*—the *passio Christi* and its being made present in the sacrament of the Eucharist cannot be understood. It is not for nothing that the Divine Office composed by Thomas for the feast of Corpus Christi contains an impressive arsenal of old covenant figures who point ahead to the Eucharist.[70] The ritual innovation remains dependent upon the old covenant's horizon of interpretation, for which reason the translation by Marie Luise Thurmair misses Aquinas's intention in this passage, when she juxtaposes the "law of fear [*Gesetz der Furcht*]" and the "meal of love [*Mahl der Liebe*]."[71]

The Sequence *Lauda Sion* will also lay stress on the point that the innovation of the new covenant is to be understood when seen against the background of the old convenant's traditions; the discontinuity separating Christian from Jewish faith is, once more, to be encompassed by a continuity in salvation history:

In figuris praesignatur,	It was prefigured in types:
Cum Isaac immolatur,	When Isaac was immolated,
Agnus Paschae deputatur	When the Pascal Lamb was sacrificed,
Datur manna patribus.	When manna was given to the fathers.

The hymn closes with a Trinitarian doxology that impressively produces the plerophoric style of diction proper to hymns. The three divine Persons are named not as Father, Son, and Spirit, but are still fittingly para-

---

69. A. Stock, *Poetische Dogmatik*, vol. 3, 316.

70. See *Ystoria sancti Thome de Aquino de Guillaume de Tocco* (1323), ed. C. le Brun-Gouanvic (Toronto: Pontifical Institute of Mediaeval Studies, 1996), 133: "Scripsit officium de corpore Christi, de mandato Vrbani, in quo omnes que de hoc sunt sacramento ueteres figuras exposuit, et ueritates que de noua sint gratia compilauit."

71. See *Gotteslob*, n. 544. In the new edition of *Gotteslob* (n. 493 [Stuttgart, 2013], 538), the translation of M.-L. Thurmair is replaced by that of O. Lumma: "Altes Zeugnis möge weichen / da der neue Brauch begann [May the old testament give way / for the new rite began]."

phrased (*genitori genitoque*).[72] In the parts of the *Summa theologiae* dealing with Trinitarian theology, Thomas explains that there is generation (*generatio*) in the divinity: "The procession of the Word in the divinity is called generation, and that Word himself proceeding is called Son."[73] Temporal, physical concepts are naturally to be kept at arm's length when dealing with the concept of generation in Trinitarian theology. In contrast with the created realm, where generation always also signifies a change from non-being to being, generation in God signifies an eternal event that indicates the relation of origin between Father and Son. From both Father and Son, however, proceeds the reciprocal bond of love, the Spirit (*procendenti ab utroque*).[74] In the hymn, a shower of predicates is lavished upon the triune God, the origin and end of created being: praise (*laus*), jubilation (*iubilatio*), salvation (*salus*), honor (*honor*), power (*virtus*), blessing (*benedictio*). The exuberance of praise corresponds to the inexpressible wonder of the gift that God gave to the faithful in the Eucharist.

An Interim Reflection

After going through the hymn in this way, I would like to conclude by emphasizing once again three considerations:

1. The hymn *Pange lingua gloriosi* illuminates—if not explicitly, then certainly implicitly—the distinct dimensions of the *corpus Christi*. It points out that there is a theological coherence between the glorified (*corpus gloriosum*), the incarnate (*verbum caro*), and the Eucharistic body of Christ (*caro* and *sanguinis Christi*). The praise of the opening stanza pertains to the glorified body, which is forever marked by the Passion. Thereafter follows a flashback to the life of Jesus, the incarnate Word.[75] The hymn places the accent on the public proclamation of the Word, while refraining from lamenting the fact that the words and parables scattered by the *verbum incarnatum* as the sower fall upon little fertile soil. It states laconically that with the institution of the Eucharist at the last supper, the life of Jesus

---

72. According to N. Lohfink, "Das 'Pange Lingua' im *Gotteslob*," 284, an allusion to Ps 2:7 and 110:3 is advanced.
73. *S. th.* I, q. 27, a. 2: "processio verbi in divinis dicitur generatio, et ipsum verbum dicitur Filius."
74. While the *processio* of the Word is understood according to an analogy with knowledge—the Father knows himself in the Word and in knowing himself knows everything else—the *processio* of the Spirit from the Father and the Son is understood according to an analogy of volition. See, on this point, *S. th.* I, q. 27, a. 3.
75. The fact that the Eucharist is a *signum rememorativum* is widened here beyond the Passion to the life of Jesus. Also, it is precisely his public preaching that met with opposition and brought about the conflict that culminated in the trial and crucifixion.

finds an astonishing conclusion (*miro clausit ordine*). Through the *verbum efficax*—spoken long ago by the *verbum caro* and spoken in his name by priests still today—the conversion of bread and wine into the body and blood of Christ takes place. The participation of the faithful in the Eucharistic *corpus Christi verum*, we might now add, builds up the body of the Church, which in scholastic theology is called the *corpus Christi mysticum*. The hymn does not articulate this connection between *corpus Christi verum* and *corpus Christi mysticum*, and it furthermore refrains from spelling out the way the New Testament employs the term *corpus Christi* as a metaphor that includes a differentiation between head (*caput*) and members (*membra*) (see *S. th.* III, q. 8). Still, on the feast of Corpus Christi the members of the *corpus Christi mysticum* extol the Eucharistic mystery of the presence of the *corpus Christi verum*, which is held up for adoration in the elevated host. In this way, an allusion is made to this connection, which Thomas will explicitly unfold in the *Summa theologiae*.[76]

2. The hymn accentuates the fact that the ritual innovation bound up with the institution of the Eucharist comes to pass within the horizon of the Jewish feast of Passover. Jesus' fidelity to the Law and the ritual prescriptions concerning meals is specifically stressed (*observata lege plene / cibis in legalibus*). To be sure, Jesus establishes a new covenant on the night of the last supper through the significant self-gift in the signs of bread and wine. And this will indeed quickly lead his disciples to a dramatic separation from the cult of the Jewish Temple. For Thomas, the figures of the old covenant that point in advance to the rite of the Eucharist retain their meaning, for they make recognizable the coherence of God's deeds in salvation history. Thomas sought to summon up their rich significance precisely in the composition of the Office for Corpus Christi, and this in order to understand more profoundly the polyvalent perspectives of the Eucharistic mystery. Thomas's scriptural hermeneutic is certainly clear in its Christological character, as is the case with scholastic theology generally.[77] Far be it from his thoughts to relativize the novelty of the new covenant. However, when it comes to Thomas, to speak of a latent or even manifest anti-Semitism is impossible, unless one simply wanted to hold the confession of Jesus as the Christ under the suspicion of anti-Semitism.[78]

---

76. See M. Grabmann, *Die Lehre des hl. Thomas von Aquin von der Kirche als Gotteswerk* (Regensburg: G.J. Manz, 1903), 267–94.

77. See M. Arias Reyero, *Thomas von Aquin als Exeget. Die Prinzipien seiner Schriftdeutung und seine Lehre von den Schriftsinnen* (Einsiedeln: Johannes-Verlag, 1971).

78. Here, see the remark of Th. Pröpper, "Wegmarken zu einer Christologie nach Auschwitz," in his *Evangelium und freie Vernunft* (Freiburg: Herder, 2001), 278: "at times the mere attempt to determine the *distinctiveness* of Christianity and give an account of it places it under the suspicion of anti-Semitism."

3. Medieval theology has often been accused of a certain myopic concentration on the aspect of the *real bodily presence* of Jesus Christ in the consecrated gifts. Indeed, we ought not to deny a concentration on the when and how of Eucharistic conversion, since it is connected to the way of framing the question that was set by the Eucharistic controversies, namely, whether Jesus Christ is present in the Eucharistic gifts *in veritate* or *in signo*. The commemoration of the salvific deeds of the Passion, resurrection, and ascension receded so often into the background that the *commemorative, actual presence* [*kommemorative Aktualpräsenz*] of Christ in the Eucharist played only a subordinated role. After a reading of the hymn *Pange lingua gloriosi*, one will be able to say that in the poetic theology of Thomas, the actual presence [*Aktualpräsenz*] of the exalted Lord (see the opening stanza) is expressed in words in the same way as the commemorative, actual presence of Jesus Christ (see the stanzas depicting his life, the last supper, and his bloody death). At the same time, the structure of the hymn follows a dynamic that tends toward the event of Eucharistic conversion—and thus the aspect of somatic real presence. The life of Jesus distills itself in the Eucharistic self-gift of Jesus Christ, as the center of the hymn introduces it: *se dat suis manibus*. On the basis of diction alone, it would be acceptable to designate as the poetic climax of the hymn the "wizardry in words" that follows in the fourth stanza, which circles around the mystery of Eucharistic conversion. Texts, however, stand within contexts which they cannot simply leave behind. The set of questions primarily set before medieval Eucharistic theology was centered around the question of how faith in the real presence of Christ in the Eucharist can be theologically ascertained and elaborated. This question, which Thomas answered discursively by working out the doctrine of transubstantiation, shapes the hymn as well, even while its poetic and linguistic form remains free of technical theological vocabulary.

6

A Poetic Theology of Gift

The Hymns *Sacris solemniis* and *Verbum supernum*

The Hymn *Sacris solemniis*

Sacris solemniis iuncta sint gaudia,
Et ex praecordiis sonent praeconia,
Recedant vetera, nova sint omnia,
Corda, voces, et opera.

At this our solemn feast let holy joys abound,
And from the inmost breast let songs of praise resound,
Let ancient rites depart and all be new around,
In every act, and voice, and heart.

Noctis recolitur cena novissima,
Qua Christus creditur agnum et azyma
Dedisse fratribus, iuxta legitima
Priscis indulta patribus.

Remember we that even, when, the Last Supper spread,
Christ, as we all believe, the Lamb, with leavenless bread,
Among his brethren shared, and thus the law obeyed,
Of all, unto their sire declared.

Post agnum typicum, expletis epulis,
Corpus Dominicum datum discipulis
Sic totum omnibus, quod totum singulis,
Eius fatemur manibus.

The typic Lamb consumed, the legal feast complete,
The Lord unto the Twelve, his body gave to eat;
The whole to all, no less, the whole to each did meet
With his own hands, as we confess.

Dedit fragilibus corporis ferculum,	He gave them, weak and frail, his flesh,
Dedit et tristibus sanguinis poculum,	their food to be;
Dicens: accipite quod trado vasculum;	On them, downcast and sad, his blood
Omnes ex eo bibite.	bestowed he:
	And thus to them he spake, "Receive this cup from me,
	And all of you this partake."
Sic sacrificium istud instituit,	So He this Sacrifice to institute did will,
Cuius officium committi voluit	And charged His priests alone that
Solis presbyteris, quibus sic congruit,	office to fulfill:
Ut sumant, et dent ceteris.	To them He did confide: to whom it pertains still
	To take, and the rest divide.
Panis angelicus fit panis hominum,	Thus Angels' Bread is made the Bread of
Dat panis caelicus figuris terminum.	man today:
O res mirabilis: manducat Dominum	The Living Bread from heaven with
Pauper, servus et humilis.	figures dost away:
	O wondrous gift indeed! Upon Lord and Master, may poor,
	Servant, and humble feed.
Te, trina Deitas unaque, poscimus,	Thee, therefore, we implore, O Godhead, One in Three,
Sic nos tu visita, sicut te colimus:	So may Thou visit us as we now worship Thee;
Per tuas semitas duc nos quo tendimus,	And lead us on Thy way, that we at last may see
Ad lucem quam inhabitas. Amen.	The light wherein Thou dwellest aye. Amen.
	[John David Chambers, 1805–93]

Observations on the Diction and Structure of the Hymn *Sacris solemniis*

The hymn *Sacris solemniis* is prayed in the Office for Matins, that is, at early dawn or in the last hours of night;[1] thus, it has somewhat the status of a hymnic overture. It includes seven strophes, each of which contains four lines. The verses are held together by a distinct rhyme scheme (A-A-A-B,

---

1. In Latin, *Matuta* is the goddess of dawn; the German designation *Mette* also derives from this Latin word. For background, see A. Baumstark, *Nocturna laus* (Münster: Aschendorff, 1957).

C-C-C-D, E-E-E-D, F-F-F-G, etc.) and follow a dactylic meter. The endings of the first two strophes are vocalic nearly without exception, while the remaining ones are consonantic. The hymn is, on the one hand, characterized by the semantic tension between old and new, as the opening stanza immediately makes clear through the chiastic placement of the attributes *vetera* and *nova*—a tension that will be taken up later.[2] Moreover, the poetic text is determined by a striking language of gift, as is indicated by the abundant derivatives of the verbs *dare* and *tradere*—sometimes in prominent positions.[3] After a festive introduction linguistically characterized by moments of alliteration and assonance,[4] there follows in the second stanza a historical reminiscence on Jesus' last supper, which—again corresponding to the chronology of the synoptics—is characterized as a Passover meal. The third strophe directs one's attention to the ritual innovation that takes place after the meal, when the body of the Lord is given to the disciples. More precisely, this self-gift of Christ is distinguished into two ritual actions: the gift of his body and the gift of his blood. The fourth strophe impressively and poetically brings out this double action by the anaphoric placement of the word *dedit*. At the same time, the stanza accentuates the gift of his blood when it quotes nearly verbatim Jesus' instruction concerning the chalice: "All of you this partake [*Omnes ex eo bibite*]." In this strophe, which makes up the compositional center of the hymn, the climax is certainly recognizable. It is not by chance that the following stanza conveys a theological commentary on the gift of Christ's blood when it takes up the term "sacrifice" (*sacrificium*). It is likewise emphasized that in the succession of time Christ wanted this ministry to be perpetuated by priests, who function, so to speak, as "instruments" of passing on (*traditio*). The two stanzas that follow distinguish themselves from what precedes, as is revealed by the change in tense and also the emphatic interjections (vocative). The fifth stanza extols the conversion of the bread of man into the bread of angels and accentuates the word *panis* to set up a thematic counterpoint to the preceding concentration on the gift of Christ's blood.[5] In the last strophe, the hymn not only flows into a doxology of the triune God, but also switches up the speaker's perspective and passes over into addressing God directly,

---

2. See the statement in v. 22, that the heavenly bread brings the end (*terminus*) to the figures.

3. See the following evidence: v. 7, *dedisse*; v. 10, *datum*; v. 13, *dedit*; v. 14, *dedit*; v. 15, *trado*; v. 20, *dent*; v. 22, *dat*. In lines 7, 13, 14, and 22, the verbs stand in a prominent position at the beginning of the verse.

4. See, in addition to the melodious rhyme on the vocalic ending "-ia," the alliteration in verses 1 and 2: "Sacris solemnis ... sint ... sonent," as well as the assonance-rich endings of the words "solemn*iis*" (v. 1) and "praecord*iis*" (v. 2) and the repetition of the prefix *prae*- in "praecordiis" and "praeconia" (v. 2).

5. See vv. 21 and 22: "*Panis* angelicus fit *panis* hominum; / dat *panis* caelicus ..."

as the emphatic invocation *"Te, trina Deitas unaque"* makes manifest right at the outset. Linguistically, what we find here are speech forms meeting that poetically produce the dialogue between those praying and God; these forms also provide forceful expression to the entreaties of those praying, that their striving for the end might attain to eternal beatitude.[6]

Theological Interpretation: Christ's Self-Gift as Ritual Innovation

A feast interrupts the everyday; it is the occasion for joy and it institutes a remembrance of origins. The first stanza of the hymn *Sacris solemniis* articulates this joy in the early morning of Corpus Christi, which is precisely the intention of Pope Urban IV's Bull *Transiturus*: to place the festive joy regarding the Sacrament of the Eucharist front and center.[7] Even in its vocabulary, the hymn picks up this intention when it points out that joy should resound (*praeconia*) from deep within (*ex praecordiis*).[8] All the poetic stops are pulled out, so to speak, in order to call forth a certain festivity. The dactylic meter, the colorful multiplicity of vowel sounds, and the phrases rich in assonance—these all contribute to the evocation of joy.[9] Those praying the hymn should join in the festal joy and support it (note the subjunctive with adhortative nuance: *sint, sonent, sint*). The old should give way, making room for the new,[10] runs the programmatic line. The polyvalence of the poetic text is revealed in its addressing here not only the typological relation between the "old" Passover ritual of Israel and the "new" Paschal lamb, Jesus Christ,[11] but also—as we read later—the *conditio humana*, which is one of fragility

---

6. Through imperatives (v. 26, *visita*; v. 27, *duc*) and personal pronouns (v. 25, *te*; v. 26, *tu, te*), the Trinitarian God is directly addressed. The verbs *poscimus, colimus*, and *tendimus* articulate the requests of those at prayer.

7. See Dorez, ed., *Registres d'Urbain IV*, 424: "Licet igitur hoc sacramentum in cotidianis missarum sollempniis frequentetur, conveniens tamen arbitramur et dignum, *ut de ipso semel saltem in anno ... memoria celebrior et sollempnior habeatur* (emphasis added). See the word-for-word identical documentation in Friedberg, ed., *Corpus iuris canonici*, vol. 2, col. 1176.

8. The Bull *Transitorus* speaks the emphatic language taken up in part by the hymn, even into its vocabulary: "O excellentissimum sacramentum, adorandum, venerandum, colendum, glorificandum, amandum et amplectandum, precipuis magnificandum laudibus, summis *preconiis* exaltandum, cunctis honorandum studiis, devotis prosequendum obsequiis, et sinceris mentibus retinendum! O memoriale nobilissimum, intimes commendandum *precordiis*, firmiter animo alligandum, diligenter in cordis reservandum utero, et meditatione ac celebratione sedula recensendum!" (Dorez, ed., *Registres d'Urbain IV*, v. 2/1, 424, emphasis added). See the slightly differing documentation in Friedberg, ed., *Corpus iuris canonici*, v. 2, col. 1176.

9. Already in the first line we find the vowels presented, "a," "i," "o," "u," and "au." The consonantal assonances, "sacris solemniis ... sint," as well as the anaphoric expressions, "praecordiis ... praeconia" work together to evoke a certain solemnity.

10. The breakthrough of what is new is accentuated syntactically by the chiastic setup: "Recedant vetera, nova sint omnia."

11. See *Pange lingua*: "et antiquum documentum / novo cedat ritui."

(*fragilibus*) and sadness (*tristibus*), which the joy of the feast ought to diminish. The emphasis placed on the new, which the opening stanza does not yet elaborate more fully, should determine everything: thinking and feeling (*corda*), words and voices (*voces*), and also deeds (*opera*).[12]

The solemnity celebrated has a specific prehistory that is worked in at this point. In the second stanza, the matter at hand is first the Old Testament background, without which the establishment of the new covenant would not be comprehensible: the feast of Passover. As we already saw in the vesper hymn *Pange lingua*, the hymn *Sacris solemniis* also expressly emphasizes that Jesus Christ did not ignore the ritual prescriptions of Israel but held to them exactly.[13] Even the time designation (*noctis*) makes this clear. Jesus celebrated the last supper with his disciples *by night* (see Mt 26:20; Mk 14:17; Lk 22:14; 1 Cor 11:23). Thus, he connects with the *nighttime* consumption of the lamb (*agnus*) and unleavened bread (*azyma*) during the flight of the Israelite people from their house of bondage in Egypt. Speaking in terms of unleavened bread not only refers to the material of the later Eucharistic sacrament,[14] but it also alludes to the typological tension between old leaven (*vetus fermentum*) and unleavened bread (*azyma*), which Paul relates to the lifestyle of Christians (see 1 Cor 5:7f.).[15] Among all the prefigurations from the old covenant, the Paschal lamb stands out, for it encompasses the three distinct aspects of a sacrament.[16] As is well known, Thomas distinguishes in his Eucharistic theology between *sacramentum tantum* (= bread and wine), *res et sacramentum* (= the true body and blood of Christ), and *res sacramenti* (= the effect of grace, or the unity of the mystical body, the Church). The diversity of figures in the old convenant are ordered by Thomas according to these aspects of the sacrament: for the *sacramentum tantum*, Melchizedek is the type, since he offered bread and wine (see Gn 14:6). Concerning the *Christus passus*, who is the *res et sacramentum*, all the sacrifices of the old covenant are prefigurations, inasmuch as they point ahead to the Passion,

---

12. Phonetically, "corda, voces, opera" all exhibit an affinity to "nova": all the words have in common that their first syllable is characterized by an "o" sound. In the Bull *Transiturus*, there is a passage containing similar motifs: "Tunc enim omnium corda et vota, ora et labia hymnos persolvant leatitae salutaris." The question of literary dependence—whether Thomas had the Bull *Transiturus* at the forefront of his mind, or contrariwise, the author of the Bull took up formulations of the Thomistic Office—does not admit of an easy historical answer. Tending to the second conjecture is C. Blume, "Das Fronleichnams-Fest. Seine ersten Urkunden und Offizien," *ThGl* 1 (1909): 337–49, here 341.

13. See also S. c. G. IV, c. 69: "Dominus autem, quamdiu fuit in mundo, legem servavit."

14. See S. th. III, q. 74, a. 4.

15. See 1 Cor 5:7f. (Vulgate): "expurgate vetus fermentum ut sitis nova consparsio sicut estis azymi etenim pascha nostrum immolatus est Christus itaque epulemur in fermento malitiae et nequitiae sed in azymis sinceritatis et veritatis."

16. See S. th. III, q. 73, a. 6, where the *agnus paschalis* is elaborated as the *praecipua figura* of the Eucharist.

especially sin offerings (Lv 23:27).[17] Finally, as for what pertains to the effect of the Eucharist, Thomas sees this anticipated in the image of manna.[18] According to Thomas, the precedence of the Paschal lamb motif consists in the fact that it unites in itself all three characteristics. First, it is eaten with unleavened bread (see Ex 12:8); second, it was sacrificed by the whole community of Israelites (see Ex 12:6); and third, the Israelites were protected from the angel of death by the lamb's blood painted on the doorposts. The readings and prayers, handed on by the fathers from of old, recall God's liberating deed (see Ex 12). The observance of the ritual prescriptions of the Law show that Jesus also places himself within the tradition of the fathers and reveals himself as a son of the Jewish people. It is notable that the disciples, with whom Jesus celebrated the last supper, are repeatedly designated as "brothers" (*fratres*). In this way, equal status is expressed, which can be related to a common belonging to the Israelite people and the observance of the Torah shared by all. But in the moment that it comes to the gift of the *corpus dominicum*, the body of the Lord, which goes beyond the horizon of the old covenant, the hymn changes the linguistic game and marks the difference between master and "disciples" (*discipuli*).

Set within the context of Passover, there follows the establishment of the new covenant. The hymn speaks emphatically of the last supper as *coena novissima*. The ritual innovation takes place—as the hymn stresses—*post agnum typicum*, that is, *after* the satiating meal.[19] The body of the Lord is given to the disciples, or more precisely: it is due to the profession of those praying (*fatemur*) that the *corpus dominicum* was given to the disciples, and indeed to each one entire, since Christ is wholly contained in each part of the gift. The hymn presupposes the teaching of concomitance, without clarifying it in any detail.[20] Christ communicates the self-gift to his own through his own hands—*se dat suis manibus*.[21] It is hardly by chance that the hands are explicitly mentioned here. It is these hands that break and share the bread. This manual act will not be insignificant for the handing on (*traditio*) of the testament—the Eucharist.

---

17. See *S. th.* I-II, q. 101, a. 4 ad 1: "per sacrificia significatur Christus immolatus."

18. In the sequence *Lauda Sion*, the manna as a prefiguration of the Eucharist is specifically taken up: "Datur manna patribus."

19. See *S. th.* III, q. 83, a. 2 ad 3: "Christus voluit ultimo hoc sacramentum discipulis tradere, ut fortius eorum cordibus imprimeretur. Et ideo *post cenam et in fine diei* hoc sacramentum consecravit et discipulis tradidit" (emphasis added).

20. The sequence *Lauda Sion* will go into it in more detail: "Fracto demum sacramento / Ne vacilles, sed memento / Tantum esse sub fragmento / Quantum toto tegitur / Nulla rei fit scissura, / Signi tantum fit fractura, / Qua nec status nec statura / Signati minuitur." See also *S. th.* III, q. 76, aa. 1 and 2.

21. As was seen earlier, the hymn *Pange lingua* runs similarly.

But to whom is the gift given? The fourth stanza, standing in the middle of the hymn, addresses the affective condition of the disciples, who see painfully before their eyes the nearing departure, indeed death, of their master. Thus, the talk of human fragility (*fragilis*) and sadness (*tristis*). The hymn shows a sense for the affective dimension of the event, through which the disciples lived and suffered on the evening before Jesus' death.[22] To the sorrows and fears of his followers, Jesus responds with a twofold gift, which is linguistically and explicitly emphasized through the anaphoric *dedit*, positioned each time at the beginning of the verse: to those in need of comfort, he gave a bit of his body (in which he is wholly contained); to those in sadness, the chalice of his blood. In connection with this, the terms *ferculum* and *poculum* merit particular attention. The word *ferculum*, which is also used in the following hymn *Verbum supernum*, is a seldom used and unusual word.[23] *Ferculum* derives from *ferre* and signifies a stretcher or also a tray for food. In the context of meaning in the hymn *Sacrum solemniis*, the Eucharistic meal becomes a sustaining support for fragile man. The background medicinal metaphor called up by the word *ferculum* (stretcher) reminds us not only of speaking of the Eucharist as "medicine of immortality" but also of the hymn *Verbum supernum*, where we read: "Da robur, fer auxilium." In contrast, the term *poculum* is used in Psalm 101:10 to designate the cup in which the one mourning mixes his drink with tears ("et poculum meum cum fletu miscebam"). This motif lends itself to being translated in such a way that the Eucharistic gift of Christ's presence transforms the cup of tears into the chalice of blessing and joy, as conjured up by the opening of the hymn: *Sacris solemniis iuncta sint gaudia*. It may be judged a special sign of divine beneficence that the giver is himself contained in the gift[24]—and the giver gives himself in the species of bread and wine. Thus, the sacrifices of the old covenant are transferred into a new unbloody rite.[25] The hymn brings out the sacrifical dimension of the event by means of the nearly verbatim working in of the *verba testamenti* (see Mt 26:27: "dedit illis dicens bibite ex eo omnes"; or, following the Roman canon: "dicens: accipite, et bi-

---

22. On this point, see *S. th.* III, q. 75, a. 5.

23. In the Vulgate, only one instance is found (Sg 3:9). See C. Blume, "Thomas von Aquin und das Fronleichnamsfest, insbesondere der Hymnus Verbum supernum," *ThGl* 3 (1911): 358–72, here 368.

24. See Dorez, *Registres d'Urbain IV*, vol. 2/1 (Paris: A. Fontemoing, 1901), 424: "Semetipsum nobis exhibuit, et transcendens omnem plenitudinem largitatis omnemque modum dilectionis excellens, tribuit se in cibum. Quam singularis et ammiranda *liberalitas, ubi donator venit in donum et datum est idem penitus cum datore!*" (emphasis added).

25. In the second Lectio of the Office for Corpus Christi, the pacification of Old Testament animal sacrifices is expressly asserted: "Quid enim hoc convivio pretiosius esse potest, in quo non carnes vitulorum et hircorum, ut olim in lege, sed nobis sumendus proponitur Christus verus Deus?" (Thomas, *Officium de festo corporis Christi*, 277).

bite ex eo omnes"). Because *all* drink from *one* chalice—a rite that differs from the Jewish feast—it is implied that all receive a share in the salvation wrought by the bloody death on the cross.

Through the double gift of the rites of bread and wine, the institution of the sacrifice (*institutio sacrificii*) is carried out—as we read in the next strophe. Only at this point do we find the term *sacrificium* in the Eucharistic hymns, a term that Thomas explicates in more detail in the *Summa theologiae*, especially in connection with the rite of the Eucharist.[26] In the first *Lectio* of the Office for Corpus Christi, we find it illustratively stated that Christ "offered his body on the altar of the Cross as a sacrifice (*hostia*) to God for our atonement"—and in view of the blood poured out, the sacrificial dimension of his death is more precisely described with the themes of ransom (*pretium*) and washing clean (*lavacrum*). The liberation from slavery and the purification from sins is purchased by the blood of Christ.[27] The ritual commemoration of the redeeming event of the cross takes place in the Eucharist, which is for this reason also called *sacrificium*. It is no accident that the hymn goes on to trace out the line of *traditio* further; it designates the very ones doing the handing on and providing the ministry of sacrifice—the *officium*—through the course of history. It is the *presbyteri* who have received their authority not from themselves but likewise as a sacramental gift.[28] They receive so that they can hand on to others—*dent ceteris*. The singular *dedit* of Jesus is carried over into the plural *dent* so that the one self-gift finds many servants among priests who then hand it on to others.[29] It would be a sort of betrayal of the gift to want to retain it for oneselves and not hand it on.

The sixth stanza praises the mystery of Eucharistic conversion. Standing at the center of attention—the word *panis* is woven in three times—is bread: the bread of men becomes the bread of angels, indeed, of heaven.[30]

---

26. See *S. th.* III, q. 83, a. 1. See also *S. th.* I-II, q. 101, a. 4 ad 2: "sacrificium novae legis, idest Eucharistia, continet ipsum Christum, qui est sanctificationis auctor: *sanctificavit enim per suum sanguinem populum*, ut dicitur ad Heb. ult. Et ideo hoc sacrificium etiam est sacramentum. Sed sacrificia veteris legis non continebant Christum, sed ipsum figurabant: et ideo non dicuntur sacramenta."

27. *Officium de festo corporis Christi*, 276: "Corpus namque suum pro nostra reconciliatione in ara crucis hostiam obtulit Deo Patri; sanguinem suum fudit in pretium simul et lavacrum, ut redempti a miserabili servitute, a peccatis omnibus mundaremur."

28. This conferral of authority is expressed in the formula of administration used at the time for sacramental Ordination, when the bishop speaks: "Receive the power (*potestas*) to offer the sacrifice in the Church for both the living and the dead." *S. th.* III, q. 82, a. 1 ad 1: "Accipe potestatem offerendi sacrificium in Ecclesia tam pro vivis quam pro mortuis." Regarding the form of the sacrament of order, see *S. th.* III (Suppl.), q. 34, a. 4 c.

29. See *S. th.* III, q. 82, a. 3: "Unde, sicut ad sacerdotem pertinet consecratio corporis Christi, ita ad eum pertinet dispensatio."

30. The motif, also encountered in the Sequence *Laudi Sion* ("Ecce panis angelorum, / factus cibus

The Eucharistic bread brings with it the end of all anticipatory images. The connection between the prefigurations and the wonderful reality of salvation is emphatically confirmed by the hymn—*o res mirabilis*—and Thomas analyzes it in another context.[31] The Old Testament and its promises are not rendered worthless and useless by Christ's coming; on the contrary, one can understand Jesus Christ and the sacrament of the Eucharist only when they are interpreted against the foil of Old Testament promises. The actual miracle, however, consists in the fact that man, whose condition is characterized by the attributes *miser* and *humilis*, takes Christ the Lord into himself when he eats (*manducat*) the *panis caelicus*, which for him is already a pledge of future glory (*futurae gloriae pignus*), as we hear in the antiphon of the Office for Corpus Christi at the Magnificat. By means of the proper *manducatio*, man is drawn into the reality of Jesus Christ.

The last stanza offers a closing doxology, which is directly addressed to the triune God: "*Te, trina Deitas unaque, poscimus.*" The longing for the vision of God expresses itself in the petition for companionship on the journey so that the end might be attained: the light that no longer knows darkness. It is once again characteristic that the eschatological dimension of the Eucharist—its character as *viaticum* for the *homo viator*—stands at the end of the hymn. Moreover, the poetic diction gives an indication of how the relation between God and man is seen. God deserves primacy and everything is ultimately to be expected from him. This primacy becomes clear in the placement of pronouns referring to God (*te, tu, tuas semitas*), which definitively break up the narrative style upheld in the first five stanzas. The pronouns each stand in the first half of the verse, followed by imperatives (*duc, visita*), which are likewise woven into the texture of the hymn only at this point and have the function of underscoring the urgency of the petition. The ones praying, however, who look for the fulfilment of their prayers, take second place to the giver. The verbs (*poscimus, colimus, tendimus*), in

---

viatorum, / vere panis filiorum, / non mittendus canibus"), can be traced back to the Psalter. See Ps 77:24f.: "et pluit illis manna ad manducandum et panem caeli dedit eis: panem angelorum manducavit homo; cibaria misit eis ad abundantiam." See the Bull *Transiturus*, in Dorez, ed., *Registres d'Urbain IV*, vol. 2/1, 423–25, here 424: "Panem enim angelorum manducavit homo."

31. In *S. th.* I-II, q. 101, a. 2, Thomas unfolds a threefold order determined by the concepts *figura / umbra, imago*, and *veritas*. Accordingly, in the *old law*, divine truth was neither revealed in itself nor was an avenue opened to reach it. Therefore, the old law had to be not only a symbol of future truth, which would be revealed in heaven, but also a symbol of Christ, who is the way to that heavenly truth. In the *new law*, by contrast, this way to truth is revealed. That means, it no longer requires figures pointing to Christ, the way to truth; at the same time, a dynamic toward eschatological truth is also written into the new law, for which reason the coming, still not revealed truth of glory (*veritas gloriae*) still requires prefiguration. See L. J. Elders, "La relation entre l'ancienne et la nouvelle Alliance, selon saint Thomas d'Aquin," *Revue Thomiste* 100 (2000): 580–602.

which their action is expressed, are each positioned at the end of the verse. This placement does not have its reason only in considerations of meter or rhyme scheme; rather, there are also theological reasons, if it is true that man is directed to the self-gift of God, to the vision of his light, which alone can bring man's longing to rest.

The Hymn *Verbum supernum*

Verbum supernum prodiens,	The heavenly Word proceeding forth,
Nec Patris linquens dexteram,	Yet leaving not his Father's side,
Ad opus suum exiens,	And going to His work on Earth,
Venit ad vitae vesperam.	Has reached at length life's eventide.
In mortem a discipulo	By false disciple to be given
Suis tradendus aemulis,	To foemen for His blood athirst,
Prius in vitae ferculo	Himself, the living Bread from heaven,
Se tradidit discipulis.	He gave to His disciples first.
Quibus sub bina specie	To them He gave, in twofold kind,
Carnem dedit et sanguinem,	His very Flesh, His very Blood:
Ut duplicis substantiae	of twofold substance man is made,
Totum cibaret hominem.	and He of man would be the Food.
Se nascens dedit socium,	By birth our fellowman was He,
Convescens in edulium;	our Food while seated at the board;
Se moriens in pretium,	He died, our ransomer to be;
Se regnans dat in praemium.	He ever reigns, our great reward.
O salutaris hostia,	O saving Victim, opening wide
Quae caeli pandis ostium;	the gate of heaven to all below:
Bella premunt hostilia,	our foes press on from every side;
Da robur, fer auxilium.	Thine aid supply, Thy strength bestow.
Uni trinoque Domino	To Thy great Name be endless praise,
Sit sempiterna gloria,	immortal Godhead, One in Three!
Qui vitam sine termino	O grant us endless length of days
Nobis donet in patria. Amen.	in our true native land with Thee.
	Amen.

[From the *Liturgia Horarum*. Trans. Neale, Caswall, et al.]

Observations on the Diction and Structure of the Hymn *Verbum supernum*

The hymn *Verbum supernum prodiens*,[32] which is prayed at Lauds in the Divine Office, is subdivided into six strophes, each of which includes four verses. Every stanza—with the exception of the fourth—follows the rhyme scheme A-B-A-B. While the verse endings in the first five stanzas are consonantic or alternatingly consonantic-vocalic, the last stanza exhibits vocalic endings throughout. To be noted are the many verbal forms in the present participle, which determine the texture of the hymn's first four strophes and are all rooted in the *verbum supernum* as subject.[33]

The hymn *Verbum supernum prodiens*[34] also gives a central place to the motif of the divine Word's *self-gift*—as shown by the various derivatives of *dare* and *tradere*[35]—and it articulates various aspects of this gift. The first strophe hints at the Trinitarian background of the divine Word's Incarnation and relocates the goal of the Incarnation to the *opus redemptionis*: the divine Word was born in order to die. The coming of the *verbum supernum* makes its way toward "life's eventide" at the end of the first stanza, and "life's eventide" will be interpreted in the second stanza under the rubric of handing oneself over (*se tradidit*). The incarnate Word—betrayed to his enemies—gave himself for his disciples in his death. This pro-existence already marks his life but also—as the third strophe reveals—the last supper. In the fourth stanza, the motifs seen up to this point run together as if in a convex mirror when the modes of self-gift in his life, at the last supper, and in his death are all bound together in a series of four participles. Simultaneously, the hymn opens up a view toward the eschatological gift—a motif that will be taken further in the following stanza. The soteriological power of the host lies not only in the fact that it offers strength and refreshment to the *homo viator* for the challenges of the present life, but also in that it opens the gate to heaven.

A break that is linguistically easy to recognize lies between the fourth and fifth strophes; it divides the hymn into two parts: whereas the first four

---

32. See my work "Leib Christi—Gabe des Lebens. Zum Opfercharakter der Eucharistie unter Rückgriff auf den Hymnus Verbum supernum des hl. Thomas von Aquin," in *Eucharistischer Kongress* [Cologne, 2013], edited by the Archdiocese of Cologne (Cologne: Erzbistum Köln, 2014), 342–56.

33. See the participles in: v. 1, *prodiens*; v. 3, *exiens*; v. 14, *convescens*; v. 15, *se moriens*; v. 16, *se regnans*. The conspicuous accumulation of participles in the fourth stanza lends itself to being interpreted as motivic constrictions—in an analogy to fugal technique. We will return to this point in the section on interpretation.

34. The hymn has even made its way into the Lutheran hymnal in the translation of Otto Riethmüller: see *Evangelisches Gesangbuch*, n. 221: "Das Wort geht von dem Vater aus."

35. See v. 6, *tradendus*; v. 8, *se tradidit*; v. 10, *dedit*; v. 13, *dedit*; v. 16, *dat*; v. 20, *da*; and v. 24, *donet*.

strophes exhibit an abundance of verbs and participles referring back to the *verbum supernum*, the fifth strophe carries out a change of subject and likewise alters the mode of speaking. Mnemonic description gives way to direct address. This is made clear by the emphatic invocation *O salutaris hostia* as well as the use of the imperative (*da—fer*). A Trinitarian closing doxology brings the hymn to an end, just as we saw with *Pange lingua* and *Sacris solemniis*.

Theological Interpretation: The Multidimensionality of Christ's Gift

The first strophe sets up a sweeping arch, which begins at the pre-existence of the divine Word, draws out the event of the Incarnation, and then—in an extremely summary fashion—brings in the life of the incarnate Word up to the threshold of death. God is not only a God in and for himself; he is a God who goes out of himself, is born as a man, and in just this way desires to be a God for and with men.[36] This dynamic comes to be clearly expressed in the selection of verbs that add up to a statement of the actions undertaken by the *verbum supernum* (*prodire—exire—venire*).[37] Just as God (*the Word*) proceeds eternally from God (*the Father*), so God (*the Word*) can go out of himself, enter into time, and communicate himself to men. Because the only-begotten son of God wanted to enable men to share in his divinity—as the first *Lectio* for the feast of Corpus Christi explains—he took up their nature in order, as God incarnate, to make them into "gods."[38] Presupposed by the *communicatio* of the divine Word with men is the *communicatio* of the divine Persons among themselves.[39] The hymn speaks to the point that the Word proceeds from the Father and does not leave the Father's right hand. Two questions are omitted here: first, the question of which divine decision motivates the act of coming forth from God, which coincides with entering into the world, and second, whether in the economy of salvation history the point in time is fittingly chosen. In contrast to

---

36. This motif is also addressed in the Bull *Transiturus*. See Dorez, ed., *Registres d'Urbain IV*, 424: "Condecens quoque caritatis liberalitas extitit et convertens operatio pietatis, ut Verbum Dei eternum, quod rationalis creaturae, carni counite homini videlicet, in edulium largiretur."
37. The first stanza is the only one in the hymn that features a verb in each line—including two derivatives of *ire* (vv. 1 and 3).
38. See *Officium de festo corporis Christi*, 276: "Unigenitus siquidem Dei Filius suae Divinitatis volens nos esse participes, naturam nostram assumpsit, ut homines deos faceret factus homo."
39. Regarding Thomas' Trinitarian theology, see G. Emery, *The Trinitarian Theology of Saint Thomas Aquinas*, trans. Francesca Aran Murphy (Oxford: Oxford University Press, 2007).

the hymn *Pange lingua*,[40] the poetry of the hymn *Verbum supernum* makes no mention of Mary, even though without her word of consent the divine Word's stepping into human history would not have been possible. Using sparing and poetically concise diction, the hymn states that the Word steps out and arrives at "life's eventide." The metaphor of evening assuredly alludes to the liturgical time of vespers as well, where the hymn has its place; but just as assuredly does it also articulate the imminent death of the Lord, which will be the precondition for new life. What the *acta et passa* are, which Thomas treated discursively in his theology of the mysteries of Jesus' life, plays only a subordinate role in the poetic space of the Eucharistic hymn. What is decisive is that the divine Word came in order to die.[41] The focus of attention rests on the setting of the end.

The second stanza then goes more into detail regarding "life's eventide" and illuminates it using significant moments taken from the pre-Passion scenes of the betrayal and the last supper. In so doing, the hymn poetically explores the ambiguity of *traditio* when, using the same word, it speaks, on the one hand, of Judas's handing Jesus over to his enemies (*tradendus aemulis*), and on the other, of Jesus' self-gift for his disciples (*se tradidit discipulis*).[42] The betrayer is not mentioned by name and instead there is merely talk of an anonymous disciple (*discipulus*). Instead of memorializing in rich imagery the scenes of violence set in motion by the betrayal—capture, scourging, crucifixion—the poem directs all of one's attention to the incarnate Word's giving himself for his disciples. As Jesus—whose name likewise remains unmentioned—was there for others in life, so is he also in death. His pro-existence makes up the common sign of both his life and his death.[43] The hymn stresses this continuity and it appears as if the *se tradidit* of his life would concentrate itself in the testament of his love.

It is not by chance that the third strophe further illuminates the self-gift of the incarnate Word with a view toward impending death. The semantic field of *traditio*, which spans handing over and self-surrender, is unfolded further in that now the gifts at the last supper are brought into view. In the twofold species of bread and wine, Jesus gives his flesh and his blood as

---

40. See the verse "fructus ventris generosi," as well as the beginning of the second strophe, "Nobis datus, nobis natus / ex intacta virgine."
41. See Augustine, *Sermo* 23 A, 3: "The Word become flesh to be able to die for us."
42. In the Divine Office, even the *Capitulum* placed before the hymn contains the semantic ambiguity of the word *tradere* when it cites the instution narrative: "Dominus Iesus in qua nocte *tradebatur*, accepit panem, et gratias agens fregit, et dixit: Accipite et manducate. Hoc est corpus meum quod pro vobis *tradetur*; hoc facite in meam commemorationem" (emphasis added).
43. See A. Hoffmann, "Die Proexistenz Jesu Christi nach Thomas," in *Thomas von Aquino. Interpretation und Rezeption. Studien und Texte*, ed. W. P. Eckert (Mainz: Matthias-Grünewald, 1974), 158–69.

he departs from his disciples. What is striking is that only at this point in the hymn do we find technical theological vocabulary woven into the poetic texture ("sub bina specie"—"duplicis substantiae"). The double species of bread and wine, which are not only gifts of creation but also artifacts of human work,[44] correspond to the double substance of flesh and blood. But the transformed gifts, the flesh and blood of Jesus Christ, bring *spiritual* hunger and thirst to rest, while simultaneously corresponding to the fundamental anthropological need for nourishment through food and drink.

The fourth strophe constitutes the climax of the poetic composition and in so doing offers a *concentrated theology of gift*, whose dynamic reaches from the Incarnation and birth of the eternal Word, through the last supper and death, and into the eschatological realm. That the hymn reaches its high point is revealed by the linguistic shape: only here are all four verses of the stanza bound together with the same rhyme (*-ium*); only here are all four verses built on the model of parallelism.[45] By means of the Incarnation and birth, the eternal Word of the Father made himself a companion of man (*socius*); he took upon himself growth and pain, hunger and thirst, joy and sadness. In the room of the last supper, the incarnate Word gave himself as food, later to die on the cross as a ransom (*pretium*) for many.[46] As the reigning exalted one (*regnans*)—one recalls here the title *rex gentium* from the hymn *Pange lingua*—he gives the prize, for which each man yearns: a life that no longer knows death (to play off the last stanza). While the divine Word's self-gift in life, at the last supper, and in death is memorialized (perfect: *dedit*), a significant change in tense takes place in the last line of the strophe (present: *dat*). The *verbum supernum*, who gave himself in various ways, gives himself now as well—and into this gift is written an eschatological dynamism, as the following stanza explains.

Nevertheless, there first occurs a caesura: although the first four strophes spoke of the divine Word (*verbum supernum*), the hymn now shifts the perspective. The sacrifice (*hostia*), in which the incarnate Word of the Father gives himself, becomes the addressee. The memorializing mode of speech (in the third person) shifts into an emphatic invocation: "O salutaris hostia." The salvific sacrifice—far from being reduced to a *thing*—is addressed as a *person*, because in it the eternal Word of the Father is present.

---

44. In the *Sentences* commentary, Thomas expressly draws out the cultural technique of baking bread. See *In IV Sent.*, d. 11, q. 2, a. 1 (n. 158): "Grana in area conculcantur, et panis in fornace decoquitur—The grains are ground on the threshing floor, and the bread is baked in the oven." On the cultural history of the host, see *Panis angelorum—Das Brot der Engel*, ed. O. Seifert (Ostfildern: Thorbecke, 2004), esp. 11–22.

45. See also the threefold anaphoric repetition of "se" (vv. 13, 15, and 16).

46. In *Pange lingua* also, the soteriological motif is brought into play: "sanguinisque pretiosi / quem in mundi pretium / fructus ventris generosi / Rex effudit gentium."

Salvific power is ascribed to the converted host.[47] It is able to open the gate to heaven; it gives strength (*robur*) and aid (*auxilium*) in the face of daily hardships. The poetic diction bundles together the references through the tonal similarity of the words placed each time at the end of the verse, *hostia*, *ostium*, and *hostilia*: the sacrament of the altar, in which the *Christus passus* gives himself as a gift, is a pledge of coming glory and a refreshment in the face of hostile afflictions.[48] The imperative, noted only at this point, shows the urgency with which the one praying pleads for help when facing the adversities of life. This very stanza, "O salutaris hostia"—which frequently was intoned at the elevation of the host in the late Middle Ages, but is so intoned only sporadically in the modern era[49]—has been set to music by such diverse composers as William Byrd, André Caplet, Luigi Cherubini, Léo Delibes, Edward Elgar, César Franck, Jan Garbarek, Charles Gounod, Franz Liszt, Gioachino Rossini, Pierre de la Rue, Camille Saint-Saens, Robert Schumann, Fernando Sor, Thomas Tallis, and Heitor Villa-Lobos, to mention but a few names.

The final Trinitarian doxology, into which the hymn flows as its conclusion, articulates the eschatological reference once again: the triune God gives life without end. The *homo viator* attains to his end when he reaches life without end (*vita sine termino*), for which the hymn holds ready a word commonly used in scholastic theology: *patria*, the land of the fathers, the homeland. In summary, we can say that all three temporal dimensions of the Eucharist are pulled together in a poetically condensed way: the *rememorative*, which keeps alive the memory of Christ's suffering; the *demonstrative*, which has strength and grace coming to the one praying for his wanderings through time (*peregrinatio*); and the *prognostic*, which points ahead to the goal, the heavenly homeland.

---

47. See *S. th.* III, q. 73, a. 4 ad 3: "dicendum quod hoc sacramentum dicitur 'sacrificium,' inquantum repraesentat ipsam passionem Christi. Dicitur autem 'hostia,' inquantum continet ipsum Christum, qui est *hostia salutaris*, ut dicitur Eph 5."

48. See the antiphon in the first Vespers of the Divine Office for Corpus Christi: "O sacrum convivium! In quo Christus sumitur, recolitur memoria passionis eius, mens impletur gratia, et futurae gloriae nobis pignus datur. Alleluia" (*Officium de festo corporis Christi*, 280).

49. See A. Heinz, "O salutaris hostia," *LThK* 7, 3rd ed. (1998) 953.

7

Commemoration—Making-Present—Expectation

The Sequence *Lauda Sion*

Observations on the Diction and Structure of the Sequence

In the Divine Office of Corpus Christi, the Sequence *Lauda Sion*—conceptualized by Geoffrey Wainwright under the rubric of *doctrinal hymn*[1]—has its place between the reading, which recites the institution narrative according to Paul (see 1 Cor 11:23–29), and the Gospel, which consists of an excerpt from the Johannine bread of life discourse (Jn 6:56–59). More precisely, the hymn presents a continuation of the Alleluia, which is sung after the Gradual and serves to prefigure the guiding verse of the Gospel.[2] The Sequence has, therefore, the character of a festive song of praise.[3]

Seeking a model for meter, rhyme scheme, and structure, Thomas may have drawn from the hymn *Laudis crucis attollamus*, which is ascribed to Adam of St. Victor or Hugh of Orléans.[4] The Sequence itself has twelve double strophes—each of the first nine has six lines, numbers ten and eleven each have eight lines, and the last has ten lines. As for the poetic meter, each stanza features two or three lines with acatalectic dimeter and each

---

1. G. Wainwright, *Doxology: The Praise of God in Worship, Doctrine and Life: A Systematic Theology* (London: Epworth Press, 1980), 203.
2. See the *Alleluia* in the Office: "Alleluia, alleluia. Caro mea vere est cibus, et sanguis meus est vere potus: qui manducat meam carnem et bibit meum sanguinem, in me manet, et ego in eo."
3. On the interpretation of the Sequence *Lauda Sion*, see J. Szövérffy, *Die Annalen der lateinischen Hymnendichtung II. Die lateinischen Hymnen vom Ende des 11. Jahrhunderts bis zum Ausgang des Mittelalters* (Berlin: E. Schmidt, 1965), 246–55; W. Breuer, *Die lateinische Eucharistiedichtung des Mittelalters von ihren Anfängen bis zum Ausgang des 13. Jahrhunderts* (Wuppertal, 1970), 244–99; J. A. Weisheipl, *Friar Thomas D'Aquino: his life, thought, and works* (Garden City, N.Y.: Doubleday, 1974), 176–85 and 400f.
4. For a comparison of the two sequences, see J. Connelly, *Hymns of the Roman Liturgy* (London: Longmans Green and Co., 1957), 125.

209

concluding line with catalectic, trochaic dimeter.[5] In general, the acatalectic verses of each strophe are connected by a rhyme, while the rhyme of the catalectic concluding verses structurally marks off every pair of strophes as a larger double strophe. The diction of the Sequence is, on the whole, rather unadorned, but it does draw partially on the vocabulary of scholastic Eucharistic theology. It likewise makes use of biblical metaphors in order to articulate referential contexts from salvation history. Notable in the style of the Sequence are the frequent anaphoric repetitions (note "*Lauda* Sion, salvatorem, / *Lauda* ducem et pastorem," or "*Sit* laus plena, *sit* sonora, *Sit* jucunda, *sit* decora," etc.), parallelisms (e.g., *Quantum* potes, *tantum* aude, or Caro *cibus*, sanguis *potus*, etc.), and the use of assonance.

The structure of the Sequence follows in a programmatic way the three tenses of past, present, and future that are interlaced in Eucharistic remembrance.[6] After an emphatic overture extolling the institution of the Eucharist, the first part of *Lauda Sion* goes into the historical origins of the sacrament and reveals the foundation of the feast of Corpus Christi. A second part unfolds the current confession of the faithful celebrating and recalls the presuppositions for properly receiving the Eucharist. Finally, a third and quite succinct part offers a sort of eschatological outlook. One can therefore affirm that the compositional principle of the hymn follows the insight that time is condensed in the Eucharist; or, put otherwise, that the Eucharist is related as *signum rememorativum* to the past, as *signum demonstrativum* to the present, and as *signum prognosticum* to the future consummation.

---

5. To explain the terms from literary criticism: a *trochee* is a metrical unit with falling rhythm and consists of a long (stressed) syllable followed by a short (unstressed) syllable. A *dimeter* (Gk: *dis* = double; *metron* = measure) is a verse made of two of the same iambic, anapestic, trochaic, etc. meters. *Acatalectic* (Gk: *akataleiktikos* = not stopping) is a verse with a complete final foot; *catalectic* (Gk: *kataleiktikos* = stopping, incomplete) is a verse whose last foot is missing one or more syllables. See the corresponding entries in G. von Wilpert, *Sachwörterbuch der Literatur*, 7th ed. (Stuttgart: A. Kröner, 1989).

6. On the three dimensions of time in the sacrament, see *S. th.* III, q. 60, a. 3. In reference to the Eucharist, we read in *S. th.* III, q. 73, a. 4: "Respondeo dicendum quod hoc sacramentum habet triplicem significationem. Unam quidem respectu praeteriti: inquantum scilicet est commemorativum Dominicae passionis, quae fuit verum sacrificium, ut supra dictum est [sc. q. 48, a. 3]. Et secundum hoc nominatur *sacrificium*.—Aliam autem significationem habet respectu rei praesentis, scilicet ecclesiasticae unitatis, cui homines congregantur per hoc sacramentum. Et secundum hoc nominatur *communio* vel *synaxis*: dicit enim Damascenus IV libro [*De fide orthodoxa* IV, c. 13], quod dicitur *communio*, *quia communicamus per ipsam Christo; et quia participamus eius carne et deitate; et quia communicamus et unimur ad invicem per ipsam*.—Tertiam significationem habet respectu futuri: inquantum scilicet hoc sacramentum est praefigurativum fruitionis Dei, quae erit in patria. Et secundum hoc dicitur *viaticum*: quia hoc praebet nobis viam illuc perveniendi."

Theological Interpretation

The first part of the hymn reads:[7]

Lauda, Sion, Salvatorem,	Praise, Zion, the Savior,
Lauda ducem et pastorem	praise the king and shepherd,
In hymnis et canticis.	in hymns and songs.
Quantum potes, tantum aude:	As much as you are able, that much dare:
Quia maior omni laude,	because [he is] greater than every praise,
Nec laudare sufficis.	you cannot adequately praise.
Laudis thema specialis,	The special theme of praise,
Panis vivus et vitalis,	the living and life-giving bread,
Hodie proponitur.	is today publicly presented:
Quem in sacrae mensa coenae,	what, on the table of the holy meal,
Turbae fratrum duodenae	to the twelve strong band of brothers,
Datum non ambigitur.	was given, is not contested.
Sit laus plena, sit sonora;	Let us praise in full, let us praise sonorously,
sit iucunda, sit decora	
mentis iubilatio.	let it be acceptable, let it be decorous,
Dies enim solemnis agitur,	the spirit's jubilation.
In qua mensae prima recolitur	For celebrated is the solemn day,
Huius institutio.	on which it is recalled the first institution of this meal.[8]
In hac mensa novi Regis,	At this table of the new King,
Novum pascha novae legis;	the new Passover of the new law
Phase vetus terminat.	Concludes the old Passover.
Vetustatem novitas,	The new puts to flight the old,
Umbram fugat veritas,	the truth likewise to shadows,
Noctem lux eliminat.	the light does 'way with night.

Prologue—Doxology and Negative Theology

The Sequence opens with a rhetorically concentrated[9] and metrically impressive (self-)summoning to praise, which borrows from the language of

---

7. Because the translation offered here is as literal as possible [based on the Latin original and matched with its German translation—Trans.], it does not attempt to imitate the poetic and metric qualities of the original. See, however, the translation in the Daily Roman Missal (Woodridge, Ill.: Midwest Theological Forum, 1993–2012), 1705–7.

8. Here and in the following, *mensa* (Lat. table) is translated metonymically as "meal."

9. In the first strophe alone, there are four instances of the lexical field "laus/laudare," which are taken up and deepened in the second and third strophes.

the Psalms.¹⁰ Unlike Holy Thursday, which commemorates Jesus' last supper before the impending Passion and therefore calls for a rather reserved pitch, the solemnity of Corpus Christi expresses gratitude and joy toward the Eucharistic sacrament bequeathed and entrusted to the faithful.¹¹ Not by chance does the vocabulary of *Lauda Sion*'s opening passage evoke a festive spirit: there is talk of praise and jubilation, of hymns and songs, and of a festive day (*dies solemnis*), and the effusive abundance of attributes orchestrates the accolade and gives it its metrical drive (*sit laus plena, sit sonora, sit iucunda, sit decora*, etc.). Taken together, all of this is intended to help the assembled faithful to attune their hearts to the joy of the solemnity.¹²
The summons to doxological rejoicing—linguistically underscored by three imperatives¹³—refers to Zion, the Church, which encompasses not only the present congregation but also the heavenly *communio sanctorum*. This reference surpassing the present is suggested by the letter to the Hebrews (12:22f.), which transfers the complex motif of "Zion"¹⁴ to the *heavenly* Jerusalem: "Sed accessistis ad Sion montem, et civitatem Dei viventis, Ierusalem caelestem, et multorum millium angelorum frequentiam."¹⁵ To relate this to the case of Corpus Christi, it means that the Church—the eschatological people of God—sings her praise to Christ, the redeemer and savior, for she owes to him all that she is.

The recipient of this hymnic praise is Jesus Christ, to whom are ascribed three essential attributes—*salvator, dux*, and *pastor*. When seen against the background of biblical salvation history, each of these attributes sounds a wide spectrum of meaning. In the old covenant, the *salvator* is first YHWH, the redeemer, who liberated his people Israel from the slavery of Egypt (Ex 20:2; Ps 81:11; etc.); but then in the new covenant as well, it is Jesus¹⁶—as

---

10. See Ps 147:12: *Lauda, Jerusalem, Sominum, lauda Deum tuum, Sion*. The imperative "lauda" is—following the linguistic style of the Psalmist—repeated anaphorically in *Lauda Sion*.

11. See the Bull *Transiturus*: "Hec est commemoratio gloriosa, que fidelium animos replet gaudio salutari, et cum infusione letitie, devotionis lacrimas subministrat. Exultamus nimirum nostram rememorando liberationem, et recolendo passionem dominicam per quam liberati sumus, vix lacrimas continemus. In hac itaque sacratissima commemoratione, adsunt nobis suaviter gaudium simul et lacrime, quia in ea et gaudemus pie lacrimantes, et lacrimamus devote gaudentes, letas habendo lacrimas et letitiam lacrimantem" (Dorez, ed., *Registres d'Urbain IV*, 423). The text's intention to commemorate the Eucharist in a festive way, is rhetorically set down in the festive linguistic style. See the nearly textually identical documentation in Friedberg, ed., *Corpus iuris canonici*, vol. 2, col. 1175.

12. See the similarly effusive diction in the final strophe of *Pange lingua gloriosi*: "Genitori Genitoque / laus et iubilatio, / salus, honor, virtus quoque / sit et benedictio; / procedenti ab utroque /compar sit laudatio. Amen."

13. V. 1, *lauda*; v. 2, *lauda*; v. 4, *aude*.

14. See J. Schreiner, "Zion," *LThK* 10, 3rd ed. (2001): 1462f.

15. Regarding this verse, see *In Hebr.* XII, l. IV (nn. 706f.).

16. See *S. th.* III, q. 37, a. 2, where the name "Jesus" is translated with savior/redeemer (*salvator*): "homini Christo hoc munus gratiae collatum erat ut per ipsum omnes salvarentur, ideo convenienter vocatum est

the name itself suggests—the one who redeemed the world by dying on the cross. Already in *Pange lingua*, Thomas made this clear and then went on to explain it later in more detail both in the introduction to the *Tertia pars* of the *Summa theologiae*[17] and in the soteriological passages of this work.[18] Moreover, Christ is expected in the parousia as the definitive liberator (Phil 3:20). Furthermore, he is the leader and shepherd (*dux et pastor*). He goes after the lost sheep (Lk 15:4–7), pastures the people of God (Mt 2:6), is there for his own as good shepherd, and even gives his life for them (Jn 10:11–13);[19] indeed at the very end, he is there "as a shepherd separates the sheep from the goats" (Mt 25:31f.). This salvific deed of God in Jesus Christ, which reaches into the eschatological dimension, is rightly to be praised *in hymnis et in canticis*. For, as the diction of the Sequence makes clear, praise is gratitude in action. Through the doubling "in hymns and songs" (*hendiaduoin*), the doxological dynamic of the prayer becomes poetically manifest to the senses, something that refers back, by the way, to a verse in the letter to the Ephesians, where a call to praise appears in similarly plerophoric style.[20]

The second part of the first double strophe takes up the scope and limits of human praise and offers no less than a brief, poetically distilled reflection on the relation between doxology and negative theology.[21] The inadequacy of prayer is expressed in the prayer itself, without the word threatening to lapse into silence: first of all, there is the finite means of language which only ever allows approaches to the infinite God.[22] At the same time, however, we could also speak here of the chasm between men

---

nomen eius Iesus, idest 'Salvator.'" Here it should also be pointed out that the Bull *Transiturus* mentions the Christological title at the very outset: Transiturus de mundo ad Patrem, *Salvator* noster Dominus Jesus Christus.... Hoc est memoriale, in quo profecto reficimur ipsius corporali presentia *Salvatoris*" (emphasis added). See Dorez, ed., *Registres d'Urbain IV*, 423.

17. See *S. th.* III, prol.: "Quia Salvator noster dominus Iesus Christus, teste Angelo: 'populum suum salvum faciens a peccatis eorum,' viam veritatis nobis in seipso demonstravit, per quam ad beatidudinem immortalis vitae resurgendo pervenire possimus, necesse est ut, ad consummationem totius theologici negotii, post considerationem ultimi finis humanae vitae et virtutem ac vitiorum, de ipso omnium Salvatore ac beneficiis eius humano generi praestitis nostra consideratio subsequatur."

18. See esp. *S. th.* III, q. 48, where the motifs of merit (*meritum*), satisfaction (*satisfactio*), sacrifice (*sacrificium*), and redemption (*redemptio*) come up in the soteriological discussion.

19. See the commentary offered in *In Io* X, l. III (nn. 1397–1400). Here, a Eucharistic and theological valence is given to the pasturing of the sheep, when it states: "nam sicut per pastorem grex gubernatur et pascitur, ita fideles per Christum spirituali cibo, et etiam corpore et sanguine suo reficiuntur."

20. See Eph 5:18–19: "Implemini Spiritu Sancto, loquentes vobismetipsis in psalmis et hymnis et canticis spiritualibus, cantantes et psallentes in cordibus vestris Domino." See the commentary in *In Eph.* V, l. VII (nn. 306–14).

21. For background, see A. Schilson, "Negative Theologie der Liturgie? Über die liturgische Erfahrung der Verborgenheit des nahen Gottes," *LJ* 50 (2000): 235–50.

22. In the Office, this motif is already addressed in the second Lectio *Manducatur*, when it states: "Suavitatem denique huius sacramenti nullus exprimere potest."

hopelessly entangled in sin and the eternal holiness of God. It is at any rate notable that the word choice of the Sequence exhibits similarities with a passage in the *Summa theologiae* that comments on the mode of religious speech, stating "that we can speak of God in a twofold way: first, in view of his essence, which is incomprehensible and ineffable and *exceeds every praise*."[23] The other sort of speaking about God is to refer to his effects. Whoever pereceives the effects of the Creator in creation is prompted to praise.[24] Thus, although the *essence* of God withdraws from being conceptually represented and even religious speech acts only inadequately attain it (*nec laudare sufficis*), still the effects of his creative and salvific actions are cause for festive gratitude and praise. Thus, the incomprehensibility of God—"si comprehendis, non est deus" (Augustine)—is itself not an inducement to become silent or to abandon religious communication. Rather, those at prayer should use all the means that language has to offer—*quantum potes, tantum aude*—in order to surpass language by means of language and to extol the ineffable God *in hymnis et canticis*. On the feast of Corpus Christi, the wonderful fact is commemorated that, in the Incarnation, the distant and unapproachable God drew near and communicated himself to man.[25] But the Son also left behind a testament of his love, which is worthy of grateful commemoration. Flowing together with the theological insight into the inadequacy of human thinking and speaking before God's infinity and perfection is a grateful astonishment that the eternal Word of the Father took on human flesh and draws close to man in the gifts of bread and wine up to the present day.

Assurance of Origin—the Eucharist as *signum rememorativum*

The second strophe leaves behind the gesture of self-summoning to praise and, in nearly academic style, states the "special theme" of the hymn: the

---

23. See *S. th.* II-II, q. 91, a. 1 ad 1: "quod de Deo dupliciter possumus loqui. Uno modo quantum ad eius essentiam. Et sic, cum sit incomprehensibilis et ineffabilis, maior est omni laude." Other passages are: *S. th.* I, q. 3, prol.: "Sed quia de Deo scire non possumus quid sit, sed quid non sit, non possumus considerare de Deo quomodo sit, sed potius quomodo non sit." Also in *Quaestiones disputatae de potentia Dei*, 7, 5 ad 14, it is asserted that the utmost point of human knowledge concerning God is to know that we do not know God: "quod [homo] sciat se Deum nescire." See J. Pieper, *The Silence of St. Thomas*, trans. John Murray, SJ, and Daniel O'Connor (South Bend, Ind.: St. Augustine's Press, 1999), 67: "Through their essences, things speak of God only imperfectly. Why? Because things are creatures and it is not possible for the creature to reveal the Creator perfectly."

24. *S. th.* II-II, q. 91, a. 1 ad 1: "secundum effectus ipsius, qui in nostram utilitatem ordinantur: et secundum hoc debetur laus Deo." On this point, see also Breuer, *Die lateinische Eucharistiedichtung*, 286.

25. Already in the first Lectio of the Divine Office, a strong emphasis is placed on God's drawing near: "Neque enim est aut fuit aliquando tam grandis natio, quae habeat deos appropinquantes sibi, sicut adest nobis Deus noster." See *Officium*, 276.

living and life-giving bread, which is publicly displayed and honored "today"—that is, on the holy feast day of the body (and blood) of Christ. The felicitous, paronomastic double indentification of the bread as *vivus et vitalis* already points ahead to the Gospel that will be recited subsequent to the Sequence (see Jn 6:56–59). In the Eucharistic discourse of John's Gospel, we find Jesus' self-identification: "I am the bread of life" (Jn 6:35, 48), or again, "I am the living bread that came down from heaven" (Jn 6:51), passages that are central for the theology of the Office for Corpus Christi. The Lord's self-description as living bread suggests the mystery of the Eucharistic real presence: on the one hand, Christ gives his flesh and blood under the species of bread and wine; on the other, whoever eats of this food and drinks of this drink receives a share in eternal life.

Furthermore, the hymn sets up a bridge from today (*hodie*) back to the then of the last supper: that Jesus broke bread and gave it to his twelve disciples as a sign of his giving up his life is held to be indubitably true (*non ambigitur*). The feast thus has an assured historical foundation and is in no way an expression of religious enthusiasm. To be noted here is that the number twelve is expressly mentioned. With Augustine and Dionysius—and in opposition to Hilary—Thomas takes as his point of departure in the *Summa theologiae* that Jesus also gave "his body and his blood" as food and drink to Judas.[26] Thomas argues that had Jesus withheld from Judas the Eucharistic gifts, he would have aggravated Judas and, in so doing, Jesus himself would have given the impetus for Judas's betrayal.

The remembrance of the historical origin of the feast is interrupted by a doxological "intermezzo" that, as already mentioned, is poetically expressed in turns of phrase employing both assonance and anaphora (*sit laus plena, sit sonora, / sit iucunda, sit decora*). The exuberant rejoicing (*mentis iubilatio*) is established specifically in the first institution (*prima institutio*), as the word *enim* leads the feast day back to the event of institution that is commemorated. At this point, we also notice that the hymn works in the motif of *mensa* multiple times: it is a table, at which Jesus gathered with his disciples (v. 10); a table, whose first institutionalization is solemnly memorialized (v. 17); a table, on which the time of old is concluded by "the new Passover of the new covenant" (vv. 19–21). The semantic of innovation[27] determines the language of the Sequence here just as much as the bringing together of antithetical figures (*vetustas* vs. *novitas*; *umbra* vs. *veritas*; *nox* vs. *lux*), which all have the function of drawing out the salvation-historical significance of

---

26. See *S. th.* III, q. 81, a. 2.
27. See the expression: "Novi Regis, / Novum pascha novae legis."

the event.[28] Even in Jesus' departing words, which are recited immediately before the Sequence in the reading from the first letter to the Corinthians, the motif of the new covenant can be heard: *Hic calix novum testamentum est in meo sanguine* (1 Cor 11:25).[29] *Lauda Sion* brings a Christological hermeneutic to the topic of the Eucharist as the new Passover between God and man, a hermeneutic that interprets the coming of Jesus Christ as the middle and fullness of time.[30] All the same, it would be false to interpret this stanza as if Thomas were expressing a radical discontinuity between Old and New Testaments. In his view of salvation history, there is rather an enduring continuity, inasmuch as the old covenant contains prefigurations of the event of salvation that took place in Christ's coming. Christ, bearing the title *Novus Rex*, did indeed establish the *Nova lex* and institute the Eucharist as *Novum Pascha*, so that the shadows (*umbrae*) and figures (*figurae*) have given way to truth (*veritas*). All the same, there is no way to understand Christ's coming adequately without the figures. For this reason, as well, the Office for Corpus Cristi is composed following the principle that as many Old Testament prefigurations as possible are to be adduced in order to show the meaning of the Eucharist. In a later strophe, three of these figures are explicitly displayed: the "sacrifice" of Isaac (Gn 22:1–19),[31] the Paschal lamb in the Exodus from Egypt (Ex 12–18),[32] and the manna in the wilderness (Ex 16). On the evening before the feast, the antiphon of the first Vespers goes further to reference Melchizedek as well.[33]

In keeping with the teaching that the sacrament is a *signum rememorativum* of the salvific deed enacted once for all,[34] the first part of the Sequence recalls the biblical and historical origin of the solemnity: the institution (*institutio*) of the sacrament at the last supper, which is extolled as the new Passover.

---

28. The hymn *Pange lingua gloriosi* also expresses the ritual innovation: "et antiquum documentum / novo cedat ritui."

29. Contemporary exegetical research has developed a differentiated picture of covenantal theology (or theologies) in the two testaments. Amidst all the diverse accentuations, there is a consensus that the "new *diatheke*" does not intend a removal of or substitution for the "old" covenant; rather, it is to be interpreted as the eschatological fulfilment of the old in Christ. It is likewise clear that, regarding Romans 9–11, the traditional forgetfulness of Israel in the Church and in theology is in need of some correction. See M. Theobald, "Kirche und Israel nach Röm 9–11," in his *Studien zum Römerbrief* (Tübingen: Mohr Siebeck, 2001), 324–49.

30. See L. J. Elders, "La relation entre l'ancienne et la nouvelle Alliance, selon saint Thomas d'Aquin," *Revue Thomiste* 100 (2000): 580–602.

31. The word *sacrificium*, which has only a subordinate status in Thomas's Eucharistic theology as well, does not appear in the hymn *Lauda Sion*. See *S. th.* II-II, q. 85, a. 1 ad 2: "Isaac vero significavit Christum inquantum ipse oblatus est in sacrificium."

32. See *S. th.* III, q. 73, a. 6, where the *agnus paschalis* is lifted up as the *praecipua figura*.

33. See *Officium de festo corporis Christi*, 275.

34. See *S. th.* III, q. 60.

Spiritual Food: The Eucharist as *signum demonstrativum*

The second sizeable section of the Sequence is devoted to the Eucharist's *meaning for the present*. The conversion of bread and wine into the flesh and blood of Jesus is called to mind as a dogma that holds even though it cannot be verified with the senses. Thereafter, it is brought out that the entire Christ is present in each of the two Eucharistic species—an assurance that the faithful receiving the sacrament *sub una specie* also receive Christ undivided. Finally, it is insistently recalled that it is in no way a matter of indifference with what disposition the faithful receive the sacrament. The motif of the reading, where unworthily receiving the Eucharist leads to judgment (see 1 Cor 11:27), is taken up and deepened in a poetic parenesis:

Quod in coena Christus gessit,	What at supper Christ carried out,
Faciendum hoc expressit	this he instructed to be done
In sui memoriam.	in his memory.
Docti sacris institutis,	Instructed by holy teaching,
Panem, vinum in salutis	we consecrate bread and wine
Consecramus hostiam.	as the sacrifice of salvation.
Dogma datur Christianis,	Dogma is given to Christians,
Quod in carnem transit panis,	that bread is changed into flesh,
Et vinum in sanguinem.	and wine into blood.
Quod non capis, quod non vides,	What you neither comprehend nor see,
Animosa firmat fides,	a strong faith establishes,
Praeter rerum ordinem.	beyond the order of things
Sub diversis speciebus,	Under diverse species,
Signis tantum et non rebus,	only signs and not things,
Latent res eximiae.	hide extraordinary things.
Caro cibus, sanguis potus,	Flesh [is] food, blood [is] drink,
manet tamen Christus totus	still Christ entire remains
sub utraque specie.	under each species.
A sumente non concisus,	For those receiving, not cut up
Non confractus, non divisus,	not broken, not divided,
Integer accipitur.	he is received entire.
Sumit unus, sumunt mille;	One receives, a thousand receive;
Quantum isti, tantum ille;	as many there are, so much is he;
Nec sumptus consumitur.	as received he is not consumed.

Sumunt boni, sumunt mali,	The good receive, the bad receive,
Sorte tamen inaequali	but their lot is unequal:
Vitae vel interitus.	life or destruction.
Mors est malis, vita bonis.	Death to the bad, life to the good,
Vide paris sumptionis	behold, from the same consumption
Quam sit dispar exitus.	follows an unequal end.
Fracto demum sacramento,	If at length the sacrament is broken,
Ne vacilles, sed memento	do not falter, but remember,
Tantum esse sub fragmento	how much is under one fragment,
Quantum toto tegitur.	as much as hidden in the whole.
Nulla rei fit scissura,	No division befalls the reality,
Signi tantum fit fractura	by which neither the status nor stature
Qua nec status nec statura	of the one signified is lessened.
Signati minuitur.	
Ecce panis angelorum,	Behold, the bread of angels,
Factus cibus viatorum,	made into the food of travelers,
Vere panis filiorum,	it is truly the bread of sons,
Non mittendus canibus.	not to be thrown to the dogs.
In figuris praesignatur,	In figures it is anticipated:
Cum Isaac immolatur,	when Isaac was sacrificed,
Agnus Paschae deputatur	the Paschal lamb was prescribed,
Datur manna patribus.	manna was given to the fathers.

What Christ did at the last supper should henceforth also be done in his memory: "Hoc facite in meam commemorationem" (1 Cor 11:24)—so runs the covenantal commission of the Lord as he departs from his disciples, something we hear recited in the reading before the Sequence. The *factum* should remain a *faciendum* for all time in order to renew the memory of Christ, his life and death. Not by chance does the hymn change perspective when it transitions from past to present, switching over to speaking in first person plural (*consecramus*). With this move, the sacrament's power to establish communion and shape life is implicitly brought into view. The Eucharist is a *signum demonstrativum*, to which Thomas attributes the effects of unity and communion.[35] Unity is ultimately not brought about by the faithful themselves, who gather to celebrate the Eucharist; nor is the

---

35. See *In IV Sent.*, d. 8, q. 1, a. 1, qa. 3 (n. 34) "Communio vel synaxis, quod idem est, inquantum scilicet homo congregatur ad unum et ad seipsum et ad alios, ei quod est maxime unum coniunctus." See *S. th.* III, q. 73, a. 4: "Aliam autem significationem habet respectu rei praesentis, scilicet ecclesiasticae unitatis, cui homines congregantur per hoc sacramentum. Et secundum hoc nominatur 'communio' vel synaxis."

memoria of Christ's suffering and death in the celebration of the Eucharist simply a historical reminiscence of a past event. *Docti sacris institutis*, that is, following the bequest of Christ, "we consecrate bread and wine as a sacrifice (*hostia*)." Taken from the gifts of creation, bread and wine are selected, prepared,[36] presented, and consecrated. In the act of consecration, however, there takes place a self-making present of Jesus Christ in and under the gifts of bread and wine. Already at the last supper, when Jesus "instituted" the sacrament (see Mk 14:22–24; Mt 26:26–28; Lk 22:19–20; 1 Cor 11:23–25), he spoke the interpretative words over bread and wine. Thomas finds this reasonable for numerous reasons. First, in view of the *usus sacramenti*, which consists of eating. If men normally nourish themselves with bread and wine, then this is sensible also for spiritual nourishment, *alimentum spirituale*. But also in view of the *passio Christi*, the double species of the sacrament is meaningful inasmuch as it symbolically represents the separation of blood from the body in the sacrifice on the cross. Finally, both signs are suitable for revealing the unity of the body that is the Church. For as bread is made from many grains and wine from many grapes, so also the Church is assembled from many members, who are united in the Eucharist in and through Christ.[37]

But—as the dogma teaches[38]—bread and wine become the flesh and blood of Jesus Christ through the recitation of the words of consecration, spoken by the ordained priest *in persona Christi*. He is the minister of the sacrament, for only he is officially authorized to speak the words of consecration.[39] With the citation of the words of institution, however, the decisive *transitus* comes to pass:[40] from bread and wine come to be the flesh and blood of Christ. The mystery of conversion, which Thomas attempted to illuminate ontologically using the concept of substantial change (*transsubstantiatio*), is not developed further within the context of the hymn. All the same, the essential elements are retained in the manner of a *doctrinal hymn*. The *transitus* is neither visible nor comprehensible; after the conversion, the

---

36. It is notable that Thomas sees a descriptive indication of Christ's Passion in the human preparation of the natural gifts of creation, which includes a transformation of wheat and grapes into bread and wine through the cultural techniques of baking and pressing. See *In IV Sent.*, d. 11, q. 2, a. 1, qa. 2 (n. 158).

37. See *In IV Sent.*, d. 11, q. 2, a. 1, qa. 2 (nn. 154–58); *S. c. G.* IV, c. 61; *In I Cor* XI, l. V; as well as *S. th.* III, q. 74, a. 1.

38. See DH 802. Although the treatment of transubstantiation in the *Sentences* commentary (*In IV Sent.*, d. 11, q. 1, a. 3 [nn. 60–114]) does not refer at all to a magisterial definition, and neither does the treatise on the Eucharist (see *S. th.* III, q. 75), the Sequence *Lauda Sion* reminds us that the Fourth Lateran Council (1215) taught the substantial change of bread and wine into the body and blood of Christ (*transsubstantiatio*).

39. See *In IV Sent.*, d. 13, a. 1, qa. 1 and 2, as well as *S. th.* III, q. 82, a. 1: "sacerdoti, cum ordinatur, confertur potestas hoc sacramentum consecrandi in persona Christi."

40. See *S. th.* III, q. 75, a. 8: "in hoc sacramento tota substantia panis transit in totum corpus Christi."

bread still looks and tastes like bread. The presence of the Lord under the Eucharistic species is therefore understandable only with the "eyes" of *faith* (*Quod non capis, quod non vides, / animosa firmat fides*).[41] Were the flesh and blood of the crucified one to be graphically tangible after the consecration, not only would faith be voided but the senses would be subjected to something quite appalling as well. Earlier in the *Sentences* commentary, Thomas staved off a crude realism, which insinuated that the *corpus Christi verum* would be "torn up and masticated with the teeth."[42] Already Ambrose had stressed that the blood of Christ is consumed in symbol so that no *horror cruoris* would arise.[43] It is this *sacramental* dimension that Thomas emphasizes in *Lauda Sion*.

With the emphasis that the signs remain after the consecration—that is, a permanence of accidents without a subject becomes a reality at the moment the substances are converted (*sub diversis speciebus, signis tantum et non rebus, latent res eximiae*)—the Sequence implicitly repudiates the doctrine of impanation, or consubstantiation, which presupposes that at the consecration the substance of the exalted Lord joins itself to the substances of bread and wine. Another reason Thomas rejects this theory of how the Lord is made present is that after the consecration a created substance would be worshipped, which amounts to an idolatrous act. If one explains the real presence with the aid of transubstantiation, then one can maintain the concerns of a realistic conception of the Eucharist without slipping into a crude sacramental realism that would hold a total identification between the Eucharistic and glorified Christ by teaching that the body of Christ is ground up with the teeth. Christ is indeed truly and substantially present—but in and under the signs of bread and wine. The flesh is given as food, the blood as drink: *Caro cibus, sanguis potus* is how the hymn condenses the Johannine statement that likewise presents the architectonic axis of the sequence.[44] In contrast, a spiritualism that denies the real presence has its

---

41. See *In IV Sent*, d. 10, q. 1, a. 1; *S. th*. III, q. 75, a. 1: "verum corpus Christi et sanguinem [est] in hoc sacramento, *neque sensu neque intellectu* deprehendi potest, sed sola fide, quae auctoritati divinae innititur." (following the textual form of the German Thomas-Ausgabe, vol. 30, 53, emphasis added; the Marietti edition differs, handing on only *neque sensu* in this passage).

42. See *In IV Sent.*, d. 10, q. 1, a. 1 (n. 14): "dicendum quod in crudelitatem sonaret et maximam irreverentiam, si corpus Christi ad modum cibi corporalis manducaretur, ut scilicet ipsum verum corpus Christi dilaniaretur et dentibus atteretur." The passage implies a critique of sensualism found in the *professio fidei* laid before Berengar of Tours by the Roman synod in 1059 (see DH 690).

43. Ambrose, *De sacr.* VI, 1 (FC 3, ed. J. Schmitz, 180): "so you also drink the symbol of the precious blood, that no revulsion before the blood (*horror cruoris*) arises."

44. The Sequence encompasses eighty verses (if one counts the Amen as its own verse, then eighty-one); line forty—*Caro cibus, sanguis potus*, which offers a prelude to the core statement of the Gospel—thus constitutes the middle.

particula veri in pointing to the continuity of the signs—concerning the bread and the wine, nothing is changed empirically by the performance of the consecration. The point of the doctrine of transubstantiation consists in its referring the process of conversion to an ontological, hence intelligible, level. The deficit of empirical verification, by contrast, continues to exist as a challenge for faith.

After this, the hymn refers to the *Christus totus* being received under both species. This may have been important for the medieval practice of administering communion, inasmuch as the chalice was withheld from the laity. They were now assured that Christ is contained whole and undivided in the species of bread, even if the theological reasoning behind this remains unexplained. The doctrine of concomitance would further disturb, and even conceptually overload, the poetic diction of a hymn that already takes risks by using theological terminology such as "thema specialis," "dogma," "consecrare," "sub utraque specie." Still, in the doctrine of concomitance, Thomas distinguishes between sacramental conversion and natural concomitance.[45] The direct end of the sacramental conversion of bread and wine is Christ's flesh and blood, but not his soul or divinity. These are contained in the converted gifts indirectly, so to speak, or as Thomas says "through natural concomitance." This is so because the divine logos has never given up the body he took on, and through the resurrection of the crucified one the soul is bound up with the glorified body. In the Eucharistic species, therefore, it is always the *totus Christus* which is present. This also applies to the two species in their relation to each other: in the converted bread, the flesh of Christ is contained *ex vi sacramenti*, the blood however, *ex naturali concomitantia*; but the contrary is the case in the converted wine, where the blood is contained *ex vi sacramenti* and Christ's flesh, *ex naturali concomitantia*.[46]

Doctrine and life, theology and spirituality are interrelated, and there-

---

45. See *In IV Sent.*, d. 10, q. 1, a. 2 (nn. 37–44); *S. th.* III, q. 76, a. 1: "Sciendum tamen quod aliquid Christi est in hoc sacramento dupliciter: uno modo, quasi *ex vi sacramenti*; alio modo, *ex naturali concomitantia*. Ex vi quidem sacramenti, est sub speciebus huius sacramenti id in quod directe convertitur substantia panis et vini praeexistens, prout significatur per verba formae, quae sunt effectiva in hoc sacramento sicut et in ceteris: puta cum dicitur, *Hoc est corpus meum, Hic est sanguis meus*. Ex naturali autem concomitantia est in hoc sacramento illud quod realiter est coniunctum ei in quod praedicta conversio terminatur. Si enim aliqua duo sunt realiter coniuncta, ubiqumque est unum realiter, oportet [sic] et aliud esse: sola enim operatione animae discernuntur quae realiter sunt coniuncta" (emphasis added).

46. See *S. th.* III, q. 76, a. 2: "Respondeo quod sub utraque specie sacramenti totus est Christus: aliter tamen et aliter. Nam sub speciebus panis est quidem corpus Christi ex vi sacramenti, sanguis autem ex reali concomitantia: sicut supra [a. 1] dictum est de anima et divinitate Christi. Sub speciebus vero vini est quidem sanguis Christi ex vi sacramenti, corpus autem Christi ex reali concomitantia: sicut anima et divinitas: eo quod nunc sanguis Christi non est ab eius corpore separatus, sicut fuit tempore passionis et mortis. Unde, si tunc fuisset hoc sacramentum celebratum, sub species panis fuisset corpus Christi sine sanguine, et sub specie vini sanguis sine corpore: sicut erat in rei veritate."

fore understanding the truths of faith yearns for a corresponding praxis. In a poetic parenesis, which occasionally has a mnemonic character, the next stanza thus concerns itself with the question of rightly receiving the Eucharist. The extraordinary accumulation of derivatives taken from *sumere* reveals, even from a purely linguistic standpoint, how the theme of eating the holy food is thrust into the foreground.[47] In connection with the Pauline word of 1 Cor 11:27–29, which warns against eating the holy bread unto judgment, the Sequence calls to mind that reception of the Eucharist is bound up with certain stipulations if it is to bear fruit. First of all, however, the hymn takes up impressive rhetoric to insist once more that Christ is received in communion undivided and whole: "*non concisus / non confractus, non divisus / integer accipitur.*" It also brings out the point that the substance of the exalted Lord remains untouched by the eating of the gifts, even should thousands upon thousands consume the Eucharistic food. This is connected with the fact that, in the eating of the gifts, it is not the substance of the exalted Lord that is assimilated to the bodily organism but, quite the reverse, it is the communicant who is taken into the living reality of Jesus Christ. He becomes what he is: a member of the body of Christ. Countless members belong to the *corpus Christi mysticum*. All the same, it is not a matter of indifference how one receives the consecrated gifts, or in what condition one encounters the Eucharistic Christ. Even if no external difference can be detected in the sacramental reception, if the good and the bad approach the sacrament in the same way, there is nevertheless a qualitative difference that leads to life or to death. Similar reception (*par sumptio*) can have greatly dissimilar results (*dispar exitus*): *Mors et malis, vita bonis*. The double outcome of judgment—death or life—is invoked here as an eschatological horizon to parenetically urge the faithful to receive communion in a worthy manner, which for Thomas means free from mortal sins. The effect of the Eucharist is dependent upon the moral disposition of the receiver.[48] Indeed, the sacrament has *in itself* the power to forgive any sin whatsoever, though Thomas holds that one receiving in a state of mortal sin is not united with Christ.[49] Receiving communion incriminates him even more. Thomas judges the situation of *peccata venialia* differently, holding that these are completely forgiven.[50] As natural food restores what strength

---

47. In verses 43–49, there are seven instances of *sumere*, or *sumptio*.
48. As is well known, this does not apply to the minister of the sacrament, for the priest does not consecrate the gifts of bread and wine from his own power but rather on the basis of having the authority to act *in persona Christi*. See *S. th.* III, q. 82, a. 5. With this as background, Thomas also emphasizes that, in view of the sacrament, a Mass celebrated by a bad priest is worth no less than one celebrated by a good one (see a. 6).
49. See *In IV Sent.*, d. 9, a. 3, qa. 2; d. 12, q. 2, qa. 2; *S. th.* III, q. 79, a. 3.
50. See *In IV Sent.*, d. 12, q. 2, a. 1 qa. 3; a. 2, qa. 1; *S. th.* III, q. 79, a. 4.

the body loses due to natural heat, so this spiritual food does the same for what is lost due to the heat of concupiscence through *peccata venialia*. For this reason, the sacrament of the Eucharist can be designated, following Ambrose, as *remedium quotidianae infirmitatis*.

The Sequence also overlays the theme of a meal (*cibus*) that is given to the *homo viator* as refreshment for the way. It summons—*ecce!*—those praying to recognize the Eucharist as the "bread of angels" (*panis angelorum*).[51] The Old Testmanet figure recalls the situation of the people of Israel in the wilderness. The manna that falls from heaven to satisfy the Israelites' hunger is named "bread of angels" in the Psalter (see Ps 77:24f.). True, eating this bread time and again quickly becomes an affliction for the Israelites; they murmur and long to return to Egypt and the meat they ate there (see Nm 11:5f.). Given this, it is notable that the later wisdom literature describes the situation positively: "You gave your people food of angels, and without their toil you supplied them from heaven with bread ready to eat, providing every pleasure and suited to every taste. For your sustenance manifested your sweetness toward your children; and the bread, ministering to the desire of the one who took it, was changed to suit everyone's liking" (Ws 16:20f.). The food given *freely* here is a miraculous food that satisfies the expectations of all. More importantly, it is an expression of God's provident love for his children. In the phrase *panis angelorum*, Thomas Aquinas sees a *figura* of the Eucharist. Precisely because this food is so precious, one may not throw it to the dogs (see Ex 22:31).

At this point in the Sequence, manna appears in the triad of figures presented in tightly interlocking poetry: the sacrifice of Isaac, the Paschal lamb, and the manna in the wilderness.[52] The shocking story of the binding of Isaac—at God's behest, the patriarch is supposed to sacrifice his only son (see Gn 22:1–19)—is read by Thomas in two directions: on the one hand, God gave this instruction in order to manifest Abraham's faith and love (*ad manifestationem fidei et amoris Abrahae*), so that his conduct would be an example (*exemplum*) to later generations; on the other, through the sacrifice of Isaac, he offered a type of Christ's death (*in significationem mortis Christi*).[53] Nevertheless, what is intimated in the *figura*—the sacrifice of Isaac is

---

51. A. Stock, "Engelbrot. Zu einer alttestamentlichen Figur," in his *Liturgie und Poesie. Zur Sprache des Gottesdienstes* (Kevelaer: Butzon & Bercker, 2010), 188–96.

52. The mention of the Paschal lamb and manna differs from the Roman canon, where the Old Testament figures of Abel, Abraham, and Melchizedek are summoned in the *Supra quae*: "sicuti accepta habere dignatus es munera pueri tui iusti *Abel*, et sacrificium Patriarchae nostri *Abrahae*: et quod tibi obtulit summus sacerdos tuus *Melchisedech*, sanctum sacrificium, immaculatam hostiam" (emphasis added).

53. See *In I Sent.*, d. 47 q. 1 a. 4 c: "et sic Deus occisionem Isaac, quae de se inordinationem habebat ex eo quod filius innocens non erat ordinatus in finem per viam occisionis a patre, ordinatam fecit, ponendo

thwarted at the last moment through angelic intervention[54]—becomes reality (*veritas*) in the Passion of Christ."God did not withhold his own Son, but gave him up for all of us (Rom 8:32). Even though Thomas does not refer back to Genesis 22 in his commentary on Romans,[55] his hymn *Lauda Sion* reveals that he nevertheless sees in the sacrifice of Isaac a prefiguration of Christ's suffering and death; moreover, this is completely in accord with the Roman canon of the Mass.[56]

The Paschal lamb, likewise cited in the Sequence, is viewed by Thomas as the most significant type of the Eucharist. In the New Testament, the motif of the lamb is expressly referred to Christ, where we read: "Christ was sacrificed as our paschal lamb" (see 1 Cor 5:7). In the *Summa theologiae*, Thomas goes further to develop a somewhat systematic ordering of the most important Old Testament figures who point ahead to the Eucharist. He initially recalls the three dimensions of the sacrament: first, *sacramentum tantum* (bread and wine); second, *res et sacramentum* (the *corpus Christi verum*); and third, *res sacramenti* (the Church as *corpus Christi mysticum*). Then he states that the first dimension was most purely expressed in the sacrifice of Melchizedek, who offered *bread and wine* (see Gn 14:18); the second dimension, the *Christus passus* contained in the sacrament, was foreshadowed by the many *sacrifices* of the old covenant, but especially by the sin offering on the day of atonement (see Lv 16); finally, the effect of spiritual strengthening finds its harbinger in the *manna* in the wilderness. All three dimensions, however, run together in the figure of the Paschal lamb, as Thomas sees it. First, the Paschal lamb is eaten together with unleavened *bread* (see Ex 12:8; connected to the *sacramentum tantum*); second, the *sacrifice* of the lamb bears on Christ's Passion (connected to the *res et sacramentum*); third, the *blood of the lamb*, which is painted on the door posts as an apotropaic sign and thus enables the exodus of the people of Israel, foreshadows the redeeming and *communio*-establishing effect of the sacrifice. The *agnus paschalis* is therefore the *praecipua figura huius sacramenti*, as Thomas summarizes.[57]

---

hunc ordinem, ut esset ad manifestationem fidei et amoris Abrahae, ut esset posteris in exemplum, et in significationem mortis Christi: et in occisionem sic ordinatam divina auctoritate licite consensit voluntas Abrahae." On Abraham as *exemplum fidei* and *pater credentium*, see *In Hebr* VIII, l. III (nn. 580–91).

54. For this reason, Thomas notes in his commentary on the Jewish feasts that the "freeing of Isaac" is solemnly commemorated in Israel. See *S. th.* I-II, q. 102, a. 4 ad 10: "In prima enim die mensis septimi erat festum tubarum, in memoriam liberationis Isaac, quando Abraham invenit arietem haerentem cornibus, quem repraesentabant per cornua quibus buccinabant."

55. See *In Rom* VIII, l. VI (nn. 712–14).

56. See also *S. th.* II-II, q. 85, a. 1 ad 2: "Isaac vero significavit Christum inquantum ipse oblatus est in sacrificium."

57. See *S. th.* III, q. 73, a. 6. See also *S. th.* I-II, q. 102, a. 5 ad 4, 5, 6; q. 103, a. 2; III, q. 46, a. 10 ad 1, 2; q. 47, a. 2 ad 1, and passim.

This triad of figures is concluded in *Lauda Sion* with the motif of manna, which is already referenced to the Eucharist in the Johannine bread of life discourse: "I am the bread of life. Your ancestors ate the manna in the wilderness, and they died. This is the bread that comes down from heaven, so that one may eat of it and not die. I am the living bread that came down from heaven. Whoever eats of this bread will live forever" (Jn 6:48–51). Unlike the manna, which satisfied hunger in the wilderness but could not preserve from death, the living bread, Christ, grants entrance into a life that no longer knows death. Thus, the transition to the eschatological dimension of the Eucharist is presented, which becomes important in the final passage of the Sequence.[58]

Escort into the Land of the Living—the Eucharist as *signum prognosticum*

Bone pastor, panis vere,	Good shepherd, you true bread,
Iesu, nostri miserere;	Jesus, have mercy on us;
Tu nos pasce, nos tuere,	put us to pasture, watch over us;
Tu nos bona fac videre	make us to see the good
In terra viventium.	in the land of the living.
Tu qui cuncta scis et vales,	You, who know and can do everything,
Qui nos pascis hic mortales,	Who pasture us mortals here:
Tuos ibi commensales,	make [us] there your table fellows,
Cohaeredes et sodales	joint heirs and companions
Fac sanctorum civium.	of the holy citizens.
Amen.	Amen.

The closing strophe of the Sequence, cited by John Paul II at the end of his encyclical on the Eucharist,[59] is governed by a uniquely eschatological dynamic; it flows into a prayer directed insistently to Christ, the good shepherd. The imploring vocative,[60] the singular invocation of Jesus' name, the abundant imperatives,[61] and the densely placed personal pronouns[62] all reveal on a merely linguistic level the change from *doctrinal hymn* to prayer.

---

58. See *In Ioan.* VI, l. VI (nn. 951–58), where the "*plus*" of the Eucharist in comparison with manna is seen in the fact that it contains what it signifies: eternal life (n. 954).
59. See John Paul II, *Ecclesia de Eucharistia*, n. 62.
60. See the vocative: v. 71, *bone pastor*; v. 71, *panis vere*; v. 72, *Jesu*.
61. See the imperatives: v. 72, *miserere*; v. 73, *pasce*; v. 73, *tuere*; v. 74, *fac videre*; v. 80, *fac*, as well as the verbs in second person singular at v. 76, *scis* and *vales*, and v. 77, *pascis*.
62. See the anaphorically repeated phrase at vv. 73 and 74, *tu nos*; and then the pronouns in v. 72, *nostri*; v. 73, *nos*; v. 76, *tu*; v. 77, *nos*.

If one describes only the texture, then it is apparent that it brings the "we" of those praying into an intimate relation to the "you" of the one adored, a relation ultimately so stable that it reaches into the sphere of final consummation.

At the beginning of the stanza, we find the invocation: *bone pastor*, which traces a structural arc back to the beginning of the Sequence, where the attribute of shepherd was earlier sounded. The address corresponds to Christ's self-description in the Gospel of John: "Ego sum pastor bonus" (Jn 10:11, 14). The good shepherd, however, is characterized by the fact that he knows his own and calls them by name,[63] indeed, that he gives his life for the sheep in order to save them. In his commentary on John's Gospel, Thomas explains that the title of shepherd belongs to Christ in a special way and establishes a connection to the Eucharist in an interesting way: as the flock is guided and led to pasture by a shepherd, so also are the faithful strengthened by Christ—by his spiritual food, that is, by his body and his blood.[64] It is no accident that Christ is apostrophized as *panis vere* in the Sequence—fitting for the occasion of Corpus Christi. In and under the form of bread, Christ, the good shepherd, is truly present and strengthens his flock, so that they do not grow weary on their way through time. The presence of the shepherd, however, challenges the faithful to turn to him and call his name. Only in this passage is the name "Jesus" invoked, to which the beginning of hymn already alluded using the soteriological title of savior and redeemer (*salvator*). The plea for mercy (*nostri miserere*), however, reflects the need for help and redemption, something perhaps rendered more clearly apparent in the light of Jesus' hidden presence. At any rate, those at prayer do not act as though they are already perfect or as if they could reach perfection by their own strength; rather, they acknowledge that their life is incomplete and in need of forgiveness and help. At the same time, and remaining with the bucolic metaphor, the faithful as "sheep" are always in danger of wandering off the path. For this reason, they ask for protection and guidance on the way.

The subsequent petition, "watch over us—*nos tuere*," requires its own commentary. Considering that the visible Eucharistic piety of the Middle Ages arose genetically out of the ever more protracted act of elevation—after the consecration, the consecrated gifts were displayed before the people in an ostentatious gesture for adoration—one then notices that the

---

63. See Jn 10:3: "et proprias oves vocat nominatim."
64. *In Ioan.* X, l. III (n. 1398): "Quod autem Christus sit pastor, manifeste ei competit: nam sicut per pastorem grex gubernatur et pascitur, ita fideles per Christum spirituali cibo, et etiam corpore et sanguine suo reficiuntur."

hymn carries out a unique reversal of perspective: it invokes the Eucharistic Christ and asks that *he* look upon the prayerful onlookers. To him, to the one looking upon them, do those prayerful onlookers raise the petition that he might grant them to look upon the goods in the land of the living. The terms related to "seeing" woven through the text are striking; they allude to the motif of the blessed vision of God (*visio beata* or *visio Dei per essentiam*)[65] and, incidentally, also characterize the final strophe of the hymn *Adoro te devote*.[66]

On the way to the *finis ultimus*, however, the Eucharist is also the *viaticum*, provision for the journey,[67] which ought to convey man into the realm of perfection. It is a matter of bridging the chasm between here (*hic*) and there (*ibi*), of Christ the shepherd accompanying the faithful into the *status gloriae*.[68] In this process, the *panis vivus et vitalis* offers a foretaste of coming glory and at the same time serves as victuals strengthening the faithful for the way into the land of the living, the *terra viventium*. There, they will be table fellows (*commensales*) with God and joint heirs (*cohaeredes*) of the promise—phrases that refer back to the New Testament letters (see Rom 8:17; Eph 2:19). Paul attests before the faithful that, as sons of God, they too will gain a share in Christ's inheritance;[69] and in the letter to the Ephesians it is emphasized that both Jews and Gentiles have access to the Father through Christ. Precisely the Gentiles will no longer have the status of guests and sojourners without rights in his kingdom; rather, they will be called co-citizens of the saints and members of the household of God.[70] In the hymn, it is only here that Thomas depicts the eschatological dimension

---

65. See J.-P. Torrell, "La vision de dieu 'per essentiam' selon Saint Thomas d'Aquin," in his *Recherches thomasiennes* (Paris: Vrin, 2000), 177–99, who at the outset points out that the term *visio beatifica* is not found at all in Thomas's work. Rarely used is *visio beatificans* (five times); more often we find Thomas speaking of *visio beata* or *visio beatorum* (thirty-eight instances); in contrast, we find abundantly used *visio Dei* (241 instances); but what is actually Thomas's typical way of speaking is *visio Dei per essentiam* (164 instances). This *modus loquendi* responds to the idea, condemned in 1241, that neither angels nor men could see God *per essentiam*. See *S. th.* I, q. 12, a. 1, where Thomas gives the distinguishing reference that *cognitio per essentiam* is eschatologically possible, but that this is not accompanied by a perfect grasp of God, that is, *comprehensio*.

66. See the strophe: "Iesu, quem velatum nunc aspicio, / quando fiet illud quod tam sitio? / te revelata cernens facie, / visu sim beatus tuæ gloriæ."

67. See *S. th.* III, q. 79, a. 2.

68. See *S. th.* III, q. 79, a. 2 ad 1: "hoc sacramentum non statim nos in gloriam introducit, sed dat nobis virtutem perveniendi ad gloriam. Et ideo viaticum dicitur."

69. See *In Rom* VIII, l. III (nn. 648f.): "Potest tamen dici quod Deus decedit nobis inquantum est in nobis per fidem: erit autem nostra haereditas, inquantum videbimus eum per speciem. Secundo describit hanc haereditatem ex parte Christi, dicens cohaeredes autem Christi, quia ipse cum sit principalis filius a quo nos filiationem participamus, ita est principalis haeres, cui in haereditate coniungimur."

70. See *In Eph* III, l. II (n. 146): "dicatur quod esse gentes cohaeredes et concorporales, et comparticipes promissionis eius, scilicet Dei patris, hoc quidem donum dedit Deus gentibus in Christo, id est per Christum, et hoc secundum operationem virtutis eius, id est per hoc quod potenter operatus est, suscitando

of the Eucharist in communal terms; otherwise, the individual longing for face-to-face vision supersedes the biblical motif of one day sitting together as table fellows at the heavenly wedding banquet.

For the sake of completeness, it should be added that Thomas illustrates the eschatological dimension of the Eucharist in the Divine Office using two further biblical texts: the first is an Old Testment text that refers to the prophet Elijah, who was strengthened in a miraculous way in order to reach the mountain of God where the theophany in the quiet whispers of the wind befell him (see 1 Kgs 19).[71] The other is in the New Testament, stemming from the Johannine bread of life discourse, which is the Gospel recited in the liturgy of the solemnity after the Sequence *Lauda Sion: Si quis manducaverit ex hoc pane, vivet in aeternum* (Jn 6:52).

Christum a morte." For background, see D. Chardonnens, "Éternité du sacerdoce du Christ et effet eschatologique de l'eucharistie," *Revue Thomiste* 99 (1999): 159–80.

71. See *Officium*, 277 (Lectio III): "Respexit Elias ad caput suum subcinericium panem: qui surgens comedit et bibit / Et ambulavit in fortitudine cibi illius / Usque ad montem Dei." This theme came up earlier in the sermon *Homo quidam fecit cenam magnam*. On this point, see: L.-J. Bataillon, "Le Sermon inédit de saint Thomas *Homo quidam fecit cenam magnam*: Introduction et édition," *Revue des sciences philosophiques et théologiques* 67 (1983): 353–69, as well as S. th. III, q. 79, a. 2 ad 1, where Elijah's miraculous food is designated a *figura* of the Eucharist as *viaticum*.

8

Hidden Presence and Contemplative Adoration

The Hymn *Adoro te devote*

The hymn *Adoro te devote*, which is offered here in the reconstruction of Robert Wielockx,[1] is not a part of the Divine Office; all the same, an investigation of Thomas's poetic theology cannot waive considering it, for it is indeed the testimony that expresses the Eucharistic spirituality of Aquinas with the greatest density and beauty.[2] Admittedly, for a long time Thomas Aquinas's authorship was called into question, because, among other reasons, there is no reference to this prayer in the biography of Aquinas flowing from the quill of William of Tocco. But now the critical edition of *Ystoria sancti Thome de Aquino de Guillaume de Tocco*, edited by Claire le Brun-Gouanvic,[3] has been able to dismantle precisely this objection by including a fourth, early version of *Ystoria*, which for a long time was not taken into consideration but is a reliable witness all the same; and in this

---

1. See R. Wielockx, "Poetry and Theology in the Adoro te deuote. Thomas Aquinas on the Eucharist and Christ's Uniqueness," in *Christ among the Mediaeval Dominicans: Representations of Christ in the Texts and Images of the Order of Preachers*, ed. K. Emery and J. Wawrykow (Notre Dame, Ind.: Notre Dame University Press, 1998), 157–74. Wielocks brought together fifty-one textual witnesses and, relying above all on the foundation of the fourth and final version of *Ystoria sancti Thome de Aquino* (William of Tocco), compiled the present form of the text. He himself discusses the deviations from the usual version of the text, which traces back to A. Wilmart. See A. Wilmart, "La tradition littéraire et textuelle de l'Adoro te devote," *RThAM* 1 (1929): 21–40 and 149–76, as well as idem, *Auteurs spirituels et texts dévots du moyen âge latin* (Paris: Études Augustiniennes, 1932), 361–414. The present form of the text diverges primarily in terms of poetic form. Whereas Wilmart hands on the hymn in strophic form, following the post-medieval editions, Wielocks retrieved the original form in fourteen couplets—a reconstruction that is also plausible on account of the rhyming couplet organization.

2. It is not by chance that J.-P. Torrell characterized the hymn *Adoro te* as St. Thomas's most beautiful prayer. See Torrell, "Adoro te. La plus belle prière de saint Thomas," *Recherches thomasiennes. Études revues et augmentées* (Paris: Vrin, 2000), 367–75.

3. *Ystoria sancti Thome de Aquino de Guillaume de Tocco* (1323), éd. critique, introd. et notes Claire le Brun-Gouanvic (Toronto: Pontifical Institute of Mediaeval Studies, 1996), c. 58, 72–75.

version, *Adoro te* is thoroughly documented as Thomas's last prayer. More precisely, it reports that on his death bed Thomas requested once more the *viaticum* and received this in tears.⁴ On this occasion, he spoke the *Adoro te devote* to set down for the last time a testimony of his faith in the real presence of Jesus Christ in the sacrament of the Eucharist. Even if this report should not be historically accurate, it would still be well contrived, for *Adoro te devote* leads into the question born of longing: when will the sacramentally *veiled* presence of Jesus Christ finally be converted into the *unveiled* face-to-face vision.

A further argument internal to the text, which is alleged against Thomas's authorship, refers to the deception of the senses: "Neither a poetic feeling nor reverence could have brought Thomas to write: *Visus, gustus, tactus / in te fallitur. Sed solus auditus / tute creditur*."⁵ In fact, the scholastic consensus at the time held that the senses could not be decieved in relation to their proper object: "sensus ... propriorum *semper verus* est."⁶ However, we should ask with Jean-Pierre Torrell whether it is reasonable "to expect the same logical rigor in a prayer, which is moreover poetic, as in a theological treatise."⁷ Furthermore, when considered more precisely, the hymn does not speak of *all* the senses being deceived; rather, it attributes to *auditus* the capacity to access the truth of the Word, which perhaps suffices "for saving the truth of sense judgment."⁸ Beyond that, the meaning of the word *fallere* need not necessarily be understood in the strong sense of *deceptio*, and having recourse to parallel texts in other hymns suggests that it is to be interpreted in the sense of a lack (*et si sensus deficit*, or *praestet fides supplementum / sensuum defectui*). Finally, in theological contexts Thomas also somtimes calls attention to the fact that the truth of the Eucharist is to be conceived as not only *praeter rationem* but also *contra sensum*.⁹

4. See *Ystoria sancti Thome de Aquino de Guillaume de Tocco* (1323), c. 58, 197–99. In the German version, offered by W. P. Eckert, the prayer is not found, since its textual basis still failed to consider the fourth traditional variant. See *Das Leben des heiligen Thomas—erzählt von Wilhelm von Tocco und andere Zeugnisse zu seinem Leben* (Düsseldorf: Patmos, 1965), 160–62.

5. Gy, *L'office*, 83. See *S. th*. III, q. 75, a. 5 ad 2: "in hoc sacramento nulla est deceptio: sunt enim secundum rei veritatem accidentia, quae sensibus diiudicantur. Intellectus autem, cuius est proprium obiectum substantia, ut dicitur in III *de Anima*, per fidem a deceptione praeservatur.—There is no deception in this sacrament; for the accidents which are discerned by the senses are truly present. But the intellect, whose proper object is substance, is preserved by faith from deception."

6. Aristotle, *De anima* (427b11; 418b18–20). See also *In IV Sent.*, d. 10, q. 1, a. 4 (n. 112): "sensus in hoc sacramento non decipitur; quia sensus non habet iudicare de substantia sed de formis sensibilibus." Nevertheless, a little later on (ibid., n. 113), the intellect as enlightened by faith is preserved, which reveals that a knowing function is ascribed to the sense of hearing—*fides e auditu* (Rom 10:18)—something also stressed in the hymn *Adoro te devote*.

7. Torrell, *Saint Thomas Aquinas*, 133f.

8. Ibid.

9. See *In IV Sent.*, d. 10, q. 1, a. 1: "et maxime meritum fidei in hoc creduntur multa in hoc sacramento quae non solum praeter rationem sunt, sed etiam contra sensum, ut videtur."

In addition to all of this, the detailed studies of Robert Wielockx have been able to further dissipate doubts regarding Thomas's authorship.[10] In particular, Wielockx brought forward three arguments for Thomas's authorship. First, of the fifty-one known textual witnesses, forty-four hand on explicitly the name of Thomas Aquinas; in contrast, no version attributes authorship of the hymn to anyone else. Second, the geography of the handwritten tradition refers to the vicinity of Naples, the place of origin for *Ystoria sancti Thome* and Thomas's last place of activity. Third, beyond the external criteria, the poetic form as well as the theological contents can corroborate the authorship of Thomas Aquinas. The hymn reads:

Adoro te devote, latens veritas,	O hidden truth, devoutly I adore Thee,
te quae sub his formis vere latitas.	who truly art within the forms before me.
Tibi se cor meum totum subicit,	To Thee my heart I bow with bended knee,
quia te contemplans totum deficit.	as failing quite in contemplating Thee.
Visus, tactus, gustus, in te fallitur,	Sight, touch, and taste in Thee are each deceived;
sed auditu solo tute creditur.	the ear alone most safely is believed.
Credo quidquid dixit dei filius,	I believe all the Son of God has spoken,
nihil veritatis verbo verius.	than Truth's own word there is no truer token.
In cruce latebat sola deitas,	God only on the Cross lay hid from view,
sed hic latet simul et humanitas.	but here lies hid at once the humanity too.
Ambo vere credens atque confitens,	And I, in both professing my belief,
peto quod petivit latro paenitens.	make the same prayer as the repentant thief.
Plagas sicut Thomas non intueor,	Thy wounds, as Thomas saw, I do not see,
deum tamen meum te confiteor.	yet Thee confess my Lord and God to be.
Fac me tibi semper magis credere,	Make me believe Thee ever more and more,
in te spem habere, te diligere.	in Thee my hope, in Thee my love to store.

---

10. Thus J.-P. Torrell, "Adoro te," 370. See his "L'authenticité de l'Adoro te devote," *RSR* 67 (1993): 79–83.

O memoriale mortis domini,	O thou Memorial of our Lord's own dying!
Panis vivus vitam præstans homini.	O Bread that living art and vivifying!
Præsta mihi semper de te vivere,	Make ever Thou my soul on Thee to live,
et te mihi semper dulce sapere.	ever a taste of Heavenly sweetness give.
Pie pellicane, Iesu domine,	O loving Pelican! O Jesus, Lord!
me immundum munda tuo sanguine.	Unclean I am, but cleanse me in Thy Blood,
Cuius una stilla salvum facere,	of which a single drop, for sinners spilt,
totum mundum posset omni scelere.	is ransom for a world's entire guilt.
Iesu, quem velatum nunc aspicio,	Jesus, whom for the present veil'd I see,
quando fiet illud quod tam sitio?	what I so thirst for, when will't be granted me?
Te revelata cernens facie,	That I may see Thy countenance unfolding,
visu sim beatus tuæ gloriæ. Amen.	and may be blest Thy glory in beholding. Amen.

(Trans. E. Caswall, slightly altered)

Observations on the Diction and Structure of the Hymn

Directing one's attention to the configuration of the final syllables, it is easily recognizable that the hymn is divided into two large, symmetrical parts: whereas verses 1–14 end *consonantically*, verses 15–28 exhibit *vocalic* endings. The further internal differentiation of the two parts can be read off of the rhyme structure. Regarding the first part of the hymn, what catches the eye is that verses 1–2 and 9–10 feature the same final rhyme (*-itas*). They border verses 3–8, which constitute three couplets standing in close thematic connection. It is likewise notable that beyond this inclusion, the first part of the hymn contains two further couplets (vv. 11–14), which can be designated a "cadenza," following Wielockx. Thus, the poetic structure follows an "inclusion with a simultaneous exclusion."[11]

The same structural principle is also exhibited in the second part of the hymn, though with a significant variation. The three couplets, vv. 15–16, 19–20, and 23–24, share an agreement on the ending rhyme figure (*-ere*). In this way, the number of including verses increases from four in the first part (vv. 1–14) to six in the second part of the hymn (vv. 15–24). Fittingly,

---

11. R. Wielockx, "Poetry and Theology in the *Adoro te devote*," 159, who likewise put forward a linguistic structural analysis of the hymn (ibid., 160–64).

the structure of the framed verses is also different. Instead of an undivided block, as is the case in the first part (vv. 3–8), the second part has two couplets separated from each other, with each being specifically framed and made quite conspicuous by emphatic invocations (vv. 17–18 and 21–22). The last four verses (25–28) form a sort of final cadenza. In the interpretation that follows, we will have to pay attention to this structure.

Theological Interpretation

The hymn begins with the verse *Adoro te devote, latens veritas*. The one praying, who pauses before the elevated host or lingers contemplatively in front of the Blessed Sacrament, begins to speak and articulates his adoration in words. He does this in a language that openly expresses the affective dimension of prayer: "devotedly—*devote*" he performs the act of adoration, which relates to a You addressed as hidden truth[12] (*latens veritas*).[13] With this, the motif characterizing the hymn's first part is designated: the presence of Jesus Christ hidden under the signs of bread and wine. The importance of this motif can be read in the fact that it is not only presented harmoniously and with chiastic crossing in the first double verse (*latens veritas—vere latitas*), but also taken up again in verses 9–10 and related to the divinity (*deitas*) and humanity (*humanitas*) of Jesus Christ. The framed verses in between (vv. 3–8) take up the question of how one can find access to this hidden truth, and they underline that the eyes of faith are required in order to read the Eucharistic signs correctly, to recognize the invisible reality of Christ in the visible.

Accentuating *hiddenness* also prevents the misunderstanding that this truth, which is Christ (see Jn 14:6), is simply available for the taking, as if one had a complete picture of it and could take possession of it. The truth is there and at the same time not there, and the accentuation of this concealment converges with the command forbidding images in the Old Testament in that it addresses the unavailability of the divine presence. The faithful response to this presence of *latens veritas* is adoration (*adoratio*)— an act that is reserved to God alone and therefore can be extended to Christ only because as man he was hypostatically united with the eternal Word of

---

12. In the familiar version, we read "hidden Godhead" (*latens deitas*). Formally speaking, the motif of *latens veritas* determines the framing double verses (vv. 1–2 and 9–10) of the first part of the hymn (note the four derivatives of *latere*), before the "cadenza" (vv. 11–14) begins.

13. It is superfluous to remark that in Thomas's view adoration is also translated into gestures. See *S. th.* II-II, q. 84, a. 3 ad 2: "ita etiam adoratio principaliter quidem in interiori Dei reverentia consistit, secundario autem in quibusdam corporalibus humilitatis signis: sicut genuflectimus nostram infirmitatem significantes in comparatione ad Deum; prosternimus autem nos quasi profitentes nos nihil esse ex nobis." In the hymn for Corpus Christi, *Pange lingua*, we hear: *Tantum ergo sacramentum / veneremur cernui.*

the Father. Jesus Christ, however, bound up his presence with the signs of bread and wine. Thus, adoration is due the Eucharist, as Augustine earlier hammered home: "And because the Lord walked here [i.e., on earth] in his flesh, he gave us this flesh for our salvation; no one, however, eats that flesh if he has not first adored it ... and not only do we not sin when we offer adoration to it, but moreover we sin by not adoring it."[14] In this respect, adoring Christ in the Eucharist has the note of being critical of idols, since it rules out adoration of finite figures. In his comments on the Decalogue, Thomas stated: "One does a great injustice to God if one equates anything with him."[15] This can be transferred to the Eucharistic and theological context: to adore Christ in the sacrament thus means to reject seeking beatitude in riches, honor, reputation, power, lust, or other created surrogates.[16] Whoever sets his heart on earthly goods enslaves himself; conversely, it is precisely the offering of right worship upon God that enables a freedom in dealing with *bona temporalia*. The difference between adoration and idolatry is thus also important in the context of Eucharistic theology, because when it comes to the elevation of the host or adoring the Blessed Sacrament, it is not a matter of worshiping the sensibly perceptible signs of bread and wine as cultic objects but rather the truth itself hidden in the signs of bread and wine. The accusation of reification and material idolatry, which had its justification when we consider certain practices of piety in the (late) Middle Ages, misses the decisive point in the doctrine of transubstantiation, according to which there is precisely no created substance remaining after the consecration, but only the substance of Christ's body.[17]

Faith as Access to the Hidden Presence of Christ

But how does the one praying obtain access to this hidden truth? The three following couplets (vv. 3–8) revolve around precisely this question. That

---

14. Augustine, *Enarrationes in Psalmos*, 98, 9 (CCSL 39, ed. D. E. Dekkers, 1385): "Et quia in ipsa carne hic ambulavit, et ipsam carnem nobis manducandam ad salutem dedit; nemo autem illam carnem manducat, nisi prius adoraverit; ... et non solum non peccemus adorando, sed peccemus non adorando."

15. "Magnum enim iniuriam Deo facit qui aliquid ei adaequat." *Collationes de decem preceptis*, in: J.-P. Torrell, *Recherches thomasiennes*, 47–117, here 73.

16. See *S. th.* I-II, q. 2. The question of whether man's beatitude (*beatitudo hominis*) could rest in riches, honor, glory, power, or any created good is answered here in the negative. For: "ultimus hominis finis est bonum increatum, scilicet Deus, qui solus sua infinita bonitate potest voluntatem hominis perfecte implere" (*S. th.* I-II, q. 3, a. 1). See also the elucidations in *S. c. G.* III, c. 27–36, as well as: A. Speer, "Das Glück des Menschen," in *Thomas von Aquin: Die Summa theologicae. Werkinterpretationen*, ed. Speer (Berlin: De Gruyter, 2005), 141–67 (Lit.).

17. Thomas's criticism of the doctrine of impanation or consubstantiation is noteworthy. Adoration of the Eucharist, which is expressed liturgically in the elevation of the consecrated gifts and the priest's genuflection, would be simply idolatrous if created substances were to remain behind in the Eucharist, for such a substance may not be honored with the adoration due to God alone. See *S. th.* III, q. 75, a. 2 ad 3.

something small—the host—could contain something infinitely great—the *totus Christus* in his divinity and humanity—is not something reason finds plausible. Nevertheless, the one at prayer professes to want to subject his whole heart (*cor meum totum*) to the divine You. A rhetoric of intimacy characterizes the hymn's diction, which expresses in an impressive way the unconditional self-surrender made by the one praying to the You of the Eucharistic Christ. The act of this self-surrender takes place because the contemplation of the hidden presence of the divine You (*te contemplans*) is unable to fathom this mystery fully.[18] Unlike theological conceptual work, which attempts to grasp the *intellectus fidei* and for that purpose employs definitional language, the poetic diction of the hymn involves the whole person at prayer and broadens the linguistic register to include affective forms of expression. In abiding contemplatively, the one at prayer professes that he cannot recognize the presence of the *corpus Christi verum* in the species of bread and wine.[19] The mystery of faith transcends the intellectual power, it exceeds as well the perceptual capacities of the senses: *Visus, tactus, gustus in te fallitur*. Only faith grants access to the truth of the Eucharistic mystery.[20] It constitutes, not surprisingly, a thematic focus of the hymn, which we now pursue further.

If one analyzes the poetic text more precisely, then four verses can be found that go into the motif of faith: first of all, it is emphasized that faith comes from *hearing* (v. 6: *auditu creditur*, see Rom 10:17: *ergo fides ex auditu*). The truth of the Eucharistic mystery cannot be reached by the avenues of sight, taste, or touch. Hearing stands in opposition to the empirical evidence of the other senses and precisely thereby institutes faith (*auditu solo*).[21] The verse seems at first to say nothing beyond this, for it dispenses with any further determination of the content or motivation of faith.

Only in the next couplet (vv. 7–8) do personal categories once again

---

18. Let it be remarked merely on the side that speaking of *totum cor* alludes to the commandment: *Diliges Dominum Deum tuum ex toto corde* (Dt 6:4).

19. In the *second* part of the hymn, the framed couplets (vv. 17–18 and vv. 21–22) do not constitute one block, as in the first part (vv. 3–8) but rather two blocks; these will then refer to the sacramental species of bread (vv. 17–18) and *wine* (vv. 21–22).

20. The deficit of empirical verification regarding Christ's real presence in the species of bread and wine was already articulated in the other hymns. In the vesper hymn *Pange lingua gloriosi*, we heard: *Et si sensus deficit / Ad firmandum cor sincerum / Sola fides sufficit*. Where the senses fall short, faith suffices: *praestet fides supplementum / sensuum defectui*. We also find in the Sequence for Corpus Christi, *Lauda Sion*, the order: *Quod non capis / Quod non vides / Animosa firmat fides*.

21. In Iacopone da Todi, we find an intertextual reference to the hymn *Adoro te devote*. See Todi, *Le Laude, secondo la stampa fiorentina del 1490*, ed. G. Ferri, 2nd ed. (Bari: Gius Laterza & Figli, 1930), 105f. (XLVI): "Li quattro sensi dicono: / Questo si è vero pane. / Solo audito resistelo, / ciascun de lor fuor remane: / so' queste visibil forme / Cristo occultato ce stane." See F. J. E. Raby, "The Date and Authorship of the Poem Adoro te devote," *Speculum* 20 (1945): 236–38.

come into play. "I believe all the Son of God has spoken—*Credo, quidquid dixit dei filius.*" The external and impersonal character of *creditur* is further specified: *credo.* The I of the one praying (first person singular) performs the act of faith, and the *credendum*, which is not further specified, is what the Son of God has spoken. That the infinite chasm between creator and creature was bridged at all is due to the Incarnation of the Son of God. In other passages, Thomas makes clear that the motive of Incarnation is the overflowing goodness (*bonitas*) of the divine essence,[22] sharing itself with others (*se aliis communicare*). Jesus Christ can therefore be designated as the incarnate *communicatio* of God. Thus, what Christ said has divine authority. And in the hymn, his consummate authority is emphatically affirmed: "Than Truth's own word there is no truer token—*nihil veritatis verbo verius.*"[23] One must not forget at this point that at the last supper, Christ himself, the word of truth, uttered the *verba testamenti*: *Hoc est corpus meum.* The truth claim bound up with this word marks a particular challenge for the faith. "Do not doubt whether it is true. Rather, accept the words of the redeemer in faith. For he is the truth and he does not lie"[24]—as Thomas quotes Cyril of Alexandria in the *Summa theologiae*, regarding the *verba testamenti*.

He considers this truth claim in the third stanza (v. 11). The couplet before that (vv. 9–10) had illuminated the motif of hiddenness and put forward a unique precision: on the cross, only the martyred man was visible—*ecce homo*—while the divinity of Christ remained veiled; in contrast, in the Eucharistic species, the humanity of Christ is also hidden. This double hiddenness of the divine and human natures of Christ in the Eucharist is believed by the one at prayer and he professes his faith openly (v. 11: *Ambo vere credens atque confitens*). The connection between faith and profession is important for the hymn (see the derivatives of *confiteri* in vv. 11 and 14).[25] An allusion to the letter to the Romans is here to be discovered, namely the passage that runs: "If you confess with your lips (*in ore tuo*) that Jesus is Lord and believe in your heart (*in corde tuo*) that God raised him from the

---

22. See *S. th.* III, q. 1. On this point, see P. Engelhardt, "Menschwerdung des Wortes und menschliches Verlangen nach Wahrheit. Ein Versuch, die grundlegende Denk- und Glaubenserfahrung des Thomas von Aquin zu erschließen," in his *Thomas von Aquin. Wegweisungen in sein Werk* (Leipzig: St. Benno Verlag, 2005), 113–30.

23. One notices the phonetic shape of this verse, which achieves an uncommonly insistent tone by means of the assonances "*veritatis verbo verius.*"

24. See *S. th.* III, q. 75, a. 1. There: Cyril, *In Luc.*, c. 22: "Non dubites an hoc verum sit, sed potius suscipe verba Salvatoris in fide; cum enim sit veritas, non mentitur."

25. See *S. th.* II-II, q. 3, a. 1, where the connection of faith and profession are understood as follows: "exterior enim locutio ordinatur ad significandum id quod in corde concipitur. Unde sicut conceptus interior eorum quae sunt fidei est proprie fidei actus, ita etiam et exterior confessio." On this point, see B. Niederbacher, *Glaube als Tugend bei Thomas von Aquin* (Munich: Kohlhammer, 2004), esp. 58ff.

dead, you will be saved" (Rom 10:9).[26] But for clarification the hymn itself brings in a biblical scene in which the saving effect of profession becomes clear. The thief, who was crucified together with Jesus, regrets his own guilt and turns to Jesus with an entreaty that includes an act of profession: "Lord, remember me when you come into your kingdom—*Domine, memento mei cum veneris / in regnum tuum*" (Lk 23:42, Vulgate).[27] The divinity of Christ was hidden to the thief; he saw only the tortured body of the crucified one, yet still he addressed his plea to the Lord: *Domine* ... For this reason, the thief becomes a figure of identification for the one praying the hymn, who makes his own the thief's desire for salvation, although he cannot even see the humanity of Christ. Not by chance does Aquinas allude to the scene of the apostle Thomas in the couplet that follows, for Thomas, as the *discipulus dubitans*,[28] demanded visible proofs and wanted first to see the wounds of the crucified Lord and place his fingers into the wounded side before he would be ready to believe. Thomas relies on the evidence of the senses, while hearing (*auditus*) is insufficient for him; he wants to be instructed through *visus* and *tactus* and only then believe.[29] When the risen one appeared for a second time to the disciples gathered together, and this time Thomas was also present, Christ granted him to see and touch his glorified body (*corpus glorificatus*). What he refused to Mary Magdalene (see Jn 20:17) he now offered to Thomas—the empirical verification Thomas desired—but not without directing the admonition to him: "Do not be unbelieving, but believing—*noli esse incredulus, sed fidelis*" (Jn 20:27). The overwhelmed Thomas puts forward a *profession*, which is taken to heart by the one praying the hymn: "My Lord and my God."[30]

In his commentary on the Gospel of John, Aquinas attests that, when faced with Christ's appearance, Thomas is immediately promoted to being a good theologian (*bonus theologus*),[31] professing the true faith. As Thomas

26. See Rom 10:9–10 (Vulgate): "quia si confitearis in ore tuo Dominum Iesum / et in corde tuo credideris quod Deus illum excitavit ex mortuis salvus eris / corde enim creditur ad iustitiam / ore autem confessio fit in salutem."
27. Here, the horizon is already widened into the eschatological—a broadening that will be taken up again in a thematic way in the hymn's concluding cadenza.
28. See *In Ioan.* XX, l. V (n. 2547).
29. See ibid. (n. 2549): "noluit credere nisi sensibili argumento; et non tamen unius sensu, sed duorum; scilicet visus ... et tactus."
30. As a sidenote, faith always also means entering into a specified *traditio*. Thus, the thief's desire and Thomas's profession are prototypical ways of acting that can and should be appropriated by later generations of faithful. See, e.g., K. Rahner, "On Christian Dying," in *Theological Investigations* 7 (London: Darton, Longman and Todd, 1971), 285–93, here 293, who takes up the conduct of the thief for a contemporary understanding of and dealing with death.
31. See *In Ioan.* XX, l. VI (n. 2562): "ponitur Thomas confessio: ubi apparet, quod statim factus est Thomas bonus theologus, veram fidem confitendo."

spells it out christologically, the exclamation "my Lord" relates to the *humanitas* of Christ, which can be seen and touched, while "my God" relates to the *divinitas* of Christ, which can be neither seen nor touched.[32] Thomas, the apostle, makes the transition from seeing to believing, but in this case seeing does not make faith null, for "Thomas saw one thing, and believed another: he saw the Man, and believing Him to be God, he made profession of his faith, saying: 'My Lord and my God.'"[33] The risen Christ concludes this scene with the word: "Blessed are those who have not seen and yet have come to believe" (Jn 20:29): *beati qui non viderunt, sed crediderunt*. And this beatitude relates "to us" as well, as is also noted in the commentary.[34] The episode about unbelieving Thomas is of use to the faithful in the future, for it disperses doubt about the resurrection of the crucified one and encourages a profession of faith in the hidden presence of the Lord under the signs of bread. In addition, Thomas notes in his commentary that it is more meritorious to believe without having seen than to believe because one has seen.[35]

But is it possible to believe from one's own resources? "The tidings I surely hear, it is faith alone that I miss,"[36] we read in Goethe's *Faust*. This is the point to which the fourth and last verse refers: that faith is itself a gift to which one has no claim, which one cannot extort but can in any case ask for. It is found already in the second part of the hymn, where we read: "Make me believe Thee ever more and more—*Fac me tibi semper magis credere*." This petition really forms the hinge between the two halves of the hymn (v. 17). Whereas the first part is devoted to the motif of hidden truth (*veritas*),[37] the second part undertakes a poetic continuation, placing the

---

32. Thomas notes astutely in his commentary: "Vidit hominem et cicatrices, et ex hoc credidit divinitatem resurgentis" (*In Ioan*. XX, l. VI [n. 2563]).

33. *S. th.* II-II, q. 1, a. 4 ad 1: "ergo dicendum est quod Thomas aliud vidit et aliud credidit. Hominem vidit et Deum credens confessus est, cum dixit: Dominus meus et Deus meus (cf. Greg., Hom. 26 in Evang., n. 8 [PL 76, 1201 A])."

34. *In Ioan*. XX, l. V (n. 2566): "et hoc specialiter ad nos pertinet. Utitur autem praeterito pro futuro propter certitudinem."

35. Ibid.: "Plus autem meretur qui credit et non vidit, quam qui videns credit." The architecture of the Freiburg Minster cathedral can be interpreted as a commentary on this insight that has taken form in stone. The roof of the Gothic cathedral is carried by fourteen columns, of which thirteen are dedicated to the twelve apostles and Paul, while one is dedicated to Christ. It is remarkable that the statue on the foremost column belongs to unbelieving Thomas. "Opposite him stands Christ, the resurrected one, who folds back his garment and shows the wound in his side, while Thomas stretches two fingers toward it." Thomas and the risen Lord meet each other right over the sanctuary, where Christ grants his hidden presence in the celebration of the Eucharist—something neither visible to the eyes nor tangible to the hands. Whoever goes to communion in the Freiburg Minster cathedral and happens upon a view of this constellation of figures is reminded of the word: "Blessed are those who have not seen and yet have come to believe." See K. Kunze, *Himmel aus Stein. Das Freiburger Münster*, 10th ed. (Freiburg: Herder, 1997), 33–35.

36. J. W. v. Goethe, *Faust. Eine Tragödie* (Hamburger Ausgabe 3), 16th ed. (Hamburg: Wegner, 1996), V. 765.

37. The semantic range of *veritas* characterizes exclusively the first part of the hymn. Note the substan-

life-giving power of this truth at the center (*vita*). Devotion to the sacramental Christ has an effect on the life of Christians.

Living in and from Christ

In the second part of the hymn, the dialogue between the one praying and the Eucharistic Christ is concentrated. What strikes the eye in looking at the diction are the emphatic vocative and the invocations of names (v. 17, *O memoriale*; v. 21, *Pie pellicane, Iesu domine*; v. 25, *Iesu*), as well as the pleading petitions in the imperative (v. 15, *fac me*; v. 19, *praesta mihi*; v. 22, *munda*).

The one praying turns to Christ anew, this time in the speech act of petitioning. Knowing that he is not in a position to imitate Christ from his own resources, he prays for help in a rhetorically insistent form.[38] The first petition pertains, as already mentioned, to the strengthening of faith. Instead of building on oneself and abandoning oneself to the *incurvatio in seipsum*, it is rather a matter of carrying out the *conversio ad Deum* ever anew, in order to be made firm in the faith. The same applies to hope (*Fac me in te spem habere*). Here, it is also clear that it is not possible for man to attain to eternal life from his own resources. What counts is placing his hope in him who overcame death by dying and thereby became our leader in life. Finally, a petition is made for the gift of love (*Fac me te diligere*). Christ held nothing back for himself but rather gave everything away, and it is he who should determine the life of the one praying, so that that one too is ready to give to others in and through Christ. Even the performative act of this petition for faith, hope, and love is an expression of devotion (note the earlier v. 3), for the one praying attempts to obtain from Christ what he himself cannot give. Thus, the life of the Christian standing in communion with Christ is finally shaped by the three theological virtues, *fides, spes*, and *caritas*. But the power to attain these virtues—this is the theological point about grace—must be given to man.[39]

The origin of grace, however, lies ultimately in the Passion of Christ. *O memoriale mortis domini* (v. 17), the hymn evokes the Lord's death, which stands at the center of the Eucharistic commemoration. Instead of describing more precisely the meaning of this event in soteriological categories,[40]

---

tive forms *veritas* and *veritatis* (vv. 1 and 8), the adjectival comparative form *verius* (v. 8), and the adverb *vere* (vv. 2 and 11).

38. Note the expressions that are almost a litany: *Fac me tibi semper* (v. 15); *praesta mihi semper* (v. 19); *et te mihi semper* (v. 20). These formulations, furthermore, express the close and lasting affinity between the human "I" and Christ.

39. It is not by chance that in the structure of the *Summa theologiae* the treatise on grace (see *S. th.* I-II, qq. 110–114) comes before the consideration of the theological virtues (II-II, qq. 1–46).

40. See *S. th.* III, q. 48 (*meritum, satisfactio, redemptio, sacrificium*). On this point, see J.-P. Torrell, *Le*

instead of memorializing the Old Testament figures of this truth, as in *Lauda Sion*,[41] Thomas inserts a hint into the structure of the text. Verses fifteen and twenty, which frame the couplet O *memoriale mortis domini*, constitute a chiastic interlacing (*me tibi semper—te mihi semper*). What this means is that the hymn itself becomes a place of remembrance, in that the cross is written into the diction in a structurally constitutive way.[42] At the last supper, when Christ was about to depart from his disciples, he gave an anticipatory interpretation of the cross, identifying himself with the broken bread. This bread, in which Christ hands himself over into the hands of others, is the "living bread" (*panis vivus*), which imparts to the one eating it a life that leads beyond death. "I am the living bread (*panis vivus*) that came down from heaven. Whoever eats of this bread will live forever" (Jn 6:51). It is for this reason that we find the prayer regarding the gift, "my soul on Thee to live" (v. 19, *semper de te vivere*) and "ever a taste of Heavenly sweetness give" (v. 20, *dulce sapere*). In the *manducatio spiritualis*, a unification with Christ takes place, and it is remarkable that Thomas elsewhere places the sense of taste (*gustus*) before the other senses, since it brings about a direct union with the perceived object. Whoever takes in the Eucharistic food is able to savor it (*dulce sapere*) and to become one with it.[43]

The whole passage (vv. 15–20)—to put it in a summary way—enacts the intimate connection between Christ and the one praying. On a linguistic level, the clustering of personal pronouns is conspicuous. The Eucharist is distinguished above the other sacraments, as Thomas emphasizes time and again, in that it contains not only the grace of Christ but Christ himself.[44] The personal pronouns designate the whole Christ (*Christus totus*),[45] not specific peculiarities belonging to him, which would then need to be expressed using possessive pronouns. In addition, Robert Wielockx called attention to the fact that Thomas incorporates into his hymn a quotation

---

Christ en ses mystères, vol. 2 (Paris: Desclée, 1999), esp. 381–428; M. Levering, *Christ's Fulfillment of Torah and Temple: Salvation according to Thomas Aquinas* (Notre Dame, Ind.: Notre Dame University Press, 2002).

41. On this point, see the Sequence *Lauda Sion*, which brings together the prefigurations of the old covenant in one stanza: "In figuris praesignatur, / Cum Isaac immolatur, / Agnus Paschae deputatur / Datur manna patribus."

42. Of course direct allusions to the cross also turn up (v. 9, *in cruce latebat*; v. 12, *latro*; v. 13, *plagas*; v. 17, *memoriale mortis*; v. 23, *tuo sanguine*; v. 24, *una stilla*).

43. In a little-noticed passage of the *Commentary on the Sentences* (*In IV Sent.*, d. 7, q. 1, a. 3, n. 76), we read: "Et ideo convenienter in figura cibi hoc sacramentum institutum est, quia inter alios sensus solus tactus est cui suum sensibile realiter coniungitur, similitudinibus tantum sensibilibus ad alios sensus per medium pervenientibus. Gustus autem tactus quidam est; et inter alia quae ad tactum pertinent, solus cibus est qui agit per coniunctionem sui ad cibatum, quia nutriens et nutritum fit unum; alia tangibilia agunt efficiendo aliquas impressiones in eo quod tangitur, sicut patet de calido, de frigido et hujusmodi."

44. See M. Morard, "L'eucharistie, clé de voûte de l'organisme sacramental chez saint Thomas d'Aquin," *Revue Thomiste* 95 (1995): 217–50.

45. See v. 15, *tibi*; v. 16, *te ... te*; v. 18, *de te*.

ADORO TE DEVOTE 241

from the book of Hosea nearly verbatim: *Sponsabo te mihi in sempiternum* (Hos 2:19, Vulgate).[46] The imagery of marriage is called upon here in order to characterize the union between the one praying and Christ. The intertextual correlation between the hymn and Hosea becomes even clearer if one notices that the line *Fac me tibi semper magis credere* (v. 20) also has a reference to faith in Hosea 2:20. There we read: *Sponsabo te mihi in fide*. What is notable here is that Thomas, unlike his contemporaries, cites Hosea 2:20 when he describes faith as the first union of the soul with God, and not only in the *Sentences* commentary,[47] but also in his exposition of the Creed.[48]

It appears as if Thomas had the text of Hosea in his ear when he wrote the hymn *Adoro te devote* and crafted the phrases *me tibi semper* and *te mihi semper*. The reciprocity of these phrases should make clear that the union of Jesus with the believer in the Eucharist finds its perfection in the union of the believer with Jesus through faith and love (*per fidem et caritatem*). Certainly, the obstacle of sin can oppose this unification, thus the cry: *"Pie pellicane, Iesu domine."* The emphatic appeal to the name of Jesus intentionally takes place where the prayer for forgiveness of sins is literally and artistically rendered (*me immundum munda tuo sanguine*). The name "Jesus" means "savior" and "redeemer" (*salvator*, see Mt 1:21), a point to which Thomas elsewhere expressly draws attention.[49] The symbol of the pelican underscores the soteriological meaning of Christ's blood. From antiquity, it was thought that the pelican would use its bill to strike a wound to its own breast in order to nourish its young with its blood or awaken them to life when they had died.[50] This self-sacrifice for one's own young is suited

46. R. Wielockx, "Poetry and Theology in the *Adoro te devote*," 167f.
47. *In IV Sent.*, d. 39, q. unica, a. 6 ad 2.
48. *In Symbolum Apostolorum prol.*, in *Opuscula theologica*, II, ed. R. M. Spiazzi (Turin-Rome: Marietti, 1954), 193 (n. 860): "Fides facit quatuor bona. Primum est quod per fidem anima coniungitur ad Deum: nam per fidem anima christiana facit quasi quoddam matrimonium cum Deo: Osee II,20: 'Sponsabo te mihi in fide.'" (cited in R. Wielockx, "Poetry and Theology in the *Adoro te devote*," 171).
49. See *S. th.* III, q. 37, a. 2, where it is set down that the names conferred by God invariably designate a gift of grace given freely by God. Regarding the name "Jesus," it is then stated: "homini Christo hoc munus gratiae collatum erat ut per ipsum omnes salvarentur, ideo convenienter vocatum est nomen eius Iesus, idest 'Salvator.'"
50. See *Physiologus*, trans./ed. Michael J. Curley (Chicago: University of Chicago Press, 2009), 9–10 (c. 6: On the Pelican); Augustine, *Enarrationes in Psalmos*, 101, 8; Isidor von Sevilla, *Origines*, 12,7, 16. Based on zoological investigations, we know today that the pelican feeds its young by pressing its bill to its breast and regurgitating fish from its throat pouch. This is probably the origin of the legend that the pelican arouses its dead young to life with blood from its opened breast, so that in connection with Is 1:2 and Jn 19:34 it could become a symbol for Christ. See H. M. Gosebrink, "Pelikan. Frömmigkeitsgeschichtlich," *LThK* 8, 3rd ed. (1999) 14. The symbol of the pelican has a prominent literary reception history. Also in Dante, it is referred to Christ: "Questi è colui che giacque sopra 'l petto / del nostro pellicano; e questi fue / d'in su la croce al grande ufficio eletto—This is the man who lay upon the breast / of Christ our Pelican; who was chosen for / the glorious duty from the very Cross" (*Divina commedia*: Paradiso 25, 112–14 [trans. A. Esolen]). A later reflection of *Adoro te devote* turns up in Paul Claudel's *Hymne de Saint Sacrement*: "Pieux Péllican, qui

for Christological adaptation, which the hymn strengthens further through the adjective *"pius*—devoted." A drop of Christ's blood would have sufficed to redeem the entire world, as the hymn has it, augmenting this motif. This augmentation, one should note, is already found nearly verbatim in the *Quaestiones quodlibetales*: "Minima gutta sanguinis Christi suffecisset ad redemptionem humani generis—the smallest drop of Christ's blood would have sufficed to redeem humankind."[51]

A Remembrance of the Future—the Longing for Unveiled Vision

The perspective of the concluding cadenza (vv. 25–28) opens up into the eschatological and voices the yearning of the one praying for the immediate vision of the risen Christ. Even if the hymn does not designate the Eucharist as a foretaste of the heavenly wedding banquet, it still expresses the dimension of the sacrament that transcends the present. The motif of hiddenness introduced right at the outset of the hymn is taken up again as a bookend and this time finds itself linked with the urgent question of the negation of this hiddenness. Moreover, what is striking is that the lone interrogative pronoun crops up in this passage (v. 26, *quando*); the question is addressed directly to Jesus (note the invocation of Jesus' name in v. 25) and it connects the tension between veiled and unveiled with the tension between present and future: "Jesus, whom for the present (*nunc*) veil'd I see, what I so thirst for, when *will't be granted* (*fiet*) me?" The personal encounter with Christ as veiled in signs provokes the question of surpassing the sacramental order. For there is a thirst, of which we are made conscious in the Eucharist precisely for the reason that the Eucharist is unable to satisfy it completely: the longing for face-to-face vision. But when this longing will be fulfilled remains an open question. The texture of the final cadenza is dominated with future and subjunctive forms,[52] and the longing articulates

---

souffrez devant nous Votre crucifixion, / Administré par les anges en pleurs qui Vous portent patène et vase, / Donnez-nous la porte de Votre flanc ainsi qu'au centurion / Afin que Vous nous soyez ouvert et que nous unissions / Notre nature à Votre hypostase" (*Oeuvre poétique* [Paris: Gallimard, 1977], 400). Cited in R. Cantalamessa, *This is My Body: Eucharistic Reflections Inspired by Adoro Te Devote and Ave Verum*, trans. A. Neame (Boston: Pauline Books and Media, 2005).

51. *Quodl.* II, q. 1, a. 2, s.c. 2. The continuation of the quotation reads: "Potuisset autem aliqua gutta sanguinis Christi effundi sine morte." Thomas ascribes the motif to Bernard of Clairvaux. See also *In III Sent.*, d. 20, q. unica, a. 3, arg. 4 and ad 4. Both instances can be called upon as text-internal witnesses of the hymn's authenticity. See Torrell, *Saint Thomas Aquinas*, 134. Admittedly, the motif of the drop of blood goes back to Nicholas of Clairvaux rather than Bernard (see PL 144, 762), a point to which R. Cantalamessa calls attention in *This is My Body*, his book of Advent sermons.

52. *S. th.* II-II, q. 76, a. 1 distinguishes three ways of speaking: first, the indicative; second, the imperative; and third, the optative. Regarding the third *modus loquendi* it is then elaborated: "Tertio modo ipsum dicere se habet ad id quod dicitur quasi expressio quaedam affectus desiderantis id quod verbo exprimitur. Et ad hoc instituta sunt verba optativi modi."

itself revealingly in terms of seeing, also in allusion to biblical references (v. 25, *aspicio*; v. 27, *revelata cernens facie*; v. 28, *visu*). The most well known passage is that from the first letter to the Corinthians (see 1 Cor 13:12), in which Paul contrasts our current vision in a mirror, obscurely (*nunc per speculum in aenigmate*), with the future vision face to face (*tunc autem facie ad faciem*). It's true, Thomas modifies the Pauline antithesis when he transposes it into the context of Eucharistic theology. It is hoped by the one praying that the body of Christ, still veiled (*velatum*) in the sign of bread, may one day be visible in an unveiled way (*revelatum*). It is interesting that the hierarchy of senses is thus altered: while the entrance into the hidden truth of the Eucharist took place by way of hearing (*auditus*), which accepted the "word of truth" in faith, the eschatological longing is focused entirely on vision (*visus*). Although the hymn itself offers little further information in this regard, Thomas seems to reason that the resurrected body of the blessed will be equipped with glorified sensory organs, which will enable humanity to perceive the exalted Christ, even if he always emphasizes as well that the *visio beata Dei* will take place in an *immediate* fashion, and thus without any representation of the imagination within the soul of the one seeing. The essence of God, the Creator, cannot be seen through any created intermediate; for this reason, God empowers the intellect of the blessed in a special way through the *lumen divinae gloriae*, so that he can be seen *essentialiter*.[53] *In statu viae*, the presence of Christ's body under the species of bread and wine remains inaccessible to the witness of the senses, whereas *in patria* the humanity of the exalted Christ, marked with the wounds of the cross, will be visible to the glorified eyes of the blessed.[54] At this point, sacramental mediation is no longer necessary: where Christ appears in his proper form (*in propria specie*) the *species sacramenti* will be obsolete.[55]

---

53. See *S. th.* I, q. 12, a. 2: "ad videndum Dei essentiam requiritur aliqua similitudo ex parte visivae potentiae, scilicet *lumen gloriae*, confortans intellectum ad videndum Deum: ... Non autem per aliquam similitudinem creatam Dei essentia videri potest, quae ipsam divinam essentiam repraesentet ut in se est." On this point, see J.-P. Torrell, "La vision de Dieu 'per essentiam' selon saint Thomas d'Aquin," in his *Recherches thomasiennes*, 177–97. On the scholastic discussions concerning the *visio beata*, see N. Wicki, *Die Lehre von der himmlischen Seligkeit in der mittelalterlichen Scholastik von Petrus Lombardus bis Thomas von Aquin* (Freiburg, Switzerland: Universitätsverlag, 1954); W. J. Hoye, "Gotteserkenntnis per essentiam im 13. Jahrhundert," in *Die Auseinandersetzungen an der Pariser Universität im XIII. Jahrhundert*, ed. A. Zimmermann (Berlin–New York: Walter de Gruyter, 1976), 269–84.

54. See *S. th.* II-II, q. 1, a. 8: "Duo autem nobis ibi videnda proponuntur: scilicet occulutm divinitatis, cuius visio nos beatos facit; et mysterium humanitatis Christi, per quem *in gloriam filiorum Dei accessum habebums*, ut dicitur *ad Rom.* 5,[2]."

55. P.-M. Gy, *La liturgie dans l'histoire*, 275–78, pointed out that the strong emphasis on the tension between faith and the vision of the blessed is a proper mark of the Eucharistic theology of Thomas Aquinas, and more precisely, of his later works (1264–74). In his contemporaries (Albert the Great, Bonaventure), this tension plays merely a subordinate role, if any at all, in the context of the Eucharist.

9

Summary

The Poetic Distillation of Eucharistic Theology in the Hymns

In the hymns—above all in those containing moments of invocation—the spiritual undercurrent of Thomas Aquinas's theology becomes manifest. The "reading master" [*Lesemeister*] and the university master is at the same time a "life master" [*Lebemeister*], to use Meister Eckhart's phrase; besides the theologian and philosopher who is a virtuoso of the scholastic technique of disputation, the prayerful poet also plays a role, being able to give utterance to his piety in the language of hymns. When it is not only silently read but also audibly spoken aloud, poetic diction generates a form of presence bound up with breath and voice. The physical presence of the spoken word, moreover, certainly has repercussions on the faithful present at the liturgy. That is to say, when the Eucharistic hymns of the Office are prayed or sung by a community, the rhythmic and vocalic effects arising in the *performance* are able to gather up the attention of the *many* and focus it on *one* thing. The concentration on the poetic word enables an entry into the joy and gratitude toward the gift of presence of the *corpus dominicum*. And it is precisely this that made up the primary intention of the solemnity inaugurated by Urban IV.[1] The common doxological performance, the celebration of joy, and the thanksgiving over the gifts received make possi-

---

1. The Bull *Transiturus* brings out the festive joy as a leitmotif. This may certainly have affective consequences, as shown by the language of tears that is worked out here: "Hec est commemoratio gloriosa, que fidelium animos replet gaudio salutari, et cum infusione letitie, devotionis lacrimas subministrat. Exultamus nimirum nostram rememorando liberationem, et recolendo passionem dominicam per quam liberati sumus, vix lacrimas continemus. In hac itaque sacratissima commemoratione, adsunt nobis suaviter gaudium simul et lacrime, quia in ea et gaudemus pie lacrimantes, et lacrimamus devote gaudentes, letas habendo lacrimas et letitiam lacrimantem." Dorez, ed., *Registres d'Urbain IV*, 423. See also Friedberg, ed., *Corpus iuris canonici*, vol. 2, col. 1175.

ble a communal experience, which realizes what is expressed in the Pauline metaphor of the body and its many members.

Vis-à-vis reflections in Eucharistic theology, the poetic *surplus* of the hymns lies in the thematic *distillation* that becomes nearly the poetic compositional principle of the hymn *Pange lingua*. First of all, Jesus' life—*nobis datus, nobis natus*—is summarized in a time-lapsed fashion and connected to the guiding image of the sower, before the outlook is scaled down and directed toward the scene of the last supper. This scene is concentrated in the self-giving of the Word to the disciples—*se dat suis manibus*. The decisive moment at which the linguistic power of the divine Word changes the gifts of bread and wine leads to the climax of the hymn, which impressively expresses the miracle of Eucharistic conversion without needing to rely on the terms taken from the theory of transubstantiation: *Verbum caro panem verum / Verbo carnem efficit*. Other assonance-rich phrases, such as *Credo quiquid dixit dei filius, / nihil veritatis verbo verius*, make recognizable the considerable poetic power at Thomas's disposal. It compresses and bundles up complex theological facts, which—to reduce it to what is essential—cajole toward discursive and interpretive unfolding.

A language that artistically subjects itself to the rules of meter and rhyme can, moreover, fulfill didactic and catechetical functions, as is precisely shown in the doctrinal hymn *Lauda Sion*. In catchy verses we find important contents of the faith transported, which ought to be impressed upon the memory of the faithful (those familiar with Latin)[2]—following the insight that there is "a living ligament between rhythmic and memorative forms in the depths of anthropology."[3] Phrases such as *Quod non capis, quod non vides, / Animosa firmat fides* use their metrical drive to fulfill very nearly the function of mnemonic verses, thereby giving a clear orientation in the face of the deficit of empirical verification regarding Christ's real presence. Other verses such as *Sumunt boni, sumunt mali / Sortet tamen inaequali / Vitae vel interitus / Mors est malis, vita bonis*, with their references to possible eschatological ramifications, serve to sharpen the awareness of the art of Eucharistic differentiation, while the unrefined misunderstanding that Christ's body suffers mastication by tooth is parried with astounding clarity by the verse, *Nulla rei fit scissura, / Signi tantum fit fractura*.

Finally, when the language of the hymns passes over into the mode of dialogue, it makes known the personal involvement of the one praying. For

---

2. See F. A. Yates, *Gedächtnis und Erinnern. Mnemonik von Aristoteles zu Shakespeare*, 4th ed. (Berlin: Akademie Verlag, 1997), 54–81 (ch. 3: "Die Gedächtniskunst im Mittelalter").

3. Zumthor, *Die Stimme und die Poesie in der mittelalterlichen Gesellschaft*, 91.

Thomas, it is does not stop at speaking "about" the Eucharist; rather, the hidden presence of the *Christus passus* in the consecrated gifts provokes a speaking "with" the Lord, who is invoked by name. The memorializing style of speech in the hymns alternates repeatedly between emphatic invocations: *Pie pellicane! Iesu, Domine!—O res mirabilis!—O Salutaris hostia*. The transformed gift—far from being reduced to a *tangible* cultic object—is called upon as a *person*, because the eternal Word of the Father is present in this gift. The sign of Eucharistic bread, which confronts the consciousness of the one at prayer, brings to mind the irreducible alterity of the divine giver; further, the fact that he held nothing back and rather in his generosity gave his very self marks the occasion for grateful wonder and exuberant joy, which breaks ground stylistically in some of the hymns in an emphatic self-summoning: *Pange, lingua ...—Sacris solemniis iuncta sint gaudia / et ex praecordiis sonent praeconia ...* Thanksgiving over the gift of Christ's presence in the *corpus dominicum* does not remain without consequences; it is translated into a gift in response: *Tibi se cor meum totum subicit, / quia te contemplans totum deficit*. The affective coloring, which runs through the eschatologically oriented strophes but is found most powerfully in the hymn *Adoro te devote*, makes clear the spiritual subtext of the conceptually sober discussion of the Eucharist in the *Sentences* commentary, the *Summa contra Gentiles*, and the *Summa theologiae*.

Regarding the contents, we always encounter in the hymns motifs that are treated extensively in Eucharistic theology, admittedly in a different manner. The *rememorative* side—the Passover, the scene of the last supper, the suffering on the cross—characterizes nearly all of the hymns. This is shown especially powerfully in *Adoro te devote*, where the cross is literally written into the poetic diction using the stylistic means of chiasmus. The text itself becomes a place of remembrance so that the reading, speaking, and praying of the hymn prompts a carrying out of the *memoriale passionis*. The salvation-historical contrast between the old and the new covenant is, moreover, a leitmotif that finds different variations in each of the Eucharistic hymns;[4] the poetic staging of the ritual innovation that took place once for all at the last supper in Jerusalem belongs to the substance of the new feast, says Thomas.[5] In order to plumb the depths of meaning surrounding the "institution" of the Eucharist, intertextual references are undertaken and prefigurations of the Eucharist are brought in, such as the sacrifice of

---

4. Only the hymn *Adoro te devote* does without this contrast.
5. See *Pange lingua*: "et antiquam documentum novo cedat ritui"; *Sacris solemniis*: "Recedant vetera, nova sint omnia"; *Lauda Sion*: "In hac mensa novi Regis / Novum Pascha novae legis / Phase vetus terminat."

Isaac, the manna, and above all the oft-encountered Paschal lamb. Standing behind this typological weaving of figures is a hermeneutic that is clearly Christological in character. The Old Testament is read in light of the New and, conversely, the qualitatively new—the fulfillment of the promises by Christ[6]—becomes clear only when seen against the background of the Old Testament testimonies. Simultaneously, the hymns, especially *Pange lingua* and *Sacris solemniis*, place great value on Jesus' faithful observance of the Law (*plene lege observata*). Together with his disciples, he fulfilled the ritual prescriptions of the Passover—and since they are sons of Israel celebrating the feast together, Thomas repeatedly works with a rhetoric of fraternity.[7] In this way, the establishment of a new meal can arise from the celebration of the Paschal meal. This new meal is distinguished by the significant twofold gesture of the Lord's self-gift, which Thomas evidently sets up to reveal precisely the asymmetry between master and disciples in the hymn *Sacris solemniis*, a point brought out by a change in terminology (*discipuli*). It is striking that Thomas's poetry does not take up the Johannine motif of foot washing, which accompanies the scene of Jesus parting from his disciples.[8] This is likely connected with the fact that the aim of Corpus Christi is not the *memoria passionis*—this is reserved to Holy Week—but rather the grateful and joyful rememberance of Christ's Eucharistic self-gift.[9] Nevertheless, the dominance of the rememorative reference to the historical origins of the Eucharist and the salvific significance of Jesus' life and death show that what Johannes Betz called the *commemorative actual presence* is certainly not relegated to the background or even suppressed. It is hardly possible to speak of a constriction or fixation on the theme of consecration or conversion within the Eucharistic hymns.

All the same, the motif of Eucharistic conversion, so central in Aquinas's Eucharistic theology, comes poetically into play. Especially in *Pange lingua*, the moment of the consecration of bread and wine into the flesh and blood of Christ is downright coincident with the poetic climax: *Verbum caro panem verum / Verbo carnem efficit*. In connection with the emphasis

---

6. See the fourth Lectio of the Divine Office, where it is expressly stated: "hoc sacramentum instituit tanquam passionis suae memoriale perenne, figurarum veterum *impletivum*" (*Officium*, 277, emphasis added).

7. See *Pange lingua*: "In supremae nocte cenae / recumbens cum fratribus, / observata lege plene /cibis in legalibus"; *Sacris solemniis*: "Noctis recolitur cena novissima, / Qua Christus creditur agnum et azyma / Dedisse fratribus, iuxta legitima / Priscis indulta patribus"; as well as *Lauda Sion*: "Quem in sacrae mensa coenae / Turbae fratrum duodenae / Datum non ambigitur."

8. See, however, his exegesis in *In Ioan*. XIII, l. II (nn. 1744–67).

9. Still, this motif is touched upon by Urban IV in the Bull *Transiturus*, where we read: "Dedit enim nobis Dominus omnia, quae subiecit sub pedibus nostris." Cited in Friedberg, ed., *Corpus iuris canonici*, vol. 2, col. 1175.

on Jesus' *somatic real presence* in the consecrated gifts, questions concerning the doctrine of concomitance are also taken into the hymns *Sacrum solemniis* and *Lauda Sion*, all the while without weighing down the diction with speculative terms. What is probably decisive here is that the Eucharistic conversion is not treated in isolation but is expressly characterized as self-gift. *Se dat suis manibus*. With this, a further theme is addressed, one that permeates the hymns *Sacris solemniis* and *Verbum supernum* like a leitmotif: self-gift as an anticipatory sign for Jesus' existence in life and death, but also for the work of the exalted one. With unsurpassable urgency, the hymn *Verbum supernum* reads:

Se nascens dedit socium,
convescens in edulium,
se moriens in pretium,
se regnans dat in praemium.

Finally, it is worth noting that in the hymns Thomas is not speaking one-sidedly to an incipient visual piety; rather, what he certainly has in view as well is the performance of the sacrament, the *usus*. The prandial and communal character given with the origins of the Eucharist in the last supper can sometimes retreat into the background in systematic Eucharistic doctrine, but in the hymns it is present through and through. This is all the more surprising given that the genesis of Corpus Christi is closely bound up with medieval visual piety. Justly, therefore, did Josef Pieper remark that whoever "reads through the texts of St. Thomas for the feast of Corpus Christi to see if he finds in them a certain separation, as if in the performance of the sacrificial meal the sacramental species of bread is there more to be shown and seen than to be eaten—such a one will not only notice nothing of all this, rather he will find conversely that *sumere* and *edere* are spoken of many times, as well as *manducatio*, *esca*, and *cibus*, that is, eating, consumption, meal, food, satiety, and, not least of all, sacrifice."[10] Several times and with great empathy, the Eucharist is brought into play as consolation and refreshment: *Dedit fragilibus ferculum. / Dedit et tristibus sanguinis poculum*. The situation of the disciples as they mourned the loss of their master can be applied paradigmatically to the time of the Church, so that the faithful striving for a Eucharistic way of life in the interim between the ascension and the parousia can receive a gift left behind for them, the *panis vivus et vitalis*, a gift accompanying and strengthening them on the way.

10. J. Pieper, *Guide to Thomas Aquinas*, trans. Richard and Clara Winston (London: Faber and Faber, 1962), 92. The palette of words could be appropriately expanded to include *mensa, commensales, coena, panis, poculum, potus, vinum, sitis, accipere, consumere, vasculum*, etc.

The hymns accentuate over and over the hiddenness of Christ's presence in the Eucharistic signs. He is there—and yet not there.[11] This dialectic of nearness and hiddenness shows at the same time a temporal tension. Unveiled and *in propria specie*, Christ the exalted one will not be seen until the face-to-face beatific vision. This eschatological dynamic, which is contained in the Eucharist as a pledge of future glory exceeding the promise, is expressed repeatedly by the hymns in visual terms. *In statu viae*, faith depends on hearing the Word in which the truth lies. *In patria*, the unbroken manifestation of the truth will be looked upon, thus rendering faith superfluous. To the extent that the hymns give this truth utterance, they direct the remembrance beyond the past and into the future. Precisely the concluding strophes of several hymns are delivered in a language of desirous longing and pertain to the *remembrance of what is still to come about*. It is accordingly not the case that the consummation has already been attained. The *homo viator* is on his way there—and the Eucharist as *viaticum* is a help and provision to arrive in the land of the living, the *terra viventium*, where the unveiled, face-to-face vision awaits him.

11. On this point, see J.-H. Tück, "Die Anwesenheit des Abwesenden. Notizen zur pneumatischen Selbstvergegenwärtigung Jesu Christi in der Eucharistie," *IKaZ Communio* 40 (2011): 38–43.

PART C

EUCHARISTIC PASSAGES

10

An Interim Reflection

Epochal Forms of Eucharistic Theology

The early Christian practice of the Lord's supper has its *historical presuppositions* in the prandial praxis of the earthly Jesus and above all his last supper "on the night he was betrayed" (1 Cor 11:23); it finds its *reason* in the upending Easter experience of the first witnesses, that the one who was crucified now lives and gives his presence anew in the form of a meal.[1] Thus, any theological reflection will necessarily return to the New Testament *traditio* of the last supper as its foundation, even if the relevant texts were assembled in the light of the Easter event. Regardless of the differences in detail, which cannot be discussed here, both threads of the tradition (both Mk 14:22–25 and Mt 26:26–29, as well as 1 Cor 11:23–26 and Lk 22:15–20) refer to one and the same *historical event*: Jesus' last supper with his disciples on the night before his death. Whether it took place on the Passover, as the synoptic tradition has it, or on the day of preparation, as the Johannine chronology suggests, can remain an open question for the moment. Instead, three main features can be drawn out for systematic theology. First, Jesus is the *host and head of the meal*. He speaks the decisive words and sets down the decisive signs; he lets those present take part in the *one* bread and the *one* cup. Second, Jesus then transforms the Jewish prayer of blessing over the Eucharistic gifts in the *berakha*, when he refers the broken bread to his body ("This is my body, which will be given for many") and the cup with wine to his blood ("This cup is the new covenant in my blood").[2] This

---

1. See Michael Theobald, "Das Herrenmahl im Neuen Testament," *ThQ* 138 (2003): 257–80. On the exegetical discussion, see section II below.
2. Thus the reconstruction of Helmut Merklein, "Erwägungen zur Überlieferungsgeschichte der neutestamentlichen Abendmahlstraditionen," in his *Studien zu Jesus und Paulus* (WUNT 43) (Tübingen: Mohr Siebeck, 1987), 157–80, here 167 and 173f.

self-identification of the giver with the gifts of bread and wine not only symbolically summarizes the pro-existence of Jesus' life but also illuminatingly anticipates his coming death. Third, and finally, Jesus bridges the way to the *eschatological meal* through prophesying his own death (see Mk 10:45), when he announces that he will not drink again of the fruit of the vine until the kingdom of God—a motif reflected in the cry of "maranatha" during the post-Easter celebration of the Lord's supper (1 Cor 16:22; see Rv 22:20; *Didache*, c. 10).

This faith in the resurrected crucified one giving his presence ever anew in the gifts of bread and wine has given rise to different readings in each epoch of the history of theology—from the patristics, through the Middle Ages, and all the way into the present. The differences are closely interwoven with the language and intellectual horizon of each time period. In what follows, the aim is not to work out a unique contribution to the problem of forms of thought.[3] Rather, what is offered here is (1) a rough overview of the way taken by the tradition of Eucharistic theology, and (2) an assessment of the meaning, but also the temporally conditioned character, of scholastic Eucharistic theology, as they can be discerned through comparison with interpretative attempts of other time periods. We find in the work of Thomas Aquinas a certain tension between categories that seem closer to the biblical witness (*se aliis communicare, dare, se tradere,* etc.) and ontological concepts going back to a (neo-)Platonic but also, and especially, Aristotelian heritage (*substantia—accidens; forma—materia;* etc.). This tension motivates the following sketch of the differing epochal forms of Eucharistic theology. The reconstruction takes place from a *typological point of view* and refers to the pertinent research findings.[4] Presupposed here is that the inculturation of the Gospel in diverse horizons of thinking cannot be read as a history of decline, as if one finds himself, since at least the early Middle Ages, ever more dis-

---

3. For background, see Walter Kasper, *Dogma unter dem Wort Gottes* (Mainz: Matthias-Grünewald, 1965); Joseph Ratzinger, *Das Problem der Dogmengeschichte in der Sicht der katholischen Theologie* (Cologne: Westdeutscher Verlag, 1966); P. Schoonenberg, "Geschichtlichkeit und Interpretation des Dogmas," in *Die Interpretation des Dogmas*, ed. Ratzinger (Düsseldorf: Patmos, 1969), 58–110; E. Schillebeeckx, *Glaubensinterpretation. Beiträge zu einer hermeneutischen und kritischen Theologie* (Mainz: Matthias-Grünewald, 1971); K. Lehmann, "Die dogmatische Denkform als hermeneutisches Problem. Prolegomena zu einer Kritik der dogmatischen Vernunft," in his *Die Gegenwart des Glaubens* (Mainz: Matthias-Grünewald, 1974), 35–53; J. Ratzinger, *Principles of Catholic Theology: Building Stones for a Fundamental Theology*, trans. Sr. Mary Frances McCarthy (San Francisco: Ignatius Press, 1987); P. Hünermann, *Dogmatische Prinzipienlehre: Glaube—Überlieferung—Theologie als Sprach- und Wahrheitsgeschehen* (Münster: Aschendorff, 2003); *Dogma und Denkform. Strittiges in der Grundlegung von Offenbarungsbegriff und Gottesgedanke*, ed. K. Müller and M. Striet (Regensburg: Pustet, 2005).

4. See J. Betz, *Eucharistie. In der Schrift und Patristik* (HDG 4/4a) (Freiburg: Herder, 1979); A. Gerken, *Theologie der Eucharistie*.

tant from the original biblical impulses;[5] nor can it be read as a progressive history of development, as if the semantic potential of biblical statements found increasingly better explication in the theological and dogmatic history that followed and, moreover, grew ever more integrated into the collective consciousness of faith. With this, it should not be ruled out "that there is an increase in knowledge within the tradition on account of historically new possibilities relating to questioning, thinking, and knowing."[6] All the same, one must still take into account that precisely because of new ways of questioning, thinking, and knowing there can also be constrictions and shadowings of the faith,[7] so that the renewed exposition of buried potential in the tradition can absolutely take place from a stance at once critical of the present and disclosive of the future.[8] Here we come up against the much-discussed question of the identity and continuity of the faith within the flux of the diverse forms in which it has been transmitted. There are answers that underestimate the complexity of the problem, such as those holding that the seed of the faith can be freed from under the husk of each way of thinking and, so to speak, extracted in a "chemically pure" way. This position forgets the fact that the deposit of faith is never abstract but is always grasped only in a linguistic form. Statements and ways of speaking are always bound up together. At the same time, *what* was theologically stated can be *retrospectively* distinguished, but not separated, from *how* it was said; it is likewise to be kept in mind that every retrospective attempt to separate the statement's content from the historically conditioned ways of speaking takes place in new ways of speaking, which cannot make the claim *per se* that they are themselves more adequate. But the hermeneutical insight into the temporally and contextually conditioned nature of each linguistic form was taken up by Pope John XXIII in his opening speech for Vatican II, when he

---

5. This view dominates in those parts of liturgical studies that look at the later concentration on the themes of consecration and Eucharistic conversion and fail to see any proper development of what lies at the core of the last supper, seeing instead a momentous constriction.

6. G. Essen and Th. Pröpper, "Aneignungsprobleme der christologischen Überlieferung. Hermeneutische Vorüberlegungen," in *Gottes ewiger Sohn. Die Präexistenz Christi*, ed. R. Laufen (Paderborn: Schöningh, 1997), 163–78, here 167.

7. See the statement of K. Rahner, *Menschsein und Menschwerdung Gottes* (Freiburg: Herder, 2005), 263: "The history of theology is certainly not simply a history of dogmatic progress but also a history of forgetting."

8. Dogmatic projects that go immediately from exegetical inspection of the so-called biblical evidence to hermeneutic interpretation and systematic exploration, without having reconstructed the mediating figures of the tradition at least in their basic features, often lose precisely their critical power with respect to the present. This critical power already lies in the tradition, even if this is only presented in the plurality of its configurations. A theology that aspires to be *scriptural* and *timely* will certainly be unable to realize its own aspiration in an adequate way if it brushes aside the classical conceptions of the theological tradition, which sought in their own time periods to think in a scriptural and timely way.

emphasized: "The substance of the ancient doctrine of the *depositum fidei* is one thing, and the way in which it is presented is another."[9]

Let it be noted here that, in going through the diverse historical forms of theological reflection on the Eucharist, two structural moments will emerge over and over again. On the one hand, there is the fact that when philosophical resources are received into the theological task, they are always partially transformed. The biblically witnessed faith, which must be communicated into new horizons of thinking and speaking, compels by its own internal logic a *transformation of these resources*.[10] On the other hand, it will become visible that in the different epochal forms of the tradition there were not only clarifications; indeed, there were also always *shadowings and abbreviations* of the Eucharistic mystery. Here too we can apply the insight that every *traddutore* is also always a *traditore*.

To be sure, when it comes to faith and the history of its tradition, one can speak of abbreviations only when one has a measure (even if provisional) with which one judges the traditional material at hand. As long as theology is *in statu viae*, it cannot take up a metahistorical standpoint, which judges quasi-*sub specie aeternitatis* the adequacy or inadequacy of categorial forms of communication in view of the truth to be attested—and, respecting the eschatological proviso, theology should not carry on as if it could do this. Certainly, it can attempt to determine more precisely the fundamental truth of Christian faith and call upon this truth as its criterion. The determination of this fundamental truth has the hermeneutic function of showing the identity of what is believed and identifying possible deficits amidst the discontinuity found in the course of tradition. There is a broad consensus that the fundamental truth of Christian faith can be expressed in the proposition that God himself acted in the person and history of Jesus and communicated himself to men. The historical self-revelation of God in Jesus Christ, which theology articulates in the linguistic terms of love, does not fall to being a datum of the past, which can be wrested from forgetfulness merely through human powers of recollection. Rather, the event of God's self-revelation is held present as love through God's pneumatically making himself present in word and sacrament. Against this background, however, the celebration of the Eucharist can be described as that happen-

---

9. John XXIII, *Eröffnungsrede*, in L. Kaufmann and N. Klein, *Johannes XXIII. Prophetie im Vermächtnis*, 2nd ed. (Freiburg-Brig: Edition Exodus, 1990), 116–50, here 136. See the reception of this distinction through the Council: *UR* II, 1.

10. At the same time, the reception of philosophical resources is often accompanied by a transformation of the understanding of faith. See B. Welte, "Die Lehrformel von Nikaia und die abendländische Metaphysik," in *Zur Frühgeschichte der Christologie. Ihre biblischen Anfänge und die Lehrformel von Nikaia*, ed. Welte (QD 51) (Freiburg: Herder, 1970), 100–117.

ing in which God's unconditional determination *for* men, as made manifest in the life and death of Jesus *for* us, is made representatively present. In listening to the word of the gospel and in receiving the Eucharistic gifts, communion with the crucified and risen Christ is accomplished ever anew—an accomplishment that likewise strengthens the communion among the faithful. This event of communion, in which the gifts of divine presence find a response in man's grateful reception, may very well not be expressed with equal adequacy by all the intellectual resources of the philosophical and theological tradition.

I

With Christianity's entrance into the Hellenistic cultural sphere,[11] a critical engagement arose, first with Greek thought.[12] Without revisiting once more the complex problem of the Hellenization of the faith, it can be said, to speak typologically, that the *real symbolic thought* of Platonism—with its distinction between exemplar and image and its conception of a hierarchically ordered cosmos—furnished the Greek fathers of the Church with a conceptual set of tools, into which the Christian faith could be translated.[13] The real symbolic thought presupposes that the reality of the idea attains to representation in the image in a veiled way. The presence of the idea in the image refers back, as it were, to the reality of the exemplar in which it participates. This referential character of the images will not escape the attentive observer; he will let himself be formed by this dynamism centering on the exemplar and step-by-step he will go back along the way out of the shadowy world and into the light of the Good.

What is central to this real symbolic way of thinking is that not only

---

11. On the history of the problem and the state of the discussion regarding the interpretational category "Hellenization," see J. Drumm, *LThK* 4, 3rd ed. (1995): 1407–09 (Lit.); F. Ricken, "Nikaia als Krisis des altchristlichen Platonismus," *ThPh* 44 (1969): 321–41; A. Grillmeier, "Hellenisierung—Judaisierung des Christentums als Deuteprinzipien der Geschichte des kirchlichen Dogmas," in *Mit ihm und in ihm*, 2nd ed. (Freiburg: Herder, 1978), 423–88; M. Lutz-Bachmann, "Hellenisierung des Christentums?" in *Spätantike und Christentum*, ed. C. Colpe (Berlin: Akademie Verlag, 1992), 77–98; P. Neuner, "Die Hellenisierung des Christentums als Modell der Inkulturation," *StZ* 213 (1995): 363–76.

12. For the complex process of receiving Hellenistic intellectual resources and its significance for the Eucharist, see J. Betz, *Die Eucharistie in der Zeit der griechischen Väter* (Freiburg: Herder, 1955 [vol. I/1] and 1964 [vol. II/1]).

13. The Hellenization thesis overlooks that along with the reception of Greek concepts came a transformation of these concepts. In this way, for example, the Council of Nicaea took up a nonbiblical concept—*homoousios*—to express the biblical conviction that the Father and Son belong equally to the concept of God, thereby revolutionizing the radically unreferential concept of God in Greek philosophy. On this point, see my essay: "Jesus Christus—Gottes Heil für uns. Eine dogmatische Skizze," in *Jesus begegnen. Zugänge zur Christologie*, ed. G. Hotze, et al. (Freiburg: Herder, 2009), 119–76, esp. 125–30.

does there exist the merely external similarity between the visible reality of the image and the invisible reality of the exemplar, but also the higher reality expresses itself in the lower, is present in it, and operates through it. When we consider the reception of this way of thinking in the Eucharistic theology of the Greek fathers, we find that the exemplar-image relation finds various applications. First of all, it is referred to the relation between the exalted Lord and the gathering of the community celebrating the Eucharist—an aspect articulated by Johannes Betz in the term "principal actual presence": the exalted Lord, the invisible exemplar, makes himself present and perceivable through the celebration of the Eucharist in the visible image. This relation is pneumatically communicated, which is why the epiclesis, as an act of calling down the spirit upon the gifts of bread and wine, is of elevated significance in the Eastern Church even until today.[14]

With the reception of the Platonic intellectual system by the Greek fathers, there took place a transformation: *anamnesis* in the context of Eucharistic theology did not designate a recollection of an idea glimpsed prior to birth and resting in itself; rather, it indicated the remembrance of the *historical* deeds of Jesus Christ for our salvation. The studies of Johannes Betz, in particular, have shown that in the pre-Ephesian tradition of Greek patristics it was the commemoration of the mystery of salvation, hence the "commemorative actual presence," that stood at the center of theological thinking on the Eucharist. Whereas in Platonism the idea is static and ahistorical, and the concept of "time" occupies an ontologically inferior status in relation to "eternity," for the Greek fathers and their Eucharistic theology, it is the exalted Lord himself who is the exemplar, one who was born, who lived and acted and attained to glory at the Father's right hand on account of his suffering and death. One can say, therefore, that the stasis of real symbolic thinking is broken up in a certain sense by the inclusion of this salvation-historical dynamic. Redemption—understood in a Christian way—is fundamentally no longer a flight from history, even if factually speaking there have always been ascetic, "flee the world" tendencies. No, redemption is man's way to salvation, a way that crucially is set in motion through history itself, is carried out in history itself, even if it is not brought to its consummation within history.

14. Through the epiclesis, the gifts of bread and wine are touched by the Holy Spirit; they are sanctified and transformed. See, for example, Cyril of Jerusalem, *Mystagogische Katechesen*, V, 7 (FC 7, ed. G. Röwekamp, 150–52); Theodore of Mopsuestia, *Katechetische Homilien*, 15, 11 (FC 17/2, ed. P. Bruns, 394–96) and 16, 25 (ibid., 440–42). Within the gathered community, the priest functions as a living icon (εἰκών) of the high priest, Christ (ibid., 15, 19). See also Chrysostom, *In Mt hom*. 82, 5 (PG 58, 744): "The holy action before us does not happen by human power. He, who accomplished it back then at that meal, also carries it out now. We only occupy the position of servants. But the one who consecrates and transforms, that is he."

The fathers, moreover, apply the concepts of a theology of image [*Bildtheologie*] (σύμβολον, εἰκών, ὁμοίωμα, τύπος) to the consecrated gifts of bread and wine.[15] With this, they give utterance to the "somatic real presence," that is, the fact that in the signs of bread and wine is present the reality of the flesh and blood of Jesus Christ himself. The conceptual scheme of exemplar and image has the merit of being able to state equally unity and difference. It is the exalted *Kyrios* who gives himself in the gifts, but he does this under the veil of symbols. The earthly priests, who preside over the offering of the Eucharist, fulfill the task of being high priests of Jesus Christ; they function as his image (εἰκών).[16] As the exemplar is not perfectly represented in the image but rather in a veiled way, so also the eschatological fullness of the exalted *Kyrios*' Eucharistic presence is still to come, but it is already given in the "medicine of immortality"[17] in seminal form.[18] Precisely this eschatological tension between "already present" and "still veiled" can be stated in the categories of real symbolic thinking, if it incorporates into itself the historical dynamism of the biblical tradition.

Indeed, with the inculturation of Christian faith into the Hellenistic cultural sphere, there took place not only a productive transformation of Platonic philosophy, inasmuch as the exemplar was referred to a datum of salvation history, but also and at the same time a certain shadowing of the fundamental impulses of the New Testament. Even if the fathers attempted to join real symbolic thinking with the dynamism of salvation history as found in biblical thinking, they still used ontological categories rather than categories of free will and history to articulate redemption through Incarnation and sanctification through the Eucharist. Biblical personalism is taken up only in a constricted way when the aspect of free appropriation and acceptance of salvation in faith is thematized rather incidentally in the context of a physical doctrine of redemption.[19]

---

15. Against a symbolic interpretation of the consecrated gifts, reservations were voiced quite early on. See Theodore of Mopsuestia, *Katechetische Homilien*, 15, 10 (FC 17/2, ed. P. Bruns, 393f.): "When he gave us the bread, he certainly did not say: 'This is the symbol (τύπος) of my body,' but rather: 'This is my body.' And likewise he certainly did not say of the cup: 'This is the symbol (τύπος) of my blood,' but rather: 'This is my blood.'" See also John of Damascus, *De fide orthodoxa*, IV, 13–15 (ed. E. M. Buytaert, 316 –18 = *Expositio fidei* [Gk], ed. B. Kotter, 197f.), who holds that, after the sanctification—μετὰ τὸ ἁγιασθῆναι—the gifts of bread and wine are no longer images (ἀντίτυπα) of Jesus Christ's body and blood.

16. Theodore of Mopsuestia, *Katechetische Homilien*, 15, 19 (FC 17/2, ed. P. Bruns), 403.

17. See Ignatius of Antioch, *Eph* 20, 2. See L. Wehr, *Arznei der Unsterblichkeit. Die Eucharistie bei Ignatius von Antiochien und im Johannesevangelium* (Münster: Aschendorff, 1987). See also Clement of Alexandria, *Quis dives salvetur* 23, 4 (Griechischen Christlichen Schriftsteller III 175, 11–13): "I am your provider, for I give myself as bread—and whoever eats of it will no longer suffer death—and I offer myself as the *drink of immortality*.

18. Gnoseologically considered, faith is required for the perception of the Eucharistic presence.

19. Betz, *Eucharistie* I/1, 308–15.

Latin patristics is no less indebted to real symbolic thinking, even if on the whole it had accents different from those of the Greek fathers and tended to draw out pastoral and practical questions. Frequently, we encounter the *topos* that the Eucharist is a refreshment for the Christian life, that it has the power to blot out sins. At the same time, the prerequisites for worthy reception of the sacrament are more prominent themes. As is often underscored, two differing ways of placing the emphases can be stated: one is the metabolic Eucharistic doctrine of *Ambrose*, which tends toward individualization, in that the personal and face-to-face posture of Christ and the believer is moved to the central place; the other, the Eucharistic theology of *Augustine*, illuminates the ecclesial dimension of the Eucharist, in that it foregrounds the body-of-Christ motif.[20] "The Eucharist is a real symbol of Christ's body, the Church; the Eucharistic bread presents the unity of the many in Christ's one body. 'Be what you see, and receive what you are.'"[21] Augustine's conception of the Eucharist oscillates between realism and symbolism. On the one hand, he can clearly accentuate the difference between sign and signified, when he says: "It is not the body you see that is eaten, and it is not the blood spilled on the cross that is drunk."[22] On the other hand, he can call attention to the identity between the historical and sacramental Christ, when he teaches the newly baptized: "The bread is the body of Christ, the cup contains the blood of Christ."[23] This need not be a contradiction if it can be presupposed that the sign really contains the reality of the signified. Ambrose of Milan shifts the balance toward realism when he emphasizes the transforming power of the *verba testamenti* in his catecheses and thus offers the first beginnings of a theory of Eucharistic conversion.[24] The *consecratio*, carried out by reciting the words of Christ, brings about the transformation of bread and wine into the flesh and blood of Jesus Christ. In the emphasis placed on the moment of consecration and

---

20. See the quintessential and famous passage in Augustine, Sermo 272 (PL 38, 1247): "Si ergo vos estis corpus Christi et membra, mysterium vestrum in mensa Dominica positum est: mysterium vestrum accipitis. Ad id quod estis, Amen respondetis, et respondendo subscribitis. Audis enim, Corpus Christi; et respondes, Amen. Esto membrum corporis Christi, ut verum sit Amen.... *Estote quod videtis, et accipite quod estis.*" See F. Hofmann, *Der Kirchenbegriff des hl. Augustinus* (Munich: Max Huber, 1933), §26: Eucharistie und Kirche, 390–413; J. Ratzinger, *Volk und Haus Gottes*, esp. 205–18 (JRGS I, 43–550, esp. 283–94).

21. Thus H. Hoping, *Mein Leib für euch gegeben*, 121, referring to Sermo 272 (PL 38, 1247).

22. Augustine, *Ennarationes in Psalmos* 98, 8 (CCSL 39, 1386).

23. Augustine, Sermo 272 (PL 38, 1246). See also A. Angenendt, *Offertorium* (Münster: Aschendorff, 2013), 66f.

24. See Ambrose, *De sacr.* IV, 14 (FC 3, ed. J. Schmitz, 142f.): "Tu forte dicis: 'Meus panis est usitatus.' Sed panis iste panis est ante verba sacramentorum; ubi accesserit consecratio, de pane fit caro Christi.... Consecratio igitur quibus verbis est et cuius sermonibus? Domini Iesu." And IV, 15 (ibid.): "non erat corpus Christi ante consecrationem, sed post consecrationem dico tibi, quia iam corpus est Christi."

the operative power of Christ's word,[25] the later concentration of Eucharistic theology on the somatic real presence is already initiated. This will lead to the anamnetic-epicletic context of the *prex eucharistia* slipping into the background, even though Ambrose certainly gave it some weight in his considerations. With this, however, the point of fracture is already marked, through which the patristic theology of image will be led into a crisis.

II

With the inculturation of the faith in the Germanic cultural realm, we find a renewed shift, which has been called the "crisis of the sacramental idea." The notion that the exemplar is really present in the image and the visible sign is the vehicle of an invisible reality becomes incomprehensible within the intellectual horizon of material realism. "The altered understanding of reality is determined by a marked turning to what is sensibly perceived. Visible reality now counts as the truth from which the symbolic is distinguished."[26] Certainly, the traditional patristic texts are intensively appropriated, but the authors are understood differently than they understood themselves. Although, in the main, the sacramental remembrance of the events of salvation stood in the foreground for the patristic authors, the medieval authors focus their theological attention primarily on the question of whether Christ is really—that is, tangibly—or "only" symbolically present in the gifts of bread and wine. The Platonic two-tiered reality—exemplar and image—is contracted to the realm of things. In certain representatives of a realistic interpretation of the Eucharist, this leads to a doctrine of an undifferentiated total identification of the historical and Eucharistic *corpus Christi*. Paschasius Radbertus, for example, writes what no Church father could have written, namely, "that we receive in the bread what hung on the cross, and we drink in the cup what flowed from the wound on Christ's side."[27] The assertion of an identity between the Eucharistic and historical body of Christ—which Radbertus clearly explains elsewhere as a mystical rather than material identity[28]—provoked the protest of theologians such as Rabanus Maurus, Gottschalk, and above all Ratramnus, who insisted more strongly on the difference between sign and signified: the consecrated

---

25. Ibid., IV, 15: "Vides ergo, quam operatorius [sic] sermo sit Christi."
26. Hoping, *Mein Leib für euch gegeben*, 193.
27. Paschasius Radbertus, *Epistola ad Fredvgardvum* (CCCM XVI, ed. B. Paulus), 151, 193–95: "immolatur pro nobis cottidie in mysterio, ut percipiamus *in pane quod pependit in cruce*, et bibamus *in calice quod manauit de latere*" (emphasis added). See also the passages in idem, *De corpore et sangvine domini*, 1,2 (CCCM XVI, ed. B. Paulus, 14,44–15,55 = PL 120, 1269 B) and 21,9 (122, 298 –302 = PL 120, 1340 C).
28. See H. Hoping, *Mein Leib für euch gegeben*, 194–213, here 197f.

gifts of bread and wine are the body and blood of Christ not *corporaliter* but *spiritualiter*. The signs (*figura, similitudo*) participate in the reality (*veritas*) but are not identical with it. In the period that followed, the rejection of an identity between Eucharistic and historical body of Christ leads to a spiritualism that involves the separation of the reality (*veritas*) and sign (*figura*), so that the consecrated gifts are merely signs of Christ's presence. With the crisis of real symbolic thinking, the question that will characterize all further Eucharistic theology gets started: whether Christ is in the Eucharistic species "only in sign" or also "truly present"—a way of framing the question which, from the perspective of real symbolic thinking, must be branded as misguided and which then breaks out with all severity in the second Eucharistic controversy.

Within the framework of a sensualistic ontology, Berengar of Tours both understated the real presence of Jesus Christ and dismissed the transformation of the gifts of bread and wine.[29] The elements "do not undergo a change of being through the consecration, but a change in meaning."[30] They become signs of the body and blood of Christ, which prompt a *spiritual* unification with the heavenly *Christus totus*, who himself cannot be called down from heaven and multiplied on the altars. Berengar's interpretation provoked not only the protest of anti-dialectic theologians but also repeated magisterial condemnations. In particular, at the Lateran Synod of 1059, a profession of faith composed by Humbert of Silva Candida was demanded of him. The document read: bread and wine, which are placed upon the altar, are, after the consecration, not only *sacramentum* but also the true body and the true blood of our Lord Jesus Christ; but these are sensibly (*sensualiter*)—not only in sacrament but also in truth—touched and broken by the priest's hands and chewed by the teeth of the faithful (*dentibus atteri*).[31] The declarative intent of this *professio* is to hold to the unreserved real presence of Jesus Christ in the Eucharist in the face of its denial by Berengar. All the same, its massive realism is itself an occasion for misunderstandings. The undifferentiated identity between sign and reality, between the Eucharistic and the exalted body of the Lord suggests that the *corpus Domini* is itself affected by the *fractio panis* and the *manducatio oralis* when the faithful receive communion. Lanfranc of Bec and above all his

---

29. See Berengar of Tours, *Rescriptum contra Lanfrannum* (CCCM 84, ed. R. B. C. Huygens) (Turnholt: Brepols, 1988).
30. J. Betz, "Eucharistie," *MySal* 4/2, 232.
31. See the *Professio fidei* laid before Berengar in 1059: "scilicet panem et vinum, quae in altari ponuntur, post consecrationem non solum sacramentum, sed etiam verum corpus et sanguinem Domini nostri Iesu Christi esse, et *sensualiter*, non solum in sacramento, sed in veritate, manibus sacerdotum tractari et frangi et fidelium *dentibus atteri*" (DH 690, emphasis added).

pupil, Guitmund of Aversa, sought to defend the formula of the *confessio* by arguing that a crude materialism can be ruled out. In so doing, they made the distinction between *substantia* and *species* and thus did the preliminary work for the later solution offered by the doctrine of transubstantiation.[32]

III

With the reception of Aristotelian concepts in high Scholasticism,[33] we arrive at a clear correction of a sensualistic understanding of the sacrament that was taught by the anti-dialectic thinkers of the eleventh century. These thinkers included Adelmann of Liège, Hugo of Langres, and Durandus of Troarn, all of whom wrote to counter Berengar's position. Bonaventure and Thomas Aquinas both explicitly criticize the crude realism found in the *professio* of 1059,[34] and they emphasize that the real presence of Jesus Christ is *sacramentally* communicated in the Eucharist. The signs remain behind without a subject even when the substance of bread and wine is converted into the substance of Christ's body and blood. In contrast to Thomas, Berengar still understood the substance of a thing as the sum of its sensibly perceptible properties, and from this sensualistic understanding of substance he came to understand that in the process of Eucharistic conversion, nothing in the *reality* of the species of bread and wine can change, although they do become symbols of Christ's body and blood. Thomas, for his part, teaches that the substance of bread and wine are changed into the substance of Jesus Christ's body and blood as a result of the consecration, while the species perceptible to the senses—the accidents of bread and wine— remain. In connection with the thirteenth-century reception of Aristotle, "substance" is not understood sensualistically but ontologically, as the intelligible essence of a reality: *Substantia ... non est visibile oculo corporali*.[35] The application of Aristotelian concepts thus in a certain way allows an ontological penetration of the process of conversion, even if Thomas admits the reservation that the divine power in this sacrament operates in a way more

---

32. See M. Vaillantcourt, "Guitmund of Aversa and the Eucharistic Theology of St. Thomas," *The Thomist* 68 (2004): 577–600.

33. See C. H. Lohr, "The Medieval Interpretation of Aristotle," in *The Cambridge History of Later Medieval History*, ed. A. Kenny, et al. (Cambridge: Cambridge University Press, 1982), 80–98; G. Wieland, "Plato oder Aristoteles? Überlegungen zur Aristoteles-Rezeption des lateinischen Mittelalters," *Tijdschrift voor Filosofie* 47 (1985): 605–30.

34. Bonaventure speaks of an "exaggerated statement" (see *In IV Sent.*, d. 12, p. 1, a. 3, q. 1: "Quamvis nimis expressa") and stresses in his *Brevoloquium* (VI, 9), that it is not acceptable to chew Christ's flesh with our teeth (*cum dentibus atteri*), for one, because it makes one cringe at the thought, and for another, because his body is immortal. See, similarly, Thomas, *In IV Sent.*, d. 10, q. 1, a. 1 (n. 14).

35. *S. th.* III, q. 76, a. 7.

sublime and hidden than could be investigated by men.³⁶ As was already made clear, the doctrine of transubstantiation pursues a middle way between crude sensualism and mere spiritualism. On the one hand, teaching that the accidents remain without a subject preserves the symbolic character of bread and wine, which is the justified concern of sensualism; on the other, the interpretation of the transformation as transubstantiation manages to assert the true and real presence of Jesus Christ's body and blood in the Eucharist and thereby conform to the *particula veri* of sacramental realism. The "theory of transubstantiation as an interpretative model manifests itself as the via media between the Scylla of mere symbolism and the Charybdis of a sensualistic realism."³⁷

The theological reception of Aristotelian philosophical resources leads, however, to a reshaping of concepts. The charge already lobbed at Thomas—that taking over categories of substance and accident distorts the truth of the *verba testamenti*—is defused by the fact that precisely fidelity to the semantic content of the *verba testamenti* themselves leads to a "transubstantiation" of Aristotelian concepts—a point we were able to demonstrate earlier. The doctrine that after the consecration the accidents of bread and wine remain without a subject (*sine subiecto*) could not be accomplished within the horizon of a strict Aristotelianism, where an ontological separation of substance and accidents is unheard of.³⁸

Even so, bound up with the reception and transformation of the terms *substantia—accidens* is also the concentration on the somatic real presence that took place in the Eucharistic doctrine of the Latin West, as already discussed.³⁹ It appears that, because of the focus on the *verba testamenti*, what is no longer quite in view is that the real presence is ultimately grounded in the self-gift of Jesus Christ on the cross. The Eucharist is indeed absolutely understood as a *memoriale passionis Jesu Christi*, though the interconnection between the self-sacrifice of Jesus Christ and his salvation-establishing

---

36. S. c. G. IV, c. 63: "Licet autem divina virtus sublimius et secretius in hoc sacramento operetur quam ab homine perquiri possit."

37. Pertinent here is B. J. Hilberath, "Eucharistie II. Historisch-theologisch," *LThK* 3 (1995): 946–48, here 947.

38. Out of fidelity to an authentic Aristotelianism, within the horizon of which a separation of substance and accidents is not conceivable, J. Wyclif rejected the doctrine of transubstantiation and declared himself for a purely symbolic interpretation along the lines of Berengar. See idem, *De Eucharistia tractatus maior*, ed. J. Loserth (London: Trubner, 1892), 29f. For this reason, he was condemned at the Council of Constance (DH 1151–53).

39. See the judgment of A. Gerken, *Theologie der Eucharistie*, 183: "The constriction of medieval theology lies ... in the fact that what is required by a New Testament point of view, namely the grounding of the somatic real presence through the self-gift of Christ on the cross, is precisely what is not accomplished in the doctrine of transubstantiation."

presence in the signs of bread and wine is scarcely explored in its own right. In the *Summa theologiae*'s treatise on the Eucharist, the rite is treated rather as an addendum and the *celebratio sacramenti* is grasped as a representative making present of the sacrifice on the cross. The ecclesial and community-establishing side of the Eucharist,[40] as well as the eschatological dynamism pointing ahead to the heavenly wedding banquet—all of this receded rather into the background in the conceptual work of theology. This holds true regardless of the fact that Thomas Aquinas certainly has a sense for this aspect, as is shown not only in his systematic theology but also and above all in his poetic theology of the Eucharist.

In the theology of the late Middle Ages, there arises in the meantime a focusing on the problem of Christ's real presence and the doctrine of transubstantiation bound up with it. Questions of natural philosophy related to the sacramental mode of making present are discussed with speculative sophistication. Within this discourse, there increasingly arise reservations concerning the subjectless accidents of bread and wine remaining behind. John Duns Scotus and, among his followers, William of Ockham and Gabriel Biel, all favor the doctrine of consubstantiation, because it—following the rational principle of parsimony—makes dispensable the additional assumption of a miracle, namely, that God's omnipotence works through a miracle to leave the species of bread and wine to stay behind without a subject. Contrary to their own theological reflections on the Eucharist, these authors formally recognize the doctrine of transubstantiation as a dogma of the Church—which reveals a certain dissociation of faith and reason.

Finally, we must mention the fatal ramifications of a certain Eucharistic theology upon pious practices.[41] "Most unfortunate, it must be admitted, was a representation of the sacrifice of the Mass only too prevalent in late medieval theology, which envisaged it as primarily an action of the Church exercised on God to promote and increase the pouring down of his benefits on men. Quite certainly, the theologians who expressed themselves in this way were well aware that the sacrifice of the Mass exists only through the free gift God made us in Christ, and therefore is itself preeminently a grace,

---

40. On this point, see H. de Lubac, *Corpus Mysticum* (Notre Dame, Ind.: University of Notre Dame Press, 2007), who can show how the connection between Church and Eucharist in the Middle Ages waned as a result of the concentration on the somatic real presence. Until the ninth century, the Eucharist was considered in the context of the doctrine of Christ and Church, and the Eucharist was designated the *corpus Christi mysticum*, which granted access to the realm of Christ. In contrast, with the crisis of the sacramental idea, the linkage between Church and Eucharist became increasingly obscure. This also became terminologically perceptible, inasmuch as now the Church was no longer designated as *corpus Christi verum*; rather, the Eucharist received this title in order to exclude a spiritual interpretation of the Eucharist.

41. See Angenendt, *Geschichte der Religiosität im Mittelalter*, 488–515.

and by no means a lever placed in man's hands to constrain God in some way or other to benefit us. But formulas of this kind were only too likely to give the ordinary people a purely magical idea of the Eucharist."[42] The thought that one offered to God the sacrifice of his Son's body and blood in the Mass, and did this to placate him, led to the formation of the whole system of Mass stipends. Altarists celebrated, and were remunerated for, votive and special Masses for the living and the dead, so that the precarious impression almost inevitably had to arise that God's freely imparted grace is a mercantile quantity that lends itself to being commercialized.[43]

IV

The recollection of Jesus' words of institution forms the starting point for the Reformation objection to these abuses. In addition to practical challenges—*communio sub utraque*, rejection of the Roman Canon, condemning veneration of the host, etc.—a theology of justification leads to a criticism of the so-called sacrificial character of the holy Mass. The sacrifice of the Mass is rejected as being a work of human self-justification. The uniqueness and sufficiency of the sacrifice on the cross requires no multiplying repetitions or completion. The doctrine of transubstantiation was also condemned as unscriptural and was criticized as "the highest sophistry."[44] While Martin Luther tried to preserve the sense of the *verba testamenti* by holding to the real presence of Christ in the Lord's supper and rooting this presence in the doctrine of the ubiquity of Christ's human nature, a purely symbolic interpretation was advocated by Zwingli, Johannes Oecolampadius, and the Sacramentarians. They interpreted the *est* tropologically and translated it into a *significat*—with the consequence that the gifts of bread and wine do indeed signify the Lord, who was sacrificed on the cross, but they do not make him substantially present.

In reaction to the Reformation theology of the Lord's supper, the Council of Trent substantially affirmed the Eucharistic theology of Thomas Aquinas.[45] But Thomas ultimately holds together the aspects of sacra-

---

42. L. Bouyer, *The Word, Church, and Sacraments in Protestantism and Catholicism* (London: Geoffrey Chapman, 1961), 65–66.
43. See A. Angenendt, *Offertorium. Das mittelalterliche Meßopfer* (Münster: Aschendorff, 2013), 401–68.
44. See Smalcald Article III, 6, in *BSLK* 452, 21. The Formula of Concord also "condemns and damns" the doctrine of transubstantiation as "papist" (see *BSLK* 801,5–11). All the same, the context makes clear that the condemnation relates to the nominalistic variant that supposes an annihilation of the substance of bread. Moreover, it is to be kept in mind that Luther himself was at times ready to allow transubstantiation to count as a received opinion (see Weimar Edition 6,456; 6,508; Weimar Edition (Letters) 10,331; but WA 10/2, 208,31 is different).
45. See F. Pratzner, *Messe und Kreuzesopfer. Die Krise der sakramentalen Idee bei Luther und in der*

ment and sacrifice, especially in seeing the representative making present of Christ's unique sacrifice on the cross as carried out in the act of consecration. In contrast, the Council of Trent considers the questions of real presence and sacrifice in two different decrees. In the decree on the holy Eucharist, it first of all strongly emphasizes the "true, real, and substantial" presence of Jesus Christ in the sacrament of the Eucharist. This takes place in opposition to the symbolistic understanding of the Lord's supper held by Zwingli, Oecolampadius, and the Sacramentarians.[46] This group rejected a real presence of Christ's body because, thinking in spatial categories, they thought it impossible that a truly substantial presence of the risen crucified one, who sits at the right hand of the Father, could be in the Eucharistic species. In rejecting a symbolistic understanding of the Eucharist, the Council of Trent joined with the Lutheran reformers, who likewise emphasized, against the enthusiasts and followers of Zwingli, that Christ is "truly, really, and substantially"[47] present in the Lord's supper.[48]

The Council of Trent gives the ontological foundation for the real presence when it states in its second step that the presence of Christ in the Eucharist takes place through a conversion (*conversio*).[49] No particular form of thought is intended to be laid down with this statement, but rather an explanatory model of the real presence is rejected that is based on a hypostatic union between Christ's human nature and the substances of bread and wine—a position the Council fathers attributed to Luther. Whether this was indeed the position of Luther may remain debatable. Luther does not teach a theory of impanation but champions the conception that at

---

mittelalterlichen Scholastik (Vienna: Herder, 1970). On the conciliar discussions and genesis of the texts, see E. Schillebeeckx, *Die eucharistische Gegenwart. Zur Diskussion über Realpräsenz* (Düsseldorf: Patmos, 1967), 18–57; J. Wohlmuth, *Realpräsenz und Transubstantiation im Konzil von Trient*, 2 vols. (Bern–Frankfurt am Main: Peter Lang, 1975).

46. See DH 1651: "Can. 1. Si quis negaverit, in sanctissimae Eucharistiae sacramento contineri vere, realiter et substantialiter, corpus et sanguinem una cum anima et divinitate Domini nostri Iesu Christi ac proinde totum Christum; sed dixerit, tantummodo in eo ut in signo vel figura, aut virtute: anathema sit."

47. See Augsburg Confession 10 (*BSLK*, 64); Apology of the Augsburg Confession 10 (*BSLK*, 247).

48. As is well known, the union of Lutherans and Reformed failed in 1529 at Marburg over the question of the Lord's supper. Luther advocated a substantial presence of Christ in the Lord's supper, but Zwingli, a virtual one. They were, however, agreed in the demand that the Lord's supper must be distributed under both species (*sub utraque specie*). The scholastic doctrine of concomitance, according to which the whole Christ (*totus Christus*) is present in each of the two species, was rejected as unscriptural, along with the Roman Catholic praxis of offering Mass for those living and dead. See J. Staedtke, "Abendmahl III/3," *TRE* 1 (1978): 106–22, here 108.

49. See DH 1652: "Can. 2. Si quis dixerit, in sacrosancto Eucharistiae sacramento remanere substantiam panis et vini una cum corpore et sanguine Domini nostri Iesu Christi, negaveritque mirabilem illam et singularem conversionem totius substantiae panis in corpus et totius substantiae vini in sanguinem, manentibus dumtaxat speciebus panis et vini, quam quidem conversionem catholica Ecclesia aptissime transsubstantiationem appellat: anathema sit."

the Lord's supper (and only for the duration of the Lord's supper) the substance of Christ's body and blood joins the substances of bread and wine.

Finally, in a third step, the Council sets down that the concept *transsubstantiatio* is "most suitable" (*aptissime*) for expressing this conversion. If one analyzes the levels of conciliar statements, then it can be stated that, first, the real presence is emphatically affirmed as an incontestable datum of *faith*. Furthermore, it is said that one cannot *think* about the real presence otherwise than that the substance of bread and of wine are converted (*conversio*) into the body and blood of Jesus Christ. Only in a last step does the *terminological* consideration take place, that this conversion is "most suitably" (*aptissime*) expressed by the term *transsubstantiatio*.[50] Even if the Council fathers at Trent saw real presence and transubstantiation as belonging together with an inner necessity, the terminological consideration *aptissime* contains nevertheless the admission of a certain relativity regarding the formulation. Already earlier it was conceded that the sacramental presence of the exalted Lord can "scarcely be expressed in words" (see DH 1636). It is therefore conceivable in principle that in other time periods another concept will be found that expresses the event of *conversio* more suitably than the concept *transsubstantiatio*. Even one who would dispute that any more fitting concept has *de facto* been found since Trent would still hardly be able to rule out the possibility *de iure*. Because the concept of transubstantiation arose only in the twelfth century—in earlier times the Eucharistic real presence was articulated in other terms (*conversio, mutatio,* etc.)—the question presents itself as to its dogmatic binding force. Is it historically conditioned and replaceable if need be? Or when it comes to the term *transsubstantiatio*, which in post-Tridentine thought was promoted as an anti-Reformation mark of identification, is it necessary in the future as well in order to explain the Eucharistic presence of Jesus Christ in a theologically apposite way? With the insight into the historicity of language and its conceptual tools, the question must at least be asked whether in this moment—when the Aristotelian notion of substance has become philosophically precarious and prone to misunderstanding in our everyday semantics[51]—it would not be appropriate to seek new and similarly adequate, possibly even complementary, expressions that are able to illuminate faith in the real presence. In connection with this, it is significant that when speaking of the presence of

---

50. See Schillebeeckx, *Die eucharistische Gegenwart*, 28–30.

51. See G. Figal, "Substanz," *RGG* 7, 4th ed. (2004) 1824–27, who points out that the Aristotelian concept of substance lost its prominence through the modern concept of subject and that "functional concepts" tend to be used in the modern era in place of "substantial concepts"—with the consequence that the concept of substance loses its force of expression.

Jesus Christ in the sacrament of the Eucharist, the Second Vatican Council avoids using the notion of transubstantiation.[52] In addition, the philosopher Robert Spaemann, who would scarcely be said to be lax regarding the magisterial tradition, has also put forward a new suggestion for an ontology corresponding to the consecration. The doctrine of transubstantiation holds an "erroneous presupposition," since it is based on the bread and wine being substances, which is not at all the case. Rather, it has to do with a mixture of ingredients, which does not itself exist independently. Spaemann thus suggests expressing the conversion of bread into the "bread of life" by means of the concept "substantiation."[53] Even this suggestion remains indebted to a classical substance ontology.

V

In the twentieth century, alternative explanatory models were worked out in order to understand the event of Eucharistic conversion. These new explanatory attempts are connected with diverse movements of renewal that led in the twentieth century to a certain "turn in understanding the Eucharist."[54] First of all, the patristic and liturgical movement, with Odo Casel's "mystery theology" at the forefront, placed thinking of the real making-present of Jesus Christ's salvific deeds once more in the center, calling this the "Paschal mystery."[55] Despite all of its merits, Casel's impulse nevertheless amounts to an (admittedly anachronistic) attempt to revitalize the real symbolic way of thinking. Beyond this movement, there were biblical-ecumenical efforts toward a reconsideration of the Eucharist, which went beyond the question of Christ's real presence to work out the prandial and communal character of the Eucharist, as well as its eschatological valence.[56] Third, because of a decided interest in updating the teaching on the Eucharist, interpretive attempts were undertaken that took up categories of a *relational ontology*

---

52. SC 5, 6, 7, 47, 48; LG 11; UR 15, 22. See also K. Lehmann and W. Pannenberg, *Lehrverurteilungen—kirchentrennend?* vol. 1 (Freiburg-Göttingen: Herder, 1986), 89–124.

53. R. Spaemann, "Substantiation. Zur Ontologie der Wandlung," *IKaZ Communio* 43 (2014): 199–202.

54. Gerken, *Theologie der Eucharistie*, 166.

55. O. Casel, *Das christliche Kultmysterium*, 4th ed. (Regensburg: Pustet, 1960). On the basics and for a criticism of Odo Casel's mystery theology, see S. Wahle, *Gottes-Gedenken* (Innsbruck: Tyrola, 2006), 95–106; H. Hoping, "Die Mysterientheologie Odo Casels und die Liturgiereform," in *Erinnerung an die Zukunft. Das Zweite Vatikanische Konzil*, ed. J.-H. Tück (Freiburg: Herder, 2013), 163–84.

56. G. Wainwright, *Eucharist and Eschatology* (London: Oxford University Press, 1971); E. Keller, *Eucharistie und Parusie. Liturgie- und theologiegeschichtliche Untersuchungen zur eschatologischen Dimension der Eucharistie anhand ausgewählter Zeugnisse aus frühchristlicher und patristischer Zeit* (Freiburg, Switz.: Universitätsverlag, 1989).

to develop alternative explanatory models (B. Welte, P. Schoonenberg, E. Schillebeeckx, J. Ratzinger). The material misunderstanding evoked by the concept of "substance" in our contemporary consciousness[57]—which understands precisely what Thomas Aquinas designated as species or accident—should be avoided and instead a contemporary interpretation should be offered, one which has recourse to categories of encounter. Connected with this, is the fact that all of the more modern interpretive suggestions regard the categories of substance and relation as equal. These attempts, which intend an explanation of the Eucharistic presence that has relational and personal contours, were discussed amidst controversy with the catchwords "transfinalisation" and "transsignification."[58]

Schoonenberg, for example, distinguishes between "informing" (e.g., road signs) and "realizing" signs that build up the community (e.g., a gift); he then likewise stresses the difference between spatial and personal presence. Spatial presence can coincide with personal absence, just as spatial distance can lead to an intensification of personal closeness. Personal closeness, however, depends on realizing signs that establish relation and communication. The primary medium of realizing signs is the body (e.g., a handshake, embrace, kiss), but in the event of spatial distance, gifts, letters, and other signs can symbolically communicate personal presence. Spatial distance can become a litmus test for people who have decided for each other in friendship or love.

A theological entry into Christ's presence in the Eucharist can be developed from these beginnings, if one bears in mind that the Eucharist is based on Jesus' departure from his disciples, his death, and his going away

---

57. On this point, see J. Ratzinger, *Die sakramentale Begründung christlicher Existenz* (1965), 3rd ed. (Meitingen-Freising: Kyrios-Verlag, 1970), 7 (*JRGS* II, 197–214, 198f.): "The concept of substance, with which the idea of conversion appears to be most intimately joined, seems to have become entirely abstract, since the bread, considered chemically and physically, presents a mixture of heterogeneous materials, which consist of an infinite myriad of atoms, which for their part fragment once again into a multiplicity of elementary particles, which—for the last time now—in the midst of the interplay of particle and wave-like properties can no longer be affirmed to have a solid substantial existence." P. Schoonenberg mentions the curiosity that a socialistic newspaper reacted to Paul VI's encyclical *Mysterium fidei* (3 September 1965) with the headline: "The Pope espouses a material presence of Christ" (Schoonenberg, *Die Interpretation des Dogmas*, 71). The example shows that a hermeneutic theology must search for new formulations precisely out of fidelity to the tradition of faith; it cannot simply repeat without commentary a form of language that has been handed on but also has become highly misunderstood.

58. See Paul VI, Encyclical Letter *Mysterium Fidei* (DH 4410–13). The encyclical presupposes—if one may apply the terminology of Schoonenberg to the text—an informing understanding of sign. See here W. Beinert, "Die Enzyklika Mysterium Fidei und neuere Auffassungen über die Eucharistie," *ThQ* 147 (1967): 159–76; Th. Freyer, "'Transssubstantiation' versus 'Transfinalisation / Transsignifikation'? Bemerkungen zu einer aktuellen Debatte," *Cath* 49 (1995): 174–95; E. Klinger, "Transsubstantiation—Transfinalisation—Transsignifikation," in *Mehr als Brot und Wein. Theologische Kontexte der Eucharistie*, ed. W. Haunerland (Würzburg: Echter, 2005), 282–98.

to the Father. The sending of the Spirit, which is enabled with Jesus' going to the Father, is the presupposition for his new pneumatic presence in the Eucharistic gifts; this kind of positive significance can thus be attributed to the absence of the exalted Christ. As the one who went away, the resurrected crucified one has the possibility of giving the faithful a realizing sign of his presence, namely by giving himself to his community in the gifts of bread and wine. In addition, the eschatological tension between "already" and "not yet" can be included, when the one who is physically absent vouchsafes his sacramental presence in the gifts, in which the promise is inherent that his having departed will one day be overcome by his "coming in glory." The prandial gifts do not exhaust themselves in being nourishment or refreshment or mere signs of community among men sharing a meal together; rather, they become realizing signs of his presence through the pneumatic self-gift of Jesus. The signs of bread and wine are transformed from the ground up by the pneumatic self-gift of Jesus Christ.[59]

All the same, one will have to defend the advocates of transsignification against the misunderstanding that they would make the personal presence of Christ dependent on the subjective consciousness of the faithful. Such an interpretation would overlook the Christological and pneumatological basis of this interpretive model: for it is *Jesus Christ* who in his Spirit vouchsafes his presence, but the offer of his presence also remains in existence when it is rejected by those to whom it is directed. *Transsignification* as a re-establishing[60] of the symbolic meaning of bread and wine would also be wrongly interpreted if one were to ascribe this meaning to an act of attribution by the believing subject in a purely horizontal way—even though it is not to be ruled out that this misunderstanding in fact exists or once existed.

VI

Taking account of these epochal forms of communicating the faith concerning Eucharistic real presence, contemporary theology stands before the task of translating this faith into the conceptual horizon of today. At the same time, it stands before the unique difficulty that within the conditions of late modernity and its strained pluralism involving different ways

---

59. P. Schoonenberg, "Inwieweit ist die Lehre von der Transsubstantiation historisch bestimmt?" *Conc*(D) 3 (1967): 305–11. It is questionable whether the criticism trained by the encyclical *Mysterium Fidei* on this new interpretation of Eucharistic real presence really hit upon the point of transsignification. The encyclical warns, certainly with good reason, against a mere symbolism, which is, however, not advocated by Schoonenberg and his conception of realizing sign.

60. See B. J. Hilberath, "Transsignifikation," *LThK* 10, 3rd ed. (2001): 177; idem, "'Substanzwandlung'—'Bedeutungswandel'—'Umstiftung,'" *Cath* 39 (1995): 133–50.

of thinking and living, there is no longer a unified conceptual horizon. To begin thinking from a unified conceptual horizon in today's world would be nearly a fiction. Against the background of this factual multiplicity of positions, which are brought under the glittering term of postmodernism,[61] there exists the temptation to proceed with the intellectual resources of the theological tradition in a selective or even eclectic way. But a selective handling of traditional resources—a *bricolage théologique*—leads practically ineluctably to incoherence and inconsistency in thinking. This is probably what Thomas Pröpper had in view when he noted: "It is unacceptable to make use of arbitrary intellectual resources in an ad hoc way: thus, for example, to conceptualize the celebration of the mysteries of faith with Platonic categories, but the Eucharistic presence of Jesus Christ with Aristotelian ones, or to understand the unity of divinity and humanity in Christ himself once more in neo-Chalcedonian terms or also speculative Hegelian concepts, while at the same time to use some resources from liberal theory to understand the events of revelation, tradition, or grace."[62]

Still, the New Testament *paradosis* of the last supper, which presents the essential *interpretandum* of all attempts at theological interpretation, does have a certain affinity for personal categories emphasizing human freedom. If one grasps the Eucharist as Jesus Christ's *self*-gift for the many[63]—a motif making up the actual nucleus of Thomas Aquinas's soteriology; if one further takes into account that this gift has addressees who, through faithfully receiving this gift, are incorporated into a community that is actualized within a ritual meal; then one pushes towards a Eucharistic theology that, in addition to the difficulty of the *verba testamenti*, takes account of the context, including the last supper and Christ's Passion, and has recourse to categories related to the person and free will. The logic of the matter centers on the statement: "Jesus Christ, the one crucified and risen, gives us himself in the signs of bread and wine." And given this logic, an interpretation of Eucharistic theology in categories of freedom seems meaningful in any event, nearly necessary even. Considering God's presence, we can hold with Thomas Pröpper that it "stems from God's free gratuity, decreed with self-determination, and this gratuity likewise *retains* its effective origin, even when it persists. God becomes able to be experienced

---

61. On this point, see H. Verweyen, *Theologie im Zeichen der schwachen Vernunft* (Regensburg: Pustet, 2000).

62. Th. Pröpper, "Zur vielfältigen Rede von der Gegenwart Gottes und Jesu Christi," in his *Evangelium und freie Vernunft*, 245–65, here 246.

63. At this point, it is noteworthy that Thomas understands *pro multis* spoken over the chalice in the sense of *pro omnibus*—and indeed relying upon 1 Jn 2:2. See *In Matth* XXVI, l. IV (n. 2202); *In I Cor* XI, l. VI (n. 681): "non solum pro multis, sed pro omnibus."

when he *gives* himself to be experienced; he is and remains present when and as long as he *wills* to be present."[64] This insight will be unfolded further in what follows here. As we do so, it will be worth taking up the intentions of Thomas Aquinas, but also updating them in rather personal and freedom-oriented categories. Already in Thomas, the terminology we find allows us to state a peculiar ambivalence. On the one hand, he has recourse to the thought of God's *communicatio* with men, in order to deduce the fittingness of the Incarnation; and from this point, he can likewise interpret the sacraments as instruments of God's communication with men. On the other hand, he rules out categorically a real relation of God (*relatio realis*) to the history of men—following the traces of Aristotelian ontology.[65] Based on the biblical evidence, however, not only are God's transcendence and his sovereignty over history to be claimed, but likewise his working in history and thus his capacity for history and willingness for relation. Therefore, in what follows the attempt is made to take up the potentialities of meaning in the categories of *communicatio* and *traditio*.

64. Pröpper, *Zur vielfältigen Rede von der Gegenwart Gottes und Jesu Christi*, 247.
65. The unmoved mover, who moves everything, is himself not moved by anything, for this would bring a moment of potency into him and thus infringe on his perfection (*actus purus*). See S. c. G. I, c. 13 and 16: "Primum agens, quod Deus est, nullam habet potentiam admixtam, sed est actus purus."

II

The Self-Gift of Jesus Christ in the Signs of Bread and Wine

> All gifts are gifts of bequeathment. Gifts of absence.
> The gift is above all what remains behind.
> It bargains for the remembrance of the giver.
>
> Botho Strauss

> Giving thanks ... is recognizing the presence of the giver in the gift.
>
> Franz von Baader

Thomas Aquinas had to sort out the set of questions given by the Eucharistic controversies of the ninth and eleventh centuries, which dealt with whether Jesus Christ is present in the Eucharist in signs (*in signo*) or in truth (*in veritate*). Thus, it appears logical that he devotes his treatise on the Eucharist first and above all to the problem of real presence. Although this concentration does not cause the disappearance of other aspects of the Eucharist—such as its prandial and communal character, its eschatological dynamic, and its liturgical celebration—it does allow them to recede into a background position. In this way, it was possible for less attentive readings to settle upon the impression that Thomas's Eucharistic theology underexposed the biblical foundations of the Eucharist by taking this approach. At the same time, Thomas certainly designated the Eucharist as *memoriale dominicae passionis*[1]—a designation that is linked with Jesus' rememora-

---

Epigraphs are from B. Strauss, *Der Untenstehende auf Zehenspitzen* (Munich: Carl Hanser Verlag, 2004), 99; and F. von Baader, *Sämtliche Werke*, v. IX (Aalen: Scientia Verlag, 1963), 387.

1. See *S. th.* III, q. 74, a. 1; q. 76, a. 2 ad 2. See *In I Cor*, XI, I.V (n. 653): "Est enim memoriale dominicae passionis, per quam sanguis Christi fuit separatus a corpore."

tive mandate (see Lk 22:19; 1 Cor 11:15, 24) and locates his Passion at the center of the Eucharistic commemoration. Thomas's focus on the somatic real presence in his Eucharistic doctrine, while something certainly to be noted, does not bring about a disappearance of the commemorative actual presence, as the explication of the concept of *passio Christi* was able to show, drawing on the soteriological passages of the *Summa theologiae*. In what follows, the theme *Gift of Presence* will now be taken up once again and explained: the Eucharistic real presence of Jesus Christ is due to the crucified and risen one pneumatically making himself present. Instead of treating directly the theme of Jesus Christ's real presence in the consecrated gifts of bread and wine and determining more precisely the mode of this sacramental making present, the first section undertakes a *biblical affirmation*. This historical flashback should show that the concentration on the *verba testamenti* does not present a regrettable aberration of Eucharistic reflection, which is then to be overcome; rather, it picks up the central element of Jesus' handing himself over, which is attested in the New Testament *paradosis* of the last supper. The last meal that Jesus shared with a select group of his disciples—the twelve as representatives of the eschatological people of God (see Mt 19:28)[2]—forms first of all the historical reference point of any Eucharistic theology. The ritual innovation inscribed by Jesus into the context of the Jewish feast and brought out repeatedly and emphatically by Thomas in his hymns consists in the significant twofold action in which Christ identified himself with the signs of bread and wine as he departed from his disciples. This action summarizing his pro-existent life also points in advance to his death. For this reason, the historical origin of the Eucharist is not exhausted in the scene of the last supper but rather encompasses Jesus' suffering and death on the cross as well—a scandalous event (see Gal 3:13) of eminently soteriological import for the eyes of faith. Jesus' disciples would certainly have interpreted the *mors turpissima* on Golgotha as a definitive capitulation were it not for the appearances of the resurrected one.[3] Only in the light of the resurrection experiences was the saving and redeeming power of Jesus' death recognized, a power already ascribed to the cross

---

2. See Th. Söding, "'Tut dies zu meinem Gedächtnis!' Das Abendmahl Jesu und die Eucharistie der Kirche nach dem Neuen Testament," in *Eucharistie. Positionen katholischer Theologie*, ed. Söding (Regensburg: Pustet, 2002), 11–58, here 25, who points out that the twelve make up the innermost circle of disciples and represent the eschatological people of God. We find a different view in M. Theobald, *Das Herrenmahl*, 263, who holds that the presence of women at Jesus' last supper was certainly probable.

3. For background, see H. Kessler, *Sucht den Lebenden nicht bei den Toten. Die Auferstehung Jesu Christi in biblischer, fundamentaltheologischer und systematischer Sicht* (Würzburg: Echter, 1995). For another perspective, see H. Verweyen, *Botschaft eines Toten? Den Glauben rational verantworten* (Regensburg: Pustet, 1997).

event by the pre-Pauline tradition of the apostolic age (1 Cor 15:3–5). Thus, beyond life and death, resurrection and ascension are also to be kept in view if one wants to explain the dimensions of the Paschal mystery[4] in an unabbreviated way and to understand adequately the crucified and resurrected one's making himself pneumatically present in the gifts of bread and wine.

Only after the *what* of the Eucharistic *memoria* is illuminated with the Paschal mystery of Jesus Christ should the *how*, that is, the mode of sacramental making-present, be placed once more in the center of theological attention. Here it will be a question of how one can take up the fundamental concerns of the doctrine of transubstantiation today, after the concept of substance has become precarious given the altered intellectual presuppositions of the late modern era, speaking both philosophically and from the perspective of everyday semantics. At the same time, an engagement with the suspicion of idolatry is in order, that is, whether or not the interpretation of the Eucharist advocated by Thomas Aquinas ties together the presence of a *person* with the presence of a *thing*. (Other important questions related to Eucharistic theology, such as ecclesiological or magisterial aspects, the liturgical-aesthetic context, or the sacrificial character of the Eucharist, will be either skipped over or treated merely in a secondary way, given the focus here on the motif *gift of presence*.)

In a third and final moment, there follow *Eucharistic Passages*, a name given to signify our taking up of further motifs of Aquinas's Eucharistic theology and poetry and translating them into the present. Instead of adducing further evidence of Eucharistic poesy, as one can find for example in Gerard Manley Hopkins and Paul Claudel; instead of working out the basic lines of Eucharistic poetry, as found laid out in the work of David Jones[5] or in the aesthetic of presence suggested by George Steiner;[6] we will

---

4. See J. Ratzinger, "40 Jahre Konstitution über die heilige Liturgie," *LJ* 53 (2003): 209–21, here 213 (*JRGS* 11, 695–711, 701): "Passover signifies the inseparability of cross and resurrection." A *theologia gloriae*, which forgets the cry of Good Friday in the joy of Easter and derails into a superficial optimism, is thus just as inadequate as a one-sided *theologia crucis*, which out of solidarity with the victims of history casts a triumphalistic suspicion on the Easter gift of new life in a sweeping fashion, thereby leading to a precarious form of denying doxology. Thomas himself justified the fittingness of the time of the Eucharist's institution in the following way: "dicendum quod imminente passione corda discipulorum magis erant affectata ad passionem, quam passione iam peracta, quando jam erant immemores pressurae passionis propter gaudium resurrectionis" (*In IV Sent.*, d. 8, q. 1, a. 2 qa. 3 [n. 93]).

5. See D. Jones, *The Anathemata: Fragments of an Attempted Writing*, 3rd ed. (London: Faber, 1972); idem, *Epoch and Artist. Selected Writings*, ed. H. Grisewood (London: Faber and Faber, 1973). That art is to be understood in analogy to the Eucharistic real presence is something Jones has made clear especially in his essay "Art and Sacrament." There we find the significant sentence: "the painter may say to himself: 'This is not a representation of a mountain, it *is* 'mountain' under the form of paint'" (*Epoch and Artist*, 170).

6. See G. Steiner, *Real Presences: Is there anything in what we say?* (London: University of Chicago Press, 1989); see also B. Strauss, *Der Aufstand gegen die sekundäre Welt. Bemerkungen zu einer Ästhetik der Anwesenheit* (Munich: Carl Hanser Verlag, 1999).

offer a series of reflections that take up once more the connection between doctrine and life, between the theology and the spirituality of the Eucharist, as indicated in the introduction. These very much fragmentary reflections can be read as sketches of a Eucharistic way of existence. The title *Eucharistic Passages* does not follow a sensibility determined by postmodern assumptions, but is rather selected for theological reasons: on the one hand, it hints at the Eucharistic conversion, which in the hymn *Lauda Sion* Thomas Aquinas extolled as *transitus* of bread and wine into the flesh and blood of Jesus Christ[7]—a *transitus* that transforms the very life of the one receiving the Eucharistic gifts. On the other hand, the title *Passages* takes up the motion inscribed into the *Passover* mystery as a passing over from death to a life that no longer knows death. "Passover is *transitus*—it is the dynamic of transcendence as such, from life to death and from death to life … from the stations of time into the new city, the final Jerusalem."[8] This movement characterizes the nature of human existence as *viator*, if it is true that each is left with "the feeling of hunger for what is to come,"[9] indeed "the ineradicable longing for the far side of the river,"[10] which Thomas designated as the *desiderium naturale in visionem Dei*. The Eucharist can be interpreted as provision for the journey, which is offered to all the baptized so that their steps (and missteps) finally reach the destination of the heavenly wedding banquet.

The Eucharist as *memoriale passionis et resurrectionis Jesu Christi*: The Interpretive Context of the Last Supper, Cross, and Resurrection

The last supper of Jesus must be hermeneutically placed within the context of Christ's life, death, and resurrection. What this reveals is that Jesus' words and signs not only distill the pro-existent stance of his life but also instantiate an interpretive anticipation of his Passion. The question of how Jesus survived his death receives its answer through the paradosis of the last supper. The brutal execution on the cross, which makes Jesus a victim of violence, is transformed from within into an act of free self-giving, something expressed by the term "sacrifice." Nevertheless, the death on the cross could have been interpreted as the definitive failure of Jesus' mission if God had

---

7. See *Lauda Sion*, v. 32: "Quod in carnem *transit* panis / Et vinum in sanguinem."
8. See J. Ratzinger, "40 Jahre Konstitution über die heilige Liturgie," 212 (*JRGS* 11, 695–711, 700).
9. P. Handke, *Langsame Heimkehr* (Frankfurt/M.: Suhrkamp, 1984), 86f.
10. Jones, *Anathemata*, 26.

not himself saved his slain witness from death and thereby ratified his message of the kingdom at hand. The gestures and words of the last supper (no longer able to be reconstructed exactly, historically speaking) point to the upcoming death as an act of pro-existent self-gift for the many; in death, Jesus' radical giving of himself over to the will of the Father takes on its ultimate shape; and in the light of the resurrection it becomes apparent that God himself was at work in this narrative.

Thomas Aquinas traces the ecclesial praxis of celebrating the Eucharist immediately back to Jesus' celebration of the last supper with his disciples. This still unbroken contact with the New Testament witnesses has become problematic as a result of the findings of historical-critical exegesis. This method has called attention to the fact that the New Testament tradition regarding the last supper is not only polymorphic in itself—something certainly well known to Thomas—but it is also already partially colored by the liturgical praxis of the early Christian celebration of the Lord's supper. The last meal of Jesus, the clearly pluriform praxis of the post-Easter Lord's supper in the congregations,[11] and the shape of the Mass in the Church's liturgy are not simply to be lumped together as one.[12] This growing exegetical awareness has led in part to a radical calling into question of the historical origins of the Eucharistic celebration. Thus, it is held that Jesus' prandial praxis can be interpreted along the lines of a prophetic cultural critique, and the shaping of the post-Easter Lord's supper traces back to the influence of Hellenistic cult mysteries. The New Testament tradition of the last supper was thus able to be presented as basically a cult legend of a Hellenized Christianity.[13] By way of contrast, it is to be recalled that the characteristic twofold gesture of the last supper account—the breaking and distributing of the bread and the drinking from the cup—cannot be

---

11. See, for example, *Didache* 9, 1–10, 7 (FC 1, ed. W. Schöllgen and W. Geerlings, 120–27); *Apostolic Constitutions*, VIII (SC 320, ed. M. Metzger, 58–60). On the question of the Eucharistic prayers without the account of the institution of the Eucharist, see F. Dünzl, "Herrenmahl ohne Herrenworte?" in *Mehr als Brot und Wein*, ed W. Haunerland, 50–72.

12. See H. B. Meyer, *Eucharistie*, 63–129, as well as the instructive sketch in R. Messner, *Einführung in die Liturgiewissenschaft* (Paderborn: Schöningh, 2001), 153–70.

13. R. Bultmann, *Theologie des Neuen Testaments*, 143–51; W. Marxsen, *Das Abendmahl als christologisches Problem*, 2nd ed. (Gütersloh: Gütersloher Verlagshaus Gerd Mohn, 1965), esp. 17–21. See also the skeptical estimation that the *verba testamenti* stem "in all likelihood from a source other than Jesus" (J. Schröter, *Das Abendmahl. Frühchristliche Deutungen und Impulse für die Gegenwart* [Stuttgart: Katholisches Bibelwerk, 2006], 132f.), as well as the bold thesis that the "intentional organization of a last supper by Jesus" is "a scholarly legend" (P. Fiedler, *Studien zur biblischen Grundlegung des jüdisch-christlichen Verhältnisses* [Stuttgart: Katholisches Bibelwerk, 2001], 22–69, here 57). In contrast, we find already emphasized by H. Merklein, *Überlieferungsgeschichte der Abendmahlstraditionen*, 169: "Whoever traces the tradition of the last supper back to the community has to explain why the community itself traced it back to Jesus, and indeed especially to his last supper."

explained from the perspective of Hellenistic cult mysteries.[14] It fits rather into the rite of Jewish feasts. This holds above all for the element that gave the Eucharist its name: the blessing (*berakha*; Mk 14:22: εὐλογήσας; 1 Cor 11:24, Lk 22:17 and 19: εὐχαριστήσας) over the bread and wine.

The New Testament witness of Jesus' last supper is not interested in offering a complete list of what took place. Unlike a procedural protocol, which tries to state meticulously and faithfully every incident, the New Testament account directs attention from the outset to the event of the Eucharistic twofold action and the eschatological outlook connected thereto. Thus, the concentration on the *verba testamenti*, which characterizes not only the Eucharistic theology of Aquinas, has a certain hold on the last supper *paradosis* found in the New Testament. Remarks concerning the place or the atmosphere of the room are omitted, just as indications of what was eaten besides bread and wine or what Jesus and his disciples discussed during the meal are also left out. Not everything is memorialized by the accounts—only what is theologically decisive. Thus the scriptural tradition regarding Jesus' last meal is based on targeted thematic selection and mnemonic accentuation.[15]

Every account of the last supper agrees that Jesus celebrated this last meal with his disciples on the night before his death; they all stress that it was a feast with bread and wine; they all place the twofold Eucharistic gesture at the center. Jesus did not simply adopt the predetermined rites of the Jewish feast—it is debated whether it was a Passover meal or not[16]—but instead transformed it through particular words and gestures. On account of these divergences from Jewish meal practices, Jesus' last meal has been described as being without analogy, indeed as a phenomenon *sui generis*.[17] Because the pro-existent stance of Jesus' life distills itself in the gestures of

---

14. See H. Schürmann, *Jesus—Gestalt und Geheimnis. Gesammelte Beiträge*, ed. K. Scholtissek (Paderborn: Bonifatius, 1994), 246: "Research in the history of religion regarding the mystery cults knows of cult meals, but it has not produced any more pertinent analogies that can explain the coming to be of this twofold Eucharistic action."

15. See Th. Söding, "'Tut dies zu meinem Gedächtnis!'" 16f.

16. On the difference of chronological indications between the synoptics (see Mk 14:12, 14, 16 and parallels: Jesus died on the feast of Passover) and Jn 19:14, 41 (Jesus died on the "day of preparation" for Passover), see Th. Söding, "Biblische Chronologie," *LThK* 2, 3rd ed. (1994): 419–20, who gives precedence to the Johannine chronology for tradition-historical reasons (Mk 14:12–16 is relatively young) and historical considerations (a crucifixion on Passover is hard to imagine under the governorship of Pontius Pilate). For another view, see J. Jeremias, *Die Abendmahlsworte Jesu*, 3rd ed. (Göttingen: Vandenhoeck & Ruprecht, 1960), who interprets the last supper as a Passover meal. Likewise P. Stuhlmacher, *Biblische Theologie des Neuen Testaments*, vol. 1: *Grundlegung: Von Jesus zu Paulus* (Göttingen: Vandenhoeck & Ruprecht, 1992), 133, and most recently L. Lies, *Mysterium fidei* (Würzburg: Echter, 2005), 11–14.

17. W. Kasper, *Das Sakrament der Einheit*, 84; H. Schürmann, *Gestalt und Geheimnis*, 251. See J. Gnilka, *Jesus von Nazareth. Botschaft und Geschichte* (Freiburg: Herder, 1990), 286: "Interpretive words, spoken to gifts brought forward, can count as something new."

offering and the interpretive words, they can be interpreted as a *summa* of his proclamation and an anticipatory construal of his death.

It is well known that diverse traditions and accentuations are reflected in the last supper *paradosis* of the New Testament and that Jesus' very own words can only be hypothetically reconstructed.[18] Still, all the New Testament witnesses converge, first, in making the point that the first part of the interpretive words over the bread run "τοῦτό ἐστιν τὸ σῶμά μου—This is my body" (see Mk 14:22; Mt 26:6; Lk 22:19; 1 Cor 11:24). A forced hermeneutic of suspicion would claim that, because of the discontinuity between pre-Easter event and post-Easter testimony, one cannot conclude to a self-utterance of the historical Jesus; the extensive agreement of textual witnesses, however, seems to me ample indication that an authentic statement of Jesus is presented here. If one takes in addition the criterion of the inner correspondence of gesture and interpretive word, then Jesus' speech act can be interpreted in the sense of a *personal self-identification*. For against the background of biblical tradition, "body" (σῶμα) does not mean some aspect of man to be anthropologically distinguished from "spirit" or "soul," but rather man's wholeness; it refers in this way to the identity of a person as constituted in a bodily way and thus standing under the mark of creatureliness. The interpretive word "This is my body," which is referred to the bread blessed, broken, and distributed to the disciples for eating, can therefore be paraphrased: "This is my very self!"[19] Or indeed: "This is my very self as a historical person in my relation to God and men."[20]

At this point, it is familiar to all that the addition "τὸ ὑπὲρ ὑμῶν [διδόμενον]—which is [given] for you" is found only in the Pauline-Lucan *paradosis* of the last supper;[21] it is not found in the Markan-Matthean (see

---

18. As is well known, the estimation of exegetes on whether the wording of the *verba testamenti* can be reconstructed from the tradition history diverges considerably. The skeptical conception that such a reconstruction is finally impossible tracks the viewpoint of R. Bultmann (see *Die Geschichte der synoptischen Tradition*, 8th ed. [Göttingen: Vandenhoeck & Ruprecht, 1970], 258ff.) and is advocated by not a few exegetes. A contrasting and more optimistic appraisal has been put forward by, above all, R. Pesch, *Das Abendmahl und Jesu Todesverständnis* (Freiburg: Herder, 1978), and more cautiously also by J. Gnilka, *Jesus von Nazareth. Botschaft und Geschichte* (Freiburg: Herder, 1990), 280–90, and by P. Stuhlmacher, *Biblische Theologie des Neuen Testaments I* (Göttingen: Vandenhoeck & Ruprecht, 1992). A middle position is occupied by H. Schürmann, *Jesus—Gestalt und Geheimnis*, esp. 241–65, as well as by Th. Söding, "Das Mahl des Herrn. Zur Gestalt und Theologie der ältesten nachösterlichen Tradition," in *Vorgeschmack*, ed. B. J. Hilberath and D. Sattler (Mainz: Matthias-Grünewald, 1995), 134–64.

19. R. Pesch, *Das Markusevangelium*, vol. 2 (Freiburg: Herder, 1977), 357.

20. As Th. Söding adds for precision: idem, "Das Mahl des Herrn," 149.

21. Lk 22:19 reads: "τὸ ὑπὲρ ὑμῶν διδόμενον," while in 1 Cor 11:24 we have only "τὸ ὑπὲρ ὑμῶν." Contrary to the assessment that "in Hebrew, or Aramaic, only one construction with the participle [is] possible" (H. Merklein, *Erwägungen zur Überlieferungsgeschiche der neutestamentlichen Abendmahlstraditionen*, 166), O. Hofius has made clear by mobilizing numerous examples from Hebrew, Aramaic, and Syriac, that the expression without a participle "τὸ ὑπὲρ ὑμῶν" can indeed be translated back into a Semitic language, which

Mk 14:22; Mt 26:26). In view of the divergence of New Testament textual witnesses, which hamper an historical reconstruction of the *ipsissima verba* of Jesus at the last supper, Heinz Schürmann called attention to the symbolic actions, the *ipsissima facta*, to interpret them in connection with the whole kingdom-of-God proclamation and the *ipsisima intentio* of Jesus.[22] If one analyzes more exactly the particular segments of the rite concerning the bread, the sense of the symbolic action emerges more clearly. First, it is a gesture of *giving*: the bread with which Jesus identifies himself is given to the disciples, which on the eve of his death implies that his upcoming death will benefit them without the "gift of his death"[23] already being more precisely determined by soteriological interpretation. When Jesus *blesses* the bread, he makes clear that the bread is referred back to God as the giver of every gift. God, the heavenly father, is the one who satisfies the petition for our daily bread (see Mt 6:11); he is also the one to whom thanks and praise are rendered for this gift. Through the blessing, in which, so to speak, the katabatic gift of God and the anabatic thanks of men run together, Jesus places the bread explicitly into the sphere of the holy, which can already be experienced through the advent of God's reign (see Mk 1:15). In the context of the meal, the fraction rite—the rite of *breaking*—prepares first of all for the sharing of bread; at the same time and in view of the impending death, it can be interpreted no less as a "hidden hint pointing to the violence of his death."[24] Finally, Jesus *distributes* the broken bread, with which he identifies himself, to the disciples, so that *all* of them eat it. This indicates that he desires to give them a share in the blessing brought about by his death. He establishes a community that not only outlasts death (see Mk 14:25) but is also co-constituted by this death. "The bread that Jesus extended to his table fellows is he himself, who gifted them with new life before God through his sacrificial death and prepared for them a place at the heavenly table."[25] Accordingly, the meal is an anticipation of the eschatological *communio* in the kingdom of God—a motif that not only is prefigured in the Old Testa-

---

could speak for the originality of the Pauline tradition. See O. Hofius, "τὸ σῶμα τὸ ὑπὲρ ὑμῶν 1 Kor 11, 24," *ZNW* 80 (1989): 80–88.

22. H. Schürmann, *Jesus—Gestalt und Geheimnis*. See also M. Theobald, *Das Herrenmahl*, 262, who begins with the "criterion of inner congruence between gesture and interpretive word."

23. Th. Söding, "'Tut dies zu meinem Gedächtnis!'": "As his life is gift, so even more is his death gift; that Jesus is the giving one shows itself definitively in his death."

24. Th. Söding, "Das Mahl des Herrn," 150. The presentation is different in Schürmann, who points to the fact that neither the usual rite of breaking bread nor the pouring out of the pitcher into the cup undergoes an interpretation as a sign. He also dismisses referring the *broken bread* to the wounded body of Jesus in death or interpreting the *red color* (nowhere mentioned) of the wine as an image of blood.

25. P. Stuhlmacher, *Biblische Theologie des Neuen Testamentes*, vol. 1, 136.

ment (see Is 25:6–8) but also occupies a special place in Jesus' proclamation (see Lk 13:29; Mt 8:11; Lk 14:34–35; Mt 22:1–14).

Something analogous can be said of the rite surrounding the cup. The usual practice has the father of the house taking his cup of wine after the meal, raising it, speaking the prayer of thanks (*birkat ha-mazon*) in the name of all, and then drinking from his own cup as a sign that now all the others sharing in the meal should drink from their own cups. Departing from this Jewish meal praxis, Jesus lets *all* present drink from *one* cup (see Mk 14:23; Lk 22:17). Precisely through this gesture is the meaning of his death as mediating salvation and establishing community emphasized. "According to early Jewish expectations, the eschatological meal of the people on Mount Zion would have the whole of Israel drinking from one single, large 'cup of salvation' (Ps 116:13), over which David speaks praise to God's glory (see Bill IV/2, 1163–1165). *Jesus had the Twelve drink from the one cup, which he handed to them, obviously in anticipation of this common drinking in the* βασιλεία. This fits together very well with the preview of the messianic meal on Zion in Mk 14:15/Lk 22:15f."[26] The corresponding interpretive words are certainly different in the two strands of tradition, but they agree in joining the *covenant motif* with the *blood motif*. In Mark's version, the words over the cup read: "τοῦτό ἐστιν τὸ αἷμά μου τῆς διαθήκης τὸ ἐκχυννόμενον ὑπὲρ πολλῶν—This is my blood of the covenant, which is poured out for many" (Mk 14:24, and slightly varying at Mt 26:28). As with the words spoken over the bread, what takes place first is a *personal self-identification* of Jesus with the cup. Once again, blood does not signify the biological, organic substance but rather stands for life. Through the explicit mention of blood, these words over the cup are certainly more strongly colored by the theology of the Passion.[27] This coloration can be conveyed by the phrase, "This is I myself in my death." Jesus gives his table fellows the utmost of what he has to give: his life, and through this very self-gift he establishes God's covenant with men. The phrase "blood of the covenant" refers back to the making of the covenant on Sinai (see Ex 24:3–8), where the people were consecrated as a covenant people by the sprinkling of blood.

---

26. Ibid., 135.

27. The symbolic content of the wine has multiple meanings when viewed against the background of biblical tradition: on the one hand, it stands for God's angry judgment (see Ps 75:9; Jer 25:15f.; Hab 2:16; Rev 14:8 and 18:3); on the other hand, it symbolizes not only the good gifts of God's creation (see Ps 104:14f; Berakhot 6:1), but also the overflowing abundance of blessings in the time of salvation (see Gen 49:11; Joel 4:18; Is 25:6; Mk 14:25; Jn 2:1–11). To the extent that, by his death, Jesus representatively takes on himself God's judgment concerning sin, his death accrues to the benefit of man. At the same time, the eschatological dimension of his symbolic act is expressed in the prophecy of his death: "I will never again drink of the fruit of the vine until that day when I drink it anew in the kingdom of God" (Mk 14:25).

In the strand of tradition coming from Paul and Luke, the words spoken over the cup (1 Cor 11:25; Lk 22:20) refer to the "new covenant," as promised in Jeremiah 31:31. This talk of a new covenant, which is singular in the Old Testament, aims not only at a renewal and universal expansion of the covenant at Sinai but also at a truly new and definitive establishment of God, by which he founds communion with himself. According to the Pauline-Lucan version of the consecratory words over the cup, this new covenant is instituted by the bloody death on the cross at Golgotha. The communal participation in the blood of Christ at the Lord's supper constitutes the new covenant people of God. For the blood is poured out for the many.[28] Through the locution "poured out for many," Jesus' impending death is placed before the background of the fourth song of the suffering servant (Is 53:10–12) and interpreted in terms of a theology of atonement: "God brings about atonement by making the suffering, which another takes upon himself, and its merits accrue to those who caused the suffering."[29]

Even if the much-debated question of which version of the words over the cup is more original must remain undecided here, both symbolic actions still show with sufficient clarity that Jesus interpreted his death as a free self-gift (*traditio*) and ascribed to it a soteriological quality, although still undetermined. Exegetical research is undecided whether a pre-Easter Jesus *could have* attributed a salvific meaning to his death at all; and if yes, whether he also factually *did* just that.[30] The objection has been voiced that with his message of the kingdom of God at hand, Jesus proclaimed an unconditional act of salvation and therefore he could not yet—shortly before his death—connect this salvation with the condition of his representative death.[31] Without going any further into the complex debate, this view can be opposed with the proposition that, faced with the looming failure of his mission, Jesus would certainly have been able to commit his life, through death, as a final means, so that by suffering a martyr's death he could call down God's eschatological salvation in a representative and atoning way— and now certainly no longer for Israel alone but also for the Gentiles.[32] For, after his collision with the Sadducee temple authorities at the latest, Jesus could have come to terms with the possibility of a violent end. If he wanted nevertheless to hold to the validity of his message (see Mt 14:25), he must

---

28. According to J. Jeremias, πολλοί is a Semitism that means "many" in the sense of "all" (see Jeremias, Art. "πολλοί," in *ThWNT* 6 [1959]: 536–45).
29. Th. Söding, "Das Mahl des Herrn," 155.
30. See H. Schürmann, "Jesu Tod als Heilstod im Kontext seiner Basileia-Verkündigung," in his *Jesus—Gestalt und Geheimnis*, 168.
31. See P. Fiedler, *Jesus und die Sünder* (Frankfurt/M.-Bern: Lang Peter, 1976), 277–81.
32. See Schürmann, *Gestalt und Geheimnis*, 259.

have then somehow reasonably integrated his death into the event of God's inbreaking kingdom. Jesus' proclamation of God's reign definitely included the proclamation of eschatological salvation for Israel. Against this background, Helmut Merklein asks:

> Can the proclamation of God's eschatological act of salvation still be maintained if this obviously proved itself to be ineffectual for Israel? Now, it is certainly conceivable that Jesus left the solution to this problem entirely to God in a formal act of trust. Had Jesus also reflected on the substantial discrepancy between his message and his death, then in fact the representative death of the suffering servant would have given a congenial model for overcoming the critical situation. With recourse to Isaiah 53, Jesus could have understood his death as expiation for the "many," that is, as atonement for Israel. Following an interpretation of this sort, it can be stated as theologically certain that even the (majority) rejection of Israel cannot call into question the efficacy of God's salvific action proclaimed by Jesus. Even with respect to the ones rejecting, God's action remains efficacious to a greater degree, in that it causes the death of the eschatological messenger to become an act of atonement. Understood in this way, Jesus' atoning death does not present an additional condition of salvation. It appears rather as a consequence of that eschatological act of salvation toward Israel, which Jesus proclaimed with his announcement of the kingdom of God.[33]

Jesus sustains his pro-existent bearing even to the point of death; his symbolic actions at the last supper suggest that he implicitly attributed a salvific meaning to his death. In addition to the continuity of signs within the discontinuity of times, the soteriology inscribed in the interpretive words is made more explicit post-Easter: "If the interpretation of Jesus' death as atoning surrender to God for men had absolutely no support in the life and death of Jesus himself, then the center of Christian faith moves dangerously close to mythology and ideology. Then by means of later preaching, God would have given a meaning to Jesus' death about which Jesus himself had no idea."[34]

---

33. H. Merklein, "Der Sühnetod Jesu nach dem Zeugnis des Neuen Testaments," in *Versöhnung in der jüdischen und in der christlichen Liturgie*, ed. H. Heinz et al. (Freiburg: Herder, 1990), 155–83; 156f. Merklein's argument seems to be unshaken by the reply of P. Fiedler, "'Beim Herrn ist die Huld, bei ihm ist Erlösung in Fülle,'" in *Israel und Kirche heute*, ed. M. Marcus et al. (Freiburg: Herder, 1991), 184–200. See also G. Häfner, "Nach dem Tod Jesu fragen. Brennpunkte der Diskussion aus exegetischer Sicht," in *Wie heute vom Tod Jesu sprechen?* ed. G. Häfner and H. Schmid, 139–90; he—unlike Fiedler—recognizes the atoning interpretation of Jesus' death as a central motif of New Testament tradition and also does not want to devalue, but still wants to dispute, the point that this interpretation can have moments of connection in Jesus' self-conception. If, however, there is in Jesus' self-conception not the faintest clue of this atoning interpretation of his death, and this interpretation should instead be based only on a post-Easter act that attributes this meaning to his death, then both a Pauline theology of the cross and also the ecclesial proclamation move into the vicinity of ideology.

34. W. Kasper, *Jesus, der Christus* (Walter Kasper Gesammelte Schriften 3) (Freiburg-Basel-Vienna: Herder, 2007), 187. Similarly H. U. von Balthasar, "Crucifixus etiam pro nobis," *IKaZ Communio* 9 (1980): 26–35, here 30.

On the other hand, Jesus' death would have been marked as the definitive failure of Jesus and his mission if God himself had not raised his slain witness from the dead. Life, death, and resurrection are therefore—as Thomas Pröpper repeatedly emphasized—to be considered as one interconnected event. "Without Jesus' proclamation, God would not have become manifest as present and unconditionally prevenient love; without his proven readiness unto death, the seriousness and irrevocable determination of this love would not have become apparent; and without his evident resurrection, the reliable fidelity and death-overcoming power of this love would not have become evident; and without all of this, God himself as origin of this love would likewise have not become manifest."[35] The words spoken at the last supper, in which the pro-existent stance of Jesus is distilled in a covenantal way, would have remained nothing but pure rhetoric were it not for the death which made good on them. The words "This is my body, given for you—This is my blood, poured out for you" are ratified on the cross and honored. Conversely, without the interpretive anticipation in the *verba testamenti* and the gestures of self-sharing, Jesus' death would have remained a semantically silent event, hence a brutal act of execution, such as has arisen countless times in man's history of violence. Through Jesus preserving the interpretive anticipation up to the point of death, the destruction of love as performed in the crucifixion becomes a place of the revelation of love *pro nobis*.

The physical absence of Jesus, which is bound up with the topos of his ascension, is the presupposition for his pneumatically qualified presence in the word of proclamation and in the sacraments, above all the Eucharist. "In virtue of the ascension, Christ is not the one absent from the world but the one present in it in a new manner."[36] The Lucan accounts of Christ's ascension (Lk 24:50–53; Act 1:9–11) tell of Jesus' visible disappearance before the eyes of his disciples. Thus, they witness an event through which the one heretofore present becomes sensibly absent, and this can be read as a narrative elaboration of the basic Christological movement that Jesus, humiliated on the cross, is exalted to the right hand of the Father (see Phil 2:6–11). Even if the ascension narratives in their form rely on legends of rapture and thus on the imaginative material of ancient cosmology, with its three-story structure—underworld, earth, heaven—nevertheless, their *theological* content is still to be held on to, that is, that the crucified Jesus enters into the

---

35. Th. Pröpper, *Evangelium und freie Vernunft*, 8.
36. J. Ratzinger, "Himmelfahrt Christi systematisch," *LThK* 5, 2nd ed. (1960): 360–62, here 361. See also H. U. von Balthasar, *Die Abwesenheiten Jesu*, in *Neue Klarstellungen*, 2nd ed. (Einsiedeln: Johannes-Verlag, 1995), 28–36.

reality of the Father. Resurrection and ascension are, theologically speaking, two sides of one event, and the term "heaven" marks Christ's arrival into the reality of everlasting life.[37]

The exaltation of the crucified one, however, is the presupposition for the mission of the Spirit, which establishes a new, pneumatically qualified form of Christ's presence among men. The fact that in the life and person of Jesus Christ, God revealed definitively and unsurpassably that he did not forget men entangled in evil but rather remembered them—this event of salvation continues in the present through the sending of the Spirit. The community of believers is the privileged place, in which is realized the gift of Christ's making himself present in the proclamation of the Word and sacramental symbolic actions (Jn 7:39, 16:7, 20:22; Eph 4:8; Rom 5:5). In the signs of bread and wine, Jesus Christ makes himself present in a pneumatic way, and this is the event so closely considered by Thomas in his Eucharistic theology.

Conversion of Gifts: "Transubstantiation" as the Risen Crucified One Making Himself Pneumatically Present

> ... transmuting the daily bread of experience into the radiant body of everliving life.
>
> James Joyce[38]

> The most beautiful waiting, that for the [Eucharistic] conversion.
>
> Peter Handke[39]

The explanatory model of transubstantiation tries to bring ontological illumination to the conversion of the species of bread and wine into the flesh and blood of Jesus Christ; it does not thereby signify any physical happening, which could be observed using empirical methods. It presupposes a concept of substance that aims at a metaphysical reality. This means: the substantial conversion that takes place in virtue of the divine Word does not refer to the level of sensible things.

From the perspective of Christian faith in creation, the doctrine of transubstantiation can be reformulated today in this way, that the substantial proper reality is withdrawn from the gifts of bread and wine by the consecration, so that they become pure signs of the *personal presence* of

---

37. See W. Kasper, "Christi Himmelfahrt," *IKaZ Communio* 12 (1983): 205–13; idem, *Jesus der Christus* (Freiburg-Basel-Vienna: Herder, 2007), 172–76; J. Ratzinger, "Himmelfahrt Christi systematisch," *LThK* 5, 2nd ed. (1960): 360–62, and H. U. von Balthasar, "Mysterium paschale," *MySal* III/2 (1969): 302–4.

38. J. Joyce, *Dubliners—A Portrait of the Artist as a Young Man* (New York: Penguin Books, 1964), 343.

39. P. Handke, *Gestern unterwegs*, 86.

Jesus Christ. Jesus Christ himself is the one who vouchsafes his nearness. His pneumatic self-presence in the signs of bread and wine results from the performative power of the words spoken by the priest not in his own name but in that of another, *in virtute et persona Christi*—*Hoc est corpus meum, quod pro vobis tradetur.*

The doctrine of transubstantiation finds itself exposed to several inquiries that are not to be ignored.[40] From the perspective of liturgical studies, it is alleged that the fixation on the formula of consecration pushed the whole performance of the Eucharistic prayer into the background. Precisely the anamnetic and epicletic character of the *prex eucharistica* should be more strongly shifted into a central position for a theological interpretation of the Eucharist. The critique of liturgical studies regarding an all-too-strong emphasis on the formula of consecration is representatively illustrated here in a statement by Reinhard Meßner: "The sanctification of the gifts into Christ's body and blood takes place on account of the prayer in its entirety, not through one formula of consecration, whether that be the words of institution ('words of consecration'), as they correspond to the understanding had by medieval and modern scholastic theology, or the epiclesis grasped one-sidedly as a petition for conversion, as sometimes envisioned by the Orthodox."[41] The doctrine that the words of institution are the *forma sacramenti* is certainly not only an "understanding had by medieval and modern scholastic theology" but a proposition defined by the magisterium of the Church (see DH 1321: *Forma huius sacramenti sunt verba Salvatoris, quibus hoc confecit sacramentum*. See also DH 1642), behind which Catholic theology—follow-

---

40. On the hermeneutical appropriation of the doctrine of transubstantiation, see among others K. Rahner, "Die Gegenwart Christi im Sakrament des Herrenmahls" (related primarily to the Council of Trent); J. Ratzinger, "Das Problem der Transsubstantiation und die Frage nach dem Sinn der Eucharistie," *ThQ* 147 (1967): 129–58 (JRGS 11, 271–98); G. Hintzen, *Die neuere Diskussion über die eucharistische Wandlung* (Frankfurt-Munich: Peter Lang Gmbh Internationaler Verlag Der Wissenschaften, 1976); L. Scheffczyk, "Die Frage nach der eucharistischen Wandlung," in *Glaube als Lebensinspiration* (Einsiedeln: Johannes-Verlag, 1980), 347–70; N. Slenczka, *Realpräsenz und Ontologie. Untersuchungen der ontologischen Grundlagen der Transsignifikationslehre* (Göttingen: Vandenhoeck & Ruprecht, 1993); see also G. Hintzen, "Personale Gegenwart des Herrn in der Eucharistie. Zu Notger Slenczkas Buch 'Realpräsenz und Ontologie,'" *Cath* 47 (1993): 210–37.

41. See R. Messner, *Einführung in die Liturgiewissenschaft* (Paderborn: Schöningh, 2001), 199. In relation to this, it may be recalled that it is not only *Jesus Christ's self-gift for us* that is pregnantly articulated in the *verba testamenti*. These words, moreover, may also count as the form of the sacrament, inasmuch as they *signify what they bring about* in an exact way: the conversion of bread and wine into the body and blood of Jesus Christ. Incidentally, Thomas Aquinas rightly pointed out in his linguistic analyses of the *verba testamenti* that the *Hoc est corpus meum* interrupts the narrative flow of the institution account and in a way expresses Christ himself as speaker. In the moment in which the priest acting *in persona Christi* (a further theme Messner calls into question, ibid., 204) recites the *verba testamenti*, he does not speak in his own name or only *in persona ecclesiae*, but rather he claims the performative power of speech had by the exalted Christ. At this point it is not hard to see that there are adequate themes to discuss, both now and in the future, for a critical and constructive exchange between dogmatic and liturgical theology.

ing a word of Karl Rahner—can no longer retreat but from which it can certainly set out. Now, one can gloss over a dogmatic statement as if it did not exist, rather than interpret it. If one quietly bids it goodbye or explains it away as obsolete, a blank space is created—as was shown recently by Michel Foucault's power-critical analyses—a void that then, whether openly or covertly, will be occupied anew. Messner's pointer, that the Eucharistic prayer in its entirety features a power to transform the gifts of bread and wine, could easily be interpreted as a suggestion to substitute for the classical theory of consecration, which incidentally is also reflected in the *Bekenntnisschriften der Evangelisch-Lutherischen Kirche*, when it states: *benedictio fit per recitationem verborum Christi* (ibid., 798). At any rate, the thought-provoking questions of *when*, *how*, and *by what means* the conversion of bread and wine into the body and blood of Christ is accomplished cannot be answered by simply looking to the liturgical and performative context, which remains quite vague. How exactly should the anamnetic and epicletic Eucharistic prayer *as a whole* have a consecratory character? There are definitely segments in the prayer that are not easily recognized as having a semantic connection to the Eucharistic conversion—for example, the intercessions.

A further point of criticism holds that treating the motif of consecration while prescinding from the liturgical context—and this is said to characterize the doctrine of transubstantiation—darkens the prandial and communal character of the Eucharist, which was the original meaning of its institution. The motif of the Eucharist being an act, an *actio*, binding all the faithful with the risen Lord who invites us to table fellowship with him, is thought to be endangered by a static and reified understanding of the Eucharist. When the consecrated host is understood as the place of Jesus Christ's presence and adored as a sort of cultic object, there inevitably takes place a devaluation, if not an entire undermining, of the covenantal commission of Jesus, "Take and eat."

Beyond this, there are reservations pertaining to the concept of *substance*. Since the re-configuring of the medieval concept of substance, the doctrine of transubstantiation elicits without fail misunderstandings and misinterpretations, so that continuing to hold to it appears anachronistic. Not only does the everyday understanding of contemporary man, shaped as it is by the natural sciences, find it problematic to designate bread and wine as substances in an ontological sense. It knows moreover that bread itself presents an artificially produced, biochemical conglomeration.[42] Ad-

---

42. Thomas certainly had the artificial character of bread and wine in view, though he simultaneously takes *substantia panis* as his point of departure. See *S. th.* III, q. 75, a. 6, obj. 1, where bread is spoken of as

SELF-GIFT OF JESUS CHRIST   289

ditionally, substance is identified with quantity and mass; it is largely construed in a materialistic way but not—as was still the case with Thomas Aquinas and scholastic theology generally—as referring to an imperceptible ontological reality.

Finally, *ecumenical* concerns are also brought onto the field. From the Orthodox side, the rightly incriminated "forgetfulness of the Spirit" in the Western theological tradition has led to a renewed awareness of the epiclesis. The disputed question was debated again and again: whether Christ's real presence takes place through the calling down of the Spirit upon the Eucharistic gifts or rather through the ordained priest's reciting the words of institution. The sharpness of the debate can perhaps be dulled if it is taken into consideration that the Spirit called down upon the gifts is none other than the Spirit *of Jesus Christ*, and that the priest does not recite the *verba testamenti* in his own name but claims rather the speech power of the exalted Christ—a power of speech that is, in the final analysis, mediated in a *pneumatic* way.[43]

Also to be taken into consideration is the protest of the reformers, which was directed not only against thoughts of sacrifice but also against the doctrine of transubstantiation. In opposition to the Eucharistic piety of the late Middle Ages, colored as it was in a monophysitic way ("God is in the host"),[44] Calvin emphasized the *humanity of Jesus* and, based on a locally conceptualized *theology of the ascension*, he disputed that Christ could be present everywhere while sitting enthroned at the Father's right hand. Calvin rejected both Luther's doctrine, which held the ubiquity of Jesus' human nature to be the foundation for the real presence, and the Catholic doctrine

---

quoddam artificiale. A little later (ibid., ad 1) we read that the *forma substantialis* of bread arises in virtue of the power of fire, which bakes the material prepared from flour and water. Today, at any rate, one would be able to grasp bread as a conglomeration of "substances" (in the plural) or elementary particles and would instead begin from an anthropologically mediated concept of meaning.

43. Furthermore, it should not be overlooked that the institution narrative in the Roman Canon leads the way with an at least "implicit epiclesis" in the *"quam oblationem."* See *S. th.* III, q. 83, a. 4, where Thomas mentions explicitly that the prayer *"quam oblationem"* precedes the act of consecration. On this point, see already Ambrose, *De sacr.* 4, 21 (FC 3, ed. J. Schmitz, 148f.): "Dicit sacerdos: 'Fac nobis, inquit, hanc oblationem scriptam, rationabilem, acceptabilem, quod est figura corporis et sanguinis domini nostri Iesu Christi. Qui pridie ....'" See also J. A. Jungmann, *Missarum sollemnia. Eine genetische Erklärung der römischen Messe*, vol. 2: *Die Opfermesse*, 5th ed. (Freiburg-Basel-Vienna: Herder, 1965), 235–38, here 238: "The formula presents the transformative petition or—looking at the essence of the matter—the *transformative epiclesis* of the Roman Mass." Referring to this assessment in a critical and historically nuanced way is R. Messner, "Probleme des eucharistischen Hochgebets," in *Erneuern und bewahren. Studien zur Messliturgie*, ed. idem et al. (Innsbruck-Vienna: Tyrolia-Verlag, 1995), 174–201, esp. 185; by means of early textual witnesses, Messner characterizes the *Hanc oblationem* as originally being a petition to accept the sacrifice, which only in the context of the medieval hermeneutic of the canon was reinterpreted as a petition for transformation or epiclesis.

44. The Eucharistic theology of Thomas is free of monophysitic tendencies, since, concerning the doctrine of concomitance, it emphasizes that the *Christus totus* is present in the sacrament according to his humanity and divinity. See *S. th.* III, q. 74, a. 4, as well as q. 76, a. 1.

of a substantial conversion of the Eucharistic gifts. Only through the *Spirit* does the exalted Christ draw up to himself whoever consumes the blessed gifts of bread and wine. This pneumatological dynamic from the bottom up undeniably breaks open a static understanding of the real presence, but it weakens the anchoring of the sacraments "here below" in the midst of the faithful and one-sidedly emphasizes the *transitus* character. What is distinctive is that Calvin sees the unification with Christ similarly at work in the reading of Scripture, in prayer, and in preaching; thus he is no longer able to specify the theological *proprium* of the Eucharistic presence. Adoration of the converted gifts and the Lord believed to be present in them appears to Calvin as problematic when seen in the light of his pneumatic-dynamic understanding of the last supper, which wholly emphasizes the *actio* of the sacramental performance.[45]

Martin Luther, as well, discarded the doctrine of transubstantiation, calling it, in the Smalcald Articles, "the highest sophistry."[46] To be sure, he also held to a substantial presence of Christ under the gifts of bread and wine,[47] in order to conform to the meaning of the *verba testamenti*; still, he connected this presence to the duration of the Eucharistic celebration. Outside the context of the liturgical service, the *usus* becomes *abusus*.[48] Adoration of the consecrated host in a monstrance, tabernacle, or a Corpus Christi procession are all suspected of being idolatrous: *Non ideo instituit sacramentum, ut adoretur, sed ut vesceremur*.[49] The rejection of transubstan-

---

45. J. Ratzinger, "Das Problem der Transsubstantiation," 136f. (*JRGS* II, 271–98, 277f.), makes out four guiding tendencies in the Eucharistic teaching of Calvin: (1) a radical *not-here* of the Lord is opposed to the undialectical *here* (in the tabernacle, in the monstrance) by the emphasis on an ascension theology; (2) the medieval understanding of the Eucharist—which had become static and for which the exposition of the consecrated host, viewing, and adoration were central marks—is replaced with a radically dynamicized understanding that centers around the assumption that man is lifted up toward Christ through the *actio sacramentalis*; (3) the emphasis on Jesus' humanity seeks to correct a nearly monophysitic tendency of medieval Eucharistic doctrine, which reaches a certain intensification in Luther's doctrine of ubiquity; (4) opposing the undialectical, localized adoration piety to adoration as elevating the heart (*sursum cor*). Notwithstanding the differences pertaining to the explanatory models of real presence, in the present ecumenical dialogue the point of departure is the fundamental consensus: that Jesus Christ gives his presence in the signs of bread and wine in the celebration of the Lord's supper.

46. See *Die Bekenntnisschriften der evangelisch-lutherischen Kirche*, 12th ed. (Göttingen: Vandenhoeck & Ruprecht, 1998), 452. In the Formula of Concord, it is dismissed as popish without further argument; in the *Solida Declaratio*, it is rejected only in passing (ibid., 977 and 983, respectively).

47. It is well known that Luther radicalized Ockham's doctrine of multivoli-presence, according to which Christ is indeed not omnipresent but still can become present at all places insofar as God wills it, transforming it to the doctrine of Christ's ubiquity, which is derived from the communication of idioms. On this point, see P. Hünermann, *Jesus Christus—Gottes Wort in der Zeit. Eine systematische Christologie* (Münster: Aschendorff, 1994), 223–52.

48. The term *usus* cannot be restricted only to the moment of reception, according to Luther; rather, it signifies the whole liturgical process and not the *sola manducatio quae ore fit* (*Solida declaratio* VII, 126).

49. Weimar Edition II, 449.

tiation in Luther feeds, first, on reservations about the conceptual acrobatics of late Scholasticism, which lost sight of the biblical foundations; second, it results from a criticism of the visual piety at the time, which was theologically legitimated to a certain extent by the explanatory model of transubstantiation. In the final analysis, Luther's reservation about the notion of transubstantiation is also philosophically motivated and is derived from that late medieval re-configuration of the concept of substance, which led to an identification of substance and quantity—a development that took on its own dynamic in modernity and was never to be slowed.[50]

Here is not the place to go into these reservations in a detailed way and address them with the requisite nuance. Instead, what will be attempted is to set up a constructive connection between the motif of *Jesus Christ's making himself present in a pneumatic way* in the gifts of bread and wine, and the foundational concerns of transubstantiation, as worked out by Thomas Aquinas.

First of all, let it be acknowledged that the doctrine of transubstantiation seeks to formulate a fact of faith—faith in the real presence of Jesus Christ—in *philosophical* terminology. Therefore, in view of contemporary misunderstandings stemming from the semantics of everyday speech, it is important to stress that the notion of substance in Thomas Aquinas is not a physicalistic or even materialistic concept, but an ontological one.[51] Whereas the concept of substance in classical physics aims at the last indivisible units as bearers of material reality, Thomas's ontology emphasizes that the *quantitas dimensiva* belongs to the category of accidents. The category of substance designates, in contrast, the self-standing of a being, not the empirical way of appearing or the spatial extension of a thing.[52] The substantial conversion that takes place in the Eucharist *cannot* therefore present a physically measurable or sensibly perceptible phenomenon. Still, by the time of the late Middle Ages the metaphysical concept of substance finds itself transformed—a development that leads definitively in Descartes to an identification of *substantia* and *quantitas* or *materia*.[53] To

---

50. See the studies of E. Iserloh, *Die Eucharistie in der Darstellung des Johannes Eck* (Münster: Aschendorff, 1950); idem, *Der Kampf um die Messe in den ersten Jahren der Auseinandersetzung mit Luther* (Münster: Aschendorff, 1952); idem, *Gnade und Eucharistie in der philosophischen Theologie des Wilhelm von Ockham* (Wiesbaden: Verlag Phillip von Zabern in Wissenschaftliche Buchgesellschaft, 1956).

51. S. th. III, q. 76, a. 5: "Dicendum est quod ... corpus Christi non est in hoc sacramento secundum proprium modum quantitatis dimensivae, sed magis secundum modum substantiae.... Unde nullo modo corpus Christi est in hoc sacramento localiter."

52. The shift in understanding of reality that takes place between the metaphysics of the high Middle Ages and the physics of the modern era is sketched in Ratzinger, "Das Problem der Transsubstantiation," 147.

53. See R. Descartes, who makes the statement "that the quantity of matter ... is no more distinct from its substance than number from the numbered things, and that its extension ... is not as an accident but as

project this spatially understood or even materialistic concept of substance back onto the thought of Thomas would thus be anachronistic and would miss the genuine meaning of his theory of transubstantiation.

Thomas emphasized that the real presence of Christ's body and blood in the sacrament of the Eucharist does not suffer to be grasped by either the senses or reason (*neque sensu neque intellectu*).[54] This empirical verification deficit is also underlined by contemporary theologians. Thus, for example, Walter Kasper writes: "All that one can feel, see, and taste externally is bread and wine; but by faith in Jesus' word we know that by the work of the Holy Spirit the actual reality withdrawn from our senses (which the Middle Ages designated as substance) is no longer bread and wine but the body and blood of Christ. This means, in biblical terms: Jesus Christ in his self-gift for us."[55] The substantial conversion, which the Eucharistic theology of High Scholasticism used to explain Christ's real presence, does not touch the sphere of what is sensibly perceptible; it would therefore amount to an absurd blurring of levels of reality if one wanted to prove "transubstantiation" through a microphysical investigation.

Unlike scientific positivism, which reduces reality to what appears to the senses, faith in God rests on the fact that there is a trans-empirical reality. This assertion of a being on the far side of or behind the appearances includes the decision for an *ontological dimension* of reality that is not encountered by the natural sciences such as chemistry and physics. If these sciences were to advocate the thesis that reality is limited to what is empirically perceptible and experimentally verifiable, they would become a reductionistic ideology that would no longer perceive itself empirically, nor would it be experimentally verifiable. In contrast, theology, which as speech about God is always simultaneously speech about the world as his creation, includes the option for an ontology, however specified.[56] For this reason,

---

its true form and its essence." See idem, *Oeuvres*, ed. Ch. Adam and P. Tannery, vol. II (Paris: Cerf, 1909), 33–36, here 36: "Mais ils ne doivent pas aussi trouver estrange, si je supose que la quantité de la matiere que j'ay décrite, ne differe non plus de sa substance, que le nombre fait des choses nombrées; & si je concois son estendue, ou la proprieté qu'elle a d'occuper de l'espace, non point comme un accident, mais comme sa vraye Forme & son Essence."

54. On this point, see the statement that the body of Christ under this sacrament cannot be seen with bodily eyes, for the body of Christ is in this sacrament *per modum substantiae*. "Substantia non est visibilis oculo corporali" (*S. th.* III, q. 76, a. 7).

55. W. Kasper, *Sakrament der Einheit. Eucharistie und Kirche* (Freiburg: Herder, 2004), 49. See also J. Ratzinger, "Das Problem der Transsubstantiation," 150: "Considered physically and chemically, there is simply nothing that takes place in the gifts—not even somewhere in the realm of the microscopic; they are, when viewed physically and chemically, exactly the same after the consecration as before it"—which in Eucharistic theology does not mean that they remain bread and wine.

56. A theology that receives approvingly philosophical concepts that radically critique ontology is no longer able to share in this option. On this topic, see also the challenge of John Paul II, *Fides et Ratio* (1998),

theological reasoning cannot conclude from the fact that nothing happens physically and chemically that nothing at all takes place or can take place.

Thomas Aquinas worked out the doctrine of transubstantiation in reliance on Aristotelian hylomorphism. In order to preserve the biblical meaning of the words of institution, Thomas modified the theory so as to speak of a permanence of subject-less accidents.[57] For the thought of Aristotle—and Thomas follows him here—it is certainly foundational that every being is composed of form and matter, and this encompasses both natural philosophy and metaphysics.[58] Vis-à-vis this Aristotelian conception, if one determines anew the notion of substance from the *viewpoint of Christian faith in creation*, then there emerge—as Joseph Ratzinger already asserted in 1965—two realms of created substance: first, a *general* notion of substance, which expresses that the whole of created being, although it is being from God and out of God, nevertheless subsists at the same time independently; thus, in a certain sense it is being from itself.[59] To be distinguished from this is a second, *more specific* meaning of substance, which designates the self-realization of independent being and is applicable to beings endowed with spirit, or persons. This distinction makes it possible to understand transubstantiation as a process in which bread and wine, belonging to the realm of created being, are re-configured and become signs of the personal presence of Jesus Christ.

At first, bread and wine take part in the general sort of substantiality belonging to every creaturely being—as contrasted with divine being. As Jesus departed from his disciples, it was no accident that he selected bread and wine,[60] food necessary for life and a drink to cheer the hearts of men, as signs for his presence. In the Eucharistic liturgy, each time the priest performs the speech act in which Jesus Christ identified himself with these gifts, a transformation of reality comes to pass. Bread and wine become the body and blood of Jesus Christ. Transubstantiation signifies here "that these things lose their creaturely self-sufficiency, that they stop standing simply in themselves, in the way attributed to creatures, and that

---

§83: "There is need for a philosophy of *genuinely metaphysical* range, capable, that is, of transcending empirical data in order to attain something absolute, ultimate and foundational in its search for truth." And further: "The word of God refers constantly to things which transcend human experience and even human thought; but this 'mystery' could not be revealed, nor could theology render it in some way intelligible, were human knowledge limited strictly to the world of sense experience."

57. See *S. th.* III, q. 75, a. 5; q. 77.

58. See C. von Bormann, W. Franzen, A. Krapiec, and L. Oeing-Hanhoff, "Form und Materie," *HWPh* 2 (1972): 977–1030, here 999–1007.

59. Herein lies the antimonistic payoff of the Christian concept of creation.

60. Strictly speaking, bread and wine are gifts of creation, which are transformed by certain human cultural techniques—in liturgical parlance, "fruit of the earth and the work of human hands."

they instead become *pure* signs of his presence among us."⁶¹ The sacramental word spoken *in persona Christi* does not effect a transformation that would be describable in physics, but rather a transubstantiation. This means, *things* that earlier stood in and for themselves now stand for something else; more precisely, they now stand for *someone* else, namely, for Jesus Christ. As Thomas Aquinas transforms Aristotelian conceptual resources and teaches a permanence of subject-less accidents, in order to correspond to the semantic content of the *verba testamenti*, so in this interpretive model the loss of substantial self-sufficiency is the presupposition for bread and wine becoming *pure* signs of the exalted Lord, and indeed, as Ratzinger emphasizes, "for Him, through Him, and in Him."⁶²

This addition is decisive for the hermeneutic development of the doctrine of transubstantiation. *First*, it makes clear that *things* belonging to the creaturely realm—bread and wine—become signs of a *person* by the event of conversion, a person who makes himself known precisely through these signs and thus also wants to be known, recognized, assimilated, and welcomed by us (see Rev 3:20). At this point, the pragmatic posture that takes in created substances as objects of the world of experience and utility becomes inadequate. To treat a person as a thing means to withhold from him the appropriate respect and to miss the possibility of encounter. The presence of a *person* demands attentiveness, which likewise calls for the involvement of the whole person, together with his affective dimensions.⁶³ But Jesus Christ is not present in and under the signs of bread and wine because the congregation decrees this change of meaning in a collective act of ascription.⁶⁴ This takes place rather—and this is the second consideration to be noted—"through Him," through his powerful Word, which is spoken by the priest *in persona Christi* and therefore is a *verbum efficax*. With respect to speaking of "pure signs of his presence," it could be alleged that this does not consider what both Thomas Aquinas⁶⁵ and, following him,

---

61. J. Ratzinger, "Das Problem der Transsubstantiation," 152.
62. Ibid.
63. This is already evident in the interpersonal realm: to receive another as a guest means expecting him with anticipatory joy, taking care of preparations, welcoming him, taking time for him, listening to him, trying to do justice to him, etc. That Eucharistic theology should therefore also furnish the *real presence of Jesus Christ* with *affective* connotations is rightly claimed by J.-Y. Lacoste, "Presence and Parousia," in *Postmodern Theology*, ed. G. Ward (Oxford: Blackwell, 2001), 394–98.
64. Such a misunderstanding is at least prone to the original and widely received interpretive suggestion by B. Welte, "Zum Verständnis der Eucharistie," in *Auf der Spur des Ewigen* (Freiburg: Herder, 1965), 459–67. Were the presence of Jesus Christ dependent upon the ascription of meaning by a human collective such as the gathered congregation of believers, then this could also be taken away at any time. The conversion would not affect reality itself but merely the human attitude with respect to reality.
65. See *In IV Sent.*, d. 10, q. 1, a. 1 (n. 12); *S. th.* III, q. 73, a. 1 ad 3: "Haec autem est differentia inter Eucharistiam et alia sacramenta habentia materiam sensibilem, quod Eucharistia continet aliquid sacrum absolute, scilicet ipsum corpus Christi." Also *S. th.* III, q. 75, a. 1 c. and *passim*.

the Council of Trent⁶⁶ emphasized, namely, that Christ himself is *contained* (*contineri*) under the species of bread and wine. For this reason, Ratzinger adds: bread and wine become signs "in Him." The theological point of this determination lies in the fact that it oddly reverses the conception that the consecrated gifts are a sort of "container" for Christ's personal presence or "matter charged with Jesus-energy," an understanding hardly able to be kept free of magical connotations.⁶⁷ But in this interpretive attempt, bread and wine lose their creaturely substantiality by being taken into Christ's personal realm of power and reality, thereby being transformed from the ground up. In this way and only in this way do they contain Christ. Unlike an illustrative symbolism, for which the signs of bread and wine reveal what lies beyond themselves, the interpretation suggested here asserts that the gifts of bread and wine are taken into the exalted Lord's sphere of reality and thereby communicate his being near us [*Bei-uns-Sein*].⁶⁸

From this attempt to develop the doctrine of transubstantiation from the vantage point of creation, and having recourse to personal categories, there emerges the following consequence for the ecumenical issue indicated at the outset: if the declarative intent of Luther's doctrine of consubstantiation consists, among other things, in the physical-chemical status of bread and wine not being altered by the speech act of the *verba testamenti*, there is in this point no difference with the doctrine of transubstantiation. Thus, Karl Rahner remarked: "If someone said: what Christ gives to his apostles is bread and his body, and he understood bread, in a sort of positivistic empiricism, as the tangible reality strictly as such and nothing more, then he would still have said nothing contradicting the Catholic dogma; he would have at most not entirely stated it."⁶⁹ Nevertheless, given the reformulation of the doctrine of transubstantiation sketched here, one could still critically mention that the notion bound up with the doctrine of consubstantiation, that Jesus Christ's substance joins the substance of bread and wine, still levels out the difference between the realms of reality. "The presence of Jesus Christ means something different than the presence of a physical figure and there-

---

66. See DH 1636: "Principio docet sancta Synodus et aperte ac simpliciter profitetur, in almo sanctae Eucharistiae sacramento post panis et vini consecrationem Dominum Iesum Christum verum Deum atque hominem vere, realiter ac substantialiter sub specie illarum rerum sensibilium *contineri*" (emphasis added). See also DH 1641 and 1651.

67. Thus recently a preacher in Freiburg in a homily for Corpus Christi.

68. See A. Gerken, "Die Gegenwart Christi in der Eucharistie," *StZ* 191 (1973): 553–62, here 558.

69. K. Rahner, "Die Gegenwart Christi im Sakrament des Herrenmahls," 371. Continuing, we read: "Only if he says: together with the substance of Christ's body is the 'substance' of bread present, *then* certainly he would have formally contradicted the Catholic dogma and would have also said something about which his experience gives no information and concerning which the Word of Christ does not teach him, but rather teaches him the opposite."

fore does not compete with it."⁷⁰ Furthermore, differences remain in view of the duration of Christ's real presence, a point to which we shall return.

At this point, Christ's sacramental presence in bread and wine can be further deepened. Thomas Aquinas speaks of a presence of Christ *secundum substantiam*.⁷¹ This substantial presence is more precisely determined by his person, by his essential selfhood, into which he integrates things from the creaturely realm in such a way that they become signs of his presence. What is present, however, "is his love, which went through the cross, a love in which he vouchsafes to us himself (his very substance), his 'you' marked by death and resurrection, as a salvific reality."⁷² If one interprets the substantial presence of Christ within the frame of a relational ontology as a presence of his pro-existent selfhood, nearness and distance are no longer understood as categories of space, like a *tangible* existence, but rather as *personal* categories aiming at the intensity and concentration of an encounter.⁷³ One can clarify this with an anthropological phenomenon repeatedly referenced in reflections on the Eucharist:⁷⁴ a man who is spatially near another can stand personally distant at the same time, and conversely a physically absent man can be personally near to another, so that he co-determines the thoughts and feelings of the other. This personal nearness, which is possible despite spatial distance and perhaps grows more intense precisely through this distance, yields an analogy from the realm of human experience. Yet it is to be borne in mind that the communication between persons—independent of the spatial distance that may separate them—cannot permanently waive material signs such as presents, letters, or pictures, which is also connected with the way human existence is bound up with the body.

As the Incarnation of the divine Logos already testifies that God entered into the reality of men, so also the guarantee of his nearness in the

---

70. J. Ratzinger, "Das Problem der Transsubstantiation," 153.

71. See *S. th.* III, q. 76, a. 5.

72. J. Ratzinger, "Das Problem der Transsubstantiation," 156, who emphasizes, against Luther's doctrine of the ubiquity of human nature, that the sacramental presence of the exalted one is not to be understood *secundum modum naturae* but rather *secundum modum personae*. The concentration of his presence depends on the intensity in which he gives himself to be received and in which he is received. It is not the ubiquity of human nature but the personal offer of his nearness that is decisive here. Simultaneously, from this personally understood nearness, Calvin's difficulty becomes apparent, which is, his local restriction of the resurrected Christ's presence to an imaginary heavenly place. "Nowhere does the resurrected one have an assignable, physically limited place. As the resurrected one, he has gone into a new mode of being and participates in God's power, in virtue of which he can give himself to his own, whenever and however he desires" (ibid., 156).

73. On this point, see A. Gerken, "Die Gegenwart Christi in der Eucharistie," 559: "A personal ontology can question further here. On account of the otherness of personal reality vis-à-vis tangible things, it can assert at once the presence and absence of Christ, a certain form of presence, that includes a certain form of absence."

74. See P. Schoonenberg, "Inwieweit ist die Lehre von der Transsubstantiation historisch bestimmt?" *Conc* 3 (1967): 305–11.

Eucharist testifies that he remains faithful to this self-binding to earthly reality. Nevertheless, the Incarnation, which places the accent on God's going into the reality of men, must be seen together with the cross and resurrection. For, with the entering of the man Jesus into the reality of God, an irreversible *transitus* took place, from death to a life that no longer knows death. It is the exalted Christ, who went through the Passion and now sits at the Father's right hand, who gives his presence in the sacrament of the Eucharist ever anew—a presence certainly not identical to face-to-face vision, the unbounded fullness of which one could designate as the pure presence of the present one. *Within the sacramental presence there remain inscribed moments of absence*; Christ is there and yet hidden. It is a tension that Thomas conceptually marks with his distinction between Christ's presence *in propria specie* and one *in specie sacramenti*; he then expresses this distinction in a poetic way in the hymn *Adoro te devote*.[75] Thus, we can apply to the Eucharistic presence this speaking of the *presence of the absent one*, which intertwines both aspects: "Christ is here and he is still hidden; he is near and still the wholly other, who imparts himself and still is not at man's disposal but rather disposes of us."[76]

To be sure, the question obtrudes, whether the presence of a person through the signs of bread and wine will not, after all, be *reified*, thus leaving the doctrine of transubstantiation to encourage idolizing the consecrated host.[77] Thinking Eucharistic presence without concessions to idolatry will most likely succeed through *thinking of the gift*, which is given inaccessibly. Eucharistic presence is then bound up with the free self-gift of the crucified and risen one. It is not to be understood as an unauthorized and producible permanence, but rather as a new kind of *advent*. Christ's coming in the Eucharist constitutes a presence in the present, which will not be taken away.

If the doctrine of transubstantiation might have encouraged a spirituality reifying the Eucharistic presence, the consecrated host offers at the same time a decisive advantage over the *immediate* consciousness of presence, as

---

75. Adopting the thinking of J. Derrida, J. Hoff inquires into the material representatives of the incarnate Word. If—so he offers for consideration—"the 'true body' of Christ is no longer to be found, can we for the time being orient ourselves only toward his secondary supplements: the 'place holders,' which remind us of this body and call to mind, above all other supplements, *the* supplement that like no other preserves the remembrance of this body—the *corpus Christi*, the *Eucharistic sacrifice*" (idem, *Spiritualität und Sprachverlust. Theologie nach Foucault und Derrida* [Paderborn: Schöningh, 2000], 168). His option, to adopt theologically the primacy, which characterizes Derrida's semiology, of the signifier over the signified, and to place "the question of the meaning of the Eucharist in parentheses," certainly marks a break with hermeneutically formulated theological conceptions, as they evolved after Vatican II.

76. J. Ratzinger, "Das Problem der Transsubstantiation," 158.

77. As already noted, Thomas sees the explanatory model of consubstantiation as exhibiting idolatrous characteristics. See *In IV Sent.*, d. II, q. 1, a. 1 (n. 24): "Esset enim idolatriae occasio, si hostiae veneratio latriae exhiberetur, substantia panis ibi remanente."

Jean-Luc Marion asserted.[78] It exists as "object," that is, it stands outside of a wandering attentiveness, and it *mediates* the relation between consciousness and the Eucharistic presence of Christ. To the extent that the faithful community becomes aware of the "thing," in which the Eucharistic presence is *embodied*, it acquires a consciousness indeed not of itself but of another, the Other *par excellence*. Peter Handke, in his *Lehre von Sainte-Victoire*, once named this Other the *Real of Reals* and thus made it indirectly clear that the sacramental presence of the absent Christ is not a product of human memory performance.[79] Spiritual idolatry, in which collective consciousness "produces" the special presence and thus threatens to become itself an idol, can be avoided by the converted gifts. In any event, the absence of a representing sign does not eliminate idolatry; rather, it places itself in danger of setting up the immediate consciousness of Eucharistic presence as an idol.

Regarding Hegel, who saw the superiority of Protestantism over Catholicism in Eucharistic consciousness without external mediation, we can see—*e contrario*—how real presence, guaranteed by an object transcending consciousness, helps precisely to avoid the highest form of idolatry. In the *Encyclopaedia*, Hegel makes clear that it is "not the nature-element in which the idea of God is embodied, and though nothing of the sort even enters as a factor into its central dogma and sole theme of a God who is known in spirit and truth." Now, what is decisive is the following explanation: "And yet in Catholicism this spirit of all truth is in actuality set in rigid opposition to the self-conscious spirit. And first of all God is in the 'host' presented to religious adoration as an *external thing*. (In the Lutheran Church, on the contrary, the host as such is not at first consecrated, but in the moment of enjoyment, i.e. in the annihilation of its externality, and in the act of faith, i.e. in the free self-certain spirit: only then is it consecrated and exalted to be present God.)"[80] Against Hegel, Marion defends the priority of the con-

---

78. See J.-L. Marion, *God without Being* (Chicago: University of Chicago Press, 1991), esp. ch. 6.
79. See P. Handke, *Die Lehre von Sainte-Victoire* (Frankfurt/M.: Suhrkamp, 1996), 66: "I would never have been able to call myself a believer, the child of old even less than me now: but wasn't there very early on a picture of pictures? ... This picture was a thing, in a particular container, in a great room. The room was the parish church, the thing was the chalice with the white wafer, which are called hosts when consecrated, and its container was the tabernacle, embedded in the altar, to be opened and closed like a revolving door.— This so-called 'Holy of Holies' [*Allerheiligste*] was for me the *Real of Reals* [*Allerwirklichste*]. The real also had its recurring moments: namely, whenever the particles of bread, which became God's body through the words of consecration, together with the chalice were secured in the tabernacle. The tabernacle opened up; the thing that was the chalice, under cloths, was placed into the colorfulness of its fabric grotto, and the tabernacle closed—and now the shining gold luster of the sealed concave vault" (emphasis original).
80. G. F. W. Hegel, *Hegel's Philosophy of Mind*, trans. William Wallace and A. V. Miller (Oxford: Oxford University Press, 1971), 157–58 (§552). A bit earlier, Hegel stated (ibid.): "The ethical life is the divine spirit as indwelling in self-consciousness, as it is actually present in a nation and its individual members. This self-consciousness retiring upon itself out of its empirical actuality and bringing its truth to con-

secrated host's externality—it allows the irreducible exteriority of presence to be perceived, which Christ imparts to us in this object (the host), in that he becomes a sacramental body in it.[81] The doctrine of transubstantiation likewise makes clear the distance between Eucharistic presence and the consciousness of the believing subject. Precisely in this separation between consciousness and the Blessed Sacrament lies the doctrine's strength. Only if the Other, who is here in his concrete sacramental corporality, is distinguished from the believing subject can he arouse the attentiveness and prayer of the latter. The duration of the Eucharistic presence, however, is owing to the gift of the crucified and risen one, an unreserved gift not to be taken back.

Jesus' making himself present in a pneumatic way in the Eucharist is a gift that is not at our disposal. This can be seen clearly in that the priest presides at the celebration of the Eucharist neither on his own authority nor because he was delegated by the congregation for this service. The primacy of Christ over the congregation comes to be expressed in a structural way in the sacrament of Ordination. "Not because one can fulfill certain functions or realizes them de facto and not because one is theologically competent or rhetorically gifted does he lead the congregation, but because he is empowered by the bishop's imposition of hands. Christ is the head of the Church; and that must remain structurally visible."[82] The abiding commissioning by Jesus Christ, which is sealed at Ordination by the episcopal imposition of hands and prayers, enables the priest to act *in persona Christi*, not special proficiencies, talents, or merits.[83] That the priest exercises the role of presider at the Eucharist is therefore "an appropriate expression of the unconditional predetermination of God's love (accomplished in Jesus' story and encountered today through him as the exalted one) and the irrevocable validity of this love in a way totally independent of our worthiness."[84]

---

sciousness has, in its faith and in its conscience, only what it has consciously secured in its spiritual actuality. The two are inseparable."

81. On this point, see F. von Baader, "Etwas zum Nachdenken bei Gelegenheit des Fronleichnamfestes in München," in idem, *Sämtliche Werke*, vol. 7, ed. F. Hoffmann (Aalen: Scientia Verlag, 1963), 241–46, here 245f.: "The God who became and remains man is for these spiritualists only a spirit, that is, a deceased one as ghost and revenant, because they do not believe in him as *nonallant*, as present; they cannot take courage in him. This is what happened to the Apostles (before Pentecost)—to name one, the spiritualistic Thomas, who, à la Kant, separated the thing in itself too sharply from the appearance until Christ himself taught him a tangible and not merely apparent (evident) kind of proof."

82. K.-H. Menke, "Gemeinsames und besonderes Priestertum," *IKaZ Communio* 28 (1999): 330–45, here 338.

83. During the liturgy at Ordination, the gesture of *prostratio* symbolically expresses the inability of the candidate to exercise the priestly charge of Jesus Christ from his own resources. On this point, see J. Ratzinger, *The Spirit of the Liturgy*, trans. John Saward (San Francisco: Ignatius Press, 2000), 188.

84. Th. Pröpper, "Zur vielfältigen Rede von der Gegenwart Gottes und Jesu Christi," *Evangelium und freie Vernunft* (Freiburg: Herder, 2001), 263.

The fact that the priest does not speak the *verba testamenti* in his own name but *in virtute et persona Christi* is moreover a fitting expression of the congregation not being able to give itself the gift of the Eucharist but receiving this gift ever anew in grateful remembrance. In this context, let us recall once more the difference, already presented by Thomas Aquinas, between liturgical ways of speaking. In most of the prayers of the liturgy, the priest speaks in his own name or *in persona ecclesiae*. At the center of the Eucharistic prayer, however, a momentous linguistic-practical change of perspective takes place, when the *narratio* of the institution narrative is interrupted and the priest goes on to speak, "This is *my* body!"[85]—quoting the words spoken by Jesus as he was parting ways with his disciples, words spoken in the mode of personal self-identification. The performative power of this speech act does not result from the priest's own power;[86] rather, it results from the exalted Lord himself as he makes himself pneumatically present, with the priest lending him in this moment his own tongue, as it were. Accordingly, what then follows is the address to the gathered faithful in the second person plural: "Do this in memory of me." But how can we suitably carry out this call to remembrance today? How can the insights brought forth by these theological reflections on the Eucharist be translated into the complexity and confusion of today's world?

---

85. On this point, see R. Sokolowski, *Eucharistic Presence: A Study in the Theology of Disclosure* (Washington, D.C.: The Catholic University of America Press, 1994), 13–21.

86. It seems to me that H. Verweyen does not have this aspect sufficiently in view. At least it appears as if he wants to trace the difference between general and specific priesthood to a difference in experience, which has something to do with the performative power of the words of consecration. "Whoever speaks these words in the I-form ('my body') not thoughtlessly and irresponsibly prattling on testifying to a making present of that body before the gathered congregation, he has an experience different from that of his hearers, however much these also follow along and participate in the making present." The power of words revert to the speaker and he realizes how little he achieves "being the body of Christ" in his own life. Precisely this frightful experience of difference could be interpreted as a "consecration of the person," who is charged with presiding over the Eucharistic celebration. Against the background of this understanding of "consecration in the echo of Jesus' words," Verweyen sees "a solid basis for deliberations on the restructuring of the introduction to the priestly ministry." See idem, *Warum Sakramente?* (Regensburg: Pustet, 2001), 115–16. Verweyen's thoughts for a deepening of priestly spirituality are undeniably stimulating and helpful. From Thomas's perspective, one should nevertheless remark that the theological point of the words of consecration is not to be comprehended only through theoretical reflections on the speech act, for the *virtus consecrativa* lies not only in the words themselves but also in the *potestas* conferred on the priest in his Ordination (on this point, see *S. th.* III, q. 82, a. 1 ad 1). He does not speak in his own name but *in persona Christi*. But he cannot arrogate to himself this linguistic competence; he must first let it be awarded to him before he can become an authorized speaker of Jesus Christ.

12

Eucharistic Passages

Thomas Aquinas "was not only a master of the page but also a master of life."[1] Prayer, scriptural meditation, and daily celebration of the Eucharist provided the form of his spirituality. As a Dominican, priest, and teacher at the University of Paris, he faced an enormous workload; despite this, he cultivated a contemplative lifestyle, which he also did not give up when he had to pass through the streets of Europe in fulfillment of the Order's commission. Even if the first signs of modernity are presaged in this mobility and restlessness—many of Thomas's works remained fragmentary—there exists nevertheless a hermeneutic difference not easily bridged between the medieval life of study and faith, which Thomas knew and practiced both at the university and in the Dominican Order, and the worlds of life and experience in late modernity. This very likely makes it impossible to reconnect directly with the theology and spirituality of Thomas. All the same, the following *Eucharistic passages* presuppose that the decisive impulses of Thomas's Eucharistic theology can be translated across the rifts of time and constructively taken up. *Gift, presence,* and *conversion* are motifs that can shape the contours of a Eucharistic lifestyle even today. The following fragments risk going beyond the characteristic style of the purely academic when they express openly the confessional moment that subterraneously determines (or should determine) every Eucharistic theology. This risk might be justified by the fact that the Eucharistic gifts of bread and wine are indeed not signs for *something* but for *someone*, who in his life and death gave everything he had to give, and who vouchsafes his presence still today, veiled in signs. If, therefore, one wanted to reflect on the Eucharist in a distant and objective way, this epistemological attitude would always miss the "object" in a certain sense. The emphatic cry, "O res mirabilis!" recalls the

---

1. Torrell, *Saint Thomas Aquinas*, xxi (and 95 as well), taking up a distinction made by Meister Eckhart.

hidden presence of the Lord in the Eucharistic gifts. The affective dimension, which finds articulation in Thomas's Eucharistic hymns, shows his personal involvement, reveals the joy and gratitude that are profoundly fitting in response to the Eucharistic self-giving of the crucified and risen one. Theology as speech *about* God (or about the conditions of the possibility of speech about God) is rooted in prayer as speech *with* God. A theology that thinks it has to be detached from the living practice of faith in prayer and liturgy for the sake of an alleged epistemological integrity quickly degenerates to an academic game, which, despite all the intellectual allure, is of hardly any relevance for a hermeneutic development of the faith. Conversely, a spirituality that opposes theological reflection as supposedly dangerous to faith derails into uncontrollable sentimentality and pious kitsch. Against this background, it will be a rewarding task to work on overcoming the diastases between scientific theology and lived spirituality, taking Thomas's systematic and poetic theology of the Eucharist as our starting point. In reference to the Eucharist, this means to inquire into how faith in the gift *par excellence*—Christ's making himself present in bread and wine—can have life-changing power today.

A Loss of the Ability to Be Present

> Nobody running at full speed has either a head or a heart.
> William Butler Yeats[2]

> The question of God in me: "Why are you not here?"
> Peter Handke[3]

A permanent lack of time and the need for arranging our day's agenda in a sovereign manner characterize the contemporary consciousness of time. In the limited episode that the life of the individual presents against the background of the universal time of the cosmos, an in-principle unlimited hunger for experience and information desires to be satisfied. The surplus of possibilities for consumption and entertainment, the accelerated pace of technological development, as well as the abundance of globally networked communication and information—all of this leads to a loss of the ability to be present. "Men *living in the present* are rare; the overwhelming majority meet us in the garment of a general concept of the present that is always in need of an overhaul," notes Botho Strauss[4]—and another poet concerned

---

2. Cited in E. Canetti, *Die Fliegenpein. Aufzeichnungen* (Munich: Carl Hanser, 1992), 93.
3. P. Handke, *Gestern unterwegs*, 400.
4. B. Strauss, *Der Untenstehende auf Zehenspitzen* (Munich: Carl Hanser, 2004), 54.

with increasing perception, attentiveness, and presence, Peter Handke, makes the appeal to himself (and his readers): "Practice the present."[5]

A lifetime is a scarce resource, and what is practically an epidemic of feverish activity defines the attitude toward life in late modern societies—and not only in the western hemisphere. The pace of innovation in the technological and industrial advances is continually on the rise—and whoever wants to find his way in the accelerating lived-in world has to become familiar with the newest thing in each case.[6] But to the ambivalence of accelerating innovation simultaneously belongs an increased half-life. Thus, wanting to keep abreast can be a strenuous undertaking, which is easily accompanied by being constantly overextended. The need to be and remain master of one's time leads at the same time to peculiar dependencies. For supremacy over time can be established only when one secures oneself against its risks—a need for security that can be satisfied only at the cost of limiting the desired space for free time.

In addition, there is the experience that the gap between one's own lifetime and the world's time diverge more and more.[7] "The more that men—following their expulsion from the lived-in world of immediate obviousness—discover the objective world with its incomprehensibly long duration, the more inevitably they discover at the same time that their lifetime is an ultra-short episode, which is limited by death, the relentless border for their vitally and cognitively unlimited appetite for the world."[8] Life is the last chance; therefore it must be optimally spent.[9] More and more should and must be accomplished and experienced, and all in less and less time. One is forced to hurry by the time limit granted to time-deficient man until an inevitable death. At the same time, the automation of industrial production has enabled man to have more time than ever before free of the burden of work. Still, there is never enough time to satisfy the hunger for experience. The more one takes part in, the more one experiences that

---

5. P. Handke, *Mein Jahr in der Niemandsbucht. Ein Märchen aus den neuen Zeiten*, 2nd ed. (Frankfurt am Main: Suhrkamp, 1994), 444. See his *Am Felsfenster morgens (und andere Ortszeiten 1982–1987)* (Munich: Deutschen Taschenbuch Verlag, 2000), 57: "By no means always gifted for the present, I"—"Not that I am incapable of thinking, it sometimes occurs to me, but rather that I am not at-tentive [*an-dächtig*], or de-liberate [*be-dächtig*]" (64)—"What is it to be Christian? Friendly attentiveness" (335).

6. See P. Borscheid, *Das Tempo-Virus. Eine Kulturgeschichte der Beschleunigung* (Frankfurt/M.: Campus, 2004); H. Lübbe, *Im Zug der Zeit. Verkürzter Aufenthalt in der Gegenwart* (Berlin-Heidelberg: Springer, 1992).

7. See H. Blumenberg, *Lebenszeit und Weltzeit* (Frankfurt/M.: Suhrkamp, 1986).

8. See O. Marquard, "Zeit und Endlichkeit," in *Skepsis und Zustimmung. Philosophische Studien* (Stuttgart: Reclam, 1994), 45–58, here 45.

9. See M. Gronemeyer, *Das Leben als letzte Gelegenheit. Sicherheitsbedürfnisse und Zeitknappheit*, 2nd ed. (Darmstadt: Wissenschaftliche Buchgesellschaft, 1996).

one *cannot* take part in everything he *could* take part in, for the choice of one implies the exclusion of the other. The angst of missing out on some crucial thing or not being able to take part in it forms a subterranean feeling of the age. Roving about on the market of possibilities, clicking from one TV channel to another, surfing all over the virtual world of the world wide web—all of this leads easily to the *loss of the ability to be present*.

Certainly, there are counterweights that compensate for the increasing rate of innovation. The development of science and technology, the internal dynamic of economic processes, and the push towards globalization bound up with these are *sui generis* indifferent to traditions and thus threaten to level the distinctive shapes of mature traditions. Never before have so many matters been put to rest and so quickly forgotten. At the same time, however, never before has so much been remembered, archived, and conserved. The "discovery of slowness" (Sten Nadolny), the discourse concerning recollection and remembrance, the constant interest in meditative techniques—these are all signs that people are seeking after antidotes for society's escalating fast pace and "escape velocity."[10] The leveling trend toward cultural amnesia and "a melting of memory" is resisted by the conscious effort to foster continuities.[11] Keeping alive the memory of the unsatisfied demands of the casualties brought about by injustice and terror is also seen and claimed as a moral task. "The faster time accelerates and global capitalism undermines old cultural traditions and institutions, the greater the importance won by cultures of remembering what is lost; these cultures always live in the language and rites of the old religions' symbolic capital."[12]

The believer can hardly pull himself from the wake of this ambivalent experience of time. The need for sovereignty over time along with chronic time scarcity also touches on the world of his everyday life and experience. In both, he might catch sight of secularized versions of a Christian understanding of time. For the fact that with Jesus' death and resurrection, faith already celebrates *within time the transformation of time* establishes a unique sort of sovereignty over time, which the believing subject can only receive in faith as given rather than produce it out of his own strategies for security. At the same time, looking for the impending *end of time* has been inscribed in Christianity from the beginning, something expressed in the cry, nearly silent today, *maranatha*. The Christian understanding of time encompasses two poles: in creation, it knows of an immemorial *beginning of time*. What has become and now is was not always so and did not become what it is of

---

10. See P. Virilio, *Fluchtgeschwindigkeit. Essay*, trans. B. Wilczek (Munich: Carl Hanser, 1996).
11. K. H. Bohrer, *Ekstasen der Zeit. Augenblick, Gegenwart, Erinnerung* (Munich: Carl Hanser, 2003), 20.
12. F. W. Graf, *Die Wiederkehr der Götter. Religion in der modernen Kultur* (Munich: Beck, 2004), 200.

itself: rather, it is due to a Creator, who in the act of creating likewise set up the beginning of time.[13] The other pole is marked by hope for the *consummation of time*: What is will not always continue the way it is, and what is to come will not simply be a lengthening of what is already seen today. Against Nietzsche's talk of a "time without a finale,"[14] faith rests on the *limitation and consummation* of time.[15]

At the same time, it is a distinguishing mark of Christianity's concept of time that the eschatological consummation of time is not a purely futuristic factor but rather is already projected into time with the first advent of Christ. The Creed does not only say that time is limited; it also holds that the omega of history has a *name*, indeed a face, Jesus Christ who, as the one to come, will not be someone other than the one who already came. Therefore, faith knows time as eschatologically qualified by the dawning of God's kingdom; it is a time in which the "already" of fulfillment and the "not yet" of promise are uniquely interwoven so that the promise is already fulfillment within the "not yet" of fulfillment.[16] This structure of the Christian concept of time has its ground in the fact that the time of salvation, contrary to all appearances, has *definitively* begun in the person and history of Jesus Christ,[17] even if it must be acknowledged in seeing the unredeemed side of the world that the universal implementation of this salvation and thus the *consummation* of history is still pending.[18] Jesus Christ already redemptively burst open the empty continuum of chronological time. In him, the future of the βασιλεία is already present. He is known therefore as the middle and fullness of time. Accordingly, the Christian concept of time is not open and evolutive but Christologically contoured.

---

13. This is the abiding insight developed by Augustine in *De civitate Dei*. See *De civitate Dei*, XI, 6: "procul dubio non est mundus factus in tempore, sed cum tempore."

14. See F. Nietzsche, *Die fröhliche Wissenschaft*, in *Kritische Studienausgabe*, vol. 3, ed. G. Colli and M. Montinari, 2nd ed. (Berlin-New York-Munich: Deutschen Taschenbuch Verlag, 1988), 343–651, here 649 [Eng. *The Gay Science*, trans W. A. Kauffman (New York: Vintage Books, 1974), 371 (in the poem "Sils Maria")].

15. J. B. Metz repeatedly made this clear, most impressively in his piece "Gott. Wider den Mythos von der Ewigkeit der Zeit," in *Ende der Zeit? Die Provokation der Rede von Gott?* ed. T. R. Peters and C. Urban (Mainz: Matthias-Grünewald, 1999), 32–49. Still, Metz's notion of limited time is *Christologically* underdetermined. On this see J.-H. Tück, "Bleibende Rückfragen an die Christologie von J. B. Metz," in *Christologie und Theodizee bei Johann Baptist Metz. Ambivalenz der Neuzeit im Licht der Gottesfrage*, 2nd ed. (Paderborn: Schöningh, 2001), 290–302, here 299f.

16. See M. Theunissen, *Negative Theologie der Zeit* (Frankfurt/M.: Suhrkamp, 1991), 321ff.

17. J. B. Metz formulates this with precision: "Speaking of the 'final' and 'definitive' word of God's commitment to humanity in Jesus Christ is itself a statement of time. It forces a logic of limited time; for 'final' and 'irrevocable'—for everyone and everything, for man and the world—can only be predicated within the horizon of limited time" (*Zum Begriff der neuen Politischen Theologie. 1967–1997* [Mainz: Matthias-Grünewald, 1997], 162).

18. See Th. Pröpper, "'Daß nichts uns scheiden kann von Gottes Liebe ...' Ein Beitrag zum Verständnis der 'Endgültigkeit' der Erlösung," in *Evangelium und freie Vernunft*, 40–56.

In the celebration of the real presence of Christ, the sacrament of the Eucharist binds the moment of remembrance with that of expectation.[19] But how is the sacramental presence to be more deeply understood? Is it a result of the memory performance of the believing subject, who, while gratefully remembering and hopefully awaiting, places himself into a relation to salvation history in the course of the liturgy? Or is the liturgy, conversely, the place where God himself enters into a relation with human time, so that the approaching of the eternal leads to a qualification of time, which is withdrawn from the believing subject's sovereign provision? How can both aspects be held together in thought if the experience of real presence is bound up with God remembering man and men recalling God's salvific deeds?[20]

A Eucharistic Consciousness of Time

> Folly, to wander around in times which are not ours
> and to forget the one that does belong to us.
>
> Blaise Pascal[21]

The experience of real presence is indissolubly bound up with a synthesizing consciousness of time, which mediates the dimensions of past and future into the present. If one thinks of Eucharistic real presence exclusively as the event of the eternal breaking into time, as the radical thwarting of a synthesizing consciousness of time, then real presence threatens to evaporate into a transitory "experience of Jesus Christ's nearness," or to a "feeling of passing by,"[22] which no longer has any point of connection in the subject itself. The concern to withdraw the approach of transcendence in the Eucharistic *memoria passionis et resurrectionis Jesu Christi* from the influence of human power and to avoid an idolization of the consecrated gifts is important; "the radical rejection of presentation or representation in favor of an empty point of entry for an ultimately nameless and storyless transcendence is hardly able to convince."[23]

---

19. See H. Hoping, "Gedenken und Erwarten. Zur Zeitstruktur christlicher Liturgie," *LJ* 30 (2000): 180–94.

20. A. Schmemann conceived of the liturgy in a striking way as a communio of reciprocal remembering: God remembers man, and men remember the salvific deeds of God, though human remembering is once more a pneumatic undertaking. See idem, *The Eucharist*, 229–45.

21. B. Pascal, *Über die Religion und über einige andere Gegenstände*, trans. E. Wasmuth (Frankfurt: Insel Verlag, 1987), 93 (Fragment 172). [Translator's note: my translation from the German.]

22. See Th. Freyer, *Sakrament—Transitus—Zeit—Transzendenz. Überlegungen im Vorfeld einer liturgisch-ästhetischen Erschließung und Grundlegung der Sakramente* (Würzburg: Echter, 1995), 15 and 107.

23. Thus the criticism of A. Schilson regarding the transitory concept of time put forward by Th. Freyer. See Schilson, "Sakramententheologie zwischen Bestandsaufnahme und Spurensuche," *LJ* 47 (1997): 99–113, here 108. Earlier, we read: "Of course, it can be asked whether the indication of God's absolute transcendence, gained from Judaism, in the form offered here does not overtake the presence of salvation, hardly

In human consciousness of time, the three modes of time—past, present, and future—are interlaced in a peculiar way.[24] From the deficient forms of this interlacing, we can read off *ex negativo* how important the successful synthesis of time is for the identity of a person and his interaction with other persons in time. Should it come to a pathological isolation of one of the three temporal dimensions, this leads to a striking curtailment of time consciousness and thus simultaneously to a loss of the ability to encounter others in an open and unburdened way. rudely simplified, we can discern three forms of deficiency.

First, if the dimension of the past interferes with the awareness of time in the moment—be it past experiences that are nostalgically conjured up time and again, or traumatic suffering that is continually projected into consciousness, or guilt weighing consciousness down—then one's relation to the present is constrained, attention is bound, and an unburdened encounter with others hardly remains possible. Second, something analogous applies to losing oneself in the future. This too amounts to a peculiar loss of the present, of reality. A person who gushes about utopian projections of another, better world or flees from present challenges into pipe dreams, which have no point of connection in reality—such a one falls prey to the present he wants to escape, all the more wholeheartedly because he no longer uses the potentialities already lying within and does not think to use them for change. But whoever lives in imaginary, ersatz worlds is likewise able to share the present and be responsive to the other only in a limited way.[25] Third, the synthesis of time consciousness fails where one is fixat-

---

of lesser importance, in the sacramental event in favor of an eschatology that evaporates into a utopia; in this way, the complementary and important category of remembrance in the sense of representation is undercut and evacuated.... The aversion, recognizable at every turn and also clearly marked, to a way of thinking oriented toward the logos of theology in favor of a transcendence, or transitus, overcoming the very same ... is hardly able to convince."

24. According to Husserl, the original consciousness of time encompasses a certain horizon of the now. What is just now past is not simply past for consciousness; as what is just now past, it is—like "a comet's tail of retentions"—*present*. Similarly, what is immediately expected is not simply nonexistent for the consciousness, inasmuch as it is not yet, but rather it is *present* as what is encroaching. Accordingly, consciousness of presence does not limit itself to a now-point without extension; rather, according to Husserl, it has a certain extension constituted by the retention of what has just ceased to be and the protention of what is just to come. To be distinguished therefrom is the act of remembrance, which brings back something long past into the present as past—it re-presents. In contrast to retention in awareness, this act of remembrance, which makes present, is called "reproduction." See E. Husserl, *Phenomenology of Inner Time Consciousness*, ed. M. Heidegger, trans. J. S. Churchill (Bloomington: Indiana University Press, 1964). On the aporia of Husserlian time theory, see M. Frank, *Was ist Neostrukturalismus?* (Frankfurt/M.: Suhrkamp, 1983): 318–25.

25. Already at the beginning of modernity, Pascal lucidly called attention to the diverse forms of fleeing from the present. See *Pensées: Thoughts on Religion and other subjects*, trans. William F. Trotter (New York: Washington Square Press, 1965), 54f.: "We do not rest satisfied with the present. We anticipate the future as too slow in coming, as if in order to hasten its course; or we recall the past, to stop its too rapid flight. So imprudent are we that we wander in the times which are not ours, and do not think of the only one which

ed on the moment and the experience of it. In a frantic effort to be up to date, in the restless running after the next event, a forgetfulness of tradition pairs up with a peculiar carelessness regarding what is to come. *Carpe diem*, which is reinterpreted on the sly to be a "consumeristic imperative" of the experiential society,[26] hides only poorly the ultimate hopelessness of an obsessive hunger for an experience prescribed by the moment. For this reason, "the unchecked search for diverting fun and faster gratification [must] perhaps be analyzed much more incisively as the exterior of despair ..., which is rooted in an incongruity of man with himself."[27]

These deficient forms of being conscious of time in life as lived can call attention to how much a successful life depends, first, on past and future not presenting an obstacle to awareness in the present, and second, on the present not taking on characteristics of forgetting both past and future by being addicted to the now. Simultaneously, it is clear that the synthesis of time consciousness must be carried out ever anew, that both past experiences and future concerns must be integrated ever anew into the present, so that conscious living is possible at all.

The Eucharist, in which these dimensions of time are interwoven, not only presupposes the ability to be present, but also helps to balance out our human consciousness of time; indeed, the Eucharist contains therapeutic potentialities that can hinder a pathological isolation of one of time's three dimensions. According to Thomas Aquinas, the Eucharist is first a *signum rememorativum*. It recalls a particular event of the past: the self-gift of Jesus Christ for us even to the point of death, his sacrifice (*sacrificium*). Already for the religious identity of Judaism, the remembrance of the Exodus event, the gift of the Torah, and the revelation at Sinai are all constitutive moments. Here it is decisive that it is not only a matter of a subjective recollection, but also and above all of a remembrance established by God himself of his salvific deeds, which are brought efficaciously into the present.[28] "In every genera-

---

belongs to us; and so idle are we that we dream of those times which are no more, and thoughtlessly overlook that which alone exists. For the present is generally painful to us. We conceal it from our sight, because it troubles us; and if it be delightful to us, we regret to see it pass away. We try to sustain it by the future, and think of arranging matters which are not in our power, for a time which we have no certainty of reaching. Let each one examine his thoughts, and he will find them all occupied with the past and the future. We scarcely even think of the present; and if we think of it, it is only to take light from it to arrange the future. The present is never our end. The past and the present are our means; the future alone is our end. So we never live, but we hope to live; and, as we are always preparing to be happy, it is inevitable we should never be so."

26. See N. Bolz, *Das konsumistische Manifest* (Munich: Wilhelm Fink, 2002).

27. M. Striet, "Gespannte Freude—oder: Wider eine verharmlosende Spiritualität der Klage," *IKaZ Communio* 33 (2004): 317–34, here 319.

28. See S. Wahle, *Gottes-Gedenken. Untersuchungen zum anamnetischen Gehalt christlicher und jüdischer Liturgie* (Innsbruck-Vienna: Tyrolia, 2006), esp. 79–87, here 85: "It is God himself, who as subject of remembering sets up a time-transcending bridge from the primordial events to the present, so that not only the 'primordial generation' but also every believing Jew belongs to the people of the Exodus."

tion, man is required to see himself as if he were the one pulled out of Egypt, for it is written: Because of what the Lord did *for me* when *I* came of Egypt (Ex 13:8)."[29] Thus, in the Christian celebration of the Paschal mystery, it is a matter of a real recollection of the death and resurrection of Jesus Christ, into which the faithful let themselves be taken. But the remembrance of Jesus' saving and redeeming deeds cannot be without consequence for dealing with the burdensome dimensions of the past, such as suffering, guilt, and grief.

Whoever believes that the Eucharist leads into contemporaneity with Christ must not repress *guilt and failure*, which threaten to weigh down the course of his life. Through the sacramental encounter with Christ, that believer is enabled to admit the painful truth about himself because Jesus Christ revealed the merciful love of God in his flesh to the point of identifying himself unconditionally with sinners. "In Jesus Christ, the sinner is able ... to stand with God against himself, because God already placed himself next to him."[30] If he lets himself be forgiven, he will be enabled by Christ to come with the burdens of his own past into the truth. This includes letting himself be defined by Christ in intersubjective conduct as well: "In Jesus Christ, man is also able—and this is the other side of the relation—to stand next to his sinful brother, because in and with Jesus Christ he is able to carry the sin of his brother."[31]

The therapeutic power of the Eucharist helps also in dealing with unhealed *wounds of the past* and unsettled *suffering*. In the Eucharistic *memoria passionis*, the *Christus passus* becomes present, the one who freely took upon himself the utmost and thus knows, from the inside, pain and the powerlessness of the humiliated. Whoever has experienced traumatic injuries at the hands of others and finds himself unable to forget and incapable of forgiving—he it is who, in the Eucharistic *communio*, encounters the crucified and risen one who himself experienced unjust suffering and who unreservedly identified himself with all those suffering in his Passion. Before Christ, the victims of discrimination and violence need not fight for their recognition as victims; Christ knows their suffering and can raise up their injured dignity so that they are strengthened in their subjecthood. Whoever believes and experiences himself embraced and recognized by Christ precisely in his hidden suffering is perhaps able to join Christ in the step of forgiveness. For in Christ he encounters the one sacrificed in violence, who prayed for his debasers while dying and thereby offered an incarnate com-

---

29. See MPes, 10, 5.
30. See P. Hünermann, "'Erlöse uns von dem Bösen.' Theologische Reflexion auf das Böse und die Erlösung vom Bösen," *ThQ* 162 (1982): 317–29, here 325.
31. Ibid.

mentary on the command to love one's enemy. Whoever encounters Christ in the converted gifts is summoned to let his unreconciled glance toward his own harassers and debasers be transformed by Christ. This can be a long, painful process, which leads in the end to a "transubstantiation" of the glance toward his own past.

In addition to guilt and suffering, there is finally *sorrow* over the irretrievability of what is past, which can interfere with and darken the present. Human memory is certainly able to bring past episodes back into consciousness and to call up earlier encounters with others; it cannot, however, bring back to life what has been. *Being present* in memory often makes us that much more painfully aware of the *absence* of what is remembered—thus the nearness of human remembrance to sadness and melancholy. The fleetingness and irretrievability of time, which cannot really be stored in man's limited memory capacity, poses the question whether all life perishes in the end and the memory thereof vanishes. *In the Eucharistic remembrance, we are reminded that the past has a future before it that is not yet manifest.* As the mistreated body of the crucified one became redemptively transformed, so in the Eucharist we receive a participation in a life that no longer knows death. The joy of Easter, which becomes present in the ritual enactment of the Paschal mystery, offers a glimpse of new life. The Eucharist can therefore be a catalyst for dealing with the past in a liberated way.

In this way, however, it leads anew into the *present*. According to Thomas, it is a *signum demonstrativum*, a sentinel for a community that did not constitute itself. It is the exalted Lord, who gathers the faithful around his word and as host invites them to the Eucharistic meal. His word interrupts the many words; it calls the listener out of the manifold dissipation and requires composure and concentration. The Eucharistic gift, in which the *Christus passus* gives himself, wants to be hospitably received not only by each individual but also and above all by the community celebrating his presence. Whoever receives the gift of the Eucharist together with others and takes time for the wholly Other will find that his own time can itself become different. Precisely when everyday life holds difficulties ready and worries entice one to flee the present, at that moment the encounter with Christ can give power and assurance, from which an increased ability to be present grows. *Da robur, da auxilium,* we find in the hymn *Verbum supernum.* Unlike forms of ecstatic religiosity, which elicit a punctiliar breaking out of the present,[32] the Eucharistic gift invites one to follow the incarna-

---

32. See H.-B. Gerl-Falkovitz, "'Esset das Lamm schnell.' Zur Antiekstase im christlichen Gottesdienst," *IKaZ Communio* 22 (1993): 217–23.

tional movement of the giver, which leads more deeply into the present. Thus, the somatic real presence of Christ in the gifts may certainly be underlined, "for the Eucharist stands in the dynamic of embodiment, of Incarnation. In opposition to Gnostic contempt for time and the body, the dynamic of the Eucharist lies in the enfleshing or the realization of love and salvation in the historical hour."[33] It is therefore fitting that receiving the body of Christ translates itself into a bodily presence for others. Here, thanksgiving means not only recognizing the presence of the giver in the gift but also reflecting his legacy and bearing witness through one's own life to the presence of the absent one.

Finally, the Eucharist is—to say it with Thomas—*signum prognosticum* and a pledge of future glory. "Where is the Life we have lost in living?" asks T. S. Eliot in one of his poems.[34] In the face of the background noise of death growing ever louder, one could opt to safeguard one's life, or extend it, or establish a remembrance of one's own name; but instead of this, the Eucharistic *communio* with Christ, the first of those to fall asleep, sets up a calm relation to one's own mortality. As a recollection of the death and resurrection of Jesus Christ, the Eucharist offers nothing less than the promise that the time seemingly lost in the life of each man will one day be found again in the remembrance of God: "All forgotten thoughts rise to the surface, at the other end of the world."[35] The *recherche du temps perdu* will attain its goal, but until then the Eucharist increases the ability to be aware of what is yet to come.

Hidden Presence and Contemplative Adoration

> Christ's Eucharistic Body is really present in the tabernacle even if no one is there to praise his presence. Our welcome is not what provides his presence; it does not confer it. Presence invites my Presence.
>
> Jean-Yves Lacoste[36]

The coming of the eternal into time, which takes place in the Eucharist, is not a punctiliar event in which the end of its duration is already present with its arrival. As Christ does not take back his self-gift, so he also does

---

33. M. Scheuer, "Wie lange noch? Zur Zeitstruktur der Eucharistie," *TThZ* 2 (2002): 106–22, here 112. On the somatophobic tendencies in cyberphilosophy and technognosis, see also: K. Müller, *Endlich unsterblich. Zwischen Körperkult und Cyberworld* (Kevelaer: Butzon & Bercker, 2011).

34. T. S. Eliot, "Choruses from the Rock," in *Collected Poems 1909–1962* (New York: Harcourt Brace Jovanovich, 1963), 147.

35. E. Canetti, *Nachträge aus Hampstead. Aufzeichnungen* (Munich: Carl Hanser, 1994), 50.

36. J.-Y. Lacoste, "Presence and Parousia," in *Postmodern Theology*, ed. G. Ward (Oxford: Blackwell, 2001), 394–98, here 396.

not take back the gift of his presence once it is given. "The Lord comes; this is his act. But it is not followed by an act of departing. We can also say it differently: the celebration of the Eucharist is a true event, a sort of breaking in of God's eternity into time. But it is not followed by a withdrawal of eternity from time, for eternity has definitively joined up with time and is evermore in the condition of blending into time; and time and space have found the means of surpassing their boundaries in Christ's gift 'for us,' 'for all.' ..."[37] As long as the species of bread and wine remain, as long as they do not cease because of *consumptio* or *corruptio*,[38] Christ remains in them.[39]

To linger in contemplative adoration before the Blessed Sacrament is a practice that arose relatively late in the history of spirituality; today it finds itself exposed to diverse questions. The (late) medieval visual piety has been charged with *reifying* the Eucharistic bread; it has been criticized for obfuscating the prandial and communal aspects of the Eucharist through increasing the veneration of the host. Just focusing on the moment of conversion,[40] which was enacted in a conspicuously sensible way through the elevation of the consecrated gifts and made acoustically perceptible even *extra muros ecclesiae* by the ringing of the Church bells was said to make the sense of the Eucharistic liturgy's whole context wither away. In the preconciliar liturgy, the priest offered the Eucharistic sacrifice on the altar, while the faithful carried out their prayers in parallel and, as a rule, made a spiritual communion. A strong feeling of personal unworthiness led to a situation in which actual reception of the Eucharist was increasingly replaced with the visual contact made during the elevation. This constriction was corrected—to state it in an abbreviated fashion—by the initiative of Pope Pius X to encourage regular reception of communion by the faithful,[41] as well as by the liturgical renewal of the twentieth century, with its new orientation toward the biblical and patristic sources of the liturgy. Furthermore, both of these developments led with good reason to giving a central place in the Church's consciousness of time to the active participation (*actuosa participatio*) by all the faithful.[42]

---

37. H. U. von Balthasar, "The Veneration of the Holy of Holies," in *Elucidations*, trans. J. Riches (San Francisco: Ignatius Press, 1998), 181–90, here 185.

38. See K. Rahner, "On The Duration of the Presence of Christ after Communion," *Theological Investigations*, vol. 4, *More Recent Writings*, trans. Kevin Smyth (Baltimore, Md.: Helicon Press, 1966), 312–20.

39. See *S. th.* III, q. 76, a. 6 ad 3: "corpus Christi remanet in hoc sacramento non solum in crastino, sed etiam in futuro, quousque species sacramentales manent; quibus cessantibus, desinit esse corpus Christi sub eis, non quia ab eis dependeat, sed quia tollitur habitudo corporis Christi ad illas species, per quem modum Deus desinit esse Dominus creaturae desinentis."

40. For background, see P. Browe, *Eucharistie im Mittelalter*, 475–509.

41. See DH 3375–83.

42. Only in passing, let it be noted that the term *actuosa participatio*, while certainly in need of

At the same time, the criticism that thinks it necessary to recognize medieval Eucharistic piety as nothing but a disastrous derailing, which has long since become obsolete, probably overlooks another aspect: the fact, already hinted at, that precisely the materiality of the Eucharistic signs guards against the misunderstanding that the sacramental presence of Christ is dependent upon the human powers of consciousness or memory found in the one praying or in the gathered community sharing the meal.[43] It is the hidden presence of Jesus Christ, which summons the presence of the one praying and shapes it, as long as he lets himself be gathered and shaped. If, conversely, the Eucharistic presence were to come about only through the attentiveness of the one praying (or of the gathered community), it would be bound to the subjective (or collective) act of ascribing some meaning, which could then also be taken away. Human consciousness would then reflect *merely itself in another* and would ultimately worship its own product. It would in fact be some form of spiritual idolatry if one worshiped what he *himself* had, in a prior solemn act, declared to be holy. For this reason, Karl Rahner objected to an interpretation of real presence based on a philosophy of consciousness, holding that "for the Catholic understanding of the faith, neither the substance of bread nor that of Christ's body can be idealistically reduced to any old meaning or sense, when Christ speaks into the dimension in which he very concretely gives his apostles food, which is his body."[44] The bread, however, is changed into the body of the Lord each time the priest carries out the consecratory speech act, engaging the exalted Lord's performative word, which imparts his presence to the Eucharist gifts. This presence cannot be produced, but can only be received with gratitude—a disposition that certainly needs to be cultivated. But recognizing the presence of the giver in the gift is called thanksgiving.

Against this backdrop, the priority of a *tangible* mediation of the Eucharistic presence can be illustrated once more. "The finger pointing of both assisting priests, their pointing with outstretched fingers toward the Eucharistic *things*, the bread and the wine, from an early Christian power in which the presence of another Great Time became everlasting."[45]

---

interpretation, is not used in the liturgical constitution *Sacrosanctum concilium* in the sense of a liturgical activism, as if there must be as many of the faithful as possible participating in as many and diverse roles as possible in the liturgical event. Instead, it is used as an interlacing of interior and exterior participation, which joins spiritual attentiveness and participation with visible forms of expression. See K. Koch, *Eucharistie. Herz des christlichen Glaubens* (Freiburg/Switzerland, 2005), 142–45.

43. This may be a misunderstanding of the doctrine of transsignification, if it is not sufficiently clearly emphasized that it is God who undertakes the "re-establishing of the meaning" of the signs of bread and wine into the body and blood of Christ. See B. J. Hilberath, Art. "Transsignifikation," *LThK* 10, 3rd ed. (2000): 177.

44. K. Rahner, "Die Gegenwart Christi im Sakrament des Herrenmahls," 378.

45. Handke, *Am Felsfenster morgens*, 487.

The material signs of bread make us aware of the irreducible exteriority of Christ's presence. Just as when receiving communion we do not simply assimilate the body of Christ into our organic life, but rather are ourselves assimilated into the mystical organism of Christ's body;[46] so also do we not place Christ in the horizon of our presence when we contemplate him in the Eucharist, but rather we are ourselves taken up into the horizon of Christ's presence, which overlaps with our time: the same Christ yesterday, today, and forever. This obviously takes place only if we allow ourselves to be taken into his presence. Whoever takes some time and places his own presence, punctuated with worries, into the presence of Christ will see his life with other eyes, or more precisely, with the eyes of the Other: "*Je Le vise et Il me vise* [I look at Him and He looks at me]."[47] In this word, we find in a nutshell the essence of Eucharistic contemplation, which today appears to have become alien to many believers.

At the same time, the presence of the Blessed Sacrament confronts us with a reality that surpasses our always limited and wandering attentiveness. It is Christ, present in the species of bread, who invites us to stay awhile. The experience of boredom that sometimes overcomes us in the celebration of the liturgy, even against our own intentions, can be transformed into an experience of condensed time through the insertion of moments of silence and stillness—namely, when our wandering consciousness lets itself be collected and shaped by Christ's presence. To the extent that we allow ourselves to take a moment with Christ, the Other, our life can itself become other, different. Everyday life, which appears unspectacular, mundane, and distant from God in its routine, can itself be transformed by consciously pausing before the signs of God's nearness *par excellence*. Contemplative Eucharistic piety always responds to the fact that in the moment of receiving the host (and in the short silence thereafter) the immeasurable is hardly to be measured, that Jesus Christ, who in his life and death did

---

46. See *In Ioan.* VI, l. VII (n. 972): "Non enim cibus iste convertitur in eum qui sumit, sed manducantem in se." See also P. Handke, *Gestern unterwegs. Aufzeichnungen November 1987 bis Juli 1990* (Frankfurt/M.: Suhrkamp, 2007), 157: "The comforted one (John) is converted entirely into the One comforting; conversely, he assimilated this One to himself, and himself to this One—and this would be the *other* supper, the *other* communion."

47. Cited in E. Schillebeeckx, *Die eucharistische Gegenwart* (Düsseldorf: Patmos, 1967), 10. For background on this word, see F. Trochu, *Der heilige Pfarrer von Ars. Johannes-Maria-Baptist Vianney (1786–1859)*, trans. J. Widlöcher (Stuttgart-Degerloch: Otto Scholz, 1952), 157, who has the curé of Ars recount the following episode: "Here in the parish there was a man who passed away several years ago. Early in the morning, before his work in the field, he left his pickax standing at the door, entered the church, and forgot himself there before his God. A neighbor, who worked the same land and had the habit of observing him, was surprised at his absence. He turned around and, thinking he could perhaps meet him in that very place, the thought came to him to go into the church. As a matter of fact, he did meet him there. 'What are you doing here for so long?' he asked him. At which the other replied: 'I'm looking at God, and God is looking at me.'"

everything for us, gives himself anew right here in sacramental form. A contemplative lingering before the hidden presence of Christ tries to balance out the fact that we can always but inadequately honor the Eucharistic gift. Eucharistic adoration should therefore be understood not as competition to the liturgical celebration of the Eucharist but as a complementary counterpart. Precisely when life is marked with hectic patterns and prevalent activism, pausing for a moment can be a salutary interruption of everyday life, leading us to see the everyday with new, transformed eyes.[48]

In recent decades, Eucharistic piety went through a change in its basic shape, which prompted Karl Rahner, as early as 1981, to designate "individual silent prayer before the tabernacle" as a good, "which also should not founder in the future, which *belongs to the past, and this past must be picked up anew by the future if it wishes to be great.*"[49] Elsewhere, he offered for consideration, that:

the tabernacle [is] certainly—theologically considered—first of all the place in which the food of life is kept safe, a food destined for consumption. But to repudiate as an outdated practice, therefore, everything that arose and still lives in the Church's Eucharistic piety, beginning in the eleventh century—this is indeed a sacrilege. Why shouldn't a Christian kneel in prayer before the body of Lord, given up for him, tomorrow as well as yesterday and today? Why shouldn't he kneel tomorrow before the sacramental signs of the Lord's death and of his own death in the Lord, which approaches him? Or tomorrow, will there not be grievousness, vanity, and death? Tomorrow, will there be only men who cowardly run away from this abyss of existence? If not, then tomorrow there will also be men who pray, kneel in adoration before the shrine of the Eucharist, gaze upon the one they have pierced, men who are ready to take up their destiny, which has entered into the Paschal mystery of Jesus.[50]

In the meditative reenactment of Jesus' unconditional self-dedication, Eucharistic adoration is moreover an impetus for letting oneself and one's

---

48. K. Rahner interpreted the Eucharist as the sacrament of everyday life. See "The Eucharistie and Our Daily Lives," *Theological Investigations*, vol. 7: *Further Theology of the Spiritual Life 1*, trans. David Bourke (London, 1971), 211–26.

49. K. Rahner, "Eucharistic Worship," *Theological Investigations*, vol. 23: *Final Writings*, trans. Joseph Donceel, SJ (New York: The Crossroad Publishing Company, 1992), 113–16, here 114, emphasis added. [Translator's note: my translation here, not Doncee1's.]

50. K. Rahner, "Christian Living Formerly and Today," *Theological Investigations*, vol. 7: *Further Theology of the Spiritual Life 1*, 3–24, here 8. [Translator's note: my translation here.] The thesis that the gesture of kneeling can no longer be communicated to our contemporaries, or the similar idea that kneelers should be abolished from the church would allow an impoverishment of liturgical expression. Those holding such positions should be reminded of the political and theological potential for resistance retained in this gesture: whoever kneels before God can confront the gods of this world. Furthermore, the hardship of confessing atheists would have to be acknowledged, which E. Canetti considered in two writings: "The hardest thing for he who doesn't believe in God is that he has no one he can thank" (*Das Geheimherz der Uhr. Aufzeichnungen 1973 –1985* [Munich: Carl Hanser, 1987], 126). And: "He has no one he could ask for grace. The proud faithless one! He can kneel before no one: his cross" (*Die Fliegenpein*, 64).

actions be configured by attentiveness to others. To communicate with Christ, to linger before the gift of his presence always means therefore letting oneself be taken into his attentive posture toward others. For whoever "does not know God's face from contemplation will not recognize it in action, not even when it shines upon him from the face of the humiliated and aggrieved."[51] Thus, communion and contemplation belong together, and a culture of Eucharistic attentiveness can help the Eucharistic meal, in which communion with Christ is celebrated, become a feast where each attends to the other and no one remains for himself.[52]

The Eucharist as the Presence of the One Absent

Suffering is the ever newly remembered presence of God.

Maurice Blondel[53]

Faith in the real presence of Jesus Christ in the Eucharist appears to contradict the widespread feeling of God's absence in downright shocking ways. This feeling is nourished in a significant way by the pressing experience of suffering, which does not appear to find an adequate answer. Not a few testaments of art and literature converge in a negative aesthetic, which gives witness to the waning of transcendence. The inscrutably perverse world of Kafka's parables, the satires on the messianic expectation in Beckett's pieces, the deformed icons of Giacometti, the poetry of Celan, extracted from silence and addressed to "no one"—all of these manifest a struggle with God's absence. "For *how long* has God hidden himself?"[54] asks Elias Canetti with a certain disquiet. Unlike the philosophical discourses of the twentieth century, where the topos of the saving nearness of God flared up as a utopian motif,[55] today it seems hardly missed anymore that one did in fact once painfully miss the salvific nearness of God (after people for centuries lived from and praised this very thing). Against this background, the liturgical celebration of Jesus Christ's real presence moves into the suspicion of

---

51. H. U. von Balthasar, *Love Alone Is Credible*, trans. D. C. Schindler (San Francisco: Ignatius Press, 2005), 109. We read further: "Moreover, the celebration of the Eucharist is an *anamnesis* and thus the contemplation in love and the communion of love with love; and only from this does a Christian *Ite Missa-Missio est!* issue forth into the world." On this point, see also J.-H. Tück, "'Glaubhaft ist nur Liebe.' Bleibende Anstöße für die Theologie der Gegenwart," *IKaZ Communio* 34 (2005): 145–63.

52. Worthwhile thoughts on the Eucharist under the rubric of waiting on or attending to others can be found in H. Verweyen, *Warum Sakramente?* (Regensburg: Pustet, 2001), 60–73.

53. M. Blondel, *Tagebuch vor Gott 1883–1894*, trans. H. U. von Balthasar (Einsiedeln: Johannes-Verlag, 1964), 232.

54. E. Canetti, *Das Geheimherz der Uhr*, 172.

55. See, for example, Th. W. Adorno's often quoted concluding reflection "Finale" [*Vom Ende*] in the *Minima moralia: Reflections from Damaged Life*, trans. E. F. N. Jephcott (New York: Verso, 2005), 247.

erecting an illusionary alternative world of salvation and peace, which indeed aesthetically beautifies the scenery of life but does not stand firm in the least against hard reality. "It could be," as George Steiner assesses, "that nothing else is available to us anymore except God's absence."[56]

Nevertheless, it would be erroneous to bid the term "real presence" farewell for this reason and replace it with a rhetorical celebration of God's absence.[57] Anyhow, the sacrament of the Eucharist is characterized by a unique hovering between presence and absence. Even in the "sign of God's nearness" *par excellence*, the moment of hiddenness has its place, so that negative theology as the advocate of the hiddenness and incomprehensibility of the divine mystery certainly comes into its own. In his hymn *Adoro te devote*, Thomas Aquinas drew out the *hidden* presence of the crucified and risen one by means of poetic resources; in the *Summa theologiae*, he determined the mode of Eucharistic presence in a conceptual way, to the effect that Christ, *absent* until the parousia *in propria specie*, is *present* in the Eucharist merely *in specie sacramenti*, hence in signs. Only by emphasizing the mediation of Christ's presence in signs was Thomas able to avoid the crudely sensorial misunderstanding that the glorified body of the Lord is itself ground up (*cum dentibus atteri*) in the reception of the Eucharist. In the withdrawal of the physical presence of Jesus' body, Thomas saw a theological advantage, because it would open up the possibility of the crucified and risen one also being interiorly close to men.[58] In the withdrawal of Christ's bodily presence lies the presupposition for a deepened pneumatic presence. "Thus the withdrawal of his being among us is the making possible of his being in us, and that means the communication of his Spirit."[59] In pneu-

---

56. G. Steiner, *Der Garten des Archimedes*, 65. See also his *Errata. Bilanz eines Lebens* (Munich: Carl Hanser, 2002), 215f.: "Such an agnosticism, broken by impulses of afflicted prayer, thankless cries to God in moments of terror and suffering, is omnipresent in the post-Darwinian, post-Nietzschean, post-Freudian Occident. Whether consciously or not, agnosticism is the established Church of modernity." In this context, see the notes: "And if God withdrew himself from creation out of shame regarding death?"—"A heaven, which from despair about men arched ever further away from them" (E. Canetti, *Nachträge aus Hampstead*, 125 and 131).

57. See E. Nordhofen, "Das Leben der Bilder," *Die Zeit* 9 (1991): 68: "Real presence, that *was* once a term that *had* played a role for the understanding of the Christian Mass" (emphasis added). It cannot be ascertained from the context whether the statement is meant as a diagnosis of the times or if should be understood in the sense of a thesis, as if it is already concluded that the term "real presence" has become obsolete for a contemporary understanding of Eucharistic theology.

58. The subtraction of the sensible presence of the body is explicitly interpreted as a pneumatological surplus in *S. th.* III, q. 57, a. 1 ad 3: "ascensio Christi in caelum, qua corporalem praesentiam suam nobis subtraxit, magis fuit utilis nobis quam praesentia corporalis fuisset." See also *In Ioan.* XIV, l. 1 (n. 1889). Reading like a commentary on this is the remarkable essay by H. U. von Balthasar, "The Absences of Jesus," *New Elucidations* (San Francisco: Ignatius Press, 1986), 46–60, who calls attention to the fact that "this last indicated presence of God, the Spirit of the Father and the Son, can become a reality only in the Son's withdrawal of his physical presence, and indeed only in its being accepted" (ibid., 48).

59. H. U. von Balthasar, "Der Erstling der neuen Welt," *IKaZ Communio* 12 (1983): 214–18, here 215.

matically making himself present, Jesus Christ binds himself to the gifts of bread and wine, which thus become signs of the *Real of Reals*.

But there is a *temporal* tension that is simultaneously peculiar to the sacramental presence: the signs vouchsafe a presence that is tentative and provisional, inasmuch as it first of all approaches to the blessed vision of God, the *visio beatificans*. There is something that is not satisfied by the sacrament: the thirst for the "inexhaustible light"[60] of glory, for the unveiled face of Jesus Christ, which Thomas expressed in a poetic language of longing and desire. In *Adoro te devote*, we read: "Iesu, quem *velatum* nunc aspicio, / quando fiet illud quod tam sitio; / te *revelata* cernens facie, / visu sim beatus tuae gloriae."

If, in addition to the eschatological provisionality of the sacramental order, one takes seriously that the Eucharist is a *memoriale mortis domini*, which is permanently referred back to the event on Golgotha, then the one present in a hidden way in the signs of bread and wine is simultaneously the one who suffered through the absence of God as no other did.[61] The crucified one suffered through the abandonment of all communication, the radical forsakenness of those dying, and, without revoking his trust in the Father, was at the end silenced in death. Since then, affliction and lamentation and even the hush of death have a place in God himself.[62] At the same time, his Passion is an expression of love that goes to the highest extreme. At its center stands the salvific nearness to the suffering and lost—salvific because the change from death to life became a reality in the unreserved abandonment for others. In Christ, the crucified *and* resurrected one, we find the point reflected that the fragment of life finds its consummation in God. In the wounds of the glorified one, we see it made visible that suffering is not forgotten, time is not extinguished but rather salvifically retained. Jesus, who held to his mission in uninterrupted faithfulness to the Father's will, even to the point of death—*se tradidit voluntarie*—experiences the radical night of God on the cross: "My God, why have you abandoned me?" (Ps 22:2). Since then, the night of God, felt heavily by so many and expressed in lamentation, has a place in God himself.[63] Therefore, the cry of the crucified one must also not be ignored in the celebration of the Paschal mystery, nor must it

---

60. On the metaphor of "inexhaustible light" (which is not found in Thomas), see J. Pieper, *The Silence of St. Thomas*, trans. John Murray, SJ, and Daniel O'Connor (South Bend, Ind.: St. Augustine's Press, 1999), 94–99.

61. Thomas himself emphasized the incomparability of Jesus' sufferings. See *S. th.* III, q. 46, a. 6.

62. See H. U. von Balthasar, *Man in History: A Theological Study* (London: Sheed and Ward, 1982), 279f.

63. See J.-H. Tück, "Höllenabstieg Christi und Hoffnung für alle. Hans Urs von Balthasars eschatologischer Vorstoß," *ThG* 49 (2006): 60–65.

founder in the exultation of Easter. "Accusations add to glory [*Anklagen zur Glorie addieren*]"[64]—writes Canetti, reminding the *theologiae gloriae* of the cracks and chasms of reality, which evoke a suffering in God and missing his salvific nearness. But the exalted Christ, who makes intercession for his own before the Father, is enduringly marked by the wounds of his Passion, the signs of his wholehearted gift of self for us. Thus, the *memoriale passionis et resurrectionis* is cut short if we overlook that in his death for the suffering and forsaken, Christ became a co-sufferer and co-forsaken, sharing in the hiddenness of God. Conversely, *communio* with the risen crucified one leads to understanding one's own suffering as *compassio* with Christ; it leads to taking this suffering upon oneself for the purpose of carrying one's cross, without slipping into a problematic glorification of suffering. In this way, suffering can become a new form of God's presence.

Anamnetic Solidarity with the Dead

> Memory is, as painful as it can be, the only thing that can bind us with the dead.
> Susan Sontag[65]

> It would, however, appear extremely inhuman, if one were not to grieve over the death of another.
> Thomas Aquinas[66]

Out of anamnetic solidarity with the dead of history, which contemporary discourses on memory demand, a salvific and redemptive power does not arise unless it is brought into the horizon of the *memoria Dei*. Before the second death, the death of oblivion, there is a time in which men can safeguard men—those who have become victims of violence and terror, who have worked for advancement of coming generations without themselves being able to participate in it—and they can strive for a better future in society through memory in a moral sense. They cannot, however, revoke death, and therein lies the powerlessness of human remembering. If one does not simply wish to consign the dead to the oblivion of forgottenness and surrender them to a cultural amnesia that abbreviates history to a history of the victors,[67] one will be able to refer to the meaning of cultic anam-

---

64. E. Canetti, *Nachträge aus Hampstead*, 163.
65. S. Sontag, *Das Leiden anderer betrachten* (Munich: Fischer, 2003), 134.
66. *In Ioan.* XI, l. V (n. 1535): "Sed valde inhumanum esse videtur quod aliquis de morte alicuius non tristetur." Going further, we read: "Sed Dominus tristari voluit, ut significet tibi quod aliquando debeas contristari—The Lord, however, wanted to grieve in order to show you that you too should grieve at the appropriate time."
67. On this point, see J. B. Metz, "Wider den Bann kultureller Amnesie," *Memoria passionis. Ein provozierendes Gedächtnis in pluralistischer Gesellschaft* (Freiburg: Herder, 2006), 123–57.

nesis, which is celebrated in the Eucharist as *memoriale passionis*. Instead of seeking happiness in a kind of loss of memory—"Blessed are the forgetful!" runs the Nietzschean slogan[68]—and instead of numbing the sorrow felt regarding the suffering of others or suppressing it in a cult of apathy, the world's history of suffering is to be referred to the memory of God, the *memoria Dei*. In the liturgical performance of the *memoria passionis, mortis et resurrectionis Jesu Christi*, what is recalled in any event is that God let himself be determined in the person and history of Jesus by the inscrutable history of suffering rather than holding himself outside of it. Precisely in his Passion, Jesus Christ identified himself with the victims of history and died for sinners in a vicarious way.[69]

The soteriological motif touched upon in the interpretive words, that Christ died for many, refers therefore not only to individuals in need of redemption, but also to the collective dimension of history, which as a history of freedom is also a history of suffering and guilt, marked by blood and tears. For the Eucharist, this means that the remembrance of Christ's Passion is combined with the remembrance of the living and the dead. As Christ, the high priest, comes before God as man's advocate, so also should the faithful advocate for others in the *commemoratio sacrificii*. As Thomas makes clear in his exposition of the rite, such advocacy in solidarity refers either to those who do not want to participate in the sacrifice of Christ, since they do not believe or have lost the faith—that they may yet convert; or likewise to those who, after sharing in Christ's sacrifice, fall back into the logic of self-love and thus betray the gift received. The community of believers gathered around the Lord's table is not closed in on itself but rather, through the mode of intercession, remains connected with others standing outside of it.[70]

Beyond this, those absent in the past, those painfully missed, and also the forgotten whose names are no longer known, are placed into the horizon of the salvific *memoria Dei*. The postulate of a universal recollective solidarity with the dead[71] can be made concrete in such a way that in celebrating the liturgical act of *commemoratio*, it is not only the individual subject who celebrates for himself but rather each celebrates it *together with* the

---

68. See H. Weinrich, *Lethe. Kunst und Kritik des Vergessens* (Munich: C. H. Beck, 1997), 160–68, here 166.

69. On the soteriological categories of "solidarity" and "representation [*Stellvertretung*]," see H. Hoping, "Stellvertretung. Zum Gebrauch einer theologischen Kategorie," *ZKaTh* 118 (1996): 345–60.

70. In an attempt to deepen this point, see my essay: "Memoriale passionis. Die Selbstgabe Jesu Christi als Anstoß zu einer eucharistischen Erinnerungssolidarität," in *Gestorben für wen? Zur Diskussion um das "pro multis,"* ed. M. Striet (Freiburg: Herder, 2007), 93–110.

71. See H. Peukert, *Wissenschaftstheorie—Handlungstheorie—fundamentale Theologie. Analysen zu Ansatz und Status theologischer Theoriebildung*, 2nd ed. (Frankfurt.: Suhrkamp, 1988), esp. 305–10.

others. The remembrance of the countless names of the human history of suffering is bound up here with the name of Jesus Christ, who not only receives the name above all names (see Phil 2:9) but is also known as the servant of God suffering *for all* and *with all* (see Is 53; Lk 24:25f.).⁷² Thus, the demand for unconditional loyalty to the dead can be met, for commemorating Christ includes in a certain way the remembrance of the dead, whose brother Christ became. In faith, the demand for universal recollective solidarity with the victims of history need not become an excessive anamnetic demand, since Christ vicariously realized this universal solidarity in his death. In this act of vicarious representation, there is no dispensation from remembering, as if in the Eucharistic remembrance Christians received a license for repressing the dead. On the contrary: they would pervert the anamnetic *communio* with the risen crucified one if they wanted to close themselves off to the suffering and the dead, with whom Christ unreservedly identified himself. They can relate themselves to Christ in an authentic way only if they are ready to let themselves be taken into his service.⁷³

The anamnetic *communio* with the risen crucified one cannot therefore be separated from the recollection of alien suffering. A cultic anamnesis that is conscious of the unconditional solidarity of Christ with the victims of history opposes itself to the social trend toward cultural amnesia, which suppresses or cynically accepts the debris resulting from the history of progress. At the same time, recollective solidarity is also not halved to the extent that the guilty and the delinquent are deleted from God's memory or underhandedly "excommunicated." By recollecting that Jesus prayed for his enemies at the moment of his death, that he went after the lost to the utmost degree to save them, the obligation arises not only to include one's own enemies in prayer but also to commend to God's saving memory history's many offenders, of whom no one thinks or wants to think anymore. Finally, a Eucharistic culture of remembrance could serve as an impetus toward atonement and rapprochement, if it enabled the faithful—where they have become guilty—to see themselves with the eyes of the injured. Such a shift in perspective, brought about by the gift of the Eucharist, would prompt a critical self-revision in those who have become guilty; this need not lead to despair, despite all the shame over deeds committed, for Christ *turns toward* the person of the sinner unconditionally, so that he is able to *turn away from* his sins. No less, moreover, can the Eucharist help believers

---

72. See K.-H. Menke, "Das Gottespostulat unbedingter Solidarität und seine Erfüllung durch Christus," *IKaZ Communio* 21 (1992): 486–99.

73. See also J.-H. Tück, *Christologie und Theodizee*, 262–65.

where injustice befalls them, where pain is inflicted upon them to the point that they no longer feel capable of forgiving—it can help them to see in the guilty one a neighbor in need of forgiveness.[74]

The "Hunger for More"—and a Joy That Remembers the Suffering of Others

The Eucharistic *memoria passionis* can be the occasion for a profound and lasting joy, one not to be confused with the ephemeral joys of everyday life: "When pleasure is past, its past; when joy is past, it is not past," notes Peter Handke.[75] In his novel *Der Große Fall* (2011), Handke tells of the surprising irruption of just this sort of joy. An actor, who is supposed to receive a prize in a big city, decides that morning to walk from just outside the city, where he spent the night, into the city center. As he crosses the forest and reaches the edge of the city, he suddenly feels a second hunger—a hunger reaching out for more than can be satisfied by food.[76] Despite the clamor in the alleyways, he hears the bells of a nearby church,[77] ringing out not only the hours but also the "meal of another time."[78] He follows the ringing and, as the only visitor, participates in a silent Mass in a recollected and reverent way. The rite and its use of forms strike him profoundly with their spell. "With the help of the Mass, the priests learn to handle things beautifully: the gentle holding of the chalice and host, the slow purification of the vessels, the turning of book pages; and the result of this beautiful way of handling things: a happiness that gives wings to the heart."[79] In *Der Große Fall*, Handke goes on to tell how "at the consecration of the bread into the body

---

74. For more detailed background of what is implied here, see M. Striet, "Versuch über die Auflehnung," in *Mit Gott streiten. Neue Zugänge zum Theodizee-Problem*, ed. H. Wagner (Quaestiones Disputatae 169) (Freiburg-Basel-Vienna: Herder, 1998), 48–89; J.-H. Tück, "Inkarnierte Feindesliebe. Der Messias Israels und die Hoffnung auf Versöhnung," in *Streitfall Christologie. Vergewisserungen nach der Shoah*, ed. H. Hoping and J.-H. Tück (Quaestiones Disputatae 214) (Freiburg-Basel-Vienna: Herder, 2005), 216–58.

75. Handke, *Am Felsfenster morgens*, 32.

76. Handke, *Der Große Fall* (Berlin: Suhrkamp, 2011), 174 (in what follows, the page numbers are cited parenthetically in the main text).

77. One often encounters the motif of bells in Handke's writings—see, as just one example, the signal of loss in *Über die Dörfer. Dramatisches Gedicht* (Frankfurt: Suhrkamp, 2002), 27f.: "Once someone explained to us: the bells do not indicate the time; rather, they remind us of eternity. Still, for the likes of us they no longer announce anything nor do they call anyone—great striker, iron casting that displaces the air, ugly brassy noise. Dogs run into the churches and drink up the holy water. No one takes care of the premises. How many things worth handing on take place here time and again ...—and no one holds on to it; nothing more will be passed on."

78. Handke, "Wie ein Gewecktwerden für einen anderen Tag," in *"Verwandeln allein durch Erzählen." Peter Handke in the Field between Theology and Literary Studies*, ed. J.-H. Tück and A. Bieringer (Freiburg: Herder, 2014), 17.

79. See P. Handke, *Phantasien der Wiederholung* (Frankfurt.: Suhrkamp, 1996), 8.

and the wine into the blood," the actor wants to let himself fall to his knees. "But in the same moment he feels a need, a longing—or was it a part of his hunger—not only to fall to his knees but fall down lengthwise and to remain lying with his face down."[80] After this scene, in which the actor wants to answer to the irruption of the presence of Christ's body and blood with an external gesture—a scene which gave the book its title—communion takes place, but for reasons unmentioned the actor does not partake; finally, there is a personally addressed final blessing: "Go in peace!" Following the silent Mass, the priest and actor sit down together in the sacristy, to chat in "mirth" over a shared meal. The Eucharistic liturgy does not remain isolated and aloof; it continues in the feast of life and leads to a deepened turning toward the world in agape.[81]

After these "revels" with the priest, the actor walks with exhilaration farther into town and feels a joy within. He wonders how this joy streaming through his consciousness differs from other previous joys. And he answers for himself: these others "pass by quickly" (186); right when they want to unfurl, they run up against the unhappiness of others—and fade away. Is one allowed to rejoice when others are unhappy? This moral self-censure forbids a joy that denounces solidarity with the poor and suffering of the world. The postulate of a mnemonic solidarity with the abased and aggrieved seems to place every joy under the suspicion of insensitivity and to nip it in the bud. Adorno writes: "The injustice committed by all cheerful art, especially by entertainment, is probably an injustice to the dead; to accumulated, speechless pain."[82] The pitiless forgetfulness belonging to the winners is rightly rejected; such winners want to blot out the traces of remembering the victims in order to be able to live undisturbed and to enjoy more. But joy is placed so much under ideological suspicion that it is not allowed to arise, since the remembrance of others' suffering is supposed to rule our consciousness. It is not only a matter of the countless victims of war and natural catastrophes, ever present in the nightly news; it is also the many moments of falling short in one's own life, which grate against the bad conscience of the actor: "My joy was not allowed to exist any longer. And finally it did not appear anymore" (187).

But when it comes to the joy following upon taking part in Mass, the

---

80. *Der Große Fall*, 180f. See Handke, *Die Lehre von Sainte-Victoire*, 21: "At that time, the consecration took place. The man, who was I, became great, and simultaneously it was demanded of him to be on his knees, or even to lie with his face down, and in all of that to be no one."

81. On the relation between Eucharist and agape in Handke, see A. Bieringer, "'Als finge ein stehengebliebenes Herz wieder zu schlagen an.' Liturgische Poesie bei Peter Handke," in *"Verwandeln allein durch Erzählen,"* ed. Tück and Bierinter, 85–100.

82. Th. W. Adorno, *Aesthetic Theory*, trans. Robert Hullot-Kentor (London: A&C Black, 2013), 54.

astounding thing is that it neither suppresses nor forgets the suffering of others. "The unhappiness became omnipresent in it, but it appeared as a part of this joy, interwoven with it rather than cancelling it out. It was a joy permeated by pain that accompanied the journeying actor, and in it, with it, and through it [as it reads in parallel to the final doxology of the Eucharistic prayer] he felt no sense of guilt and no prick of conscience at all: it was not his personal joy that carried him, nor did it have to do with him alone, but rather it surpassed him. This painful joy was a unanimous one" (188). This joy cannot be made but can only be gratefully received. It comes—in Handke's lapidary formulation—"from a purification, through a ceremony and a togetherness—even if it was just as a pair" (189).

What Peter Handke relates here in poetic language shows that the transformation of the gifts in the Eucharistic liturgy can become a gift of transformation: through gathering, remembering, and participating, everyday awareness can win back a lost joy in faith, which is not bounded off from the suffering of others. One could nearly speak of a transubstantiation of awareness, which is due to the hidden presence of Christ. The unintended joy that arrives after celebrating the Eucharist does not betray those who suffer; rather it confronts them with a broadened sensibility regarding life: "If one rejoices, then one already fears overlooking solidarity with the many who suffer. I don't have any right to rejoice, people think, in a world where there is so much misery, so much injustice."[83] But we must not confuse the joy of Easter, the triumph of the resurrected Lord over death, with a triumphalism insensitive to suffering. Suppressing the joy of Easter with an attitude that refuses doxology would be fatal, for it remains tethered to the Passion on Golgotha and the experience of the dark night of the soul. On the cross, through his crying out to God and his being silenced in death, Jesus took his place with those beaten and battered. Even as the resurrected one, he is marked by the traces of suffering; as the scars of the glorified one reveal, he has passed through pain and negativity. Even today, he draws near and imparts through the *gift of his presence* a quiet joy that is different from and more than the glittering allure of the culture of mere fun and fleeting experience. As Vatican II puts it in *Gaudium et Spes* (§62), art and literature have to do with "revealing man's place in history and in the universe; with illustrating the miseries and joys, the needs and strengths of man." If this is true, then integrating the outside perspectives of literature, art, and music can—as shown by our sporadic glance at Peter Handke's work,[84] or for

---

83. J. Ratzinger, *Salt of the Earth: The Church at the End of a Millenium: A Conversation with Peter Seewald*, trans. Adrian Walker (San Francisco: Ignatius Press, 1997), 36.

84. For more a more detailed treatment, see my essay: "'Wandlung—die Urform der Wirklichkeit'—

example the compositions of Olivier Messiaen[85]—remind theology of a largely forgotten dimension of the Eucharist: *joy*.

Infidelity and Betrayal

> Even my bosom friend in whom I trusted, who ate of my bread, has lifted the heel against me.
>
> Ps 41:9

> a discipulo / suis tradendus aemulis
>
> Thomas Aquinas, *Verbum supernum*

Although the last supper has a testamentary character and in it Jesus joined his presence to the signs of bread and wine, it is itself surrounded by gestures of infidelity and betrayal, which are rarely perceived in current Eucharistic theology. The disciples quarrel over the question, who among them is the greatest (see Lk 22:24–30); the farewell scene brings out latent feelings of envy and rivalry, with the guests fighting for the master's nearness. Judas, one of the twelve, quits the *convivium* in order to hand over his Lord to the high priests in return for thirty pieces of silver (see Mt 26:14–16). Later, he will take his own life in despair over this deed; in the garden of Gethsemane, the disciples fall asleep instead of waiting and watching with Jesus, who meanwhile prays in mortal fear (see Mt 26:36–46). At the nighttime capture, the sign of friendship, a kiss, is perverted into a sign of betrayal (see Mt 26:48f.); at the moment of danger, all the disciples abandon Jesus and take flight (see Mk 14:50); Peter, who had earlier assured Christ of his faithfulness unto death (Mt 26:33–35), denies his Lord three times (see Mt 26:69–75) and can only weep bitterly over his cowardice as the cock crows. In his analysis of the Passion, Aquinas subsumed even these events into the concept of *traditio*.[86] One could see implied in this that the events of ecclesial handing on are accompanied from the beginning by moments of incomprehension, infidelity, and betrayal.

The history of Christianity is burdened by incidents in which precisely the Eucharist, the *sacramentum caritatis*, has become an occasion for hate or violent excesses. Even this should not be forgotten in the ritual celebration

---

Spuren einer eucharistischen Poetik bei Peter Handke," in *"Verwandeln allein durch Erzählen,"* ed. Tück and Bieringer, 29–53.

85. On Olivier Messiaen, see J.-R. Kars, "Olivier Messiaen—ein Musiker der Freude," *IKaZ Communio* 33 (2004): 359–73; as well recently: Dorothee Brunner, "Hörendes Verweilen vor dem Allerheiligsten. Olivier Messiaens Orgelwerk 'Livre du Saint Sacrement,'" *IKaZ Communio* 42 (2013): 307–16, here 314: "In *Livre de Saint Sacrement* it is precisely the attitudes of gratitude and joy are emphasized in tonally effusive and compositionally unconventional ways."

86. See *S. th.* III, q. 47.

of the *memoria passionis*. In the Middle Ages, the Jewish people were collectively charged with Judas's betrayal and the accusation of murdering God was raised against them. They were alleged—for the first time in 1290 in the city of Paris[87]—to have maliciously defiled the hosts and thus pogroms, persecution, and murder were legitimated.

Even earlier than this, the sacrament of unity was compromised by the controversy over leavened or unleavened bread and which was to be used for the Eucharistic celebration. Shortly before the Great Schism between the Eastern and Western Church in 1054, the controversy came to a head. Leo of Ohrid and Patriarch Michael Kerularios decisively reject the use of unleavened bread and justify their rejection by an anti-Semitic argument: "the lifeless yeast of the Jewish custom could not have enabled an ecclesial, sacramental life."[88] They based themselves on the Johannine chronology, according to which the last supper took place the evening before Passover (see Jn 13:1)—thus, without unleavened bread. Their polemic went so far that they deny the validity of the Eucharist in the Western Church on account of its use of unleavened bread.[89] Against this, Cardinal Humbert of Silva Candida insisted on the Western Church's rite and the use of unleavened bread for the Eucharistic celebration; he appealed to Christ's example as attested in the synoptic chronology (see Mt 26:17; Mk 14:12; Lk 22:7, referring to Ex 12:15). To diminish this controversy's Church-dividing character, Thomas Aquinas, like Anselm of Canterbury before him, devoted himself to the problem and offered an intermediary solution. He taught that the only requirement is to use wheat bread and that the question of leavened or unleavened bread can be left to the custom of the Church.[90]

Beyond this, the conflict triggered by the Reformers concerning the correct exegesis of the *verba testamenti* led to divisions. At the Marburg Colloquy, Luther and Zwingli disagreed over the interpretation of the words of institution, thus shattering the Reformation's unity; for centuries, a lack of unity was found between the Lutherans, who held to the real presence, and the Reformed, who supported rather a symbolic interpretation. Although they were agreed in their insistence on distributing communion under both species, and although they rejected both the doctrine of transubstantiation and the Euharist's sacrificial character, still they could not come to unity on the question of real presence. The fact that the "sacrament

---

87. See M. Eder, "Hostienfrevel," *LThK* 5, 3rd ed. (1993): 290.
88. See M. Petzold, "Azymenstreit," *LThK* 1, 3rd ed. (1993): 1326–28.
89. A. Bayer, *Spaltung der Christenheit. Das sogenannte Morgenländische Schisma von 1054* (Cologne: Böhlau Verlag, 2002), 63–72.
90. See *S. th.* III, q. 74, a. 4.

of unity" could drive, of all things, such fierce altercations and even bloody religious conflicts led Michel de Montaigne to note with exaggeration in his *Essais:* "How many and weighty conflicts were brought upon the world by the contentious meaning of this one syllable, 'hoc.'"[91] The Eucharistic controversies of the Reformation period are, despite all the ecumenical convergence, still not overcome, even today. Admittedly, Protestants of the Lutheran, Reformed, and United churches were able to unite at the Leuenberg Agreement in 1973, where they decided for fellowship at the pulpit and at the table following the model of unity in reconciled diversity. All the same, the scandal of the *one* table of the Lord being divided continues, since the differences between the Catholic Church and the Churches of the East remain.

Furthermore, although Jesus and the apostles descended from Israel according to the flesh, the time of National Socialism found the Church turning its back on the persecuted Jews, notwithstanding the exemplary conduct of individual persons and groups. Notable theologians abnegated the Jewish heritage in Christianity and ennobled the Nazi racial doctrine theologically.[92] In the churches, the Eucharistic liturgy was celebrated, without any corresponding protest against the destruction of synagogues and eradication of Jewish life.

Finally, the manifold forms of failure and guilt *within the Church* itself are to be reflected upon. Regarding the gap between the poor churches of Latin America, Africa, and Asia and the rich churches in the developed countries of the West,[93] it ought to be called to mind that whenever some suffer scarcity while others live in superabundance, the ethos of sharing—which belongs to the core of Eucharistic culture since Paul's criticism of the Corinthian practice of the Lord's supper—is damaged. If Christians neglect to think of each other when they celebrate the supper of the Lord, they impair the remembrance of Jesus Christ himself and threaten to replace the cultic anamnesis with a cult of apathy. This applies as well to the

---

91. Montaigne, *Essais*, ed. H. Lüthy (Zürich: Manesse, 1953), 451f. Pascal, too, notes: "Que je hais ces sottises, de ne pas croire l'Eucharistie, etc.! Si l'Évangile est vrai, si Jésus-Christ est Dieu, quelle difficulté y a-t-il là?" (*Pensées* [Saint-Etienne: Editions la Bibliothèque Digitale, 1971])—"How I *hate* this stupidity of not believing in the Eucharist, etc." (*Penseés*, trans. Trotter, fragment 224). As if hate could serve a rapprochement concerning the sacrament of love.

92. See only M. Schmaus, *Begegnungen zwischen katholischem Christentum und nationalsozialistischer Weltanschauung* (Münster: Aschendorff, 1933); K. Adam, "Deutsches Volkstum und katholisches Christentum," *ThQ* 114 (1933): 40–63; idem, "Jesus, der Christus, und wir Deutsche," *Wissenschaft und Weisheit* 10 (1943): 74–103 and ibid. 11 (1944): 10–23.

93. See J. B. Metz, "Brot des Überlebens. Das Abendmahl der Christen als Vorzeichen einer anthropologischen Revolution," in *Jenseits bürgerlicher Religion. Reden über die Zukunft des Christentums* (Mainz: Grünewald Kaiser, 1980), 51–70.

many persecuted Christians, who are exposed to oppression and violence, and thus are in need of support.

The list of failures, guilt, and breakdowns can easily be lengthened; it casts a shadow on the handing on of the Eucharist and requires continual purification and rehabilitation.[94] Believers who receive the Eucharist today place themselves not only in the impressive line of confessors and witnesses but also in the line of *traditores*, who have denied and betrayed Christ. The remembrance of the diverse history of the Church's guilt is not to be confused with self-deprecation. It presents a preventative to moral arrogance or triumphalistic self-righteousness, for no one who believes, or believes he believes, is beyond the risk of incomprehension and betrayal. Insight into one's own fallibility is an occasion for a personal examination of conscience and critical self-revision. Encountering the Eucharistic Christ and accepting his self-gift always mean as well admitting one's *own* need for forgiveness: "*Iesu Domine / me immundum munda tuo sanguine*"—we hear in the hymn *Adoro te devote*. But whoever is aware of his own need for forgiveness will not refuse forgiveness to others. Thus, an indicator of a Eucharistic lifestyle would be a readiness for reconciliation where human relations appear to be definitively messy. Regarding the ecclesial handling of the Church's burden of guilt in history, John Paul II launched a *purificazione della memoria* by means of the great petitions for forgiveness in the year 2000; the consistent development of this can contribute to a purification of *traditio*.[95] The potential of the Eucharistic tradition lies in handing on the gift of love in such a way that the Church, in and through her subjects, the faithful, can herself become an attractive sign of the presence of the absent One in the world.

---

94. George Tabori's story *Mutters Courage* points to a further semantic nuance of the word "hand over [*übergeben*]." As Tabori tries to show in *Mutters Courage*, the betrayal of the Gospel in the Third Reich took on characteristics that were unappetizing to the point of vomiting. See idem, *Mutters Courage*, trans. U. Grützmacher-Tabori (Berlin: Klaus Wagenbach, 2003), 7–33, esp. 31–32.

95. See International Theological Commission, *Memory and Reconciliation: The Church and the Faults of the Past* (1999).

"Theophagy" and Transformation

> The God-eater and his hunger.
> Elias Canetti[96]
>
> The "otherness" that enters into us, makes us other.
> George Steiner[97]
>
> per Eucharistiam manducamus Christum.
> Thomas Aquinas[98]

Man lives by eating and drinking. Loss of appetite is a sign of crisis, for taking up nourishment—transforming the other into the self—is necessary for life, and this from the very beginning. Even a baby, by crying, signals its mother that it wants to be nursed, to have its hunger satisfied, that it needs closeness. Man needs the other and rarely realizes that he can live only with the help of another life; no one is sufficient unto himself. This basic anthropological need, with the elementary dependence man has on food and drink, is taken up into the Eucharist; at the same time, it is transposed into a spiritual key. The sacramental remembrance of Christ's suffering is inscribed by the rite of eating and drinking into the body of the one performing the remembrance.[99] The Eucharist nourishes, strengthens, and "quickens" the spirit of man. Thomas Aquinas made this clear in his considerations on the economy of the sacraments—and Goethe was not alone in followed him on this point, when he wrote: "The sacraments are the highest part of religion, the symbols to our senses of an extraordinary divine favor and grace. In the last supper, earthly lips are to receive a divine being embodied, and in the form of earthly fare they participate in a heavenly one."[100]

Man does not live on bread alone—he hungers for God (see Ps 42:1f.). God, however, who took up a *communicatio* with men once for all in Christ and his Spirit, gives himself in the mode of food, so that spiritual hunger will be satisfied. To be sure, there is immediately a difference to be marked out when compared to the banquets put on by men for one another. To wit,

---

96. E. Canetti, *Das Geheimherz der Uhr. Aufzeichnungen 1973–1985* (Munich: Carl Hanser, 1987), 86. See also the drastic writing in B. Strauss, *Der Untenstehende auf Zehenspitzen*, 44: "The human longing for an edible God." Reading like a theological commentary on this is G. Bachl, *Eucharistie—Macht und Lust des Verzehrens* (St. Ottilien: EOS, 2008).

97. G. Steiner, *Von realer Gegenwart. Hat unser Sprechen Inhalt?* (Munich: Carl Hanser, 1990), 248.

98. *S. th.* III, q. 73, a. 5 ad 1.

99. See *Officium de festo corporis Christi*, lect. II, 276f.: "Ut autem tanti beneficii iugis in nobis maneret memoria, corpus suum in cibum et sanguinem suum in potum sub specie panis et vini sumendum fidelibus dereliquit."

100. See J. W. von Goethe, *The Auto-Biography of Goethe: Truth and Poetry: From My Own Life*, trans. John Oxenford (London: H. G. Bohn, 1874), 245–48, here 245 [translation slightly modified].

unlike exquisite foods, which—artfully prepared and adeptly arranged—satisfy culinary and aesthetic needs, the unleavened wheat bread,[101] from which the host is prepared, retracts the dimension of being sensibly affected. Already the rite of the bread, which Jesus adopted from the Jewish feast and provided with a new interpretation, gets along with a plain gesture: a piece of bread broken and distributed to the guests present. Through this contrast with a meal of satiety, which was able very early on to take on opulent, not to mention excessive, traits, it becomes clear that the Eucharistic food is not a select form of "gastro-eroticism."[102] Around the turn of the first millennium, the widely instituted stylization of the Eucharist bread into a *hostia oblata*, connected technologically to the advent of the baking iron, certainly brought along the disadvantage that it pushed the communal and prandial character of the Eucharistic celebration into the background. The many pre-stamped hosts in the bowl make superfluous the rite of breaking *one* bread and distributing it to *all*. At the same time, however, the stylization of the bread into a host also has the advantage of reducing the culinary aesthetic to almost nil. "The host of unleavened bread (*azyme*) is thin and, as distinct from leavened bread, good for breaking, without particles breaking off. This is an advantage hardly to be underestimated, if one considers that the whole body of the Lord is present even in the smallest part of the consecrated host. The white color of the host is a sign of the purity of the sacrifice. Finally, in the host, the bread-like character of the sacrificial offering recedes quite into the background."[103] The last aspect certainly encourages the visual piety of the Middle Ages. It is not a matter of taste and appreciation, not a matter of "the experience of that explosion of gustatory nuances, which accompanies the first bite of a delectable dish."[104] The senses are obviously to be directed to something else. While virtually nothing takes place in the *sumptio* on the level of the senses, something indeed takes place at a spiritual level, "that beyond which nothing greater can be thought": the most intimate union of man with Christ, the wholly Other, who joined his presence to this small piece of bread.

Something analogous pertains to the rite of the chalice. It is not a matter of deploying wine as a stimulant of religious ecstasy or initiating Dio-

---

101. See *S. th.* III, q. 74, aa. 3 and 4.
102. On this point, see O. Paz, *Der menschenfreundliche Menschenfresser* (Frankfurt/M.: Suhrkamp 1981), 136–69; A. F. Méndez, "Göttliche Speise. Gastroerotik und eucharistisches Verlangen," *Conc(D)* 41 (2005): 128–36.
103. See M. Währen, "Zur Geschichte der Hostienbäckerei," in *Panis angelorum. Kulturgeschichte der Hostie*, ed. O. Seifert (Ostfildern: Thorbecke, 2004), 16f.
104. H. U. Gumbrecht, *Diesseits der Hermeneutik* (Frankfurt: Suhrkamp, 2004), 119.

nysian orgies. The well-dosed amount of wine used in the Eucharistic celebration offers a *symbolic* foretaste of the heavenly wedding banquet and is a *symbolic* anticipation of eschatological *communio* in the kingdom of God; but it is not already this very thing.[105] It is no accident that Thomas employed affective categories for the Eucharistic unification with Christ and transposed the vocabulary of tasting and savoring to a spiritual level.[106] In his answer to the question whether it is fitting that Christ gave himself in the mode of food to the disciples remaining behind, Thomas emphasized that the sense of taste (*gustus*) is the only one in the range of senses that accomplishes a direct union with its object. This is the aspect of union that matters, assimilation or *incorporatio*, and not the select satisfaction of needs, which remains within the horizon of the self. For Eucharistic communion does not aim at the assimilation of the thing but rather at union with a person."Just as there cannot be a meal without a sacrifice, since eating is the assimilation of something that is eaten in the process ... , so also the Eucharist cannot be exclusively a meal of remembrance for the person of Jesus and his proclamation. The Eucharist is the presence of the crucified one in the sacramental form of a meal, in the eating of bread and the drinking of wine, which are not only marks of the word of proclamation, but the body and blood of Christ, that is, Christ himself for us in his death."[107]

A second difference that contrasts with everyday eating is to be noted: whoever receives the body of Christ is not satisfied but rather finds his longing for definitive union further intensified."We are creatures of a great thirst. Bent on coming home to a place we have never known."[108] As the hymn *Adoro te devote* recalls, there is a thirst made conscious in the Eucharist pre-

---

105. At the time of his ministry, Jesus was classified by some as a "glutton and a drunkard" (see Mt 11:19; Lk 7:34). His banquets can be understood as prophetic symbolic actions. He sat at table equally with tax collectors and sinners, Pharisees and Sadducees, rich and poor—a sign that could be understood as a symbol of hope for the perfect reign of God, when seen against the background of Old Testament prophecy (Is 24:23; 25:6ff.) and early Jewish apocalyptic (äthHen 25:6ff.). The motif of banquets also plays an important role in Jesus' parables. At the same time, Jesus' last supper goes beyond this tradition of banquets, in that it establishes a new beginning in the sign of the Passion and death. For the time of his absence—the absence of the bridegroom (see Mt 9:15; Mk 2:20; Lk 5:35)—Jesus institutes the Eucharist as a sign of his presence in the gifts of bread and wine. The ritual commemoration of his suffering, however, is anti-ecstatic and points symbolically to the eschatological joy of consummation, in which Christ's presence will no longer be communicated in signs.

106. See *S. th.* III, q. 79, a. 1 ad 2:"ex virtute huius sacramenti anima spiritualiter reficitur, per hoc quod anima delectatur, et quodammodo inebriatur dulcedine bonitatis divinae: secundum illud *Cant.* 5; *Comedite, amici, et bibite; et inebriamini, carissimi.*—The soul is spiritually nourished through the power of this sacrament, by being spiritually gladdened, and as it were inebriated with the sweetness of the Divine goodness, according to Cant 5:1:"Eat, O friends, and drink, and be inebriated, my dearly beloved."

107. H. Hoping, "Wie heute vom Tod Jesu sprechen? Der Opfertod Jesu als Mitte des christlichen Glaubens," in *Wie heute vom Tod Jesu sprechen?* ed. G. Häfner and H. Schmid (Freiburg: Katholische Akademie, 2002), 81–101, here 98f.

108. G. Steiner, *Grammars of Creation* (London: Yale University Press, 2001), 20.

cisely because the sacrament cannot satisfy it: the longing for face-to-face vision. In addition, the process of "eating God" is not to be confused with the biochemical assimilation of what is received.[109] The act of communion would be a sacred cannibalism only if the interpretation of the earlier mentioned massive realism—teaching an undifferentiated total identification between the historical and the Eucharistic Christ—were right. What is eaten and what is drunk, however, are the transformed gifts of bread and wine, which Aquinas's theory of conversion holds as accidents without a subject, maintained in existence also to avoid a *horror cruoris*. Accordingly, communion with Christ is mediated in signs. The "substantial" presence of the giver in the gift leads to a transformation of the receiver, which could be designated as a "moral transubstantiation,"[110] following Maurice Blondel. For in the act of communion, Christ, the Other, is not simply assimilated and inscribed into the ego-logically shaped horizon of the self. In contrast to the eating of normal food, which is biochemically assimilated through the digestive organs of our body, receiving the body and blood of Christ causes us to be taken up into the reality of his life. It is not we who change Christ but he who transforms us, if we allow ourselves to be transformed, following the insight of Thomas: " ... corporeal food is changed into the substance of the person nourished; but spiritual food changes man into itself."[111] Much like the the change of the gifts through Jesus Christ's pneumatically making himself present, a spiritual incorporation into the body of Christ takes place in those who receive the Eucharist, changing them. In this way, the *conversion of the gifts* becomes a *gift of conversion* for those who hospitably receive them.

The tendency to receive the Eucharist unreflectively—and who can absolve himself from this?—is therefore to be counteracted by a Eucharistic culture of *cortesía*, which supports taking time to gratefully welcome him who comes not with any gift, but who gives himself and wants to do so. In the context of a spreading *fast food culture*, which undermines the com-

---

109. Merely in passing, let it be hinted at that the gifts of bread and wine are products of human culture, the emergence of which already includes a *re-shaping* of natural source materials. The artist and poet David Jones was alert to this circumstance when he noted: "Let it be understood that [the priest] was not to speak these words over grapes and wheat, but over things that already stood under the jurisdiction of the Muse, that are themselves artifacts made by means of various arts following a *recta ratio*: the art of the mill, baking table, oven, wine press, and barrel. Without handicraft, therefore, we could not have control over the minimal conditions in order to obey the command: 'Do this in memory of me.' Where there is handicraft, there is also the Muse, and whoever uses the signs of bread and wine cannot escape their presence. There must firstly be something made by us, before it can become a sign for the one who made us. He himself sets down this point in the room of the last supper. Without artifacts, no Christian religion" (Jones, *Anathemata*, 35).

110. Blondel, *Tagebuch vor Gott*, 219. See also the note: "My God, let me be as good bread and then speak over me the words of consecration!" (ibid., 35).

111. *S. th.* III, q. 73, a. 3 ad 2. See Augustine, *Conf.* VII, 10: "Cibus sum grandium: cresce et manducabis me, nec tu me mutabis sicut cibum tuae carnis, sed tu mutaberis in me."

munal dimension of eating and is oriented toward "gulping down" one's foodstuffs, an attentiveness toward others and taking time for one another ought to be strengthened anew. "'One must certainly eat,' does not mean in the first place taking something into oneself and containing it, but rather *learning* to eat and *giving* to eat, that is, learning to give the other something to eat. One never eats alone. This is the rule of 'one must certainly eat.' It is a law of boundless hospitality."[112]

Communion is always linked with the readiness to let oneself be determined by Christ, to make his disposition one's own, to be there for others, to have time for them. In a journal entry addressing this context, Maurice Blondel noted:

Strangely magnificent words. *Ut ventri esca et escis venter, ita corpus Domino et Dominus corpori. Dominus corpori.* God is there for our body. Jesus is Jesus only to perfect us in Him, and we are only to merge into His divine humanity. God needs our bodies as food for His love, as the substance of His mystical body, as the single life-giving part of His creation; everything else is dead: *et hunc et has destruet.* God and man are in exchange. God treats man as if man were His God: they are to each other reciprocal end and means, as befits an organism, which lives according to the same determination. God expects from man that he contribute to fulfilling all justice: but God's body in us is not the animalistic life; it is the ethical life, the doing.[113]

Friendship with Christ and *Communio*

> As I see it, contemplative prayer is simply an intimate sharing between friends. It's about frequently taking time to be alone with the one who loves us.
>
> Teresa of Ávila[114]

No one can live without friendship. Each of us depends on being able to share with others the *secreta cordis*—and conversely also to be taken into the trust of others.[115] Following Aristotle, Thomas Aquinas emphasizes that friendship is characterized by reciprocal benevolence (*mutua benevolentia*). This benevolence may not remain hidden to friends but must be openly and recognizably articulated. As is well known, he distinguishes three forms of friendship: friendship of utility (*amicitia utilis*), friendship of desire (*amicitia delectabilis*), and friendship in the good (*amicitia honesti*).

---

112. J. Derrida, "Man muss wohl essen," *Auslassungspunkte. Gespräche* (Vienna: Passagen Verlag, 1998), 267–98, here 293.

113. Blondel, *Tagebuch vor Gott*, 150f.

114. Teresa of Avila, *Teresa of Ávila: The Book of My Life*, trans. Mirabai Starr (Boston: New Seeds, 2007), 53 (= Santa Teresa de Jesús, *Libro de la vida*, ed. O. Steggink [Madrid: Castalia, 1986], VIII, 5).

115. See Thomas, *In Ioan.* XV, l. 3 (n. 2016): "Verum enim amicitiae signum est quod amicus amico suo cordis secreta revelet."

The highest form of friendship, that in the good, is present where the other is loved *for the sake of himself*; thus, there is not an instrumental reduction of the relation of friendship. Unlike Aristotle, for whom the thought of friendship with God was unthinkable, since within his philosophical theology he was unable to conceive of a common basis between the divine and the human,[116] Thomas grounded the possibility of friendship with God in God's turning toward men. God himself establishes the *communicatio* with men through Jesus Christ; the communication of his divine life sets up the basis for friendship with him.[117] The word from the Johannine farewell discourse functions as a biblical point of reference: "I do not call you servants any longer, because the servant does not know what the master is doing; but I have called you friends, because *I have made known to you everything* that I have heard from my Father" (Jn 15:15). Accordingly, nothing is held back in the divine *communicatio*, so that the unreserved communication of the Father's message constitutes friendship with God. Even so, this friendship is subject to its own dynamic. *In statu viae*, it does not bear primarily upon the sensibly affected nature of man, as is always the case in friendships between men. Contact with God and the exalted Christ takes place, as Thomas comments, on the spiritual level and is imperfect and fragmentary until the unconditional and perfect friendship with God can be realized *in patria*.

In the scene of the last supper, Jesus instituted an abiding memorial of his friendship not least because he wanted to help his disciples by bridging the precarious interim of his absence, the time between the ascension and the parousia.[118] In the times of bodily absence, bread and wine guarantee his presence in signs. Thus, the Eucharist as *sacramentum caritatis* is simultaneously *signum amicitiae*. Relations of friendship, however, are relations of freedom, which normally establish a preferential relation based on reciprocal sympathy and common intentions. As Christ gave his life freely for his friends, so he expects of his friends that they remember him, that they faithfully preserve his legacy, that they make the absent friend present ever anew in their life witness.[119] Unlike fleeting acquaintanceships, interpersonal

---

116. See Aristotle, *Nic. Eth.* 1159a: "but if the distance is very great, as is the case with God, then there cannot be friendship anymore."

117. *S. th.* II-II, q. 23, a. 1. See R. Egenter, *Gottesfreundschaft. Die Lehre von der Gottesfreundschaft in der Scholastik und Mystik des 12. und 13. Jahrhunderts* (Augsburg: Dr. Benno Filser Verlag, 1928), 52–89.

118. See *S. th.* III, q. 73, a. 5: "ea quae ultimo dicuntur, maxime ab amicis recedentibus, magis memoriae commendantur: praesentim quia tunc magis *inflammatur affectus ad amicos*"—and Thomas continues—"ea vero ad quae magis afficimur, profundis animo imprimuntur" (emphasis added). See also *In IV Sent.*, q. 1, a. 1 ad 4 (n. 98).

119. See *In Ioan.* XV, l. 3 (n. 2011): "Signum ex parte discipulorum, quod sunt amici Christi, est observatio mandatorum eius."

friendship requires time, "for it carries beyond the present moment and keeps memory as much as it anticipates."[120] It holds entirely true for Christians that it is a sign of lived friendship with Christ when they recall his words and deeds with gratitude, let themselves and their lives be shaped in a practical way by his instructions, and anticipate a common future. Of course, daily consciousness will normally be dominated by other things, which at least push friendship with Christ thematically into the background; at the same time, no obstacles should be set up in opposition to his coming—speaking metaphorically—so that when we are not here, he can act as a friend who is familiar enough to dwell with us even in our absence (see Rev 3:20). The current and, on our side, ever fragmentary friendship lived with Christ has a sensible and material support in the signs of bread and wine, which recall our absentmindedness and dissipation to his presence ever anew.

Admittedly, it would be a false understanding of Eucharistic friendship with Christ if it were conceived as a privilege of religious interiority, as a private relationship of pious souls. Friendship with Christ cannot be exclusive; it cannot set up an elite circle, which remains restricted to only the like-minded. Rather, it pushes toward expansion, it is aimed at being aware of and attending to others, strangers, the disadvantaged, all as friends of Christ (without therefore immediately incorporating them into one's community). This is a sociological idiosyncracy of the community that gathers in the Church: it includes young and old, healthy and sick, rich and poor— or as Peter Handke described it: "At communion in the Church, I saw the 'people': what became entirely perceptible was the greatness and smallness of the people, of the young and old, the bright and witless, the normal and insane ('Praise O tongue, the mystery of the glorious body and the precious blood')."[121] All who gather here and as the many members form the one body of Christ; they show their readiness to let themselves be taken into the life reality of Christ. In his life and death, Jesus Christ raised up God's definitive Yes to men—through union with Christ, every believer is therefore summoned to participate in this Yes toward the other, precisely where barriers to communication exist, where quarrelsome coercion is present. To the extent that the individual believer enters into friendship with Christ, he grows into the community of those who are Christ's friends and want to be such. *Communio* is therefore an implication of friendship with Christ. Or, put otherwise: friendship with Christ can be authentically lived only as a *communio* of friends and companions of Christ. "This is my command-

---

120. J. Derrida, *Politics of Friendship*, trans. George Collins (New York: Verso, 1997), 14–15.
121. P. Handke, *Die Geschichte des Bleistifts* (Frankfurt: Suhrkamp, 1985), 231.

ment, that you love one another as I have loved you" (Jn 15:12). For the self-understanding of Christians, what emerges from this is an ecclesiological norm for conduct: "We know love by this, that he laid down his life for us—and we ought to lay down our lives for one another" (1 Jn 3:16).[122] But also those who consciously reject friendship with Christ are, from his viewpoint, to be seen and treated as potential friends. "One should consider all men as if they had just received the Eucharist, as they should always be: Christ in them, they in Christ."[123]

Homecoming—the Eucharist as Passage from Death to Life

> It is the facticity of death … that makes us "guest workers," *frontaliers*, in the boarding-houses of life.
> George Steiner[124]

> Was not in fact a homecoming possible?
> Peter Handke[125]

> Being continually ready to receive the Eucharist or to die, this is one and the same thing. Death is the last, the perfect, the eternal communion.
> Maurice Blondel[126]

Human life unfolds along the slope of mortality. The definitive departure from others, the experience of sickness and age are precursors of coming death. "For contemporary, western man, even if he is fit as a fiddle, the thought of death begets a sort of *background noise*, which fills his brain as soon as his plans and wishes become fewer. With advancing age, the presence of this noise becomes more and more insistent; it can be compared to a dull rustling that is sometimes accompanied by a crunching. In other time periods, the background noise was generated by waiting for the Lord's kingdom; today, it is generated by waiting for death."[127] Whoever does not drown out this noise with the lulling products of consumerism will be confronted with the question of whether at the very end *nothing*

---

122. See H.-J. Klauck, "Kirche als Freundesgemeinschaft? Auf Spurensuche im Neuen Testament," *MThZ* 42 (1991): 1–14.
123. M. Blondel, *Tagebuch vor Gott*, 193.
124. G. Steiner, *Real Presences: Is There Anything in What We Say?* (London: University of Chicago Press, 1989), 140.
125. P. Handke, *Die morawische Nacht. Erzählung* (Frankfurt/M.: Suhrkamp, 2008), 262.
126. M. Blondel, *Tagebuch vor Gott*, 129.
127. M. Houellebecq, *Elementarteilchen*, trans. U. Wittmann (Berlin: DuMont, 1999), 92. See also the remark by B. Strauss, *Der Untenstehende auf Zehenspitzen*, 78: "In earlier times, men feared the afterlife; today, death."

stands or whether there is a *life beyond death*. Confessing atheists anticipate the goal of their journey in a certain way when they believe that their lives must be placed within the horizon of a definitive hopelessness. Should it be shown at the end that everything is *nothing* (although where would this consciousness be which could ascertain this end?), then the strategy of radical self-relativization would make complete sense: to practice already here and now the separation from oneself, from others, and from the world.[128] But the thought of a total extinguishing of human consciousness, as fascinating as it appears to be for many contemporaries, still provokes queries: Are there not moments appearing in the course of living out one's conscious life that contain a promise beyond death? What about love, which in the unconditional affirmation of the other refuses to relinquish him to death? What about the demand for justice, which for the sake of the dead cannot and does not want to allow past injustices to rest?

The limit concept of nothingness recalls how futile it is to want to secure immortality in the progress of time. All attempts to mark one's own name into the fleeting material of history in a lasting way—like the urge of the artist to immortalize himself in his work, or the striving of politicians to get into the annals of history through "historical" deeds, or the ambition of scientists to make a name for themselves through their books—are ultimately vanity. One need only hold before his eyes that a lifetime (along with one's own epoch) is at best a short episode within the world's history. But: "How can one live knowing that all will die?"[129]

In view of the hopelessness of this question, one can protest against death or try to suppress it, but despite every protest and suppression, one will ultimately be unable to flee from it. A life that cannot be broken by death exceeds man's power over the world. It must come from *somewhere else*—the omnipotent fantasies of certain bio-engineers notwithstanding.[130] No philosophy "can restore to the status of a rounded, meaningful whole this fragment of earthly life, slipping away as it is toward death ... : the shattered image can only be restored by God."[131] Faith confesses God as the God of the living, who called the being of creatures *out of nothing*, who preserves

---

128. On the strategy of self-relativization, the "mystical" receding from oneself, see E. Tugendhat, *Egozentrizität und Mystik. Eine anthropologische Studie* (Munich: C. H. Beck, 2003).

129. A. Schmemann, *The Journals of Father Alexander Schmemann 1973–1983*, trans. Juliana Schmemann (Crestwood, N.Y.: St. Vladimir's Seminary Press, 2000), 15.

130. On this point, see the remarkable essay by F. Kamphaus, "Der 'Neue Mensch': Über unchristliche Spielarten einer christlichen Vision," in his *Um Gottes willen—Leben. Einsprüche* (Freiburg: Herder, 2004), 15–25.

131. H. U. von Balthasar, *Mysterium Paschale: The Mystery of Easter*, trans. Aidan Nichols, OP (Edinburgh: Ignatius Press, 1990), 12.

them in life and will not hand them over to the abyss of death at the end of time. The life of man is not a caprice of fate, a fleeting episode of evolution; it does not peter out into nothingness but rather runs up to the judging and restoring encounter with the crucified and risen one, who calls each by name and grants them to enter with him and others into the truth. Still, not wanting to hastily overplay the severity of death, it must be immediately added that the God of life shared in human life even into the frightfulness of death. "He, who is our life, himself descended to the extreme, suffered our death and slew it out of the abundance of his life."[132] In this *transitus* of death to a life that no longer knows death, a hope is established, that all names are ultimately listed in the *memoria Dei*. In the words of Erik Peterson: "As God cannot forget himself, so also must his not being able to forget himself be realized in the resurrection."[133] In this remembering of God, however, there takes place the definitive *re-membering*, the re-incorporating of the *disiecta membra* into the eschatological body of the Lord.

In the Eucharist, those who believe receive already here and now a participation in the gift of the life that no longer knows death. The Eucharist is *viaticum*, which helps the *homo viator* to keep the end of his journey in view, to not go astray on the streets of life but rather to hold in view the land of the living—the *terra viventium*. The question: "When I am no longer a traveler, who will I then be?"[134] refers to the hereafter of the pilgrimage, to a destination into which the "off-ramp to infinitude"[135] will run. To let oneself be given the *panis vivus et vitalis* as provision for the journey is already to receive a foretaste of this end while walking and—at least as in a beginning—to grow into the disposition of overcoming death given by the "chief of life."[136] Eucharistic identity, which does not cling to life but receives it as a gift, communes already now with the giver, who went ahead of us to prepare our dwelling place in the Father's house. It sees itself as referred to the gifts of inheritance—the bread and wine—and allows itself to be captured in faith by the hidden presence of the *Christus passus*. If the act of believing involves the believer handing himself over—*credere* is associated with *cor dare*—and if learning by rote presents an *apprendre par coeur* beyond cognitive effort, then even the passerby of the late modern world can be captivated in faith

---

132. Augustine, *Conf.*, IV, 19: "Et descendit huc ipsa vita nostra et tulit mortam nostram et occidit eam de abundantia vitae suae."

133. E. Peterson, *Marginalien zur Theologie und andere Schriften* (Würzburg: Echter, 1995), 141.

134. P. Handke, *Gestern unterwegs. Aufzeichnungen November 1987 bis Juli 1990* (Frankfurt: Suhrkamp, 2007), 553.

135. P. Handke, *Mein Jahr in der Niemandsbucht*, 2nd ed. (Frankfurt: Suhrkamp, 2004), 918.

136. See A. Schmemann, *The Journals of Father Alexander Schmemann 1973–1983*, 27: "What is real culture? Communion. Participation in that which conquered time and death."

by the mystery, despite the distance in time and the unfamiliarity of metaphors, through the slow re-petition and co-petition of St. Thomas Aquinas's Eucharistic hymns. This captivation not only includes grateful wonder at the hidden presence of the host in the gifts of bread and wine, but also is borne by a yearning one day to be table fellows—*commensales*—at the eternal wedding feast of the lamb and co-heirs of the kingdom—*cohaeredes*. Thomas gave poetic voice to this yearning at the end of the Sequence *Lauda Sion*:

> Bone pastor, panis vere,
> Jesu, nostri miserere;
> Tu nos pasce, nos tuere,
> Tu nos bona fac videre
> In terra viventium.
> Tu qui cuncta scis et vales,
> Qui nos pascis hic mortales:
> Tuos ibi commensales,
> Cohaeredes et sodales
> Fac sanctorum civium.
> Amen.

BIBLIOGRAPHY

I. Primary Sources

1. Thomas Aquinas

In Sent.   Scriptum super libros sententiarum magistri Petri Lombardi episcopi Parisiensis. Edited by P. Mandonnet, vols. 1–2. Paris: P. Lethielleux, 1929.
Scriptum super sententiis magistri Petri Loardi. Recogn. atque iterum ed. M. F. Moos. Vol. 3. Paris: P. Lethielleux, 1933. Vol. 4. Paris: P. Lethielleux, 1947.

S.c.G.   Summa contra gentiles—editions:
Leonina, vols. 13–15 (with commentary by Sylvester of Ferrara). Rome, 1918, 1926 and 1930.
Marietti (Textus Leoninus diligenter recognitus). Edited by C. Pera, P. Marc, P. Caramello. 3 vols. Rome, 1961 and 1967.
Wissenschaftliche Buchgesellschaft. 4 vols. Edited and translated by K. Allgaier. Latin text provided, with remarks, by L. Gerken. Darmstadt, 2001.
Summa contra Gentiles. Translated into English and edited by A. C. Pegis, J. F. Anderson, V. J. Bourke, C. J. O' Neil. 5 vols. Notre Dame, Ind.: University of Notre Dame Press, 1975.

S. th.   Summa theologiae—editions:
Leonina, vols. 4–11. Rome, 1888–1903 (I: vols. 4–5; I–II: vols. 6–7; II–II: vols. 8–10; III: vol. 11; Suppl.: vol. 12)—identical with the Marietti Edition. 3 vols. Edited by P. Caramello. Rome, 1956.
Die Deutsche Thomas-Ausgabe: Vollständige, ungekürzte deutschlateinische Ausgabe der Summa theologica. Translated by the Dominicans and Benedictines of Germany and Austria. Heidelberg-Graz-Cologne-Vienna: Pustet /Styra, 1933–.
Summa theologica. Edited by the Fathers of the English Dominican Province. 5 vols. Westminster, Md.: Christian Classics, 1981.
Summa theologica. Latin-English version edited by T. Gilby and T. C. O'Brien. 60 vols. Cambridge: Cambridge University Press, 1964–73.

In Math.   Super Evanglium S. Matthaei Lectura. Edited by P. Raphaelis Cai. Rome: Marietti, 1951.

In Ioan.	*Super Evangelium S. Ioannis Lectura.* Edited by P. Raphaelis Cai. Rome: Marietti, 1952. *Commentary on the Gospel of John.* 3 vols. Translated by James A. Weisheipl and Fabian R. Larcher. Edited by Daniel Keating and Matthew Levering. Thomas Aquinas in Translation. Washington, D.C.: The Catholic University of America Press, 2010.
In Rom.	*Super Epistolas S. Pauli Lectura.* Edited by P. Raphaelis Cai. 2 vols. Rome: Marietti, 1953.
In Phys.	*In octo libros physicorum Aristotelis expositio.* Edited by P. M. Maggiòlo. Rome: Marietti, 1954. *Commentary on Aristotle's Physics.* Translated by Richard J. Blackwell, Richard J. Spath, and W. Edmund Thirlkel. Aristotelian Commentary Series. Notre Dame, Ind.: Dumb Ox Books, 1999.
In Met.	*In duodecim libros metaphysicorum Aristotelis expositio.* Edited by M.-R. Cathala and R. M. Spiazzi. Rome: Marietti, 1950. *Commentary on Aristotle's Metaphysics.* Translated by John P. Rowan. Aristotelian Commentary Series. Notre Dame, Ind.: Dumb Ox Books, 1995.
In De Anima	*In Aristotelis librum de anima commentarium.* Edited by A. M. Pirotta. Rome: Marietti, 1948. *Commentary on Aristotle's De anima.* Translated by Robert C. Pasnau. New Haven, Conn.: Yale University Press, 1999.
Officium	*Officium de festo corporis Christi ad mandatum Urbani Papae IV dictum Festum instituentis.* In *Opuscula theologica II*, edited by R. M. Spiazzi, 275–81. Rome: Marietti, 1954. *The Aquinas Prayer Book: The Prayers and Hymns of Saint Thomas Aquinas.* Translated by Robert Anderson and Johann Moser. Sophia Institute, 2000. (Includes *Officium de festo Corporis Christi* and many of the prayers composed by St. Thomas, such as *Adoro te devote* and *Pange lingua*.)
Homo	*Homo quidam fecit cenam magnam.* Edited by L.-J. Bataillon. *RSPhTh* 58 (1974): 451–56.
In De Trin.	*In librum Boethii De trinitate expositio.* Translated into English by Armand Maurer, as *The Division and Methods of the Sciences: Questions V and VI of His Commentary on the De Trinitate of Boethius.* Mediaeval Sources in Translation 3. 4th ed. Toronto: Pontifical Institute of Mediaeval Studies, 1986. And *Faith, Reason and Theology: Questions I–IV of His Commentary on the De Trinitate of Boethius.* Mediaeval Sources in Translation 32. Toronto: Pontifical Institute of Mediaeval Studies, 1987.
De decem praec.	*Collationes de decem preceptis.* In *Recherches thomasiennes: Études revues et augmentées*, edited by Jean-Pierre Torrell, 47–117. Bibliothèque thomiste 52. Paris: Vrin, 2000.

2. Further Primary Sources

Abaelard, Peter. *Theologia scholarium.* In: idem. *Opera theologica.* Cura et studio E. M. Buytaert, vol. 3. Corpus Christianorum: Continuatio Mediaevalis 13. Turnholt: Brepols Publishers, 1987.

Abbaudus. *De fractione corporis Christi.* PL 166, 1341–1348.

BIBLIOGRAPHY 343

Albert the Great. *Opera omnia* = Alberti Magni Opera omnia: ex editione Lugdunensi religiose castigata, et pro auctoritatibus ad fidem Vulgatae versionis accuratiorumque patrologiae textuum revocata, auctaque B. Alberti vita ac bibliographia operum a PP. Quétif et Echard exaratis, etiam revisa et locupletata, cura ac labore Augusti Borgnet. Paris: Vivès, 1890–.

Alexander III. *Die Sentenzen Rolands nachmals Papstes Alexander III*. First published by Fr. Ambrosius M. Gietl. Freiburg i. Br.: Herder'sche Verlagshandlung, 1891. Later printing: Amsterdam: Rodopi Bv Editions, 1969.

Alexander of Hales. *Quaestiones disputatae 'antequam esset frater', nunc primum ed. studio et cura Pp. Collegii S. Bonaventurae*. Bibliotheca Franciscana scholastica medii aevi 20. Quaracchi, Florentiae: Ex Typographia Collegii S. Bonaventurae, 1960.

Amalarius of Metz (Amalarius Metensis). *Liber Officialis*. Edited by J. M. Hanssens (Opera liturgica omnia 2 = Studi e testi 139). Città del Vaticano: Biblioteca Apostolica Vaticana, 1967. Translated into English by Eric Knibbs as *On the Liturgy*. Cambridge, Mass.: Harvard University Press, 2014.

Ambrose. *De Sacramentis—De Mysteriis. Über die Sakramente—Über die Mysterien. Lateinisch—Deutsch*. Translated by J. Schmitz, CSSR. Fontes Christiani 3. Freiburg-Basel-Vienna: Herder, 1990. Translated into English by Roy J. Deferrari, as *The Sacraments* and *The Mysteries* in *Theological and Dogmatic Works*. Fathers of the Church 44. Washington, D.C.: The Catholic University of America Press, 1963.

Anselm of Canterbury. *Cur Deus homo. Warum Gott Mensch geworden. Lateinisch—Deutsch*, edited by F. S. Schmitt. 5th ed. Munich: Kösel, 1993. Translated into English as *Why God Became Man* in *Anselm of Canterbury: The Major Works*. Oxford University Press, 1998. Reprint 2008.

Aristotle. *Ethica Nicomachea, recogn. brevique adnotatione critica instruxit I. Bywater*, Reprint of the 1894 edition. Oxford: E Typographeo Clarendoniano, 1979.

———. *Metaphysik*. 2 vol. Greek–German, translated by H. Bonitz, edited by H. Seidl (Greek text taken from the edition of W. Christ). 3rd ed. Hamburg: Meiner, 1991.

———. *Physik: Vorlesung über die Natur—Über die Seele*. Translated by H. G. Zekl and W. Theiler, edited by H. Seidl. Hamburg: Meiner, 1995.

Augustinus, Aurelius (Augustine). *Confessionum libri XIII, quos post Martinvm Skutella iterum ed. Lvcas Verheijen—cura et studio B. Dombart* (Opera 1,1 = Corpus Christianorum: Series Latina 27). Turnholt: Brepols, 1981. Translated into English by Vernon J. Bourke. Fathers of the Church 21. Washington, D.C.: The Catholic University of America Press, 1953. Reprint 2008.

———. *De Civitate Dei*, libri 1–10, cura et studio B. Dombart (Opera 14,1 = Corpus Christianorum: Series Latina 47). Turnholt: Brepols, 1955. Translated into English by Gerald G. Walsh, Demetrius B. Zema [Books I–VII], and G. Monahan [Books VIII–XVI] as *The City of God*. Fathers of the Church 12 and 13. Washington, D.C.: The Catholic University of America Press, 1950, 1952. Reprint 2008.

———. *De Civitate Dei*, libri 11–22, cura et studio B. Dombart (Opera 14,2 = Corpus Christianorum: Series Latina 48). Turnholt: Brepols, 1955. Translated into English by G. Monahan [Books VIII–XVI] and Gerald G. Walsh [Books XVII–XXII] as *The City of God*. Fathers of the Church 13 and 14. Washington, D.C.: The Catholic University of America Press, 1952, 1954. Reprint 2008.

———. *De doctrina christiana; De vera religione*, cura et studio K. D. Daur (Opera 4,1 =

Corpus Christianorum: Series Latina 32). Turnholt: Brepols, 1996. *De doctrina christiana* translated into English by John J. Gavigan as *Christian Instruction* in Fathers of the Church 2. Washington, D.C.: The Catholic University of America Press, 1950. Reprint 2002. *De vera religione* translated into English by Edmund Hill, OP, Ray Kearney, Michael G. Campbell, and Bruce Harbert in *The Works of Saint Augustine*, vol. I/8. Hyde Park, N.Y.: New City Press, 2005.

———. *De Trinitate* libri XV, libri 1–12, cura et studio W. J. Mountain (Opera 16,1 = Corpus Christianorum: Series Latina 50). Turnholt: Brepols, 1968. Translated into English by Stephen McKenna as *The Trinity*. Fathers of the Church 45. Washington, D.C.: The Catholic University of America Press, 1963. Reprint 2002.

———. *Enarrationes in Psalmos*, cura et studio D. E. Dekkers et I. Fraipant (Opera 10/1–3 = Corpus Christianorum: Series Latina 38–40). Turnholt: Brepols, 1956. Translated into English as *Expositions on the Psalms*. 6 vols. The Works of Saint Augustine, vol. III/15–20. Hyde Park, N.Y.: New City Press.

———. *Epistulae* LVI–C, cura et studio Kl. D. Daur (Opera 3,2 = Corpvs Christianorvm: Series Latina 31A). Turnholt: Brepols, 2005. Translated into English by Wilfrid Parsons. Fathers of the Church 12, 18, 20, 30, 32. Washington, D.C.: The Catholic University of America Press. Reprint 2008.

———. *In Iohannis evangelium tractatus CXXIV*, cura et studio R. Willems (Opera 8 = Corpus Christianorum: Series Latina 36). Turnholt: Brepols, 1990. Translated into English by John W. Rettig. Fathers of the Church 78, 79, 88, 90, 92. Washington, D.C.: The Catholic University of America Press, 1988, 1988, 1993, 1994, 1995.

Bartholomew of Lucca. *Historia ecclesiastica nova, nebst Fortsetzung bis 1329*. Edited by O. Clavuot and Ludwig Schmugge. Monumentum Germaniae Historica: Scriptores 39. Hanover: Hahnsche Buchhandlung, 2009.

Bede, the Venerable. *In Lucae evangelium expositio: In Marci evangelium expositio*, cura et studio D. Hurst. (Opera 2,3 = Corpus Christianorum: Series Latina 120). Turnholt: Typographi Brepols, 1960. Translated into English by Lawrence T. Martin and David Hurst as *Homilies on the Gospel*. 2 vols. Kalamazoo, Mich.: Cistercian Publications, 1991.

Berengar of Tours. *Rescriptum contra Lanfrannum*. Edited by R. B. C. Huygens. Corpus Christianorum: Continuatio Mediaevalis 84. Turnholti: Brepols, 1988.

Biel, Gabriel. *Sacrosancti Canonis Missae expositio pia & catholica. viro M. Gabriele Biel, sacrae Theologiae professore in Epitomen contracta, ac recens explosis mendis enchiridij forma edita.* (Bibliotheca Palatina, ed. Leonard Boyle and Elmar Mittler, H2155/H2156.) Antverpiae: Bellerus, 1556.

Bonaventure. *Commentaria in quatuor libros sententiarum magistri Petri Lombardi*. 4 vols.: 1. In primum librum sententiarum. Quaracchi, 1883. 2. In secundum librum sententiarum. Quaracchi, 1885. 3. In tertium librum sententiarum. Quaracchi, 1887. 4. In quartum librum sententiarum. Quaracchi, 1889.

———. *Breviloquium*. In *Opera omnia*, vol. 5. Quaracchi, 1891. Translated, with an introduction and glossary, by Marianne Schlosser. Christliche Meister 52. Freiburg: Johannes Verlag 2002. Translated into English by Dominic Monti. St. Bonaventure, N.Y.: Franciscan Institute Publications, 2005.

Chrysostom, John. *Enarratio in epistulam ad Hebraeos*. In PG 63, 9–236.

Cyprian, Thascius Caecilius. *Opera omnia*, vol. 1 (Corpus scriptorum ecclesiasticorum Latinorum 3). Reprint of the 1868 edition, Vindobonae 1965. Partial English translation by

Roy J. Deferrari as *Treatises*. Fathers of the Church 36. Washington, D.C.: The Catholic University of America Press, 1956. Reprint 2007.

Cyril of Jerusalem. *Explanatio in Lucae evangelium*, in PG 72, 475–950.

———. *Mystagogicae Catecheses: Mystagogische Katechesen*. Greek–German, translated by G. Röwekamp. Fontes Christiani 7. Freiburg-Basel-Vienna: Herder, 1992. Translated into English by Leo P. McCauley, SJ, as *Mystagogical Catecheses* in *The Works of Saint Cyril of Jerusalem*, vol. 1. The Fathers of the Church 61. Washington, D.C.: The Catholic University of America Press, 1969. Reprint 2005.

Descartes, René. *Oeuvres*. Edited by Ch. Adam and P. Tannery. Vol. XI. Paris: Cerf, 1909. Translated into English as *The Philosophical Writings of Descartes*. 3 vols. Cambridge University Press, 1985 (vols. 1–2) and 1991 (vol. 3).

The Didache (Text, Translation, and Commentary). Translated by Aaron Milavec. Collegeville, Minn.: Liturgical Press, 2003.

Pseudo-Dionysius the Areopagite. *De coelesti hierarchia*. Edited by Günter Heil and Adolf Martin Ritter. Corpus Dionysiacum 2; Patristische Texte und Studien 36. Berlin–New York: De Gruyter, 1991.

Duns Scotus, John. *Opera omnia* (= *Joannis Duns Scoti doctoris subtilis Ordinis Minorum Opera omnia*. Editio nova iuxta editionem Waddingi XII tomos continentem a Patribus Franciscanis de observantia accurate recognita. Paris: Vivès, 1891–. Partial English translations: John Duns Scotus. *Opera philosophica*. 5 vols. St. Bonaventure, N.Y.: The Franciscan Institute, 1997 (vols. 3–4), 1999 (vol. 1), 2004 (vol. 2), 2006 (vol. 5).

Gregory the Great. *Registrum epistularum*. Vol. 2: Libri 8–14. Edited by D. Norberg. In S. Gregorii Magni opera; Corpus Christianorum: Series Latina 140a. Turnholt 1982.

Gui, Bernardo. *Vita S. Thomae Aquinatis* (Fontes vitae S. Thomae Aquinatis III—Documents inédits publiés par la *Revue Thomiste*). Edited by D. Prümmer, o. O. 1926.

Guimundus. *De corporis et sanguinis Christi veritate in Eucharistia*. PL 149, 1427–1512.

Hilary of Poitiers. *La trinité, tome II: livres IV–VIII*. Texte critique par P. Smulders, traduction et notes par G. M. de Durand, Ch. Morel, et G. Pelland. Sources Chrétiennes 448. Paris: Cerf, 2000. Translated into English by Stephen McKenna as *The Trinity*. Washington, D.C.: The Catholic University of America Press, 1954. Reprint 2002.

Hippolytus. *Apostolische Überlieferung—Traditio apostolica*. Edited by. W. Geerlings. Fontes Christiani 1. Freiburg-Basel-Vienna: Herder, 1990. Translated into English by A. C. Stewart as *On the Apostolic Tradition*. Yonkers, N.Y.: St. Vladimir's Seminary Press, 2015.

Hugh of Saint Victor. *De sacramentis christianae fidei*. PL 176, 173–618. Translated into English by Roy J. Deferrari as *On the Sacraments of the Christian Faith*. Cambridge, Mass.: Mediaeval Academy of America, 1951.

Innocent III. *De sacro altaris mysterio*. PL 217, 773–916.

Isidore of Seville. *Isidori Hispalensis Episcopi Etymologiarvm sive Originvm libri XX*, recogn. brevique adnot. critica instruxit W. M. Lindsay. 2 vols. Oxonii: E Typographeo Clarendoniano, 1957.

Ivo of Chartres. *Panormia*. PL 161, 1037–1344.

Jacopone da Todi. *Le Laude, secondo la stampa fiorentina del 1490*. Edited by G. Ferri. 2nd ed. Bari: Gius Laterza & Figli, 1930. Translated into English by S. Hughes and E. Hughes as *Jacopone da Todi: The Lauds*. New York: Paulist Press, 1982.

John of Damascus. *De fide orthodoxa*. Latin–English. *Versions of Burgundio and Cerbanus*. Edited by E. M. Buytaert. Franciscan Institute Publications: Text Series 8. New York: Franciscan Institute, 1955.

Lanfranc of Canterbury. *De corpore et sanguine Domini.* PL 150, 407–442. Translated into English by Mark G. Vallaincourt as *On the Body and Blood of the Lord.* The Fathers of the Church: Medieval Continuation 10. Washington, D.C.: The Catholic University of America Press, 2009.

Leo the Great. *Sermons.* Vol. 3. Edited by R. Dolle. Sources Chrétiennes 74. 2nd ed. Paris: Cerf, 1976. Translated into English by Jane Patricia Freeland as *Sermons.* Fathers of the Church, vol. 93. Washington, D.C.: The Catholic University of America Press, 1996. Reprint 2015.

Lombard, Peter. *Libri IV sententiarum, studio ed cura PP. Collegii S. Bonaventurae in lucem editi.* Vol. 2: Liber III et IV. 2nd ed. Ad Claras Aquas/prope Florentiam: Ex Typographia Collegii S. Bonaventurae, 1916. English–Latin edition: *The Sentences* in 4 volumes. Mediaeval Sources in Translation 42, 43, 45, 48. Toronto: Pontifical Institute of Mediaeval Studies, 2007, 2008, 2008, 2011.

Luther, Martin. *De captivitate Babylonica ecclesiae praeludium* (1520). In *Werke*, vol. 6. Weimar: Hermann Böhlau, 1888. Translated into English by Erik H. Hermann as *The Babylonian Captivity of the Church, 1520.* Minneapolis, Minn.: Fortress Press, 2016.

Ockham, Guilelmus de [William of Ockham]. *Quaestiones in librum quartum sententiarum (Reportatio).* In *Opera theologica*, vol. 7. St. Bonaventure, N.Y.: Franciscan Institute Publications, 1984.

Physiologus. Greek/German. Translated by O. Schönberger. Stuttgart: Philipp Reclam, 2001. Translated into English by Michael J. Curley. Austin: University of Texas Press, 1979.

Radbertus, Paschasius. *De corpore et sanguine domini.* Cum appendice Epistola ad Fredugardum. Cura et studio Bedae Paulus. Corpus Christianorum: Continuatio Mediaevalis 16. Turnholt: Brepols, 1969.

Ratramnus. *De corpore et sanguine Domini.* Edited by J. N. Bakhuizen van den Brink. Amsterdam: North Holland Publishing Co., 1974.

Teresa of Jesus: *Libro de la vida.* Edited by Otger Steggink. Clásicos Castalia 154. Madrid: Castalia, 1986. Translated into English by Mirabai Starr as *Teresa of Ávila: The Book of My Life.* Boston: New Seeds, 2007.

Tertullian. *Ad martyras.* Edited by V. Bulhart and J. W. Ph. Borleffs. Corpus Scriptorum Ecclesiasticorum Latinorum 76. Vindobonae: Hoelder, Pichler, Tempsky, 1957, 1–8. Translated into English by Rudolph Arbesmann, Sister Emily Joseph Daly, and Edwin A. Quain as *To the Martyrs*, in *Disciplinary, Moral, and Ascetical Works.* Fathers of the Church 40. Washington, D.C.: The Catholic University of America Press, 1959.

Theodore of Mopsuestia. *Katechetische Homilien.* Translated by P. Bruns. Fontes Christiani 17,1 and 2. Freiburg-Basel-Vienna: Herder, 1994 (vol. 1), 1995 (vol. 2). Translated into English as *Catechetical Homilies* in *Theodore of Mopsuestia.* The Early Church Fathers. London and New York: Routledge, 2009.

Urban IV. *Transiturus de hoc mundo* (Bull), in *Corpus iuris canonici. Editio lipsensis secunda.* Edited by E. Friedberg. Vol. 2: Decretalium collectiones, colls. 1174–77. Leipzig: Bernhard Tauchnitz, 1881

William of Tocco. *Ystoria sancti Thome de Aquino* (1323). Édition critique, introduction et notes Claire le Brun-Gouanvic. Toronto: Pontifical Institute of Mediaeval Studies, 1996. German translation by W. P. Eckert as *Das Leben des heiligen Thomas von Aquino und andere Zeugnisse zu seinem Leben.* Düsseldorf: Patmos, 1965.

Wycliff, John. *De Eucharista tractatus maior.* Edited by J. Loserth. London: Trübner, 1892.

II. Auxiliary Texts and Anthologies

Analecta Hymnica Medii Aevi. 55 vols. Leipzig 1886–1922.

Browe, Petrus. *Textus antiqui de festo Corporis Christi: Opuscula et textus*. Series liturgica 4. Münster: Aschendorff, 1934.

Corpus iuris canonici—post Aemilii Ludouici Richteri curas ad librorum manu sriptorum et ed. romanae fidem recogn. et adnotatione critica instruxit Aemilius Friedberg. Vol. 1: *Decretum Gratiani*, 2nd ed. Leipzig 1879. Vol. 2: *Decretalium collectiones. Decretales Gregorii P. IX.*, 2nd ed. Leipzig 1881.

Denzinger, Heinrich, ed. *Kompendium der Glaubensbekenntnisse und kirchlichen Lehrentscheidungen*. Edited by Peter Hünermann, translated into German and expanded by Helmut Hoping. 40th ed. Freiburg: Herder, 2005. Translated into English by Robert Fastiggi and Anne Englund Nash as *Compendium of Creeds, Definitions, and Declarations on Matters of Faith and Morals*. 43rd ed. San Francisco: Ignatius Press, 2012.

Die Bekenntnisschriften der evangelisch-lutherischen Kirche. 12th ed. Göttingen: Vandenhoeck & Ruprecht, 1998 (= BSLK).

Döpp, Siegmar, and Wilhelm Geerlings, eds. *Lexikon der antiken christlichen Literatur*. 3rd ed. Freiburg: Herder, 2002.

Dorez, Léon, ed. *Les Registres d'Urbain IV. Recueil des bulles de ce pape, publiées ou analysés d'après les manuscrits originaux du Vatican*. Bibliothèque des écoles françaises d'Athènes et de Rome: sér. 2, 13. Vol. 2/ 1. Paris: A. Fontemoing, 1901.

Reichert, Benedictus Maria, ed. *Acta Capitulorum generalium Ordinis Praedicatorum*. Vol. 2. Rome: Nabu Press, 1899.

Schott, Anselm. *Das vollständige Römische Messbuch, lateinisch und deutsch, mit allgemeinen und besonderen Einführungen im Anschluss an das Messbuch*. Edited by the Benedictines of Archabbey Beuron. 13th ed. Freiburg: Herder, 1954.

Schütz, Ludwig. *Thomas-Lexikon*. 2nd ed. Stuttgart: Frommann-Holzboog, 1983.

Stock, Alex. *Lateinische Hymnen*. Berlin: Insel Verlag, 2012.

Wilpert, Gero von. *Sachwörterbuch der Literatur*. Kröners Taschenausgabe 231. 7th ed. Stuttgart: Alfred Kröner, 1989.

III. Secondary Liturature: Thomas Aquinas and the Scholastics

Angenendt, Arnold. *Geschichte der Religiosität im Mittelalter*. Darmstadt: Wissenschaftliche Buchgesellschaft, 2001.

———. *Offertorium. Das mittelalterliche Meßopfer*. Münster: Aschendorff, 2013.

Ardley, Gavin. "The Physics of Local Motion." *The Thomist* 17 (1954): 145–85.

Arias Reyero, Maximino. *Thomas von Aquin als Exeget: Die Prinzipien seiner Schriftdeutung und seine Lehre von den Schriftsinnen*. Einsiedeln: Johannes-Verlag, 1971.

Avril, François. "Une curieuse illustration de la Fête-Dieu: L'iconographie du Christ pretre élevant l'hostie et sa diffusion." In *Rituels: Mélanges offerts à P.-M. Gy*, edited by P. de Clerck and E. Palazzo. Paris: Cerf, 1990.

Backes, Ignaz. *Die Christologie des hl. Thomas von Aquin und die griechischen Kirchenväter*. Paderborn: Ferdinand Schöningh, 1931.

Bataillon, Louis-J. "Le sermon inédit de Saint Thomas *Homo quidam fecit cenam mangnam*." *RSPhTh* 67 (1983): 353–69.

Beckermann, Wolfgang. "Überblicksrezension zu E. Panofsky, Gotische Architektur und Scholastik." *Concilium Medii Aevi* 1 (1998): 1000–1013.

Bell, Thomas J. "The Eucharistic Theologies of *Lauda Sion* and Thomas Aquinas's *Summa Theologiae*." *The Thomist* 57 (1993): 163–85.

Bendel-Maidl, Lydia. *Tradition und Innovation: Zur Dialektik von historischer und systematischer Perspektive in der Theologie: Am Beispiel von Transformationen in der Rezeption des Thomas von Aquin im 20. Jahrhundert.* Religion—Geschichte—Gesellschaft 27. Münster: LIT Verlag, 2004.

Berceville, Gilles. "Le sacerdoce du Christ dans le Commentaire de l'épître aux Hébreux de saint Thomas d'Aquin." *Revue Thomiste* 99 (1999): 143–58.

Berchtold, Christoph. *Manifestatio veritatis: Zum Offenbarungsbegriff bei Thomas von Aquin.* Münster-Hamburg-London: LIT Verlag, 2000.

Berger, David. "'S. Thoma praesertim magistro ...' Überlegungen zur Aktualität des Thomismus." *Forum Katholische Theologie* 15 (1999): 180–92.

———. *Thomas von Aquin und die Liturgie.* 2nd ed. Cologne: Books on Demand, 2000. Translated into English by C. Grosz as *Thomas Aquinas and the Liturgy.* Naples, Fla.: Sapientia Press, 2005.

———. *Was ist ein Sakrament? Der heilige Thomas von Aquin und die Sakramente im Allgemeinen.* Respondeo 16. Siegburg: Franz Schmitt, 2004.

Blanche, Francis A. "Le vocabulaire de l'argumentation et la structure de l'article dans les ouvrages de S. Thomas." *RSPhTh* 14 (1925): 167–87.

Blume, Clemens. "Das Fronleichnamsfest: Seine ersten Urkunden und Offizien." *ThGl* 1 (1909): 337–49.

———. "Thomas von Aquin und das Fronleichnamsfest, insbesondere der Hymnus Verbum supernum." *ThGl* 3 (1911): 358–72.

Bonino, Serge-Thomas. "Le sacerdoce comme institution naturelle selon saint Thomas d'aquin." *Revue Thomiste* 99 (1999): 33–57.

Bormann, C. von, W. Franzen, A. Krapiec, and L. Oeing-Hanhoff. "Form und Materie." *HWPh* 2 (1972): 977–1030.

Bouëssé, Humbert. "La causalité efficiente instrumentale de l'humanité du Christ et des sacraments chrétiens." *Revue Thomiste* 39 (1934): 370–93.

Boyle, John F. "The Twofold Division of St. Thomas's Christology in the *Tertia Pars*." *The Thomist* 60 (1996): 439–47.

Bracken, W. Jerome. "Thomas Aquinas and Anselm's Satisfaction Theory." *Angelicum* 62 (1985): 503–30.

———. "Of What Benefit to Himself Was Christ's Suffering? Merit in Aquinas's Theology of the Passion." *The Thomist* 65 (2001): 385–407.

Breuer, Werner. *Die lateinische Eucharistiedichtung des Mittelalters.* Wuppertal: Henn, 1970.

Brock, Stephen L. "St. Thomas and the Eucharistic Conversion." *The Thomist* 65 (2001): 529–65.

Browe, Peter. "Die scholastische Theorie der eucharistischen Verwandlungswunder." *ThQ* 110 (1929): 305–32.

———. "Die Verehrung der Eucharistie im Mittelalter." Munich: Sankt Meinrad Reprintverlag, 1933.

———. *Die Eucharistie im Mittelalter: Liturgiehistorische Forschungen in kulturwissenschaftlicher Absicht.* Edited by H. Lutterbach and Th. Flammer. Münster: LIT Verlag, 2003.

Burkard, Dominik. "Nähe und Distanz: Eucharistische Frömmigkeit im Mittelalter." In *Mehr als Brot und Wein: Theologische Kontexte der Eucharistie*, edited by W. Haunerland, 73–96. Würzburg: Echter, 2005.
Candler, Peter M. "Liturgically Trained Memory: A Reading of Summa Theologiae III.83." *Modern Theology* 20 (2004): 423–45.
Caprioli, Mario. "Il sacerdozio di cristo nella Somma teologica e nel Commento Super Epistolam ad Hebraeos." *Studi tomistici* 45 (1992): 96–105.
Catao, Bernard. *Salut et redemption chez S. Thomas d'Aquin: L'acte sauveur du Christ*. Paris: Aubier, 1965.
Cathrein, Viktor. "Gottesliebe und Verdienst nach der Lehre des hl. Thomas." *ZAM* 6 (1931): 15–32.
Cessario, Romanus. *Christian Satisfaction in Aquinas: Towards a Personalist Understanding*. Washington, D.C.: University Press of America, 1982.
———. *The Godly Image: Christ and Satisfaction in Catholic Thought from Anselm to Aquinas*. Petersham, Mass.: St. Bede's Publications, 1990.
Chardonnens, Denis. "Éternité du sacerdoce du Christ et effet eschatologique de l'eucharistie: La contribution de saint Thomas à un thème de théologie sacramentaire." *Revue Thomiste* 99 (1999): 159–80.
Chenu, Marie-Dominique. *Toward Understanding Saint Thomas*. Translated by A.-M. Landry and D. Hughes. Chicago: Regnery Publishing, 1964.
———. "Pour une anthropologie sacramentelle." *La Maison-Dieu* 119 (1974): 83–100.
———. "Le plan de la Somme théologique de Saint Thomas." *Revue Thomiste* 47 (1939): 93–107.
———. *Introduction à l'étude de saint Thomas d'Aquin*. Publications de l'Institut d'Etudes Médiévales 11. Montréal: Institut d'Études Médiévales, 1950. Translated into German and edited by O. H. Pesch as *Das Werk des hl. Thomas von Aquin*. 2nd ed. Graz-Vienna-Cologne: Kerle, 1982.
Congar, Yves. "'Traditio' und 'Sacra doctrina' bei Thomas von Aquin." In *Kirche und Überlieferung*, edited by J. Betz and H. Fries, 170–210. Freiburg: Herder, 1960.
———. "Vision de l'Église chez Thomas d'Aquin." *RSPhTh* 62 (1978): 523–42.
Connelly, Joseph. *Hymns of the Roman Liturgy*. London: Newman Press, 1957.
Cottiaux, Jean. *L'office Liégeois de la Fête-dieu: sa valeur et son destin*. Louvain: Liège, 1963.
———. *Sainte Juliana de Cornillon, promotrice de la Fête-Dieu: Son pays, son temps, son message*. Lüttich: Carmel de Cornillon, 1991.
Courth, Franz. *Trinität in der Scholastik*. HDG 2/1b. Freiburg: Herder, 1985.
Craig, William L. "Aquinas on God's Knowledge of Future Contingents." *The Thomist* 54 (1990): 33–79.
Crockett, William R. *Eucharist: Symbol of Transformation*. New York: Liturgical Press, 1989.
Cross, Richard. "Aquinas on Nature, Hypostasis, and the Metaphysics of the Incarnation." *The Thomist* 60 (1996): 171–202.
Dander, Franz. "Grundsätzliches zur Auffassung der Freundschaft nach der Lehre des hl. Thomas von Aquin." *ZAM* 6 (1931): 132–45.
Dauphinais, Michael, and Matthew Levering. *Knowing the Love of Christ: An Introduction to the Theology of St. Thomas Aquinas*. Notre Dame, Ind.: University of Notre Dame Press, 2002.
Descourtieux, Patrick. "Theologie und Liturgie der Eucharistie beim hl. Thomas von Aquin." *UVK* 8 (1978): 18–23.

Diekamp, Franz. *Katholische Dogmatik nach den Grundsätzen des heiligen Thomas von Aquin.* Edited by K. Jüssen. 12th ed. Münster: Sarto, 1954.

Dittoe, John T. "Sacramental Incorporation into the Mystical Body." *The Thomist* 9 (1946): 469–514.

Dondaine, Antoine. "Les 'Opuscula Fratris Thomae' chez Ptolémé de Lucques." *Archivum Fratrum Praedicatorum* 31 (1961): 150–54.

Dondaine, Hyacinthe F. "La définition des sacrements dans la *Somme théologique*." *RSPhTh* 31 (1947): 213–28.

———. "À propos d'Avicenne et de Saint Thomas: De la causalité dispositive à la causalité instrumentale." *Revue Thomiste* 51 (1951): 441–53.

Dörnemann, Holger. *Freundschaft als Paradigma der Erlösung: Eine Reflexion auf die Verbindung von Gnadenlehre, Tugendlehre und Christologie in der Summa Theologiae des Thomas von Aquin.* Bonner dogmatische Studien 27. Würzburg: Echter, 1997.

Egenter, Richard. *Gottesfreundschaft. Die Lehre von der Gottesfreundschaft in der Scholastik und Mystik des 12. und 13. Jahrhunderts.* Augsburg: Dr. Benno Filser Verlag, 1928.

Elders, Leo. *Die Metaphysik des Thomas von Aquin.* 2 vols. Salzburg: Pustet, 1985. Translated by J. Dudley into English as *The Metaphysics of Being of St. Thomas Aquinas in a Historical Perspective.* Leiden: Brill, 1993.

———. "La relation entre l'ancienne et la nouvelle Alliance, selon saint Thomas d'Aquin." *Revue Thomiste* 100 (2000): 580–602.

Emery, Gilles. "Le fruit ecclésial de l'eucharistie chez saint Thomas d'Aquin." *Nova et Vetera* 72 (1997): 25–40.

———. *La théologie trinitaire de saint Thomas d'Aquin.* Paris: Cerf, 2004. Translated into English as *The Trinitarian Theology of Saint Thomas Aquinas.* Translated by F. Aran Murphy. Oxford: Oxford University Press, 2007.

———. *The Trinity: An Introduction to Catholic Doctrine on the Triune God.* Translated by Matthew Levering. Washington, D.C.: The Catholic University of America Press, 2011.

Engelhardt, Paulus. *Thomas von Aquin: Wegweisungen in sein Werk.* Dominikanische Quellen und Zeugnisse 6. Leipzig: St. Benno Verlag, 2005.

Ernst, Stephan. "Die bescheidene Rolle der Demut: Christliche und philosophische Grundhaltungen in der speziellen Tugendlehre (S. th. II-II, q. 161)." In *Thomas von Aquin: Die Summa theologiae: Werkinterpretationen*, edited by A. Speer, 343–76. Berlin–New York: De Gruyter, 2005.

Finkenzeller, Josef. *Die Lehre von den Sakramenten im allgemeinen: Von der Schrift bis zur Scholastik.* HDG IV/1a. Freiburg: Herder, 1980.

Franz, Adolph. *Die Messe im deutschen Mittelalter: Beiträge zur Geschichte der Liturgie und des religiösen Volkslebens.* Freiburg: Herder, 1902.

Frutsaert, E. "La définition du sacrement dans S. Thomas." *Nouvelle Revue Théologique* 55 (1928): 401–9.

Garrigues, Jean-Miguchel. "Les prérogatives inaliénables du peuple juif selon saint Thomas commentant saint Paul." *Revue Thomiste* 103 (2003): 145–58.

Geenen, G. "L'usage des 'auctoritates' dans la doctrine du baptême chez S. Thomas d'Aquin." *Ephemerides theologicae lovaniensis* 15 (1938): 279–329.

———. "L'adage 'Eucharistia est sacramentum ecclesiasticae unitatis' dans les œuvres et la doctrine de S. Thomas d'Aquin." In *Eucaristia y la Paz: Congreso eucarístico internacional* (1952), 275–81. Sesiones de estudio 1. Barcelona: Planas, 1953.

Geiselmann, Josef Rupert. *Die Eucharistielehre der Vorscholastik*. Forschungen zur christlichen Literatur- und Dogmengeschichte 15. Paderborn: Schöningh, 1926.
Ghellinck, Joseph de. "Eucharistie au XIIe siècle en occident." In *Dictionnaire de Théologie Catholique* V/2 (1913): 1233–1302.
Gierens, Michael. "Zur Lehre des heiligen Thomas über die Kausalität der Sakramente." *Scholastik* 9 (1934): 321–45.
Glorieux, Palémon. "Le mérite du Christ selon saint Thomas." *RevSR* 10 (1930): 622–49.
Gössmann, Elisabeth. "Der Christologietraktat in der Summa Halensis, bei Bonaventura und Thomas von Aquin." *MThZ* 12 (1961): 175–91.
Goering, Joseph. "The Invention of Transubstantiation." *Traditio* 46 (1991): 147–70.
Grabmann, Martin. "Die Theologie der eucharistischen Hymnen des hl. Thomas." *Der Katholik* 82 (1902): 385–99.
———. *Die Lehre des heiligen Thomas von Aquin als Gotteswerk: Ihre Stellung im thomistischen System und in der Geschichte der mittelalterlichen Theologie*. Regensburg: Manz, 1903.
Gy, Pierre-Marie. "L'office du Corpus Christi et S. Thomas d'Aquin: État d'une recherche." *RSPhTh* 64 (1980): 491–504.
———. "Le texte original de la Tertia Pars de la *Somme théologique* de S. Thomas d'Aquin dans l'apparat critique de l'édition léonine: Le cas de l'eucharistie." *RSPhTh* 65 (1981): 608–16.
———. "L'office du Corpus Christi et la théologie des accidents eucharistiques." *RSPhTh* 66 (1982): 81–86.
———. "La relation au Christ dans l'Eucharistie selon Bonaventura et S. Thomas d'Aquin." In *Sacrements de Jésus Christ*, edited by J. Doré, 69–103. Paris: Desclée, 1983.
———. *La Liturgie dans l'histoire*. Paris: Éditions Saint-Paul, 1990.
———. "Avancées du traité de l'eucharistie de S. Thomas dans la Somme par rapport aux Sentences." *RSPhTh* 77 (1993): 219–28.
Häussling, Angelus. "Literaturbericht zu Fronleichnam." *JVK* 9 (1986): 228–40.
Hedwig, Klaus. "Über das 'Jetzt' (nunc) bei Thomas von Aquin." *PhJ* 109 (2002): 114–29.
———. "'Efficiunt, quod figurant': Die Sakramente im Kontext von Natur, Zeichen und Heil." In *Thomas von Aquin: Die Summa theologiae: Werkinterpretationen*, edited by A. Speer, 401–25. Berlin: De Gruyter, 2005.
Heinzmann, Richard. "Der Plan der Summa Theologiae des Thomas von Aquin in der Tradition der frühscholastischen Systembildung." In *Thomas von Aquino: Interpretation und Rezeption: Studien und Texte*, edited by W. P. Eckert, 455–69. Mainz: Matthias-Grünewald, 1974.
———. "Die Theologie auf dem Weg zur Wissenschaft: Zur Entwicklung der theologischen Systematik in der Scholastik." *MThZ* 25 (1974): 1–17.
———. "Anima unica forma corporis: Thomas von Aquin als Überwinder des platonisch-neuplatonischen Dualismus." *PhJ* 93 (1986): 236–59.
Hödl, Ludwig. "Die confessio Berengarii von 1059." *Scholastik* 37 (1962): 370–94.
———. "Der Transsubstantiationsbegriff in der scholastischen Theologie des 12. Jahrhunderts." *Recherches de Théologie ancienne et médiévale* 31 (1964): 230–59.
Hoffmann, Adolf M. "Die Stufen der Sanctificatio sacramentalis." *DT* 52 (1938): 129–60.
———. "Der Begriff des Mysteriums bei Thomas von Aquin." *DT* 53 (1939): 30–60.
———. "Die Proexistenz Jesu Christi nach Thomas." In *Thomas von Aquino: Interpretation und Rezeption: Studien und Texte*, edited by W. P. Eckert, 158–69. Walberberger Studien

der Albertus-Magnus-Akademie: Philosophische Reihe 5. Mainz: Matthias-Grünewald, 1974.

Hoogland, Mark-Robin. *God, Passion and Power: Thomas Aquinas on Christ Crucified and the Almightiness of God*. Leuven: Peeters, 2003.

Hoping, Helmut. *Weisheit als Wissen des Ursprungs: Philosophie und Theologie in der* Summa contra gentiles *des Thomas von Aquin*. Freiburg: Herder, 1997.

Horst, Ulrich. "Über die Frage einer heilsökonomischen Theologie bei Thomas von Aquin." *MThZ* 12 (1961): 97–111.

———. *Die Diskussion um die Immaculata Conceptio im Dominikanerorden: Ein Beitrag zur Geschichte der theologischen Methode*. Paderborn: Schöningh, 1987.

Horst, Ulrich, and Barbara Faes de Mottoni. "Die Zwangstaufe jüdischer Kinder im Urteil scholastischer Theologen." *MThZ* 40 (1989): 173–99.

Humbrecht, Thierry-Dominique. "L'eucharistie, 'représentation' du sacrifice du Christ selon saint Thomas." *Revue Thomiste* 98 (1998): 355–86.

Jamros, Daniel P. "Satisfaction for Sin: Aquinas on the Passion of Christ." *Irish Theological Quarterly* 56 (1990): 307–28.

Jorissen, Hans. *Die Entfaltung der Transsubstantiationslehre bis zum Beginn der Hochscholastik*. Münsterische Beiträge zur Theologie 28/1. Münster: Aschendorff, 1965.

———. "Wandlungen des philosophischen Kontextes als Hintergrund der frühmittelalterlichen Eucharistiestreitigkeiten." In *Streit um das Bild: Das Zweite Konzil von Nizäa (787) in ökumenischer Perspektive*, edited by J. Wohlmuth. Bonn: Bouvier, 1989.

———. *Der Beitrag Alberts des Großen zur theologischen Rezeption des Aristoteles am Beispiel der Transsubstantiationslehre*. Münster: Aschendorff, 2002.

Käppeli, Thomas. "Una raccolta di predicheaatribuite a S. Thommaso d'Aquino." *Archivum Fratrum Praedicatorum* 13 (1943): 59–94.

Keaty, Anthony W. "Thomas's Authority for Identifying Charity as Friendship: Aristotle or John 15?" *The Thomist* 62 (1998): 581–601.

Kühn, Ulrich. *Via caritatis: Theologie des Gesetzes bei Thomas v. Aquin*. Göttingen: Vandenhoeck and Ruprecht, 1965.

Laarmann, Matthias. "Transsubstantiation." *HWPh* 10 (1998): 1349–1358.

———. "Transsubstantiation: Begriffsgeschichtliche Materialien und bibliographische Notizen." *Archiv für Begriffsgeschichte* 41 (1999): 119–50.

Lambot, Cyrille. "L'office de la Fête-Dieu: Aperçus nouveaux sur ses origines." *Revue bénédictine* 54 (1942): 61–123.

Lambot, Cyrille, and Paul-Irénée Fransen. *L'office de la Fête-Dieu primitive: Textes et melodies retrouvés*. Maredsous: Éditions de Maredsous, 1946.

La Soujeole, Benoît-Dominique de. "Les *tria munera Christi*: Contribution de saint Thomas à la recherche contemporaine." *Revue Thomiste* 99 (1999): 59–74.

Leclercq, Jacques. *L'amour des lettres et le désir de Dieu*. Paris: Cerf, 1957. Translated into German by J. Stöber and N. Stöber as *Wissenschaft und Gottverlangen: Zur Mönchstheologie des Mittelalters*. Düsseldorf: Patmos, 1963.

Lécuyer, Joseph. "La causalité efficiente des mystères du Christ selon saint Thomas." *Doctor Communis* 6 (1953): 91–120.

———. "Réflexions sur la théologie du culte selon saint Thomas." *Revue Thomiste* 55 (1955): 339–62.

Levering, Matthew. "Israel and the Shape of Thomas Aquinas's Soteriology." *The Thomist* 63 (1999): 65–82.

———. *Christ's Fulfillment of Torah and Temple: Salvation according to Thomas Aquinas.* Notre Dame: University of Notre Dame Press, 2002.

Liske, Michael-Thomas. "Kann Gott reale Beziehungen zu den Geschöpfen haben? Logisch-theologische Betrachtungen im Anschluss an Thomas von Aquin." *ThPh* 68 (1993): 208–28.

Lohfink, Norbert. "Das 'Pange Lingua' im 'Gotteslob.'" *Bibel und Liturgie* 76 (2003): 276–85.

Lohaus, Gerd. *Die Geheimnisse des Lebens Jesu in der* Summa Theologiae *des heiligen Thomas von Aquin.* Freiburger theologische Studien 131. Freiburg: Herder, 1985.

Lohr, Charles H. "The Medieval Interpretation of Aristotle." In *The Cambridge History of Later Medieval History,* edited by A. Kenny, 80–92. Cambridge: Cambridge University Press, 1982.

Louis, René. "Saint Thomas liturgiste." *Revue des Jeunes* 10 (1920): 558–83.

Luscombe, David E. *The Influence of Abaelard's Thought in the Early Scholastic Period.* Cambridge: Cambridge University Press, 1969.

Macy, Gary. "The Dogma of Transubstantiation in the Middle Ages." *Journal of Ecclesiastical History* 45 (1994): 11–41.

Maidl, Lydia. *Desiderii interpres: Genese und Grundstruktur der Gebetstheologie des Thomas von Aquin.* Veröffentlichungen des Grabmann-Instituts 38. Paderborn: Schöningh, 1994.

Mandonnet, Pierre. "Thomas d'Aquin lecteur à la curie romaine: Chronologie du séjour (1259–1268)." In *Xenia Thomistica a plurimis orbis catholici viris eruditis praeparata quae sancto Thomae Aquinati doctori communi et angelico anno ab eius canonizatione sexcentesimo,* edited by L. Theissling, vol. 3, 9–40. Rome: Typis Polyglottis Vaticanis, 1925.

Marschler, Thomas. *Auferstehung und Himmelfahrt Christi in der scholastischen Theologie bis zu Thomas von Aquin.* 2 vols. Beiträge zur Geschichte der Philosophie und Theologie des Mittelalters 64. Münster: Aschendorff, 2003.

———. "Das Hohepriestertum Jesu Christi nach dem hl. Thomas von Aquin." *Doctor Angelicus* 3 (2003): 143–64.

Martelet, Gustave. "Theologie und Heilsökonomie in der Christologie der 'Tertia.'" In *Gott in Welt,* edited by J. B. Metz et al., vol. 2, 3–42. Freiburg-Basel-Vienna: Herder, 1964.

McCord Adams, Marilyn. "Aristotle and the Sacrament of the Altar: A Crisis in Medieval Aristotelianism." *Canadian Journal of Philosophy,* Supplementary Volume XVII (1992): 195–249.

McCou, James F. "The Doctrine of Transubstantiation from Berengar through Trent." *Harvard Theological Review* 61 (1968): 385–430.

Megivern, James J. *Concomitance and Communion: A Study in Eucharistic Doctrine and Practise.* Fribourg-New York: Herder, 1963.

Menessier, J. "L'idée du sacré et le culte chrétien d'après S. Thomas." *RSPhTh* 19 (1930): 63–82.

———. "Les réalités sacrées dans le culte chrétien d'après S. Thomas." *RSPhTh* 20 (1931): 276–86, 453–71.

Metz, Johann Baptist. *Christliche Anthropozentrik: Über die Denkform des Thomas von Aquin.* Munich: Kösel, 1962.

Metz, Wilhelm. *Die Architektonik der* Summa Theologiae *des Thomas von Aquin: Zur Gesamtansicht des thomasischen Gedankens.* Hamburg: Meiner, 1998.

Mitzka, Franz. "Das Wirken der Menschheit Christi zu unserem Heil nach dem hl. Thomas von Aquin." *ZKaTh* 69 (1947): 189–208.

Morard, Martin. "Les expressions 'corpus mysticum' et 'persona mystica' dans l'œuvre de saint Thomas d'Aquin." *Revue Thomiste* 95 (1995): 653–64.

———. "L'eucharistie, clé de voûte de l'organisme sacramental chez saint Thomas d'Aquin." *Revue Thomiste* 95 (1995): 217–50.

Morgott, Franz. *Der Spender der heiligen Sacramente nach der Lehre des heiligen Thomas von Aquin: Eine theologische Studie.* Freiburg: Herder, 1886.

Morin, Germain. "L'office cistercien pour la Fête-Dieu comparé avec celui de saint Thomas d'Aquin." *Revue bénédictine* 27 (1910): 236–46.

Mostert, Walter. *Menschwerdung: Eine historische und dogmatische Untersuchung über das Motiv der Inkarnation des Gottessohnes bei Thomas von Aquin.* Tübingen: Mohr Siebeck, 1978.

Müller, Ewald. *Das Konzil von Vienne 1311–1312: Seine Quellen und seine Geschichte.* Vorreformationsgeschichtliche Forschungen 12. Münster: Aschendorff, 1934.

Nau, Paul. *Le mystère du Corps et du Sang du Seigneur: La messe d'après saint Thomas d'Aquin, son rite d'après l'historie.* Solesmes: Abbaye Saint-Pierre, 1976.

Neunheuser, Burkhard. *Eucharistie in Mittelalter und Neuzeit.* Handbuch der Dogmengeschichte vol. 4/4b. Freiburg: Herder, 1963.

Niederbacher, Bruno. *Glaube als Tugend bei Thomas von Aquin.* Munich: Kohlhammer, 2004.

Nissing, Hanns-Gregor. *Sprache als Akt bei Thomas von Aquin.* Leiden-Boston: Brill Academic Publishers, 2006.

Oeing-Hanhoff, Ludger. "Zur thomistischen Freiheitslehre." *Scholastik* 31 (1956): 161–82.

———. "Thomas von Aquin und die gegenwärtige katholische Theologie." In *Thomas von Aquino: Interpretation und Rezeption: Studien und Texte*, edited by W. P. Eckart, 245–306. Mainz: Matthias-Grünewald Verlag, 1974.

O'Meara, Thomas F. *Thomas Aquinas, Theologian.* Notre Dame, Ind.: Notre Dame University Press, 1997.

Panofsky, Erwin. *Gothic Architecture and Scholasticism.* Latrobe, Penn.: Archabbey Publications, 1948.

Patfoort, Albert. "Le vrai visage de la satisfaction du Christ selon saint Thomas: Une étude de la Somme théologique." In *Ordo sapientiae et amoris: Image et message de Saint Thomas d'Aquin à travers les récentes études historiques, herméneutiques et doctrinales*, edited by C.-J. Pinto de Oliveira, 247–66. Fribourg: Éditions Universitaires, 1993.

Perger, Mischa von. "Theologie und Werkstruktur bei Thomas von Aquin: Wilhelm Metz' Studie zur Summa theologiae." *FZThPh* 48 (2001): 191–208.

Pesch, Otto Hermann. "Besinnung auf die Sakramente: Historische und systematische Überlegungen und ihre pastoralen Konsequenzen." *FZThPh* 18 (1971): 266–321.

———. "Sittengebote, Kultvorschriften, Rechtssatzungen: Zur Theologiegeschichte von Summa Theologiae I-II 99, 2–5." In *Thomas von Aquino: Interpretation und Rezeption: Studien und Texte*, edited by W. P. Eckert, 488–518. Walberberger Studien: Philosophische Reihe 5. Mainz: Matthias-Grünewald Verlag, 1974.

———. "Theologie des Wortes Gottes bei Thomas von Aquin." *ZThK* 66 (1969): 437–65.

———. "Um den Plan der Summa Theologiae des hl. Thomas von Aquin: Zu Max Secklers neuem Deutungsversuch." In *Thomas von Aquin*, edited by K. Bernath, vol. 1, 411–37. Darmstadt: Wissenschaftliche Buchgesellschaft, 1978.

———. *Thomas von Aquin: Grenze und Größe mittelalterlicher Theologie: Eine Einführung.* Mainz: Matthias-Grünewald, 1988.

———. "Thomas von Aquino/Thomismus/Neuthomismus." *TRE* 33 (2002): 433–74.

Pickstock, Catherine. "Thomas Aquinas and the Quest for the Eucharist." *Modern Theology* 15 (1999): 159–80.

Pieper, Josef. *Philosophia negativa: Zwei Versuche über Thomas von Aquin.* Munich: Warrington Verlag, 1953. Translated into English by John Murray, SJ, and Daniel O'Connor as *The Silence of St. Thomas.* South Bend, Ind.: St. Augustine's Press, 1999.

———. *Hinführung zu Thomas von Aquin.* Munich: Kösel, 1958. Translated into English by Richard and Clara Winston as *Guide to Thomas Aquinas.* London: Faber and Faber, 1962.

Pinto de Oliveira, Carlos-Josaphat, ed. *Ordo sapientiae et amoris: Image et message de Saint Thomas d'Aquin à travers les récentes études historiques, herméneutiques et doctrinales.* Fribourg: Éditions Universitaires, 1993.

Prouvost, Géry. *Thomas d'Aquin et les thomismes: Essai sur l'histoire des thomismes.* Cogitatio fidei 195. Paris: Cerf, 1996.

Raby, Frederic J. E. "The Date and Authorship of the Poem *Adoro te devote*." *Speculum* 20 (1945): 236–38.

Rahner, Karl. "Bekenntnis zu Thomas von Aquin." In *Schriften zur Theologie*, vol. 10, 11–20. Einsiedeln: Benzinger Verlag, 1972. Translated into English as "On Recognizing the Importance of Thomas Aquinas." In *Theological Investigations*, vol. 13, *Theology, Anthropology, Christology*, 3–12. New York: Darton, Longman and Todd, Ltd., 1975.

———. "Einleitende Bemerkungen zur allgemeinen Sakramentenlehre bei Thomas von Aquin." In *Schriften zur Theologie*, vol. 10, 392–404. Einsiedeln: Benzinger Verlag, 1972. Translated into English as "Introductory Observations on Thomas Aquinas' Theology of the Sacraments in General." In *Theological Investigations*, vol. 14, *Ecclesiology, Questions in the Church, The Church in the World*, 149–60. New York: Darton, Longman and Todd, Ltd., 1976.

Remy, Gérard. "Le Christ médiateur dans l'œuvre de saint Thomas." *Revue Thomiste* 93 (1993): 182–233.

———. "Sacerdoce et médiation chez saint Thomas." *Revue Thomiste* 99 (1999): 101–18.

Reinhold, Georg. *Die Lehre von der örtlichen Gegenwart beim hl. Thomas von Aquin.* Vienna: H. Kirsch, 1893.

Röhrig, Hermann-Josef. "'Realisierende Zeichen' oder 'Zeichen einer heiligen Sache': Das Sakramentsverständnis des hl. Thomas von Aquin als Anfrage an gegenwärtige Sakramententheologie." *Lebendiges Zeugnis* 58 (2003): 101–16.

Rubin, Miri. *Corpus Christi: The Eucharist in Late Medieval Culture.* Cambridge: Cambridge University Press, 1991.

Ruello, Francis. *La Christologie de Thomas d'Aquin.* Théologie historique 76. Paris: Beauchesne Editions, 1987.

Sabra, George. *Thomas Aquinas' Vision of the Church: Fundamentals of an Ecumenical Ecclesiology.* Tübinger Theologische Studien 27. Mainz: Matthias-Grünewald Verlag, 1987.

Schachten, Winfried H. *Ordo salutis: Das Gesetz als Weise der Heilsvermittlung: Zur Kritik des hl. Thomas von Aquin an Joachim von Fiore.* Beiträge zur Geschichte der Philosophie und Theologie des Mittelalters, N.F. 20. Münster: Aschendorff, 1980.

Scheffczyk, Leo. "Die Stellung des Thomas von Aquin in der Entwicklung der Lehre von den Mysteria Vitae Christi." In *Renovatio et Reformatio*, edited by M. Gerwing and G. Ruppert, 44–70. Münster: Aschendorff, 1986.

———. "'Satisfactio non efficax nisi ex caritate': Zur Frage nach dem Grund der Erlösung in Tod und Auferstehung Jesu Christi." *Annales theologici* 1 (1987): 73–94.

Scheller, Emil J. *Das Priestertum Christi im Anschluß an den hl. Thomas von Aquin: vom Mysterium des Mittlers in seinem Opfer und unserer Anteilnahme.* Paderborn: Schöningh, 1934.

Schenk, Richard. "Tod und Theodizee: Ansätze zu einer Theologie der Trauer bei Thomas von Aquin." *FKTh* 10 (1994): 161–76.
Scheuer, Manfred. *Weiter-Gabe: Heilsvermittlung durch Gnadengaben in den Schriftkommentaren des Thomas von Aquin.* Würzburg: Echter, 2001.
———. "Aliis communicare: Zum Offenbarungsverständnis des Thomas von Aquin." In *"Wozu Offenbarung?" Zur philosophischen und theologischen Begründung von Religion,* edited by B. Dörflinger et al., 60–83. Paderborn: Schöningh, 2006.
Schillebeeckx, Edward. *De sacramentale heilseconomie: Theologische bezinning op S. Thomas' sacramentenleer in het licht van de traditie en van de hedendaagse sacramentenproblematiek.* Antwerpen: 't Groeit, 1952. Translated into French as *L'économie sacramentelle du salut. Réflexion théologique sur la doctrine sacramentaire de saint Thomas, à la lumière de la tradition et de la problématique sacramentelle contemporaine.* Fribourg: Academic Press Fribourg, 2004.
———. *Christus: Sakrament der Gottbegegnung.* Mainz: Matthias-Grünewald Verlag, 1960. Translated into English by N. D. Smith as *Christ the Sacrament of the Encounter with God.* New York: Sheed and Ward, 1963.
———. "Hin zu einer Wiederentdeckung der christlichen Sakramente: Ritualisierung religiöser Momente im alltäglichen Leben." In *Interdisziplinäre Ethik: Grundlagen, Methoden, Bereiche,* edited by A. Holderegger and J.-P. Wils, 309–39. Freiburg-Vienna: Herder, 2001.
Schilson, Arno. "Symbol und Mysterium als liturgiewissenschaftliche Grundbegriffe." In *Liturgische Theologie,* edited by H. Hoping and B. Jeggle-Merz, 57–84. Paderborn: Schöningh, 2004.
Schneider, Theodor. *Zeichen der Nähe Gottes: Grundriß der Sakramententheologie.* 6th ed. Mainz: Matthias-Grünewald Verlag, 1992.
Schockenhoff, Eberhard. *Bonum hominis: Die anthropologischen und theologischen Grundlagen der Tugendethik des Thomas von Aquin.* Mainz: Matthias-Grünewald Verlag, 1987.
———. "Die Liebe als Freundschaft des Menschen mit Gott: Das Proprium der Caritaslehre des Thomas von Aquin." *IKaZ Communio* 36 (2007): 232–46.
Schultes, Reginald M. "Die Wirksamkeit der Sakramente." *Jahrbuch für Philosophie und spekulative Theologie* 20 (1906): 409–49.
Seckler, Max. *Das Heil in der Geschichte: Geschichtstheologisches Denken bei Thomas von Aquin.* Munich: Kösel, 1964.
Seckler, Max. "Das Haupt aller Menschen." In *Die schiefen Wände des Lehrhauses: Katholizität als Herausforderung,* 26–39. Freiburg: Herder, 1988.
Sedlmayr, Petrus. "Die Lehre des hl. Thomas von den accidentia sine subjecto remanentia." *DT* (F) 3–12 (1934): 315–26.
Seidl, Horst. "Zum Substanzbegriff der katholischen Transsubstantiationslehre." *FKTh* 11 (1995): 1–18.
Shanley, Brian J. "St. Thomas, Onto-Theology and Marion." *The Thomist* 60 (1996): 617–25.
Speer, Andreas, ed. *Thomas von Aquin: Die Summa theologiae: Werkinterpretationen.* Berlin: De Gruyter, 2004.
———. "Das Glück des Menschen." In *Thomas von Aquin: Die Summa theologiae: Werkinter-pretationen,* 141–67. Berlin: De Gruyter 2005.
Stufler, Johann. "Bemerkungen zur Lehre des hl. Thomas über die virtus instrumentalis." *ZKaTh* 42 (1918): 719–62.
Szövérffy, Josef. *Die Annalen der lateinischen Hymnendichtung.* Vol. 2, *Die lateinischen Hymnen vom Ende des 11. Jahrhunderts bis zum Ausgang des Mittelalters.* Die lyrische Dichtung des Mittelalters 2. Berlin: Schmidt-Verlag, 1965.

Ternus, Joseph. "Dogmatische Untersuchungen zur Theologie des hl. Thomas über das Sakrament der Weihe." *Scholastik* 7 (1932): 161–86, 354–386, and *Scholastik* 8 (1933): 161–202 (continuation).
Torrell, Jean-Pierre. "L'authenticité de l'*Adoro te devote*." *RSR* 67 (1993): 79–83.
———. *Initiation à Saint Thomas d'Aquin: sa personne et son oeuvre*. Paris: Cerf: 1993. 2nd ed. 2002; 3rd ed. 2015. Translated into English by Robert Royal as *Saint Thomas Aquinas*. Vol. 1, *The Person and His Work*. Washington, D.C.: The Catholic University of America Press, 1996. 2nd ed. 2005.
———. "*Ecclesia Iudaeorum*: Quelques jugements positifs de saint Thomas à l'égard des juifs et de judaisme." In *Les Philosophies morales et politiques au Moyen Age*, edited by B. C. Bazán, E. Andújar, and L. G. Sbbrocchi, vol. 3, 1732–41. New York–Ottawa: Legas, 1996.
———. *Saint Thomas d'Aquin, maître spirituel*. Initiation 2; Vestigia 19. Fribourg: Cerf, 1996. Translated into English as *Saint Thomas Aquinas*. Vol. 2, *Spiritual Master*, translated by Robert Royal. Washington, D.C.: The Catholic University of America Press, 2003.
———. "Le Christ dans la 'spiritualité' de saint Thomas." In *Christ among the Medieval Dominicans: Representations of Christ in the Texts and Images of the Order of Preachers*, edited by K. Emery and J. Wawrykow, 197–219. Notre Dame, Ind.: Notre Dame University Press, 1998.
———. *Le Christ en ses mystères. La vie et l'œuvre de Jésus selon Thomas d'Aquin*. Jésus et Jésus-Christ 78/79. 2 vols. Paris: Desclée, 1999.
———. "Le sacerdoce du Christ dans la *Somme de théologie*." *Revue Thomiste* 99 (1999): 75–100.
———. "*Adoro te*: La plus belle prière de saint Thomas." In *Recherches thomasiennes: Études revues et augmentées*, 367–75. Paris: Librairie Philosophique, 2000.
———. "La vision de dieu 'per essentiam' selon Saint Thomas d'Aquin." In *Recherches thomasiennes: Études revues et augmentées*, 177–99. Paris: Librairie Philosophique, 2000.
———. "Le semeur est sorti pour semer: L'image du Christ pêcheur chez frère Thomas d'Aquin." In *Recherches thomasiennes: Études revues et augmentées*, 357–66. Paris: Librairie Philosophique, 2000.
Travers, Jean. *Valeur sociale de la liturgie d'après Thomas d'Aquin*. Lex orandi 5. Paris: Cerf, 1946.
Tschipke, Theophil. *Die Menschheit Christi als Heilsorgan der Gottheit*. Freiburg: Herder & Co., 1940.
Tück, Jan-Heiner. "Die Sequenz *Lauda Sion* als poetische Verdichtung der Eucharistietheologie des Thomas von Aquin." *ThGl* 93 (2003): 475–97.
———. "Verborgene Gegenwart und betrachtendes Verweilen: Zur poetischen Theologie des Hymnus *Adoro te devote*." *IKaZ Communio* 34 (2005): 401–18.
Urban, Wolfgang. "Das eucharistische Brot in den Fronleichnamshymnen des Thomas von Aquin." In *Panis Angelorum—Das Brot der Engel: Kulturgeschichte der Hostie*, edited by O. Seifert. Ostfildern: Thorbecke, 2004.
VanRoo, William A. "The Resurrection of Christ: Instrumental Cause of Grace." *Gregorianum* 39 (1958): 271–83.
Vaillancourt, Mark G. "Guitmund of Aversa and the Eucharistic Theology of St. Thomas." *The Thomist* 68 (2004): 577–600.
Venard, Olivier-Thomas. *Thomas d'Aquin: Poète théologien*. 2 vols. Genf: Ad Solem, 2003–2004.
Vonier, Anscar. *A Key to the Doctrine of the Eucharist*. Bethesda, Md.: Zaccheus Press, 2003.

Walsh, Liam G. "Liturgy in the Theology of St. Thomas." *The Thomist* 38 (1974): 557–83.

———. "The Divine and the Human in St. Thomas' Theology of Sacraments." In *Ordo sapientiae et amoris*, edited by C.-J. Pinto de Oliveira, 321–51. Fribourg: Éditions Universitaires, 1993.

Wawrykow, Joseph P. *God's Grace and Human Action: "Merit" in the Theology of Thomas Aquinas*. Notre Dame, Ind.: University of Notre Dame Press, 1995.

———. "Wisdom in the Christology of Thomas Aquinas." In *Christ among the Medieval Dominicans: Representations of Christ in the Texts and Images of the Order of Preachers*, edited by K. Emery and J. Wawrykow, 175–96. Notre Dame, Ind.: University of Notre Dame Press, 1998.

Wéber, Édouard-Henri. "L'incidence du traité de l'eucharistie sur la métaphysique de s. Thomas d'Aquin." *RSPhTh* 77 (1993): 195–218.

Weisheipl, James A. *Friar Thomas d'Aquino: His Life and Works*. Garden City, N.Y.: Doubleday, 1974. Revised edition, Washington, D.C.: The Catholic University of America Press, 1983.

Wicki, Nikolaus. *Die Lehre von der himmlischen Seligkeit in der mittelalterlichen Scholastik von Petrus Lombardus bis Thomas von Aquin*. Freiburg, Switzerland: Universitätsverlag, 1954.

Wiederkehr, Dietrich. "Spannungen in der Christologie des Thomas von Aquin." *FZThPh* 21 (1974): 392–419.

Wieland, Georg: "Plato oder Aristoteles? Überlegungen zur Aristoteles-Rezeption des lateinischen Mittelalters." *Tijdschrift voor Filosofie* 47 (1985): 605–30.

Wielockx, Robert. "Poetry and Theology in the *Adoro te deuote*: Thomas Aquinas on the Eucharist and Christ's Uniqueness." In *Christ among the Mediaeval Dominicans: Representations of Christ in the Texts and Images of the Order of Preachers*, edited by K. Emery and J. Wawrykow, 157–74. Notre Dame, Ind.: University of Notre Dame Press, 1998.

Wilmart, André. "La tradition littéraire et textuelle de 'L'adoro te devote.'" *Recherches de Théologie ancienne et médiévale* 1 (1929): 21–40, 149–76.

———. *Auteurs spirituels et texts dévots du moyen âge latin*. Paris: Études Augustiniennes, 1932.

Winter, Stephan. *Eucharistische Gegenwart: Liturgische Redehandlung im Spiegel mittelalterlicher und analytischer Sprachtheorie*. Ratio fidei 13. Regensburg: Pustet, 2002.

Zawilla, Ronald. "The Biblical Sources of the *Historiae Corporis Christi* attributed to Thomas Aquinas." PhD diss., University of Toronto, 1985.

Zimmermann, Albert. "'Ipsum enim est nihil est' (Aristoteles, Periherm. I, c. 3): Thomas von Aquin über die Bedeutung der Kopula." In *Der Begriff Repraesentatio im Mittelalter*, 282–95. Berlin: De Gruyter, 1971.

———, ed. *Die Auseinandersetzung an der Pariser Universität im XIII. Jahrhundert*. Berlin–New York: De Gruyter, 1976.

———. "Glaube und Wissen." In *Thomas von Aquin*, edited by A. Speer, 271–97. Berlin: De Gruyter, 2005.

Zumthor, Paul. *Die Stimme und die Poesie in der mittelalterlichen Gesellschaft*. Munich: Fink, 1994.

IV. Further Secondary Literature

Adam, Karl. *Die Eucharistielehre des hl. Augustinus*. Paderborn: Schöningh, 1908.

———. "Deutsches Volkstum und katholisches Christentum." *ThQ* 114 (1933): 40–63.

———. "Jesus, der Christus, und wir Deutsche (Teil 1)." *WuW* 10 (1943): 74–103

———. "Jesus, der Christus, und wir Deutsche (Teil 2)." *WuW* 11 (1944): 10–23.
Adorno, Theodor W. *Minima moralia. Reflexionen aus dem beschädigten Leben*. Frankfurt: Suhrkamp, 1987. Translated into English by E. F. N. Jephcott as *Minima moralia. Reflections from Damaged Life*. New York: Verso, 2005.
———. *Aesthetic Theory*, translated by R. Hullot-Kentor. London: A & C Black, 2013.
Aubert, Roger. "Die Enzyklika 'Aeterni patris' und die weiteren päpstlichen Stellungnahmen zur christlichen Philosophie." In *Christliche Philosophie im katholischen Denken des 19. und 20. Jahrhunderts*. Vol. 2, *Rückgriff auf scholastisches Erbe*, edited by E. Coreth, 310–32. Graz: Styria, 1988.
Austin, John L. *How to Do Things with Words*. Cambridge: The William James Lectures, 1962.
Baader, Franz von. *Sämtliche Werke*. Edited by F. Hoffmann. 16 vols. Reprint of the Leipzig edition 1851–60. Aalen: Scientia Verlag, 1963.
Bachl, Gottfried. *Eucharistie—Macht und Lust des Verzehrens*. Spuren—Essays zu Kultur und Glaube. St. Ottilien: EOS Verlag, 2008.
Balthasar, Hans Urs von. "Theologie und Heiligkeit." In *Verbum Caro: Skizzen zur Theologie I*, 195–225. Einsiedeln: Johannes-Verlag, 1960. Translated into English by Arthur V. Littledale and Alexander Dru as "Theology and Sanctity." In *Explorations in Theology*. Vol. 1, *The Word Made Flesh*, 181–209. San Francisco: Ignatius Press, 1989.
———. *Glaubhaft ist nur Liebe*. Christ heute, Reihe 5, 1. Einsiedeln: Johannes-Verlag, 1963. Translated into English by D. C. Schindler as *Love Alone Is Credible*. San Francisco: Ignatius Press, 2005.
———. "Mysterium paschale." *MySal* III/2 (1969): 302–4.
———. "Christus, Gestalt unseres Lebens." *Geist und Leben* (1970): 173–80.
———. *Theodramatik*. Vol. 2/2, *Die Personen in Christus*. Einsiedeln: Johannes Verlag, 1978. Translated into English by Graham Harrison as *Theo-Drama: Theological Dramatic Theory*. Vol. 3, *The Dramatis Personae: The Person in Christ*. San Francisco: Ignatius Press, 1992.
———. "Verehrung des Allerheiligsten." In *Klarstellungen*, 111–16. 4th ed. Einsiedeln: Johannes-Verlag, 1978. Translated into English by J. Riches as "The Veneration of the Holy of Holies." In *Elucidations*, 181–90. San Francisco: Ignatius Press, 1998.
———. "Crucifixus etiam pro nobis." *IKaZ Communio* 9 (1980): 26–35.
———. "Der Erstling der neuen Welt." *IKaZ Communio* 12 (1983): 214–18.
———. *Das Ganze im Fragment. Aspekte der Geschichtstheologie*. 2nd ed. Einsiedeln: Benzinger Verlag, 1990. Translated into English by W. G. Doepel as *Man in History: A Theological Study*. London: Sheed and Ward, 1982.
———. *Theologie der drei Tage*. Einsiedeln: Benzinger Verlag, 1990. Translated into English by Aidan Nichols, O.P. as *Mysterium Paschale: The Mystery of Easter*. Edinburgh: T&T Clark, 1990.
———. "Die Abwesenheiten Jesu." In *Neue Klarstellungen*, 23–36. Einsiedeln: Johannes-Verlag, 1995. Translated into English by Mary Theresilde Skerry as "The Absences of Jesus." In *New Elucidations*, 46–60. San Francisco: Ignatius Press, 1986.
Barth, Karl. *Kirchliche Dogmatik III/3: Die Lehre von der Schöpfung*. Zollikon-Zürich: Evangelischer Verlag Zollikon, 1950. Translated into English as *Church Dogmatics III/3: The Doctrine of Creation*. Edited by G. W. Bromiley and T. F. Torrance. Edinburgh: T&T Clark Ltd., 1960.
Bauke-Ruegg, Jan. *Theologische Poetik und literarische Theologie? Systematisch-theologische Streifzüge*. Zurich: Theologischer Verlag, 2004.

Baumstark, Anton. *Nocturna laus: Typen frühchristlicher Vigilienfeier und ihr Fortleben vor allem im römischen und monastischen Ritus.* Liturgiewissenschaftliche Quellen und Forschungen 32. Edited by O. Heiming. Münster: Aschendorff, 1957.

Bayer, Axel. *Spaltung der Christenheit. Das sogenannte Morgenländische Schisma von 1054.* Cologne: Böhlau Verlag, 2002.

Beinert, Wolfgang. "Die Enzyklika Mysterium Fidei und neuere Auffassungen über die Eucharistie." *ThQ* 147 (1967): 159–76.

———. "Zum Beispiel Transsignifikation." *ThPQ* 118 (1970): 313–26.

Beinert, Wolfgang, ed. *Glaubenszugänge: Lehrbuch der katholischen Dogmatik.* 3 vols. Paderborn: Schöningh, 1995.

Betz, Johannes. *Die Aktualpräsenz der Person und des Heilswerkes Jesu im Abendmahl nach der vorephesinischen, griechischen Patristik.* Freiburg: Herder, 1955.

———. *Die Eucharistie in der Zeit der griechischen Väter.* Vol. I/1, *Die Aktualpräsenz der Person und des Heilswerkes Jesu im Abendmahl nach der vorephesinischen griechischen Patristik.* Freiburg: Herder, 1955.

———. "Eucharistie als zentrales Mysterium." *MySal* IV/2 (1973): 231–43.

———. *Eucharistie in der Schrift und der Patristik.* HDG IV/4a. Freiburg: Herder, 1979.

Beumer, Johannes. "Amalar von Metz und sein Zeugnis für die Gestalt der Meßliturgie seiner Zeit." *ThPh* 50 (1975): 416–26.

Bloch, Ernst. *Erbschaft dieser Zeit: Erweiterte Ausgabe.* Frankfurt: Suhrkamp, 1962. Translated into English by Neville and Stephen Plaice as *Heritage of Our Times.* Berkeley/Los Angeles: Wiley, 1991.

Blondel, Maurice. *Carnets intimes.* Vol. 1. Paris: Cerf, 1961. Translated into German by H. U. von Balthasar as *Tagebuch vor Gott 1883–1894.* Einsiedeln: Johannes-Verlag, 1964.

Blume, Clemens. *Unsere Liturgischen Lieder: Das Hymnar der altchristlichen Kirche.* Regensburg: Pustet, 1932.

Blumenberg, Hans. *Lebenszeit und Weltzeit.* Frankfurt: Suhrkamp, 1986.

Bohrer, Karl-Heinz. *Ekstasen der Zeit: Augenblick, Gegenwart, Erinnerung.* Munich: Carl Hanser, 2003.

Bolz, Norbert. *Das konsumistische Manifest.* Munich: Wilhelm Fink, 2002.

Borscheid, Peter. *Das Tempo-Virus: Eine Kulturgeschichte der Beschleunigung.* Frankfurt: Campus, 2004.

Bouyer, Louis. *The Word, Church, and Sacraments in Protestantism and Catholicism.* London: Geoffrey Chapman, 1961. Reprint San Francisco: Ignatius Press 2004.

———. "Von der jüdischen zur christlichen Liturgie." *IKaZ Communio* 7 (1978): 509–19.

Bultmann, Rudolf. *Die Geschichte der synoptischen Tradition.* Forschungen zur Religion und Literatur des Alten und Neuen Testaments 29 (= N.F. 12). 8th ed. Göttingen: Vandenhoeck & Ruprecht, 1970. Translated into English by J. Marsh as *The History of the Synoptic Tradition.* 2nd ed. Oxford: Blackwell, 1968.

Cantalamessa, Raniero. *This is My Body: Eucharistic Reflections Inspired by Adoro Te Devote and Ave Verum.* Translated into English by A. Neame. Boston: Pauline Books and Media, 2005.

Casel, Odo. *Das christliche Kultmysterium.* 4th ed. Regensburg: Pustet, 1960. Translated into English as *The Mystery of Christian Worship.* Edited by Burkhard Neunheuser. Milestones in Catholic Theology. New York: Crossroad Publishing Company, 1999.

———. *Mysterientheologie: Ansatz und Gestalt.* Selected and introduced by Arno Schilson. Regensburg: Pustet, 1986.

Cassidy, D. C. "Is Transubstantiation without Substance?" *Religious Studies* 30 (1994): 193–99.
Courth, Franz. *Die Sakramente: Ein Lehrbuch für Studium und Praxis*. Freiburg: Herder, 1995.
Curtius, Ernst Robert. *Europäische Literatur und lateinisches Mittelalter*. 11th ed. Tübingen: Francke, 1993. Translated into English by W. R. Trask as *European Literature and the Latin Middle Ages*. Princeton, N.J.: Princeton University Press, 1991.
Derrida, Jacques. *Politiques de l'amitié*. Paris: Editions Galilée, 1994. Translated into Engish by George Collins as *Politics of Friendship*. New York: Verso, 1997.
——. "'Man muss wohl essen' oder die Berechnung des Subjekts." In *Auslassungs-punkte: Gespräche*, 267–98. Vienna: Passagen Verlag, 1998.
Dölger, Franz Joseph. *Sol salutis: Gebet und Gesang im christlichen Altertum mit besonderer Rücksicht auf die Ostung in Gebet und Liturgie*. Liturgiegeschichtliche Forschungen 4/5. 2nd ed. Münster: Aschendorff, 1925.
Dumoutet, Edouard. *Le désir de voir l'hostie et les origines de la dévotion au Saint-Sacrement*. Paris: Beauchesne, 1926.
Essen, Georg, and Thomas Pröpper. "Aneignungsprobleme der christologischen Überlieferung: Hermeneutische Vorüberlegungen." In *Gottes ewiger Sohn: Die Präexistenz Christi*, edited by R. Laufen, 163–78. Paderborn: Schöningh, 1997.
Faber, Eva-Maria. *Einführung in die katholische Sakramentenlehre*. Darmstadt: Wissenschaftliche Buchgesellschaft, 2002.
Fiedler, Peter. *Jesus und die Sünder*. Beiträge zur biblischen Exegese und Theologie 3. Frankfurt-Bern: Lang Peter, 1976.
——. "Beim Herrn ist die Huld, bei ihm ist Erlösung in Fülle." In *Israel und Kirche heute: Beiträge zum christlich-jüdischen Dialog*, edited by M. Marcus et al., 184–200. Freiburg: Herder, 1991.
——. *Studien zur biblischen Grundlegung des jüdisch-christlichen Verhältnisses*. Stuttgart: Katholisches Bibelwerk, 2001.
Frank, Manfred. *Was ist Neostrukturalismus?* Frankfurt: Suhrkamp, 1983. Translated into English by Sabine Wilke and Richard Gray as *What Is Neostructuralism?* Theory and History of Literature 45. Minneapolis: University of Minnesota Press, 1989.
Freyer, Thomas. *Sakrament—Transitus—Zeit—Transzendenz: Überlegungen im Vorfeld einer liturgisch-ästhetischen Erschließung und Grundlegung der Sakramente*. Bonner dogmatische Studien 20. Würzburg: Echter, 1995.
——. "'Transsubstantiation' versus 'Transfinalisation/Transsignifikation'? Bemerkungen zu einer aktuellen Debatte." *Catholica* 49 (1995): 174–95.
——. "'Sakrament'—was ist das?" *ThQ* 178 (1998): 39–51.
Fuchs, Ottmar, and Peter Hünermann. "Kommentar zum Dekret über die Priesterausbildung *Optatam totius*." In *Eine andere Barmherzigkeit: Zum Verständnis der Erlösungslehre Anselms von Canterbury*, edited by Gerhard Gäde. Bonner dogmatische Studien 3. Würzburg: Echter, 1989.
——. *Herders Theologischer Kommentar zum Zweiten Vatikanischen Konzil*. Vol. 3. Freiburg: Herder, 2005.
Gäde, Gerhard. *Eine andere Barmherzigkeit: Zum Verständnis der Erlösungslehre Anselms von Canterbury*. Bonner dogmatische Studien 3. Würzburg: Echter, 1989.
Gerhards, Albert, and Klemens Richter, eds. *Das Opfer: Biblischer Anspruch und liturgische Gestalt*. Quaestiones disputatae 186. Freiburg-Basel-Vienna: Herder, 2000.
Gerl-Falkovitz, Hanna-Barbara. "'Esset das Lamm schnell': Zur Antiekstase im christlichen Gottesdienst." *IKaZ Communio* 22 (1993): 217–23.

Gerken, Alexander. "Die Gegenwart Christi in der Eucharistie: Analyse und Interpretation neuerer Deutungen der Realpräsenz." *StZ* 191 (1973): 553–62.

———. *Theologie der Eucharistie*. Munich: Kösel, 1973.

Gessel, Wilhelm. *Eucharistische Gemeinschaft bei Augustinus*. Würzburg: Augustinus-Verlag, 1966.

Gnilka, Joachim. *Jesus von Nazareth: Botschaft und Geschichte*. Freiburg: Herder, 1990. Translated into English by Siegfried S. Schatzmann as *Jesus of Nazareth: Message and History*. Peabody, Mass.: Hendrickson Publishers, 1997.

Grabmann, Martin. *Die Geschichte der katholischen Theologie seit dem Ausgang der Väterzeit*. 2nd ed. Darmstadt: Wissenschaftliche Buchgesellschaft, 1961.

———. *Die Lehre des hl. Thomas von Aquin von der Kirche als Gotteswerk*. Regensburg: G. J. Manz, 1903.

Graf, Friedrich Wilhelm. *Die Wiederkehr der Götter: Religion in der modernen Kultur*. Munich: C.H. Beck, 2004.

Grane, Leif. "Luthers Kritik an Thomas von Aquin in De captivitate Babylonica." *ZKG* 80 (1969): 1–13.

Greshake, Gisbert. "Erlösung und Freiheit: Zur Neuinterpretation der Erlösungslehre Anselms von Canterbury." *ThQ* 153 (1973): 323–45.

Grillmeier, Alois. "Hellenisierung—Judaisierung des Christentums als Deuteprinzipien der Geschichte des kirchlichen Dogmas." In *Mit ihm und in ihm*. 2nd ed. Freiburg: Herder, 1978.

Gronemeyer, Marianne. *Das Leben als letzte Gelegenheit: Sicherheitsbedürfnisse und Zeitknappheit*. 2nd ed. Darmstadt: Wissenschaftliche Buchgesellschaft, 1996.

Gumbrecht, Hans Ulrich. *Production of Presence: What Meaning Cannot Convey*. Stanford University Press, 2004.

Habermas, Jürgen. "Im Gespräch mit E. Mendieta." In *Befristete Zeit*, edited by J. Manemann, 190–209. Jahrbuch Politische Theologie 3. Münster: LIT Verlag, 1999.

Häfner, Gerd. "Nach dem Tod Jesu fragen: Brennpunkte der Diskussion aus neutestamentlicher Sicht." In *Wie heute vom Tod Jesu sprechen?* edited by G. Häfner and H. Schmid, 139–90. Freiburg: Katholische Akademie, 2002.

Harnack, Adolf von. *Lehrbuch der Dogmengeschichte*. Vol. 3. Tübingen: J. C. B. Mohr, 1932. (Reprinted from 3rd ed., 1889.)

Harnoncourt, Philipp. *Gesamtkirchliche und teilkirchliche Liturgie: Studien zum liturgischen Heiligenkalender und zum Gesang im Gottesdienst unter besonderer Berücksichtigung des deutschen Sprachgebiets*. Untersuchungen zur praktischen Theologie 3. Freiburg: Herder, 1974.

Hegel, Georg Friedrich Wilhelm. *Enzyklopädie der philosophischen Wissenschaften im Grundrisse*. 1830. Vol. 20 of *Gesammelte Werke (Akademieausgabe)*. Edited by W. Bonsiepen. Hamburg: Felix Meiner Verlag, 1992. Translated into English by William Wallace and A. V. Miller as *Hegel's Philosophy of Mind*. Oxford: Oxford University Press, 1971.

Henrix, Hans Hermann, and Rolf Rendtorff, eds. *Die Kirchen und das Judentum: Dokumente von 1945–1985*. 2nd ed. Gütersloh-Paderborn: Kaiser, 1989.

Hilberath, Bernd Jochen. "'Substanzwandlung'—'Bedeutungswandel'—'Umstiftung.'" *Catholica* 39 (1985): 133–50.

Hilberath, Bernd Jochen, and Theodor Schneider. "Eucharistie: Systematisch." In *Neues Handbuch Theologischer Grundbegriffe*, edited by P. Eicher, 313–23. Munich: Kösel, 2005.

Hintzen, Georg. *Die neuere Diskussion über die eucharistische Wandlung: Darstellung, kritische Würdigung, Weiterführung.* Disputationes theologicae 4. Frankfurt-Munich: Peter Lang Gmbh Internationaler Verlag Der Wissenschaften, 1976.

———. "Personale Gegenwart des Herrn in der Eucharistie: Zu Notger Slenczkas Buch 'Realpräsenz und Ontologie.'" *Catholica* 47 (1993): 210–37.

Hörisch, Jochen. *Brot und Wein: Die Poesie des Abendmahls.* Frankfurt: Suhrkamp, 1992.

Hoff, Johannes. *Spiritualität und Sprachverlust: Theologie nach Foucault und Derrida.* Paderborn: Schöningh, 1999.

Hofius, Ottfried. "Τὸ σῶμα τὸ ὑπὲρ ὑμῶν—1Kor11,24." *ZNW* 80 (1989): 80–88.

Hoffmann, Franz. *Der Kirchenbegriff des hl. Augustinus.* Munich: Max Hueber, 1933.

Hoping, Helmut. "Stellvertretung: Zum Gebrauch einer theologischen Kategorie." *ZKaTh* 118 (1996): 345–60.

———. "Gedenken und Erwarten: Zur Zeitstruktur christlicher Liturgie." *LJ* 50 (2000): 180–94.

———. "Wie heute vom Tod Jesu sprechen? Der Opfertod Jesu als Mitte des christlichen Glaubens." In *Wie heute vom Tod Jesu sprechen?* edited by G. Häfner and H. Schmid, 81–101. Freiburg: Katholische Akademie., 2002.

Hoping, Helmut, and Birgit Jeggle-Merz, eds. *Liturgische Theologie: Aufgaben systematischer Liturgiewissenschaft.* Paderborn: Ferdinand Schöningh, 2004.

Hünermann, Peter. "'Erlöse uns von dem Bösen': Theologische Reflexion auf das Böse und die Erlösung vom Bösen." *ThQ* 162 (1982): 317–29.

———. *Jesus Christus—Gottes Wort in der Zeit: Eine systematische Christologie.* Münster: Aschendorff, 1994.

———. *Dogmatische Prinzipienlehre: Glaube—Überlieferung—Theologie als Sprach- und Wahrheitsgeschehen.* Münster: Aschendorff, 2003.

Husserl, Edmund. *Phänomenologie des inneren Zeitbewusstseins.* Edited by M. Heidegger. 3rd ed. Tübingen: Meiner, 2000. Translated into English by J. S. Churchill as *Phenomenology of Inner Time Consciousness.* Edited by M. Heidegger. Bloomington: Indiana University Press, 1964.

International Theological Commision. *Erinnern und versöhnen: Die Kirche und die Verfehlungen in ihrer Vergangenheit: Ansprache und Vergebungsbitten.* Translated by G. L. Müller. 3rd ed. Freiburg: Johannes, 2000. The official English translation is available on the CDF page of the Vatican website as *Memory and Reconciliation: The Church and the Faults of the Past.*

Iserloh, Erwin. *Die Eucharistie in der Darstellung des Johannes Eck.* Münster: Aschendorff, 1950.

———. *Der Kampf um die Messe in den ersten Jahren der Auseinandersetzung mit Luther.* Münster: Aschendorff, 1952.

———. *Gnade und Eucharistie in der philosophischen Theologie des Wilhelm von Ockham.* Wiesbaden: Verlag Phillip von Zabern in Wissenschaftliche Buchgesellschaft, 1956.

Jaeschke, Walter. *Die Vernunft in der Religion: Studien zur Grundlegung der Religionsphilosophie Hegels.* Spekulation und Erfahrung, Abt. 2, Untersuchungen 4. Stuttgart-Bad Cannstatt: Frommann-Holzboog, 1986. Translated into English by J. Michael Stewart and Peter C. Hodgson as *Reason in Religion: The Foundations of Hegel's Philosophy of Religion.* Berkeley: University of California Press, 1990.

Jeremias, Joachim. *Die Abendmahlsworte Jesu.* 4th ed. Göttingen: Vandenhoeck & Ruprecht, 1967. Translated into English by Norman Perrin as *The Eucharistic Words of Jesus.* New York: Scribner, 1966.

John Paul II. *Fides et Ratio*. Verlautbarungen des Apostolischen Stuhls 135. Bonn, 1998. The official English translation as *Fides et Ratio* is available on the Vatican website.

———. *Ecclesia de Eucharistia*. Verlautbarungen des Apostolischen Stuhls 159. Bonn, 2003. The official English translation as *Ecclesia de Eucharistia* is available on the Vatican website.

Jüngel, Eberhard. "Gottes Passage: Schwellenängste und weihnachtliche Selbstvergessenheit." *Neue Zürcher Zeitung* (Supplement: Literatur und Kunst), December 24, 2005.

Jüngel, Eberhard, and Karl Rahner. *Was ist ein Sakrament?* Freiburg: Herder, 1971.

Jungmann, Josef Andreas. "Das Pater noster im Kommunionritus." *ZKaTh* 58 (1934): 552–71.

———. *Missarum sollemnia: Eine genetische Erklärung der römischen Messe*. 2 vols. 5th ed. Freiburg-Basel-Vienna: Herder, 1965. Translated into English by F. A. Brunner as *The Mass of the Roman Rite: Its Origins and Development*. London and New York: Burns and Oates, 1959.

Kamphaus, Franz. "Der 'Neue Mensch': Über unchristliche Spielarten einer christlichen Vision." In *Um Gottes willen—Leben: Einsprüche*. Foreword by Heinz-Günther Stobbe. Freiburg-Basel-Vienna: Herder, 2004.

Kasper, Walter. *Dogma unter dem Wort Gottes*. Mainz: Matthias Grünewald, 1965.

———. "Christi Himmelfahrt." *IKaZ Communio* 12 (1983): 205–13.

———. "Einheit und Vielheit der Aspekte der Eucharistie: Zur neuerlichen Diskussion um Grundgestalt und Grundsinn der Eucharistie." In *Theologie und Kirche*, 300–320. Mainz: Matthias-Grünewald, 1987. Translated by Margaret Kohl as *Theology and Church*. New York: Crossroad Publishing, 1989.

———. *Sakrament der Einheit. Eucharistie und Kirche*. Freiburg-Basel-Vienna: Herder, 2004. Translated into English by Brian McNeil as *Sacrament of Unity: The Eucharist and the Church*. New York: Crossroad Publishing, 2004.

———. *Jesus, der Christus*. Walter Kasper Gesammelte Schriften 3. Freiburg-Basel-Vienna: Herder, 2007. Translated into English by V. Green as *Jesus the Christ*. London: Burns and Oates, 1976.

Kaufmann, Ludwig and Nikolaus Klein. *Johannes XXIII: Prophetie im Vermächtnis*. 2nd ed. Freiburg-Brig: Edition Exodus, 1990.

Kehl, Medard. *Eschatologie*. 3rd ed. Würzburg: Echter, 1996.

———. *Die Kirche. Eine katholische Ekklesiologie*. Würzburg: Echter, 1992.

Keller, Ernst. *Eucharistie und Parusie: Liturgie- und theologiegeschichtliche Untersuchungen zur eschatologischen Dimension der Eucharistie anhand ausgewählter Zeugnisse aus frühchristlicher und patristischer Zeit*. Freiburg/Switzerland: Universitäts-Verlag, 1989.

Kessler, Hans. *Die theologische Bedeutung des Todes Jesu: Eine traditionsgeschichtliche Untersuchung*. Düsseldorf: Patmos, 1970.

———. *Erlösung als Befreiung*. Düsseldorf: Patmos, 1972.

———. *Sucht den Lebenden nicht bei den Toten: Die Auferstehung Jesu Christi in biblischer, fundamentaltheologischer und systematischer Sicht: Neuausgabe mit ausführlicher Erörterung der aktuellen Fragen*. Würzburg: Echter, 1995.

Kienzler, Klaus. "Die Erlösungslehre Anselms von Canterbury: Aus der Sicht des mittelalterlichen jüdisch-christlichen Religionsgesprächs." In *Versöhnung in der jüdischen und christlichen Liturgie*, edited by H. Heinz, 88–116. Freiburg: Herder, 1990.

Klinger, Elmar. "Transsubstantiation—Transfinalisation—Transsignifikation." In *Mehr als Brot und Wein: Theologische Kontexte der Eucharistie*, edited by W. Haunerland, 282–98. Würzburg: Echter, 2005.

Koch, Günter. *Sakramentenlehre*. In *Glaubenszugänge. Lehrbuch der Katholischen Dogmatik*, vol. 3, edited by W. Beinert. Paderborn: Schöningh, 1995.

Kolping, Adolf. "Amalar von Metz und Florus von Lyon: Zeugen eines Wandels im liturgischen Mysterienverständnis in der Karolingerzeit." *ZKaTh* 73 (1951): 424–64.

Kranemann, Benedikt, et al. *Wiederkehr der Rituale*. Stuttgart: Kohlhammer, 2004.

Kunzler, Michael. *Die Liturgie der Kirche*. AMATECA 10. Paderborn: Bonifaitus, 1995. Translated into English as *The Church's Liturgy*. London, New York: Continuum, 2001.

Kuschel, Karl-Josef. *Im Spiegel der Dichter: Mensch, Gott und Jesus in der Literatur des 20. Jahrhunderts*. Düsseldorf: Patmos Verlag, 1997. Translated into English by John Bowden as *Poet as Mirror: Human Nature, God and Jesus in Twentieth-Century Literature*. London: SCM Press, 1999.

Kutzer, Mirja. *In Wahrheit erfunden: Dichtung als Ort theologischer Erkenntnis*. Regensburg: Pustet, 2006

Lacoste, Jean-Yves. "Presence and Parousia." In *Postmodern Theology*, edited by Graham Ward, 394–98. Oxford: Blackwell, 2001.

Landgraf, Artur Michael. *Écrits théologiques de l'école d'Abélard. Textes inédits Louvain*. Spicilegium sacrum Lovaniense 14. Louvain: Spicilegium Sacrum Lovaniense, 1934.

Langenhorst, Georg. *Theologie und Literatur: Ein Handbuch*. Darmstadt: Wissenschaftliche Buchgesellschaft, 2005.

Lehmann, Karl. "Die dogmatische Denkform als hermeneutisches Problem: Prolegomena zu einer Kritik der dogmatischen Vernunft." In *Die Gegenwart des Glaubens*, 35–53. Mainz: Matthias Grünewald, 1974.

Lehmann, Karl, and Wolfhart Pannenberg. *Lehrverurteilungen kirchentrennend?* Vol. 1, *Rechtfertigung, Sakramente und Amt im Zeitalter der Reformation und heute*. Freiburg-Göttingen: Herder, 1986. Translated into English by Margaret Kohl as *The Condemnations of the Reformation Era: Do They Still Divide?* Minneapolis: Fortress Press, 1990.

Lengeling, Emil Joseph. *Liturgie—Dialog zwischen Gott und Mensch*. Edited and revised by K. Richter. 2nd ed. Freiburg: Herder, 1991.

Lesch, Walter, ed. *Theologie und Ästhetische Erfahrung: Beiträge zur Begegnung von Religion und Kunst*. Darmstadt: Wissenschaftliche Buchgesellschaft, 1994.

Lies, Lothar. *Mysterium fidei*. Würzburg: Echter, 2005.

———. "Zur Eucharistielehre von Johannes Betz (1914–1984)." *ThPh* 128 (2006): 53–80.

Lubac, Henri de. *Corpus mysticum: Kirche und Eucharistie im Mittelalter*. Einsiedeln: Johannes Verlag, 1969. Translated into English by Gemma Simmons, CJ, with Richard Price and Christopher Stephens, as *Corpus mysticum: The Eucharist and the Church in the Middle Ages: Historical Survey*. Edited by Laurence Paul Hemming and Susan Frank Parsons. Notre Dame, Ind.: Notre Dame University Press, 2007.

Lübbe, Hermann. *Im Zug der Zeit: Verkürzter Aufenthalt in der Gegenwart*. Berlin-Heidelberg-New York: Springer, 1992.

Lustiger, Jean-Marie. *Gotteswahl: Jüdische Herkunft—Übertritt zum Katholizismus—Zukunft von Kirche und Gesellschaft*. With Jean-Louis Missika and Dominique Wolton. Munich-Zürich: Sankt Ulrich, 1992. Translated into English by Rebecca Howell Balinski as *Choosing God, Chosen by God: Conversations with Jean-Marie Lustiger*. San Francisco: Ignatius Press, 1991.

Lutz-Bachmann, Matthias. "Hellenisierung des Christentums?" In *Spätantike und Christentum*, edited by C. Colpe, 77–98. Berlin: Akademie Verlag, 1992.

Manemann, Jürgen, ed. *Befristete Zeit*. Jahrbuch Politische Theologie 3. Münster: LIT Verlag, 1999.

Marin, Louis. *La parole mangée et autres essais théologico-politiques*. Paris: Boreal, 1986. Translated into English by Mette Hjort as *Food for Thought*. Baltimore: Johns Hopkins University Press, 1997.

Marion, Jean-Luc. *Dieu sans l'être*. Paris: Presses Universitaires De France, 1982. Translated into English by Thomas A. Carlson as *God without Being*. Chicago: University of Chicago Press, 1991.

Marquard, Odo. *Schwierigkeiten mit der Geschichtsphilosophie*. 4th ed. Frankfurt: Suhrkamp Verlag, 1994.

———. "Zeit und Endlichkeit." In *Skepsis und Zustimmung: Philosophische Studien*, 45–58. Stuttgart: Reclam, 1994.

Marxsen, Willi. *Das Abendmahl als christologisches Problem*. 2nd ed. Gütersloh: Gütersloher Verlagshaus Gerd Mohn, 1965. Translated into English by Paul J. Achtemeier and Lorenz Nieting as *The Lord's Supper as a Christological Problem* in *The Beginnings of Christology*. Philadelphia: Fortress Press, 1979.

Méndez, Angel F. "Göttliche Speise: Gastroerotik und eucharistisches Verlangen." *Concilium* 41 (2005): 128–36.

Menke, Karl-Heinz. "Das Gottespostulat unbedingter Solidarität und seine Erfüllung durch Christus." *IKaZ Communio* 21 (1992): 486–99.

———. "Gemeinsames und besonderes Priestertum." *IKaZ Communio* 28 (1999): 330–45.

Merklein, Helmut. "Der Sühnetod Jesu nach dem Zeugnis des Neuen Testaments." In *Versöhnung in der jüdischen und in der christlichen Liturgie*, edited by H. Heinz et al., 155–83. Freiburg: Herder, 1990.

———. "Erwägungen zur Überlieferungsgeschichte der neutestamentlichen Abendmahlstraditionen." In *Studien zu Jesus und Paulus*, 157–80. Wissenschaftliche Untersuchungen zum Neuen Testament 43. Tübingen: Mohr Siebeck, 1987.

Messner, Reinhard. *Die Meßreform Martin Luthers und die Eucharistie der Alten Kirche: Ein Beitrag zu einer systematischen Liturgiewissenschaft*. Innsbrucker theologische Studien 25. Innsbruck: Tyrolia, 1989.

———. "Zur Hermeneutik allegorischer Liturgieerklärung." *ZKaTh* 115 (1993): 284–319, 415–34.

———. "Probleme des eucharistischen Hochgebets." In *Erneuern und bewahren: Studien zur Messliturgie*, edited by R. Messner et al., 174–201. Innsbruck-Vienna: Tyrolia, 1995.

———. *Einführung in die Liturgiewissenschaft*. Paderborn: Schöningh, 2001.

Metz, Johann Baptist. "Brot des Überlebens: Das Abendmahl der Christen als Vorzeichen einer anthropologischen Revolution." In *Jenseits bürgerlicher Religion: Reden über die Zukunft des Christentums*, 51–69. Mainz-Munich: Grünewald-Kaiser, 1980.

———. *Zum Begriff der neuen Politischen Theologie: 1967–1997*. Mainz: Matthias-Grünewald, 1997.

———. *Memoria passionis: Ein provozierendes Gedächtnis in pluralistischer Gesellschaft: In Zusammenarbeit mit Johann Reikerstorfer*. Freiburg: Herder, 2006.

Meuffels, Hans Otmar. *Kommunikative Sakramententheologie*. Freiburg-Basel-Vienna: Herder, 1995.

Meyer, Hans Bernhard. *Eucharistie: Geschichte, Theologie, Pastoral: Mit einem Beitrag von Irmgard Pahl*. Handbuch der Liturgiewissenschaft 4. Regensburg: Pustet, 1989.

Moos, Alois. *Das Verhältnis von Wort und Sakrament in der deutschsprachigen Theologie des 20. Jahrhunderts.* Paderborn: Bonifatius, 1993.

Müller, Klaus, and Magnus Striet, eds. *Dogma und Denkform: Strittiges in der Grundlegung von Offenbarungsbegriff und Gottesgedanke.* Regensburg: Pustet, 2005.

Müller, Klaus. *Endlich unsterblich. Zwischen Körperkult und Cyberworld.* Kevelaer: Butzon & Bercker, 2011.

Neuner, Peter. "Die Hellenisierung des Christentums als Modell der Inkulturation." *Stimmen der Zeit* 213 (1995): 363–76.

Newman, Barbara. *The Life of Juliana of Mont-Cornillon.* Matrologia Latina 13. Toronto: Cistercian Publications, 1990.

Nietzsche, Friedrich. *Die fröhliche Wissenschaft.* Vol. 3 of *Kritische Studienausgabe: 15 Bände,* edited by G. Colli and M. Montinari, 343–651. 2nd ed. Berlin–New York–Munich: dtv Verlagsgesellschaft, 1988. Translated into English by Walter Kauffman as *The Gay Science.* New York: Vintage Books, 1974.

Nocke, Franz-Josef. *Sakramententheologie: Ein Handbuch.* Düsseldorf: Patmos, 1997.

Osborne, Kenan B. *Christian Sacraments in a Postmodern World: A Theology for the Third Millenium.* New York: Paulist Press International, 1999.

Pascal, Blaise. *Pensées sur la religion, et sur quelques autres sujets, l'ed. de Port-Royal (1670) et ses compl. (1678–1776) prés. par G. Couton et J. Jehasse.* Images et témoins de l'âge classique 2. Facsimile edition. Saint-Etienne: Editions la Bibliothèque Digitale, 1971. Translated into English by William F. Trotter as *Pensées: Thoughts on Religion and Other Subjects.* New York: Washington Square Press, 1965.

Pesch, Otto Hermann. "Gottes Wort in der Geschichte." In *Katholische Dogmatik aus ökumenischer Erfahrung.* Vol. I/1, *Wort Gottes und Theologie, Christologie,* 735–62. Ostfildern: Matthias-Grünewald, 2008.

Pesch, Rudolf. *Das Markusevangelium.* Vol. 2, *Kommentar zu Kap. 8,27–16,20.* Herders theologischer Kommentar zum Neuen Testament 2. Freiburg: Herder, 1977.

Pesch, Rudolf. *Das Abendmahl und Jesu Todesverständnis.* Freiburg: Herder, 1978.

Peters, Tiemo Rainer, and Claus Urban, eds. *Ende der Zeit? Die Provokation der Rede von Gott: Dokumentation einer Tagung mit Joseph Kardinal Ratzinger, Johann Baptist Metz, Jürgen Moltmann und Eveline Goodman-Thau in Ahaus.* Mainz: Matthias-Grünewald, 1999.

Peterson, Erik. *Heis theos: Epigraphische, formgeschichtliche und religionsgeschichtliche Untersuchungen.* Forschungen zur Religion und Literatur des Alten und Neuen Testaments 41 (= N. F. 24). Göttingen: Vandenhoeck & Ruprecht, 1926.

———. *Marginalien zur Theologie und andere Schriften, mit einer Einführung von Barbara Nichtweiss.* Ausgewählte Schriften 2. Würzburg: Echter, 1995.

Peukert, Helmut. *Wissenschaftstheorie—Handlungstheorie—fundamentale Theologie: Analysen zu Ansatz und Status theologischer Theoriebildung.* 2nd ed. Frankfurt: Suhrkamp, 1988. Translated into English by James Bohman as *Science, Action, and Fundamental Theology: Toward a Theology of Communicative Action.* Cambridge, Mass.: MIT Press, 1986.

Pohle, Joseph. *Lehrbuch der Dogmatik.* Newly revised by Michael Gierens. Vol. 3. 8th ed. Paderborn: Schöningh Verlag, 1933. Translated into English by Arthur Preuss as *God: The Author of Nature and the Supernatural.* London: Herder, 1916.

Pratzner, Ferdinand. *Messe und Kreuzesopfer: Die Krise der sakramentalen Idee bei Luther und in der mittelalterlichen Scholastik.* Vienna: Herder, 1970.

Pröpper, Thomas. *Erlösungsglaube und Freiheitsgeschichte: Eine Skizze zur Soteriologie.* 3rd ed. Munich: Kösel, 1991.

———. *Evangelium und freie Vernunft: Konturen einer theologischen Hermeneutik*. Freiburg: Herder, 2001.

Rahner, Karl, and Angelus Häussling. *Die vielen Messen und das eine Opfer: Eine Untersuchung über die rechte Norm der Messehäufigkeit*. Quaestiones disputatae 31. 2nd ed. Freiburg 1966. Translated into English by William Joseph O'Hara as *The Celebration of the Eucharist*. London: Herder, 1968.

Rahner, Karl. "Die Gegenwart Christi im Sakrament des Herrenmahls nach dem katholischen Bekenntnis im Gegenüber zum evangelisch-lutherischen Bekenntnis." *Catholica* 12 (1959): 105–28.

———. *Kirche und Sakramente*. Quaestiones disputatae 10. Freiburg: Herder, 1960. Translated into English by William Joseph O'Hara as *Church and Sacraments*. London: Herder and Herder, 1974.

———. "Über die Dauer der Gegenwart Christi nach dem Kommunionempfang." In Vol. 4 of *Schriften zur Theologie*, 387–97. Einsiedeln: Benzinger, 1960. Translated into English by Kevin Smyth, "On the Duration of the Presence of Christ after Communion." In *Theological Investigations*. Vol. 4, *More Recent Writings*, 312–20. Baltimore: Helicon Press 1966.

———. "Eucharistie und alltägliches Leben." In Vol. 7 of *Schriften zur Theologie*, 204–20. Einsiedeln: Benzinger, 1966. Translated into English by David Bourke as "The Eucharist and Our Daily Lives." In *Theological Investigations*. Vol. 7, *Further Theology of the Spiritual Life 1*, 211–26. London: Darton, Longman and Todd, 1971.

———. "Frömmigkeit früher und heute." In Vol. 7 of *Schriften zur Theologie*, 11–31. Einsiedeln: Benzinger 1966. Translated into English by David Bourke as "Christian Living Formerly and Today." In *Theological Investigations*. Vol. 7, *Further Theology of the Spiritual Life 1*, 3–24. London: Darton, Longman and Todd, 1971.

———. "Über das christliche Sterben." In Vol. 7 of *Schriften zur Theologie*, 273–80. Einsiedeln: Benzinger, 1966. Translated into English by David Bourke as "On Christian Dying." In *Theological Investigations*. Vol. 7, *Further Theology of the Spiritual Life 1*, 285–93. London: Darton, Longman and Todd, 1971.

———. "Eucharistische Anbetung." In Vol. 16 of *Schriften zur Theologie*, 300–304. Einsiedeln: Benzinger, 1984. Translated into English by Joseph Donceel, S.J. as "Eucharistic Worship." In *Theological Investigations*. Vol. 23, *Final Writings*, 113–16. New York: Crossroad Publishing, 1992.

———. *Menschsein und Menschwerdung Gottes: Studien zur Grundlegung der Dogmatik, zur Christologie, theologischen Anthropologie und Eschatologie*. Edited by Herbert Vorgrimler. Freiburg: Herder, 2005.

Ratzinger, Joseph. *Volk und Haus Gottes in Augustins Lehre von der Kirche*. 1954. 2nd ed. St. Ottilien: Herder, 1992.

———. *Die erste Sitzungsperiode des Zweiten Vatikanischen Konzils: Ein Rückblick*. Cologne: Bachem, 1963. Translated into English in *Theological Highlights of Vatican II*. New York: Paulist Press, 1966. Rev. ed., 2009.

———. *Die sakramentale Begründung christlicher Existenz*. Meitingen: Kyrios-Verlag, 1965. Translated into English in *Collected Works: Theology of the Liturgy*. San Francisco: Ignatius Press, 2014.

———. *Das Problem der Dogmengeschichte in der Sicht der katholischen Theologie*. Cologne: Westdeutscher Verlag, 1966.

———. "Das Problem der Transsubstantiation und die Frage nach dem Sinn der Eucharistie." *ThQ* 147 (1967): 129–58.

———. *Theologische Prinzipienlehre: Bausteine zur Fundamentaltheologie*. Munich: Erich Wewel Verlag, 1982. Translated into English by Sr. Mary Francis McCarthy as *Principles of Catholic Theology: Building Stones for a Fundamental Theology*. San Francisco: Ignatius Press, 1987.

———. *Salt of the Earth: The Church at the End of a Millenium: A Conversation with Peter Seewald*. Translated by Adrian Walker. San Francisco: Ignatius Press, 1997.

———. *Der Geist der Liturgie. Eine Einführung*. Freiburg-Basel-Vienna: Herder, 2000. Translated into English by John Saward as *The Spirit of the Liturgy*. San Francisco: Ignatius Press, 2000.

———. *Gott ist uns nah—Eucharistie: Mitte des Lebens*. Edited by Stephan O. Horn and Vinzenz Pfnür. 2nd ed. Augsburg: Sankt Ulrich, 2002. Translated into English by Henry Taylor. *God Is Near Us: The Eucharist, the Heart of Life*. San Francisco: Ignatius Press, 2003.

———. "40 Jahre Konstitution über die heilige Liturgie." *LJ* 53 (2003): 209–21.

Ratzinger, Joseph / Benedict XVI. *Eschatologie: Tod und ewiges Leben*. New edition. Regensburg: Pustet, 2007. Translated into English by Michael Waldstein as *Eschatology: Death and Eternal Life*. 2nd ed. Washington, D.C.: The Catholic University of America Press, 2007.

———. *Predigten, Ansprachen und Grußworte im Rahmen der Apostolischen Reise von Papst Benedikt XVI. nach Köln anlässlich des XX. Weltjugendtages*. Edited by Sekretariat der Deutschen Bischofskonferenz. Verlautbarungen des Apostolischen Stuhls 169. Bonn: Libreria Editrice Vaticana, 2005.

Reiser, Michael. "Eucharistische Wissenschaft: Eine exegetische Betrachtung zu Joh 6,26.59." In *Vorgeschmack: Ökumenische Bemühungen um die Eucharistie*, edited by B. J. Hilberath and Dorothea Sattler, 164–77. Mainz: Matthias-Grünewald, 1995.

Ricken, Frido. "Nikaia als Krisis des altchristlichen Platonismus." *ThPh* 44 (1969): 321–41.

Ruster, Thomas. *Wandlung: Ein Traktat über Eucharistie und Ökonomie*. Mainz: Matthias-Grünewald, 2006.

Sala, Giovanni B. "Transsubstantiation oder Transsignifikation?" *ZKaTh* 92 (1970): 1–34.

Sattler, Dorothea. "Wandeln Worte Wirklichkeit? Nachdenkliches über die Rezeption der Sprechakttheorie in der (Sakramenten-)Theologie." *Catholica* 51 (1997): 125–38.

Schaede, Stephan. *Stellvertretung. Begriffsgeschichtliche Studien zur Soteriologie*. Tübingen: Mohr Siebeck, 2004.

Scheffczyk, Leo. "Die Frage nach der eucharistischen Wandlung." In *Glaube als Lebensinspiration*, 347–70. Einsiedeln: Johannes-Verlag, 1980.

Scheuer, Manfred. "Wie lange noch? Zur Zeitstruktur der Eucharistie." *TThZ* (2002): 106–22.

Schilson, Arno. *Theologie als Sakramententheologie: Die Mysterientheologie Odo Casels*. 2nd ed. Mainz: Matthias-Grünewald, 1987.

———. "Sakramententheologie zwischen Bestandsaufnahme und Spurensuche: Eine Umschau." *LJ* 47 (1997): 99–128.

———. "Negative Theologie der Liturgie? Über die liturgische Erfahrung der Verborgenheit des nahen Gottes." *LJ* 50 (2000): 235–50.

Schillebeeckx, Edward. *Christus—Sakrament der Gottbegegnung*. 2nd ed. Mainz: Matthias-Grünewald, 1965. Translated into English by Mark Schoof and Laurence Bright as *Christ, the Sacrament of the Encounter with God*. New York: Rowman and Littlefield, 1963.

———. *Die eucharistische Gegenwart: Zur Diskussion über die Realpräsenz*. Theologische Perspektiven. Düsseldorf: Patmos, 1967.

———. *Glaubensinterpretation: Beiträge zu einer hermeneutischen und kritischen Theologie*. Mainz: Matthias-Grünewald, 1971.

Schlier, Heinrich. "Johannes 6 und das johanneische Verständnis der Eucharistie." In *Das Ende der Zeit: Exegetische Aufsätze und Vorträge III*, 102–23. Freiburg: Herder, 1971.

Schmaus, Michael. *Begegnungen zwischen katholischem Christentum und nationalsozialistischer Weltanschauung*. Münster: Aschendorff, 1933.

———, ed. *Aktuelle Fragen zur Eucharistie*. Munich: Hueber, 1960.

Schmemann, Alexander. *The Journals of Father Alexander Schmemann 1973–1983*. Translated by Juliana Schmemann. Crestwood, N.Y.: St. Vladimir's Seminary Press, 2000.

———. *Eucharistie: Sakrament des Gottesreiches*. Translated by Matthias Mühl. Freiburg: Johannes Verlag, 2005. Translated into English by Paul Kachur as *The Eucharist: Sacrament of the Kingdom*. Crestwood, N.Y. : St. Vladimir's Seminary Press, 1987. Reprinted 2003.

Schneider, Theodor. *Zeichen der Nähe Gottes: Grundriss der Sakramententheologie*. 7th ed. Mainz: Matthias-Grünewald, 1998.

———, ed. *Handbuch der Dogmatik*. 2 vols. Mainz: Matthias-Grünewald, 1992.

Schoonenberg, Piet. "Inwieweit ist die Lehre von der Transsubstantiation historisch bestimmt?" *Concilium* 3 (1967): 305–11.

———. "Geschichtlichkeit und Interpretation des Dogmas." In *Die Interpretation des Dogmas*, 58–110. Düsseldorf: Patmos, 1969.

Schreiner, Klaus. "Juliana von Lüttich (1193–1258): Eine Frau 'in den Liliengärten des Herrn.'" *Zur Debatte* 38 (2008): 41–43.

Schröer, Henning, Gotthard Fermor, and Harald Schroeter, eds. *Theopoesie: Theologie und Poesie in hermeneutischer Sicht*. Hermeneutica 7. Rheinbach: CMZ Verlag, 1998.

Schröter, Jens. *Das Abendmahl. Frühchristliche Deutungen und Impulse für die Gegenwart*. Stuttgart: Katholisches Bibelwerk, 2006.

Schulte, Raphael. "Die Einzelsakramente als Ausgliederung des Wurzelsakraments." *MySal* IV/2 (1973): 46–155.

Schulz, Hans-Joachim. "Interpretation durch liturgischen Vollzug: 'Transsubstantiation' und 'Transsignifikation' in liturgiewissenschaftlicher Sicht." In *Sprache und Erfahrung als Problem der Theologie*, edited by Wolfgang Beinert, 61–77. Paderborn: Ferdinand Schöningh, 1978.

Schupp, Franz. *Glaube—Kultur—Symbol. Versuch einer kritischen Theorie sakramentaler Praxis*. Düsseldorf: Patmos, 1974.

Schürmann, Heinz. *Jesus—Gestalt und Geheimnis: Gesammelte Beiträge*. Edited by Klaus Scholtissek. Paderborn: Bonifatius, 1994.

Searle, John R. *Speech Acts: An Essay in the Philosophy of Language*. Cambridge: Cambridge University Press, 1969.

Seidl, Horst. "Zum Substanzbegriff der katholischen Transsubstantiationslehre." *FKTh* 11 (1995): 1–16.

Seifert, Oliver, ed. *Panis angelorum—Das Brot der Engel: Kulturgeschichte der Hostie*. Ostfildern: Thorbecke, 2004.

Semmelroth, Otto. *Die Kirche als Ursakrament*. Mainz: Josef Knecht, 1963. Translated into English by Emily Schossberger as *Church and Sacrament*. Notre Dame, Ind.: Fides, 1965.

———. "Die Kirche als Sakrament des Heils." *MySal* IV/1 (1972): 309–56.

Servais, Jacques. "'Weisheit, Wissen und Freude': Zur Überwindung einer verhängnisvollen Diastase." In *Die Kunst Gottes verstehen: Hans Urs von Balthasars theologische Provokationen*, edited by Magnus Striet and Jan-Heiner Tück, 320–48. Freiburg: Herder, 2005.

Simonis, Walter. *Ecclesia visibilis et invisibilis: Untersuchungen zur Ekklesiologie und Sakramentenlehre in der afrikanischen Tradition von Cyprian bis Augustinus*. Frankfurt: Knecht, 1970.

Slenczka, Notger. *Realpräsenz und Ontologie: Untersuchungen der ontologischen Grundlagen der Transsignifikationslehre*. Göttingen: Vandenhoeck & Ruprecht, 1993.

Sobrino, Jon. *Christ the Liberator: A View from the Victims*. Translated by Paul Burns. New York: Orbis, 2001.

Söding, Thomas. "Das Mahl des Herrn: Zur Gestalt und Theologie der ältesten nachösterlichen Tradition." In *Vorgeschmack*, edited by B. J. Hilberath and Dorothea Sattler, 134–64. Mainz: Matthias-Grünewald, 1995.

———. "'Tut dies zu meinem Gedächtnis!' Das Abendmahl Jesu und die Eucharistie der Kirche nach dem Neuen Testament." In *Eucharistie: Positionen katholischer Theologie*, 11–58. Regensburg: Pustet, 2002.

Sölle, Dorothee. *Leiden*. Freiburg-Basel-Vienna: Herder, 1973. Reprinted 1993. Translated into English as *Suffering*. Philadelphia: Fortress Press, 1975.

Sokolowski, Robert. *Eucharistic Presence: A Study in the Theology of Disclosure*. Washington D.C.: The Catholic University of America Press, 1993.

Staedtke, Joachim. "Abendmahl III/3." *TRE* 1 (1978): 106–22.

Stegemann, Ekkehard W. "Wie im Angesicht des Judentums vom Tod Jesu sprechen? Vom Prozess Jesu zu den Passionserzählungen der Evangelien." In *Wie heute vom Tod Jesu sprechen?* edited by Gerd Häfner and Hansjörg Schmid, 23–52. Freiburg: Katholische Akademie, 2002.

Steger, Christian. *Nur neugotisch? Das pastorale Programm im historischen Kirchenbau 1870 bis 1914*. Regensburg: Pustet, 2013.

Steiner, George. *Real Presences: Is there anything in what we say?* London: University of Chicago Press, 1989.

———. *No Passion Spent: Essays 1978–1995*. New Haven: Yale University Press, 1996.

———. *Errata: An Examined Life*. London: Yale University Press, 1997.

———. *Grammars of Creation: Originating in the Gifford lectures for 1990*. London: Yale University Press, 2001.

———. *Lessons of the Masters. The Charles Eliot Norton Lectures 51*. Cambridge, MA: Harvard University Press, 2005.

Stock, Alex. *Poetische Dogmatik: Christologie*. Vol. 3, *Leib und Leben*. Paderborn: Schöningh, 1998.

———. *Poetische Dogmatik: Christologie*. Vol. 4, *Figuren*. Paderborn: Schöningh, 2001.

———. *Liturgie und Poesie: Zur Sprache des Gottesdienstes*. Kevelaer: Butzon & Bercker, 2011.

Stohr, Albert. "Die Hauptrichtungen der spekulativen Trinitätslehre in der Theologie des 13. Jahrhunderts." *ThQ* 106 (1925): 113–35.

Striet, Magnus. "Versuch über die Auflehnung: Philosophisch-theologische Überlegungen zur Theodizeefrage." In *Mit Gott streiten: Neue Zugänge zum Theodizee-problem*, edited by Harald Wagner, 48–89. Quaestiones disputatae 169. Freiburg-Basel-Vienna: Herder, 1998.

———. *Offenbares Geheimnis: Zur Kritik der negativen Theologie*. ratio fidei 14. Regensburg: Pustet 2002.

———. "Gespannte Freude—oder: Wider eine verharmlosende Spiritualität der Klage." *IKaZ Communio* 33 (2004): 317–34.

Striet, Magnus, and Jan-Heiner Tück, eds. *Die Kunst Gottes verstehen: Hans Urs von Balthasars theologische Provokationen*. Freiburg: Herder, 2005.

Strobel, Regula. "Feministisch-theologische Kritik an Kreuzestheologien." *KatBl* 123 (1998): 84–90.

Stuhlmacher, Peter. *Biblische Theologie des Neuen Testaments*. Vol. 1, *Grundlegung: Von Jesus zu Paulus*. Göttingen: Vandenhoeck & Ruprecht, 1992.

Theobald, Michael. "Kirche und Israel nach Röm 9–11." In *Studien zum Römerbrief*, 324–49. Tübingen: Mohr Siebeck, 2001.

———. "Das Herrenmahl im Neuen Testament." *ThQ* 138 (2003): 257–80.

Theunissen, Michael. *Negative Theologie der Zeit*. Frankfurt: Suhrkamp, 1991.

Tillard, Jean-Marie R. *L'Eucharistie—Pâque de l'église*. Unam Sanctam 44. Paris: Éditions du Cerf Bourges, 1964. Translated into English by Dennis L. Wienk as *The Eucharist: Pasch of God's People*. Staten Island, N.Y.: Society of St. Paul, 1967.

Trochu, Francis. *The Curé d'Ars, St. Jean-Marie-Baptiste Vianney (1786–1859)*. Translated by Dom Ernest Graf, OSB. Charlotte, N.C.: TAN Books, 2007.

Tück, Jan-Heiner. *"Gelobt seist du, Niemand": Paul Celans Dichtung—eine theologische Provokation*. Frankfurt: Josef Knecht, 2000.

———. *Christologie und Theodizee bei Johann Baptist Metz: Ambivalenz der Neuzeit im Licht der Gottesfrage*. 2nd ed. Paderborn: Schöningh, 2001.

———. "'Glaubhaft ist nur Liebe': Bleibende Anstöße für die Theologie der Gegenwart." *IKaZ Communio* 34 (2005): 145–63.

———. "Inkarnierte Feindesliebe: Der Messias Israels und die Hoffnung auf Versöhnung." In *Streitfall Christologie: Vergewisserungen nach der Shoah*, edited by Helmut Hoping and Jan-Heiner Tück, 216–58. Quaestiones disputatae 214. Freiburg-Basel-Vienna: Herder, 2005.

———. "Höllenabstieg Christi und Hoffnung für alle: Hans Urs von Balthasars eschatologischer Vorstoß." *ThG* 49 (2006): 60–65.

———. "Memoriale passionis: Die Selbstgabe Jesu Christi als Anstoß zu einer eucharistischen Erinnerungssolidarität." In *Gestorben für wen? Zur Diskussion um das "pro multis,"* edited by Magnus Striet, 93–110. Theologie kontrovers. Freiburg: Herder, 2007.

———. "Die Kunst, es nicht gewesen zu sein: Die Krise des Sündenbewusstseins als Anstoß für die Soteriologie." *Stimmen der Zeit* 226 (2008): 579–89.

———. "Jesus Christus—Gottes Heil für uns: Eine dogmatische Skizze." In *Jesus begegnen: Zugänge zur Christologie*, edited by G. Hotze et al., 119–76. Theologische Module. Freiburg: Herder, 2009.

———. *Hintergrundgeräusche: Liebe, Tod und Trauer in der Gegenwartsliteratur*. Ostfildern: Matthias-Grünewald, 2010.

———. *Erinnerung an die Zukunft. Das Zweite Vatikanische Konzil*. 2nd ed. Freiburg: Herder, 2013.

———, and Andreas Bieringer, eds. *"Verwandeln allein durch Erzählen." Peter Handke im Spannungsfeld von Theologie und Literaturwissenschaft*. Freiburg: Herder, 2014.

Tugendhat, Ernst. *Egozentrizität und Mystik: Eine anthropologische Studie*. Munich: C. H. Beck, 2003. Translated into English by Alexei Procyshyn and Mario Wenning as *Egocentricity and Mysticism: An Anthropological Study*. New York: Columbia University Press, 2016.

Verweyen, Hansjürgen. "Die Einheit von Gerechtigkeit und Barmherzigkeit bei Anselm von Canterbury." *IKaZ Communio* 14 (1985): 52–55.

———. *Botschaft eines Toten? Den Glauben rational verantworten*. Regensburg: Friedrich Pustet, 1997.

———. *Gottes letztes Wort*. 3rd ed. Regensburg: Pustet, 2000.

———. *Theologie im Zeichen der schwachen Vernunft*. Regensburg: Pustet, 2000.

———. *Warum Sakramente?* Regensburg: Pustet, 2001.

Virilio, Paul. *Fluchtgeschwindigkeit: Essay*. Translated into English by Julie Rose as *Open Sky*. London: Verso, 2008.

Vorgrimler, Herbert. "Liturgie—ein Bild der Kirche: Anfragen der systematischen Theologie." In *Heute Gott feiern: Liturgiefähigkeit des Menschen und Menschenfähigkeit der Liturgie*, edited by Benedikt Kranemann et al., 39–56. Freiburg: Herder, 1999.

Wahle, Stephan. *Gottes-Gedenken: Untersuchungen zum anamnetischen Gehalt christlicher und jüdischer Liturgie*. Innsbruck-Vienna: Tyrolia, 2006.

Wainwright, Geoffrey. *Doxology: The Praise of God in Worship, Doctrine and Life: A Systematic Theology*. London: Oxford University Press, 1980.

———. *Eucharistic and Eschatology*. New York: Oxford University Press, 1981.

Wehr, Lothar. *Arznei der Unsterblichkeit: Die Eucharistie bei Ignatius von Antiochien und im Johannesevangelium*. Neutestamentliche Abhandlungen; N. F. 18. Münster: Aschendorff, 1987.

Weinrich, Harald. *Lethe. Kunst und Kritik des Vergessens*. Munich: C. H. Beck, 1997. Translated into English by Steven Rendall as *Lethe: The Art and Critique of Forgetting*. Ithaca, N.Y.: Cornell University Press, 2004.

Welte, Bernhard. "Zum Referat von Leo Scheffczyk." In *Aktuelle Fragen zur Eucharistie*, edited by Michael Schmaus, 190–94. Munich: Hueber, 1960.

———. "Zum Verständnis der Eucharistie." In *Auf der Spur des Ewigen*, 459–67. Freiburg: Herder, 1965.

———. "Die Lehrformel von Nikaia und die abendländische Metaphysik." In *Zur Frühgeschichte der Christologie: Ihre biblischen Anfänge und die Lehrformel von Nikaia*, edited by Bernhard Welte, 100–117. Quaestiones disputatae 51. Freiburg: Herder, 1970.

Wendenbourg, Dorothea. "Den falschen Weg Roms zu Ende gegangen? Zur gegenwärtigen Diskussion über Martin Luthers Gottesdienstreform und ihr Verhältnis zu den Traditionen der Alten Kirche." *ZThK* 94 (1997): 437–67.

Wenz, Gunther. *Einführung in die evangelische Sakramentenlehre*. Darmstadt: Wissenschaftliche Buchgesellschaft, 1988.

Werbick, Jürgen. *Soteriologie*. Leitfaden Theologie. Düsseldorf: Patmos, 1990.

Wohlmuth, Josef. *Realpräsenz und Transsubstantiation im Konzil von Trient: Eine historisch-kritische Analyse der Canones 1–4 der Sessio XIII*. 2 vols. Frankfurt et al.: Peter Lang, 1975.

Wohlmuth, Josef. "Eucharistie—Feier des Neuen Bundes." In *Christologie der Liturgie*, edited by Klemens Richter and Benedikt Kranemann, 187–206. Quaestiones disputatae 159. Freiburg-Basel-Vienna: Herder, 1995.

———. "Eucharistie als liturgische Feier der Gegenwart Jesu Christi: Realpräsenz und Transsubstantiation im Verständnis katholischer Theologie." In *Eucharistie: Positionen katholischer Theologen*, edited by Thomas Söding, 87–119. Regensburg: Pustet, 2002.

Yates, Francis A. *The Art of Memory*. Chicago: University of Chicago Press, 1966. Reprinted 2001.

Zenger, Erich. *Das Erste Testament: Die jüdische Bibel und die Christen*. Düsseldorf: Patmos, 1991.

V. Literary Works

Boccaccio, Giovanni. *Vita di Dante*. Vol. 3 of *Tutte le opere*. Edited by Vittore Branca. Mailand: Mondadori, 1974. Translated into German by Otto Freiherr von Taube as *Das Leben Dantes*. 5th ed. Frankfurt: Insel Verlag, 1987. Translated into English by George R. Carpenter as *A Translation of Giovanni Boccaccio's Life of Dante*. New York: Grolier Club, 1900.

Calderón de la Barca, Pedro. *Autos Sacramentales Alegóricos Y Historiales Del Insigne Poeta Español Don Pedro Calderon De La Barca ... Obras Pósthumas Que Del Archivo De La Villa De Madrid Saca Originales a Luz Don Pedro De Pando Y Mier*. En Madrid: En La Imprenta De Manuel Ruiz De Murga, 1718. Translated into German and edited by Franz Lorinser as *Geistliche Festspiele*. Vol. 7. Regensburg: Manz, 1888.

Canetti, Elias. *Das Geheimherz der Uhr: Aufzeichnungen 1973–1985*. Munich: Carl Hanser, 1987. Translated into English by Joel Agee as *The Secret Heart of the Clock*. New York: Farrar, Strauss, and Giroux, 2005.

———. *Die Fliegenpein: Aufzeichnungen*. Munich: Carl Hanser, 1992. Translated into English by H. F. Broch de Rothermann as *The Agony of Flies* [bilingual edition]. New York: Farrar, Strauss, and Giroux, 1994.

———. *Nachträge aus Hampstead: Aufzeichnungen*. Munich: Carl Hanser, 1994. Translated into English by John Hargraves as *Notes from Hampstead*. New York: Farrar, Strauss, and Giroux, 1994.

———. *Aufzeichnungen 1992–1993*. Munich: Carl Hanser, 1996.

Claudel, Paul. *Oeuvre poétique*. Introduction by Stanislas Fumet, text established and annotated by Jacques Petit. Bibliothèque de la Pléiade 125. Paris: Gallimard, 1977.

Dante Alighieri. *Divina commedia—Die Göttliche Komödie*. Vol. 3, *Paradiso*. Translated by H. Federmann. Berlin-Leipzig: Cotta, 1929. Translated into English by Anthony Esolen as *Paradise*. New York: Modern Library, 2004.

Eliot, T. S. *Collected Poems 1909–1962*. New York: Harcourt Brace Jovanovich, 1963.

Goethe, Johann Wolfgang von. *Aus meinem Leben: Dichtung und Wahrheit*. Berliner Ausgabe 13. 4th ed. Berlin: Akademie Verlag, 1976. Translated into English by John Oxenford as *The Auto-Biography of Goethe: Truth and Poetry: From My Own Life*. London: H. G. Bohn, 1874.

———. *Faust. Eine Tragödie*. In *Werke*. Vol. 3, *Dramatische Dichtungen I*, edited by Erich Trunz, 9–364. Hamburger Ausgabe in 14 Bänden. 16th ed. Hamburg: Wegner, 1996.

Handke, Peter. *Langsame Heimkehr*. Frankfurt: Suhrkamp, 1984. Translated by Ralph Manheim as "The Long Way Round" in *The Slow Homecoming*. New York: Farrar, Strauss, and Giroux, 1985. Reprinted 2011.

———. *Die Geschichte des Bleistifts*. Frankfurt: Suhrkamp, 1985.

———. *Mein Jahr in der Niemandsbucht: Ein Märchen aus den neuen Zeiten*. 2nd ed. Frankfurt: Suhrkamp, 1994. Translated by Krishna Winston as *My Year in the No-Man's-Bay*. New York: Farrar, Strauss, and Giroux, 1998.

———. *Die Lehre von Sainte-Victoire*. Frankfurt: Suhrkamp, 1996. Translated by Ralph Manheim as "The Lesson of Mount Sainte-Victoire" in *The Slow Homecoming*. New York: Farrar, Strauss, and Giroux, 1985. Reprinted 2011.

———. *Phantasien der Wiederholung*. Frankfurt: Suhrkamp, 1996.

———. *Am Felsfenster morgen (und andere Ortszeiten 1982–1987)*. Munich: dtv, 2000.

———. *Über die Dörfer. Dramatisches Gedicht*. Frankfurt: Suhrkamp, 2002. Translated by Michael Roloff as *Walk about the Villages*. New York: Ariadne Press, 1996.

———. *Gestern unterwegs: Aufzeichnungen November 1987 bis Juli 1990*. Frankfurt: Suhrkamp, 2007.

———. *Die morawische Nacht: Erzählung*. Frankfurt: Suhrkamp, 2008. Translated by Krishna Winston as *The Moravian Night*. New York: Farrar, Strauss, and Giroux, 2017.

———. *Der Große Fall*. Berlin: Suhrkamp, 2011.

Houellebecq, Michel. *Les particules élémentaires*. Paris: Flammarion, 1983. Translated into English by Frank Wynne as *The Elementary Particles*. New York: Knopf, 2001.

Jones, David. *The Anathemata: Fragments of an Attempted Writing*. 3rd ed. London: Faber and Faber, 1972. Translated into German by Cordelia Spaemann as *Anathemata: Fragmente eines Schreibversuchs*. Freiburg: Herder, 1988.

———. *Epoch and Artist: Selected Writings*. Edited by Harman H. Grisewood. London: Faber and Faber, 1973.

Joyce, James. *Dubliners—A Portrait of the Artist as a Young Man*. New York: Penguin Books, 1964.

Montaigne, Michel de. *Essais*. Edited by Herbert Lüthy. Zürich: Manesse, 1953.

Paz, Octavio. *Der menschenfreundliche Menschenfresser*. Frankfurt: Suhrkamp, 1981.

Sontag, Susan. *Regarding the Pain of Others*. New York: Penguin, 2003.

Strauss, Botho. *Der Aufstand gegen die sekundäre Welt: Bemerkungen zu einer Ästhetik der Anwesenheit*. Munich: Carl Hanser Verlag, 1999.

———. *Der Untenstehende auf Zehenspitzen*. Munich: Carl Hanser, 2004.

Tabori, George. *Mutters Courage*. Translated into German by Ursula Grützmacher-Tabori. Berlin: Klaus Wagenbach, 2003.

INDEX

Abelard, Peter, 24
Adoro te devote, 54, 76, 227, 246, 297, 317, 318, 328, 331–32; authorship, 229–31; the Beatific Vision, 242–43; faith, 234–39; in general, 229–43; and Hosea, 240–41; pelican image in, 241–42; and petition, 239–242; Real Presence, 234–35; structure, 232–33; text, 231–32; theological virtues, 239; transubstantiation, 234
Albert the Great, 48, 69, 73, 105, 129, 144, 148n220, 243n52
Anointing of the sick. *See* Extreme Unction
Anselm of Canterbury: *Cur Deus homo*, 100–1; doctrine of satisfaction, 16, 17, 100–1, 112; necessity of redemption, 101, 102, 104
Ambrose of Milan, 61–62, 67, 76, 81, 84, 220, 223, 260–61
Aristotle, 5, 13, 32, 43, 75, 92, 293; friendship in, 183, 333–34; ontological concepts, 17, 51, 254, 263–64, 273
Augustine: on the Eucharist, 60, 92, 141, 157–8, 234, 260; on sacraments, 31; on sacrifice, 121, 132
Aquinas, Thomas: and authenticity of hymns, 167–73; *Commentary on the Book of Hebrews*, 135–37; as a Dominican, 301–2; and Eucharistic theology, 198; on the Order of the Mass, 148–55; as a poet, 162–63

Baptism: and procreation, 49; sacrament of, 48; and sin, 124–25
de la Barca, Calderón, 163,
beginners, theology for, 23
Berengar of Tours, 56n2, 60, 65, 72–73, 139, 146, 165, 178, 262, 263
Betz, Johannes, xiv, 14, 57, 88, 247, 258
Blondel, Maurice, 332, 333
Bonaventure, 42, 48, 105, 129, 163, 171, 172, 263

Calvin, John, 289–90
Casel, Odo, 269

Christology, 26n14, 27–29, 31, 44n91
Clement V, Pope, 167–69
Confirmation, 48, 49
Corpus Christi: history of, 165–167; Office of, 167–74, 201, 215, 216, 228; Solemnity of, 212, 248
Council of Trent, 54, 72, 266–67, 295
creation, 26, 75, 83–84, 92–93, 100, 207, 286, 293

Dante Alighieri, 12, 163–64
Descartes, René, 291

ecclesiology, 28, 114–15; and the Eucharist, 155–58, 219, 222, 265–66, 278, 294, 300; and sin, 124
Eliot, T. S., 311
eschatology: and the Eucharist, 202, 225–28, 249, 281–82, 331, 336–39; and the Passion, 126, 204, 284; and time, 305
Eucharist: and adoration, 311–16; and alternative formulae, 83–86; annihilation, theory of, 70–72; and anthropophagy, 60n19, 60n20, 63–64, 65, 65n44, 65n45, 76, 97, 180n13, 220, 261–62, 332; and commemorative actual presence, 94, 258; communal character of, 50; and concomitance, 86, 88; consecration of, 90–91; controversies, 56n2; and communio, 333–36; and divisions, 325–28; and ecumenism, 289; as *exemplum*, 140–42; form of, 78–83; and friendship, 333–36; in general, 51; and Germanic theology, 261–63; and Hellenism, 257–61; and the Holy Spirit, 154; impanation/consubstantiation, theory of, 66–70; 84n121, 220, 234n14; and the last supper, 96–100, 187, 277–86; and love, 127, 158; and mystagogy, 148–55; and the Old Covenant, 308–09; and the Paschal Lamb, 224; and priesthood, 259; and the problem of Real Presence, 59–66; and the Reformation, 266–69; relation to other sacraments, 51–52;

377

378 INDEX

Eucharist (cont.)
  Real Presence in, 59–66, 79, 94–96, 127n127, 286–87, 291–292, 316–19; and representation of the Passion, 97–98, 155–59; as sacrifice, 133–34, 136, 137, 138–43; and Scholastic theology, 86–88, 263–66; and the senses, 75–76; and solidarity with the dead, 319–22; somatic real presence, 259, 264; and spiritualism, 87, 262; as spiritual nourishment, 50; and symbolic action, 143–47; and theophagy, 329–33; and time, 306–11; and transfinalisation, theory of, 270; and transsignification, theory of, 270–71; transubstantiation, theory of, 55–59, 72–77, 219–220, 264, 268, 286–300; and twentieth-century theology, 269–71; and typology, 62–63
Extreme Unction, 50

Fides et Ratio, 4

grace, salvation and, 113–14
good, self-communication of, 27
Guitmund of Aversa, 56n2, 72, 87n128, 263

Handke, Peter, xix, 298, 303, 322–25, 335, 338n134
Hegel, G.F.W., 298
hymns: and authenticity, 167–73; in general, 163–164, 173–74
Hugh of St. Victor, 24, 39, 42n83, 45

idealism, 3
Innocent III, Pope, 144
instrument: conjoined, 27, 45; separated, 28, 45

Jesus Christ: and the ascension, 276, 285–86; and collective guilt of Jews in death, 111, 175–76, 326; effects of his Passion, 123–26, 143; efficient causes of his Passion, 105–9; fittingness of his Passion, 104–5; human nature of, 27; and hylomorphism, 293; hypostatic union, 27; the Incarnation of, 296–97; life of, 27–28; and the last supper, 253–54; necessity of his Passion, 101–11; and the Old Covenant, 120–22, 132–33, 189–90, 198–99, 212–13, 215–16, 224, 246–47; person of, 27; and preaching, 182–86; priesthood, 128–37; his Resurrection, 179–82, 276, 286; self-gift of, 28, 94, 97, 99, 100–11, 120, 187–91, 204, 207–8, 271, 272, 277–78, 281, 283, 297; soteriological categories of his Passion, 112–26

Joachim of Fiore, 41
John XXIII, Pope, 255–56
John Paul II, Pope: on Christ's priesthood, 128, and *Ecclesia de Eucharistia*, 225; and the Jubilee Year, 328; recommendation of Aquinas, 4
Joyce, James, 164
Juliana of Liège, 165

Kasper, Walter, 279n17, 284n34, 286n37, 292

Lanfranc of Bec, 72, 139–40, 262–63
last supper: and Hellenism, 278–79; historical-critical approaches to, 278, 280; and Jewish practices, 279–80; and the Old Covenant, 282; and Pauline-Lucan interpretation, 280–81, 283
Lauda Sion: 73, 87, 164, 190, 240, 245, 248, 277, 339; and anthropophagy, 220; and concomitance, 221; and doxology, 211–13; in general, 209–28; the Good Shepherd in, 226; and impanation, theory of, 220; and Jesus as living bread, 214–16; negative theology in, 213–14; and the Passover, 223; and praxis, 221, 222, 223; and real presence, 218–19, 221; and spiritualism, 220–21; structure of, 209–10; text of, 211, 217–18, 225; and transubstantiation, 220; and eschatology, 225–28
Leo the Great, 28
Leo XII, Pope, 2
Luther, Martin, 67, 68n53; and consubstantiation, 295; and the Eucharist, 266–69, 289–91

Mariology, 27
Marion, Jean-Luc, 298–99
Matrimony, 51
medieval theology, 193, 226–27, 254, 265, 287, 289, 312, 313, 330
mystery theology. *See* Casel, Odo

neoplatonic thought, 26
neo-Scholasticism, 5
neo-scholastic theology, 128
new covenant, sacraments of, 41
Nietzsche, Frederick, 305, 320
Nostra Aetate, 110–11

old covenant, sacraments of, 40
Optatam Totius, 3
Order, sacrament of. *See* Ordination
Ordination: and the Eucharist, 89–93, 99, 299–300; in general, 48, 51

INDEX 379

Pange lingua: 62, 163, 173, 198, 206, 245, 247; and Anti-Semitism, 175–76, 192; and the Body of Christ, 191–92; Christ's life in, 182–86; and doxology, 179–82; and Eucharistic presence, 187–89; and evangelization, 184–85; and fulfillment of the Old Covenant, 180–81, 186, 187, 189–90; in general, 175–93; and Mary, 183–84; and the Passover, 187, 192; and the real presence, 193; and self-gift of Christ, 182–183, 187; structure of, 177–78; text of, 176–77; and thanksgiving, 189–91; theology of, 178–93; and the Trinity, 190–91

Penance: in general, 48, 50, 117–18; and sin, 124–25

Patristics: Greek, 257–59; Latin, 260–61

Pesch, Otto Hermann, 25, 30, 118, 123, 173

Pieper, Josef, 248

Pius X, Pope, 31

Pius XI, Pope, 3

Plato, philosophy of, 257–59

Pröpper, Thomas, 272–73, 285

Rahner, Karl, xiv, 1, 6, 288, 287n40, 295, 312n38, 313, 315

Ratzinger, Joseph, xiv, 6, 270, 276n4, 277n8, 285n36, 297n40, 290n45, 292n55, 293, 295, 296n70, 296n72, 297n76, 299n83

Reginald of Piperno, 28

Rite of the Mass: and the *epiclesis*, 289; and solidarity with the dead, 319–22; and suffering of others, 323–25

sacrament(s): anthropological dimension of, 28, 38–39, 49–50, 52; and the body, 38–39, 49; divine institution of, 35; divine pact theory of, 42–43, 53; divine pedagogy of, 41; ecclesial dimension of, 31, 39; fittingness of, 37–39; form of, 78–83; in general, 28, 30; as instrumental cause, 31, 38, 42–47, 53; liturgical context of, 30; matter and form of, 34, 36; minister of, 46–47; natural, 40(n73); necessity of, 37; number of, 48–49, 52; and Christ's Passion, 45–46; personal dimension of, 30; recipient of, 47–48; relation to Christology, 31, 36, 38, 44–45, 53; elation to the Passion, 124–26; and salvation history, 34, 39–42; and the senses, 34–35, 75; as sign, 31, 33; and sin, 45, 49; and time, 33–34; validity of, 36, 46–48, 53–54

sacramental grace, 53

sacramental theology: of Aquinas, 29, 89; medieval, 30, 57. *See also individual sacraments by name*

Sacris solemniis: 158, 247, 248; and eschatology, 202; and fulfillment of the Old Covenant, 201–2; in general, 194–203; and the Passover, 198–99; and self-gift theology, 197–203; and sacrifice, 201; and structure, 195–97; text of, 194–95

Scholasticism: and the Eucharist, 86–88, 147, 263–66, 291, 292; in general, 23, 29, 30

Schillebeeckx, Edward, xiv, 75, 270

Schoonenberg, Piet, 270

science of faith, 23

Scotus, John Duns, 265

Second Vatican Council, 3–4, 128, 143, 255–56; and *Gaudium et spes*, 324

sign(s): material, 30

soteriology, 27; and the Eucharist, 94–95, 137, 158–59, 272, 284, 320; and *meritum*, 112–15; and the Passion, 112–23, 204, 207–08; and *redemptio*, 115–23, 180; *sacrificium*, 115–23; and *satisfactio*, 115–23; and sin, 100–101

Spaemann, Robert, 269

Studiorem Ducem, 3

summae, 23

Summa theologiae: *exitus-reditus* in, 25–26, 27; priesthood in, 128–37; salvation history in, 24, 26; Scripture in, 26; structure of, 23, 26–27

systematic theology, 128

theology, 25; and history, 254–57; of image, 259; and modern life, 301–6

Thomism: neo-Thomism, 2, 4; magisterial support of, 2–5

Torrell, Jean-Pierre: in general, 115, 129, 230; and historicity of the Office of Corpus Christi, 172–73

Transiturus, Papal Bull, 166–67, 169–72, 197, 244n1

Tübingen School, 2

Urban IV, Pope, 166–68, 197, 244

Vatican II. *See* Second Vatican Council

Verbum, 92–93

Verbum supernum: 158–59, 200, 248, 310; in general, 203–8; and pre-Passion details, 206; and salvation, 207–8; and self-gift of Christ, 204–8; and structure, 204–5; text of, 203; and the Word of God, 205–6

A Gift of Presence: The Theology and Poetry of the Eucharist in Thomas Aquinas was designed in Adobe Jenson Pro with Cinzel display type and composed by Kachergis Book Design of Pittsboro, North Carolina. It was printed on 60-pound Natures Book Natural and bound by Thomson-Shore of Dexter, Michigan.

www.ingramcontent.com/pod-product-compliance
Lightning Source LLC
Chambersburg PA
CBHW031229290426
44109CB00012B/217